WS-BPEL 2.0 for SOA Composite Applications with Oracle SOA Suite 11*g*

Define, model, implement, and monitor real-world BPEL business processes with SOA-powered BPM

Matjaz B. Juric

with Marcel Krizevnik

BIRMINGHAM - MUMBAI

WS-BPEL 2.0 for SOA Composite Applications with Oracle SOA Suite 11*g*

First published: September 2010

Production Reference: 1010910

Published by Packt Publishing Ltd.
32 Lincoln Road
Olton
Birmingham, B27 6PA, UK.

ISBN 978-1-847197-94-8

www.packtpub.com

Cover Image by Tina Negus (tina_manthorpe@sky.com)

Credits

Author
Matjaz B. Juric

Co-Author
Marcel Krizevnik

Reviewers
Harish Gaur
Clemens Utschig-Utschig

Acquisition Editor
James Lumsden

Development Editor
Wilson D'souza

Technical Editors
Neha Damle
Vinodhan Nair

Indexer
Rekha Nair

Editorial Team Leader
Gagandeep Singh

Project Team Leader
Priya Mukherji

Project Coordinator
Prasad Rai

Proofreader
Sandra Hopper

Graphics
Nilesh R. Mohite

Production Coordinator
Kruthika Bangera
Adline Swetha Jesuthas

Cover Work
Kruthika Bangera

Foreword

Before the advent of SOA, integration was nothing less than an IT nightmare. Any integration project imposed a tremendous financial and resource burden on the IT department. In many cases, integration was solved with point solutions: here a database link, there a file transfer.

With SOA, things started to look better. SOA allowed organizations to take on integration challenges head-on. SOA provided an opportunity for organizations to build services once and reuse everywhere. Reusability fastened the implementation timelines and reduced the maintenance costs.

As SOA started becoming mainstream and the de-facto choice for standards-based integration, organizations have started expanding their SOA footprint and its use. SOA is no longer just about faster integration. With SOA and the advent of BPM, organizations are now looking to optimize inefficient processes, bring agility through a rules-driven approach, determine visibility into key business metrics, and empower business users to participate in the SOA lifecycle, and so on. These requirements go beyond a simple integration between two applications. SOA is fast becoming an approach to drive IT agility.

However, this expanded role of SOA is not without its own perils. For SOA to optimize business processes, drive agility, and improve visibility, organizations have to bring several technologies together—orchestration engine, rules engine, process modeling tools, process monitoring tools, and data service bus. With different tools from different vendors, the integration challenge has moved to a new level now. Before integrating processes and data, organizations have to first integrate tools and technologies. In short, the solution is now the new problem.

This is where Oracle SOA Suite brings sanity back in the integration landscape. Oracle SOA Suite 11*g* has been created to provide a unified and integrated experience throughout the entire SOA lifecycle. It has been designed with a goal of shielding developers, IT operations, and business users from underlying infrastructure complexity and providing an experience they would have gotten had they used just one single tool. Oracle SOA Suite 11*g* brings together an orchestration engine (BPEL Process Manager), a rules engine (Oracle Business Rules), modeling tools (JDeveloper integration with BPA Suite), a process monitoring tool (Oracle BAM), and a data service bus (Oracle Service Bus). But, what makes Oracle SOA Suite really stand apart is how integrated this stack is.

When you read this book, you will see how developers don't have to leave their unified console to business SOA applications and work with all SOA artifacts (processes, rules, activity sensors, services, XML, SQL). Similarly, IT administrators have a single application to install, cluster, and manage their entire SOA deployment, greatly simplifying their duties. And the good news is everything is standards based.

As you start building SOA applications, this book will be your trustworthy companion. Along with how-to tutorials, you will also get to hear interesting insights on competing standards, architecture patterns, and best practices. This book is a true successor of Oracle BPEL. We would like to thank Matjaz for putting this together.

May SOA force be with you!

Clemens Utschig-Utschig, Sr. Principal Product Manager, Oracle SOA Suite

Harish Gaur, Director, Product Management, Oracle Fusion Middleware

Markus Zirn, VP Product Management, Oracle Fusion Middleware

About the Authors

Matjaz B. Juric holds a Ph.D. in computer and information science. He is a professor at the university and head of the Cloud Computing and SOA Competence Center. Matjaz is Java Champion and Oracle ACE Director. He has more than 15 years of work experience. He has authored/coauthored *Business Process Driven SOA using BPMN and BPEL, Business Process Execution Language for Web Services* (English and French editions), *BPEL Cookbook: Best Practices for SOA-based integration and composite applications development* (award for best SOA book in 2007 by SOA World Journal), *SOA Approach to Integration, Professional J2EE EAI, Professional EJB, J2EE Design Patterns Applied, and .NET Serialization Handbook*. He has published chapters in *More Java Gems* (Cambridge University Press) and in *Technology Supporting Business Solutions* (Nova Science Publishers). He has also published in journals and magazines, such as SOA World Journal, Web Services Journal, Java Developer's Journal, Java Report, Java World, EAI Journal, Theserverside.com, OTN, ACM journals, and presented at conferences such as OOPSLA, Java Development, XML Europe, OOW, SCI, and others. He is a reviewer, program committee member, and conference organizer. Matjaz has been involved in several large-scale projects.

In cooperation with IBM Java Technology Centre, he worked on performance analysis and optimization of RMI-IIOP, an integral part of the Java platform. Matjaz is also a member of the BPEL Advisory Board.

My efforts in this book are dedicated to my family. Special thanks to my dear beautiful Ana. Thanks to my friends at SOA, Cloud Computing Center, and at Packt Publishing.

Marcel Krizevnik is a researcher at the University of Maribor, where he is preparing a Ph.D. in computer and information science. Marcel started his career as a software developer of chemistry information systems. Now, his main research areas are service-oriented architecture and cloud computing. He is also a member of the SOA Competency Center and Cloud Computing Center. In the last three years, he has been involved in several SOA technology projects.

I would like to thank my dear and beautiful Lucija for standing beside me throughout my career and while writing this book.

About the Reviewers

Harish Gaur has more than thirteen years of experience in the enterprise software industry, including more than seven years at Oracle. He is currently the Director of Product Management for Fusion Middleware at Oracle. In his current role, he works closely with strategic customers implementing SOA and BPM using Oracle Fusion Middleware. He is co-author of *BPEL Cookbook* (2007) and *Fusion Middleware Patterns* (September, 2010).

Before Oracle, he worked as a Solution Specialist with Vitria Technology, educating customers about the benefits of Business Process Management. Prior to that, he helped Fortune 500 companies architect scalable integration solutions using EAI tools like webMethods and CrossWorlds (now IBM).

Harish holds an engineering degree in Computer Science and has an MBA from Haas School of Business, UC Berkeley.

Clemens Utschig-Utschig works as Platform Architect for the SOA Product Management team at Oracle Headquarters, USA.

As a native Austrian, he started his career years back at the local consulting branch, helping customers designing their next generation JEE and SOAs, as well as doing crisis management for projects abroad.

Since his transfer almost five years ago into engineering, Clemens is responsible for cross-product integration and strategic standards, as well as being a member of Oracle's SOA platform steering committee. In his current role, he serves on the OASIS TC for Service Component Architecture (SCA) and supports customers all around the world on their journey towards implementing enterprise-wide SOA.

In 2006 Clemens co-founded the "Masons-of-SOA", an inter-company network founded by architects of Oracle Germany, Opitz, SOPEra (Eclipse Project Swordfish founders), and EDS, with the mission of spreading knowledge, fostering discussion, and supporting SOA programs across companies and borders.

Table of Contents

Appendix A

This chapter is not present in the book but is available as a free download from: `http://www.packtpub.com/sites/default/files/downloads/7948_AppendixA.pdf`

Appendix B

This chapter is not present in the book but is available as a free download from: `http://www.packtpub.com/sites/default/files/downloads/7948_AppendixB.pdf`

Preface

Business Process Execution Language for Web Services (BPEL, WS-BPEL, or BPEL4WS) is the commonly accepted standard for defining business processes with composition of services. It is the cornerstone of **Service-Oriented Architecture** (**SOA**). With its ability to define executable and abstract business processes, it plays an important role in business process management. BPEL is supported by a majority of software vendors including Oracle, IBM, Microsoft, SAP, and others.

This book explains the role of BPEL when building SOA composite applications with Oracle SOA Suite 11*g*. It explains the BPEL 2.0 standard, the role of BPEL in SOA, and provides a step-by-step guide to designing and developing BPEL processes. The book also covers several related technologies and products, such as **Oracle Business Activity Monitoring** (**Oracle BAM**), **Oracle Service Bus** (**OSB**), **Oracle Service Registry** (**OSR**), **Oracle Business Process Analysis Suite** (**Oracle BPA Suite**), and **Oracle Business Process Management Suite** (**Oracle BPM Suite**).

What this book covers

Chapter 1, Introduction to BPEL and SOA, provides a detailed introduction to BPEL and Service-Oriented Architecture (SOA). It discusses business processes and their automation, explains the role of BPEL, Web Services, and **Enterprise Service Bus** (**ESB**) in SOA, provides insight into business process composition with BPEL, and explains the most important features.

Chapter 2, Service Composition with BPEL, discusses the composition of Web Services with BPEL. The chapter introduces the core concepts of BPEL and explains how to define synchronous and asynchronous business processes with BPEL. The reader gets familiar with the BPEL process structure, partner links, sequential and parallel service invocation, variables, conditions, and so on.

Chapter 3, Advanced BPEL, goes deeper into BPEL specifications and covers advanced features for implementing complex business processes. Advanced activities, scopes, fault handling, compensations, event handling, correlation sets, concurrent activities and links, process lifecycle, dynamic partner links, and other BPEL 2.0 features are covered in detail.

Chapter 4, Using BPEL with Oracle SOA Suite 11g, explains how to develop, deploy, test and manage BPEL processes as part of SOA composite applications in Oracle SOA Suite 11*g* using Oracle SOA Composite Editor, Oracle BPEL Component Designer, and Oracle Enterprise Manager Console.

Chapter 5, BPEL Extensions, Dynamic Parallel Flow, Dynamic Partner Links, Notification Service, Java Embedding, and Fault Management Framework and *Chapter 6, Entity Variables, Master and Detail Processes, Security, and Business Events in BPEL,* take a detailed look at several advanced topics of using BPEL with Oracle SOA Suite 11*g*, such as dynamic parallel flows, dynamic partner links, Java embedding, fault management framework, entity variables, master and detail processes, security policies, business events, and more.

Chapter 7, Human Interactions in BPEL, explains how to enable human interaction in BPEL processes using the Human Task service component. The chapter discusses Oracle Human Workflow architecture and features. The reader gets familiar with how to design a human task, how to create ADF-based human task web forms, and how to access and act on tasks using the Oracle BPM Worklist Application.

Chapter 8, Monitoring BPEL Processes with BAM, discusses how to capture and monitor real-time information about the execution of business activities to improve business process effectiveness. It explains the Oracle BAM architecture and features. The chapter also discusses how to use data objects, sensors, sensor actions, monitoring objects, and how to build BAM dashboard.

Chapter 9, BPEL with Oracle Service Bus and Service Registry, explains how to ensure loose coupling between different components of the SOA architecture by using the Oracle Service Bus (OSB) and Oracle Service Registry (OSR). The chapter explains the OSB and OSR architecture and features. The reader gets familiar with how to publish business entities and services to OSR using the Registry Control console, how to import and export resources between OSB and OSR using the Oracle Service Bus Console, how to create OSB projects, business and proxy services. The chapter also covers some advanced features of OSB, such as service-result caching and monitoring.

Chapter 10, BPMN to BPEL Round-tripping with BPA Suite and SOA Suite, explains how to eliminate the semantic gap between IT and process models through automated translation between BPMN and BPEL using Oracle Business Process Analysis Suite (Oracle BPA Suite) and Oracle SOA Suite. The chapter discusses Oracle BPA Suite architecture and features and how various constructs map between BPMN and BPEL. The reader gets familiar with how to model a BPMN business process, how to convert a BPMN model into a BPEL Blueprint, how to import the generated BPEL code in JDeveloper, and how to propagate changes from BPEL code back to the BPMN model.

Chapter 11, Integrating BPEL with BPMN using BPM Suite, presents an interesting new feature provided by Oracle Business Process Management Suite 11*g* (Oracle BPM Suite 11*g*) - the BPMN 2.0 service engine. It allows direct execution of BPMN 2.0 processes, without the need to transform them to BPEL. The chapter discusses Oracle BPM Suite architecture and features, and demonstrates how both, BPMN and BPEL processes can be used inside a single SOA composite application.

Appendix A, WS-BPEL 2.0 Syntax Reference, provides a syntax reference for the WS-BPEL Web Services Business Process Execution Language Version 2.0, OASIS Standard as defined in the specification dated April 11, 2007.

Appendix B, BPEL 1.1 Syntax Reference, provides a syntax reference for the BPEL (BPEL4WS) version 1.1 as defined in the specification dated May 5th, 2003.

Appendix A, WS-BPEL 2.0 Syntax Reference and *Appendix B, BPEL 1.1 Syntax Reference* are not present in the book but are available as a free download from the following links:

- `http://www.packtpub.com/sites/default/files/downloads/7948_AppendixA.pdf`
- `http://www.packtpub.com/sites/default/files/downloads/7948_AppendixB.pdf`

What you need for this book

To develop and test the examples in this book, you need to have Oracle SOA Suite 11*g* Patch Set 2 (11.1.1.3) installed on your system. For *Chapter 9,* you also need Oracle Service Bus 11*g* (11.1.1.3) and Oracle Service Registry 11*g* (11.1.1.2), and for *Chapter 10,* you need Oracle BPA Suite 11*g* (11.1.1.2).

Who this book is for

This book is aimed at SOA architects and developers involved in the design, implementation, and integration of composite applications and end-to-end business processes. The book provides comprehensive coverage of WS-BPEL 2.0 for implementing business processes and developing SCA composite applications, dealing with the issues of composition, orchestration, transactions, coordination, and security. This book uses Oracle SOA Suite 11*g* and related Oracle products. To follow this book, you need to have basic a knowledge of XML, Web Services, and Java EE.

Conventions

In this book, you will find a number of styles of text that distinguish between different kinds of information. Here are some examples of these styles, and an explanation of their meaning.

Code words in text are shown as follows: "For example, if we select the `Business Process simulator` filter, we only see information related to performing business process simulations."

A block of code is set as follows:

```
<assign>
  <copy>
    <from variable="InsuranceBResponse" />
    <to variable="InsuranceSelectionResponse" />
  </copy>
</assign>
```

When we wish to draw your attention to a particular part of a code block, the relevant lines or items are set in bold:

```
<process ...>
  <sequence>

  <!-- Wait for the incoming request to start the process -->
  <receive ... />

  <!-- Invoke a set of related services, one by one -->
  <invoke ... />
  <invoke ... />
  <invoke ... />
      ...
  </sequence>
</process>
```

New terms and **important words** are shown in bold. Words that you see on the screen, in menus or dialog boxes for example, appear in the text like this: "The **Create database** dialog opens".

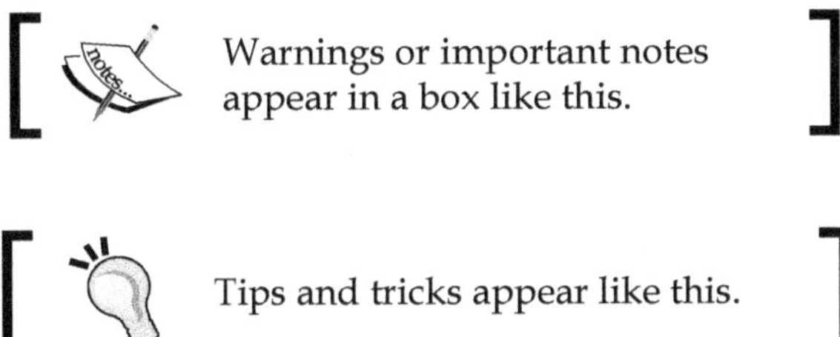

Warnings or important notes appear in a box like this.
Tips and tricks appear like this.

Reader feedback

Feedback from our readers is always welcome. Let us know what you think about this book—what you liked or may have disliked. Reader feedback is important for us to develop titles that you really get the most out of.

To send us general feedback, simply send an e-mail to `feedback@packtpub.com`, and mention the book title via the subject of your message.

If there is a book that you need and would like to see us publish, please send us a note in the **SUGGEST A TITLE** form on `www.packtpub.com` or e-mail `suggest@packtpub.com`.

If there is a topic that you have expertise in and you are interested in either writing or contributing to a book, see our author guide on `www.packtpub.com/authors`.

Customer support

Now that you are the proud owner of a Packt book, we have a number of things to help you to get the most from your purchase.

Downloading the example code for this book

You can download the example code files for all Packt books you have purchased from your account at `http://www.PacktPub.com`. If you purchased this book elsewhere, you can visit `http://www.PacktPub.com/support` and register to have the files e-mailed directly to you.

Errata

Although we have taken every care to ensure the accuracy of our content, mistakes do happen. If you find a mistake in one of our books—maybe a mistake in the text or the code—we would be grateful if you would report this to us. By doing so, you can save other readers from frustration and help us improve subsequent versions of this book. If you find any errata, please report them by visiting `http://www.packtpub.com/support`, selecting your book, clicking on the errata submission form link, and entering the details of your errata. Once your errata are verified, your submission will be accepted and the errata will be uploaded on our website, or added to any list of existing errata, under the Errata section of that title. Any existing errata can be viewed by selecting your title from `http://www.packtpub.com/support`.

Piracy

Piracy of copyright material on the Internet is an ongoing problem across all media. At Packt, we take the protection of our copyright and licenses very seriously. If you come across any illegal copies of our works, in any form, on the Internet, please provide us with the location address or website name immediately so that we can pursue a remedy.

Please contact us at `copyright@packtpub.com` with a link to the suspected pirated material.

We appreciate your help in protecting our authors, and our ability to bring you valuable content.

Questions

You can contact us at `questions@packtpub.com` if you are having a problem with any aspect of the book, and we will do our best to address it.

1
Introduction to BPEL and SOA

BPEL (Business Process Execution Language for Web Services, also WS-BPEL, BPEL4WS) is a language used for the composition, orchestration, and coordination of Web Services. It provides a rich vocabulary for expressing the behavior of business processes. In this chapter, we will introduce BPEL, define its role with regard to **Service-Oriented Architecture** (SOA), and explain the process-oriented approach to SOA and the role of BPEL. We shall also provide short descriptions of the most important BPEL servers—the run-time environments for the execution of business processes specified in BPEL. We will also compare BPEL to other business process languages. In this chapter, we will:

- Discuss the role of business processes and their automation
- Discuss business and IT alignment
- Examine SOA, its concepts, and BPEL
- Look at the SOA building blocks, such as services, Enterprise Service Bus, Registry and Repository, Human Task Support, Process Monitoring, Rule Engine, and Adapters
- Mention SOA governance
- Look at BPEL features
- Distinguish between Orchestration and Choreography
- Examine the relation of BPEL to other languages
- Overview BPEL Servers and SOA platforms
- Discuss the future of BPEL

Why business processes matter

Enterprise applications and information systems have become fundamental assets to companies. Companies rely on them to be able to perform business operations. Enterprise information systems can improve the efficiency of businesses through the automation of business processes. The objective of almost every company is that the applications it uses should provide comprehensive support for business processes. This means that applications should align with business processes closely.

A business process is a collection of coordinated service invocations and related activities that produce a business result, either within a single organization or across several.

Although this requirement does not sound very difficult to fulfill, real-world situations show us a different picture. Business processes are usually dynamic in nature. Companies have to improve and modify, act in an agile manner, optimize and adapt business processes to their customers, and thus improve the responsiveness of the whole company. Every change and improvement in a business process has to be reflected in the applications that provide support for them.

It is most likely that companies have to live with very complex information system architectures consisting of a heterogeneous mix of different applications that have been developed over time using different technologies and architectures. These existing applications (often called legacy applications) are a vital asset in each company and core business usually depends on them. Replacing them with newly developed applications would be very costly and time consuming and usually would not justify the investment.

On the other hand, existing applications have several limitations. Probably the most important fact is that the majority of older applications have been developed from the functional perspective and have addressed the requirements of a single domain. Therefore, such applications typically do not provide support for the whole business process. Rather they support one, or a few activities, in a process. Such applications provide support for certain functions or tasks only. For an information system to provide complete support for business processes, it has to be able to use the functionalities of several existing applications in a coordinated and integrated way.

The consequence is that users need to switch between different applications to fulfill tasks and also perform some tasks manually. The flow of the tasks is in the heads of users, not in the information system, and this has several disadvantages, such as:

- Limited insight into the way business activities are performed
- Difficulties in tracing current status and progress

- Difficulties in monitoring key performance indicators

Existing applications have often been developed using older technologies, languages, and architectures, which are by definition less flexible to change. Tightly coupled applications, constructed of interrelated modules, which cannot be differentiated, upgraded, or refactored with a reasonable amount of effort, place important limitations on the flexibility of such applications. This is why such applications are sometimes called stovepipe applications.

Let us summarize—on one side we have the business system, which consists of business processes. Business processes define the order of activities and tasks that produce a specific business result. Business processes have to be flexible in order to adapt to customer requirements, to market demand, and to optimize operations.

On the other side, we have the information system with multiple existing applications. Existing applications have important business logic implemented, which a company relies upon to perform business operations. Existing applications are also difficult to modify and adapt because they have not been developed in a flexible way that would allow modifying application parts quickly and efficiently. This is shown in the following figure:

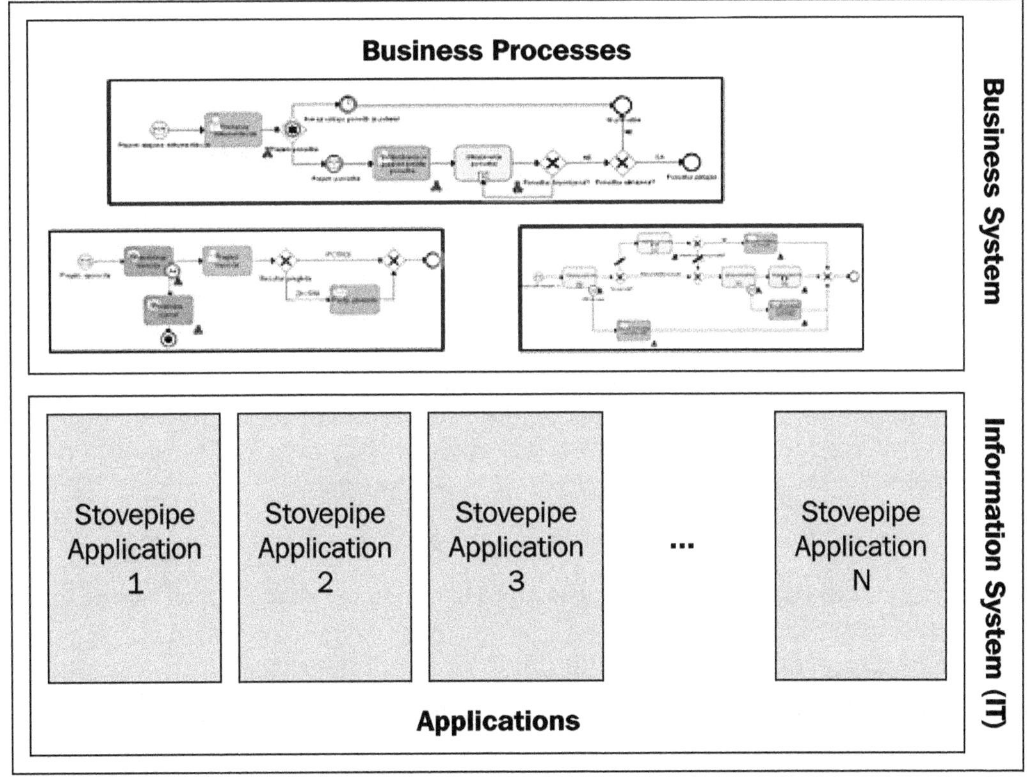

Business and IT alignment

The business system usually evolves with a different pace to that of the information system. Over time, this has resulted in an important loss of alignment between the business system and the information system. This has resulted in applications that do not fully support business tasks, and which have again hindered the evolution of business processes. The consequence has been less flexible and adaptable organizations with less competitive power in the market. Only companies where applications can be quickly and efficiently adapted to changing business needs can stay competitive in the global market.

The loss of alignment between the business and IT has a name—IT gap. An IT gap is a common occurrence in almost every company. It is mainly a consequence of the inability of application developers to modify and adapt the applications to business requirements quickly and efficiently.

The main reason probably hides in the fact that in the past neither programming languages and technologies nor architectural design could have anticipated changes. Existing applications had been designed to last. They had been developed in a tightly coupled fashion, which makes changes to specific parts of applications very difficult. Because of dependencies such changes usually have several, often unpredictable, consequences. In addition to the complexity and size of the modification, an important factor is also the state of the application being modified. If an application has a well-defined architecture and has been constructed keeping in mind future modifications, then it will be easier to modify. However, each modification to the application makes its architecture less robust with respect to future changes. Applications that have been maintained for several years and have gone through many modifications usually do not provide robust architecture anymore (unless they have been refactored constantly). Modifying them is difficult, time consuming, and often results in unexpected errors.

Modifying existing applications therefore requires time. This means that an information system cannot react instantly to changes in business processes—rather it requires time to implement, test, and deploy the modifications. This time is sometimes referred to as the IT *gap time*. It is obvious that the gap time should be as short as possible. However, in the real world this is (once again) not always the case.

We have seen that there are at least three important forces that have to be considered:

- Alignment between the business and IT, which is today seen as one of the most important priorities.
- Complexity of existing applications and the overall IT architecture. Modifying them is a complex, difficult, error-prone, and time-consuming task.

- Indispensability of existing applications. Companies rely upon existing applications and very often their core business operations would be jeopardized if existing applications fail.

This makes the primary objective of information systems—to provide timely, complete, and easy to modify support for business processes—even more difficult to achieve.

Service-Oriented Architecture

We have seen that the lack of alignment between business and IT is a common occurrence in almost every company. Achieving the alignment by modifying existing applications is in most cases not successful for two reasons:

- Complexity of the IT architecture, which makes modifying existing applications difficult and time consuming
- Existing applications must not fail because companies rely on them for everyday business.

The alignment of business and IT is very difficult to achieve using traditional approaches. However, if a mediation layer between the business and the information system is introduced, the alignment between business and IT becomes more realistic—meet the Service-Oriented Architecture.

To manage problems related to changing requirements, developments in technology, and integration of different methods have been proposed and used over time. A Service-Oriented Architecture is the latest architectural approach related to the integration, development, and maintenance of complex enterprise information systems.

SOA is not a radically new architecture, but rather the evolution of well-known distributed architectures and integration methods. Integration between applications has evolved from early days into well-defined integration methods and principles, often referred to as **Enterprise Application Integration** (**EAI**). EAI initially focused on the integration of applications within enterprises (intra-EAI). With the increasing need for integration between companies (business-to-business), the focus of EAI has been extended to inter-EAI.

SOA improves and extends the flexibility of earlier integration methods (EAI) and distributed architectures, and focuses on the reusability of existing applications and systems, efficient interoperabilities and application integrations, and the composition of business processes out of services (functionalities) provided by applications. An important objective of SOA is also the ability to apply changes in the future in a relatively easy and straightforward way.

SOA defines the concepts, architecture, and process framework, to enable the cost-efficient development, integration, and maintenance of information systems by reducing complexity, and stimulation of integration and reuse. Let us look at the definition of SOA, as provided by Bernhard Borges, Kerrie Holley, and Ali Arsanjani:

> *SOA is the architectural style that supports loosely coupled services to enable business flexibility in an interoperable, technology-agnostic manner. SOA consists of a composite set of business-aligned services that support a flexible and dynamically re-configurable end-to-end business processes realization using interface-based service descriptions.*

The following figure shows SOA as a mediator that aligns business and IT more closely. The end-to-end automation of business processes with BPEL fills the gap towards the business system. The services fill the gap towards the information system.

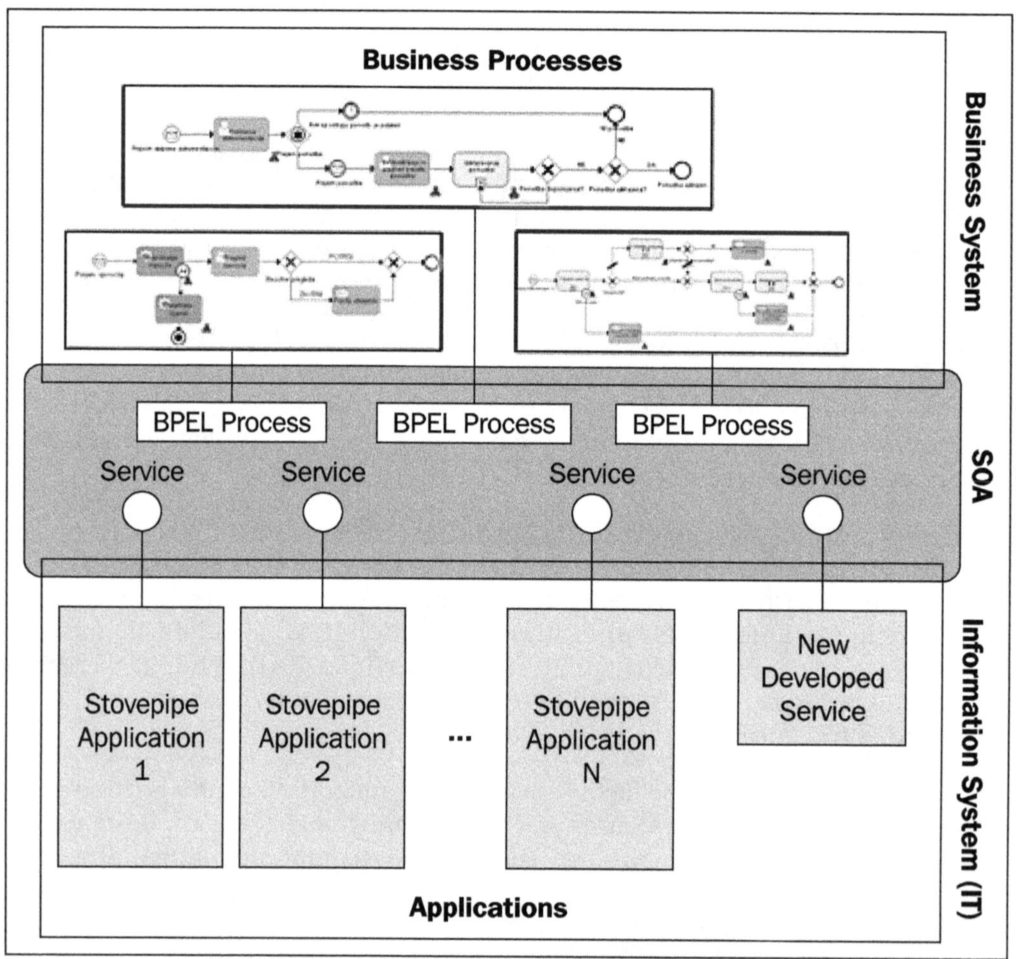

A Service-Oriented Architecture has several goals, but the two most important goals are to:

- Provide end-to-end automation of business processes. To achieve end-to-end automation of business processes, SOA introduces a special language—BPEL (Business Process Execution Language).
- Provide a flexible, adaptable IT architecture, where applications are modularized, consolidated, decoupled, and where business logic is contained in autonomous, encapsulated, loosely coupled, and reusable components called services.

Let's look at these two goals more closely.

BPEL

From the perspective of business systems, it is important that IT provides applications that support business processes from the beginning to the end (or end-to-end). Such support however has to be flexible, so that business processes can be modified quickly.

In SOA this is achieved by introducing a specialized language for business process execution—BPEL. BPEL is the most popular, commonly accepted specialized language for business process automation, and the main topic of this book. BPEL is a special language, designed to execute business processes using a special server—the process server. BPEL promises to achieve the holy grail of enterprise information systems—to provide an environment where business processes can be developed in an easy and efficient manner, directly executed, monitored, and quickly adapted to the changing needs of enterprises without too much effort.

Services

Achieving adaptable and flexible IT architecture is another important objective of SOA. SOA enables us to develop a modular, loosely coupled architecture which can overcome the difficulties of existing architectures.

The end-to-end automation of business processes can only be successful if sound, robust, and reliable applications are available underneath. This goal can only be achieved by developing a flexible architecture, where applications consist of modules. In SOA, modules are called services.

Services should be autonomous and be able to work in different contexts. They should be reusable and loosely coupled. They should be encapsulated and expose the operations through interfaces. Finally, the application architecture should be consolidated, which means that for a specific functionality only one service should exist.

In SOA, services become the main building blocks of the overall IT architecture. Services guide us into good development practices and away from monolithic, tightly coupled applications. They enable better and more efficient integration. Services enable us to modify and adapt the applications faster, with less effort, and with less negative consequences.

Services are also the main building blocks of BPEL processes. They are the executable artifacts. Those services that expose high-level, coarse-grained operations are called business services. The operations in business services usually represent distinct business activities. They are used in business processes; more exactly, BPEL uses business services to execute process activities. In other words, BPEL processes are compositions of business services. Business services provide the functionality, while BPEL processes contain the process flow.

Business services should be designed in a reusable manner, which means that a single business service can be used by more than one BPEL process. It also means that only one business service with the same functionality should exist in the system, which leads to consolidation.

Although services in SOA are one of the most important building blocks, we should not forget about the architecture. Services will fulfill the promises only if they adhere to the architecture. Architectural design should therefore be the key priority.

How to develop services

There are several possibilities in which we can develop services. They are:

- Developing services from scratch. This is appropriate for functionalities that are new and not yet covered by existing applications.
- Exposing the functionality of existing applications through services. It is particularly important to reuse the logic in existing applications and to integrate new solutions with existing applications. Today, several possibilities exist for exposing existing applications through services, such as facades, adapters, mediators, and so on.
- Using services provided by a third party.

The ability to expose existing applications is particularly important because it enables those who will adopt SOA, to reuse their existing IT assets. Existing applications have an enormous amount of business logic, which should be exposed and reused. SOA provides a standardized way to expose and access the functionalities (business logic) of existing applications through services.

From the technical perspective, services can be developed using a variety of distributed architectures. The requirement to expose the functionalities of applications and access them remotely has resulted in several distributed architectures and middleware products over time. The latest distributed architecture is Web Services. Web Services are the most suitable distributed architecture for exposing the functionality of applications as services.

SOA concepts

SOA is more than just a set of technologies. SOA is not directly related to any technology, although it is most often implemented with Web Services. Web Services are the most appropriate technology for SOA realization. However, using Web Services is not adequate to build SOA. We have to use Web Services according to the concepts that SOA defines.

The most important SOA concepts are:

- Services and service abstraction
- Self-describing, standardized interfaces with coarse granulation
- Exchange of messages
- Support for synchronous and asynchronous communication
- Loose coupling
- Reusability
- Service registries and repositories
- Quality of Service
- Composition of services into business processes

Services

Services provide business functionalities, such as an application for business travel, an application for a loan, and so on. This differs considerably from technology-oriented functionalities, such as retrieving or updating a table in a database. Services in SOA must provide business value, hide implementation details, and be autonomous. They should be abstract and autonomous. Service consumers are software entities, which call the service and use its functionality.

Interfaces

Service consumers access the service through its interface. The interface of a service defines a set of public operation signatures. The interface is a contract between the service provider and a service consumer. The interface is separated from the implementation, is self-describing, and platform independent. Interface description provides a basis for the implementation of the service by the service provider and a basis for the implementation of the service consumers. Each interface defines a set of operations. In order to define business services, we need to focus on the correct granulation of operations, and we should standardize interfaces. SOA services are best modeled with coarse granulation.

Messages

Operations are defined as a set of messages. Messages specify the data to be exchanged and describe it in a platform- and language-independent way using schemas. Services exchange only data, which differs considerably from object-oriented and component approaches, where behavior (implementation code) can also be exchanged. Operations should be idempotent (an operation is idempotent if repeated invocations have the same effect as one invocation). WSDL is a service description language that meets SOA criteria.

Synchronicity Service consumers access services through the service bus. This can be either a transport protocol, such as SOAP, or an ESB. Service consumers can use synchronous or asynchronous communication modes to invoke the operations of services. In synchronous mode, a service operation returns a response to the service consumer after the processing is complete. The service consumer has to wait for the completion. Usually we use the synchronous mode with operations in order to complete processing in a short time. In an asynchronous mode, a service operation does not return a response to the consumer, although it may return an acknowledgement so that the consumer knows that the operation has been invoked successfully. If a response is needed, usually a callback from the service to the consumer is used. In such a scenario, a correlation between messages is needed.

Loose Coupling

Through the self-describing interfaces, coarse granulation, exchange of data structures, and support for synchronous and asynchronous communication modes, a loose coupling of services is achieved. Loosely coupled services are services that expose only the necessary dependencies and reduce all kinds of artificial dependencies. This is particularly important when services are subject to frequent changes. Minimal dependencies assure us that there will be minimal number of changes required to other services when one service is modified. Such an approach improves robustness, makes systems more resilient to change, and promotes the reuse of services.

Reusability

SOA is about the consolidation of functionalities. Therefore, the common goal is to have a single service for each business functionality. In other words, we should not allow having more than one service with equal or similar functionalities. To achieve this it is essential to reuse services in different contexts. Reuse is not easy to achieve. First, we have to develop services that are general enough to be useful in different scenarios. Second, developers should first look at existing services, before developing a new one. If an existing service fulfills the need, they should reuse it. Reuse is fostered by registries and repositories.

Registries and repositories

To simplify and automate searching for the appropriate service, services are maintained in service registries, which act as directory listings. Service providers publish services in registries; service consumers look up the services in the registries. Lookup can be done by name, service functionality, or business process properties. UDDI is an example of a service registry. Service registries can improve reuse. In addition to registries, repositories are becoming important for storing artifacts, such as WSDL interfaces, XML schemas, and so on. Registries and repositories play an important role in SOA governance.

Quality of Service

Services usually have associated Quality of Service attributes. Such attributes include security, reliable messaging, transaction, correlation, management, policy, and other requirements. The infrastructure must provide support for these attributes. Quality of Service attributes are often important in large information systems. In Web Services, Quality of Service attributes are covered by WS-* specifications, such as WS-Security, WS-Addressing, WS-Coordination, and so on. Quality of Service is also provided by the ESB.

Composition of services into business processes

The final, and probably the most important, SOA concept is the composition of services into business processes. Services are composed in a particular order and follow a set of rules to provide support for business processes. The composition of services allows us to provide support for business processes in a flexible and relatively easy way. It also enables us to modify business processes quickly and therefore provide support to changed requirements faster and with less effort. For composition, we will use a dedicated language, BPEL, and an engine on which business process definitions will be executed. Only when we reach the level of service composition can we realize all the benefits of SOA.

SOA building blocks

Let us now have a closer look at the SOA building blocks that enable us to realize the above-mentioned concepts:

- **BPEL**: This is for business process automation with service composition.
- **Services**: This is for achieving modular and flexible architecture. For service development, Web Services technology is usually used.
- **Enterprise Service Bus (ESB)**: This provides a means for services and processes to communicate, and enables management and control over the communication. ESB is the backbone of SOA.
- **Registries and repositories**: These are central directories of services and useful for locating and reusing services, as well as SOA governance.
- **Human task support**: Business processes often involve human interaction. SOA supports human interactions in different ways, such as **WS-HumanTask** and **BPEL4People**. Human task support is related to Identity Management.
- **Process monitoring or Business Activity Monitoring (BAM)**: This allows the monitoring of the execution of processes, such as total execution time, average execution time, execution time of certain activities, and so on. It also allows us to monitor the **Key Performance Indicators (KPIs)**, which is particularly interesting for management, as it allows them to understand better how the business operations perform.
- **Business Rules Management Systems (BRMS) or Rule Engine**: This is a central place for managing business rules. With BRMS we can put business rules into a central location instead of hard coding them.
- **Adapters**: These provide easy access not only to external systems, such as ERP, CRM, SCM, but also DBMS systems.

A very important aspect of SOA is SOA governance. SOA is a complex architecture, which has to be governed in order to be consistent. SOA governance is a set of activities related to control over services and processes in SOA. Typical activities are related to managing service portfolios and lifecycles, ensuring service consistency, and monitoring service performance.

The full architecture of SOA is shown in the following figure:

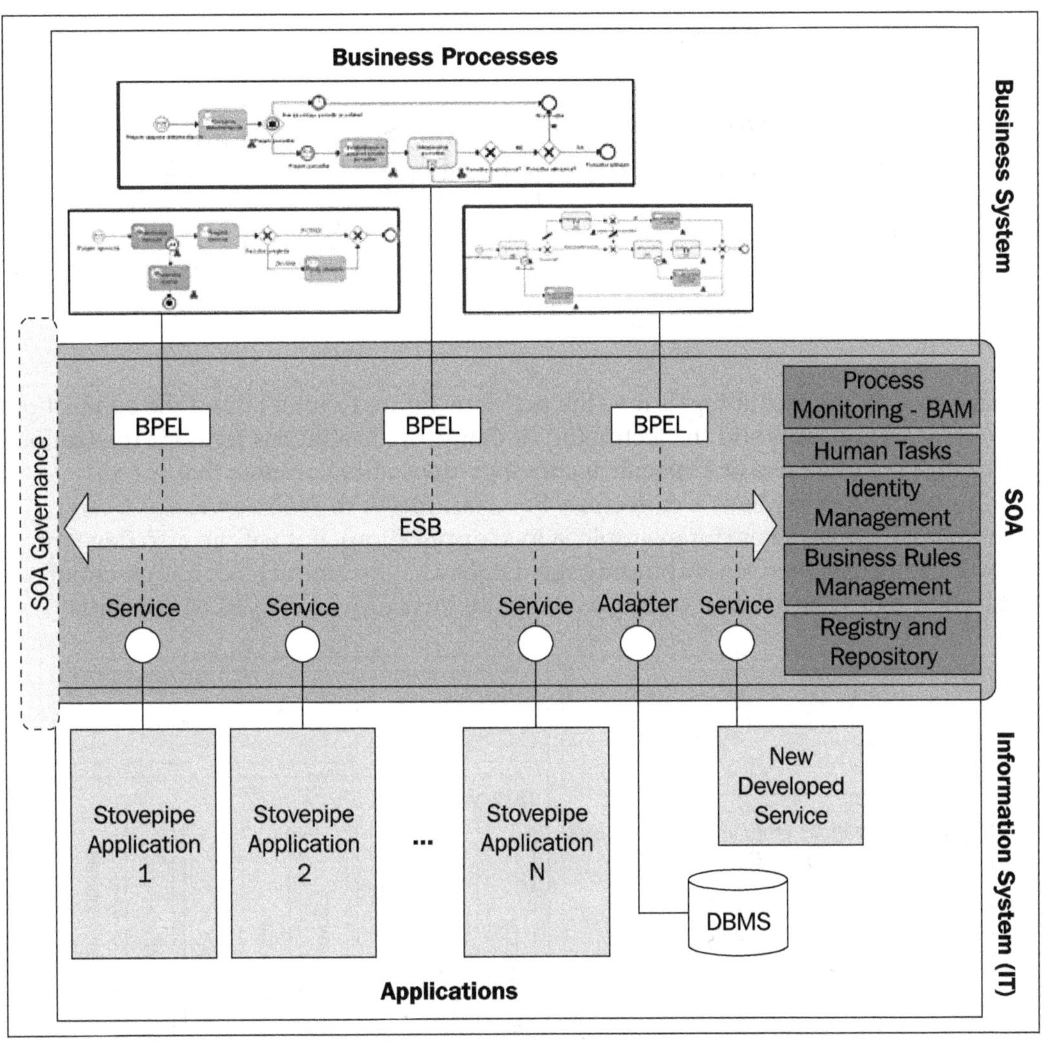

The next figure shows the technology view of SOA and positions the above-mentioned concepts:

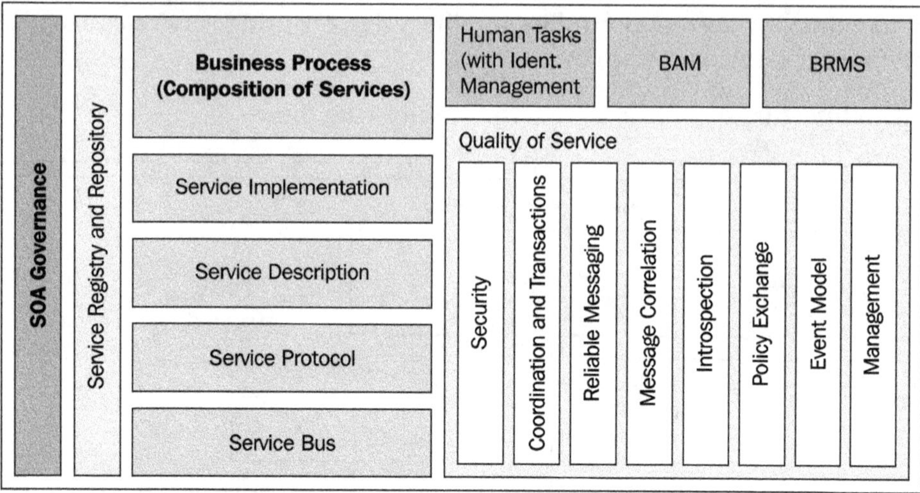

Let us now add the technologies into the previous figure to understand the connection between SOA concepts and the technologies that provide a means for their realization. Notice that the mere use of a specific technology does not guarantee that we are building an SOA-compliant architecture. For example, with Web Services we can develop business services (for example, a loan application), but we can also develop technology-focused services (updating the database, for example). So, it is essential that technologies are used according to the guidelines provided by SOA concepts.

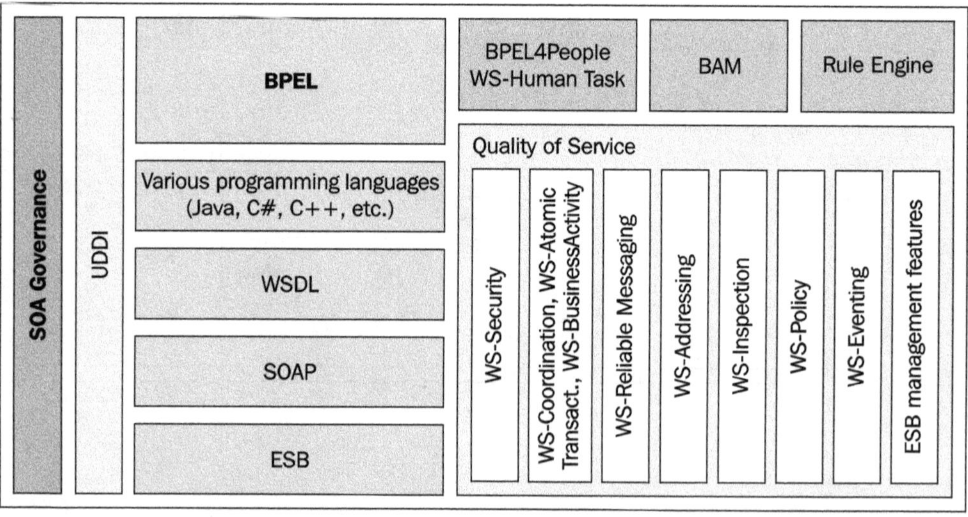

For this figure, we can have two views. The bottom-up view of SOA sees different applications exposing their functionalities through business services. This enables access to functionalities (services) of different existing and newly developed applications in a standard way. Access to services is important because a typical enterprise has a large number of applications that have to be integrated.

Developing business services, either through reuse of existing applications or by new development, is not sufficient. We also need to compose services into business processes—this is the second, the top-down, or process-oriented approach to SOA. We would obviously prefer a relatively simple and straightforward way to compose and modify business processes. This is where BPEL becomes important.

BPEL for process automation

Services in SOA are composed into aggregate services. We compose services until the aggregate services provide support for the whole business processes. Business processes are thus defined as a collection of activities through which services are invoked. For the outside world (that is, for the clients) a business process looks like any other service. In real-world scenarios we will usually create two kinds of business processes—those that will contain services from within the enterprise only, and those that will consume services provided by several companies. With service composition, we can use services provided by business partners in our processes, and business partners can use our services in their processes.

For example, a business process for booking business travel will invoke several services. In an oversimplified scenario, the business process will require us to specify the employee name, destination, dates, and other travel details. Then the process will invoke a service to check the employee's status. Based on the employee status, it will select the appropriate travel class. Then it will invoke the services of several airline companies (such as American Airlines, Delta Airlines, and so on) to check the airfare price and buy the one with the lowest price. The structure of services composed in the business process is shown in the following figure. In *Chapter 2*, we will discuss this example in detail and show how to define this process using BPEL.

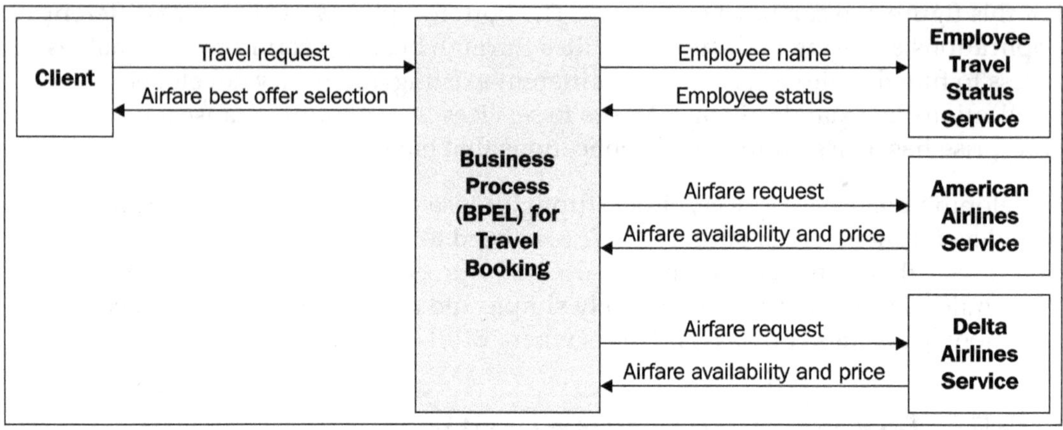

From the perspective of our business process, we do not care whether the service for checking the employee status accesses a legacy system, a database directly, or retrieves the status in any other way. We also do not care whether the services of airline companies are composed of other, lower-level services. From the perspective of the client (for our business process), the client sees the process as any other service and does not care whether the process is implemented through composition of other services, or some other way. *This stimulates reuse and further composition.* Real-world business processes will usually be much more complicated than our example. Usually they will contain several services and invoke their operations either in sequence or in parallel. They will also contain flow logic, handle faults, take care of transactions and message correlation, and so on.

The composition of services into business processes requires the definition of collaboration activities and data-exchange messages between involved Web Services. WSDL provides the basic technical description and specifications for messages that are exchanged. However, the description provided by WSDL does not go beyond simple interactions between the client (sender) and the web service (receiver). These interactions may be stateless, synchronous, or asynchronous. These relations are inadequate to express, model, and describe the complex compositions of multiple Web Services in business activities, which usually consist of several messages exchanged in a well-defined order. In such complex compositions, synchronous and asynchronous messages can be combined, and interactions are usually long running, often involving state information that has to be preserved. An important aspect is also the ability to describe how to handle faults and other exceptional situations. Given the limitations of WSDL, we need a mechanism to describe the composition of Web Services into more complex processes.

The composition of services into business processes could be realized using one of the well-known programming languages (Java, C#, and so on), but it turns out that the composition of services somehow differs from traditional programming. With composition, we merge functionalities (services) into larger services and processes. In other words, we do programming in the large, which differs from traditional programming in the small. Programming in the large refers to the representation of the high-level state transition logic of a system. Using programming languages, such as Java, C#, and so on, for composition often results in inflexible solutions, particularly because there is no clear separation between the process flow and the business logic, which should not be tightly coupled.

In addition to these facts, the composition of business processes has other specific requirements, such as support for many process instances, long-running processes, compensation, and so on. All this makes the use of dedicated solutions reasonable. This is why over the years several proprietary **BPM** (**Business Process Management**) products have been developed, such as **Dralasoft Workflow** and **TIBCO Business Process Management.** The disadvantage of using proprietary BPMs is that these are traditionally niche products, sold from a top-down perspective to large business users. Such products are usually expensive and bound to a certain provider. This is why we need BPEL.

BPEL is equally important for SOA as SQL is for databases.

Web Services

Web Services are the latest distributed technology and, as we will see, the most suitable technology for the realization of SOA. They have become the commonly used technology for interoperability and the integration of applications and information systems. Web Services provide the technological foundation for achieving interoperability between applications using different software platforms, operating systems, and programming languages. They are built on XML. While XML is the de facto standard for data-level integration, Web Services are becoming the de facto standard for service-level integrations between and within enterprises.

From the technological perspective, Web Services are a distributed architecture. The distributed computing paradigm started with **DCE** (**Distributed Computing Environment**), **RPC** (**Remote Procedure Call**), and messaging systems, also called message-oriented middleware (products such as MQSeries, MSMQ, and so on). Then distributed objects and **ORBs** (**Object Request Brokers**) such as CORBA (**Common Object Request Broker Architecture**), **DCOM** (**Distributed Component Object Model**), and **RMI** (**Remote Method Invocation**) emerged. Based on these, component models, such as **EJB** (**Enterprise Java Beans**), **COM+** (**Component Object Model**), .NET Enterprise Services, and **CCM** (**CORBA Component Model**) have been developed. RPC, ORBs, and component models share a similar communication model, which is based on a synchronous operation invocation. Messaging systems are based on an asynchronous communication model.

How Web Services differ from their predecessors

Web Services are similar to their predecessors, but also differ from them in several aspects. Web Services are the first distributed technology to be supported by all major software vendors. Therefore, they are the first technology that fulfills the promise of universal interoperability between applications running on disparate platforms. The fundamental specifications that Web Services are based on are **SOAP** (**Simple Object Access Protocol**), **WSDL** (**Web Services Description Language**), and **UDDI** (**Universal Description, Discovery, and Integration**). SOAP, WSDL, and UDDI are XML based, making Web Services protocol messages and descriptions human readable.

From the architectural perspective, Web Services introduced several important changes compared to earlier distributed architectures:

- Web Services support loose coupling through operations that exchange data only. This differs from component and distributed object models, where behavior can also be exchanged.
- Operations in Web Services are based on the exchange of XML-formatted payloads. They are a collection of input, output, and fault messages. The combination of messages defines the type of operation (one-way, request/response, solicit response, or notification). This differs from previous distributed technologies. For more information, please refer to the WSDL and XML Schema specifications (XML spec: `http://www.w3.org/TR/REC-xml/` and WSDL spec: `http://www.w3.org/TR/wsdl`).
- Web Services provide support for asynchronous as well as synchronous interactions.
- Web Services introduce the notion of endpoints and intermediaries. This allows new approaches to message processing.
- Web Services are stateless. They do not follow the object paradigm.

- Web Services utilize standard Internet protocols such as **HTTP (Hyper Text Transfer Protocol)**, **SMTP (Simple Mail Transfer Protocol)**, **FTP (File Transfer Protocol)**, and **MIME (Multipurpose Internet Mail Extensions)**. So, connectivity through standard Internet connections, even those secured with firewalls, is less problematic.

Web Services technology stack

In addition to several advantages, Web Services also have a couple of disadvantages. One of them is performance, which is not as good as that of distributed architectures that use binary protocols for communication. The other is that plain Web Services do not offer infrastructure and Quality of Service (QoS) features, such as security, transactions, and others, which have been provided by component models for several years. Web Services fill this important gap by introducing additional specifications:

- **WS-Security**: Addresses authentication and message-level security, and enables secure communication with Web Services.
- **WS-Coordination**: Defines a coordination framework for Web Services and is the foundation for WS-AtomicTransaction and WS-BusinessActivity.
- **Transactions specifications (WS-AtomicTransaction** and **WS-BusinessActivity**): Specify support for distributed transactions with Web Services. AtomicTransaction specifies short duration, ACID transactions, and BusinessActivity specifies longer-running business transactions, also called compensating transactions.
- **WS-ReliableMessaging**: Provides support for reliable communication and message delivery between Web Services over various transport protocols.
- **WS-Addressing**: Specifies message coordination and routing.
- **WS-Inspection**: Provides support for the dynamic introspection of web service descriptions.
- **WS-Policy**: Specifies how policies are declared and exchanged between collaborating Web Services.
- **WS-Eventing**: Defines an event model for asynchronous notification of interested parties for Web Services.

Because of their flexibility, interoperability, and other features, Web Services are regarded as the most appropriate technology for exposing the functionalities of applications as services and are therefore the most appropriate technology for realization of SOA. Because of their wide support by all major software vendors, Web Services provide the possibility to use the same technology to expose services implemented in a variety of different applications ranging from mainframe-based legacy applications to the modern multitier applications.

Enterprise Service Bus

While Web Services are an appropriate technology for SOA, some other aspects need to be considered, such as:

- In most enterprises, Web Services are not the only middleware solution used. Usually enterprises already have one or more middleware products, such as messaging systems and ORBs. Enterprises cannot afford to replace them overnight with Web Services. Therefore, there is a need to integrate different middleware products, and provide interoperability with Web Services.
- In order to provide connectivity between services, the use of SOAP in complex environments is not adequate. In such environments, we need ways to connect, mediate, manage, and control the services and particularly the communication between them.
- SOAP over HTTP might not be robust enough for heavy enterprise use. Enterprise information systems require dependable, robust, and secure service infrastructure.

The ESB is the software infrastructure, acting as an intermediary layer of middleware that addresses the above-mentioned requirements. An ESB adds flexibility to the communication between services, and simplifies the integration and reuse of services. An ESB makes it possible to connect services implemented in different technologies (such as EJBs, messaging systems, CORBA components, and legacy applications) in an easy way. An ESB can act as a mediator between different, often incompatible protocols and middleware products.

The ESB provides a robust, dependable, secure, and scalable communication infrastructure between services. It also provides control over the communication and control over the use of services, including:

- **Message interception capabilities**: This allows us to intercept requests to services and responses from services, and apply additional processing to them. In this manner, the ESB acts as an intermediary.
- **Routing capabilities**: This allows us to route the messages to different services based on their content, origin, or other attributes.
- **Transformation capabilities**: These allow us to transform messages before they are delivered to services. For XML-formatted messages, such transformations are usually done using **XSLT** (**Extensible Stylesheet Language Transformations**) or XQuery engines.
- **Control over the deployment, usage, and maintenance of services**: This allows logging, profiling, load balancing, performance tuning, charging for use of services, distributed deployment, on-the-fly reconfiguration, and so on.

- **Other important management features**: These include the definition of correlation between messages, definition of reliable communication paths, definition of security constraints related to messages and services, and so on.

ESB features

The ESB enables the communication and management of services, along with providing answers related to the usage of services in complex enterprise information systems. In such environments, support for the centralized, declarative, and well-coordinated management of services and their communication is required. Because of existing middleware, the integration of different middleware products and interoperability with other services is required.

The ESB is important because it represents the communication backbone for services. Using ESB for communication, we can get rid of point-to-point connections between services and processes. ESB also simplifies the transition between development, test, and production environments.

The most important features of ESB are service routing, transformation and enhancement, protocol transformation, service mapping, security, and Quality of Service.

- Message routing enables us to route messages to a specific service provider in a declarative manner based on the message content, user type, channel, or other rules.
- Message transformation enables us to transform the input and output messages. Usually this is related to XML transformation using XSLT.
- Message enhancement enables us to add data to the message or remove data, so that they conform to the requirements of the service provider and service consumer.
- Protocol transformation is the ability to automatically transform the protocol based on the service provider and service consumer preferences. For example, a service consumer might use SOAP, while the service uses JMS. Protocol transformation can also optimize performance and switch to an optimized protocol for collocated services.
- Service mapping enables us to map a service to a specific service implementation. This is usually an extension of WSDL bindings.

- Security enables us to secure services and the transportation layer used for the exchange of messages. For securing services, authentication and authorization are important; for securing the exchange of messages, encryption is usually applied.
- Quality of Service allows us to define specific parameters of service communication, such as reliability, bandwidth, availability, and so on. Quality of Service assurance is the baseline for the definition of **Service Level Agreements** (**SLAs**).

Currently, there are several products in the market that claim to provide ESB functionality. A good ESB should provide at least Quality of Service support at enterprise level, including reliability, fault-tolerance, and security. If provided by an ESB, services can depend on these features and do not need to implement them themselves. The ESB should also allow the configuration of any combination of these Quality of Service features and provide flexibility.

An ESB should provide support for a variety of technologies on which services are implemented. In addition to Web Services, an ESB should provide connectors for a broad range of technologies, such as Java EE and .NET components, messaging middleware, legacy applications, and TP monitors. The ESB needs to provide flexibility to bind any combination of services without technological constraints. It should also support a combination of different interaction models, such as queuing, routing, and so on, without changing the services or requiring code writing.

An ESB should make services broadly available. This means that it should be easy to find, connect, and use a service irrespective of the technology it is implemented in. With a broad availability of services, an ESB can increase reuse and can make the composition of services easier. Finally, an ESB should provide management capabilities, such as message routing, interaction, and transformation, which we have already described.

An ESB that provides these features becomes an essential part of the SOA. It provides several benefits, including increased flexibility, reduced deployment, development, and maintenance costs, along with increased reliability and manageability.

The following figure shows the relation between BPEL, ESB, and services:

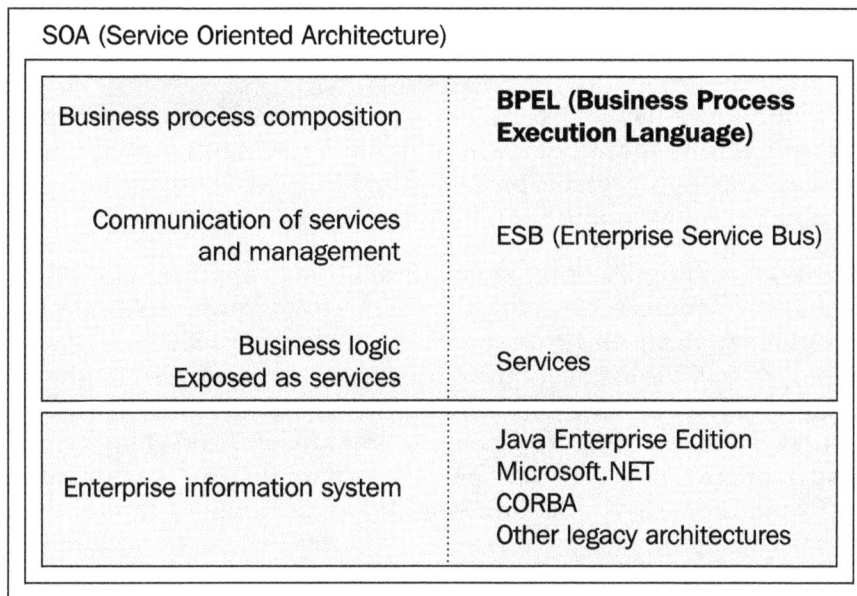

SOA (Service Oriented Architecture)

Business process composition	**BPEL (Business Process Execution Language)**
Communication of services and management	ESB (Enterprise Service Bus)
Business logic Exposed as services	Services
Enterprise information system	Java Enterprise Edition Microsoft.NET CORBA Other legacy architectures

Registry and repository

We have already seen that SOA consists of services and processes. The more applications that we implement following SOA concepts, the more services we will have. Managing services becomes a challenging task. This includes aspects such as:

- How many services do we have?
- Does a service with a specific functionality already exist?
- Where is the service deployed?
- Which versions of the service exist?
- Who are the consumers (clients) of a specific service?
- What is the interface definition (WSDL) of a service?

Registries and repositories help to answer these and similar questions. They have become an essential part of each SOA architecture. Registries and repositories are used to register services in a central location. Once registered, we can search and locate appropriate services. The more metadata about a service we include, the better search capabilities a registry and repository can provide.

A rule of thumb is that once we have more than 50 services we will desperately start needing the registry and repository. However, sometimes it might be wise to introduce it from the beginning because once developers get used to a certain development process, it will be very difficult to change their behavior.

In addition to the above-mentioned questions, registries and repositories play an important role in service reuse. Somewhat simplifying things, reuse on a service level means that we compose executable processes (in BPEL) and reuse as many services as possible instead of developing them from scratch.

Registries and repositories also play an important role in the deployment process. In professional development it is usual to have three environments—development, test, and production. When an application is ready for production use, this requires that it is deployed into the production environment. The controlled deployment of processes requires that a process starts to use a production version of services instead of development or test versions. If links to services are hard coded into the BPEL processes, such migrations can be very painful, as it might (in a worst-case scenario) require the manual change of URL addresses. When deploying a service we might want to know which processes use this service because we might want to retest those processes.

The understanding of the role of registries and repositories in SOA has changed considerably over the years. A few years ago, we believed that a relatively simple registry, UDDI, would cover all the needs. Today, we have identified that a registry alone is not powerful enough for SOA because in many cases it makes sense to store service metadata as well (WSDL interfaces, XSD schemas, and so on).Therefore, today we talk about registries and repositories.

A powerful registry and repository should have the following features:

- Classification capabilities to categorize and classify services and processes based on one or more classification schemas. This simplifies queries and enables easier locations for the most appropriate services for reuse.
- Governance functions that should enable the definition of proprietary service/process lifecycles, together with the conditions to go from one stage of the lifecycle to another. Stage transitions can trigger automatic actions, such as validators.
- Access control that defines *who* can do *which* operations on the registry and repository, and on the registered services/processes. Such access control could be based on **XACML (eXtensible Access Control Markup Language**).
- User, programming, and administration interfaces.

Registries and repositories also play an important role in SOA governance.

Human task support and identity management

Business processes often involve human interaction. SOA, therefore, has to provide support for human tasks. Human tasks are sometimes called user interactions. Human tasks in business processes can be simple, such as approving certain tasks or decisions, or complex, such as delegation, renewal, escalation, nomination, or chained execution. Task approval is the simplest, and probably the most common, human task. If the situation is more complex, a business process might require several users to make approvals, either in sequence or in parallel. In sequential scenarios, the next user often wants to see the decision made by the previous user. Sometimes, (particularly in parallel human tasks) users are not allowed to see the decisions taken by other users. This improves the decision potential. Sometimes one user doesn't even know which other users are involved, or whether any other users are involved at all.

A common scenario for involving more than one user is escalation. Escalation is typically used in situations where an activity doesn't fulfill a time constraint. In such a case, a notification is sent to one or more users. Escalations can be chained, going first to the first-line employees and advancing to senior staff if the activity is not fulfilled.

Sometimes it's difficult or impossible to define in advance which user should perform an interaction. In this case, a supervisor might manually nominate the task to other employees; the nomination can also be made by a group of users or by a decision-support system.

In other scenarios, a business process may require a single user to perform several steps that can be defined in advance or during the execution of the process instance. Even more-complex processes might require that one workflow is continued with another workflow.

Human tasks can include data entries or process management issues, such as process initiation, suspension, and exception management. This is particularly true for long-running business processes, where, for example, user exception handling can prevent costly process termination and related compensation for those activities that have already been successfully completed.

As a best practice for human tasks, it's usually not wise to associate human tasks directly to specific users. It's better to connect tasks to roles and then associate those roles with individual users. This gives business processes greater flexibility, allowing any user with a certain role to interact with the process and enabling changes to users and roles to be made dynamically. To be able to do this, we need to have an identity management system, where users, roles, and groups are managed. This can be a simple LDAP or a more sophisticated system.

To interleave human tasks with BPEL processes we can use a workflow service, which interacts with BPEL processes using standard WSDL interfaces, as any other service. This way, the BPEL process can assign user tasks and wait for responses by invoking the workflow service using the same syntax as for any other service. The BPEL process can also perform more complex operations such as updating, completing, renewing, routing, and escalating tasks.

To standardize the explicit inclusion of human tasks in BPEL processes the BPEL4People (WS-BPEL Extension for People) specification has been proposed. BPEL4People introduces people activities and people links into BPEL. People activity is a new BPEL activity used to define user interactions, in other words, tasks that a user has to perform. For each people activity, the BPEL server must create work items and distribute them to users who are eligible to execute them. To specify human tasks the WS-Human Task specification has been proposed.

Process Monitoring or Business Activity Monitoring

One of the key elements for process control is Process Monitoring or Business Activity Monitoring (BAM). The key objective of BAM is to provide a complete insight into business process execution. BAM allows for the monitoring of KPIs, such as total execution time, average execution time, the execution time of certain activities, and so on. This allows us to better understand how the business processes perform.

Business Activity Monitoring is the real-time observation of key performance indicators.

The most important component of BAM is time. Time is crucial because BAM shows the actual near real-time information on process execution. This way, a company can react quickly and efficiently to changes reflected through process execution.

BAM solutions can provide other useful information. They can show us how many process instances are active at a specific time, how long on average it takes to complete a process, which users (employees) have started how many process instances, and so on.

Note that BAM is not related to automatic activities (those implemented by services) only. It can be used with human activities as well. In such a case, we can use BAM to observe the productivity of employees.

BAM is not only a system that displays interesting information about processes, but also consolidates data gathered from different, often independent sources. Connecting these data with past data enables BAM to identify critical situations in process execution or even automatically or semi-automatically solve some frequent critical problems. The ultimate goal of each BAM user is to optimize the process execution, to improve the process efficiency, and to sense important events and react.

The BAM user interface (dashboard) should be simple and present information and data in an easy and understandable way. It should hide all the complexity behind the scenes. Usually a typical BAM user interface uses graphical elements, graphs, and colors to present the data. The next screenshot shows an example of a BAM user interface:

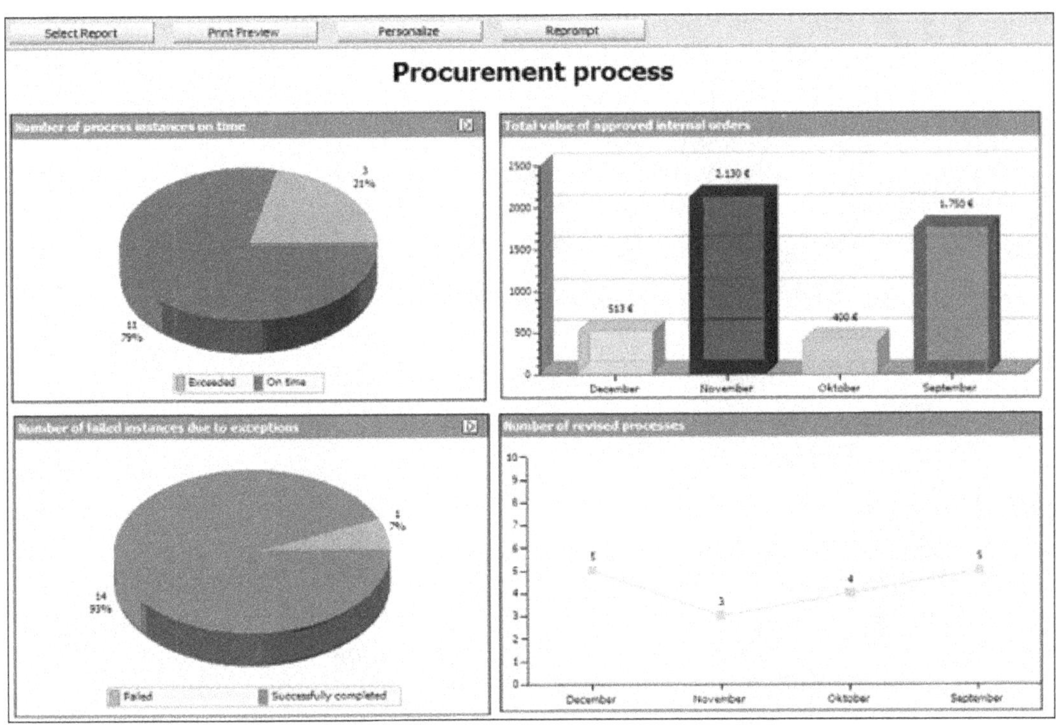

In the previous screenshot, we can see the BAM dashboard showing different important information for decision makers. In addition to the dashboard, another important part of the BAM is the decision-support module. A module such as this can use decision methods, business intelligence, or simulations for support and can help decision makers take the right decision at the right time, which can improve business efficiency.

Business Rules Management Systems (BRMS) or Rule Engine

Business rules are part of almost every business application. Experiences have shown that business rules change, sometimes very often. Today, business rules are usually coded into different applications and are tightly coupled with the implementation of an application system. Changing business rules is therefore often very difficult and requires modifications to applications. Each modification requires that the developer change the code. After that, testing and deployment has to be done.

The same business rules are often implemented in several applications. Therefore, if a rule changes, the major challenge becomes to identify which applications this business rule is coded into and to modify each application where such a rule has been used.

Business rules are also very common in business processes. **Business Rules Management Systems (BRMS)** or Rule Engines are meant to provide a central location for storing, executing, and managing business rules. Instead of hard-coding business rules into the executable code (whether BPEL, Java, C#, and so on), we place business rules into the BRMS, where:

- Business rules can be reused from different processes, services, and applications
- User-friendly interfaces exist, which enable us to change and modify business rules

Adapters

Adapters in SOA are meant to simplify the integration with external systems, such as ERP, CRM, SCM, and others. Without adapters we would need to manually expose functionality out of such systems, for example by developing corresponding Web Services. As such systems usually have rich functionalities, it would require a considerable amount of time and effort to develop the integration interfaces and services. Additionally, when such a system is upgraded, we would need to modify the integration services.

Adapters automate this procedure and provide tools to integrate with such systems in an easy way. Examples of adapters are adapters for SAP, Oracle, PeopleSoft, Salesforce, or some other popular system. Adapters are also useful for accessing database data directly. Such adapters automate the development of data services. Examples include adapters for Oracle, DB2, SQL Server, and so on.

Adapters differ in the level of sophistication. The simplest adapters are just API wrappers that expose the interfaces of the external systems as a service (usually as a web service). More sophisticated adapters can have smart fault handling mechanisms, can capture events on both sides, allow synchronous and asynchronous interactions, take care of load balancing, performance, scalability, security, and so on.

When deploying an SOA platform, it makes sense to check whether it provides adapters for the systems that we have deployed in our information system. With adapters, accessing the functionality of such systems will most likely be much simpler than without.

Service Component Architecture

So far we have seen that SOA applications are composite applications that consist of several components, such as services, BPEL processes, ESB mediation, rules, adapters, and so on. All these components have to work together and support one or more composite applications.

Service Component Architecture (**SCA**) defines a programming model for composite SOA applications. SCA is based on the idea of service composition (orchestration). SCA provides a model for the composition of services and for the creation of service components, including the reuse of existing applications within SCA composites.

The basic building blocks of SCA are *components*. Every SCA application is built from one or more components. Components can be implemented in a programming language, such as Java, C++, C, or they can be implemented as BPEL processes. SCA provides a generalized definition of a component.

Components offer their business functions for use by other components as services. Implementations may depend on services provided by other components. Such dependencies are called *references*. Implementations can have *properties* through which the business function can be influenced. The component configures the implementation by providing values for the properties and by *wiring* the references to services provided by other components. An SCA component is represented as follows:

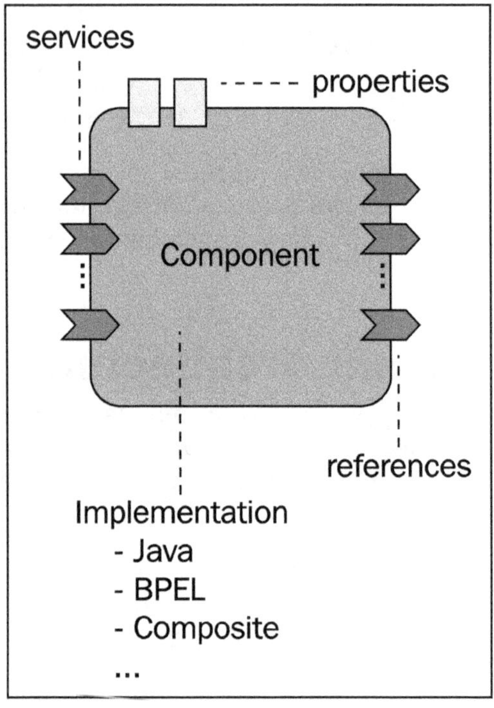

Service components are assembled into applications, called *composites*. Composites can contain components, services, references, properties, and wiring. Composites themselves can also be used as components and can provide services. They can depend on references and expose properties.

Composites can be used within other composites. This allows a hierarchical construction of composite business applications, where high-level services are implemented by sets of lower-level services. The following example shows an SCA composite:

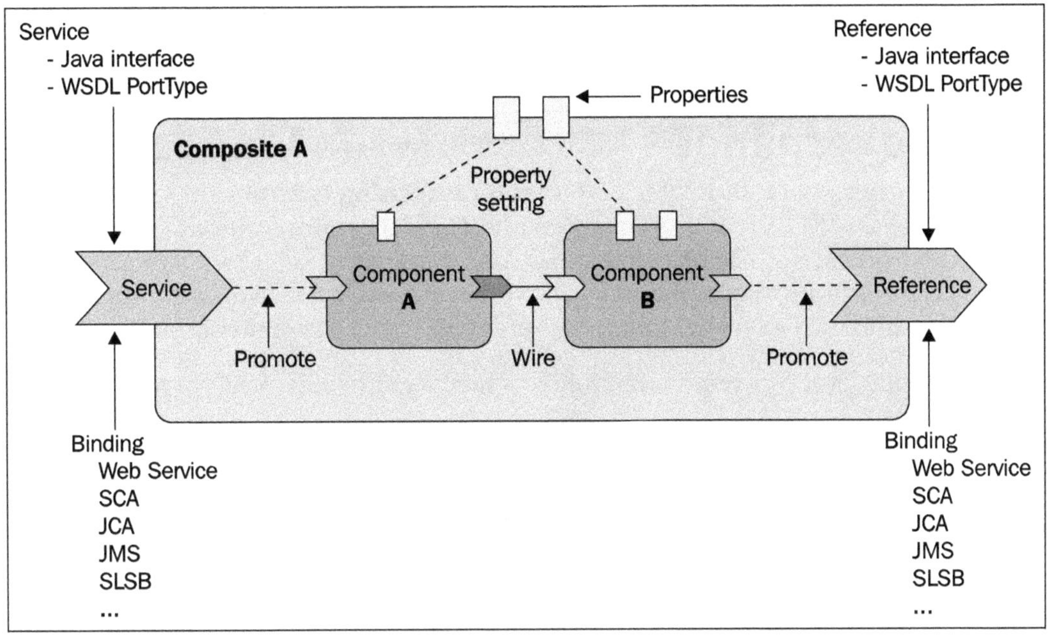

Composites are deployed within an *SCA Domain*. An SCA Domain represents an area of business functionality with the related services. The SCA Domain diagram is shown in the next figure:

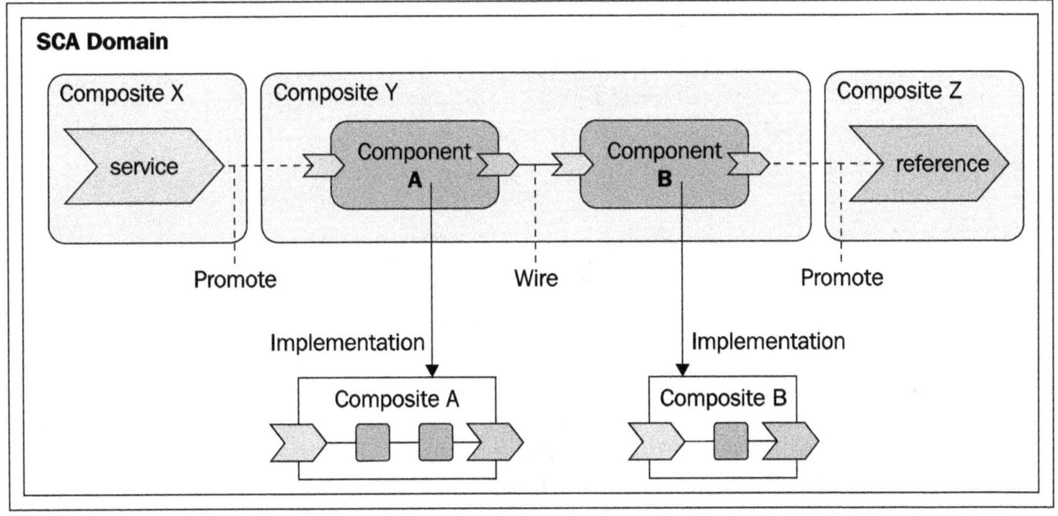

We will use the SCA and composites in *Chapter 4*, when we start to develop composite applications.

SOA governance

SOA governance is a set of related activities for exercising control over services and processes in SOA. SOA is a distributed architecture where applications consist of services and processes. The objective of SOA governance is assurance that all services and processes within an information system will adhere to the overall architecture. SOA governance has to address many different aspects, among them:

- Services and processes must follow specific guidelines, best practices, and patterns
- Services should not be duplicated
- Services are reused and reusable
- The portfolio of services is managed, including the development of new services and modifications of existing services
- Versioning of services and processes is defined
- Service lifecycle is defined
- Deployment practices are defined
- Consistency of services is monitored
- Quality of Services is ensured

SOA governance is an essential element of a successful SOA implementation. Without governance, SOA will most likely fail to deliver its value to the stakeholders. To learn more about SOA governance, have a look at *SOA Governance* by Todd Biske, Packt Publishing.

Understanding BPEL

The general adoption of business process automation solutions requires a standard foundation and a specialized language for composing services into business processes that provide the ability to express business processes in a standardized way, using a commonly accepted language. BPEL is such a language and is quickly becoming the dominant standard. The main goal of BPEL is to standardize the process of automation between Web Services.

With BPEL we can define business processes that make use of services and business processes that externalize their functionality as services.

Within enterprises, BPEL is used to standardize enterprise application integration and extend the integration to previously isolated systems. Between enterprises, BPEL enables easier and more effective integration with business partners. BPEL stimulates enterprises to further define their business processes, which in turn leads to business process optimization, re-engineering, and the selection of the most appropriate processes, thus further optimizing the organization. Definitions of business processes described in BPEL do not influence existing systems. BPEL is the key technology in environments where functionalities already are, or will be, exposed via Web Services. With increases in the use of web service technology, the importance of BPEL will rise further.

IBM, BEA, and Microsoft developed the first version of BPEL in August 2002. Since then SAP and Siebel have joined in, which has resulted in several modifications and improvements and the adoption of version 1.1 in March 2003. In April 2003, BPEL was submitted to **OASIS** (**Organization for the Advancement of Structured Information Standards**) for standardization purposes, where the **WSBPEL TC** (**Web Services Business Process Execution Language Technical Committee**) has been formed. Many vendors have joined the WSBPEL TC (`http://www.oasis-open.org/committees/tc_home.php?wg_abbrev=wsbpel`) since. This has led to even broader acceptance in industry. In April 2007, BPEL version 2.0 was approved by OASIS after quite a long preparation period.

BPEL represents a convergence of two early workflow languages—**WSFL** (**Web Services Flow Language**) and **XLANG**. WSFL was designed by IBM and is based on the concept of directed graphs. XLANG was designed by Microsoft and is a block-structured language. BPEL combines both approaches and provides a rich vocabulary for the description of business processes.

In this book, we will use BPEL version 2.0.

BPEL uses an XML-based vocabulary to specify and describe business processes. BPEL version 2.0 utilizes the WSDL 1.1, XML Schema 1.0, XPath 1.0, and XSLT 1.0 specifications. Familiarity with them is helpful for learning BPEL.

BPEL features

With BPEL we can define simple and complex business processes. To a certain extent, BPEL is similar to traditional programming languages. It offers constructs, such as loops, branches, variables, assignments, and so on that allow us to define business processes in an algorithmic way. BPEL is a specialized language focused on the definition of business processes. It is an execution language for business processes, not a modeling language. Therefore, on one hand it offers constructs, which make the definition of processes relatively simple and on the other hand, it is less complex than traditional programming languages, which simplifies learning.

The most important BPEL constructs are related to the invocation of services. BPEL makes it easy to invoke operations of services either synchronously or asynchronously. We can invoke operations either in sequence or in parallel. We can also wait for callbacks. BPEL provides a rich vocabulary for fault handling, which is very important, as robust business processes need to react to failures in a smart way. BPEL also provides support for long-running process and compensation, which allows undoing partial work done by a process that has not finished successfully. Listed below are the most important features that BPEL provides. With BPEL we can:

- Describe the logic of business processes through composition of services
- Compose larger business processes out of smaller processes and services
- Handle synchronous and asynchronous (often long-running) operation invocations on services, and manage callbacks that occur at later times
- Invoke service operations in sequence or parallel
- Selectively compensate completed activities in case of failures
- Maintain multiple long-running transactional activities, which are also interruptible
- Resume interrupted or failed activities to minimize work to be redone
- Route incoming messages to the appropriate processes and activities
- Correlate requests within and across business processes
- Schedule activities based on the execution time and define their order of execution
- Execute activities in parallel and define how parallel flows merge based on synchronization conditions
- Structure business processes into several scopes
- Handle message-related and time-related events

Orchestration and choreography

Depending on the requirements, the composition of services can address private or public processes, for which the following two terms are used:

- Orchestration
- Choreography

In **orchestration**, a central process takes control over the involved services and coordinates the execution of different operations on the services involved in the operation. This is done as per the requirements of the orchestration. The involved services do not know (and do not need to know) that they are involved in a composition and that they are a part of a higher business process. Only the central coordinator of the orchestration knows this, so the orchestration is centralized with explicit definitions of operations and the order of invocation of services. Orchestration is usually used in private business processes and is schematically shown as follows:

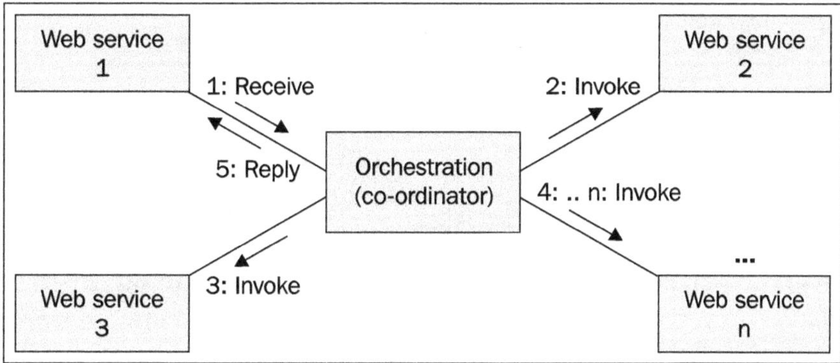

Choreography, on the other hand, does not rely on a central coordinator. Rather, each service involved in the choreography knows exactly when to execute its operations and whom to interact with. Choreography is a collaborative effort focused on the exchange of messages in public business processes. All participants of the choreography need to be aware of the business process, operations to execute, messages to exchange, and the timing of message exchanges. Choreography in services composition is as shown in the following figure:

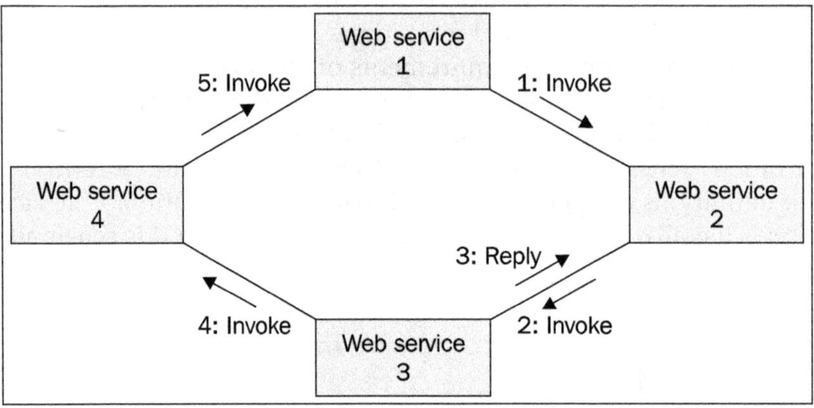

From the perspective of composing services to execute business processes, orchestration has an advantage over choreography. Orchestration is a more flexible paradigm, although the line between orchestration and choreography is vanishing. Orchestration has the following advantages:

- We know exactly who is responsible for the execution of the whole business process
- We can incorporate services, even those that are not aware that they are a part of a business process
- We can also provide alternative scenarios when faults occur

BPEL provides support for orchestration and choreography through executable and abstract business processes.

Executable and abstract processes

With BPEL, we can describe business processes in two distinct ways:

- We can specify the exact details of business processes. Such processes are called **executable business processes** and follow the orchestration paradigm. They can be executed by an orchestration engine.
- We can specify the public message exchange between parties only. Such processes are called **abstract business processes**. They do not include the internal details of process flows and are not executable. They follow the choreography paradigm.

Executable business processes are processes that comprise a set of existing services and specify the exact algorithm of activities and input and output messages. Such processes are executable by BPEL engines. Executable processes are important because they are the direct answer to the problem of business process automation through IT that we have discussed earlier in this chapter. With BPEL executable processes, we are able to specify the exact algorithm of service composition in a relatively simple and straightforward way, and execute it on a BPEL-compliant engine. Executable processes fill the gap between the business process specifications and the code responsible for their execution.

When we define an executable business process in BPEL, we actually define a new web service that is a composition of existing services. The interface of the new BPEL composite web service uses a set of port types, through which it provides operations like any other web service. To invoke an executable business process, we have to invoke the resulting composite web service. You can see that executable business processes are the most important way of using BPEL. In the majority of cases, BPEL is used to specify executable processes.

Abstract business processes, on the other hand, are not executable. They specify public message exchange between parties only—the externally observable aspects of process behavior. The description of the externally observable behavior of a business process may be related to a single service, or a set of services. It might also describe the behavior of a participant in a business process. Abstract processes will usually be defined for two scenarios:

- To describe the behavior of a service without knowing exactly in which business process it will take part
- To define collaboration protocols among multiple parties and precisely describe the external behavior of each party

Abstract processes are rarely used. The most common scenario is to use them as a template to define executable processes. Abstract processes can be used to replace sets of rules usually expressed in natural language, which are often ambiguous. In this book, we will first focus on executable processes and come back to abstract processes in *Chapter 3*.

Relation of BPEL to other languages

BPEL is not the only language for business process execution. Before we start discussing the technical aspects of BPEL, let us overview the relation of BPEL to other languages. Recently, several orchestration and choreography languages have been proposed. The most important orchestration languages include:

- **XLANG and the new version XLANG/s** from Microsoft
- **WSFL** (**Web Services Flow Language**) from IBM
- **BPML** (**Business Process Modeling Language**) from BPMI.org, the Business Process Management Initiative
- **BPSS** (**Business Process Specification Schema**), part of the ebXML framework
- **YAWL** (**Yet Another Workflow Language**), an open source workflow language

The most important choreography languages include:

- **WSCL** (**Web Services Conversation Language**) from HP, submitted to W3C
- **WSCI** (**Web Services Choreography Interface**), co-developed by Sun, SAP, BEA, and Intalio and submitted to W3C
- **WS-CDL** (**Web Services Choreography Description Language**), at the time of writing a W3C Candidate Recommendation

In addition to orchestration and choreography languages, which have primarily been designed to provide machine executable representations of business processes, we also have to mention the business process modeling notations. These are used to define business process models and are essential for **BPM** (**Business Process Management**). The most popular and well-known is the BPMN (Business Process Modeling Notation). BPMN is becoming an important part of SOA.

The following figure shows a timeline of the mentioned languages, as they have been developed:

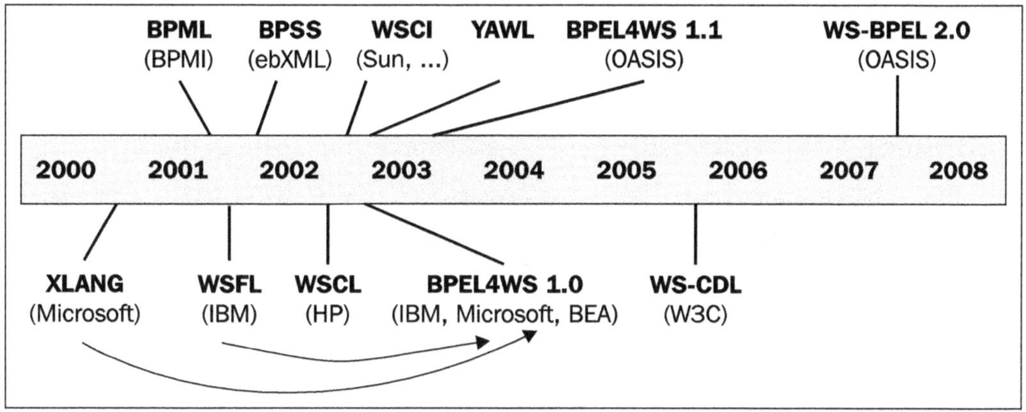

We have already mentioned that BPEL represents a convergence of XLANG and WSFL and it shares and further develops the concepts of those languages. In the following sections we will briefly describe these languages.

XLANG

XLANG has been one of the early orchestration languages. It has been developed with the objective of achieving clear separation between processes and implementations. It is a Microsoft proprietary language and not fully documented. It has been used in Microsoft BizTalk. XLANG and its successor XLANG/s can be viewed as messaging languages with some of the expression capabilities of C#. However, code is not portable between XLANG/s and C#.

XLANG/s specifies high-level constructs that are used to define and execute business processes. The semantics embodied in XLANG/s are a reflection of those defined in BPEL. Although XLANG is thought of as a predecessor of BPEL, Microsoft continues to use XLANG/s in their BizTalk Server. Instead of moving to BPEL in BizTalk, Microsoft provides a conversion between XLANG/s and BPEL.

WSFL

WSFL is also one of the early XML-based orchestration languages. It has been developed by IBM to be a part of the Web Services technology stack. WSFL supports two types of service compositions. First is the flow model, which specifies the exact interactions between services (a process). Such a flow model is executable. The second type is the global model, which specifies the overall interaction of services and is abstract. This is very similar to BPEL-executable and abstract processes.

As we have already mentioned, WSFL has, together with XLANG, provided a basis for BPEL. Unlike Microsoft, IBM has moved to BPEL as their main language for service composition and provides full support for BPEL in their various products, such as in IBM WebSphere Process Server.

BPML

BPML has been developed by BPMI.org (Business Process Management Initiative). Intalio has played an important role, and has been the initiator of BPML. BPML is a meta-language for modeling business processes and provides an abstract execution model for describing collaborations and transactions. It defines a formal model for expressing abstract and executable processes, and supports:

- Data management
- Conformity
- Exception handling
- Operation semantics

BPML can describe a process in a specific language, defined on top of the extensible BPML scheme. Business processes are defined as groups of flows (control flows, data flows, and event flows). Formatting features, security rules, and transactional contexts can also be defined. BPML offers support for synchronous and asynchronous distributed transactions and can be used for the process components of existing applications.

Comparing BPML to BPEL shows that both share similar roots in Web Services and leverage other Web Services specifications, particularly WS-Security, WS-Coordination, and WS-Transactions. BPML, however, supports modeling more complex business processes through its support for advanced semantics such as nested processes and complex compensated transactions. BPML can therefore be regarded as a superset of BPEL. The extensions of BPEL with business rules, task management, human interactions, and so on are defined in BPXL (Business Process eXtension Layers).

The fact that both BPEL and BPML share the same idioms and have similar syntax has resulted in BPML being discontinued in favor of BPEL. BPEL has over the years gained much broader support by software vendors than BPML.

ebXML BPSS

Electronic Business using eXtensible Markup Language (ebXML) is a framework that provides a set of technologies, BPSS being one of them. ebXML has been developed under the initiative of OASIS and UN/CEFACT and consists of the following technologies:

- **Messaging**: Uses SOAP with attachments for communication between partners.
- **Registry and repository**: Similar to UDDI registry, but offers additional functionality through the repository.
- **Core components**: Used for construction of business documents.
- **CPP (Collaboration Protocol Profile)**: Used to express a partner profile.
- **CPA (Collaboration Protocol Agreement)**: Used to express an agreement between partners.
- **BPSS**: Used for the specification of business processes.

BPSS covers the same domain as BPEL. The BPSS approach to process specification follows the choreography pattern and is therefore comparable to abstract BPEL processes. In addition to specifying the process logic, BPSS also specifies the communication protocol details.

BPSS is designed around the concept of business transactions, which is, however, not fully conformant with the Web Services Transactions specifications. A BPSS business transaction is used to describe the message exchange between two abstract roles—the sender and the responder. Each message consists of an XML document and optional attachments, which can be XML or binary. For each responding message, we specify whether it is a positive or negative message. Each message is associated with a business transaction protocol. Collaboration in BPSS can be bilateral or multi-party and is described by the business transaction protocol.

We can see that BPSS is not a direct alternative to BPEL and is used in environments where ebXML is applied. For more information on ebXML, refer to the following books:

- *ebXML: Concepts and Application* by Brian Gibb and Suresh Damodaran, John Wiley & Sons
- *ebXML: The New Global Standard for Doing Business over the Internet* by Alan Kotok and David RR Webber, SAMS

- *ebXML Simplified: A Guide to the New Standard for Global E-Commerce* by Eric Chiu, John Wiley & Sons

YAWL

YAWL has been developed by Eindhoven University of Technology and Queensland University of Technology. Subsequently, several companies have contributed to the language. The objective of YAWL has been to develop a language that would support workflow patterns with a formal specification. YAWL is based on Petri nets. The formal semantics of YAWL enables the static analysis of the language, which is supported by a tool. The language itself is supported by software that is developed as open source under an LGPL. It includes the execution engine, graphical editor, and an application for human tasks.

Similar to BPEL, YAWL is an executable language for processes (workflows). The main advantage of YAWL is its support for workflow patterns. The major difference is how both languages have been developed. BPEL has been driven by a standardization committee under OASIS and has gained large industry support. Today, most major vendors provide support for BPEL. YAWL on the other hand, has only one implementation. More on YAWL can be found on `http://www.yawl-system.com/`.

WSCL

WSCL has been developed by HP. In contrast to previously mentioned languages, WSCL has focused on the choreography aspect rather than on the orchestration. It has been designed to describe business-level conversations or public processes, supported by corresponding services. WSCL specifies the XML documents being exchanged, and the allowed sequencing of these document exchanges. WSCL is not a direct alternative to BPEL, as it does not support executable process orchestrations, as BPEL does. It is somehow similar to BPEL abstract processes.

HP has submitted WSCL to W3C, where it has become a W3C Note in 2002. Since then it has not gained much support from software vendors, therefore WSCL does not play an important role in SOA. The WSCL specification is accessible at `http://www.w3.org/TR/wscl10/`.

WSCI

WSCI version 1.0 has been developed by Sun, BEA, SAP, and Intalio. WSCI is a choreography language for describing the flow of messages exchanged by Web Services in the context of a process. It allows us to describe the observable behavior of a web service in a message exchange. WSCI also describes the collective message exchange among interacting Web Services, providing a global and message-oriented view of a process involving multiple Web Services.

In WSCI, message exchange is described from the viewpoint of each web service. Each exchange can be qualified by message correlations, transaction descriptions, and location capabilities. WSCI therefore describes the observable behavior of Web Services. However, WSCI does not address the definition of the processes driving the message exchange. It also does not address the definition of the internal behavior of each web service.

Since WSCI follows the choreography pattern and does not address defining executable business processes, it compares directly only to BPEL abstract processes. WSCI has a cleaner interface, which makes it a little easier to learn than BPEL. The WSCI specification has also been submitted to W3C, which has published it as a W3C Note. Further, W3C has formed a WS-Choreography working group, which will address the choreography of Web Services, but has only released the requirements specification so far.

WSCI has not gained industry support comparable to BPEL. The industry consensus seems to support BPEL. The WSCI specification is accessible at `http://www.w3.org/TR/wsci/`.

WS-CDL

WS-CDL is a language for specifying the choreography of collaborating services. It targets the composition of interoperable collaborations between services. With WS-CDL we can specify the peer-to-peer collaboration of Web Services through the definition of their observable behavior. We can define sets of rules that define how, and in what order, different services should act together. Such specification provides a flexible systemic view of the process.

WS-CDL is positioned as a complementary language to BPEL (and other business process languages). While BPEL focuses on the behavior specification of a specific business partner, WS-CDL focuses on the description of message interchanges between business partners. WS-CDL provides the global model needed by BPEL processes to ensure that the behavior of endpoints is consistent across all cooperating services.

A business partner can use the WS-CDL choreography specification to verify if their internal processes have their outside behavior defined in a way that will allow them to participate in choreography. WS-CDL choreography specifications can be used to generate public interfaces, for example, specified using BPEL abstract processes. WS-CDL specifications are also useful at runtime to verify the execution of message exchange between business partners.

As WS-CDL is a complementary language to BPEL we cannot make a direct comparison. However, WS-CDL differs considerably from BPEL. With WS-CDL we define the message flows exchanged by all partners, while with BPEL we focus on message flow and the behavior of a specific partner—that is, on the internal behavior of a business process. The WS-CDL description of message flows is done from a general perspective, while BPEL specifies message exchange from the point of view of a specific partner. A BPEL process specifies activities that are executed. WS-CDL specifies reactive rules, which are used by all participants of a collaboration.

At the time of writing, WS-CDL has been a W3C Candidate Recommendation, dated 9 November 2005. Since then WS-CDL has not gained much industry support, as no major vendor supports it. At the time of writing, only two small vendors provided tools. The WS-CDL specification is accessible at `http://www.w3.org/TR/ws-cdl-10/`.

BPMN

BPMN is a graphical notation for specifying business processes. It is the most comprehensive notation for process modeling so far. BPMN has initially been developed by BPMI. In 2005, BPMI merged with **OMG (Object Management Group)**. The current version of BPMN is 1.2. BPMN version 2.0 is currently a work in progress.

We use BPMN to draw business process diagrams. Such diagrams present the activities and tasks of a process and their relations. The diagram uses flowchart concepts to represent the logic of business processes.

BPMN is a graphical-visual language and uses a set of graphical elements. Activities are represented as rectangles and decisions are diamonds. BPMN successfully joins the simplicity of the diagrams with the expressive power, which allows BPMN to be used for complex processes and specification of details.

To model the diagrams, BPMN defines four categories of elements:

- Flow objects, which are activities, events, and gateways. Activities can be tasks or subprocesses. Events can be triggers or results. Three types of events are supported—start, intermediate, and end. Gateways control the divergence of sequential flows into concurrent flows and their convergence back to sequential flow.
- Connecting objects are used to connect together flow objects. Connectors are sequence flows, message flows, and associations.
- Swim lanes are used to organize activities into visual categories in order to illustrate different responsibilities or functional capabilities. Pools and lanes can be used for swim lanes.
- Artifacts are used to add specific context to the business processes that are modeled. Data objects are used to show how data is produced or required by the process. Groups are used to group together similar activities or other elements. Annotations are used to add text information to the diagram. We can also define custom artifacts.

BPMN can be used to model parts of processes or whole processes. Processes can be modeled at different levels of fidelity. BPMN is equally suitable for internal (private) business processes and for public (collaborative) business-to-business processes.

The most important goals when designing BPMN have been:

- To develop a notation that will be useful and understandable at all levels of BPM. In business process modeling, different people are involved, from business users, business analysts, process owners, to the technical architects and developers. The goal of BPMN has been to provide a graphical that, which is simple to understand, but powerful enough to model business processes into the required details.
- The semantic gap between the business process models and the information technology (application software) has been quite large with existing technologies. There has been no clear definition of how one relates to the other. The goal of BPMN has been to enable automatic transformation into the executable code—into BPEL and vice-versa. Therefore, BPMN has been designed specifically to provide such transformation.

Particularly because of the ability to automatically transform BPMN process models in executable BPEL processes, BPMN today plays an important role in SOA development. Modeling of a business process using BPMN is usually the first step. After the model is complete, such a process is transformed into BPEL to be executed on a process server. Today several tools for major vendors such as Oracle and IBM provide such automatic transformation, usually in both directions, which enables round-tripping between model (BPMN) and executable process representation (BPEL).

For more information on BPMN, refer to the following:

- *Business Process Driven SOA using BPMN and BPEL* by Matjaz B. Juric and Kapil Pant, Packt Publishing
- *BPMN Specification*, `http://www.bpmn.org/`

BPEL servers overview

BPEL servers provide a runtime environment for executing BPEL business processes. Today BPEL servers are usually part of the SOA platform, which in addition to the BPEL server includes other elements of a complete SOA environment—application server, ESB, registry and repository, human tasks support, process monitoring, BRMS (Rule Engine), and adapters. Often a development environment is included and sometimes a process modeling tool is also available. Most advanced SOA platforms support the automatic translation of business models into executable BPEL processes.

Most SOA platforms have been developed on top of modern software platforms, particularly Java Enterprise Edition and Microsoft .NET. BPEL servers leverage Java Enterprise Edition or .NET application server environments, where they can make use of the services provided by application servers, such as security, transactions, scalability, integration with databases, components such as **EJBs** (**Enterprise Java Beans**) and **COM+** (**Component Object Model**), messaging systems such as **JMS** (**Java Message Service**) or **MSMQ** (**Microsoft Message Queue**), and so on.

The most important commercial SOA platforms with BPEL servers are listed below:

- Oracle SOA Suite (BPEL Process Manager) (`http://www.oracle.com/technologies/soa/soa-suite.html`)
- Oracle Sun Java Composite Application Platform Suite (`http://developers.sun.com/javacaps/`)
- IBM WebSphere (WebSphere Process Server) (`http://www.ibm.com/software/solutions/soa/`)

- TIBCO ActiveMatrix (ActiveMatrix BusinessWorks) (`http://www.tibco.com/products/soa/default.jsp`)
- InterSystems Ensemble (`http://www.intersystems.com/ensemble/index.html`)
- Fujitsu Interstage (Business Process Manager) (`http://www.fujitsu.com/global/services/software/interstage/`)
- Hitachi uCosminexus Service Platform (`http://www.hitachi.co.jp/Prod/comp/soft1/global/prod/cosminexus/sol/sp/sp_view.html`)
- Software AG webMethods (`http://www.softwareag.com/Corporate/products/wm/default.asp`)
- Intalio BPM (`http://www.intalio.com/products/bpm/`)
- Fiorano SOA Platform (`http://www.fiorano.com/products/fsoa/products_fioranosoa.php`)
- Active Endpoints ActiveVOS (`http://www.activevos.com/`)
- OpenLink Virtuoso Universal Server (`http://virtuoso.openlinksw.com/`)
- Parasoft BPEL Maestro (`http://www.parasoft.com/jsp/products/home.jsp?product=BPEL`)
- PolarLake Integration Suite (`http://www.polarlake.com/`)

Microsoft also provides an SOA platform, although Microsoft does not use the acronym SOA as often as the other suppliers. Microsoft's SOA is built around Windows Workflow Foundation, Windows Communication Foundation, and Microsoft BizTalk (process server). In contrast to most of the other vendors, Microsoft does not support BPEL natively (yet). Microsoft BizTalk, at the time of writing, still uses XLANG/s, the Microsoft proprietary orchestration language. However, it allows for the import and export of BPEL.

An important supporter of SOA is SAP. SAP Enterprise Service-Oriented Architecture (Enterprise SOA) has been defined by SAP as "an open architecture for adaptive business solutions". Enterprise SOA is enabled by the SAP NetWeaver platform. SAP has positioned Enterprise SOA to deliver the benefits offered by service-oriented architecture, including enabling both flexibility and business efficiency. Most of SAP products, such as mySAP ERP, mySAP CRM, and mySAP SRM, are built upon Enterprise SOA.

There are also a few open source implementations:

- JBoss Enterprise SOA Platform (Red Hat) (`http://www.jboss.com/products/platforms/soa/`)
- Open ESB (`https://open-esb.dev.java.net/`)

- ActiveBPEL Engine (`http://www.activebpel.org/`)
- bexee BPEL Execution Engine (`http://sourceforge.net/projects/bexee`)
- Apache Agila (`http://wiki.apache.org/agila/`), formerly known as Twister

In the following chapters we will use Oracle SOA Suite platform, including JDeveloper and Oracle BPEL Process Manager. Please keep in mind however that BPEL is an open specification therefore it does not differ between the products. BPEL code is portable between different BPEL servers. This holds true as long as you are not using some vendor-specific extensions. Therefore, in the next chapters we will first look at standard BPEL. Then, we will look how to use BPEL using Oracle SOA Suite.

The future of BPEL

OASIS has been responsible for the further development of BPEL since April 2003. An OASIS technical committee, called WSBPEL TC, has been formed for the development of a new BPEL version, called WS-BPEL 2.0. The technical committee, which supervises and influences further development of BPEL, has many new members. This ensures that BPEL will be extended with new features and also ensures continuity of development. The number of participants involved in BPEL shows that industry support is large and still increasing. More information on WSBPEL TC can be found at `http://www.oasis-open.org/committees/tc_home.php?wg_abbrev=wsbpel`.

Summary

In this chapter, we have become familiar with BPEL, its role in the SOA, and basic concepts related to service composition and the definition of business processes. BPEL provides a rich vocabulary for defining processes and has several features not found in programming languages. This makes BPEL the preferred choice for composition of services. Major software vendors support BPEL and open source implementations exist. Based on comparison to other technologies and languages, we have seen that BPEL plays an important role in service composition.

BPEL fits very well into the SOA, and with BPEL, we can define executable business processes and abstract business processes. Executable processes are the most important and allow us to define the exact order in which services are composed.

In the next chapter, we will look at BPEL and learn how to define a BPEL process.

2
Service Composition with BPEL

In this chapter, we will get familiar with BPEL concepts, and discuss composing services with BPEL. We will look at how to develop executable business processes. In a nutshell, we will:

- Discuss service composition with BPEL
- Explain how business processes are defined in BPEL
- Get familiar with core concepts including:
    - The structure of BPEL process definitions
    - Invoking services
    - Synchronous and asynchronous processes
    - Partner links
    - The role of WSDL
    - Important activities and other constructs
    - Define an example BPEL process

Developing business processes with BPEL

BPEL uses an XML-based vocabulary that allows us to specify and describe business processes. BPEL is a programming language. Most development environments that support BPEL, such as Oracle JDeveloper, IBM WebSphere Integration Developer, or Eclipse *usually* provide a visual editor, where we can compose BPEL processes by dragging and dropping the BPEL activities in a visual way. However, the majority of tools also allow a switch to the source view, where you can enter the BPEL code directly. A BPEL visual representation is generated out of BPEL code. In this chapter we will look at the BPEL code.

With BPEL, you can describe business processes in two distinct ways:

- **Executable business processes**: They specify the exact details of business processes and can be executed by a BPEL process server. In the majority of cases, we will use BPEL to specify executable processes.
- **Abstract business processes**: They process templates or public message exchange between parties, without including the specific details of process flows. They are not executable and are rarely used.

This chapter focuses on executable business processes. Abstract business processes are covered in the next chapter.

Executable business processes are processes that comprise a set of services. When we describe a business process in BPEL, we actually define a new service that is a composition of existing services. The interface (WSDL) of the new BPEL composite service uses a set of port types, through which it provides operations like any other service. To invoke a business process described in BPEL, we must invoke the resulting composite service.

In a typical scenario, the BPEL business process receives a request. To fulfill it, the process then invokes the involved services and finally responds to the original caller. Because the BPEL process communicates with other services, it relies heavily on the WSDL description of the services invoked by the composite BPEL service.

Anyone developing BPEL processes requires a good understanding of WSDL and other related technologies. BPEL introduces WSDL extensions, which enable us to accurately specify relations between several services in the business process. These relations are called **partner links**. The following figure shows a BPEL process and its relation to services (partner links):

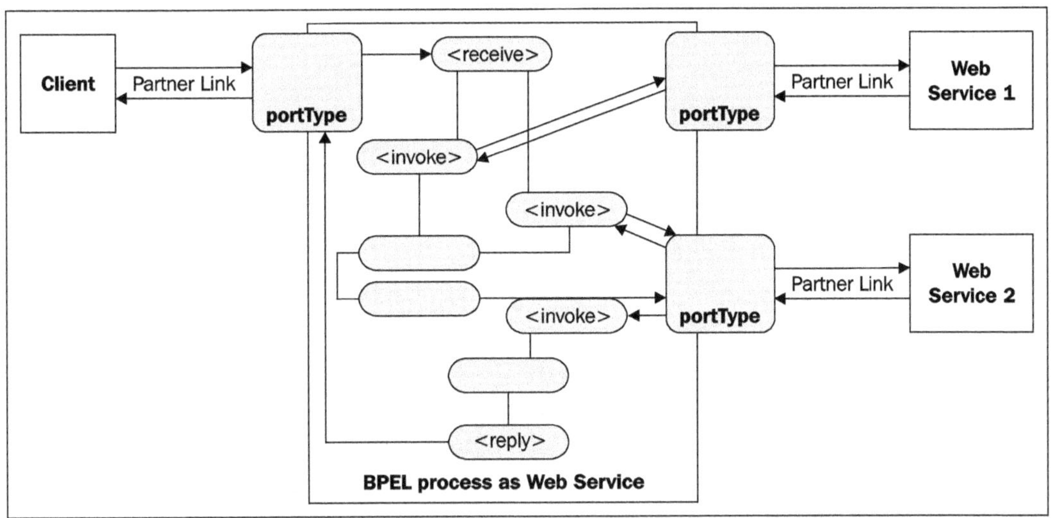

Any BPEL process specifies the exact order in which participating services should be invoked. This can be done sequentially or in parallel. With BPEL, we can express conditional behavior; for example, a service invocation can depend on the value of a previous invocation. We can also construct loops, declare variables, copy, assign values, define fault handlers, and so on. By combining all these constructs, we can define complex business processes in an algorithmic manner. We can describe deterministic as well as non-deterministic flows. Because business processes are essentially graphs of activities, it is sometimes useful to express them using a modeling notation, such as **BPMN** (**Business Process Modeling Notation**) or **UML** (**Unified Modeling Language**) activity diagrams. BPEL is not a modeling language for processes, but an execution language for processes and orchestration of services. To understand how business processes are defined in BPEL, we look at the core concepts in the next section.

Core concepts

A BPEL process consists of steps. Each step is called an **activity**. BPEL supports basic and structured activities. Basic activities represent basic constructs and are used for common tasks, such as those listed below:

- Invoking other Web Services, using `<invoke>`
- Waiting for the client to invoke the business process by sending a message, using `<receive>` (receiving a request)
- Generating a response for synchronous operations, using `<reply>`
- Manipulating data variables, using `<assign>`

- Indicating faults and exceptions, using `<throw>`
- Waiting for some time, using `<wait>`
- Terminating the entire process, using `<exit>`

We can then combine these and other basic activities and define complex flows that specify exactly the steps of a business process. To combine basic activities, BPEL supports several structured activities. The most important are:

- Sequence (`<sequence>`), for defining a set of activities that will be invoked in an ordered sequence
- Flow (`<flow>`), for defining a set of activities that will be invoked in parallel
- Conditional construct (`<if>`), for implementing branches
- While, repeat, and for each (`<while>`, `<repeatUntil>`, `<forEach>`), for defining loops
- The ability to select one of a number of alternative paths, using `<pick>`

Each BPEL process will also define partner links, using `<partnerLinks>`, and declare variables, using `<variables>`.

To provide an idea of how a BPEL process looks, we show a very simple BPEL process, which selects the best insurance offer from several.

We first declare the partner links to the BPEL process client (called `client`) and two insurance services (called `insuranceA` and `insuranceB`):

```
<?xml version="1.0" encoding="utf-8"?>
<process name="InsuranceSelectionProcess"
  targetNamespace="http://packtpub.com/bpel/example/"
  xmlns=
    "http://docs.oasis-open.org/wsbpel/2.0/process/executable"
  xmlns:ins="http://packtpub.com/bpel/insurance/"
  xmlns:com="http://packtpub.com/bpel/company/" >

<partnerLinks>
  <partnerLink name="client"
    partnerLinkType="com:selectionLT"
    myRole="insuranceSelectionService"/>

  <partnerLink name="insuranceA"
    partnerLinkType="ins:insuranceLT"
    myRole="insuranceRequester"
    partnerRole="insuranceService"/>

  <partnerLink name="insuranceB"
    partnerLinkType="ins:insuranceLT"
```

```
        myRole="insuranceRequester"
        partnerRole="insuranceService"/>
</partnerLinks>
```

Next, we declare variables for the insurance request (`InsuranceRequest`), insurance A and B responses (`InsuranceAResponse`, `InsuranceBResponse`), and for the final selection (`InsuranceSelectionResponse`):

```
<variables>
  <!-- input for BPEL process -->
  <variable name="InsuranceRequest"
    messageType="ins:InsuranceRequestMessage"/>
  <!-- output from insurance A -->
  <variable name="InsuranceAResponse"
    messageType="ins:InsuranceResponseMessage"/>
  <!-- output from insurance B -->
  <variable name="InsuranceBResponse"
    messageType="ins:InsuranceResponseMessage"/>
  <!-- output from BPEL process -->
  <variable name="InsuranceSelectionResponse"
    messageType="ins:InsuranceResponseMessage"/>
</variables>
```

Finally, we specify the process steps. First we wait for the initial request message from the client (`<receive>`). Then we invoke both insurance services (`<invoke>`) in parallel using the `<flow>` activity. The insurance services return the insurance premium. Then we select the lower amount (`<if>`) and return the result to the client (the caller of the BPEL process) using the `<reply>` activity:

```
<sequence>

  <!-- Receive the initial request from client -->
  <receive partnerLink="client"
    portType="com:InsuranceSelectionPT"
    operation="SelectInsurance"
    variable="InsuranceRequest"
    createInstance="yes" />

  <!-- Make concurrent invocations to Insurance A and B -->
  <flow>

    <!-- Invoke Insurance A service -->
    <invoke partnerLink="insuranceA"
      portType="ins:ComputeInsurancePremiumPT"
      operation="ComputeInsurancePremium"
      inputVariable="InsuranceRequest"
      outputVariable="InsuranceAResponse" />
```

```
      <!-- Invoke Insurance B service -->

      <invoke partnerLink="insuranceB"
        portType="ins:ComputeInsurancePremiumPT"
        operation="ComputeInsurancePremium"
        inputVariable="InsuranceRequest"
        outputVariable="InsuranceBResponse" />

    </flow>

    <!-- Select the best offer and construct the response -->
    <if>
     <condition>
        $InsuranceAResponse.confirmationData/ins:Amount &lt;=
        $InsuranceBResponse.confirmationData/ins:Amount
      </condition>
      <!-- Select Insurance A -->
      <assign>
        <copy>
          <from variable="InsuranceAResponse" />
          <to variable="InsuranceSelectionResponse" />
        </copy>
      </assign>

      <else>
      <!-- Select Insurance B -->
        <assign>
          <copy>
            <from variable="InsuranceBResponse" />
            <to variable="InsuranceSelectionResponse" />
          </copy>
        </assign>
      </else>
    </if>

    <!-- Send a response to the client -->
    <reply partnerLink="client"
      portType="com:InsuranceSelectionPT"
      operation="SelectInsurance"
      variable="InsuranceSelectionResponse"/>

  </sequence>

  </process>
```

In the coming sections, we will explain the different parts of the BPEL process and the syntax of various BPEL activities.

As BPEL processes are exposed as services, we need a WSDL for the BPEL process.

Because each BPEL process is a service, each BPEL process needs a WSDL document too. This is more or less obvious. As mentioned, a client will usually invoke an operation on the BPEL process to start it. With the BPEL process WSDL, we specify the interface for this operation. We also specify all message types, operations, and port types a BPEL process offers to other partners. We will show WSDL for the BPEL process later in this chapter.

Invoking services

A BPEL process definition is written as an XML document using the `<process>` root element. Within the `<process>` element, a BPEL process will usually have the top-level `<sequence>` element. Within the sequence, the process will first wait for the incoming message to start the process. This wait is modeled with the `<receive>` construct. Then the process will invoke the related services, using the `<invoke>` construct. Such invocations can be done sequentially or in parallel. If we want to make them sequential, we simply write an `<invoke>` for each invocation and the services will be invoked in that order. This is shown in the following code excerpt:

```
<process ...>
  <sequence>

  <!-- Wait for the incoming request to start the process -->
  <receive ... />

  <!-- Invoke a set of related services, one by one -->
  <invoke ... />
  <invoke ... />
  <invoke ... />
      ...
  </sequence>
</process>
```

Here we have not shown the full syntax of `<receive>`, `<invoke>`, and other activities, which require that we specify certain attributes. This is explained later in this chapter, after we have become familiar with the basic structure of BPEL documents.

To invoke services concurrently, we can use the `<flow>` construct. In the example below, the three `<invoke>` operations would perform concurrently:

```
<process ...>
  <sequence>
  <!-- Wait for the incoming request to start the process -->
  <receive ... />
  <!-- Invoke a set of related services, concurrently -->
    <flow>
       <invoke ... />
       <invoke ... />
       <invoke ... />
    </flow>
  </sequence>
</process>
```

We can also combine and nest the `<sequence>` and `<flow>` constructs, which allows us to define several sequences executing concurrently. In the following example we have defined two sequences, one consisting of three invocations, and one with two invocations. Both sequences would execute concurrently:

```
<process ...>
  <sequence>
    <!-- Wait for the incoming request to start the process -->
    <receive ... />
    <!-- Invoke two sequences concurrently -->
      <flow>
      <!-- The three invokes below execute sequentially -->
        <sequence>
          <invoke ... />
          <invoke ... />
          <invoke ... />
        </sequence>
        <!-- The two invokes below execute sequentially -->
        <sequence>
          <invoke ... />
          <invoke ... />
        </sequence>
      </flow>
  </sequence>
</process>
```

Invoking asynchronous services

We just explained how to invoke synchronous service operations. There are actually two major types of service operations:

- **Synchronous request/reply service operations**: Here we send a request and wait for the reply. Such operations usually do not require much time to process; therefore, it is reasonable for the sender (client) to wait for the reply. They are shown in the following figure:

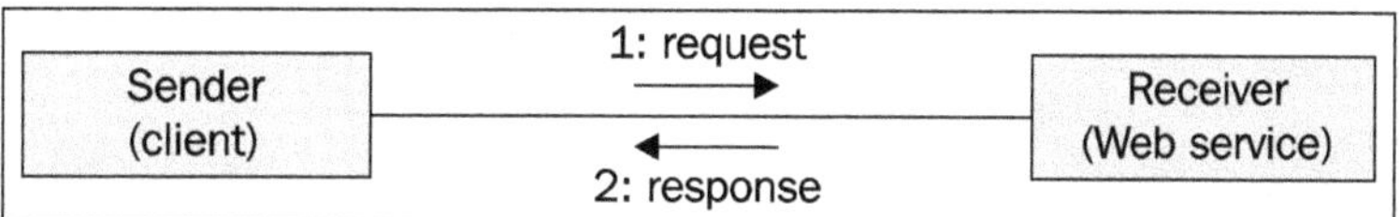

- **Asynchronous service operations**: Usually, such operations perform processing that requires a longer time to finish. Therefore, they do not block the sender for the duration of the operation. If such operations require that results are sent back to the client, they usually perform callbacks. This is shown in the following figure:

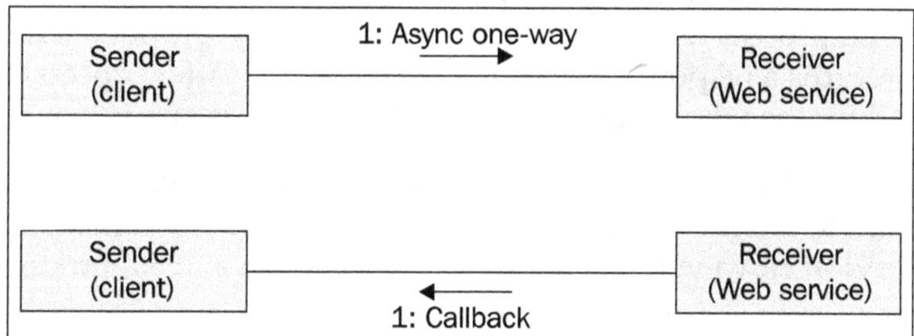

Callbacks usually need to be related to original requests. We call this **message correlation**. Message correlation can be achieved automatically with WS-Addressing, or with BPEL correlation sets, which we will cover in *Chapter 3*.

Using the `<invoke>` construct, we can invoke both types of operations—synchronous and asynchronous. If we invoke a synchronous operation, the business process waits for the reply. We do not need to use an explicit construct to retrieve the reply.

With asynchronous operations, `<invoke>` only takes care of the first part—for the operation invocation. To receive a result (if one is returned to the client), we need to use a separate construct, `<receive>`. With `<receive>`, the business process waits for the incoming message. Between the `<invoke>` and `<receive>` we could do some other processing instead of waiting for the reply, as is the case with synchronous operations. The code excerpt below shows how to invoke asynchronous operations:

```
<process ...>
  <sequence>

    <!-- Wait for the incoming request to start the process -->
    <receive ... />

    <!-- Invoke an asynchronous operation -->
    <invoke ... />

    <!-- Do something else... -->

    <!-- Wait for the callback -->
    <receive ... />
  </sequence>
</process>
```

Just like synchronous operations, we can use asynchronous `<invoke>`/`<receive>` pairs within `<flows>` to perform several concurrent invocations.

Synchronous/Asynchronous business processes

We have already mentioned that the BPEL-modeled business process is exposed as a service. The BPEL process itself can be synchronous or asynchronous. A synchronous BPEL process returns a response to the client immediately after processing and the client is blocked for the whole duration of the BPEL process execution.

An asynchronous BPEL process, on the other hand, does not block the client. To return a result to the client, an asynchronous process uses a callback, similar to any other service. However, it is not required that such a BPEL process returns a response.

This brings us to the conclusion that the type of BPEL process we choose is very important. Most real-world processes are long running, so we model them as asynchronous. However, there may also be processes that execute in a relatively short time, or processes where we want the client to wait for completion. We model such processes as synchronous.

How do synchronous and asynchronous processes differ in the BPEL specification? We know that both first wait for the initial message, using a `<receive>`. Both also invoke other services, either synchronously or asynchronously. However, a synchronous BPEL process will return a result after the process has completed. Therefore, we use a `<reply>` construct at the end of the process, as shown in the following excerpt:

```
<process ...>
  <sequence>
    <!-- Wait for the incoming request to start the process -->
    <receive ... />
    <!-- Invoke a set of related services -->
        ...
    <!-- Return a synchronous reply to the caller (client) -->
    <reply ... />
  </sequence>
</process>
```

An asynchronous BPEL process does not use the <reply> clause. If such a process has to send a reply to the client, it uses the <invoke> clause to invoke the callback operation on the client's port type. Remember that an asynchronous BPEL process does not need to return anything.

```
<process ...>
  <sequence>
    <!-- Wait for the incoming request to start the process -->
    <receive ... />
    <!-- Invoke a set of related services -->
    <!-- Invoke a callback on the client (if needed) -->
    <invoke ... />
  </sequence>
</process>
```

We will come back to the <invoke>, <receive>, and <reply> activities a little later to describe the whole syntax, including the necessary attributes. First, however, we have to introduce the concept of partner links and partner link types.

Understanding links to partners

From what have we said until now, we can see that BPEL processes interact with external services in two ways:

- The BPEL process invokes operations on other services.
- The BPEL process receives invocations from clients. One of the clients is the user of the BPEL process, who makes the initial invocation. Other clients are services, for example, those that have been invoked by the BPEL process but make callbacks to return replies.

Links to all parties BPEL interacts with are called **partner links**. Partner links can be links to services that are invoked by the BPEL process. These are sometimes called **invoked partner links**. Partner links can also be links to clients, and can invoke the BPEL process. Such partner links are sometimes called **client partner links**. Note that each BPEL process has at least one client partner link, because there has to be a client that first invokes the BPEL process.

Usually a BPEL process will also have at least one invoked partner link because it will most likely invoke at least one service. The process invokes other services using the `<invoke>` activity, where it has to specify the operation name and the port type used for invocation, as we will see later. Invoked partner links may, however, become client partner links. This is usually the case with asynchronous services, where the process invokes an operation. Later the service (partner) invokes the callback operation on the process to return the requested data.

BPEL treats clients as partner links for two reasons. The most obvious reason is support for asynchronous interactions. In asynchronous interactions, the process needs to invoke operations on its clients. This is used for modeling asynchronous BPEL processes. Such processes also invoke the callback on the initial caller, as mentioned in the previous section.

The second reason is based on the fact that the BPEL process can offer services. These services, offered through port types, can be used by more than one client. The process may wish to distinguish between different clients and only offer them the functionality they are authorized to use. For example, an insurance process might offer a different set of operations to car-insurance clients than to real-estate-insurance clients. To sum up, partner links describe links to partners, where partners might be:

- Services invoked by the process
- Services that invoke the process
- Services that have both roles—they are invoked by the process and they invoke the process

We have already described the first two scenarios. Let us now have a closer look at the third scenario—a typical asynchronous callback. Here a service offers a `portType A`, through which the BPEL process invokes the operations on that service. The BPEL process also has to provide a `portType` through which the service invokes the callback operation—let us call that `portType B`. This is shown in the following figure:

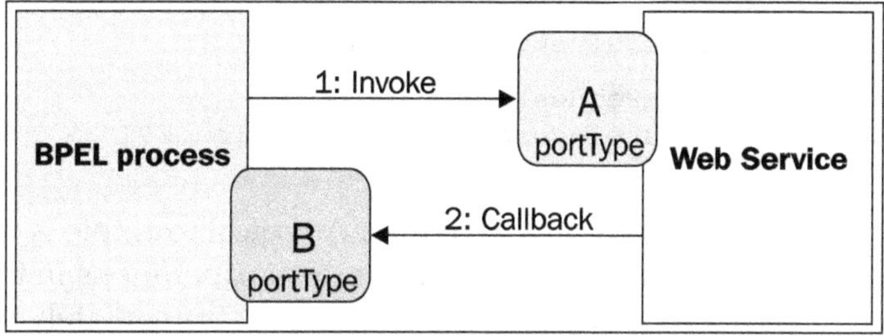

From the viewpoint of the BPEL process, the process requires `portType A` on the service and provides `portType B` to the service. From the perspective of the service, the service offers `portType A` to the BPEL process and requires `portType B` from the process.

Partner link types

Describing situations where the service is invoked by the process, and vice versa, requires selecting a certain perspective. We can select the process perspective and describe the process as requiring the `portType A` on the service and providing the `portType B` to the service. Alternatively, we select the service perspective and describe the service as offering `portType A` to the BPEL process and requiring `portType B` from the process.

To overcome this limitation, BPEL introduces partner link types. They allow us to model such relationships as a third party. We are not required to take a certain perspective; rather, we just define roles. A partner link type must have at least one role and can have at most two roles. The latter is the usual case. For each role we must specify a `portType` that is used for interaction.

[A partner link type declares how two parties interact and what each party offers.]

In the following example, we define a `partnerLinkType` called `insuranceLT`. It defines two roles, the `insuranceService` and the `insuranceRequester`. The `insuranceService` offers the `ComputeInsurancePremiumPT` port type from the namespace `ins`, qualified by the corresponding URI (the namespace declarations are not shown here). The `insuranceRequester` offers the `ComputeInsurancePremiumCallbackPT` port type from the `com` namespace. As the name implies, the latter port type is used for the callback operation. The following declaration specifies the service and the callback roles:

```
<partnerLinkType name="insuranceLT"
  xmlns="http://docs.oasis-open.org/wsbpel/2.0/plnktype">
```

```
    <role name="insuranceService"
      portType="ins:ComputeInsurancePremiumPT"/>

    <role name="insuranceRequester"
      portType="com:ComputeInsurancePremiumCallbackPT"/>

</partnerLinkType>
```

Sometimes we may not need to specify two roles. A typical example is when we use synchronous request/response operations. If the operations in the `ComputeInsurancePremiumPT` port type returned results immediately, there would be no need for a callback. We would only need a single role, which is done as follows:

```
<partnerLinkType name="insuranceLT"
  xmlns="http://docs.oasis-open.org/wsbpel/2.0/plnktype">

  <role name="insuranceService"
    <portType="ins:ComputeInsurancePremiumPT"/>

</partnerLinkType>
```

If we specify only one role, we express willingness to interact with the service, but do not place any additional requirements on the service. In the first example, however, where we have specified two roles, we require that the insurance service supports the `ComputeInsurancePremiumCallbackPT` port type.

It is important to understand that the partner link types are not part of the BPEL process specification document. This is reasonable because partner link types belong to the service specification and not the process specification. They can therefore be placed in the WSDL document that describes the partner service or the BPEL process. Partner link types use the WSDL extensibility mechanism, so they can be a part of a WSDL document.

Shown below is a skeleton of the WSDL document with the `partnerLinkType` section. It specifies types, messages, port types, and partner link types. It does not, however, show the bindings and the service sections because the BPEL execution environment usually automatically generates these:

```
<?xml version="1.0" encoding="UTF-8" ?>
<definitions
  xmlns:http="http://schemas.xmlsoap.org/wsdl/http/"
  xmlns:soap="http://schemas.xmlsoap.org/wsdl/soap/"
  xmlns:xs="http://www.w3.org/2001/XMLSchema"
  xmlns:soapenc="http://schemas.xmlsoap.org/soap/encoding/"
  xmlns:ins="http://packtpub.com/bpel/insurance/"
  xmlns:com="http://packtpub.com/bpel/company/"
  targetNamespace="http://packtpub.com/bpel/company/"
  xmlns="http://schemas.xmlsoap.org/wsdl/"
  xmlns:plnk="http://docs.oasis-open.org/wsbpel/2.0/plnktype" >

  <import ... />
```

```
<types>
  <xs:schema ... >
    ...
  </xs:schema>
</types>
<message ... >
  <part ... />
  ...
</message>
<portType name="ComputeInsurancePremiumPT">
  <operation name="...">
    <input message="..." />
  </operation>
</portType>
<portType name="ComputeInsurancePremiumCallbackPT">
  <operation name="...">
    <input message="..." />
  </operation>
</portType>
...
<plnk:partnerLinkType name="insuranceLT">
  <plnk:role name="insuranceService"
    portType ="ins:ComputeInsurancePremiumPT"/>
  <plnk:role name="insuranceRequester"
    portType ="ins:ComputeInsurancePremiumCallbackPT"/>
</plnk:partnerLinkType>
</definitions>
```

Sometimes existing services will not define a partner link type. Then we can wrap the WSDL of the service and define partner link types ourselves.

Now that we have become familiar with the partner link types and know where to place their declarations, it is time to go back to the BPEL process definition, more specifically to the partner links.

Defining partner links

We have already described the role of partner links in BPEL process specifications. However, we have not yet explained how to define partner links because we first had to get familiar with partner link types.

Partner links are concrete references to services that a BPEL business process interacts with. They are specified near the beginning of the BPEL process definition document, just after the `<process>` tag. Several `<partnerLink>` definitions are nested within the `<partnerLinks>` element:

```
<process ...>
  <partnerLinks>
    <partnerLink ... />
    <partnerLink ... />
      ...
  </partnerLinks>
  <sequence>
      ...
  </sequence>
</process>
```

For each partner link, we have to specify:

- `name`: Serves as a reference for interactions via that partner link
- `partnerLinkType`: Defines the type of the partner link
- `myRole`: Indicates the role of the BPEL process itself
- `partnerRole`: Indicates the role of the partner
- `initializePartnerRole`: Indicates whether the BPEL engine should initialize the partner link's partner role value. This is an optional attribute and should only be used with partner links that specify partner role.

We define both roles (`myRole` and `partnerRole`) only if the `partnerLinkType` specifies two roles. If the `partnerLinkType` specifies only one role, the `partnerLink` also has to specify only one role—we omit the one that is not needed.

Let us go back to our previous example, where we have defined the `insuranceLT` partner link type. To define a `partnerLink` called `insurance`, characterized by the `insuranceLT` `partnerLinkType`, we need to specify both roles because it is an asynchronous relation. The role of the BPEL process (`myRole`) is described as **insurance requester** and the partner role is described as **insurance service**. The definition is shown in the following code excerpt:

```
<partnerLinks>
  <partnerLink name="insurance"
    partnerLinkType="tns:insuranceLT"
    myRole="insuranceRequester"
    partnerRole="insuranceService"/>
</partnerLinks>
```

BPEL process tag

Now that we are more familiar with BPEL, let's focus on the `<process>` tag. This delimits the root element of the BPEL document. The `<process>` tag requires that we specify certain attributes. We have to specify the following at least:

- `name`: Specifies the name of the BPEL business process
- `targetNamespace`: Specifies the target namespace for the business process definition
- `xmlns`: The namespace used by BPEL is `http://docs.oasis-open.org/wsbpel/2.0/process/executable`

Usually, we also specify one or more additional namespaces to reference other involved namespaces, for example, those used by services. Here is a typical process declaration tag:

```
<process name="InsuranceSelectionProcess"
  targetNamespace="http://packtpub.com/bpel/example/"
  xmlns="http://docs.oasis-open.org/wsbpel/2.0/process/executable"
  xmlns:ins="http://packtpub.com/bpel/insurance/"
  xmlns:com="http://packtpub.com/bpel/company/" >
```

We can also specify additional attributes for the `<process>` tag, including:

- `queryLanguage`: Specifies which query language is used for node selection in assignments, properties, and other uses. The default is XPath 1.0 (`urn:oasis:names:tc:wsbpel:2.0:sublang:xpath1.0`). However, another language can be specified, such as XPath 2.0 or XQuery. The available options are determined by what is supported by a given BPEL engine.
- `expressionLanguage`: Specifies which expression language is used in the process. The default is XPath 1.0 (`urn:oasis:names:tc:wsbpel:2.0:sublang:xpath1.0`).
- `suppressJoinFailure`: Determines whether to suppress join failures (`yes` or `no`). The default is `no`. Join failures are explained in *Chapter 3*.

- `exitOnStandardFault`: Defines how the process should behave when a standard fault occurs. We can specify `yes` if we want the process to exit on a standard fault (other than `bpel:joinFailure`), or `no` if we want to handle the fault using a fault handler. The default is `no`.

Variables

The BPEL business model processes the exchange of messages between involved services. Messages are exchanged as operations are invoked. When the business process invokes an operation and receives the result, we often want to store that result for subsequent invocations, use the result as is, or extract certain data. BPEL provides variables to store and maintain the state.

> Variables are used to store messages that are exchanged between business process partners or to hold data that relates to the state of the process.

Variables can also hold data that relates to the state of the process, but will never be exchanged with partners. Specifically, variables can store WSDL messages, XML schema elements, or XML schema simple types. Each variable has to be declared before it can be used. When we declare a variable, we must specify the variable name and type. To specify type we have to specify one of the following attributes:

- `messageType`: A variable that can hold a WSDL message
- `element`: A variable that can hold an XML schema element
- `type`: A variable that can hold an XML schema simple type

The declaration of variables is gathered within the `<variables>` element. The following example shows three variable declarations. The first one declares a variable with the name `InsuranceRequest`, which holds WSDL messages of type `ins:InsuranceRequestMessage`. The second declaration defines a variable `PartialInsuranceDescription` that can hold XML elements of type `ins:InsuranceDescription`. The last variable declaration is for variable `LastName`, which can hold XML schema `string` type data. The first two declarations assume that the corresponding `messageType` and `element` have been declared in the WSDL (these declarations are not shown here):

```
<variables>
  <variable name="InsuranceRequest"
    messageType="ins:InsuranceRequestMessage"/>
  <variable name="PartialInsuranceDescription"
    element="ins:InsuranceDescription"/>
  <variable name="LastName" type="xs:string"/>
</variables>
```

You can declare variables globally at the beginning of a BPEL process declaration document or within scopes. Here we focus on globally-declared variables and discuss scopes in the next chapter. The following example shows the structure of a BPEL process that uses variables:

```
<process ...>
  <partnerLinks>
      ...
  </partnerLinks>
  <variables>
    <variable ... />
    <variable ... />
      ...
  </variables>
  <sequence>
      ...
  </sequence>
</process>
```

Providing the interface to BPEL processes: <invoke>, <receive>, and <reply>

At the beginning of this section, we became familiar with the `<invoke>`, `<receive>`, and `<reply>` activities. With `<invoke>`, the BPEL process invokes operations on other services, while with `<receive>`, it waits for incoming messages (that is, operation invocations). With `<receive>`, the business process usually waits for the initial message to start the process. Another typical use of `<receive>` is to wait for callbacks. With `<reply>`, a BPEL process can send a response, if the process is modeled as synchronous.

All three activities use the same three basic attributes:

- `partnerLink`: Specifies which partner link will be used
- `portType`: Specifies the used port type
- `operation`: Specifies the name of the operation to invoke (`<invoke>`), to wait to be invoked (`<receive>`), or the name of the operation which has been invoked but is synchronous and requires a reply (`<reply>`)

For each BPEL activity we can specify a `name` attribute. We use the `name` attribute to provide names for activities. In most BPEL activities the `name` attribute is optional, but we can add it to improve the readability of the code.

<invoke>

The `<invoke>` operation supports two other important attributes. When the business process invokes an operation on the service, it sends a set of parameters. These parameters are modeled as input messages with services. To specify the input message for the invocation, we use the `inputVariable` attribute and specify a variable of the corresponding type.

If we invoke a synchronous request/response operation, it returns a result. This result is again a message, modeled as an output message. To store it in a variable, `<invoke>` provides another attribute, called the `outputVariable`.

The following code excerpt shows an example of the `<invoke>` clause. We specify that the BPEL process should invoke the synchronous operation `ComputeInsurancePremium` on port type `ins:ComputeInsurancePremiumPT` using the `insuranceA` partner link, providing the input from variable `InsuranceRequest`, and storing output in the `InsuranceAResponse` variable:

```
<invoke partnerLink="insuranceA"
  portType="ins:ComputeInsurancePremiumPT"
  operation="ComputeInsurancePremium"
  inputVariable="InsuranceRequest"
  outputVariable="InsuranceAResponse" >
</invoke>
```

<receive>

Let us now take a closer look at the `<receive>` activity. We have said that `<receive>` waits for the incoming message (operation invocation), either for the initial to start the BPEL process, or for a callback. Usually, the business process needs to store the incoming message, and it can use the `variable` attribute to specify a suitable variable.

Another attribute for `<receive>` activity is the `createInstance` attribute, which is related to the business process lifecycle and instructs the BPEL engine to create a new instance of the process. Usually, we specify the `createInstance="yes"` attribute with the initial `<receive>` activity of the process to create a new process instance for each client. We discuss this attribute in more detail in the next chapter.

Another optional attribute for `<receive>` activity is `messageExchange`, which is used to disambiguate the relationship between inbound message activities and `<reply>` activities. We will discuss message exchange in *Chapter 3*.

The following example shows a `<receive>` that waits for the `SelectInsurance` operation on port type `com:InsuranceSelectionPT` using the `client` partner link. Because this is the initial `<receive>` activity, the `createInstance` attribute is used. The client request is stored in the `InsuranceRequest` variable as follows:

```
<receive partnerLink="client"
  portType="com:InsuranceSelectionPT"
  operation="SelectInsurance"
  variable="InsuranceRequest"
  createInstance="yes" >
</receive>
```

<reply>

Finally, let's look at the `<reply>` clause. As we already know, `<reply>` is used to return the response for synchronous BPEL processes. `<reply>` is always related to the initial `<receive>` through which the BPEL process started. Using `<reply>`, we can return the answer, which is the normal usage, or we can return a fault message. Returning a fault message using `<reply>` is discussed in *Chapter 3*. We can also specify a message exchange.

When we use `<reply>` to return a response for a synchronous process, we have to define only one additional attribute—the name of the variable where the response is stored. The following example shows a reply on an initial receive operation. It uses the `client` partner link and provides a response for the `SelectInsurance` operation on `ins:InsuranceSelectionPT` port type. The return result is stored in the `InsuranceSelectionResponse` variable. Please notice that the same `partnerLink`, `portType`, and `operation` name have been used in the initial `<receive>` clause:

```
<reply partnerLink="client"
  portType="com:InsuranceSelectionPT"
  operation="SelectInsurance"
  variable="InsuranceSelectionResponse" >
</reply>
```

The three activities, `<invoke>`, `<receive>`, and `<reply>` support additional functionality. They all support correlations, and `<invoke>` also supports fault handlers and compensation handlers. We will discuss these in *Chapter 3*.

Assignments

The variables in the business process hold and maintain the data. We used variables in `<invoke>`, `<receive>`, and `<reply>` to specify the input and output messages for invoking operations on partner services. In this section, we get familiar with how to copy data between variables.

To copy data between variables, expressions, and partner link endpoint references, BPEL provides the `<assign>` activity. Within it, we can perform one or more `<copy>` commands. For each `<copy>`, we have to specify the source (`<from>`) and the destination (`<to>`). The syntax of an assignment is presented below:

```
<assign>
  <copy>
    <from ... />
    <to ... />
  </copy>
  <copy>
    <from ... />
    <to ... />
  </copy>
        ...
</assign>
```

There are several choices for the `<from>` and `<to>` clauses. To copy values from one variable to the other, we have to specify the `variable` attribute in the `<from>` and `<to>` elements. This is shown in the following example, where we have copied a value from the `InsuranceAResponse` variable to the `InsuranceSelectionResponse` variable:

```
<assign>
  <copy>
    <from variable="InsuranceAResponse" />
    <to variable="InsuranceSelectionResponse" />
  </copy>
</assign>
```

This copy can be performed only if both variables are of same type, as in our example `ins:InsuranceResponseMessage`, or if the source type is a subtype of the destination type.

Variables can be of three types:

- WSDL message types
- XML schema elements
- XML schema primitive types

If a variable holds a WSDL message, which is common, we can further refine the copy by specifying the part of the message we would like to copy. WSDL messages consist of parts (more on WSDL can be found at `http://www.w3.org/TR/wsdl`). Presented below is a simple message (defined in the WSDL document) that consists of two parts—the `insuredPersonData` part and the `insuranceDetails` part. Both parts are specified with the corresponding XML schema complex types (not shown here):

```
<message name="InsuranceRequestMessage">
  <part name="insuredPersonData"
    element="ins:InsuredPersonData" />
  <part name="insuranceDetails" element="ins:InsuranceDetails" />
</message>
```

Now suppose that we get a variable of type `ins:InsuredPersonDataType` from invoking another service, which has the following message declaration in its WSDL and uses the same namespace:

```
<message name="InsuredPersonDataRequestMessage">
  <part name="insuredPersonData"
    element="ins:InsuredPersonData" />
</message>
```

Our BPEL process would declare two variables, `InsuranceRequest` and `InsuredPersonRequest`, with the declaration shown below:

```
<variables>
  <variable name="InsuranceRequest"
    messageType="ins:InsuranceRequestMessage"/>
  <variable name="InsuredPersonRequest"
    messageType="ins:InsuredPersonDataRequestMessage"/>
</variables>
```

Now we could perform a copy from the `InsuredPersonRequest` variable to the `insuredPersonData` part of the `InsuranceRequest` variable, using the following assignment:

```
<assign>
  <copy>
    <from variable="InsuredPersonRequest" part="insuredPersonData" />
    <to variable="InsuranceRequest" part="insuredPersonData" />
  </copy>
</assign>
```

We could also perform a copy in the opposite direction. In addition to specifying the part, we can also specify the exact path to the element we require. To specify the path, we have to write a query, using the selected query language specified within the <process> tag.

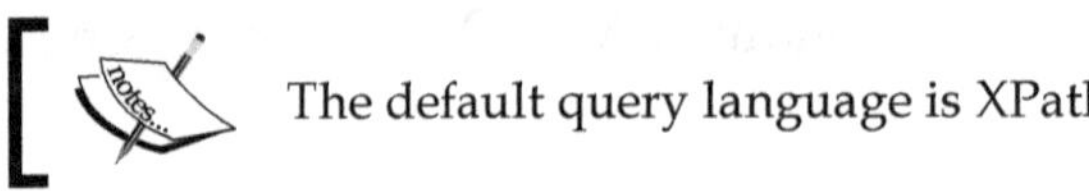

The default query language is XPath 1.0.

In our previous example, suppose the ins:InsuredPersonData is defined as follows:

```
<xs:element name="InsuredPersonData">
  <xs:complexType>
    <xs:sequence>
        <xs:element name="FirstName" type="xs:string" />
        <xs:element name="LastName" type="xs:string" />
        <xs:element name="Address" type="xs:string" />
        <xs:element name="Age" type="xs:int" />
    </xs:sequence>
  </xs:complexType>
</xs:element>
```

We could perform a copy from the LastName variable to the InsuranceRequest variable, to the message part insuredPersonData, and to the last name:

```
<assign>
  <copy>
    <from variable="LastName" />
    <to variable="InsuranceRequest"
      part="insuredPersonData">
        <query>ins:LastName</query>
    </to>
  </copy>
</assign>
```

The location path must select exactly one node.

We can also use the <assign> activity to copy expressions to variables. Expressions are written in the selected expression language; the default is XPath 1.0. We specify the expression within the <from> element. The following example shows how to copy a constant string to the LastName variable:

```
<assign>
  <copy>
```

```
      <from>string('Juric')</from>
      <to variable="LastName"/>
    </copy>
  </assign>
```

We are not restricted to such simple expressions. We can use any valid XPath 1.0 expressions (or the expressions of the selected expression language). For more information, refer to the XPath 1.0 specification: `http://www.w3.org/TR/xpath`.

Another possibility is to copy a literal XML complex element to the `InsuredPersonRequest` variable. In this case, we can specify the source XML directly:

```
<assign>
  <copy>
    <from>
      <literal>
        <insuredPersonData
                   xmlns="http://packtpub.com/bpel/insurance/">
          <FirstName>Matjaz B.</FirstName>
          <LastName>Juric</LastName>
          <Address>Ptuj</Address>
          <Age>30</Age>
        </insuredPersonData>
      </literal>
    </from>
    <to variable="InsuredPersonRequest" part="insuredPersonData" />
  </copy>
</assign>
```

We can specify two optional attributes for the `<copy>` activity:

- `keepSrcElementName`: Specifies whether the element name of destination will be replaced by the element name of the source. The default is `no`.
- `ignoreMissingFromData`: Specifies whether the BPEL engine should ignore missing data in the `<from>` part of the copy assignment (and not raise a fault). The default is `no`.

  We can also specify an optional attribute for the `<assign>` activity.
- `validate`: If set to `yes`, the assign activity will validate all variables being modified by the `<assign>`. The default is `no`.

Validating variables

Sometimes, particularly after assignments (if we did not use validation in assignments), it makes sense to validate the variables against their associated XML schemas and WSDL definitions. We can validate the variables explicitly using the `<validate>` activity.

It is very simple to validate variables. We just have to list all variable names that we would like to validate. We separate the variable names with space. The syntax is as follows:

```
<validate variables="BPELVariableNames" />
```

For example, if we would like to validate variables `InsuredPersonRequest`, `InsuranceRequest`, and `PartialInsuranceDescription`, we would write the following:

```
<validate variables="InsuredPersonRequest InsuranceRequest
  PartialInsuranceDescription " />
```

Accessing variables in expressions

We can access BPEL variables from XPath expressions. This is particularly useful in `<copy>` assignments, where we would like to access specific nested elements. We access BPEL variables in XPath using the `$` operator. We will look at the three types of variables (variables can be of a `messageType`, `element`, or `type`).

Let us first look at `messageType` variables. Let us assume that we have the following definition of a variable:

```
<variables>
  <variable name="InsuredPersonRequest"
     messageType="ins:InsuredPersonDataRequestMessage"/>
</variables>
```

Where the WSDL message and the corresponding XML schema look as follows:

```
<message name="InsuredPersonDataRequestMessage">
  <part name="insuredPersonData"
    element="ins:InsuredPersonData" />
</message>
<xs:element name="InsuredPersonData">
  <xs:complexType>
    <xs:sequence>
        <xs:element name="FirstName" type="xs:string" />
        <xs:element name="LastName" type="xs:string" />
        <xs:element name="Address" type="xs:string" />
```

```
        <xs:element name="Age" type="xs:int" />
    </xs:sequence>
  </xs:complexType>
</xs:element>
```

We can access such variables from XPath in the following way:

```
$variableName.messagePart/ns:node/ns:node…
```

For example, if we would like to access the `LastName` from the `InsuredPersonRequest` variable, we would need to write:

```
$InsuredPersonRequest.insuredPersonData/ins:LastName
```

Let us now look at an example, where the variable contains an XML element. Let us assume that we have the following definition of a variable:

```
<variables>
  <variable name="PartialInsuranceDescription"
    element="ins:InsuranceDescription"/>
</variables>
```

Where the XML schema looks as follows:

```
<xs:element name="InsuranceDescription">
  <xs:complexType>
    <xs:sequence>
          <xs:element name="Code" type="xs:string" />
          <xs:element name="Description" type="xs:string" />
          <xs:element name="ValidFrom" type="xs:date" />
    </xs:sequence>
  </xs:complexType>
</xs:element>
```

We can access such variables from XPath in the following way:

```
$variableName/ns:node/ns:node…
```

For example, if we would like to access the `Description` from the `PartialInsuranceDescription` variable, we would need to write:

```
$PartialInsuranceDescription/ins:Description
```

Finally, let us look at an example, where the variable contains an XML type. Let us assume that we have the following definition of a variable:

```
<variables>
  <variable name="Address" type="ins:AddressType"/>
</variables>
```

Where the XML schema looks as follows:

```
<xs:complexType name="AddressType">
  <xs:sequence>
    <xs:element name="Street" type="xs:string" />
    <xs:element name="Number" type="xs:int" />
    <xs:element name="City" type="xs:string" />
  </xs:sequence>
</xs:complexType>
```

We can access such variables from XPath in the following way:

```
$variableName/ns:node/ns:node...
```

For example, if we would like to access the `Street` from the `Address` variable, we would write:

```
$Address/ins:Street
```

XSLT transformations

Using the assignments to copy data from one variable to another is useful. However, if we deal with complex XML schemas and have to perform transformations between different schemas, using the `<copy>` construct alone would be very time consuming. A much better approach would be to use XSLT transformations.

The `<assign>` activity provides support for XSLT transformations. We can invoke an XSLT transformation from an assignment using the `bpel:doXslTransform()` function. The `bpel:doXslTransform()` is a XPath extension function. The syntax is as follows:

```
bpel:doXslTransform('style-sheet-URI', node-set,
                    ('xslt-parameter', value)*)
```

The first parameter is the URI that points to the XSLT stylesheet. We have to provide a `string` literal and cannot use a variable here because the BPEL server has to statically analyze the XSLT stylesheet.

The second parameter is the node set on which the XSLT transformation should be performed. Here we provide an XPath expression. In most cases, we will provide a variable (as described in the previous section).

Optionally, we can specify XSLT parameters (if our XSLT stylesheet requires parameters). We always specify parameters in pairs: first the name of the parameter, then the value. The value can be an XPath expression (for example, a BPEL variable). We can specify several pairs of parameters.

For example, we can use an XSLT transformation to transform the data stored in the `PersonData` variable and copy the result of the transformation to the `InsuredPersonRequest` variable:

```
<assign>
  <copy>
    <from>
        bpel:doXslTransform(
          "http://packtpub.com/xslt/person.xsl", $PersonData)
    </from>
    <to variable="InsuredPersonRequest" />
  </copy>
</assign>
```

Conditions

We have to get familiar with one more construct before we are ready to start developing our BPEL processes. In a business process specification, we usually have to make choices based on conditions. In BPEL, conditional branches are defined with the `<if>` activity. The `<if>` activity can have several `<elseif>` branches and one `<else>` branch. The following example shows the structure of the `<if>` activity:

```
<if>
  <condition> boolean-expression </condition>
  <!-- some activity -->
  <elseif>
    <condition> boolean-expression </condition>
    <!-- some activity -->
  </elseif>
  <elseif>
    <condition> boolean-expression </condition>
    <!-- some activity -->
  </elseif>
    ...
  <else>
      <!-- some activity -->
  </else>
</if>
```

The Boolean expressions for `<condition>` elements are expressed in the selected query language. Since the default query language is XPath 1.0, we can use any valid XPath expression that returns a Boolean value.

Variables are usually used in conditions. We access variables in conditions in the same way as in assignments. We have described it in the previous section.

Let us define a conditional branch, based on the age of the insured person. Suppose we want to make three different activities, based on the ages from 0-25, 26-50, and 51 and above. The BPEL would look as follows:

```
<if>
  <condition>
    $InsuranceRequest.insuredPersonData/ins:Age &gt; 50
  </condition>
  <!-- perform activities for age 51 and over -->

  <elseif>
    <condition>
      $InsuranceRequest.insuredPersonData/ins:Age &gt; 25
    </condition>
    <!-- perform activities for age 26-50 -->
  </elseif>

  <else>
    <!-- perform activities for age 25 and under -->
  </else>
</if>
```

Activity names

For each BPEL activity, such as `<if>`, `<invoke>`, `<reply>`, `<sequence>`, and so on, we can specify a name by using the `name` attribute. This attribute is optional and can be used with all basic and structured activities. For instance, the Employee Travel Status web service invocation activity could be named `EmployeeTravelStatusSyncInv`; this is shown in the code excerpt below. We will see that naming activities is useful on several occasions, for example, when invoking inline compensation handlers or when synchronizing activities.

```
...
<invoke name="EmployeeTravelStatusSyncInv"
  partnerLink="employeeTravelStatus"
  portType="emp:EmployeeTravelStatusPT"
  operation="EmployeeTravelStatus"
  inputVariable="EmployeeTravelStatusRequest"
  outputVariable="EmployeeTravelStatusResponse" />
...
```

Activity names also improve the readability of BPEL processes.

Documentation

To include documentation into the BPEL code, we can use the <documentation> construct. We can add this construct to any BPEL activity. For example, we could add documentation to the above-mentioned <invoke> activity:

```
...
<invoke name="EmployeeTravelStatusSyncInv"
  partnerLink="employeeTravelStatus"
  portType="emp:EmployeeTravelStatusPT"
  operation="EmployeeTravelStatus"
  inputVariable="EmployeeTravelStatusRequest"
  outputVariable="EmployeeTravelStatusResponse">
    <documentation>
        Invoking the Employee Travel Status service to get the
          travel class for an employee.
    </documentation>
</invoke>
...
```

Now we know enough to start writing BPEL business process definitions. In the next section, we will write a sample BPEL business process to get familiar with using the core concepts.

BPEL business process example

To demonstrate how business processes are described with BPEL, we will define a simple business process for business travels. Let us consider the business travel process. We describe an oversimplified scenario, where the client invokes the business process, specifying the name of the employee, the destination, the departure date, and the return date. The BPEL business process first checks the employee travel status. We will assume that a service exists through which such a check can be made. Then the BPEL process will check the price for the flight ticket with two airlines—American Airlines and Delta Airlines. Again we will suppose that both airline companies provide a service through which such checks can be made. Finally, the BPEL process will select the lower price and return the travel plan to the client.

For the purpose of this example, we first build a synchronous BPEL process, to maintain simplicity. This means that the client will wait for the response. Later in this chapter, we modify the example and make the BPEL process asynchronous. We will assume that the service for checking the employee travel status is synchronous. This is reasonable because such data can be obtained immediately and returned to the caller.

To acquire the plane ticket prices we use asynchronous invocations. Again, this is reasonable because it might take a little longer to confirm the plane travel schedule. We assume that both airlines offer a service and that both Web Services are identical (provide equal port types and operations). This assumption simplifies our example. In real-world scenarios, you will usually not have the choice about the services but will have to use whatever services are provided by your partners. If you have the luxury of designing the Web Services along with the BPEL process, consider which is the best interface. Usually we use asynchronous services for long-lasting operations and synchronous services for operations that return a result in a relatively short time. If we use asynchronous services, the BPEL process is usually asynchronous as well.

In our example, we first develop a synchronous BPEL process that invokes two asynchronous airline Web Services. This is legal, but not recommended in real-world scenarios since the client may have to wait for an arbitrarily long time. In the real world, the solution would be to develop an asynchronous BPEL process, which we will cover later in this chapter.

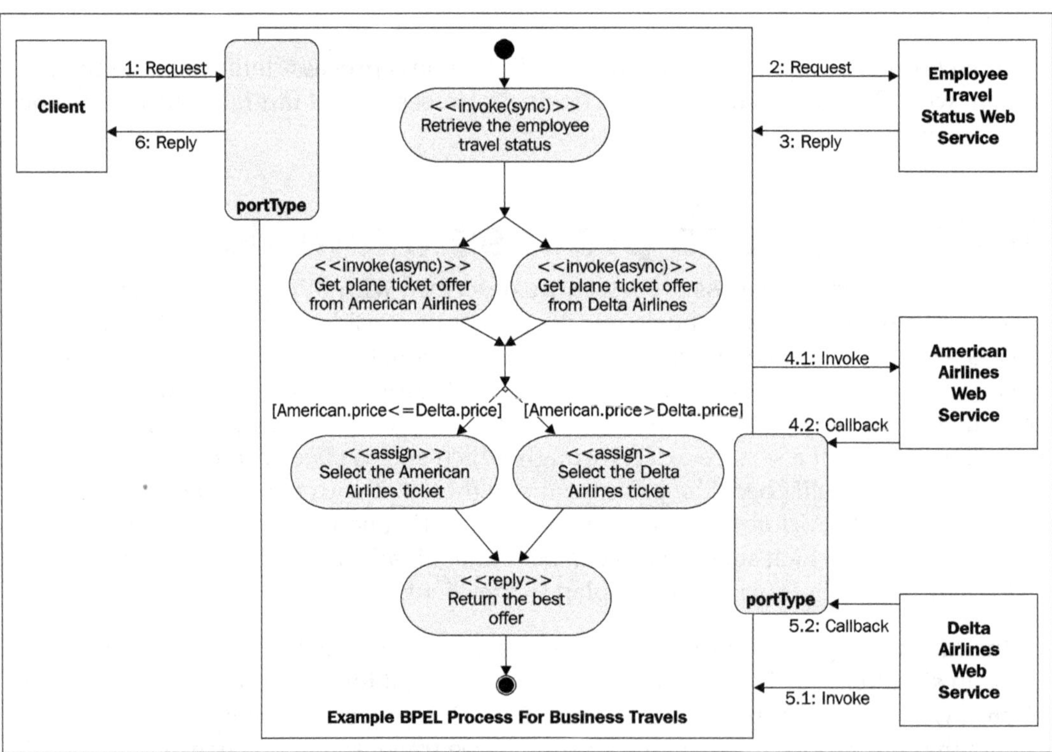

We invoke Web Services of both airlines concurrently and asynchronously. This means that our BPEL process will have to implement the callback operation (and a port type), through which the airlines will return the flight ticket confirmation.

Finally, the BPEL process returns the best airline ticket to the client. In this example, to maintain simplicity, we will not implement any fault handling, which is crucial in real-world scenarios. This topic is discussed in the next chapter.

Let's start by presenting the BPEL process activities using a UML activity diagram. In each activity, we have used the stereotype to indicate the BPEL operation used.

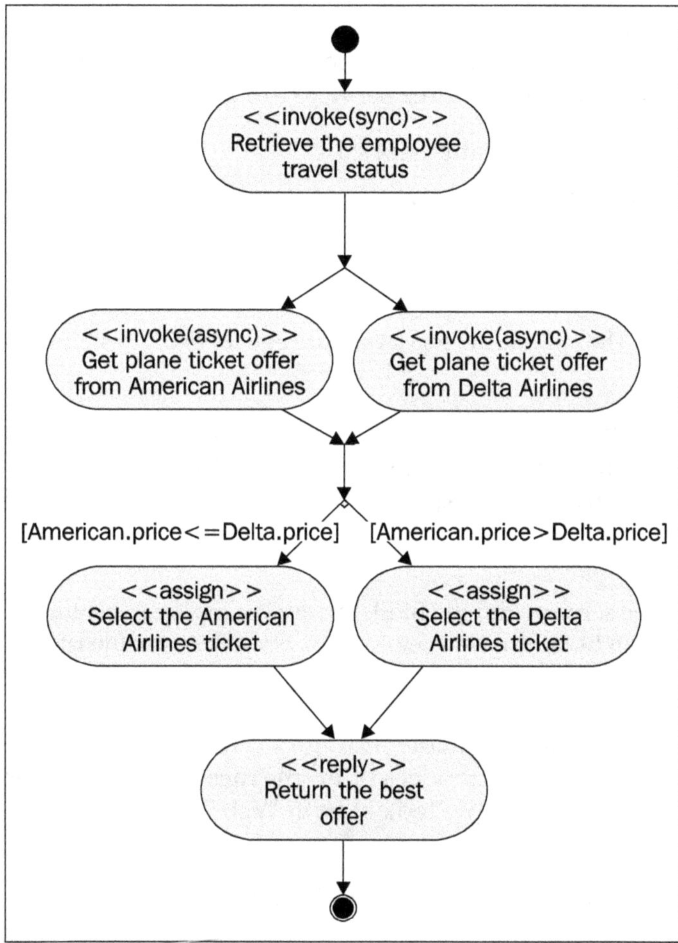

Although the presented process might seem very simple, it will offer a good start for learning BPEL. To develop the BPEL process, we will go through the following steps:

- Get familiar with the involved services
- Define the WSDL for the BPEL process
- Define partner link types

- Define partner links
- Declare variables
- Write the process logic definition

Involved services

Before we can start writing the BPEL process definition, we have to get familiar with all services invoked from our business process. These services are sometimes called partner services. In our example, three services are involved:

- The Employee Travel Status service
- The American Airlines service
- The Delta Airlines service

The two airline services share equal WSDL descriptions.

The services used in this example are not *real*, so we will have to write WSDLs and even implement them to run the example. In real-world scenarios we would obviously use real Web Services exposed by partners involved in the business process.

The services and the BPEL process example can be downloaded from `http://www.packtpub.com`. The example runs on the Oracle SOA Suite.

Web Service descriptions are available through WSDL. WSDL specifies the operations and port types Web Services offer, the messages they accept, and the types they define. We will now look at both Web Services.

Employee Travel Status service

Understanding the services that a business process interacts with is crucial to writing the BPEL process definition. Let's look into the details of our Employee Travel Status service. It provides the `EmployeeTravelStatusPT` port type through which the employee travel status can be checked using the `EmployeeTravelStatus` operation. The operation will return the travel class an employee can use—economy, business, or first. This is shown in the following figure:

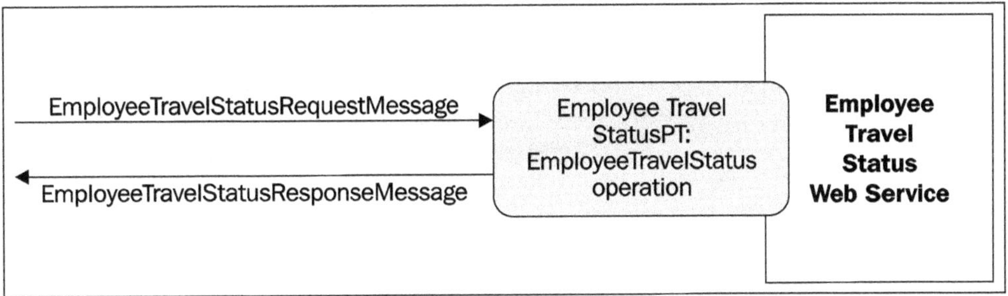

The operation is a synchronous request/response operation as we can see from the WSDL:

```
<?xml version="1.0" encoding="utf-8" ?>
<definitions
  xmlns:http="http://schemas.xmlsoap.org/wsdl/http/"
  xmlns:soap="http://schemas.xmlsoap.org/wsdl/soap/"
  xmlns:xs="http://www.w3.org/2001/XMLSchema"
  xmlns:soapenc=
    "http://schemas.xmlsoap.org/soap/encoding/"
  xmlns:tns="http://packtpub.com/service/employee/"
  targetNamespace="http://packtpub.com/service/employee/"
  xmlns="http://schemas.xmlsoap.org/wsdl/"
  xmlns:plnk="http://docs.oasis-open.org/wsbpel/2.0/plnktype">
...
<portType name="EmployeeTravelStatusPT">
  <operation name="EmployeeTravelStatus">
    <input message="tns:EmployeeTravelStatusRequestMessage" />
    <output message="tns:EmployeeTravelStatusResponseMessage" />
  </operation>
</portType>
...
```

The `EmployeeTravelStatus` operation consists of an input and an output message. To maintain simplicity, the fault is not declared. The definitions of input and output messages are also a part of the WSDL:

```
...
<message name="EmployeeTravelStatusRequestMessage">
  <part name="employee" element="tns:Employee" />
</message>

<message name="EmployeeTravelStatusResponseMessage">
  <part name="travelClass" element="tns:TravelClass" />
</message>
...
```

The `EmployeeTravelStatusRequestMessage` message has a single part—`employee` of element `Employee` with type `EmployeeType`, while the `EmployeeTravelStatusResponseMessage` has a part called `travelClass`, of element `TravelClass` and type `TravelClassType`. The `EmployeeType` and the `TravelClassType` types are defined within the WSDL under the `<types>` element:

```
...
<types>
  <xs:schema elementFormDefault="qualified"
    targetNamespace="http://packtpub.com/service/employee/">
    <xs:complexType name="EmployeeType">
        <xs:sequence>
            <xs:element name="FirstName" type="xs:string" />
            <xs:element name="LastName" type="xs:string" />
            <xs:element name="Department" type="xs:string" />
        </xs:sequence>
    </xs:complexType>
    <xs:element name="Employee" type="EmployeeType"/>
...
```

`EmployeeType` is a complex type and has three elements: first name, last name, and department name. `TravelClassType` is a simple type that uses the enumeration to list the possible classes:

```
...
    <xs:simpleType name="TravelClassType">
        <xs:restriction base="xs:string">
            <xs:enumeration value="Economy"/>
            <xs:enumeration value="Business"/>
            <xs:enumeration value="First"/>
        </xs:restriction>
    </xs:simpleType>
    <xs:element name="TravelClass" type="TravelClassType"/>
  </xs:schema>
</types>
...
```

Now let us look at the airline service.

Airline service

The Airline Service is an asynchronous web service. Therefore, it specifies *two* port types. The first, `FlightAvailabilityPT`, is used to check the flight availability using the `FlightAvailability` operation. To return the result, the service specifies the second port type, `FlightCallbackPT`. This port type specifies the `FlightTicketCallback` operation.

Although the Airline Service defines two port types, it only implements the `FlightAvailabilityPT`. `FlightCallbackPT` is implemented by the BPEL process, which is the client of the web service. The architecture of the service is schematically shown as follows:

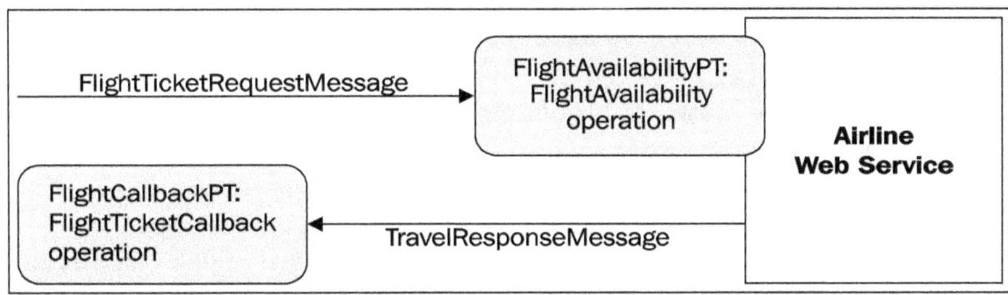

Flight Availability port type

`FlightAvailability` is an asynchronous operation, containing only the input message.

```
<?xml version="1.0" encoding="utf-8" ?>
<definitions xmlns:http="http://schemas.xmlsoap.org/wsdl/http/"
  xmlns:soap="http://schemas.xmlsoap.org/wsdl/soap/"
  xmlns:xs="http://www.w3.org/2001/XMLSchema"
  xmlns:soapenc="http://schemas.xmlsoap.org/soap/encoding/"
  xmlns:emp="http://packtpub.com/service/employee/"
  xmlns:tns="http://packtpub.com/service/airline/"
  targetNamespace="http://packtpub.com/service/airline/"
  xmlns="http://schemas.xmlsoap.org/wsdl/"
  xmlns:plnk="http://docs.oasis-open.org/wsbpel/2.0/plnktype">
...
  <portType name="FlightAvailabilityPT">
    <operation name="FlightAvailability">
      <input message="tns:FlightTicketRequestMessage" />
    </operation>
  </portType>
...
```

The definition of the input message is shown as follows. It consists of two parts—the `flightData` part and the `travelClass` part:

```
<message name="FlightTicketRequestMessage">
  <part name="flightData" element="tns:FlightRequest" />
  <part name="travelClass" element="emp:TravelClass" />
</message>
```

The `travelClass` part is the same as that used in the Employee Travel Status service. The `flightData` part is of element `FlightRequest`, which is defined as follows:

```
...
<types>
  <xs:schema elementFormDefault="qualified"
    targetNamespace="http://packtpub.com/service/airline/">

    <xs:complexType name="FlightRequestType">
      <xs:sequence>
          <xs:element name="OriginFrom" type="xs:string" />
          <xs:element name="DestinationTo" type="xs:string" />
          <xs:element name="DesiredDepartureDate" type="xs:date" />
          <xs:element name="DesiredReturnDate" type="xs:date" />
      </xs:sequence>
    </xs:complexType>
    <xs:element name="FlightRequest" type="FlightRequestType"/>
...
```

`FlightRequestType` is a complex type and has four elements through which we specify the flight origin and destination, the desired departure data, and the desired return date.

Flight Callback port type

The Airline Service needs to specify another port type for the callback operation through which the BPEL process receives the flight ticket response messages.

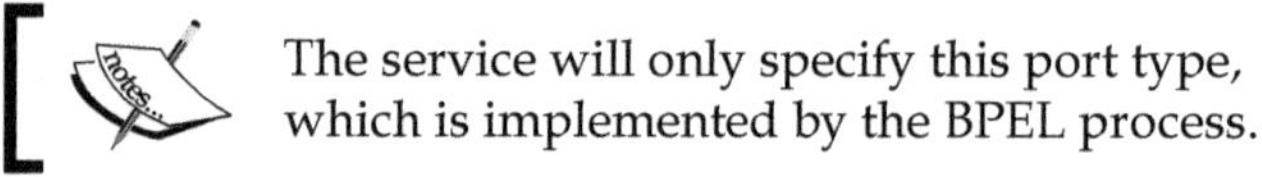

The service will only specify this port type, which is implemented by the BPEL process.

We define the `FlightCallbackPT` port type with the `FlightTicketCallback` operation, which has the `TravelResponseMessage` input message:

```
...
<portType name="FlightCallbackPT">
  <operation name="FlightTicketCallback">
```

```
      <input message="tns:TravelResponseMessage" />
    </operation>
  </portType>
  ...
```

TravelResponseMessage consists of a single part called confirmationData:

```
  ...
  <message name="TravelResponseMessage">
    <part name="confirmationData" element="tns:FlightConfirmation" />
  </message>
  ...
```

FlightConfirmation is of type FlightConfirmationType, which is a complex type used for returning the result. It includes the flight number, travel class, price, departure and arrival date and time, and the approved flag. It is declared as follows:

```
      <xs:complexType name="FlightConfirmationType">
        <xs:sequence>
           <xs:element name="FlightNo" type="xs:string" />
           <xs:element name="TravelClass" type="tns:TravelClassType" />
           <xs:element name="Price" type="xs:float" />
           <xs:element name="DepartureDateTime" type="xs:dateTime" />
           <xs:element name="ReturnDateTime" type="xs:dateTime" />
           <xs:element name="Approved" type="xs:boolean" />
        </xs:sequence>
      </xs:complexType>
      <xs:element name="FlightConfirmation"
        type="FlightConfirmationType"/>
    </xs:schema>
  </types>
```

Now that we are familiar with both services, we can define the BPEL process. Remember that our BPEL process is an actual web service. Therefore, we first have to write the WSDL for the BPEL process.

WSDL for the BPEL process

The business travel BPEL process is exposed as a service. We need to define the WSDL for it. The process will have to receive messages from its clients and return results. So it has to expose a port type that will be used by the client to start the process and get the reply. We define the `TravelApprovalPT` port type with the `TravelApproval` operation, as shown in the following figure:

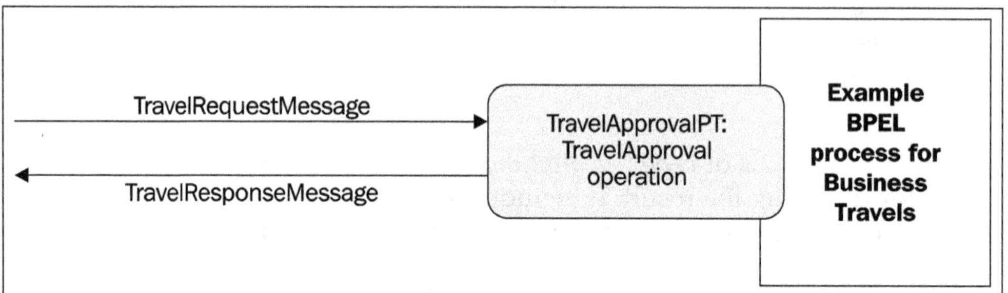

We have already said that the BPEL process is synchronous. The `TravelApproval` operation will be of synchronous request/response type.

```
<?xml version="1.0" encoding="utf-8" ?>
<definitions xmlns:http="http://schemas.xmlsoap.org/wsdl/http/"
  xmlns:soap="http://schemas.xmlsoap.org/wsdl/soap/"
  xmlns:xs="http://www.w3.org/2001/XMLSchema"
  xmlns:soapenc="http://schemas.xmlsoap.org/soap/encoding/"
  xmlns:emp="http://packtpub.com/service/employee/"
  xmlns:aln="http://packtpub.com/service/airline/"
  xmlns:tns="http://packtpub.com/bpel/travel/"
  targetNamespace="http://packtpub.com/bpel/travel/"
  xmlns="http://schemas.xmlsoap.org/wsdl/"
  xmlns:plnk="http://docs.oasis-open.org/wsbpel/2.0/plnktype">
...
  <portType name="TravelApprovalPT">
    <operation name="TravelApproval">
        <input message="tns:TravelRequestMessage" />
        <output message="aln:TravelResponseMessage" />
    </operation>
  </portType>
...
```

We also have to define messages. The `TravelRequestMessage` consists of two parts:

- `employee`: The employee data, which we reuse from the Employee Travel Status service definition
- `flightData`: The flight data, which we reuse from the airline service definition

```
...
<import namespace="http://packtpub.com/service/employee/"
  location="./Employee.wsdl"/>
<import namespace="http://packtpub.com/service/airline/"
  location="./Airline.wsdl"/>
...
<message name="TravelRequestMessage">
  <part name="employee" element="emp:Employee" />
  <part name="flightData" element="aln:FlightRequest" />
</message>
...
```

For the output message, we use the same message used to return the flight information from the airline service: the `TravelResponseMessage` defined in the `aln` namespace. This is reasonable because the BPEL process will get the `TravelResponseMessage` from both airlines, select the most appropriate (the cheapest), and return the same message to the client. As we have already imported the Airline WSDL, we are done.

When writing the WSDL for the BPEL process, we usually do not define the binding (`<binding>`) and the service (`<service>`) sections. These are usually generated by the BPEL execution environment (BPEL server).

Before we can start writing the BPEL process, we still need to define partner link types.

Partner link types

Partner link types represent the interaction between a BPEL process and the involved parties, which includes the services the BPEL process invokes and the client that invokes the BPEL process.

In our example, there are three different partners—the client, the employee travel status service, and the airline service. Ideally, each service should define the corresponding partner link types (in the WSDL). In real-world scenarios, this may not be the case. Then we can wrap the partner web service with a WSDL that imports the WSDL of the service and defines the partner link types. We define three partner link types, each in the corresponding WSDL of the service:

- `travelLT`: This is used to describe the interaction between the BPEL process client and the BPEL process itself. This interaction is synchronous. This partner link type is defined in the WSDL of the BPEL process.
- `employeeLT`: This is used to describe the interaction between the BPEL process and the Employee Travel Status service. This interaction is synchronous too. This partner link type is defined in the WSDL of the Employee service.

- `flightLT`: This describes the interaction between the BPEL process and the Airline Service. This interaction is asynchronous and the Airline Service invokes a callback on the BPEL process. This partner link type is defined in the WSDL of the Airline Service.

We already know that each partner link type can have one or two roles and for each role we must specify the `portType` it uses. For synchronous operations, there is a single role for each partner link type because the operation is only invoked in a single direction.

For example, the client invokes the `TravelApproval` operation on the BPEL process. Because it is a synchronous operation, the client waits for completion and gets a response only after the operation is completed.

Note that if `TravelApproval` were an asynchronous callback operation, we would have to specify two roles. The first role would describe the invocation of the `TravelApproval` operation by the client. The second role would describe the invocation of a callback operation. This callback operation would be invoked by the BPEL process and would call the client to return the result. We will make our example process asynchronous later in this chapter. Remember that there is an asynchronous relationship between the BPEL process and the Airline Service.

As we have already figured out, we need three partner link types. In the first two we have to specify a single role because they deal with synchronous operations. In the third we need to specify both the roles because it is asynchronous.

Partner link types are defined within a special namespace (`http://docs.oasis-open.org/wsbpel/2.0/plnktype`). The reference to this namespace has to be included first as follows:

```
<definitions xmlns:http="http://schemas.xmlsoap.org/wsdl/http/"
  xmlns:soap="http://schemas.xmlsoap.org/wsdl/soap/"
  xmlns:xs="http://www.w3.org/2001/XMLSchema"
  xmlns:soapenc="http://schemas.xmlsoap.org/soap/encoding/"
  xmlns:emp="http://packtpub.com/service/employee/"
  xmlns:aln="http://packtpub.com/service/airline/"
  xmlns:tns="http://packtpub.com/bpel/travel/"
  targetNamespace="http://packtpub.com/bpel/travel/"
  xmlns="http://schemas.xmlsoap.org/wsdl/"
  xmlns:plnk="http://docs.oasis-open.org/wsbpel/2.0/plnktype">
...
```

Now we can add the definitions for the partner link types. First, we define the `travelLT` link type in the BPEL process WSDL. This is used by clients to invoke the BPEL process. The only role required is the role of the travel service (our BPEL process). The client uses the `TravelApprovalPT` port type to communicate with the BPEL service:

```
...
<plnk:partnerLinkType name="travelLT">
  <plnk:role name="travelService"
    portType="tns:TravelApprovalPT" />
</plnk:partnerLinkType>
...
```

The second link type is `employeeLT`. It is used to describe the communication between the BPEL process and the Employee Travel Status service and is defined in the WSDL of the Employee service. The interaction is synchronous, so we need a single role, called `employeeTravelStatusService`. The BPEL process uses the `EmployeeTravelStatusPT` on the Employee service:

```
...
<plnk:partnerLinkType name="employeeLT">
  <plnk:role name="employeeTravelStatusService"
             portType="tns:EmployeeTravelStatusPT" />
</plnk:partnerLinkType>
...
```

The last partner link type is `flightLT`, used to describe the communication between the BPEL process and the Airline Service. This communication is asynchronous. The BPEL process invokes an asynchronous operation on the Airline Service. The web service, after it has completed the request, invokes a callback on the BPEL process. Therefore, we need two roles:

- The first role describes the role of the Airline Service to the BPEL process, which is the airline service (`airlineService`). The BPEL process uses the `FlightAvailabilityPT` port type to make the asynchronous invocation.
- The second role describes the role of the BPEL process to the Airline Services. For the Airline Service, the BPEL process is an airline customer, thus the role name is `airlineCustomer`. The Airline Service uses the `FlightCallbackPT` port type to make the callback.

This partner link type is defined in the WSDL of the Airline service:

```
...
<plnk:partnerLinkType name="flightLT">
  <plnk:role name="airlineService"
             portType="tns:FlightAvailabilityPT" />
```

```
    <plnk:role name="airlineCustomer"
               portType="tns:FlightCallbackPT" />
  </plnk:partnerLinkType>
  ...
```

Understanding partner link types is crucial for developing a BPEL process specification. Sometimes it helps to make a diagram of all the interactions. Once the partner link types are defined, we have finished the preparation phase and are ready to start writing the business process definition.

Business process definition

The BPEL business process definition specifies the order of activities that have to be performed within a business process. Typically, a BPEL process waits for an incoming message, which starts the execution of the business process. This incoming message is usually the client request. Then a series of activities occur, either sequentially or in parallel. These activities include:

- Invoking operations on other services
- Receiving results from other services
- Conditional branching, which influences the flow of the business process
- Looping
- Fault handling
- Waiting for certain events to occur

In our example process, we do not cover all these aspects. We will leave loops, faults, and waits for the next chapter. Before we start defining our business process, let's have a quick look at the sequence diagram. It shows the messages exchanged between the involved parties.

The following parties are involved:

- The client that will invoke the BPEL process
- The BPEL process itself
- The Employee Travel Status service
- Two airline web services, American and Delta

The client initiates the BPEL process by sending an input message, `TravelRequest`. This is a synchronous call. Then the BPEL process invokes the Employee Travel Status service, sending the `EmployeeTravelStatusRequest` message. Because this is a synchronous invocation, it waits for the `EmployeeTravelStatusResponse` message. Then the BPEL process makes concurrent asynchronous invocations of both airline Web Services by sending them the `FlightTicketRequest` message. Both airline Web Services make a callback, sending the `TravelResponse` message. The BPEL process then selects the more appropriate airline and returns the reply message `TravelResponse` to the initial client. See the following sequence diagram:

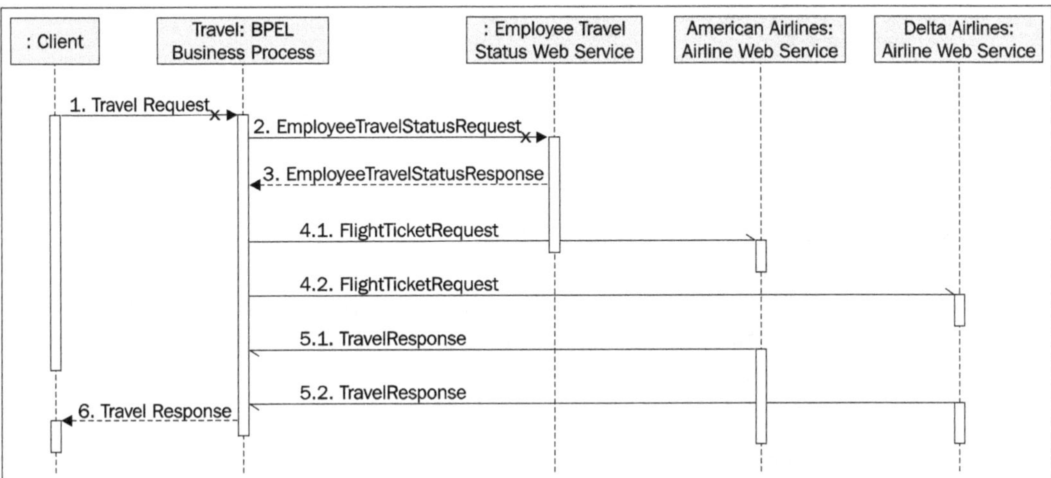

In real-world scenarios, we do not define synchronous BPEL processes that use asynchronous Web Services, since the client may have to wait an arbitrarily long time. We would rather select an asynchronous BPEL process. In this example, we use the synchronous example to maintain simplicity. The next section shows how to define an asynchronous BPEL process.

Understanding and knowing the exact details of a business process is crucial. Otherwise, we will not be able to specify it using BPEL.

Now we are ready to start writing the BPEL process definition. Each BPEL definition contains at least four main parts:

- The initial `<process>` root element with the declaration of namespaces
- The definition of partner links, using the `<partnerLinks>` element
- The declaration of variables, using the `<variables>` element
- The main body where the actual business process is defined; this is usually a `<sequence>` that specifies the flow of the process

BPEL process outline

We start with an empty BPEL process outline that presents the basic structure of each BPEL process definition document:

```
<process name="Travel" ... >
  <partnerLinks>
    <!-- The declaration of partner links -->
  </partnerLinks>

  <variables>
    <!-- The declaration of variables -->
  </variables>

  <sequence>
    <!-- The definition of the BPEL business process main body -->
  </sequence>
</process>
```

Let us first add the required namespaces. Here we have to define the target namespace and the namespaces to access the Employee and Airline WSDLs and the BPEL process WSDL. We also have to declare the namespace for all the BPEL activity tags (here the default namespace, so we do not have to qualify each BPEL tag name). The BPEL activity namespace must be `http://docs.oasis-open.org/wsbpel/2.0/process/executable`.

```
<process name="Travel"
  targetNamespace="http://packtpub.com/bpel/travel/"
  xmlns="http://docs.oasis-open.org/wsbpel/2.0/process/executable"
  xmlns:trv="http://packtpub.com/bpel/travel/"
  xmlns:emp="http://packtpub.com/service/employee/"
  xmlns:aln="http://packtpub.com/service/airline/" >
...
```

Partner links

Next we have to define the partner links. Partner links define different parties that interact with the BPEL process. Each partner link is related to a specific `partnerLinkType` that characterizes it. Each partner link also specifies up to two attributes:

- `myRole`: Indicates the role of the business process itself
- `partnerRole`: Indicates the role of the partner

The partner link can specify a single role, which is usually the case with synchronous request/response operations. In our example, we define four roles. The first partner link is called `client` and is characterized by the `travelLT` partner link type. The `client` invokes the business process. We need to specify the `myRole` attribute to describe the role of the BPEL process. In our case, this is the `travelService`.

```
...
<partnerLinks>
  <partnerLink name="client"
    partnerLinkType="trv:travelLT" myRole="travelService"/>
...
```

The second partner link is called `employeeTravelStatus` and is characterized by the `employeeLT` partner link type. It is a synchronous request/response relationship between the BPEL process and the service; we again specify only one role. This time it is the `partnerRole` because we describe the role of the service, which is a partner to the BPEL process.

```
...
  <partnerLink name="employeeTravelStatus"
    partnerLinkType="emp:employeeLT"
    partnerRole="employeeTravelStatusService"/>
...
```

The last two partner links correspond to the airline services. Because they use the same type of service, we specify two partner links based on a single partner link type, `flightLT`. Here we have asynchronous callback communication; therefore, we need two roles. The role of the BPEL process (`myRole`) to the airline web service is `airlineCustomer`, while the role of the airline (`partnerRole`) is `airlineService`.

```
...
  <partnerLink name="AmericanAirlines"
    partnerLinkType="aln:flightLT"
    myRole="airlineCustomer"
    partnerRole="airlineService"/>

  <partnerLink name="DeltaAirlines"
    partnerLinkType="aln:flightLT"
    myRole="airlineCustomer"
    partnerRole="airlineService"/>
</partnerLinks>
```

Variables for the Travel Process

Variables are used to store messages and to reformat and transform them. We usually need a variable for every message sent to the partners and received from the partners. Looking at the sequence diagram, this would mean eight variables for our example. However, notice that the messages sent to both Airline Services are identical. So, we only need seven variables. Let's call them `TravelRequest`, `EmployeeTravelStatusRequest`, `EmployeeTravelStatusResponse`, `FlightDetails`, `FlightResponseAA`, `FlightResponseDA`, and `TravelResponse`.

For each variable we have to specify the type. We can use a WSDL message type, an XML schema simple type, or an XML schema element. In our example, we use WSDL message types for all variables:

```
...
<variables>
  <!-- input for this process -->
  <variable name="TravelRequest"
    messageType="trv:TravelRequestMessage"/>
  <!-- input for the Employee Travel Status service -->
  <variable name="EmployeeTravelStatusRequest"
    messageType="emp:EmployeeTravelStatusRequestMessage"/>
  <!-- output from the Employee Travel Status service -->
  <variable name="EmployeeTravelStatusResponse"
    messageType="emp:EmployeeTravelStatusResponseMessage"/>
  <!-- input for American and Delta services -->
  <variable name="FlightDetails"
     messageType="aln:FlightTicketRequestMessage"/>
  <!-- output from American Airlines -->
  <variable name="FlightResponseAA"
    messageType="aln:TravelResponseMessage"/>
  <!-- output from Delta Airlines -->
  <variable name="FlightResponseDA"
     messageType="aln:TravelResponseMessage"/>
  <!-- output from BPEL process -->
  <variable name="TravelResponse"
    messageType="aln:TravelResponseMessage"/>
</variables>
...
```

BPEL process main body

The process main body may contain only one top-level activity. Usually, this is a `<sequence>` that allows us to define several activities that will be performed sequentially. Other possibilities for this activity include `<flow>`, through which several activities can be performed concurrently. We can also specify `<while>` to indicate loops, or `<scope>` to define nested activities. However, we usually use `<sequence>` and nest other activities within the sequence.

Within the sequence, we first specify the input message that starts the business process. We do this with the `<receive>` construct, which waits for the matching message. In our case, this is the `TravelRequest` message. Within the `<receive>` construct, we do *not* specify the message directly. Rather we specify the partner link, the port type, the operation name, and optionally the variable that holds the received message for consequent operations.

We link the message reception with the client partner, and wait for the `TravelApproval` operation to be invoked on port type `TravelApprovalPT`. We store the received message in the `TravelRequest` variable as follows:

```
...
<sequence>

<!-- Receive the initial request for business travel from client -->
  <receive name="ReceiveInitialRequest" partnerLink="client"
    portType="trv:TravelApprovalPT" operation="TravelApproval"
    variable="TravelRequest" createInstance="yes" />
...
```

As already mentioned, `<receive>` waits for the client to invoke the `TravelApproval` operation and stores the incoming message and parameters about the business trip into the `TravelRequest` variable. Here, the variable name is the same as the message name, but this is not necessary.

Next, we need to invoke the Employee Travel Status service. Before this, we have to prepare the input for this service. Looking at the WSDL of the Employee service, we can see that we have to send a message consisting of the employee part. We can construct such a message by copying the employee part of the message that the client sent. We write the corresponding assignment:

```
...
<!-- Prepare the input for the Employee Travel Status Service -->
<assign name="PrepareInputForEmployeeWS">
  <copy>
    <from variable="TravelRequest" part="employee"/>
    <to variable="EmployeeTravelStatusRequest" part="employee"/>
```

```
    </copy>
  </assign>
  ...
```

Now we can invoke the Employee Travel Status service. We make a synchronous invocation, for which we use the `<invoke>` activity. We use the `employeeTravelStatus` partner link and invoke the `EmployeeTravelStatus` operation on the `EmployeeTravelStatusPT` port type. We have prepared the input message in the `EmployeeTravelStatusRequest` variable. Because it is a synchronous invocation, the call waits for the reply and stores it in the `EmployeeTravelStatusResponse` variable:

```
...
<!-- Synchronously invoke the Employee Travel Status Service -->
<invoke name="InvokeEmployeeWS"
  partnerLink="employeeTravelStatus"
  portType="emp:EmployeeTravelStatusPT"
  operation="EmployeeTravelStatus"
  inputVariable="EmployeeTravelStatusRequest"
  outputVariable="EmployeeTravelStatusResponse" />
...
```

The next step is to invoke both Airline Web Services. Again, we first prepare the required input message (which is equal for both Web Services). The `FlightTicketRequest` message consists of two parts:

- `flightData`: This is retrieved from the client message (`TravelRequest`)
- `travelClass`: This is retrieved from the `EmployeeTravelStatusResponse` variable

Therefore, we write an assignment with two copy elements:

```
...
<!-- Prepare the input for AA and DA -->
<assign name="PrepareInputForAAandDA">
  <copy>
    <from variable="TravelRequest" part="flightData"/>
    <to variable="FlightDetails" part="flightData"/>
  </copy>
  <copy>
    <from variable="EmployeeTravelStatusResponse"
      part="travelClass"/>
    <to variable="FlightDetails" part="travelClass"/>
  </copy>
</assign>
...
```

The input data includes the data that needs to be passed to the Airline Web Services. Since it is in the same format, we can pass it directly (using a simple copy). In the real world, we usually need to perform a transformation. We could do that using XPath expressions with `<assign>`, use a transformation service (such as an XSLT engine), or use the transformation capabilities provided by specific BPEL servers.

Now we are ready to invoke both Airline Web Services. We will make concurrent asynchronous invocations. To express concurrency, BPEL provides the `<flow>` activity. The invocation to each web service will consist of two steps:

1. The `<invoke>` activity is used for the asynchronous invocation.
2. The `<receive>` activity is used to wait for the callback.

We use `<sequence>` to group both activities. The two invocations differ only in the partner link name. We use `AmericanAirlines` for one and `DeltaAirlines` for the other. Both invoke the `FlightAvailability` operation on the `FlightAvailabilityPT` port type, sending the message from the `FlightDetails` variable.

The callback is received using the `<receive>` activity. Again, we use both partner link names. The `<receive>` activity waits for the `FlightTicketCallback` operation to be invoked on the `FlightCallbackPT` port type. We store the resulting message in the `FlightResponseAA` and the `FlightResponseDA` variables respectively:

```
...
<!-- Make a concurrent invocation to AA in DA -->
<flow name="InvokeAAandDA">
  <sequence>
  <!--Async invoke of the AA web service and wait for the callback-->

    <invoke name="InvokeAA"
      partnerLink="AmericanAirlines"
      portType="aln:FlightAvailabilityPT"
      operation="FlightAvailability"
      inputVariable="FlightDetails" />

    <receive name="ReceiveCallbackFromAA"
      partnerLink="AmericanAirlines"
      portType="aln:FlightCallbackPT"
      operation="FlightTicketCallback"
      variable="FlightResponseAA" />

  </sequence>

  <sequence>
  <!--Async invoke of the DA web service and wait for the callback-->
```

```
    <invoke name="InvokeDA"
      partnerLink="DeltaAirlines"
      portType="aln:FlightAvailabilityPT"
      operation="FlightAvailability"
      inputVariable="FlightDetails" />

    <receive name="ReceiveCallbackFromDA"
      partnerLink="DeltaAirlines"
      portType="aln:FlightCallbackPT"
      operation="FlightTicketCallback"
      variable="FlightResponseDA" />

  </sequence>

</flow>
...
```

At this stage of the process, we have two ticket offers. In the next step, we have to select one. For this, we use the `<if>` activity:

```
...
<!-- Select the best offer and construct the TravelResponse -->
<if name="SelectBestOffer">

  <condition>
    $FlightResponseAA.confirmationData/aln:Price &lt;=
      $FlightResponseDA.confirmationData/aln:Price
  </condition>

  <!-- Select American Airlines -->
  <assign>
    <copy>
        <from variable="FlightResponseAA" />
        <to variable="TravelResponse" />
    </copy>
  </assign>

  <else>
  <!-- Select Delta Airlines -->
    <assign>
        <copy>
            <from variable="FlightResponseDA" />
            <to variable="TravelResponse" />
        </copy>
    </assign>
  </else>
</if>
...
```

In the `<if>` element, we check whether the offer from American Airlines (`FlightResponseAA`) is equal or better than the offer from Delta (`FlightResponseDA`). For this, we access the BPEL variable from XPath using the `$` operator. The price is located inside the `confirmationData` message part, which is the only message part, but we still have to specify it. We also have to specify the node to locate the price element. Here, this is a simple XPath 1.0 expression.

If the American Airlines offer is better than Delta (or equal), we copy the `FlightResponseAA` variable to the `TravelResponse` variable (which we finally return to the client). Otherwise, we copy the `FlightResponseDA` variable.

We have come to the final step of the BPEL business process—to return a reply to the client using the `<reply>` activity. Here we specify the same partner link as in the initial receive client. We also specify the same port type and operation name. The variable that holds the reply message is `TravelResponse`.

```
...
<!-- Send a response to the client -->
    <reply name="SendResponse"
      partnerLink="client"
      portType="trv:TravelApprovalPT"
      operation="TravelApproval"
      variable="TravelResponse"/>
  </sequence>
</process>
```

With this, we have concluded our first business process specification in BPEL. You can see that BPEL is not very complicated and allows a relatively easy and natural specification of business processes. The consumption of other services is also relatively easy if you are familiar with WSDL. In the next section, we modify our BPEL process to make it asynchronous.

Asynchronous BPEL example

Our first BPEL business process example was synchronous because this was the easiest case. However, in the real world, we will mostly use asynchronous processes. Most business processes are long running. It makes no sense for a client to wait (and be blocked) for the entire duration of the process. A much better alternative is to model the BPEL process as asynchronous. This means that the client invokes the process, and when the process completes, it performs a callback to the client. This has a few consequences:

- For the BPEL process to be able to perform a callback to the client, the client must be a service and implement a certain port type (usually defined by the BPEL process WSDL)

- The partner link type for the client will have to specify two roles
- The BPEL process will not <reply> to the client. Rather it will <invoke> the callback

Let us now focus on our business process and modify it for asynchronous invocation, presented in the next sequence diagram. We have to perform the following steps:

1. Modify the BPEL process WSDL, where the operation invoked by the client will now have only the input message.
2. Define the client port type and the operation, which the BPEL process will invoke for the callback. We will do this in the WSDL of the BPEL process.
3. Modify the partner link type, where we will add the second role.
4. Modify the BPEL process specification. We have to modify the partner link and replace the <reply> activity with an <invoke>.

The modified sequence diagram is shown as follows. It is very similar to the previous example, except that the initial travel request is asynchronous and the final answer is delivered as a callback.

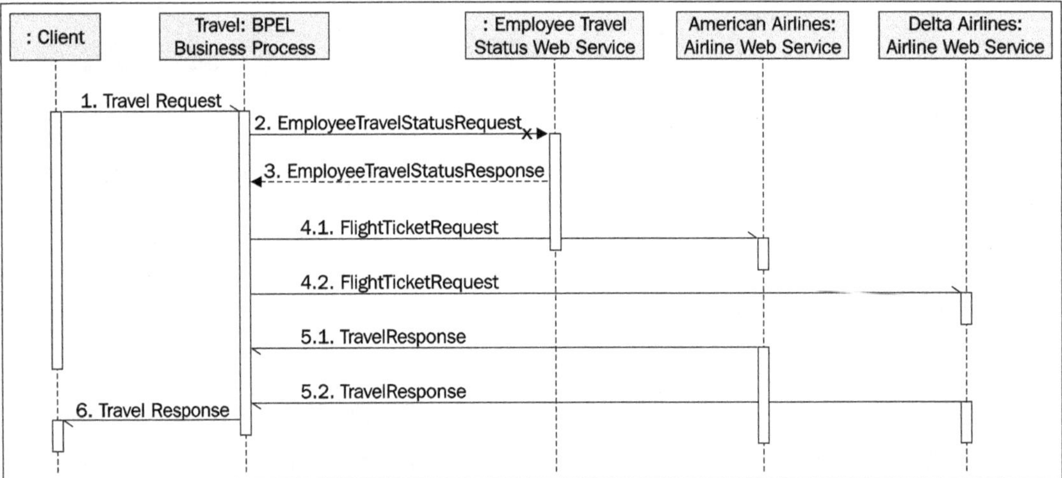

Modify the BPEL Process WSDL

The modified WSDL for the BPEL process will have to specify the `TravelApprovalPT` port type, which will now specify an input message only. It will also have to declare the `ClientCallbackPT` port type, used to return the result to the client (asynchronously, using a callback). This is shown in the following figure:

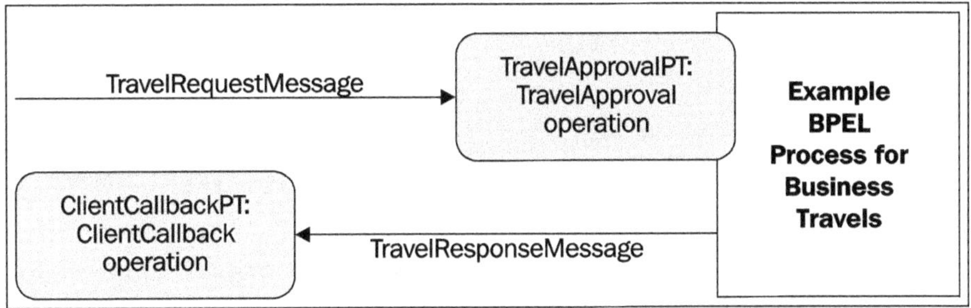

Let us first modify the `TravelApprovalPT` port type used for client interaction, which will now define only the input message:

```
...
<portType name="TravelApprovalPT">
  <operation name="TravelApproval">
    <input message="tns:TravelRequestMessage" />
  </operation>
</portType>
...
```

Next we define the client callback port type (`ClientCallbackPT`) with the `ClientCallback` operation. The response message is `TravelResponseMessage`. Notice that the WSDL only specifies this port type, which is implemented by the client.

```
...
<portType name="ClientCallbackPT">
  <operation name="ClientCallback">
    <input message="aln:TravelResponseMessage" />
  </operation>
</portType>
...
```

Modify partner link types

We need to modify the partner link type for the interaction with the BPEL process, called the `travelLT` link type. We have to add the second role, `travelServiceCustomer`, which characterizes the client to which the BPEL process will perform a callback on the `ClientCallbackPT` port type. This is done in the WSDL of the BPEL process:

```
<plnk:partnerLinkType name="travelLT">
  <plnk:role name="travelService"
    portType="tns:TravelApprovalPT" />
```

```
    <plnk:role name="travelServiceCustomer"
      portType="tns:ClientCallbackPT" />
  </plnk:partnerLinkType>
```

Modify the BPEL process definition

Finally, we modify the BPEL process definition. Here we first have to modify the client partner link, where we have to specify the second role—the `partnerRole`. Here, this is `travelServiceCustomer`, which characterizes the BPEL process client.

```
<partnerLinks>
  <partnerLink name="client"
    partnerLinkType="trv:travelLT"
    myRole="travelService"
    partnerRole="travelServiceCustomer"/>
...
```

Next, we change the last activity of the BPEL process. We replace the `<reply>` activity with the `<invoke>` callback. For the callback, we use the client partner link and invoke the `ClientCallback` operation on the `ClientCallbackPT` port type. The message signature has not changed, so we use the same variable as before, `TravelResponse`.

```
...
    <!-- Make a callback to the client -->
    <invoke name="SendResponse"
      partnerLink="client"
      portType="trv:ClientCallbackPT"
      operation="ClientCallback"
      inputVariable="TravelResponse" />
  </sequence>
</process>
```

Our BPEL process is now asynchronous!

To execute a BPEL process, we need a runtime environment. In *Chapter 1* we provided an overview of BPEL servers. Later chapters give a detailed description of the Oracle SOA Suite.

You can download both the synchronous and asynchronous BPEL process examples with the corresponding services from `http://www.packtpub.com`. They can be deployed to the Oracle SOA Suite using JDeveloper. For more information on Oracle SOA Suite and JDeveloper, refer to *Chapter 4*.

Summary

In this chapter, you have become familiar with the basic concepts of service composition with BPEL. BPEL is an XML-based language for business process definition. Each process has a set of activities and interacts with partner services. The BPEL process is also a service.

With BPEL, we can define executable and abstract business processes. In this chapter, we have focused on executable processes. They define exactly the activities of the processes and can be executed on a BPEL-compliant server. We have overviewed the basic concepts of BPEL, described how to invoke services synchronously and asynchronously, and discussed the role of WSDL. BPEL processes can be synchronous or asynchronous and we have overviewed both options. Web Services with which a BPEL process interacts are called partner services. Therefore, we have explained the concepts of partner link types and partner links.

We have overviewed the most important activities for invoking operations, receiving messages, and returning replies to clients. We have also become familiar with variables and assignments. With this theoretical knowledge, we defined two example BPEL processes for business travel. We developed a synchronous and then an asynchronous process.

3
Advanced BPEL

In the previous chapter, we covered the basics of BPEL and provided an introduction to the structure of business processes. We are now familiar with defining business processes, invoking web service operations sequentially and in parallel, defining partner links, defining variables, and assigning values. However, using BPEL for complex real-world business processes requires additional functionality. Sometimes, the activities of a business process need to be performed in loops. Often activities might have links that would affect the execution order. This is usually the case with concurrent flows. Sometimes, we will have to wait either for a message event or an alarm event to occur.

One very important aspect of business process modeling is fault handling. Particularly in business processes that span multiple enterprises and use web services over the Internet, we can assume that faults will occur quite often due to various reasons, including broken connections, unreachable web services, unavailability of services, and so on. If business processes do not finish successfully, we might need a way to undo the partial work. This is called compensation and is one of the features of BPEL.

In this chapter, we will look at these and other advanced BPEL features including:

- BPEL activities not covered in the previous chapter, such as loops, delays, and process termination
- Fault handling
- Scopes and isolation
- Compensation
- Events and event handlers
- Concurrent activities and links
- The business process lifecycle
- Correlations and message properties

- Dynamic partner links
- Abstract business processes
- Generating BPEL from BPMN diagrams

Advanced activities

In the previous chapter, we familiarized ourselves with important BPEL activities, including invoking web service operations (`<invoke>`), receiving messages from partners (`<receive>`), returning results to process clients (`<reply>`), declaring variables (`<variable>`), updating variable contents (`<assign>`), sequential and concurrent structured activities (`<sequence>` and `<flow>`), and conditional behavior (`<if>`).

However, these activities are not sufficient for complex real-world business processes. Therefore, in the first part of this chapter we will become familiar with the other important activities offered by BPEL, particularly activity names, loops, delays, empty activities, and process termination. We will not discuss concrete use cases where these activities can be used, because they are well known to developers. We will, however, use these activities later in the chapter, where we will present some examples. Let us first look at loops.

Loops

When defining business processes, we will sometimes want to perform a certain activity or a set of activities in a loop, for example, perform a calculation or invoke a partner web service operation several times, and so on.

BPEL supports the following three types of loops:

- `<while>` loops
- `<repeatUntil>` loops
- `<forEach>` loops

The `<while>` and `<repeatUntil>` loops are very similar to other programming languages. The `<forEach>` loop, on the other hand, provides the ability to start the loop instances in parallel.

Loops are helpful when dealing with arrays. In BPEL, arrays can be simulated using XML complex types where one or more elements can occur more than once (using the `maxOccurs` attribute in the XML Schema definition). To iterate through multiple occurrences of the same element, we can use XPath expressions.

Let us now look at the <while> loop.

While

The <while> loop repeats the enclosed activities until the Boolean condition no longer holds true. The Boolean condition is expressed through the condition element, using the selected expression language (the default is XPath 1.0). The syntax of the <while> activity is shown in the following code excerpt:

```
<while>
  <condition> boolean-expression </condition>

   <!-- Perform an activity or a set of activities enclosed by
        <sequence>,
        <flow>, or other structured activity -->

</while>
```

Let us consider a scenario where we need to check flight availability for more than one person. Let us also assume that we need to invoke a web service operation for each person, similar to the example in Chapter 2. In addition to the variables already present in the example, we would need two more NoOfPassengers to hold the number of passengers, and Counter to use in the loop. The code excerpt with variable declarations is shown as follows:

```
<variables>
   ...
   <variable name="NoOfPassengers"
             type="xs:int"/>
   <variable name="Counter"
             type="xs:int"/>
   ...
</variables>
```

We also need to assign values to the variables. The NoOfPassengers can be obtained from the Employee Travel web service. In the following code, we initialize both variables with static values:

```
<assign>
  <copy>
    <from>number(5)</from>
    <to variable="NoOfPassengers"/>
  </copy>
  <copy>
    <from>number(0)</from>
    <to variable="Counter"/>
  </copy>
</assign>
```

The loop to perform the web service invocation is shown in the following code excerpt. Please remember that this excerpt is not complete:

```
<while>
  <condition>$Counter &lt; $NoOfPassengers</condition>
  <sequence>
    <!-- Construct the FlightDetails variable with passenger data
    -->
    ...
    <!-- Invoke the web service -->
    <invoke partnerLink="AmericanAirlines"
          portType="aln:FlightAvailabilityPT"
          operation="FlightAvailability"
          inputVariable="FlightDetails" />
    <receive partnerLink="AmericanAirlines"
          portType="trv:FlightCallbackPT"
          operation="FlightTicketCallback"
          variable="FlightResponseAA" />
    ...
    <!-- Process the results ... -->
    ...
    <!-- Increment the counter -->
    <assign>
      <copy>
        <from>$Counter + 1</from>
        <to variable="Counter"/>
      </copy>
    </assign>
  </sequence>
</while>
```

Repeat Until

The `<repeatUntil>` loop repeats the enclosed activities until the Boolean condition becomes true. The Boolean condition is expressed through the `condition` element, the same way as in `<while>` loop. The syntax of the `<repeatUntil>` activity is shown in the following code excerpt:

```
<repeatUntil>
   <!-- Perform an activity or a set of activities enclosed by
        <sequence>,
        <flow>, or other structured activity -->
```

```
    <condition> boolean-expression </condition>
  </repeatUntil>
```

A similar example of a loop as in the previous section, but using `<repeatUntil>` is shown as follows:

```
<repeatUntil>

  <sequence>

    <!-- Construct the FlightDetails variable with passenger data
    -->
    ...
    <!-- Invoke the web service -->
    <invoke partnerLink="AmericanAirlines"
          portType="aln:FlightAvailabilityPT"
          operation="FlightAvailability"
          inputVariable="FlightDetails" />

    <receive partnerLink="AmericanAirlines"
          portType="trv:FlightCallbackPT"
          operation="FlightTicketCallback"
          variable="FlightResponseAA" />

    ...
    <!-- Process the results ... -->
    ...
    <!-- Increment the counter -->
    <assign>
      <copy>
        <from>$Counter + 1</from>
        <to variable="Counter"/>
      </copy>
    </assign>
  </sequence>

  <condition>$Counter &gt;= $NoOfPassengers</condition>
</repeatUntil>
```

For Each

The `<forEach>` loop is a `for` type loop, with an important distinction. In BPEL, the `<forEach>` loop can execute the loop branches in parallel or serial. The serial `<forEach>` is very similar to the `for` loops from various programming languages, such as Java. The parallel `<forEach>` executes the loop branches in parallel (similar to `<flow>`), which opens new possibilities in relatively simple parallel execution (for example, invocation of services).

The `<forEach>` loop requires us to specify the BPEL variable for the counter (`counterName`), the `startCounterValue`, and the `finalCounterValue`. The `<forEach>` loop will execute (`finalCounterValue - startCounterValue + 1`) times.

The `<forEach>` loop requires that we put all activities, which should be executed within the branch, into a `<scope>`. A `<scope>` allows us to group related activities. We will discuss them in detail later in this chapter.

The syntax of `<forEach>` is shown as follows:

```
<forEach counterName="BPELVariableName" parallel="yes|no">

   <startCounterValue>unsigned-integer-expression</startCounterValue>
   <finalCounterValue>unsigned-integer-expression</finalCounterValue>

   <scope>
      <!-- The activities that are performed within forEach have to be
           nested
           within a scope. -->
   </scope>

</forEach>
```

Such `<forEach>` loops will complete when all branches (`<scope>`s) have completed.

A similar example of a loop as in the previous section is shown next:

```
<forEach counterName="Counter" parallel="no">

  <startCounterValue>number(1)</startCounterValue>
  <finalCounterValue>$NoOfPassengers</finalCounterValue>

  <scope>
    <sequence>

      <!-- Construct the FlightDetails variable with passenger
           data -->
      ...

      <!-- Invoke the web service -->
      <invoke partnerLink="AmericanAirlines"
          portType="aln:FlightAvailabilityPT"
          operation="FlightAvailability"
          inputVariable="FlightDetails" />

      <receive partnerLink="AmericanAirlines"
          portType="trv:FlightCallbackPT"
          operation="FlightTicketCallback"
          variable="FlightResponseAA" />

      ...
```

```
          <!-- Process the results ... -->
          ...
        </sequence>
      </scope>
    </forEach>
```

Sometimes it would be useful if the <forEach> loop would not have to wait for all branches to complete. Rather, it would wait so that at least some branches complete. In <forEach>, we can specify that the loop will complete after at least N branches have completed. We do this using the <completionCondition> . We specify the number N of <branches>. The <forEach> will complete after at least N branches have completed. We can specify if we would like to count only successful branches or all branches. We do this using the successfulBranchesOnly attribute. If set to yes, only successful branches will count. If set to no (default), successful and failed branches will count. The syntax is shown below:

```
<forEach counterName="BPELVariableName" parallel="yes|no">
   <startCounterValue>unsigned-integer-expression</startCounterValue>
   <finalCounterValue>unsigned-integer-expression</finalCounterValue>
   <completionCondition>      <!-- Optional -->
      <branches successfulBranchesOnly="yes|no">
         unsigned-integer-expression
      </branches>
   </completionCondition>
   <scope>
      <!-- The activities that are performed within forEach have to be
           nested
           within a scope. -->
   </scope>
</forEach>
```

Delays

Sometimes a business process may need to specify a certain delay. In BPEL, we can specify delays either for a specified period of time or until a certain deadline is reached, by using the <wait> activity. Typically, we could specify delays to invoke an operation at a specific time; or wait for some time and then invoke an operation; for example, we could choose to wait before we pool the results of a previously initiated operation or wait between iterations of a loop.

The `<wait>` activity can be as follows:

- `for`: We can specify duration; we specify a period of time.

```
<wait>
  <for> duration-expression </for>
</wait>
```

- `until`: We can specify a deadline; we specify a certain date and time.

```
<wait>
  <until> deadline-expression </until>
</wait>
```

Deadline and duration expressions

To specify deadline and duration expressions, BPEL uses lexical representations of corresponding XML Schema data types. For deadlines, these data types are either `dateTime` or `date`. For duration, we use the `duration` data type. The lexical representation of expressions should conform to the XPath 1.0 (or the selected query language) expressions. The evaluation of such expressions should result in values that are of corresponding XML Schema types: `dateTime` and `date` for deadline and `duration` for duration expressions.

All three data types use lexical representation inspired by the ISO 8601 standard, which can be obtained from the ISO web page `http://www.iso.ch`. ISO 8601 lexical format uses characters within the date and time information. Characters are appended to the numbers and have the following meanings:

- `C` represents centuries
- `Y` represents years
- `M` represents months
- `D` represents days
- `h` represents hours
- `m` represents minutes
- `s` represents seconds. Seconds can be represented in the format `ss.sss` to increase precision
- `Z` is used to designate **Coordinated Universal Time** (**UTC**). It should immediately follow the time of day element

For the `dateTime` expressions, there is another designator:

- `T` is used as time designator to indicate the start of the representation of the time.

Examples of deadline expressions are shown in the following code excerpts:

```
<wait>
  <until>'2004-03-18T21:00:00+01:00'</until>
</wait>
<wait>
  <until>'18:05:30Z'</until>
</wait>
```

For duration expressions, the following characters can also be used:

- `P` is used as the time duration designator. Duration expressions always start with `P`.
- `Y` follows the number of years.
- `M` follows the number of months or minutes.
- `D` follows the number of days.
- `H` follows the number of hours.
- `S` follows the number of seconds.

To specify a duration of 4 hours and 10 minutes, we use the following expression:

```
<wait>
  <for>'PT4H10M'</for>
</wait>
```

To specify the duration of 1 month, 3 days, 4 hours, and 10 minutes, we need to use the following expression:

```
<wait>
  <for>'P1M3DT4H10M'</for>
</wait>
```

The following expression specifies the duration of 1 year, 11 months, 14 days, 4 hours, 10 minutes, and 30 seconds:

```
<wait>
  <for>'P1Y11M14DT4H10M30S'</for>
</wait>
```

Empty activities

When developing BPEL processes, you may come across instances where you need to specify an activity as per rules, but you do not really want to perform the activity. For example, in `<if>` activities, we need to specify an activity for each branch. However, if we do not want to perform any activity for a particular case, we can specify an `<empty>` activity. Not specifying any activity in this case would result in an error, because the BPEL process would not correspond to the BPEL schema. Empty activities are also useful in fault handling, when we need to suppress a fault.

The syntax for the `empty>` element is rather straightforward:

```
<empty/>
```

Ending a process

BPEL provides the `<exit>` activity to immediately end a business process before it has finished. We can use it to immediately terminate processes that are in execution. Often we use `<exit>` in conditional branches, where we need to exit a process when certain conditions are not met.

The `<exit>` activity ends the current business process instance and no fault and compensation handling is performed. Process instances, faults, and compensations are discussed later in this chapter.

The syntax is very simple and is shown as follows:

```
<exit/>
```

Now that we have become familiar with loops, delays, empty activities, and process termination (which we will use in examples in the rest of this chapter), we will go on to fault handling.

Fault handling and signaling

Business processes specified using BPEL will interact with their partners through operation invocations of web services. Web services are based on loosely coupled **Service-Oriented Architecture** (**SOA**). The communication between web services is done over Internet connections that may or may not be highly reliable. Web services could also raise faults due to logical errors and execution errors arising from defects in the infrastructure. Therefore, BPEL business processes will need to handle faults appropriately. BPEL processes may also need to signal faults themselves. Fault handling and signaling is an important aspect of business processes designed using BPEL.

Faults in BPEL can arise in various situations such as the following:

- When a BPEL process invokes a synchronous web service operation, the operation might return a WSDL fault message, which results in a BPEL fault.
- A BPEL process can explicitly signal (throw) a fault.
- A fault can be thrown automatically, for example, when a join failure has occurred. We will discuss join failures later in this chapter.
- The BPEL server might encounter error conditions in the runtime environment, network communications, or any other such reason. BPEL defines several standard faults; these are listed in Appendix A.

WSDL faults

WSDL faults occur due to synchronous operation invocations on partner web services. In WSDL, such faults are denoted with the `<fault>` element within the `<operation>` declaration. In BPEL, WSDL faults are identified by the qualified name of the fault and the target namespace of the corresponding port type used in the operation declaration.

In the Synchronous Business Travel Process example in the previous chapter, we have used the `TravelApproval` operation on the `TravelApprovalPT` port type with input and output messages. This is shown in the WSDL excerpt as follows:

```
...
<portType name="TravelApprovalPT">
  <operation name="TravelApproval">
    <input message="tns:TravelRequestMessage" />
    <output message="aln:TravelResponseMessage" />
  </operation>
</portType>
...
```

To add fault information to the operation, we first need to define a corresponding message. For simplicity, this message will be of the `xs:string` type:

```
...
<message name="TravelFaultMessage">
  <part name="error" type="xs:string" />
</message>
...
```

Now we will add the fault declaration to the operation signature shown previously:

```
...
<portType name="TravelApprovalPT">
  <operation name="TravelApproval">
    <input message="tns:TravelRequestMessage" />
    <output message="aln:TravelResponseMessage" />
    <fault name="fault" message="tns:TravelFaultMessage" />
  </operation>
</portType>
...
```

WSDL does not require that we use unique fault names within the namespace used to define the operation. This implies that faults that have the same name and are defined within the same namespace will be considered as the same fault in BPEL. Keep this in mind when designing services that can potentially become partners of BPEL business processes, because this can lead to conflicts in fault handling during execution.

Signaling faults

A business process may sometimes need to explicitly signal a fault. For such a situation, BPEL provides the `<throw>` activity. It has the following syntax:

```
<throw faultName="name" />
```

BPEL does not require that we define fault names in advance, prior to their use in the `<throw>` activity. This flexible approach can also be error-prone because there is no compile-time checking of fault names. Therefore, a typo could result in a situation where a misspelled fault might not be handled by the designated fault handler.

Faults can also have an associated variable that usually contains data related to the fault. If such a variable is associated with the fault, we need to specify it when throwing the fault. This is done by using the optional `faultVariable` attribute as shown here:

```
<throw faultName="name" faultVariable="variable-name" />
```

The following example shows the most straightforward use of the `<throw>` activity, where a `WrongEmployeeName` fault is thrown—no variable is needed. Remember that fault names are not declared in advance:

```
<throw faultName="WrongEmployeeName" />
```

The faults raised with the `<throw>` activity have to be handled in the BPEL process. Fault handling is covered later in this chapter. Faults that are not handled will *not* be automatically propagated to the client as is the case in modern programming languages (Java, for example). Rather, the BPEL process will terminate abnormally. Sometimes, however, we may want to signal faults to clients.

Signaling faults to clients in synchronous replies

A BPEL process offers operations to its clients through the `<receive>` activity. If the process wants to provide a synchronous request/response operation, it sends a `<reply>` activity in response to the initial `<receive>`. Remember that the type of the operation is defined in the WSDL document of the BPEL process. A synchronous request/response operation is defined as an operation that has an input and an output message and an optional fault message.

If such an operation has the fault part specified, we can use the `<reply>` activity to return a fault instead of the output message. The syntax of the `<reply>` activity in this case is as follows:

```
<reply partnerLink="partner-link-name"
       portType="port-type-name"
       operation="operation-name"
       variable="variable-name"     <!-- optional -->
       faultName="fault-name" >
</reply>
```

When we specify a fault name to be returned through the `<reply>` activity, the variable name is optional. If we specify a variable name, then the variable has to be of the fault message type as defined in WSDL.

Example

Let's modify the BPEL process definition in the synchronous travel example and signal the fault (`TravelFaultMessage`) to the client by using the `<reply>` activity.

First, we need to declare an additional variable that will hold the fault description to return to the client. The variable is of the `TravelFaultMessage` type:

```
...
<variables>
   ...
   <!-- fault to the BPEL client -->
   <variable name="TravelFault"
                    messageType="trv:TravelFaultMessage"/>
</variables>
...
```

Then we return the fault to the BPEL process client. We will need to check if something went wrong in the travel process. For the purpose of this example, we will check whether the selected flight ticket has been approved. This information is stored in the `confirmationData` part of the `TravelResponse` variable in the `Approved` element (see the previous chapter for the complete schema definition). Note that this is an oversimplification but it demonstrates how to return faults. We can use an `<if>` activity to determine whether the ticket is approved; then we construct the fault variable and use the `<reply>` activity to return it to the client. This is shown in the following code:

```
...
<!-- Check if the ticket is approved -->
<if>

  <condition>
     $TravelResponse.confirmationData/aln:Approved='true'
  </condition>

  <!-- Send a response to the client -->
  <reply partnerLink="client"
       portType="trv:TravelApprovalPT"
       operation="TravelApproval"
       variable="TravelResponse"/>

  <else>
    <sequence>

        <!-- Create the TravelFault variable with fault
             description -->
      <assign>
         <copy>
           <from>string('Ticket not approved')</from>
           <to variable="TravelFault" part="error" />
         </copy>
      </assign>

      <!-- Send a fault to the client -->
      <reply partnerLink="client"
           portType="trv:TravelApprovalPT"
           operation="TravelApproval"
           variable="TravelFault"
           faultName="fault" />
    </sequence>
  </else>
</if>
```

If the ticket is not approved, the following fault is signaled to the client:

```
<TravelFault>
  <part name="error">
    <error xmlns="http://packtpub.com/bpel/travel/">
       Ticket not approved
    </error>
  </part>
</TravelFault>
```

We have seen that signaling faults in synchronous replies is easy. Let us now discuss signaling faults in asynchronous scenarios.

Signaling faults to clients in asynchronous scenarios

If an asynchronous BPEL process needs to notify the client about a fault, it cannot use the `<reply>` activity. Remember that in asynchronous scenarios the client does not wait for the reply—rather the process uses a callback. To return a fault in callback scenarios, we usually define additional callback operations on the same port type. Through these callback operations, we can signal that an exceptional situation has prevented normal completion of the process.

To demonstrate how faults can be propagated to the client using a callback operation, we will use the asynchronous travel process example. First, we need to modify the travel BPEL process WSDL and introduce another operation called `ClientCallbackFault`. This operation consists of an input message called `tns:TravelFaultMessage`. The message is of the `string` type (similar to the synchronous example). The declaration of the operation and the message is shown in the following code excerpt:

```
...
<message name="TravelFaultMessage">
  <part name="error" type="xs:string" />
</message>

<portType name="ClientCallbackPT">
  <operation name="ClientCallback">
    <input message="aln:TravelResponseMessage" />
  </operation>

  <operation name="ClientCallbackFault">
    <input message="tns:TravelFaultMessage" />
  </operation>

</portType>
...
```

We can use the `<if>` activity to determine whether the ticket has been approved, as in the synchronous example. If the ticket is not approved, however, we `<invoke>` the `ClientCallbackFault` operation instead of using the `<reply>` activity to signal the fault to the client. This is shown in the following code excerpt:

```
...
<!-- Check if the ticket is approved -->
<if>

  <condition>
     $TravelResponse.confirmationData/aln:Approved='true'
  </condition>

  <!-- Make a callback to the client -->
  <invoke partnerLink="client"
          portType="trv:ClientCallbackPT"
          operation="ClientCallback"
          inputVariable="TravelResponse" />

  <else>

    <sequence>
      <!-- Create the TravelFault variable with fault
           description -->
      <assign>
         <copy>
           <from>string('Ticket not approved')</from>
           <to variable="TravelFault" part="error" />
         </copy>
      </assign>

      <!-- Send a fault to the client -->
      <invoke partnerLink="client"
              portType="trv:ClientCallbackPT"
              operation="ClientCallbackFault"
              inputVariable="TravelFault" />

    </sequence>

  </else>
</if>
```

In the next section, we will look at how to handle faults thrown in BPEL processes.

Handling faults

Now that we are familiar with how faults are signaled, let us consider how the business process handles faults. When a fault occurs within a business process (this can be a WSDL fault, a fault thrown by the BPEL process, or any other type of fault), it means that the process may not complete successfully. The process can complete successfully only if the fault is handled within a scope. Scopes are discussed in the next section.

Business processes handle faults through fault handlers.

A business process can handle a fault through one or more fault handlers. Within a fault handler, the business process defines custom activities that are used to recover from the fault and recover the partial (unsuccessful) work of the activity in which the fault has occurred.

The fault handlers are specified before the first activity of the BPEL process, after the partner links and variables. The overall structure is shown in the following code excerpt:

```
<process ...>
   <partnerLinks>
      ...
   </partnerLinks>
   <variables>
      ...
   </variables>
   <faultHandlers>

      <catch ... >
         <!-- Perform an activity -->
      </catch>
      <catch ... >
         <!-- Perform an activity -->
      </catch>
      ...
      <catchAll>
         <!-- catchAll is optional -->
         <!-- Perform an activity -->
      </catchAll>
   </faultHandlers>
```

```
    <sequence>
       ...
    </sequence>
</process>
```

We can see that within the fault handlers we specify several <catch> activities where we indicate the fault that we would like to catch and handle. Within a fault handler, we have to specify at least one <catch> or a <catchAll> activity. Of course, the <catchAll> activity can be specified only once within a fault handler.

Usually, we will specify several <catch> activities to handle specific faults and use the <catchAll> to handle all other faults. The <catch> activity has two attributes, of which we have to specify at least one:

- `faultName`: Specifies the name of the fault to be handled.
- `faultVariable`: Specifies the variable type used for fault data. Additionally, we can specify one of the following attributes (both are optional, but we may specify one, not both).
- `faultMessageType`: Specifies the WSDL message type of the fault to be handled.
- `faultElement`: Specifies the XML element type of the fault to be handled.

The flexibility of <catch> activities is high and several variations are permissible. The most common are listed as follows:

```
<faultHandlers>

   <catch faultName="trv:TicketNotApproved" >
      <!-- First fault handler -->
      <!-- Perform an activity -->
   </catch>
   <catch faultName="trv:TicketNotApproved"
          faultVariable="TravelFault" >
      <!-- Second fault handler -->
      <!-- Perform an activity -->
   </catch>
   <catch faultVariable="TravelFault" >
      <!-- Third fault handler -->
      <!-- Perform an activity -->
   </catch>
   <catchAll>
      <!-- Perform an activity -->
   </catchAll>
</faultHandlers>
```

We can see that fault handlers in BPEL are very similar to try/catch clauses found in modern programming languages.

Selection of a fault handler

Let us consider the fault handlers listed previously and discuss the scenarios for which the `<catch>` activities will be selected:

- The first `<catch>` will be selected if the `trv:TicketNotApproved` fault has been thrown and the fault carries no fault data.
- The second `<catch>` will be selected if the `trv:TicketNotApproved` fault has been thrown and carries data of type matching that of the `TravelFault` variable.
- The third `<catch>` will be selected if a fault has been thrown whose fault variable type matches the `TravelFault` variable type and whose name is *not* `trv:TicketNotApproved`.
- In all other cases, the `<catchAll>` will be selected.

We can see that the selection of the `<catch>` activity within fault handlers is quite complicated. It may even happen that a fault matches several `<catch>` activities. Therefore, BPEL specifies exact rules to select the fault handler that will process a fault:

- For faults without associated fault data, the fault name will be matched. The `<catch>` activity with a matching `faultName` will be selected, if present; otherwise, the default `<catchAll>` handler will be used, if present.
- For faults with associated fault data, a `<catch>` activity specifying a matching `faultName` value and `faultVariable` value will be selected, if present. Otherwise, a `<catch>` activity with no specified `faultName` and a matching `faultVariable` will be selected, if present. Otherwise, the default `<catchAll>` handler will be used, if present.

The `<catchAll>` activity will execute only if no other `<catch>` activity has been selected.

If no `<catch>` is selected and `<catchAll>` is not present, the fault will be re-thrown to the immediately enclosing scope, if present. Otherwise, the process will terminate abnormally. This situation is similar to explicitly terminating the process using the `<exit>` activity.

Synchronous example

Let's go back to the synchronous BPEL travel process example to add a fault handlers section. We need to define a fault handler that will simply signal the fault to the client. In real-world scenarios, a fault handler can perform additional work to try to recover the work done by an activity or retry the activity itself.

To signal the fault to the client, we use the same `TravelFaultMessage` message that we defined in the previous section. Here is an excerpt from the WSDL:

```
...
<message name="TravelFaultMessage">
  <part name="error" type="xs:string" />
</message>
<portType name="TravelApprovalPT">
  <operation name="TravelApproval">
    <input message="tns:TravelRequestMessage" />
    <output message="aln:TravelResponseMessage" />
    <fault name="fault" message="tns:TravelFaultMessage" />
  </operation>
</portType>
...
```

We define a fault handler and add a `<faultHandlers>` section immediately after the `<variables>` definition and before the `<sequence>` activity, as shown next. The fault handler for the `trv:TicketNotApproved` fault is defined with the associated `TravelFault` variable. This handler will use the `<reply>` activity to signal the fault to the BPEL client. We will also provide a default `<catchAll>` handler, which will first create a variable and then use the `<reply>` activity to signal the fault to the client:

```
...
<faultHandlers>
   <catch faultName="trv:TicketNotApproved"
          faultVariable="TravelFault">
   <reply partnerLink="client"
            portType="trv:TravelApprovalPT"
            operation="TravelApproval"
            variable="TravelFault"
            faultName="fault" />

   </catch>
   <catchAll>
     <sequence>
```

```
        <!-- Create the TravelFault variable -->
        <assign>
          <copy>
            <from>string('Other fault')</from>
            <to variable="TravelFault" part="error" />
          </copy>
        </assign>

        <reply partnerLink="client"
               portType="trv:TravelApprovalPT"
               operation="TravelApproval"
               variable="TravelFault"
               faultName="fault" />
    </sequence>

  </catchAll>

</faultHandlers>
...
```

We also have to modify the process itself. Instead of replying to the client (<reply>) in the <if> activity if the ticket has not been approved, we will simply throw a fault, which will be caught by the corresponding fault handler. The fault handler will also catch other possible faults:

```
...
<!-- Check if the ticket is approved -->
<if>

  <condition>
     $TravelResponse.confirmationData/aln:Approved='true'
  </condition>

  <!-- Send a response to the client -->
  <reply partnerLink="client"
       portType="trv:TravelApprovalPT"
       operation="TravelApproval"
       variable="TravelResponse"/>

  <else>

    <sequence>
      <!-- Create the TravelFault variable with fault
                                            description -->
      <assign>
         <copy>
           <from>string('Ticket not approved')</from>
           <to variable="TravelFault" part="error" />
```

```
                </copy>

            </assign>

            <!-- Throw fault -->
            <throw faultName="trv:TicketNotApproved"
                    faultVariable="TravelFault" />
          </sequence>

        </else>
      </if>
      ...
```

Faults that are not handled by the BPEL process result in abnormal termination of the process and are not propagated to the client. In other words, unhandled faults do not cross service boundaries unless explicitly specified using a `<reply>` activity as we did in our example. This differentiates BPEL from Java and other languages where unhandled exceptions are propagated to the client.

Asynchronous example

In asynchronous BPEL processes, faults are handled in the same way as in synchronous processes by using `<faultHandlers>`. We need to define a fault handler that, in our example, will simply forward the fault to the client. We cannot, however, use the `<reply>` activity to signal the fault to the client. Instead, we need to define an additional callback operation and use the `<invoke>` activity, as we did in our previous example. In this example, we will use the same fault callback operation as in the previous asynchronous example:

```
...
<message name="TravelFaultMessage">
  <part name="error" type="xs:string" />
</message>

<portType name="ClientCallbackPT">
  <operation name="ClientCallback">
    <input message="aln:TravelResponseMessage" />
  </operation>

  <operation name="ClientCallbackFault">
    <input message="tns:TravelFaultMessage" />
  </operation>

</portType>
...
```

Now, we will define the <faultHandlers> section. The difference to the synchronous example will be that we will use the <invoke> activity to invoke the newly defined operation instead of the <reply> activity to propagate the fault to the client:

```
...
<faultHandlers>

   <catch faultName="trv:TicketNotApproved"
          faultVariable="TravelFault">

     <!-- Make a callback to the client -->
     <invoke partnerLink="client"
             portType="trv:ClientCallbackPT"
             operation="ClientCallbackFault"
             inputVariable="TravelFault" />
   </catch>

   <catchAll>

     <sequence>
       <!-- Create the TravelFault variable -->
       <assign>
         <copy>
           <from>string('Other fault')</from>
           <to variable="TravelFault" part="error" />
         </copy>
       </assign>

       <invoke partnerLink="client"
               portType="trv:ClientCallbackPT"
               operation="ClientCallbackFault"
               inputVariable="TravelFault" />
     </sequence>

   </catchAll>

</faultHandlers>
...
```

Another important question related to fault handling is how the BPEL process can be notified of faults that occurred in asynchronously invoked partner web service operations. A typical example is the invocation of the American and Delta Airlines web services in our example. To invoke the operation, we used the <invoke> activity and then a <receive> activity to wait for the callback.

BPEL provides a way to wait for more than just one message (operation call) using the `<pick>` activity, which is described later in this chapter in the *Managing events* section. By using `<pick>` instead of `<receive>`, our BPEL process can wait for several incoming messages. One of these can be a message for regular callback; others can be messages that signal fault conditions. With `<pick>`, we can even specify a timeout for receiving a callback. For further information on these issues, please see the *Managing events* section.

Propagating faults

In fault handlers, we might want to propagate a fault that we have caught to a higher-level fault handler. For example, a fault handler of a nested scope catches a fault. However, it is a type of fault that it will not handle. Rather, it will propagate it to the fault handler of a higher-level scope.

To achieve this, we can use the `<rethrow>` activity. This is used to rethrow the fault caught by the fault handler. `<rethrow>` can be used only within a fault handler (`<catch>` and `<catchAll>`).

The syntax is simple:

```
<rethrow />
```

Default fault handler

If a `<catchAll>` fault handler for any fault is not defined for any given `<scope>`, the BPEL engine implicitly creates a default fault handler. The default fault handler will compensate all inner scopes (compensation is covered later in this chapter) and rethrow the fault to the upper scope.

The default implicit fault handler looks like this:

```
<catchAll>
   <sequence>
      <compensate />
      <rethrow />
   </sequence>
</catchAll>
```

Inline fault handling

The loosely coupled model of web services and the use of Internet connections for accessing them make the invocation of operations on web services particularly error prone. Numerous situations can prevent a BPEL process from successfully invoking a partner web service operation, such as broken connections, unavailability of web services, changes in the WSDL, and so on.

Such faults can be handled in the general `<faultHandlers>` sections. However, a more efficient way is to handle faults related to the `<invoke>` activity directly and not rely on the general fault handlers. The `<invoke>` activity provides a shortcut to achieve this—inline fault handlers.

Inline fault handlers can catch WSDL faults for synchronous operations, and also other faults related to the runtime environment, communications, and so on.

The syntax for inline fault handlers in the `<invoke>` activity is similar to the syntax of the `<faultHandlers>` section. As shown in the following code excerpt, we can specify zero or more `<catch>` activities and we can also specify a `<catchAll>` handler. The only difference is that in inline `<catch>` activities, we have to specify a fault name. Optionally, we may specify the fault variable:

```
<invoke ... >
   <catch faultName="fault-name" >
      <!-- Perform an activity -->
   </catch>
   ...
   <catch faultName="fault-name"
          faultVariable="fault-variable"
      <!-- Perform an activity -->
   </catch>
   ...
   <catch faultName="fault-name"
          faultVariable="fault-variable"
          faultMessageType="WSDL-message" <!-- Optional one or the
                                               other -->
          faultElement="XML-element" >
      <!-- Perform an activity -->
   </catch>
   ...
   <catchAll>
      <!-- Perform an activity -->
   </catchAll>
</invoke>
```

The following code excerpt shows an inline fault handler for invoking the Employee Travel Status web service from our BPEL travel process example. Please notice that this also requires modifying the Employee Travel Status WSDL and declaring an additional fault message for the operation. As this code is similar to what we did in previous examples, it is not repeated here again. The following code excerpt demonstrates inline fault handling. The rules for which the catch activity will be selected are the same as for stand-alone fault handlers and have been discussed in the previous section:

```
<invoke partnerLink="employeeTravelStatus"
        portType="emp:EmployeeTravelStatusPT"
        operation="EmployeeTravelStatus"
        input Variable="EmployeeTravelStatusRequest"
        outputVariable="EmployeeTravelStatusResponse" >

   <catch faultName="emp:WrongEmployeeName" >
      <!-- Perform an activity -->
   </catch>

   <catch faultName="emp:TravelNotAllowed"
          faultVariable="FaultDesc" >
      <!-- Perform an activity -->
   </catch>

   <catchAll>
      <!-- Perform an activity -->
   </catchAll>

</invoke>
```

This brings us to the thought that it would be useful if we could specify more than one `<faultHandlers>` section in a BPEL process. It would be great if we could specify different fault handlers sections for different parts of the process, particularly for complex processes. This is possible if we use scopes, described in the next section. We will see that inline fault handling of the `<invoke>` activity is equal to enclosing the `<invoke>` activity in a local scope.

Scopes

Scopes provide a way to divide a complex business process into hierarchically organized parts—scopes. Scopes provide behavioral contexts for activities. In other words, scopes address the problem that we identified in the previous section and allow us to define different fault handlers for different activities (or sets of activities gathered under a common structured activity, such as `<sequence>` or `<flow>`). In addition to fault handlers, scopes also provide a way to declare variables and partner links that are visible only within the scope. Scopes also allow us to define local correlation sets, compensation handlers, event handlers, termination handler, and message exchanges. We will discuss these topics later in this chapter.

The following code excerpt shows how scopes are defined in BPEL. We can specify `<partnerLinks>`, `<messageExchanges>`, `<variables>`, `<correlationSets>`, `<faultHandlers>`, `<compensationHandler>`, `<terminationHandler>`, and `<eventHandlers>` locally for the scope. All are optional:

```
<scope>
   <partnerLinks>
      <!-- Partner link definitions local to scope. -->
   </partnerLinks>
   <messageExchanges>
      <!-- Message exchanges local to scope.
           Discussed later in this chapter. -->
   </messageExchanges>
   <variables>
      <!-- Variable definitions local to scope. -->
   </variables>
   <correlationSets>
      <!-- Correlation sets local to scope.
           Discussed later in this chapter. -->
   </correlationSets>
   <faultHandlers>
      <!-- Fault handlers local to scope. -->
   </faultHandlers>
   <compensationHandler>
      <!-- Compensation handlers local to scope.
           Discussed later in this chapter. -->
   </compensationHandler>
   <terminationHandler>
      <!-- Termination handler local to scope.
           Discussed later in this chapter. -->
   </terminationHandler>
```

```
    <eventHandlers>
       <!-- Event handlers local to scope.
            Discussed later in this chapter. -->
    </eventHandlers>

    activity
 </scope>
```

Each scope has a primary activity. This is similar to the overall process structure, where we have said that a BPEL process also has a primary activity. The primary activity, often a `<sequence>` or `<flow>`, defines the behavior of a scope for normal execution. Fault handlers and other handlers define the behavior for abnormal execution scenarios.

The primary activity of a scope can be a basic activity such as `<invoke>`, or it can be a structured activity such as `<sequence>` or `<flow>`. Enclosing the `<invoke>` activity with a scope and defining the fault handlers is equivalent to using inline fault handlers. The inline fault handler shown in the previous section is equal to the following scope:

```
<scope>

   <faultHandlers>

     <catch faultName="emp:WrongEmployeeName" >
        <!-- Perform an activity -->
     </catch>

     <catch faultName="emp:TravelNotAllowed"
            faultVariable="Description" >
        <!-- Perform an activity -->
     </catch>

     <catchAll>
        <!-- Perform an activity -->
     </catchAll>

   </faultHandlers>

   <invoke partnerLink="employeeTravelStatus"
           portType="emp:EmployeeTravelStatusPT"
           operation="EmployeeTravelStatus"
           inputVariable="EmployeeTravelStatusRequest"
           outputVariable="EmployeeTravelStatusResponse" >

   </invoke>
</scope>
```

If the primary activity of a scope is a structured activity, it can have many nested activities where the nesting depth is arbitrary. The scope is shared by all nested activities. A scope can also have nested scopes with arbitrary depth.

The variables defined within a scope are only visible within that scope. Fault handlers attached to a scope handle faults of all nested activities of a scope. By default behavior, faults not caught in a scope are re-thrown to the enclosing scope. Scopes in which faults have occurred are considered to have ended abnormally even if a fault handler has caught the fault and not re-thrown it.

Similarly as for the `<process>`, we can define the `exitOnStandardFault` for a scope as well. If set to *no*, which is the default, the scope can handle the faults using the corresponding fault handlers. If set to *yes*, then the scope must exit immediately if a fault occurs (similarly as if it would reach an `<exit>` activity). If we do not set this attribute, it inherits the value from its enclosing `<scope>` or `<process>`.

Example

To demonstrate how scopes can be used in BPEL processes, we will rewrite our asynchronous travel process example and introduce three scopes:

- In the first scope, we will retrieve the employee travel status (`RetrieveEmployeeTravelStatus`).
- In the second scope, we will check the flight availability with both airlines (`CheckFlightAvailability`).
- In the third scope, we will call back to the client (`CallbackClient`).

We will also declare those variables that are limited to a scope locally within the scope. This will reduce the number of global variables and make the business process easier to understand. The major benefit of scopes is the capability to define custom fault handlers, which we will also implement. The high-level structure of our travel process will be as follows:

```
<process ...>

   <partnerLinks/>...</partnerLinks>
   <variables>...</variables>

   <faultHandlers>
      <catchAll>...</catchAll>
   </faultHandlers>

   <sequence>
      <!-- Receive the initial request for business travel from
                                                        client -->
```

```
    <receive .../>
    <scope name="RetrieveEmployeeTravelStatus">
      <variables>...</variables>
      <faultHandlers>
        <catchAll>...</catchAll>
      </faultHandlers>
      <sequence>
        <!-- Prepare the input for Employee Travel Status Web
             Service -->
        <!-- Synchronously invoke the Employee Travel Status Web
             Service -->
        <!-- Prepare the input for AA and DA -->
      </sequence>
    </scope>
    <scope name="CheckFlightAvailability">
      <variables>...</variables>
      <faultHandlers>
        <catchAll>...</catchAll>
      </faultHandlers>
      <sequence>
        <!-- Make a concurrent invocation to AA and DA -->
        <flow>
          <!-- Async invoke the AA web service and wait for the
                                                   callback -->
          <!-- Async invoke the DA web service and wait for the
                                                   callback -->
        </flow>
        <!-- Select the best offer and construct the TravelResponse
                                                                -->
      </sequence>
    </scope>
    <scope name="CallbackClient">
      <faultHandlers>...</faultHandlers>
      <!-- Check if the ticket is approved -->
    </scope>
  </sequence>
</process>
```

To signal faults to the BPEL process client, we will use the `ClientCallbackFault` operation on the client partner link, which we defined in the previous section. This operation has a string message, which we will use to describe the fault. In real-world scenarios, the fault message is more complex and includes a fault code and other relevant information.

Let us start with the example. The process declaration and the partner links have not changed:

```
<process name="Travel"
         targetNamespace="http://packtpub.com/bpel/travel/"
         xmlns="http://docs.oasis-
                    open.org/wsbpel/2.0/process/executable"
         xmlns:trv="http://packtpub.com/bpel/travel/"
         xmlns:emp="http://packtpub.com/service/employee/"
         xmlns:aln="http://packtpub.com/service/airline/" >

   <partnerLinks>

      <partnerLink name="client"
                   partnerLinkType="trv:travelLT"
                   myRole="travelService"
                   partnerRole="travelServiceCustomer"/>

      <partnerLink name="employeeTravelStatus"
                   partnerLinkType="emp:employeeLT"
                   partnerRole="employeeTravelStatusService"/>

      <partnerLink name="AmericanAirlines"
                   partnerLinkType="aln:flightLT"
                   myRole="airlineCustomer"
                   partnerRole="airlineService"/>

      <partnerLink name="DeltaAirlines"
                   partnerLinkType="aln:flightLT"
                   myRole="airlineCustomer"
                   partnerRole="airlineService"/>

   </partnerLinks>
   ...
```

The variables section will now define only global variables. These are `TravelRequest`, `FlightDetails`, `TravelResponse`, and `TravelFault`. We have reduced the number of global variables, but we will have to declare other variables within scopes:

```
...
<variables>
   <!-- input for this process -->
   <variable name="TravelRequest"
             messageType="trv:TravelRequestMessage"/>
   <!-- input for the Employee Travel Status web service -->
   <variable name="FlightDetails"
             messageType="aln:FlightTicketRequestMessage"/>
   <!-- output from BPEL process -->
   <variable name="TravelResponse"
             messageType="aln:TravelResponseMessage"/>
   <!-- fault to the BPEL client -->
   <variable name="TravelFault"
             messageType="trv:TravelFaultMessage"/>
</variables>
...
```

Next, we define the global fault handlers section. Here, we use the `<catchAll>` activity, through which we handle all faults not handled within scopes. We will signal the fault to the BPEL client:

```
...
<faultHandlers>

   <catchAll>

     <sequence>
         <!-- Create the TravelFault variable -->
         <assign>
           <copy>
             <from>string('Other fault')</from>
             <to variable="TravelFault" part="error" />
           </copy>
         </assign>

         <invoke partnerLink="client"
                 portType="trv:ClientCallbackPT"
                 operation="ClientCallbackFault"
                 inputVariable="TravelFault" />
     </sequence>

   </catchAll>

</faultHandlers>
...
```

The main activity of the BPEL process will still be <sequence>, and we will also specify the <receive> activity to wait for the incoming message from the client:

```
...
<sequence>
   <!-- Receive the initial request for business travel from client
   -->
   <receive partnerLink="client"
            portType="trv:TravelApprovalPT"
            operation="TravelApproval"
            variable="TravelRequest"
            createInstance="yes" />
...
```

First scope

Now let's define the first scope for retrieving the employee travel status. Here, we will first declare two variables needed for the input and output messages for web service operation invocation:

```
...
   <scope name="RetrieveEmployeeTravelStatus">
     <variables>
        <!-- input for the Employee Travel Status web service -->
        <variable name="EmployeeTravelStatusRequest"
           messageType="emp:EmployeeTravelStatusRequestMessage" />
        <!-- output from the Employee Travel Status web service-->
        <variable name="EmployeeTravelStatusResponse"
          messageType="emp:EmployeeTravelStatusResponseMessage" />
     </variables>
...
```

Next, we will define the fault handlers section for this scope. We will use the <catchAll> activity to handle all faults, including Employee web service WSDL faults, communication faults, and other run-time faults. We will signal all faults to the client, although in real-world scenarios, we could invoke another web service or perform other recovery operations:

```
...
     <faultHandlers>

       <catchAll>

         <sequence>
             <!-- Create the TravelFault variable -->
```

```
                <assign>
                  <copy>
                    <from>
                       string('Unable to retrieve employee travel
                                                          status')
                    </from>
                    <to variable="TravelFault" part="error" />
                  </copy>
                </assign>

                <invoke partnerLink="client"
                        portType="trv:ClientCallbackPT"
                        operation="ClientCallbackFault"
                        inputVariable="TravelFault" />
                <exit/>
            </sequence>
          </catchAll>
        </faultHandlers>
    ...
```

Next, we will start a sequence (which is the main activity of the scope) and prepare the input variable, invoke the Employee web service, and prepare the input for both airlines' web services:

```
    ...
        <sequence>
             <!-- Prepare the input for the
                  Employee Travel Status Web Service -->
             <assign>
               <copy>
                 <from variable="TravelRequest" part="employee"/>
                 <to variable="EmployeeTravelStatusRequest"
                                              part="employee"/>
               </copy>
             </assign>
             <!-- Synchronously invoke the
                  Employee Travel Status Web Service -->
             <invoke partnerLink="employeeTravelStatus"
                     portType="emp:EmployeeTravelStatusPT"
                     operation="EmployeeTravelStatus"
                     inputVariable="EmployeeTravelStatusRequest"
                     outputVariable="EmployeeTravelStatusResponse" />
             <!-- Prepare the input for AA and DA -->
             <assign>
```

```
            <copy>
              <from variable="TravelRequest" part="flightData"/>
              <to variable="FlightDetails" part="flightData"/>
            </copy>
            <copy>
              <from variable="EmployeeTravelStatusResponse"
                     part="travelClass"/>
              <to variable="FlightDetails" part="travelClass"/>
            </copy>
          </assign>

       </sequence>
     </scope>
...
```

Second scope

In the second scope, we check the flight availability with both airlines' web services. First, we declare two variables for storing output from both web service operations:

```
...
   <scope name="CheckFlightAvailability">

     <variables>
       <!-- output from American Airlines -->
       <variable name="FlightResponseAA"
                 messageType="aln:TravelResponseMessage"/>
       <!-- output from Delta Airlines -->
       <variable name="FlightResponseDA"
                 messageType="aln:TravelResponseMessage"/>
     </variables>
...
```

Next, we define the fault handlers section, where we use the <catchAll> activity similar to that in the first scope:

```
...
     <faultHandlers>

       <catchAll>

         <sequence>
             <!-- Create the TravelFault variable -->
             <assign>
               <copy>
```

```
                <from>
                   string('Unable to invoke airline web service')
                </from>
                <to variable="TravelFault" part="error" />
              </copy>
            </assign>

            <invoke partnerLink="client"
                    portType="trv:ClientCallbackPT"
                    operation="ClientCallbackFault"
                    inputVariable="TravelFault" />
            <exit/>

          </sequence>
        </catchAll>
      </faultHandlers>
   ...
```

The main activity of the second scope will be a <sequence>, in which we will first concurrently invoke both airlines' web services using a <flow> activity and then select the best offer using a <if> activity:

```
   ...
      <sequence>

           <!-- Make a concurrent invocation to AA and DA -->
           <flow>

             <sequence>
               <!-- Async invoke of the AA web service
                    and wait for the callback -->

               <invoke partnerLink="AmericanAirlines"
                   portType="aln:FlightAvailabilityPT"
                   operation="FlightAvailability"
                   inputVariable="FlightDetails" />

               <receive partnerLink="AmericanAirlines"
                   portType="aln:FlightCallbackPT"
                   operation="FlightTicketCallback"
                   variable="FlightResponseAA" />

             </sequence>

             <sequence>
               <!-- Async invoke of the DA web service
                    and wait for the callback -->

               <invoke partnerLink="DeltaAirlines"
                   portType="aln:FlightAvailabilityPT"
                   operation="FlightAvailability"
```

```
                inputVariable="FlightDetails" />

            <receive partnerLink="DeltaAirlines"
                portType="aln:FlightCallbackPT"
                operation="FlightTicketCallback"
                variable="FlightResponseDA" />

          </sequence>

        </flow>

        <!-- Select the best offer and construct the
             TravelResponse -->
        <if>

          <condition>
             $FlightResponseAA.confirmationData/aln:Price &lt;=
             $FlightResponseDA.confirmationData/aln:Price
          </condition>
          <!-- Select American Airlines -->
          <assign>
             <copy>
                <from variable="FlightResponseAA" />
                <to variable="TravelResponse" />
             </copy>
          </assign>

          <else>
             <!-- Select Delta Airlines -->
             <assign>
               <copy>
                 <from variable="FlightResponseDA" />
                 <to variable="TravelResponse" />
               </copy>
             </assign>
          </else>
        </if>

      </sequence>
    </scope>
...
```

Third scope

In the third scope, we call back to the BPEL client. For this scope we do not need additional variables. However, we define a fault handler to handle the `TicketNotApproved` fault. Therefore, we explicitly specify the fault name and the fault variable. Note that we do not use the `<catchAll>` activity in this fault handlers section, so all unhandled faults will be re-thrown to the main process fault handler:

```
...
     <scope name="CallbackClient">
       <faultHandlers>

         <catch faultName="trv:TicketNotApproved"
                faultVariable="TravelFault">
           <!-- Make a callback to the client -->
           <invoke partnerLink="client"
                   portType="trv:ClientCallbackPT"
                   operation="ClientCallbackFault"
                   inputVariable="TravelFault" />
         </catch>
       </faultHandlers>
...
```

The main activity of this scope is the `<if>` activity, where we check if the flight ticket has been approved:

```
...
       <!-- Check if the ticket is approved -->
       <if>

         <condition>
            $TravelResponse.confirmationData/aln:Approved='true'
         </ condition>

         <!-- Make a callback to the client -->
         <invoke partnerLink="client"
                 portType="trv:ClientCallbackPT"
                 operation="ClientCallback"
                 inputVariable="TravelResponse" />

         <else>

           <sequence>
                <!-- Create the TravelFault variable
                     with fault description -->
```

```
                <assign>
                   <copy>
                     <from>string('Ticket not approved')</from>
                     <to variable="TravelFault" part="error" />
                   </copy>

                </assign>

                <!-- Throw fault -->
                <throw faultName="trv:TicketNotApproved"
                       faultVariable="TravelFault" />
           </sequence>

         </else>
       </if>

     </scope>

  </sequence>

</process>
```

Isolated scopes

For each scope we can specify whether we require concurrency control over shared variables, partner links, and dependency links. We will need such control if, in our scenario, more than one instance uses shared variables concurrently. This can occur, for example, if we use a parallel <forEach> loop, which starts several parallel branches of the same <scope>.

Scopes that require concurrency control are called **isolated scopes**. In isolated scopes, it is ensured that the results of the scope will be equal if all conflicting activities on all shared variables and partner links are done in any possible sequence. This guarantees that there will be no conflicting situations if several concurrent scopes access the same set of shared variables. Conflicting operations are in this case all read/write and write-only activities, such as assignments, incoming messages stored in variables, and so on. The semantics of isolated scopes are similar to the *serializable* transaction isolation level.

We denote a scope as isolated using the optional attribute `isolated` and setting it to `yes`. The default value of this attribute is `no`. Isolated scopes must not contain other isolated scopes (but may contain scopes that are not marked as isolated). The fault handlers (and other handlers) associated with the scope also share the isolation. The following code excerpt shows how to declare a scope as isolated:

```
<scope isolated="yes" >
   ...
</scope>
```

Compensation

Compensation, or undoing steps in the business process that have already completed successfully, is one of the most important concepts in business processes. Let us discuss the compensation on our travel process and suppose that in addition to checking the flight availability, our business process would also have to confirm the flight tickets, make the payments, reserve a hotel room, and make the payment for the hotel room. If the business travel is canceled (for various reasons) the reservation and payment activities would have to be undone—compensated. In business processes, the compensation behavior must be explicitly defined. Therefore, when defining the BPEL process, we would have to explicitly define how to compensate the flight ticket confirmation, how to compensate the flight ticket payment, and so on.

The goal of compensation is to reverse the effects of previous activities that have been carried out as part of a business process that is being abandoned.

Compensation is related to the nature of most business processes, which are long running and use asynchronous communication with loosely coupled partner web services. Business processes are often sensitive in terms of successful completion because the data they manipulate is sensitive. As they usually span multiple partners (often multiple enterprises), special care has to be taken that business processes either fully complete their work or that the partial (not fully completed) results are undone—compensated.

In enterprise information systems, processes that have not been able to finish all their activities and need to undo the partial work are usually handled with transactions, more exactly with the ACID distributed transaction model, such as X/Open DTP (Distributed Transaction Processing). **ACID** stands for **Atomicity**, **Consistency**, **Isolation**, and **Durability** and defines a transaction model that uses data locking and isolation. Such a model works perfectly well in trusted domains within enterprises under the prerequisite that the duration of transactions can be relatively short.

The problem with business processes is that they usually last a long time, sometimes several hours, sometimes even a few days. This is much too long for the ACID model, because we cannot afford to lock certain data for such a long time and to isolate the access to these data.

In business processes, compensation is used instead of ACID to reverse the effects of an unfinished process. Compensation requires that an activity specifies a reverse activity, which can be invoked if it is necessary to undo the effect of that activity. BPEL supports the concept of compensation with the ability to define compensation handlers, which are specific to scopes, and calls this feature **Long-Running Transactions** (**LRT**).

The concept of compensation and LRTs as defined by BPEL is independent of any transaction protocol and can be used with various business transaction protocols. As BPEL is bound to web services, it is, however, reasonable to expect that in most cases the LRTs will be used with the WS-BusinessActivity (WS-Transaction) specification. The BPEL specification even defines a detailed model of BPEL LRTs based on WS-BusinessActivity concepts.

It is very important to understand that compensation differs from fault handling. In fault handling, a business process tries to recover from an activity that could not finish normally because an exceptional situation has occurred. The objective of compensation, on the other hand, is to reverse the effects of a previous activity or a set of activities that have been carried out successfully as part of a business process that is being abandoned. Note that the order in which compensation activities are run is often important. BPEL addresses this aspect with scopes.

Compensation handlers

To define the compensation activities, BPEL provides compensation handlers. Compensation handlers gather all activities that have to be carried out to compensate another activity. Compensation handlers can be defined as follows:

- For the scope
- Inline for the `<invoke>` activity

BPEL 2.0 does not support compensation handlers on the process level anymore. The reason is that such compensation handlers had to be invoked from outside the process, which was difficult and not very practical.

The compensation handler for the scope is defined immediately after the fault handlers section, as shown in the next code excerpt:

```
<scope>
   <partnerLinks>
      <!-- Partner link definitions local to scope. -->
   </partnerLinks>

   <messageExchanges>
      <!-- Message exchanges local to scope.
```

```
            Discussed later in this chapter. -->
    </messageExchanges>
    <variables>
       <!-- Variable definitions local to scope. -->
    </variables>
    <correlationSets>
       <!-- Correlation sets local to scope.
            Discussed later in this chapter. -->
    </correlationSets>
    <faultHandlers>
       <!-- Fault handlers local to scope. -->
    </faultHandlers>
    <compensationHandler>
      <!-- Compensation activity
           (or several activities within a <sequence>, <flow>,
           or other structured activity) -->
    </compensationHandler>
    <terminationHandler>
       <!-- Termination handler local to scope.
            Discussed later in this chapter. -->
    </terminationHandler>
    <eventHandlers>
       <!-- Event handlers local to scope.
            Discussed later in this chapter. -->
    </eventHandlers>
    activity
</scope>
```

Sometimes, it is reasonable to define a compensation handler for each `<invoke>` activity. We could define a scope for each `<invoke>`. However, BPEL provides a shortcut where we can inline the compensation handler rather than explicitly using an immediately enclosing scope. This is similar to the inline capability of fault handlers. The syntax is shown as follows:

```
<invoke ... >
  <compensationHandler>
    <!-- Compensation activity
         (or several activities within a <sequence>, <flow>,
         or other structured activity) -->
  </compensationHandler>
</invoke>
```

The syntax of the compensation handler is the same for all three cases; we specify the activity that has to be performed for compensation. This can be a basic activity such as `<invoke>` or a structured activity such as `<sequence>` or `<flow>`.

Example

Let us suppose that within a business process we will invoke a web service operation through which we will confirm the flight ticket. The compensation activity would be to cancel the flight ticket. The most obvious way to do this is to define the inline compensation handler for the `<invoke>` activity, as shown in the following example:

```
<invoke name="TicketConfirmation"
        partnerLink="AmericanAirlines"
        portType="aln:TicketConfirmationPT"
        operation="ConfirmTicket"
        inputVariable="FlightDetails"
        outputVariable="Confirmation" >

  <compensationHandler>

     <invoke partnerLink="AmericanAirlines"
             portType="aln:TicketConfirmationPT"
             operation="CancelTicket"
             inputVariable="FlightDetails"
             outputVariable="Cancellation" />

  </compensationHandler>

</invoke>
```

Let us now suppose that the business process performs two operations in a sequence. First it confirms the ticket and then makes the payment. To compensate these two activities, we could define an inline compensation handler for both `<invoke>` activities. Alternatively, we could also define a scope with a dedicated compensation handler, as shown in the example that follows:

```
<scope name="TicketConfirmationPayment" >

   <compensationHandler>

      <sequence>
         <invoke partnerLink="AmericanAirlines"
              portType="aln:TicketConfirmationPT"
              operation="CancelTicket"
              inputVariable="FlightDetails"
              outputVariable="Cancellation" />

         <invoke partnerLink="AmericanAirlines"
              portType="aln:TicketPaymentPT"
              operation="CancelPayment"
```

```
                inputVariable="PaymentDetails"
                outputVariable="PaymentCancellation" />
        </sequence>
      </compensationHandler>
      <sequence>
         <invoke partnerLink="AmericanAirlines"
              portType="aln:TicketConfirmationPT"
              operation="ConfirmTicket"
              inputVariable="FlightDetails"
              outputVariable="Confirmation" />
         <invoke partnerLink="AmericanAirlines"
              portType="aln:TicketPaymentPT"
              operation="PayTicket"
              inputVariable="PaymentDetails"
              outputVariable="PaymentConfirmation" />
      </sequence>
   </scope>
```

Which approach is better depends on the nature of the business process. In most cases, we will define inline compensation handlers or compensation handlers within scopes. In the global BPEL process compensation handler, we will usually invoke compensation handlers for specific scopes and thus define the order in which the compensation should perform. Let's have a look at how to invoke a compensation handler.

Default compensation handler

If a <compensationHandler> is not defined for any given <scope>, the BPEL engine implicitly creates a default compensation handler, which compensates all inner scopes:

```
<compensationHandler>
   <compensate />
</compensationHandler>
```

Invoking compensation handlers

Compensation handlers can be invoked only after the activity that is to be compensated has completed normally. If we try to compensate an activity that has completed abnormally, nothing will happen because an <empty> activity will be invoked. This is useful because it is not necessary to track the state of activities to know which can be compensated and which cannot.

BPEL provides two activities to invoke a compensation handler:

- <compensate> activity to start compensation on all inner scopes
- <compensateScope> activity to start compensation on a specified inner scope

Usually, we invoke <compensateScope> and <compensate> activities from a fault handler.

<compensateScope> and <compensate> activities can only be used within <catch>, <catchAll>, <compensationHandler>, and <terminationHandler>.

The syntax is simple and is shown next. The <compensateScope> activity has a `target` attribute through which we specify which scope should be compensated. We have to specify the name of the scope:

```
<compensateScope target="name" />
```

To invoke the compensation handler for the `TicketConfirmationPayment` scope (shown in the previous section), we could simply write:

```
<compensateScope target="TicketConfirmationPayment" />
```

To start compensation on all inner scopes, we use the <compensate> activity. It starts compensation on all inner scopes that have already completed successfully, in default order. The syntax is very simple:

```
<compensate/>
```

We also invoke the inline compensation handler of the <invoke> activity in the same way.

If we invoke a compensation handler for a scope that has no compensation handler defined, the default handler invokes the compensation handlers for the immediately enclosed scopes in the reverse order of completion (remember that the order in which compensations are performed is often important).

Compensation handlers can be explicitly invoked only from the following:

- The fault handler of the scope that immediately encloses the scope for which compensation should be performed
- The compensation handler of the scope that immediately encloses the scope for which compensation should be performed

When a compensation handler is invoked, it sees a frozen snapshot of all variables as they were when the scope being compensated was completed.

In the compensation we can use the same variables as in regular activities and these variables will have the same values as when the activity being compensated is finished. This means that the compensation handler cannot update live data in the variables the BPEL process is using. The compensation handler cannot affect the global state of the business process.

Termination handler

When a BPEL process instance is executing, there are several scenarios which require that the currently executed activity of a process is terminated, for example:

- When a fault handler is invoked, it disables the scope's event handlers and implicitly terminates all enclosed activities.
- A fault in the fault handler causes the termination of all running contained activities.
- When the `<completionCondition>` is fulfilled for a parallel `<forEach>` activity, all still running directly enclosed `<scope>` activities are terminated.

This is called forced termination. Termination handler provides the ability for scopes to control the forced termination. The syntax of a termination handler is listed as follows:

```
<terminationHandler>
   activity
</terminationHandler>
```

In a termination handler we can use the same range of activities as in a fault handler. We can use the `<compensateScope>` or `<compensate>` activities. However, in a termination handler we cannot throw any fault. If an uncaught fault occurs within the termination handler, it is not rethrown to the next enclosing scope.

Default termination handler

If a custom `<terminationHandler>` for the scope is not present, the BPEL engine will generate a default termination handler. The default termination handler will trigger the compensation. This is convenient, as it does not require to always define a termination handler. The default termination handler has the following syntax:

```
<terminationHandler>
   <compensate />
</terminationHandler>
```

Managing events

A business process may have to react on certain events. We already know that a business process specified in BPEL usually waits for an incoming message using the `<receive>` activity. This incoming message is the event that activates the whole process. A business process also often invokes web service operations asynchronously. For such operations, results are returned using callbacks. The BPEL process often waits for callback messages, which are also events.

Using the `<receive>` activity, we can wait for an exactly specified message on a certain port type. Often, however, it is more useful to wait for more than one message, of which only one will occur. Let us go back to our example, where we invoked the `FlightAvailability` operation and waited for the `FlightTicketCallback` callback. In a real-world scenario, it would be very useful to wait for several messages, `FlightTicketCallback` being one of them. The other messages could include `FlightNotAvaliable`, `TicketNotAvaliable`, and so on.

Even more useful would be to specify that we will wait for the callback for a certain period of time (for example, five minutes). If no callback is received, we continue the process flow. This is particularly useful in loosely coupled service-oriented architectures, where we cannot rely on web services being available all the time. This way, we could proceed with the process flow even if American Airlines' web service does not return an offer—we would then invoke another airline web service operation.

In most business processes, we will need to react on two types of events:

- **Message events**: These are triggered by incoming messages through operation invocation on port types.
- **Alarm events**: These are time related and are triggered either after a certain duration or at a specific time.

Pick activity

BPEL provides the <pick> activity through which we can specify that the business process awaits the occurrence of one of a set of events. Events can be message events handled using the <onMessage> activity and alarm events handled using the <onAlarm> activity. For each event, we then specify an activity or a set of activities that should be performed.

The syntax of the <pick> activity is shown as follows:

```
<pick>

   <onMessage ...>
      <!-- Perform an activity -->
   </onMessage>

   <onMessage ...>
      <!-- Perform an activity -->
   </onMessage>

   ...

   <onAlarm ...>
      <!-- Perform an activity -->
   </onAlarm>

   ...

</pick>
```

Within <pick>, we can specify several <onMessage> elements and several <onAlarm> elements. The <onAlarm> elements are optional (we can specify zero or more), but we have to specify at least one <onMessage> element.

Message events

Both elements take additional attributes. The <onMessage> element is identical to the <receive> activity, and has the same set of attributes. We have to specify the following attributes:

- partnerLink: Specifies which partner link will be used for the invoke, receive, or reply, respectively
- portType: Specifies the used port type
- operation: Specifies the name of the operation to wait for being invoked
- variable: Specifies the name of the variable used to store the incoming message

We can also specify message exchanges, correlation, and from-parts, but we will discuss this later in this chapter.

The basic syntax of <onMessage> is shown in the following code excerpt:

```
<pick>
   <onMessage partnerLink="name"
              portType="name"
              operation="name"
              variable="name">

      <!-- Perform an activity or a set of activities enclosed by
           <sequence>, <flow>, etc. or throw a fault -->

   </onMessage>

   ...

</pick>
```

Alarm events

The <onAlarm> element is similar to the <wait> element. We can specify the following:

- A duration expression using a <for> duration expression
- A deadline expression using an <until> deadline expression

For both expressions, we use the same literal format as for the <wait> activity described earlier in this chapter.

Often, we will use the <onAlarm> event to specify duration. A typical example is for a business process to wait for the callback for a certain amount of time, for example, 15 minutes. If no callback is received, the business process invokes another operation or throws a fault. The deadline approach is useful, for example, if the business process should wait for a callback until an exactly specified time and then throw a fault or perform a backup activity.

The following code excerpt shows examples of both with hard-coded times/dates:

```
<pick>
   <onMessage ...>
      <!-- Perform an activity -->
   </onMessage>
   ...
   <onAlarm>
      <for>'PT15M'</for>
```

```
        <!-- Perform an activity or a set of activities enclosed by
             <sequence>, <flow>, etc. or throw a fault -->

     </onAlarm>

  </pick>
  <pick>
     <onMessage ...>
        <!-- Perform an activity -->
     </onMessage>
     ...
     <onAlarm>
        <until>'2004-03-18T21:00:00+01:00'</until>

        <!-- Perform an activity or a set of activities enclosed by
             <sequence>, <flow>, etc. or throw a fault -->

     </onAlarm>
  </pick>
```

Instead of hard-coding the exact date and time or the duration, we can use a variable.

Example

Going back to our travel example, we could replace the `<receive>` activity, where the business process waited for the `FlightTicketCallback`, with the `<pick>` activity, where the business process will also wait for the `FlightNotAvaliable` and `TicketNotAvaliable` operations and throw corresponding faults. The business process will wait no more than 30 minutes, when it will throw a `CallbackTimeout` fault. The code excerpt is shown as follows:

```
<pick>
    <onMessage partnerLink="AmericanAirlines"
               portType="aln:FlightCallbackPT"
               operation="FlightTicketCallback"
               variable="FlightResponseAA">
       <empty/>
       <!-- Continue with the rest of the process -->
    </onMessage>

    <onMessage partnerLink="AmericanAirlines"
               portType="aln:FlightCallbackPT"
               operation="FlightNotAvaliable"
               variable="FlightFaultAA">
       <throw faultName="trv:FlightNotAvaliable"
              faultVariable="FlightFaultAA"/>
    </onMessage>
```

```
        <onMessage partnerLink="AmericanAirlines"
                   portType="aln:FlightCallbackPT"
                   operation="TicketNotAvaliable"
                   variable="FlightFaultAA">
           <throw faultName="trv:TicketNotAvaliable"
                  faultVariable="FlightFaultAA"/>
        </onMessage>

        <onAlarm>
           <for>'PT30M'</for>
           <throw faultName="trv:CallbackTimeout" />
        </onAlarm>
    </pick>
```

For this example to work, we also need to declare the `FlightFaultAA` variable and to modify the Airline web service WSDL to add the `FlightNotAvaliable` and `TicketNotAvaliable` callback operations. This is not shown here but can be seen from the example, which can be downloaded from the Packt Publishing website.

Event handlers

The `<pick>` activity is very useful when we have to specify that the business process should wait for events. Sometimes, however, we would like to react on events that occur while the business process executes. In other words, we do not want the business process to wait for the event (and do nothing else but wait). Instead, the process should execute, and still listen to events and handle them whenever they occur.

For this purpose BPEL provides event handlers. If the corresponding events occur, event handlers are invoked concurrently with the business process. Typical usage of event handlers is to handle a cancellation message from the client. For example, in our travel process we could define an event handler that would allow the BPEL process client to cancel the travel at any time.

We can specify event handlers for the whole BPEL process as well as for each scope. Event handlers for the whole process are specified immediately after the compensation handlers and before the main process activity, as shown next:

```
<process ...>

   <partnerLinks>
      ...
   </partnerLinks>

   <variables>
      ...
   </variables>
```

```
      <faultHandlers>
         ...
      </faultHandlers>
      <compensationHandler>
         ...
      </compensationHandler>
      <eventHandlers>
         <onEvent ...>
            <!-- Perform activities -->
         </onEvent>
         ...
         <onAlarm ...>
            <!-- Perform activities -->
         </onAlarm>
         ...
      </eventHandlers>
      activity
   </process>
```

Event handlers for the scope are also specified after compensation handlers.

The syntax of the event handler section is similar to the syntax of the <pick> activity. Instead of <onMessage>, the message event in <eventHandlers> is called <onEvent>. The most notable difference is that in <eventHandlers> we can specify zero or more <onEvent> handlers and/or zero or more <onAlarm> handlers. An event handler must contain at least one <onEvent> or <onAlarm> element.

<onEvent>

The <onEvent> element indicates that the event handler will wait for a message to arrive. The interpretation of the <onEvent> is very similar to a <receive> activity. The syntax of an <onEvent> handler is shown as follows:

```
<eventHandlers>
   <onEvent partnerLink="name"
            portType="name"      <!-- Optional -->
            operation="name"
            messageType="name"  <!-- Optional -->
            element="name"       <!-- Optional -->
            variable="name"      <!-- Optional -->
            messageExchange="name">  <!-- Optional -->
      <correlations>             <!-- Optional -->
```

```
            <correlation set="name" initiate="yes|join|no"? />
         </correlations>
         <fromParts>                    <!-- Optional -->
            <fromPart part="name" toVariable="name" />
         </fromParts>
         <scope>
            <!-- Perform activities -->
         </scope>
      </onEvent>
      ...
   </eventHandlers>
```

We have to specify the following:

- `partnerLink` of the partner link service that can send the message
- `operation` that is invoked by the partner in order to cause the event

The operation specified in the `<onEvent>` event handler can be a one-way or a request/response operation. If it is a request/response operation, the event handler should use a `<reply>` activity to send the response.

We can specify other attributes, which are optional. Often, we will also specify:

- `portType` over which the operation that causes the event will be invoked.
- `variable`, which identifies a variable local to the event handler that will contain the message received from the partner. For a variable, we can specify the `messageType` or the `element` (depending on the type of variable). The type of the variable must be the same as the type of the input message causing the event.

We can also specify message exchange, correlations, and from parts, which we will discuss later in this chapter.

We put all activities that should occur within the event handler into a `<scope>`.

Message events (`<onEvent>`) in event handlers can occur multiple times, even concurrently, while the corresponding scope is active. We have to take care of concurrency and use isolated scopes if necessary.

Example

Let us go back to the example and define the event handler that will allow the BPEL process client to cancel the travel at any time. The difficult part here is to define the appropriate activities to be performed when the client does the cancellation. The simplest solution is to terminate the process, as shown in the following example:

```
<process name="Travel" ... >

   ...
   <eventHandlers>

      <onEvent partnerLink="client"
               portType="trv:TravelApprovalPT"
               operation="CancelTravelApproval"
               messageType="trv:TravelRequestMessage"
               variable="TravelRequest" >

         <scope>
            <exit/>
         </scope>
      </onEvent>

   </eventHandlers>
   ...
</process>
```

In the real world, we would want to undo some work when a cancellation actually occurs. We could use compensation handlers; however, we would need to structure the activities into scopes and compensate the scopes.

<onAlarm>

The `<onAlarm>` element indicates a time-driven event. There are three possibilities:

- We can specify a time duration after which the event will be signaled. We use a `<for>` expression for this.
- We can specify a specific point in time (deadline) when the alarm will be fired. We use an `<until>` expression for this. Please note that only one of these two expressions may occur in any `<onAlarm>` event.
- We can also specify a repeating duration event. In this case, an alarm will be fired repeatedly each time the duration period expires. We use a `<repeatEvery>` expression for this.

The syntax of an <onAlarm> handler is shown as follows:

```
<eventHandlers>
   <onAlarm>
      <for>duration-expression</for>            <!-- Optional -->
      <until>deadline-expression</until>        <!-- Optional -->
      <repeatEvery>                             <!-- Optional -->
         duration-expression
      </repeatEvery>
      <scope>
         <!-- Perform activities -->
      </scope>
   </onAlarm>
   ...
</eventHandlers>
```

We can specify the <repeatEvery> expression on its own or with either the <for> or the <until> expression. If we specify the <repeatEvery> expression alone, the clock for the first duration starts at the point in time when the parent scope starts. If we specify the <repeatEvery> expression with either the <for> or the <until> expression, the first alarm is not fired until the time specified in the <for> or <until> expression expires. After that, it is fired repeatedly at the interval specified by the <repeatEvery> expression. The duration for the <repeatEvery> is calculated when the parent scope starts.

Example

The following example shows an alarm using a duration expression of 12 hours. We could use variable data to specify the duration instead of hard-coding it.

```
<process name="Travel" ... >

   ...
   <eventHandlers>
      <onAlarm>
         <for>'PT12H'</for>
         <scope>
            <exit/>
         </scope>
      </onAlarm>
   </eventHandlers>
   ...
</process>
```

Other usage scenarios depend on the actual business process. Note that the examples shown for the process could also be defined within scopes. As the code differences are minimal, these examples are not shown.

The event handlers associated with the scopes are enabled when the associated scope starts. The event handlers associated with the global BPEL process are enabled as soon as the process instance is created. This brings us to the process lifecycle, which we will discuss in the next section.

Business process lifecycle

A business process specified in BPEL has a well-defined structure. It usually waits for the client to invoke the process. This is done using the `<receive>` activity, as we have seen in the previous chapter. A business process can also use the `<pick>` activity to wait for the initial incoming message. Then the business process typically invokes several operations on partner web services and waits for partners to invoke callback operations. The business process also performs some logic, such as comparison and calculation of certain values. The business process terminates after all activities have been performed.

We can see that each BPEL process has a well-defined lifecycle. To communicate with partners, BPEL uses web services. Web services provide a stateless model for operation invocation. This means that a web service does not provide a common approach to store client-dependent information between operation invocations. For example, consider a shopping cart where a client uses an `add` operation to add items to the cart. Of course, there could be several simultaneous clients using the shopping cart through the web service. We would like each client to have its own cart. To achieve this using web services, each client would have to pass its identity for each invocation of the `add` operation. This is because the web services model is a stateless model—a web service does not distinguish between different clients.

For business processes, a stateless model is inappropriate. Let us consider the business travel scenario where a client sends a travel order, through which it initiates the business process. The process then communicates with several web services and first sends a ticket approval to the client. Later, it sends a hotel approval and an invoice. There are usually several concurrent clients using the business travel process. Also, a single client can start more than one interaction with the business process. The business process has to remember each interaction in order to know to whom to return the results. In contrast to stateless web services, BPEL business processes are stateful and typically long-running interactions.

BPEL business processes are stateful and support long-running interactions with a well-defined lifecycle. For each interaction with the process, a process instance is created. Therefore, we can think of the BPEL process definition as a template for creating process instances. This is similar to the class-object relation where classes represent templates for creating objects at runtime.

In BPEL, we do not create instances explicitly as we would in programming languages (there is no `new` command, for example). Rather, the creation is implicit and occurs when the process receives the initial message that starts the process. This can happen within the `<receive>` or `<pick>` activities, so both activities provide an attribute called `createInstance`. Setting this attribute to `yes` indicates that the occurrence of that activity causes a new instance of the business process to be created.

We usually annotate the initial `<receive>` or `<pick>` of each business process with the `createInstance` attribute. Going back to our business travel example, this is shown in the following excerpt:

```
...
<sequence>
   <!-- Receive the initial request for business travel from client
   -->
   <receive partnerLink="client"
            portType="trv:TravelApprovalPT"
            operation="TravelApproval"
            variable="TravelRequest"
            createInstance="yes" />
 ...
```

If, however, we would like to specify more than one operation, we can use a special form of the `<pick>` activity. Using `<pick>`, we can specify several operations and receiving any one of these messages will result in business process instance creation. We specify the `createInstance` attribute for the `<pick>` activity. However, we can only specify `<onMessage>` events; `<onAlarm>` events are not permitted in this specific form.

The following example shows the initial business process activity, which waits for the `TravelApproval` or `TravelCancellation` operations. Receiving one of these messages results in business process instance creation:

```
...
<pick createInstance="yes">
   <onMessage partnerLink="client"
            portType="trv:TravelApprovalPT"
            operation="TravelApproval"
```

```
                   variable="TravelRequest" >

             <!-- Perform activities -->

          </onMessage>

          <onMessage partnerLink="client"
                   portType="trv:TravelCancellationPT"
                   operation="TravelCancellation"
                   variable="TravelCancel" >

             <!-- Perform activities -->

          </onMessage>

       </pick>
```

A business process can be terminated normally or abnormally. **Normal termination** occurs when all business process activities complete. **Abnormal termination** occurs either when a fault occurs within the process scope, or a process instance is terminated explicitly using the `<exit>` activity.

In more complex business processes, more than one start activity could be enabled concurrently. Such start activities are required to use correlation sets.

Correlation and message properties

Business processes use a stateful model. When a client starts a business process, a new instance is created. This instance lives for the duration of the business process. Messages sent to the business process (using operations on port types and ports) need to be delivered to the correct instance of the business process. We would expect this to be provided by the runtime environment, such as a BPEL server. This is the case if an appropriate transport mechanism can be used, such as WS-Addressing. However, in some cases where several partners are involved (for example if the BPEL process calls service A, which calls service B, and service B makes a direct callback to the BPEL process), or a lightweight transport mechanism is used that does not provide enough information to explicitly identify instances (such as JMS), manual correlation is required. In such cases, we will have to use specific business data, such as flight numbers, social security numbers, chassis number, and so on.

BPEL provides a mechanism to use such specific business data to maintain references to specific business process instances and calls this feature **correlation**. Business data used for correlation is contained in the messages exchanged between partners. The exact location usually differs from message to message—for example, the flight number in the message from the passenger to the airline might be in a different location than in the confirmation message from the airline to the passenger. To specify which data is used for correlation, message properties are used.

Message properties

Messages exchanged between partner web services in a business process usually contain application-specific data and protocol-specific data. Application-specific data is the data related to the business process. In our example, such data includes the employee name, employee travel status, travel destination, and dates. To actually transfer this data (as SOAP messages, for example) additional protocol-specific data has to be added, such as security context, transaction context, and so on. In SOAP, protocol-specific data is usually gathered in the `Header` section and application-specific data in the `Body` section of a SOAP message. However, not all protocols differentiate application- and protocol-specific data.

In business processes, we will always need to manipulate application-specific data, and sometimes even protocol-specific data. BPEL provides a notion of **message properties**, which allow us to associate relevant data with names that have greater significance than just the data types used for such data.

For example, a chassis number can be used to identify a motor vehicle in a business process. The chassis number will probably appear in several messages and it will always identify the vehicle. Let us suppose that the chassis number is of type `string`, because a chassis number consists of numbers and characters. Naming it with a global property name `chassisNo` gives this string a greater significance than just the data type `string`.

Examples of such globally significant data are numerous and include social security numbers, tax payer numbers, flight numbers, license plate numbers, and so on. These data can be denoted as properties whose significance goes beyond a single business process and can therefore be used for correlation. Other properties will be data significant for a single business process only, such as uniform identifiers, employee numbers, and so on.

Message properties have global significance in business processes and are mapped to multiple messages. So, it makes sense to name them with global property names.

Message properties are defined in WSDL through the WSDL extensibility mechanism, similarly to partner link types. The namespace used for property declaration within WSDL is: `http://docs.oasis-open.org/wsbpel/2.0/varprop`. The syntax is simple and shown next. We have to define a property name and its type:

```
<wsdl:definitions
      xmlns:vprop="http://docs.oasis-open.org/wsbpel/2.0/varprop"
      ... >
   ...
```

```
    <vprop:property name="name" type="type-name" />
    ...
</wsdl:definitions>
```

Let's go back to our travel process example. The flight number is such a significant data element that it makes sense to define it as a property in the Airline web service WSDL:

```
<definitions xmlns:xs="http://www.w3.org/2001/XMLSchema"
        xmlns:emp="http://packtpub.com/service/employee/"
        xmlns:tns="http://packtpub.com/service/airline/"
        targetNamespace="http://packtpub.com/service/airline/"
        xmlns="http://schemas.xmlsoap.org/wsdl/"
        xmlns:plnk="http://docs.oasis-open.org/wsbpel/2.0/plnktype"
        xmlns:vprop="http://docs.oasis-open.org/wsbpel/2.0/varprop" >
    ...
    <vprop:property name="FlightNo" type="xs:string" />
    ...
</definitions>
```

Mapping properties to messages

Properties are parts of messages, usually embedded in the application-specific part of messages. To map a property to a specific element (or even attribute) of the message, BPEL provides **property aliases**. With property aliases, we map a property to a specific element or attribute of the selected message part. We can then use the property name as an alias for the message part and the location. This is particularly useful in abstract business processes where we focus on message exchange description.

Property aliases are defined in WSDL. The syntax is shown next:

```
<wsdl:definitions ...
      xmlns:vprop="http://docs.oasis-open.org/wsbpel/2.0/varprop"
      ... >
    ...
    <vprop:propertyAlias propertyName="property-name"
                         messageType="message-type-name"
                         part="message-part-name"
                         type="type-name"
                         element="element-name">
       <vprop:query>
          query
       </vprop:query>
```

```
    </vprop:propertyAlias>
    ...
</wsdl:definitions>
```

We have to specify the property name, the message type, and the message part, or type, or element. More specifically, to define a property alias, we must use one of the following combinations: `messageType` and `part`, `type`, or `element`. We also have to specify the query expression to point to the specific element or attribute. The query expression is written in the selected query language; the default is XPath 1.0.

We now define the property alias for the flight number property defined in the previous section. In our travel process example, we have defined the `TravelResponseMessage` in the airline WSDL:

```
...
<message name="TravelResponseMessage">
  <part name="confirmationData" element="tns:FlightConfirmation" />
</message>
...
```

The `FlightConfirmationType` has been defined as a complex type with the `FlightNo` element of type `xs:string` being one of the elements. For the complete WSDL with the type definition please look in *Chapter 2, Service Composition with BPEL*. To define the alias, we write the following code:

```
<definitions xmlns:xs="http://www.w3.org/2001/XMLSchema"
        xmlns:emp="http://packtpub.com/service/employee/"
        xmlns:tns="http://packtpub.com/service/airline/"
        targetNamespace="http://packtpub.com/service/airline/"
        xmlns="http://schemas.xmlsoap.org/wsdl/"
        xmlns:plnk="http://docs.oasis-open.org/wsbpel/2.0/plnktype"
        xmlns:vprop="http://docs.oasis-open.org/wsbpel/2.0/varprop" >
    ...
    <vprop:property name="FlightNo" type="xs:string" />
    ...
    <vprop:propertyAlias propertyName="tns:FlightNo"
                         messageType="tns:TravelResponseMessage"
                         part="confirmationData">

       <vprop:query>
           /confirmationData/FlightNo
       </vprop:query>
    </vprop:propertyAlias>
    ...
</definitions>
```

With this, we have defined a global property `FlightNo` as an alias for the `confirmationData` part of the `FlightConfirmationType` message type on the location specified by the `query`.

Extracting properties

To extract property values from variables, BPEL defines an extension function called `getVariableProperty`, which is defined in the standard BPEL namespace. The function takes two parameters, the variable name and the property name, and returns the node that represents the property. The syntax is shown as follows:

```
bpws:getVariableProperty ('variableName', 'propertyName')
```

To extract the `FlightNo` property from the `TravelResponse` variable, we write the following:

```
bpws:getVariableProperty ('TravelResponse', 'FlightNo')
```

The use of properties increases flexibility in extracting relevant data from the message compared to accessing variables. Using properties, we do not have to specify the exact location of the data (such as flight number), but rather use the property name. If the location changes, we only have to modify the property definition.

Properties and assignments

Properties can also be used in assignments, which is particularly useful in abstract processes. We can copy a property from one variable to another using the `<assign>` activity, as shown in the following code excerpt:

```
<assign>
   <copy>
      <from variable="variable-name" property="property-name"/>
      <to variable="variable-name" property="property-name"/>
   </copy>
</assign>
```

To copy the `FlightNo` property from the `FlightResponseAA` variable to the `TravelResponse` variable, we write the following:

```
<assign>
   <copy>
      <from variable="FlightResponseAA" property="FlightNo"/>
      <to variable="TravelResponse" property="FlightNo"/>
   </copy>
</assign>
```

Correlation sets

Now that we are familiar with properties, let's go back to the problem of correlation of messages. Correlation in BPEL uses the notion of properties to assign global names to relevant data used for correlation messages (such as flight number) and to define aliases through which we specify the location of such data in messages.

A set of properties shared by messages and used for correlation is called a **correlation set**.

When correlated messages are exchanged between business partners, two roles can be defined. The partner that sends the first message in an operation invocation is the **initiator** and defines the values of the properties in the correlation set. Other partners are **followers** and get the property values for their correlation sets from incoming messages. Both initiator and followers must mark the first activity that binds the correlation sets.

A correlation set is used to associate messages with business process instances. Each correlation set has a name. A message can be related to one or more correlation sets. The initial message is used to initialize the values of a correlation set. The subsequent messages related to this correlation set must have property values identical to the initial correlation set. Correlation sets in BPEL can be declared globally for the whole process or within scopes. The syntax is shown next:

```
<correlationSets>
  <correlationSet name="correlation-set-name"
                  properties="list-of-properties"/>
  <correlationSet name="correlation-set-name"
                  properties="list-of-properties"/>
  ...
</correlationSets>
```

An example of a correlation set definition named `VehicleOrder` that includes two properties `chassisNo` and `engineNo` is shown next:

```
<correlationSets>
  <correlationSet name="VehicleOrder"
                  properties="tns:chassisNo tns:engineNo"/>
</correlationSets>
```

Going back to our example, let's define a correlation set named `TicketOrder` with a single property, `FlightNo`:

```
<process ... >
   <partnerLinks>...</partnerLinks>
   <variables>...</variables>
   <correlationSets>
      <correlationSet name="TicketOrder"
                      properties="aln:FlightNo"/>
   </correlationSets>
   ...
```

Using correlation sets

We can use correlation sets in `<invoke>`, `<receive>`, `<reply>`, `<onMessage>` parts of `<pick>` activities, and `<onEvent>` parts of event handlers. To specify which correlation sets should be used, we use the `<correlation>` activity nested within any of the above-mentioned activities. The syntax is shown as follows:

```
<correlations>
   <correlation set="name"
                initiate="yes|join|no"     <!-- Optional -->
                pattern="request|response|request-response" />
</correlations>
```

We must specify the name of the correlation set used and indicate whether the correlation set should be initiated. If we want that the activity (such as `<receive>`) initiates the correlation set, we have to set the `initiate` to `yes`. If we want that the activity initiates the correlation set if the correlation set is not yet initiated, then we have to set the `initiate` to `join`. The default value of the `initiate` attribute is `no`.

When we use the correlation with the `<invoke>` activity and when the operation invoked is a request/response operation, we must specify the `pattern` attribute to indicate the direction in which the correlation applies. The `request` value specifies that the correlation applies to outbound messages, `response` to inbound, and `request-response` to both messages. Please notice that we can use the `pattern` attribute for request/response operation only. We should not use it for one-way operations.

The following example shows how to use correlation sets in a scenario where the BPEL process first checks the flight availability using an asynchronous <invoke> and then waits for the callback. The callback message contains the flight number (FlightNo), and is used to initiate the correlation set. Next, the ticket is confirmed using a synchronous <invoke>. Here the correlation set is used with the out-in pattern. Finally, the result is sent to the BPEL process client using a callback <invoke> activity. Here the correlation set is used with the out pattern:

```
...
<sequence>
   ...
   <!-- Check the flight avaliablity -->
   <invoke partnerLink="AmericanAirlines"
       portType="aln:FlightAvailabilityPT"
       operation="FlightAvailability"
       inputVariable="FlightDetails" />
   <!-- Wait for the callback -->
   <receive partnerLink="AmericanAirlines"
       portType="aln:FlightCallbackPT"
       operation="FlightTicketCallback"
       variable="TravelResponse" >
       <!-- The callback includes flight no
            therefore initiate correlation set -->
       <correlations>
          <correlation set="TicketOrder"
                       initiate="yes" />
       </correlations>
   </receive>
   ...
   <!-- Synchronously confirm the ticket -->
   <invoke partnerLink="AmericanAirlines"
       portType="aln:TicketConfirmationPT"
       operation="ConfirmTicket"
       inputVariable="FlightRespnseAA"
       outputVariable="Confirmation" >
       <!-- Use the correlation set to confirm the ticket -->
       <correlations>
          <correlation set="TicketOrder"
                       pattern="request-response" />
       </correlations>
   </invoke>
   ...
   <!-- Make a callback to the client -->
```

```
        <invoke partnerLink="client"
            portType="trv:ClientCallbackPT"
            operation="ClientCallback"
            inputVariable="TravelResponse" >
            <!-- Use the correlation set to callback the client -->
            <correlations>
               <correlation set="TicketOrder"
                            pattern="request" />
            </correlations>

        </invoke>
    </sequence>
</process>
```

Concurrent activities and links

In business processes, activities often occur concurrently. In BPEL, such concurrent activities are modeled using the `<flow>` activity. Activities within `<flow>` start concurrently as soon as the `<flow>` is started. The `<flow>` completes when all nested activities complete. Gathering nested activities within `<flow>` is straightforward and very useful for expressing concurrency scenarios that are not too complicated. We have used it in the examples in this and the previous chapter.

To express more complex concurrency scenarios, `<flow>` provides the ability to express synchronization dependencies between activities. In other words, we can specify which activities can start and when (depending on other activities) and define dependencies that are more complex than those expressed with a combination of `<flow>` and `<sequence>` activities. For example, we will often specify that a certain activity or several activities cannot start before another activity or several activities have finished. We express synchronization dependencies using the `<link>` construct. For each link we specify a name. Links have to be defined within the `<flow>` activity. Link definitions are gathered within a `<links>` element. This is shown in the following code excerpt:

```
<flow>
   <links>
      <link name="TravelStatusToTicketRequest" />
      <link name="TicketRequestToTicketConfirmation" />
   </links>
   ...
</flow>
```

These links can now be used to link activities together. For actual linking, we use standard elements that can be used with any BPEL activity.

Sources and targets

For each BPEL activity, whether basic or structured, we can specify two **standard elements** for linking activities and expressing synchronization dependencies. These two standard elements are nested within the activity:

- `<source>` is used to annotate an activity as being a source of one or more links
- `<target>` is used to annotate an activity as being a target of one or more links

Every link declared within `<flow>` must have exactly one activity within the flow as its `<source>`. It must also have exactly one activity within the flow as its `<target>`.

> A link's target activity can be performed only after the source activity has been finished.

The syntax of the `<source>` element is shown below. We have to specify the link name, which has to be defined within the `<flow>` activity. Optionally, we can specify the transition condition. We will say more on transition conditions later in this section. If the transition condition is not specified, the default value is `true`. We can specify one or more `<source>` elements within the `<sources>` element:

```
<sources>
   <source linkName="name">
      <transitionCondition>      <!-- Optional -->
         boolean-expression
      </transitionCondition>
   </source>
</sources>
```

The syntax of the `<target>` element is also quite simple. We only have to specify the link name. Optionally, we can specify a join condition. We will discuss join conditions later. If no join condition is specified, the default join condition is the disjunction (logical or) of all incoming link statuses for this activity. For the beginning, we will use targets with the default join condition. We can specify one or more `<target>` elements within the `<target>` element. The syntax is as shown next:

```
<targets>
   <joinCondition>           <!-- Optional -->
      boolean-expression
```

```
        </joinCondition>
        <target linkName="name" />
    </targets>
```

Example

Let's now consider the business travel example. There the process had to invoke the Employee Travel Status web service first (synchronous invocation) to get the employee travel class information. Then, it asynchronously invoked the American and Delta Airlines' web services to get flight ticket information. Finally, the process selected the best offer and sent the callback to the BPEL client.

In Chapter 2, we used a combination of `<sequence>` and `<flow>` activities to control the execution order. These two activities allowed us to perform basic synchronization, but they are not appropriate for expressing complex synchronization scenarios. In such scenarios, we should use links.

To demonstrate how to use links, let's use the business travel example, but keep in mind that the scenario of our example is simple enough to be expressed using a combination of `<flow>` and `<sequence>` activities without the need for links. We will use the example for simplicity reasons. In the real world, we use links only where the scenario is so complex that it cannot be expressed using a combination of `<flow>` and `<sequence>` activities.

We have modified the asynchronous travel example and gathered all activities except the initial `<receive>` and the final `<invoke>` within a single `<flow>` activity. We have also added the `name` attribute to each activity. Although this attribute is optional, we have added it because it simplifies understanding which activities have to be linked:

```
<process name="Travel"
         ... >

   <partnerLinks>
      ...
   </partnerLinks>

   <variables>
      ...
   </variables>

   <sequence>

      <!-- Receive the initial request for business travel from client
      -->
      <receive name="InitialRequestReceive"
               partnerLink="client"
               portType="trv:TravelApprovalPT"
```

```
        operation="TravelApproval"
        variable="TravelRequest"
        createInstance="yes" />

<flow>

  <!-- Prepare the input for the Employee Travel Status Web
                                                  Service -->
  <assign name="EmployeeInput">
    <copy>
      <from variable="TravelRequest" part="employee"/>
      <to variable="EmployeeTravelStatusRequest"
                                            part="employee"/>
    </copy>
  </assign>

  <!-- Synchronously invoke the Employee Travel Status Web
                                                  Service -->
  <invoke name="EmployeeTravelStatusSyncInv"
          partnerLink="employeeTravelStatus"
          portType="emp:EmployeeTravelStatusPT"
          operation="EmployeeTravelStatus"
          inputVariable="EmployeeTravelStatusRequest"
          outputVariable="EmployeeTravelStatusResponse" />

  <!-- Prepare the input for AA and DA -->
  <assign name="AirlinesInput">
    <copy>
      <from variable="TravelRequest" part="flightData"/>
      <to variable="FlightDetails" part="flightData"/>
    </copy>
    <copy>
      <from variable="EmployeeTravelStatusResponse"
            part="travelClass"/>
      <to variable="FlightDetails" part="travelClass"/>
    </copy>
  </assign>

  <!-- Async invoke of the AA web service and wait for the
                                                  callback -->

  <invoke name="AmericanAirlinesAsyncInv"
          partnerLink="AmericanAirlines"
          portType="aln:FlightAvailabilityPT"
          operation="FlightAvailability"
```

```
        inputVariable="FlightDetails" />


<receive name="AmericanAirlinesCallback"
         partnerLink="AmericanAirlines"
         portType="aln:FlightCallbackPT"
         operation="FlightTicketCallback"
         variable="FlightResponseAA" />

<!-- Async invoke of the DA web service and wait for the
                                                    callback -->

<invoke name="DeltaAirlinesAsyncInv"
        partnerLink="DeltaAirlines"
        portType="aln:FlightAvailabilityPT"
        operation="FlightAvailability"
        inputVariable="FlightDetails" />

<receive name="DeltaAirlinesCallback"
         partnerLink="DeltaAirlines"
         portType="aln:FlightCallbackPT"
         operation="FlightTicketCallback"
         variable="FlightResponseDA" />

<!-- Select the best offer and construct the TravelResponse-->
<if>
<condition>
     $FlightResponseAA.confirmationData/aln:Price &lt;=
     $FlightResponseDA.confirmationData/aln:Price
  </condition>
  <!-- Select American Airlines -->
  <assign>
     <copy>
       <from variable="FlightResponseAA" />
       <to variable="TravelResponse" />
     </copy>
  </assign>

  <else>
     <!-- Select Delta Airlines -->
     <assign>
       <copy>
         <from variable="FlightResponseDA" />
         <to variable="TravelResponse" />
```

```
            </copy>
          </assign>
       </otherwise>
     </if>

   </flow>

   <!-- Make a callback to the client -->
   <invoke name="ClientCallback"
           partnerLink="client"
           portType="trv:ClientCallbackPT"
           operation="ClientCallback"
           inputVariable="TravelResponse" />

</sequence>

</process>
```

Note that all activities gathered within `<flow>` will start concurrently, which is not what we want. We therefore use links to express dependencies. First, we identify the dependencies:

- The input for the Employee web service (`EmployeeInput`) has to be prepared before the Employee web service can be invoked (`EmployeeTravelStatusSyncInv`).
- The invocation (`EmployeeTravelStatusSyncInv`) of the Employee web service has to be finished before the input for both airlines' web services can be prepared (`AirlinesInput`).
- The input for both airlines' web services has to be prepared (`AirlinesInput`) before the process can invoke the web services of both airlines (`AmericanAirlinesAsyncInv` and `DeltaAirlinesAsyncInv`).
- The invocation of the American Airlines web service (`AmericanAirlinesAsyncInv`) has to be finished before the callback can be received (`AmericanAirlinesCallback`).
- The invocation of the Delta Airlines web service (`DeltaAirlinesAsyncInv`) has to be finished before the callback can be received (`DeltaAirlinesCallback`).
- Both callbacks (from American and Delta Airlines: `AmericanAirlinesCallback` and `DeltaAirlinesCallback`) have to be received before the best offer can be selected (`BestOfferSelect`).

Let us now name the links. We will need the following eight links:

- The link from the `EmployeeInput` to `EmployeeTravelStatusSyncInv`
- The link from the `EmployeeTravelStatusSyncInv` to the `AirlinesInput` preparation
- Two links form the `AirlinesInput` preparation to `AmericanAirlinesAsyncInv` and `DeltaAirlinesAsyncInv`
- The link from `AmericanAirlinesAsyncInv` to the receive callback `AmericanAirlinesCallback`
- The link from `DeltaAirlinesAsyncInv` to the receive callback `DeltaAirlinesCallback`
- The link from `AmericanAirlinesCallback` to `BestOfferSelect`
- The link from `DeltaAirlinesCallback` to `BestOfferSelect`

We have to define the links within the `<flow>` activity, as shown in the following code excerpt:

```
<flow>

  <links>

    <link name="EmployeeInputToEmployeeTravelStatusSyncInv" />
    <link name="EmployeeTravelStatusSyncInvToAirlinesInput" />
    <link name="AirlinesInputToAmericanAirlinesAsyncInv" />
    <link name="AirlinesInputToDeltaAirlinesAsyncInv" />
    <link name="AmericanAirlinesAsyncInvToAmericanAirlinesCall
               back" />
    <link name="DeltaAirlinesAsyncInvToDeltaAirlinesCallback"/>
    <link name="AmericanAirlinesCallbackToBestOfferSelect" />
    <link name="DeltaAirlinesCallbackToBestOfferSelect" />

  </links>
...
```

The dependency of links and activities is shown in the following activity diagram:

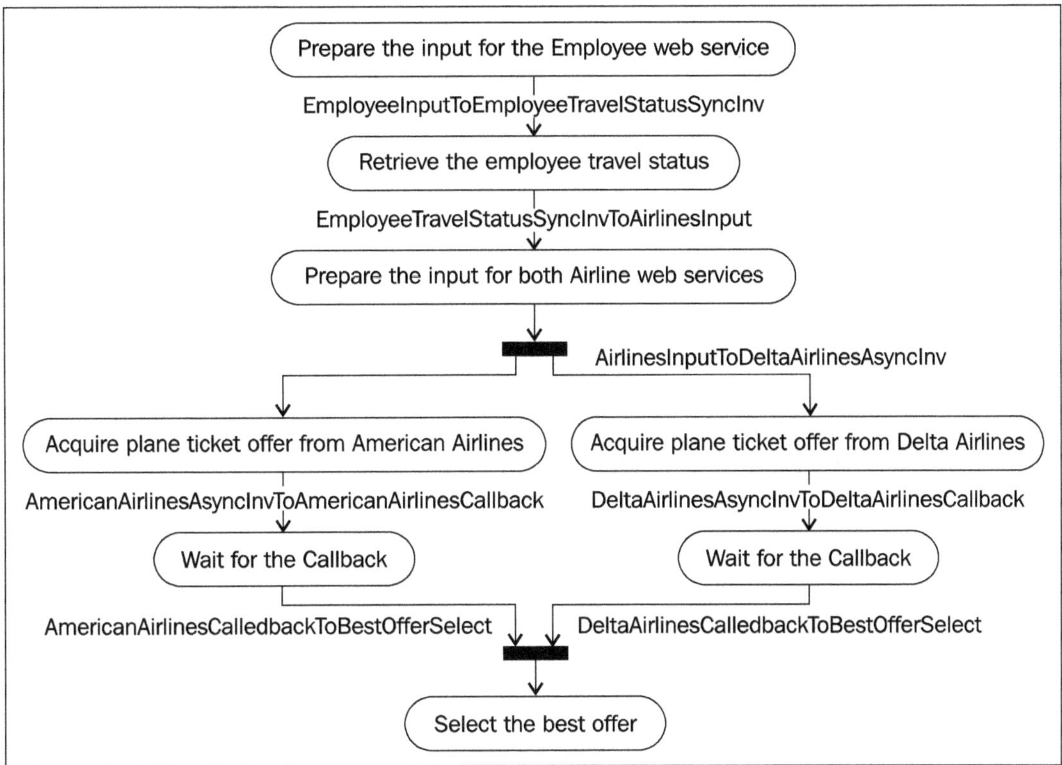

Let us now add the `<source>` and `<target>` elements to the BPEL process activities:

```
...
    <!-- Prepare the input for the Employee Travel Status Web
                                                     Service -->
    <assign name="EmployeeInput">

      <sources>
        <source
         linkName="EmployeeInputToEmployeeTravelStatusSyncInv" />
      </sources>

      <copy>
        <from variable="TravelRequest" part="employee"/>
        <to variable="EmployeeTravelStatusRequest"
                                  part="employee"/>
      </copy>
    </assign>
```

```
<!-- Synchronously invoke the Employee Travel Status Web
                                                Service -->
<invoke name="EmployeeTravelStatusSyncInv"
        partnerLink="employeeTravelStatus"
        portType="emp:EmployeeTravelStatusPT"
        operation="EmployeeTravelStatus"
        inputVariable="EmployeeTravelStatusRequest"
        outputVariable="EmployeeTravelStatusResponse" >

  <targets>
    <target
     linkName="EmployeeInputToEmployeeTravelStatusSyncInv" />
  </targets>
  <sources>
    <source
     linkName="EmployeeTravelStatusSyncInvToAirlinesInput" />
  </sources>

</invoke>

<!-- Prepare the input for AA and DA -->
<assign name="AirlinesInput">

  <targets>
    <target
     linkName="EmployeeTravelStatusSyncInvToAirlinesInput" />
  </targets>
  <sources>
    <source
        linkName="AirlinesInputToAmericanAirlinesAsyncInv" />
   <source linkName="AirlinesInputToDeltaAirlinesAsyncInv" />
  </sources>

  <copy>
    <from variable="TravelRequest" part="flightData"/>
    <to variable="FlightDetails" part="flightData"/>
  </copy>
  <copy>
    <from variable="EmployeeTravelStatusResponse"
          part="travelClass"/>
    <to variable="FlightDetails" part="travelClass"/>
  </copy>
</assign>
```

```
<!-- Async invoke of the AA web service and wait for the
     callback -->

<invoke name="AmericanAirlinesAsyncInv"
        partnerLink="AmericanAirlines"
        portType="aln:FlightAvailabilityPT"
        operation="FlightAvailability"
        inputVariable="FlightDetails" >

  <targets>
    <target
        linkName="AirlinesInputToAmericanAirlinesAsyncInv" />
  </targets>
  <sources>
    <source
linkName="AmericanAirlinesAsyncInvToAmericanAirlinesCallback" />
  </sources>

</invoke>

<receive name="AmericanAirlinesCallback"
         partnerLink="AmericanAirlines"
         portType="aln:FlightCallbackPT"
         operation="FlightTicketCallback"
         variable="FlightResponseAA" >

  <targets>
    <target
linkName="AmericanAirlinesAsyncInvToAmericanAirlinesCallback" />
  </targets>
  <sources>
    <source
    linkName="AmericanAirlinesCallbackToBestOfferSelect" />
  </sources>

</receive>

<!-- Async invoke of the DA web service and wait for the
                                              callback -->

<invoke name="DeltaAirlinesAsyncInv"
        partnerLink="DeltaAirlines"
        portType="aln:FlightAvailabilityPT"
        operation="FlightAvailability"
        inputVariable="FlightDetails" >
```

```
    <targets>
     <target linkName="AirlinesInputToDeltaAirlinesAsyncInv" />
    </targets>
    <sources>
      <source
     linkName="DeltaAirlinesAsyncInvToDeltaAirlinesCallback" />
    </sources>

  </invoke>

  <receive name="DeltaAirlinesCallback"
           partnerLink="DeltaAirlines"
           portType="aln:FlightCallbackPT"
           operation="FlightTicketCallback"
           variable="FlightResponseDA" >

    <targets>
      <target
   linkName="DeltaAirlinesAsyncInvToDeltaAirlinesCallback" />
    </targets>
    <sources>
      <source linkName="DeltaAirlinesCallbackToBestOfferSelect"
                                                            />
    </sources>

  </receive>

 <!-- Select the best offer and construct the TravelResponse-->
  <if>

    <targets>
      <target
        linkName="AmericanAirlinesCallbackToBestOfferSelect" />
      <target linkName="DeltaAirlinesCallbackToBestOfferSelect"
                                                             />
    </targets>

    <condition>
       $FlightResponseAA.confirmationData/aln:Price &lt;=
       $FlightResponseDA.confirmationData/aln:Price
    </condition>            <!-- Select American Airlines -->
    <assign>
       <copy>
          <from variable="FlightResponseAA" />
          <to variable="TravelResponse" />
```

```
          </copy>
        </assign>

        <else>
          <!-- Select Delta Airlines -->
          <assign>
            <copy>
              <from variable="FlightResponseDA" />
              <to variable="TravelResponse" />
            </copy>
          </assign>
        </otherwise>
      </if>

    </flow>
```

With this we have defined synchronization dependencies between activities. Note that according to the BPEL specification, every link within the <flow> activity must have exactly one activity within the flow as its source and exactly one activity within the flow as its target. This prevents us from using the same link as the source or target of two activities.

Transition conditions

A <source> element specifies that a certain activity defines an outgoing link. When BPEL processes are executed, outgoing links are evaluated after the activity has finished. Each outgoing link can have a positive or negative status. This status is important when the decision is made to start the linked activity (denoted with <target>).

In our example, the `AmericanAirlinesCallback` <receive> activity defines an outgoing link `AmericanAirlinesCallbackToBestOfferSelect`. This link is the incoming link of the `BestOfferSelect` <if> activity. The `BestOfferSelect` <if> activity has another incoming link, `DeltaAirlinesCallbackToBestOfferSelect`, which is the outgoing link of the `DeltaAirlinesCallback` <receive> activity.

After the `AmericanAirlinesCallback` <receive> activity has finished, the outgoing `AmericanAirlinesCallbackToBestOfferSelect` link is evaluated. More precisely, the <transitionCondition> expression of the outgoing link is evaluated. If the <transitionCondition> is evaluated to `true`, the link status is positive. Otherwise, it is negative.

We have already mentioned that the `<source>` element has an optional nested element called `<transitionCondition>`. We have also mentioned that if the element is omitted, a default value of `true` is used. In our previous example, therefore, the outgoing link status was always `true`.

Let's now modify the example and explicitly add the transition condition. The outgoing link will be positive only if the flight ticket is approved. This is signaled using the `Approved` element of the `FlightConfirmationType` complex type, which is the `confirmationData` part of the `TravelResponseMessage` message, used for the `FlightResponseAA` and `FlightResponseDA` variables (see the previous chapter for corresponding WSDL definitions).

We will extract the `Approved` element from the `confirmationData` part of the message stored in the `FlightResponseAA` variable. The code is shown as follows:

```
...
<!-- Receive the callback -->
<receive name="AmericanAirlinesCallback"
         partnerLink="AmericanAirlines"
         portType="aln:FlightCallbackPT"
         operation="FlightTicketCallback"
         variable="FlightResponseAA" >

  <targets>
    <target
linkName="AmericanAirlinesAsyncInvToAmericanAirlinesCallback" />
  </targets>
  <sources>
    <source
      linkName="AmericanAirlinesCallbackToBestOfferSelect">
      <transitionCondition>
       $FlightResponseAA.confirmationData/aln:Approved='true'
      </transitionCondition>
    </source>
  </sources>
</receive>
...
```

We will do the same for the `DeltaAirlinesCallback` `<receive>` activity:

```
...
<!-- Receive the callback -->
<receive name="DeltaAirlinesCallback"
         partnerLink="DeltaAirlines"
         portType="aln:FlightCallbackPT"
         operation="FlightTicketCallback"
```

```
            variable="FlightResponseDA" >

      <targets>
        <target
       linkName="DeltaAirlinesAsyncInvToDeltaAirlinesCallback" />
      </targets>
      <sources>
        <source
            linkName="DeltaAirlinesCallbackToBestOfferSelect">
          <transitionCondition>
           $FlightResponseDA.confirmationData/aln:Approved='true'
          </transitionCondition>
        </source>
      </sources>
    </receive>
    ...
```

Both outgoing links are now evaluated using the transition conditions and statuses can be determined.

Join conditions and link status

The `AmericanAirlinesCallbackToBestOfferSelect` and the `DeltaAirlinesCallbackToBestOfferSelect` are the incoming links for the `BestOfferSelect` `<if>` activity. In order to start the `BestOfferSelect` activity:

- The status of both incoming links has to be determined. As we already know, the status is determined using the `<transitionCondition>` expression.
- The join condition for the `BestOfferSelect` activity has to be evaluated.

The join condition is specified using the standard element called `<joinCondition>`. This element may be specified for each activity that is the target of a link (has at least one incoming link). If no `<joinCondition>` is specified, the default (for the default expression language XPath 1.0) is the logical disjunction (logical `or`) of the link status of all incoming links of this activity. In other words, if the `<joinCondition>` is not explicitly defined, all incoming link statuses are evaluated and the status of at least one incoming link has to be positive. The consequence of evaluating all incoming link statuses is the synchronization of all incoming activities.

In our example, the default (implicit) join condition for the `BestOfferSelect` is, therefore, a disjunction of both incoming link statuses, the `AmericanAirlinesCallbackToBestOfferSelect` and the `DeltaAirlinesCallbackToBestOfferSelect`. The join condition will be evaluated to `true` if at least one of the airlines has approved the flight tickets. Please notice that the incoming link statuses of both links will be evaluated prior to the decision.

Sometimes, the default disjunction will not fit our needs and we will want to define our own join condition. To do this we will use the `<joinCondition>` element. We have to specify this element for the target link activity as the first element under `<targets>`. In our example, we would define the `<joinCondition>` for the `BestOfferSelect` `<if>` activity.

For the `<joinCondition>`, we can specify any valid Boolean expression using the selected expression language (the default is XPath 1.0). Often, we will also want to check the status of the incoming links. We can access the link statuses in a similar way as variables (`$link`). The link status returns `true` if the status of the link is positive and `false` if the status of the link is negative. In `<joinCondition>`, we can only access the status of links that target the join condition's enclosing activity. We cannot access any other variable.

Suppose that instead of the disjunction of link statuses, we would rather use a conjunction. Then, we would define the following `joinCondition`:

```
...
<!-- Select the best offer and construct the TravelResponse
-->
<if>

  <targets>
    <joinCondition>
      $AmericanAirlinesCallbackToBestOfferSelect and
      $DeltaAirlinesCallbackToBestOfferSelect
    </joinCondition>
    <target
      linkName="AmericanAirlinesCallbackToBestOfferSelect" />
  <target linkName="DeltaAirlinesCallbackToBestOfferSelect"/>
  </targets>

  <condition>
     $FlightResponseAA.confirmationData/aln:Price &lt;=
     $FlightResponseDA.confirmationData/aln:Price
  </condition>              <!-- Select American Airlines -->

...
```

Join failures

Join conditions are evaluated before the activity is started. In our example, the join condition would be evaluated to `true` only if both link statuses (`AmericanAirlinesCallbackToBestOfferSelect` and `DeltaAirlinesCallbackToBestOfferSelect`) are positive. Positive join condition is required for starting the activity.

If a join condition evaluates to false, a standard bpel:joinFailure fault is thrown. A bpel:joinFailure can be thrown even if a join condition is not explicitly specified. In our previous example (before explicitly specifying the join condition), the default join condition would be used and would be evaluated to false if both link statuses were negative. This would be the case if neither American nor Delta Airlines would approve the flight ticket.

Suppressing join failures

Sometimes, it would be more useful if instead of throwing a bpel:joinFailure fault the activity would simply not be performed without any fault thrown. BPEL provides an attribute through which we can express this behavior. The attribute is called suppressJoinFailure and is a standard attribute that can be associated with each activity (basic or structured). The value of the attribute can be either yes or no. The default is no.

In our example, we could suppress join failure for selecting the best offer <if> activity as shown below:

```
...
<!-- Select the best offer and construct the TravelResponse
-->
<if suppressJoinFailure="yes" >

  <targets>
    <joinCondition>
      $AmericanAirlinesCallbackToBestOfferSelect and
      $DeltaAirlinesCallbackToBestOfferSelect
    </joinCondition>
    <target
      linkName="AmericanAirlinesCallbackToBestOfferSelect" />
    <target
         linkName="DeltaAirlinesCallbackToBestOfferSelect" />
  </targets>

  <condition>
     $FlightResponseAA.confirmationData/aln:Price &lt;=
     $FlightResponseDA.confirmationData/aln:Price
  </condition>              <!-- Select American Airlines -->

...
```

Please notice that in the above example the suppressJoinFailure="yes" is an attribute of the <if> activity, not the actual condition. The condition is defined within the <condition> expression.

This means that if even one link status is negative, the activity will not be performed and no fault will be thrown—in other words, the activity would be silently skipped. Skipping the activity is equivalent to catching the fault locally with an `<empty>` fault handler.

The consequence of skipping an activity is that outgoing links become negative. This way, the next activity figures out that the previous activity has been skipped. In our example, the activity to select the best offer does not have outgoing links.

The default value of the `suppressJoinFailure` attribute is `no`. This is because in simple scenarios without complex graphs, such behavior is preferred. In simple scenarios, links without transition conditions are often used. Here the developers often do not think about join conditions. Suppressing join failures would lead to unexpected behavior where activities would be skipped.

In complex scenarios with networks of links, the suppression of join failures can be desirable. If such behavior is desirable for the whole BPEL process, we can set the `suppressJoinFailure` attribute to `yes` in the first process element (often a `<sequence>`). Skipping activities with join conditions evaluated to false and setting the outgoing link statuses to negative is called **dead-path-elimination**. The reason is that in complex networks of links with transition conditions, such behavior results in propagating the negative link status along entire paths until a join condition is reached that evaluates to `true`.

With this, we have concluded our discussion on concurrent activities, links, and transition conditions. In the next section, we discuss dynamic partner links.

Dynamic partner links

So far we have discussed BPEL processes where all partner links have been defined at the design time and related to actual web services. We have used a single partner link for each web service we have communicated with.

In an advanced BPEL process, we might want to define the partner link endpoint references at runtime. This means that the BPEL process will dynamically determine which actual web service it will use for a certain invocation, based on the variable content. This is particularly useful in scenarios where the BPEL process communicates with several web services that have the same WSDL interface. This has been the case for our travel process example where American and Delta Airlines' web services shared the same interface.

To understand how we can define partner link endpoint references dynamically at run time, let us look at how endpoint references are represented in BPEL. BPEL uses endpoint references as defined by the WS-Addressing. For each BPEL process instance and for each partner role in a partner link, a unique endpoint reference is assigned. We already know that this assignment can take place at deployment or at runtime. To make such an assignment at runtime, we use the `<assign>` activity. There are several ways in which we can use this. We can copy from one partner link to another using the following syntax:

```
<assign>
    <copy>

      <from partnerLink="name"
            endpointReference="myRole|partnerRole"/>
      <to partnerLink="name"/>

    </copy>
</assign>
```

In the `<from>` activity, we have to specify the endpoint role `myRole` or `partnerRole`, while in the `<to>` activity, we always copy to the `partnerRole`. We can also copy a partner link to a variable:

```
<assign>
    <copy>

      <from partnerLink="name"
            endpointReference="myRole|partnerRole"/>
      <to variable="varName"/>

    </copy>
</assign>
```

The most interesting, however, is to copy a variable, expression, or XML literal to a partner link. This way, we can store the partner link endpoint reference in a variable and copy it to the partner link at runtime, thus selecting the service, which will be invoked dynamically. The syntax for copying a variable to partner link is shown next:

```
<assign>
    <copy>

      <from variable="varName"/>
      <to partnerLink="name"/>

    </copy>
</assign>
```

The partner link endpoint reference in BPEL is represented as service reference container `<sref:service-ref>`. This container is used as an envelope to wrap the actual endpoint reference value.

For the actual endpoint reference, the WS-Addressing `wsa:EndpointReference` XML element is used. The `wsa` namespace URL is `http://schemas.xmlsoap.org/ws/2004/08/addressing`. The `wsa:EndpointReference` element is of type `wsa:EndpointReferenceType` and has the following structure:

```
<EndpointReference xmlns="http://schemas.xmlsoap.org/ws/2004/08/
addressing">

<Address>ServiceURL</Address>
<ReferenceProperties>…</ReferenceProperties>        <!-- optional -->
<ReferenceParameters>…</ReferenceParameters>        <!-- optional -->
<PortType>PortTypeName</PortType>                   <!-- optional -->
<ServiceName PortName="…">ServiceName</ServiceName> <!-- optional -->

</EndpointReference>
```

We can see that the endpoint reference `<Address>` is the only required element. The `<Address>` should include a valid URL of the partner link service.

To dynamically assign an endpoint reference to a partner link, we have to declare a variable of element type `<sref:service-ref>` and copy it to the partner link. Alternatively, we can hardcode the address into the BPEL process and copy the XML literal to the partner link. This is shown in the following example. It is assumed that a service is available on the specified URL:

```
<assign>
    <copy>

      <from>
        <literal>
          <sref:service-ref
             xmlns:sref="http://docs.oasis-
                                    open.org/wsbpel/2.0/serviceref">
            <EndpointReference
           xmlns="http://schemas.xmlsoap.org/ws/2004/08/addressing">
              <Address>
                http://www.soa.si/default/AmericanAirline
              </Address>
            </EndpointReference>
          </sref:service-ref>
        </literal>
```

```
        </from>
        <to partnerLink="Airline"/>

      </copy>
  </assign>
```

With this, we have concluded the discussion on dynamic partner links. Please refer to Chapter 4 for a working demo.

Message exchanges

In scenarios where operations are invoked using the request/response pattern, we always have a situation where an inbound message activity has to be related with a reply activity. The inbound message activity can be a `<receive>`, `<onMessage>`, or `<onEvent>`. The reply activity is always a `<reply>`. In most cases, the BPEL engine will figure out itself which reply activity relates to which inbound message activity. However, if there can be more than one pair of inbound message activities (`<receive>`, `<onMessage>`, or `<onEvent>`) and `<reply>`, we have to explicitly mark the pairing relationship. We do this using message exchanges.

To use message exchanges, we first have to declare them. We declare message exchanges immediately after partner links. We can declare message exchanges for the process or for each individual scope:

```
<messageExchanges>
   <messageExchange name="name" />
   <messageExchange name="name" />
   ...
</messageExchanges>
```

To explicitly specify the pairing, we use the `messageExchange` attribute on the following activities:

- `<receive>`, `<onMessage>`, or `<onEvent>`for inbound messages
- `<reply>` for outbound messages

For example, let's suppose we would like to explicitly denote a message exchange called `TravelExchange`. First, we have to declare it:

```
...
    <messageExchanges>
      <messageExchange name="TravelExchange" />
    </messageExchanges>
    ...
```

Next, we have to add the `messageExchange` attribute to the corresponding inbound and outbound activities. In our case, we use `<receive>` and `<reply>`:

```
<receive partnerLink="client"
         portType="trv:TravelApprovalPT"
         operation="TravelApproval"
         variable="TravelRequest"
         messageExchange="TravelExchange" />
...

<reply partnerLink="client"
       portType="trv:TravelApprovalPT"
       operation="TravelApproval"
       variable="TravelResponse"
         messageExchange="TravelExchange" />
```

From-parts and to-parts

In BPEL, activities such as `<invoke>`, `<receive>`, `<reply>`, and so on, deal with messages. An `<invoke>` activity will send a message to the service that is being invoked and will also receive a message from that service as a response (if we use request/response operation). A `<receive>` operation will wait for an incoming message. A `<reply>` activity will send a response message. Usually these messages are stored in BPEL variables. For example, for an `<invoke>` activity, we can specify the `inputVariable` and `outputVariable` attributes.

BPEL, however, provides an alternative. Instead of using variables, we can deal with WSDL messages directly and specify how to store and extract them from BPEL variables. This alternative approach is particularly useful if the messages have multiple parts (please refer to Chapter 2 or the WSDL specification for discussion on message parts). If we use the `inputVariable` and `outputVariable` attributes, then the whole message is stored into a single variable. With the alternative approach, we can store and extract each message part separately. This gives us additional flexibility, as we can store different parts to different variables or only store some parts of the message.

To specify how message parts should be stored and extracted, we use the `<fromParts>` and `<toParts>` activities.

<fromParts>

The `<fromParts>` activity is used to specify how to store the different message parts to BPEL variables. We can specify `<fromParts>` in the following BPEL activities that receive messages:

- `<receive>`
- `<onMessage>` (within `<pick>`)
- `<onEvent>` (within `<eventHandlers>`)
- `<invoke>` (for receiving the response in request/response operations)

The syntax is equal for all mentioned activities. The `<fromParts>` is always nested within one of the mentioned BPEL activities. We have to specify the message part name (part) and the BPEL variable name to which the message part will be stored. We can specify as many parts as we like, as shown next:

```
<fromParts>
   <fromPart part="name" toVariable="BPELVariableName" />
   <fromPart part="name" toVariable="BPELVariableName" />
   ...
</fromParts>
```

If we specify parts, we must not specify the variable attributes (such as `inputVariable` and `outputVariable`).

For example, if we would like to use the `<fromParts>` within a `<receive>` activity, we could use it like this:

```
<receive partnerLink="AmericanAirlines"
    portType="aln:FlightCallbackPT"
    operation="FlightTicketCallback" >
    <correlations>
       <correlation set="TicketOrder"
                    initiate="yes" />
    </correlations>

    <fromParts
       <fromPart part="confirmationData"
                 toVariable="TravelResponse" />
    </fromParts>

</receive>
```

<toParts>

The `<toParts>` serves a very similar purpose as `<fromParts>`, except that it specifies which BPEL variables will map to which message part. The `<toParts>` activity is used to specify the mapping of outbound messages. We can specify `<toParts>` in the following BPEL activities:

- `<reply>`
- `<invoke>`

The syntax is shown as follows:

```
<toParts>
   <toPart part="name" fromVariable="BPELVariableName" />
   <toPart part="name" fromVariable="BPELVariableName" />
   ...
</toParts>
```

If we specify parts, we must not specify the variable attributes (such as `inputVariable` and `outputVariable`).

For example, if we would like to use the `<toParts>` within an `<invoke>` activity, we could use it as shown below:

```
<invoke partnerLink="AmericanAirlines"
    portType="aln:FlightAvailabilityPT"
    operation="FlightAvailability"
    inputVariable="FlightDetails" >

   <toParts>
     <toPart part="flightData"
             fromVariable="FlightDataDetails" />
     <toPart part="travelClass"
             fromVariable="FlightTravelClass" />
   </toParts>

</invoke>
```

In the next section, we discuss abstract business processes.

Abstract business processes

Although the BPEL name suggests that this is a language for specifying executable business processes, BPEL supports both executable business processes and abstract business processes. Abstract business processes are partially specified processes that are not intended to be executed. As abstract processes are not executable, the question is: What are they useful for? There are several use cases where abstract business processes can be useful. The BPEL specification defines two such cases:

- Abstract processes can be used as templates, which hide execution details and have extension points for adding behavior
- Abstract processes can be used to describe the externally observable service behavior

There can be other use cases for abstract processes.

The most common scenario is to use abstract processes as a template to define executable processes. Abstract processes can be used to replace sets of rules usually expressed in natural language, which is often ambiguous. This reduces misunderstandings and errors. An abstract process can define the process flow, but will not include all the execution details such as service endpoint details, variable manipulation, and so on. Such details can be added later when the abstract process is used as a template for developing an executable process.

The second possibility for using abstract processes is for describing the externally observable service behavior. This is useful for describing public process behavior without the exact details of how the process executes. Such abstract business processes specify public message exchange between parties only. An abstract business process should provide a complete description of external behavior relevant to a partner or several partners it interacts with.

The description of the externally observable behavior of a business process may be related to a single service or a set of services. It might also describe the behavior of a participant in a business process. In the latter case, the abstract processes of all partners must be coupled together, usually using a separate global protocol structure description. We can describe the externally observable behavior of a service even though we do not know exactly in which business process it will take part. In this scenario, we will use partner links with `myRole` attributes only. With such an abstract process, we can provide a service behavioral description that does not place any requirements on the partners except that they respect the behavior of the web service.

Second, we can use an abstract process to define collaboration protocols among multiple parties and precisely describe the external behavior of each party. Such abstract processes will usually be defined by large enterprises to define protocols for their partners, or by vertical standards organizations such as RosettaNet, to define business protocols for their domains.

Abstract processes are defined in the `http://docs.oasis-open.org/wsbpel/2.0/process/abstract` namespace. They must specify the `abstractProcessProfile` attribute of the `<process>` tag. This attribute denotes which profile is used. We have mentioned two profiles:

- Abstract process profile for templates, identified as `http://docs.oasis-open.org/wsbpel/2.0/process/abstract/simple-template/2006/08`
- Abstract process profile for observable behavior, identified as `http://docs.oasis-open.org/wsbpel/2.0/process/abstract/ap11/2006/08`

Although abstract processes are not executable, they can use all the constructs from the executable processes, which we have described in this and the previous chapter. For the activities, we use opaque expressions and omit some syntactic details. For example, when defining a partner link, we do not have to specify all the attributes:

```
<partnerLinks>
   <partnerLink name="EmployeeTravelStatus"
      partnerLinkType="##opaque"
      myRole="##opaque"
      partnerRole="##opaque">
   </partnerLink>
</partnerLinks>
```

We can also use opaque attributes with variable declarations, for example:

```
<variables>
   <variable name="TravelStatus" element="##opaque" />
</variables>
```

The same holds true for other activities, such as `<invoke>`, `<receive>`, `<reply>`, and so on. An example of `<invoke>` is listed as follows:

```
<invoke partnerLink="EmployeeTravelStatus"
        operation="##opaque"
        inputVariable="##opaque"/>
```

Abstract processes may omit the `createInstance` attribute of the initial `<receive>` or `<pick>` activity, which is mandatory for executable processes.

Although abstract processes look useful, at the time of writing this book they have not been widely used and tools did not provide any substantial support for abstract processes. It seems that in the majority of cases, BPEL is to be used for executable processes.

Generating BPEL from BPMN diagrams

Throughout the chapter we have seen that BPEL is a high-level language for specifying business processes. BPEL is an executable language but not a modeling language. If you try to model processes in BPEL, this will likely not be successful, as BPEL requires many details, such as variable assignments, endpoints, and so on. All these details are usually not necessary when we model business processes.

In the past, several notations have been used to model processes. Flow diagrams and block diagrams have been representatives of the first generation notations. Then, more sophisticated notations have been defined, such as **EPC** (**Event Process Chain**) and **eEPC** (**Extended Event Process Chain**). UML activity diagrams have also been used. A few years ago a new notation, called **Business Process Modeling Notation** (**BPMN**) has been developed. Business Process Modeling Notation is the most comprehensive notation for process modeling so far. It has been developed under the hood of **OMG** (**Object Management Group**).

BPMN has been developed with BPEL and SOA in mind. The most important information in our context is the ability to generate BPEL from BPMN models automatically. This is extremely important, as it enables full-lifecycle support for business processes. Automatic generation of BPEL out of BPMN and round-tripping between BPMN and BPEL enables that business process models and their executable representation stay in sync. This approach also reduces the workload, as it does not require to develop BPELs from scratch.

Today, several SOA platforms provide support for automatic generation of BPEL from BPMN. Later in this book, we will show how BPEL can be generated out of BPMN using Oracle BPA Suite. Be aware, however, that we have to follow certain rules when designing BPMN models in order to be able to automatically translate them to BPEL. For more information, please refer to the book *"Business Process Driven SOA using BPMN and BPEL", August 2008, ISBN 1847191460, Packt Publishing.*

Summary

We have seen that BPEL is an efficient language for describing business processes. It provides support for the complexities of real-world business process implementations but is still relatively easy to learn and use. In this chapter, we have become familiar with the advanced concepts of BPEL, such as loops, process termination, delays, and deadline and duration expressions. We have addressed fault handling, which is a very important aspect of each business process. Particularly in BPEL processes, which use loosely coupled web services for partner operations, faults can occur quite often. We have discussed scopes, which enable us to break the process into several parts. Each part or scope can have its own variables, correlation sets, fault handlers, compensation handlers, and event handlers. In addition, scopes can provide concurrency control through isolation.

Another very important aspect of business processes is compensation. In business processes, consistency has to be preserved even if a process is abandoned. As business processes are often long running and span several partners, the usage of ACID transactions is not reasonable. BPEL therefore supports the concept of compensation. The goal of compensation is to reverse the effects of previous activities that have been carried out as part of a business process that is being abandoned. We have become familiar with compensation handlers and how to invoke them. Next, we have discussed events and have seen that a business process has to react on message events, which happen when an operation is invoked on the process, and on alarm events, which can occur at a specific time or after certain duration.

We have also addressed complex business processes with many concurrent activities and have seen that BPEL provides links, which enable concurrency control and synchronization using source and target links. Then we have discussed transition and join conditions, and link statuses. We have seen why and when join failures are thrown and how to eliminate dead paths using join failure suppression.

We have discussed the business process lifecycle and process instances and have focused on correlation of messages, another important aspect of BPEL processes. Correlation uses correlation sets to associate messages with business process instances, and is related to message properties. Message properties have global significance in business processes and are mapped to multiple messages. We have become familiar with dynamic partner links. Finally, we have discussed abstract business processes and mentioned the BPMN to BPEL round-tripping. With this we have covered all the advanced aspects of BPEL.

4
Using BPEL with Oracle SOA Suite 11*g*

In this chapter, we will get familiar with developing and executing BPEL processes in the Oracle SOA Suite 11*g*, which is currently one of the most powerful BPEL environments with good support for deployment, execution, and management of business processes defined in BPEL. We will get familiar with all stages of the BPEL process lifecycle. We will look at the BPEL Component Designer, which is a JDeveloper plug-in that represents a rich graphical development environment for implementing and testing BPEL processes and deploying the SOA composites, and thus eases the development and maintenance of BPEL processes considerably. We will also show how to deploy composite applications using the command-line utility and how to manage and test deployed composites using Oracle Enterprise Manager Console. We use version 11*g* PatchSet 2 (11.1.1.3.0) of the SOA Suite products in this book.

> Oracle SOA Suite 11*g* PS2 supports BPEL 2.0. However, BPEL 2.0 is only supported at runtime and not in JDeveloper. BPEL 2.0 support in Oracle SOA Suite 11*g* PS2 is not yet production ready, so by default, BPEL version 1.1 is used. However, we can write BPEL 2.0 code in text mode (graphical mode is currently not supported). Therefore, for the examples in this chapter, we will use BPEL 1.1 and BPEL 2.0.

In this chapter, we will discuss the following:

- Overview and architecture of the BPEL design-time and runtime environment
- Building composite applications with SOA Composite Editor
- Development of processes with BPEL Component Designer
- Process deployment within SOA composites

- Management and debugging of processes with the use of Enterprise Manager Console
- Development and deployment of BPEL 2.0 processes

Overview

The Oracle SOA Suite 11*g* PS 2 (11.1.1.3.0) fully supports BPEL versions 1.1 and 2.0; however, version 2.0 is only supported at runtime and is not yet production ready. At the time of writing this book, we cannot use graphical editor for the development of BPEL 2.0 processes. In addition to standard BPEL support, Oracle also provides extensions to BPEL in the form of new activities (such as FlowN) and XPath functions. Oracle extensions are described in detail in Chapters 5 and 6. As Oracle SOA Suite 11*g* follows the SCA-compliant approach for building SOA composite applications, BPEL processes can be implemented and deployed only as part of a composite application. Every BPEL process is therefore a service component inside an SOA composite application.

We will look at the four major parts:

- BPEL Component Designer
- BPEL Service Engine
- Database
- Enterprise Manager Console

BPEL Component Designer

BPEL Component Designer enables the development of BPEL processes in a graphical environment without having to write BPEL code by hand. BPEL Component Designer supports three different views:

1. **BPEL view**: We can implement a BPEL process (graphical or text mode) using this view.
2. **Monitor view**: This enables us to define monitoring objects, sensors, and sensor actions, which are used to collect **KPI** (**Key Performance Indicators**) about business activity execution, so that we can show this data on the **BAM** (**Business Activity Monitoring**) dashboard.
3. **BPA view**: This is used to open BPEL blueprints that were automatically generated from BPMN models, using Oracle **BPA** (**Business Process Analysis**) Suite.

Instead of writing code, we drag and drop activities into the process. We can add partner links and locate services. We can also use function and copy wizards, XPath expression builder, and XSLT mapper. By using JDeveloper, we can easily deploy the developed processes as composites. This eases the development and maintenance of BPEL processes considerably. BPEL Component Designer internally uses BPEL as its native format. BPEL Component Designer is available as part of the SOA Composite Editor plug-in for JDeveloper. We will discuss SOA Composite Editor and BPEL Component Designer later in this chapter.

BPEL Service Engine

The BPEL Service Engine is the runtime environment where the BPEL processes are deployed and executed. In Oracle SOA Suite 11*g*, the BPEL Service Engine is part of the Service Infrastructure, such as the new BPMN 2.0 Service Engine. In fact, both engines share a common process core, which provides common engine functionality. Some of the key functionalities performed by the process core include the following:

- Manage security
- Generate audit trails
- Invoke services
- Manage persistence

In addition to full BPEL 1.1 and BPEL 2.0 support, Oracle SOA Suite 11*g* also provides support for version control. This enables development of several versions of composites that can be deployed side by side. This feature is important in real-world scenarios because business processes evolve over time. Having an effective versioning support simplifies the management.

Another very important feature is **dehydration**. In previous chapters, we have explained that business processes can be long-running because the involved partners might not be able to react instantly to the requests. This happens particularly in asynchronous scenarios where a business process invokes a partner web service (using the `<invoke>` activity) and then waits for the response (using the `<receive>` or `<pick>` activities or `<onMessage>` within event handlers). While waiting for the response, the Oracle engine can store the process (and its state) in the database, thus freeing up server resources. This is called dehydration. When the engine receives the response, it first restores the process with its state from the database (**hydration**) and then continues with the execution of the process. In real-world scenarios, where many business processes might be running side by side, the dehydration capability is important, as it reduces the demands on hardware performance.

Oracle SOA Suite 11*g* also provides support for clustering. **Clustering** increases server reliability because fail-over can be configured on the engine. Clustering also improves scalability with load balancing. These features are very important in real-world usage of the product and are provided by the fabric, except the message recovery, which is BPEL process core specific.

Database

The database is used for storing messages and the state of process instances (dehydration). Oracle SOA Suite 11*g* provides support for different databases. Usually, Oracle Database or other production-quality DBMS systems such as IBM DB2 or Microsoft SQL Server are used.

Enterprise Manager Console (EM)

Unlike in Oracle SOA Suite 10*g*, where BPEL Process Manager had its own console (Oracle BPEL Console), Oracle SOA Suite 11*g* provides a unified web-based management console for managing and monitoring SOA infrastructure and all deployed services and composite applications—the Oracle Enterprise Manager Fusion Middleware Control Console (shorter form is Enterprise Manager Console, or EM Console).

The most important features of the EM console are as follows:

- Managing the SOA infrastructure and the service engines
- Deploying and un-deploying composite applications
- Testing of deployed services and composites
- End-to-end instance tracking
- Visual process flows
- Audit trails
- Debugging views of composites
- Performance tuning
- Error hospital
- Unit tests
- Attaching and detaching of policies (security, logging, and so on)

As a composite application can contain several BPEL processes (and/or other service components), it is very convenient to be able to deploy, test, debug, and manage the composite application as one unit, without the need to open multiple web-based consoles. We will show the practical use of EM Console later in this chapter.

Building composite applications with SOA Composite Editor

SOA Composite Editor is a JDeveloper plug-in that follows the SCA standard as a way to assemble services, service components, and references into a single SOA composite application (composite). The details of a composite are stored in the **composite.xml** file. However, we do not need to edit that file by hand; instead, we can use the visual SOA Composite Editor, which allows us to simply drag-and-drop service components and binding components from the **Component Palette** to the composite diagram. Following is the screenshot of an SOA composite application, opened in the SOA Composite Editor. The composite shown is implemented by a single BPEL process service component, which uses three external Web Services (references). The composite defines one service (Web Service binding component), through which other applications can invoke the composite.

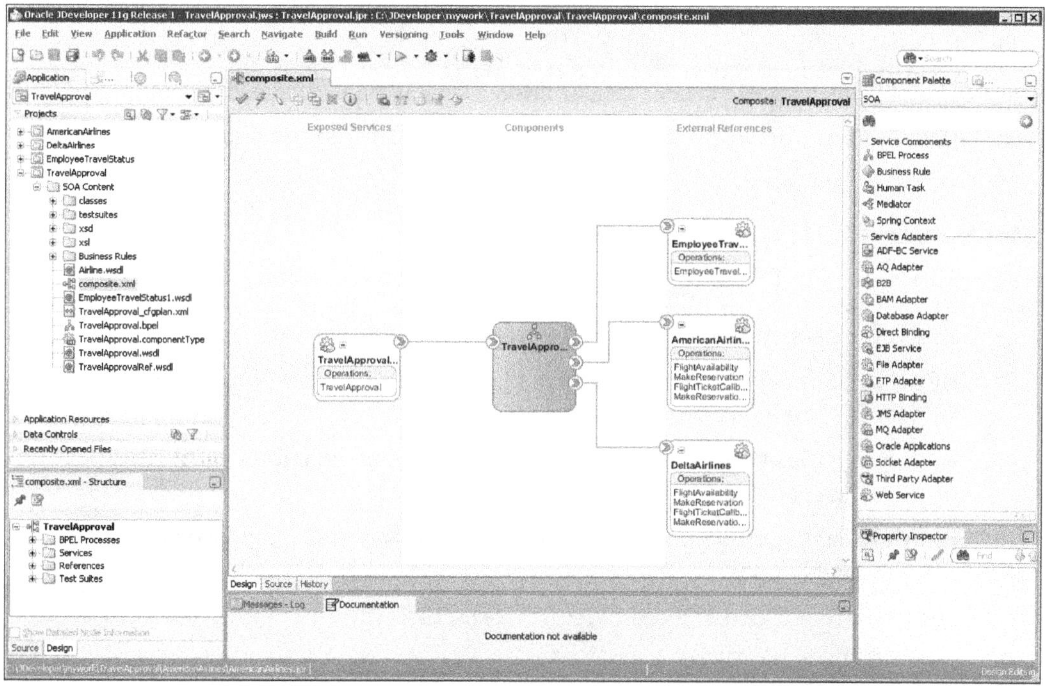

We can see that a composite application consists of three vertical swimlanes: **Exposed Services**, **Components**, and **External References**. The **Components** lane represents the implementation of the composite and can contain only service components. Service components are the main building blocks of composite applications and can be implemented using heterogeneous technologies. We can add service components by simply dragging them from the **Component Palette**. The left lane (**Exposed Services**) represents the entry point to the composite for the outside world. Each composite can define one or more services, which specify how the composite can be invoked. Each composite application can also use external services (references). These appear in the **External References** lane. Both service binding components and reference binding components can be dragged-and-dropped from the **Component Palette** (from the **Service Adapters** list) to the composite diagram.

There are two approaches when building an SOA composite application. They are listed as follows:

- **Top-Down**: We first create a contract (WSDL interface), which is used to define how the SOA composite will be exposed to the outside world, and then add service components and implement the composite. This approach is usually called the contract-driven approach. We will demonstrate this approach later in this chapter.
- **Bottom-Up**: Sometimes, we first want to implement service components and then create appropriate services on an as-needed basis. If we do not define a custom interface when adding a new service component, the service binding component with an auto-generated interface is added automatically by Oracle JDeveloper. This approach works well when IT must react to a change.

Service components

Oracle SOA Suite 11*g* PS 2 supports the following types of service components:

- BPEL Process enables us to orchestrate web services into business processes.
- BPMN Process provides full support for modeling and implementation of BPMN 2.0 business processes.
- Business Rules enable us to externalize business decisions from the application code.
- Human Task enables human interaction inside business processes.
- Mediator is used for routing of events and messages between service components. It can also be used for transformation between different types of messages.
- Spring Context enables us to use Java code inside a composite.

Service infrastructure provides a corresponding service engine for each type of service component; therefore, all service engines can interact in a single composite.

Binding components

Binding components specify how communication between SOA composite applications and the external world should be done. There are two types of binding components:

- **Services**: They describe how the composite will be available to the service consumers (clients). Services define the interface of the composite (provided functionality) and technical information about protocols (SOAP/HTTP, JCA adapter, and so on). A composite can have one or more services.
- **References**: These are external services that provide functionality which is used to implement SOA composite application.

Binding components provided by Oracle SOA Suite 11*g* PS 2 are detailed in the following table:

Binding component	Description
`Web Service`	Exposes the SOA composite as a Web Service available through SOAP. When used as a reference, it enables us to invoke external SOAP Web Services.
`HTTP Binding`	Enables us to expose the SOA composite or invoke an external service through HTTP POST and GET operations.
`JCA Adapters`	Through the use of JCA Adapters, we are able to connect services and references with different technologies and applications. JCA Adapters include Database Adapter, File Adapter, FTP Adapter, JMS Adapter, AQ Adapter, MQ Adapter, and Socket Adapter.
`B2B Service`	Enables secure and reliable exchange of messages between SOA composite applications and organization trading partners by connecting to Oracle B2B.
`ADF-BC Service`	Enables us to connect to Oracle Application Development Framework (ADF) Business Components services by using Service Data Objects (SDO) for message exchange.
`Oracle Applications`	Oracle Application Adapter enables us to communicate with Oracle Applications.

Binding component	Description
`BAM Adapter`	Enables composite application to directly send data about business events to the BAM server.
`EJB Service`	Enables us to integrate EJBs (Enterprise JavaBeans) with SOA composite applications. Integration can be achieved through the use of Service Data Objects (SDO) parameters or java interfaces. Integration of Enterprise JavaBeans with Oracle SOA Suite through java interfaces eliminates the need for WSDL file definitions.
`Direct Binding Service`	Enables an SOA composite application to be invoked and exchange messages over **Remote Method Invocation** (**RMI**). When used as a reference, we have to select a reference target. Possible values are Oracle SOA Composite (direct binding with another SOA composite) and Oracle Service Bus (direct binding with Oracle Service Bus).

Wires

Wires are part of the SCA standard and are used to define message communication between service components and binding components. When wiring components, we have to be familiar with the following rules and restrictions:

- We can wire two components by dragging a wire from the reference handle arrow icon of the first component (it appears on the right side) to the service handle icon of the second component (it appears on the left side), or vice versa. However, this can be done only if the reference and the service of both components match. The match implies the same interface and callback interface.
- We can connect service binding components to service components, services components to other service components, and service components to reference binding components.
- A specific service component can be wired with one or more binding components; however, there are some exceptions. For example, a mediator can only have one inbound service. We also cannot connect a business rule to an external service, as business rules do not support references.
- We cannot wire components with different interfaces. If two components have different interfaces, we have to use a mediator service component to perform a transformation between the interfaces.
- When a reference is added to the BPEL service component, the corresponding partner link is automatically created.

- If we delete a service component or binding component, all associated wires are also deleted, and related service components update their metadata. For example, if we delete a reference connected to a BPEL service component, the BPEL partner link is also deleted.
- If we delete a wire, the component's outbound reference is also deleted and the component updates its metadata (deletes the partner link, deletes routing rules, and so on).

Development of BPEL processes in JDeveloper

To develop a composite application with a BPEL process, we have to follow these steps:

1. Define the XML schemas that will be used by the BPEL process.
2. Define the WSDL interface for the BPEL process.
3. Create a new SOA application and an SOA project inside it.
4. Open the SOA Composite editor, where we drag the BPEL process service component to the Components lane of the SCA diagram. We expose the BPEL processes as a service, using the WSDL interface.
5. Implement the BPEL process using BPEL Component Designer.

We will demonstrate the development of BPEL process on the TravelApproval BPEL process example that we have developed in *Chapter 2, Service Composition with BPEL*. The process that we will use in this chapter is slightly different from the one that we have already implemented. However, the only important difference is that at the end we also make a reservation of the selected flight ticket. Let us have a look at the process activity diagram.

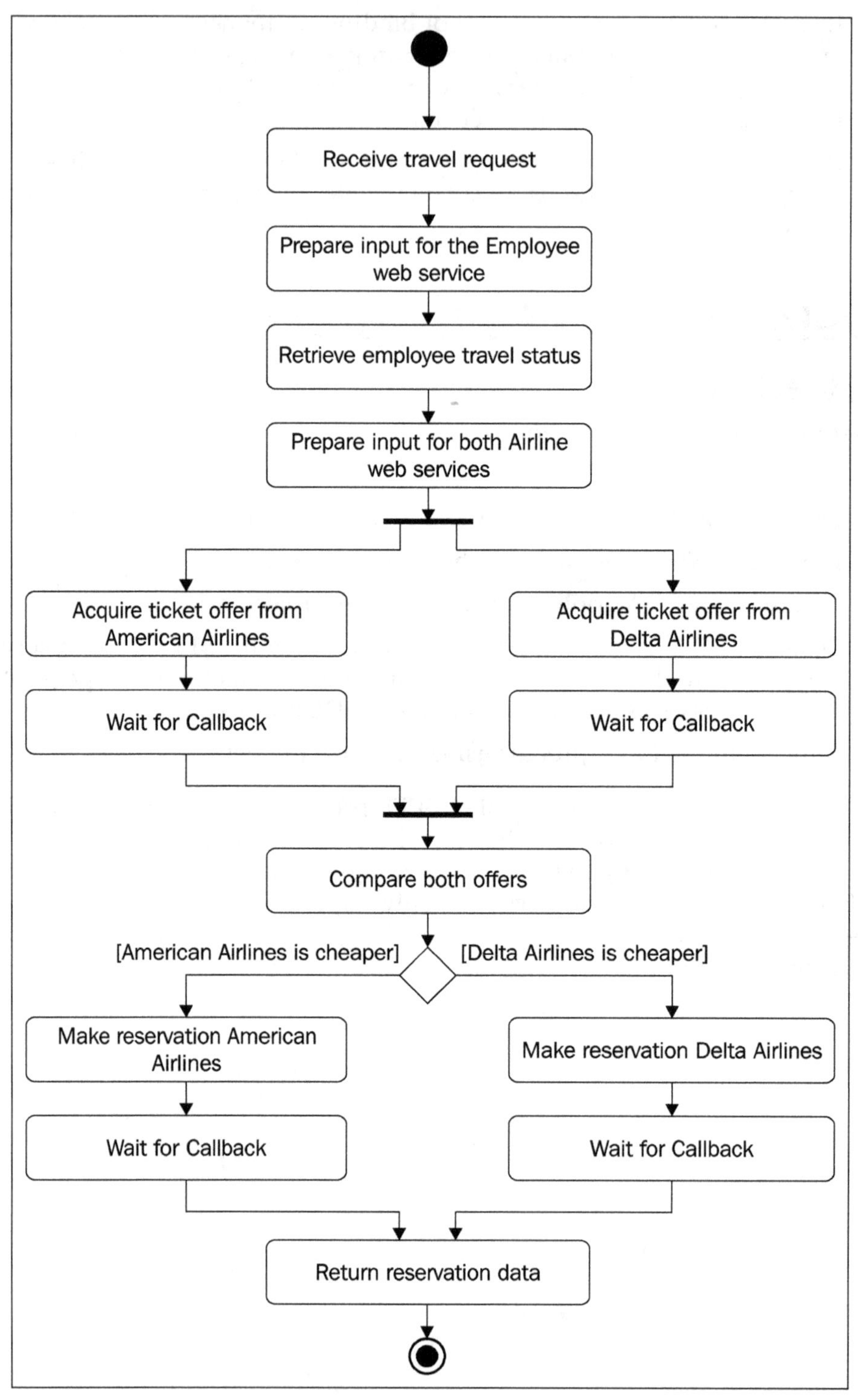
Receive travel request
Prepare input for the Employee web service
Retrieve employee travel status
Prepare input for both Airline web services
Acquire ticket offer from American Airlines
Acquire ticket offer from Delta Airlines
Wait for Callback
Wait for Callback
Compare both offers
[American Airlines is cheaper]
[Delta Airlines is cheaper]
Make reservation American Airlines
Make reservation Delta Airlines
Wait for Callback
Wait for Callback
Return reservation data

We will follow the Top-Down approach for building our composite application. Therefore, we will first define the XML schemas and WSDL interface of the composite. We will not show the source code of BPEL and WSDL files, as they have already been shown in previous chapters. They can also be downloaded from `http://www.packtpub.com`.

Defining XML schemas

JDeveloper provides support for XML schemas by providing XML Schema Editor. This editor is not specific to SOA; therefore, XML schemas are usually created as part of a separate project. By using XML Schema Editor we can create new, and edit existing, XML schemas. XML Schema Editor also provides a validator of the XML schemas. We can define schemas in graphical mode (XML Schema Visual Editor) using simple drag-and-drop operations.

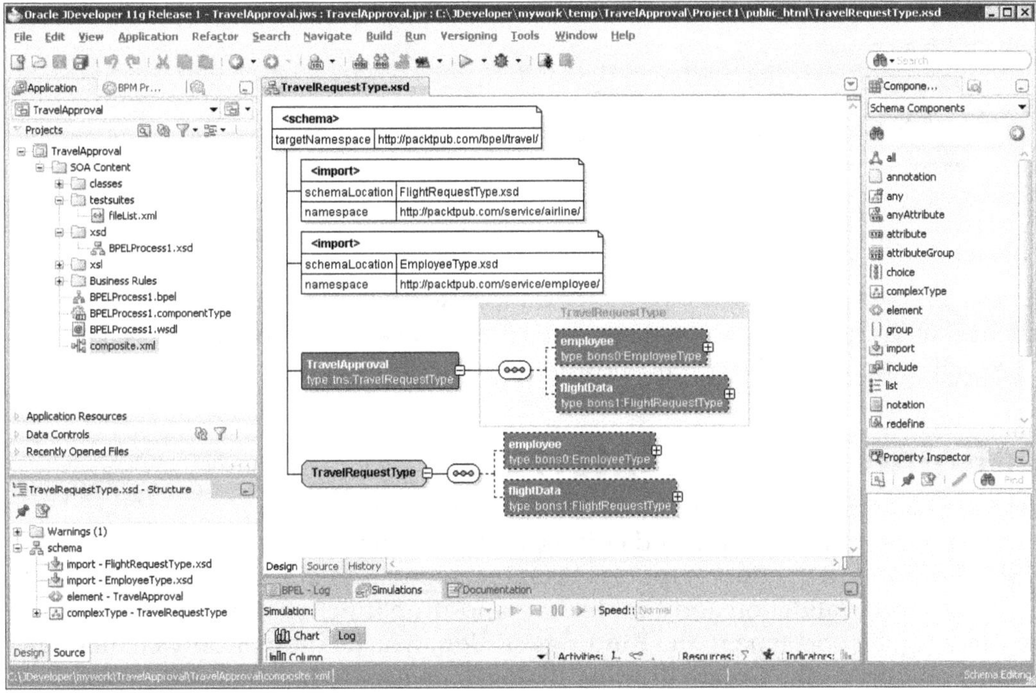

However, we can also switch to the source code and edit the XML schema by hand.

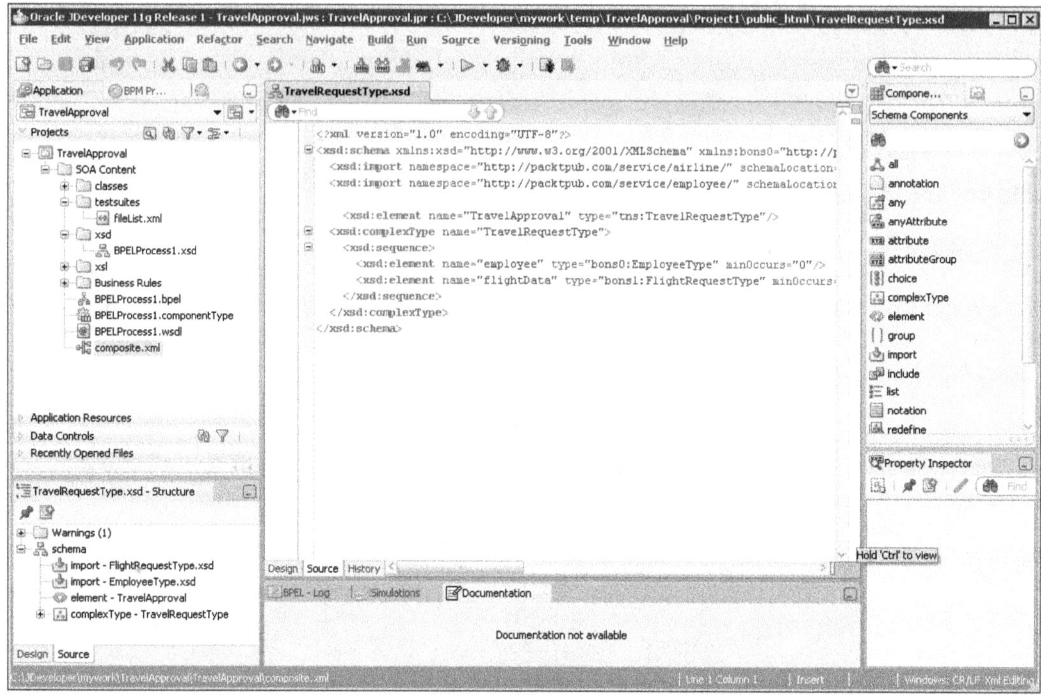

For our TravelApproval BPEL process example, we have to create several XML schemas with complex types and elements that will be used to define messages in the WSDL interface of the composite application.

Defining a WSDL interface

Next, we have to define a WSDL interface for our composite application. JDeveloper provides support for creating and editing WSDL documents by providing the rich WSDL Editor. WSDL Editor supports visual manipulation of the WSDL documents. It also supports validation and simple drag-and-drop functionality. For example, we can drag the port type to the **Bindings** section, which automatically creates new binding and opens the **Create Binding** dialog. However, when building WSDL interfaces for composite applications, we do not create bindings and services, as these are automatically generated during deployment of the composite.

For our TravelApproval BPEL process example, we create a new `TravelApproval.wsdl` document. For the definition of WSDL message parts, we use previously developed XML schemas. We will define one port type (`TravelApprovalPT`) only, as we want to build a synchronous BPEL process. The port type specifies one operation (`travelApproval`). We will also add the Partner Link Type (`travelLT`) with one role (`travelService`). However, it is not necessary to add the Partner Link Type, as if it does not exist, it is automatically generated when we create the BPEL process.

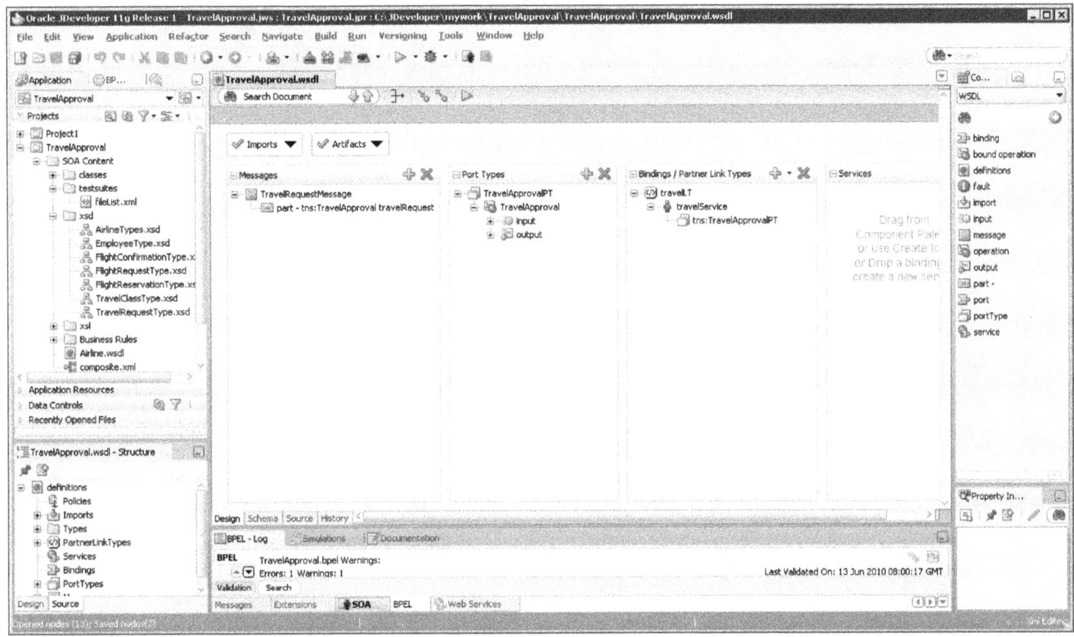

If we want to edit a WSDL document in text mode, we can open the **Source** tab in WSDL Editor.

Creating an SOA composite application

For this example, we will create a new SOA application. The wizard automatically creates a new SOA project inside the application. We set the name of the project to `TravelApproval`.

> In order to create and deploy SOA composite applications and projects, we first have to install the Oracle SOA Composite Editor extension for JDeveloper.

Then we have to set the composite name and choose a composite template. By choosing the **Composite With BPEL Process** template, we could create a composite which would already contain a BPEL process service component. However, we select the **Empty Composite** template. We will add the BPEL process by dragging it from the **Component Palette**.

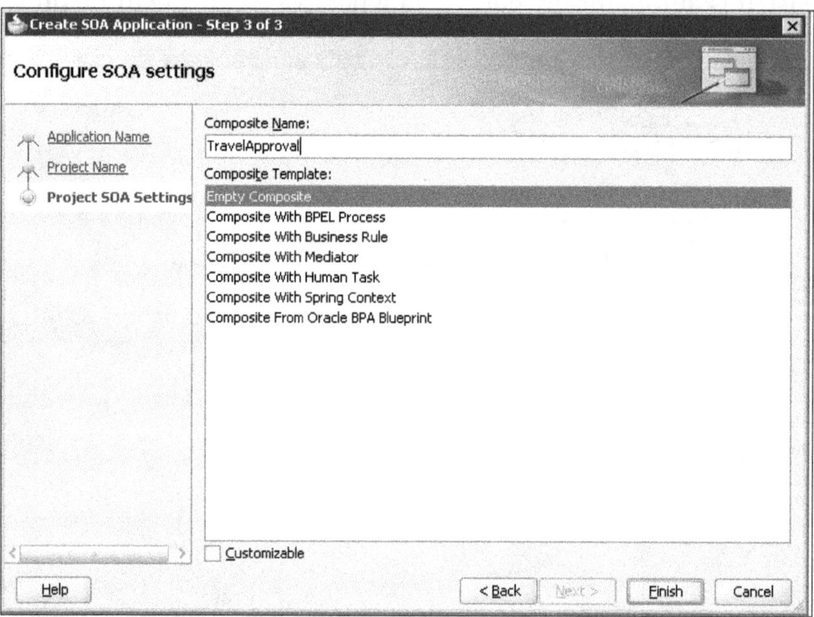

When the project is created, SOA Composite Editor is automatically opened. Our composite application currently contains no service components, because we selected the **Empty Composite** template.

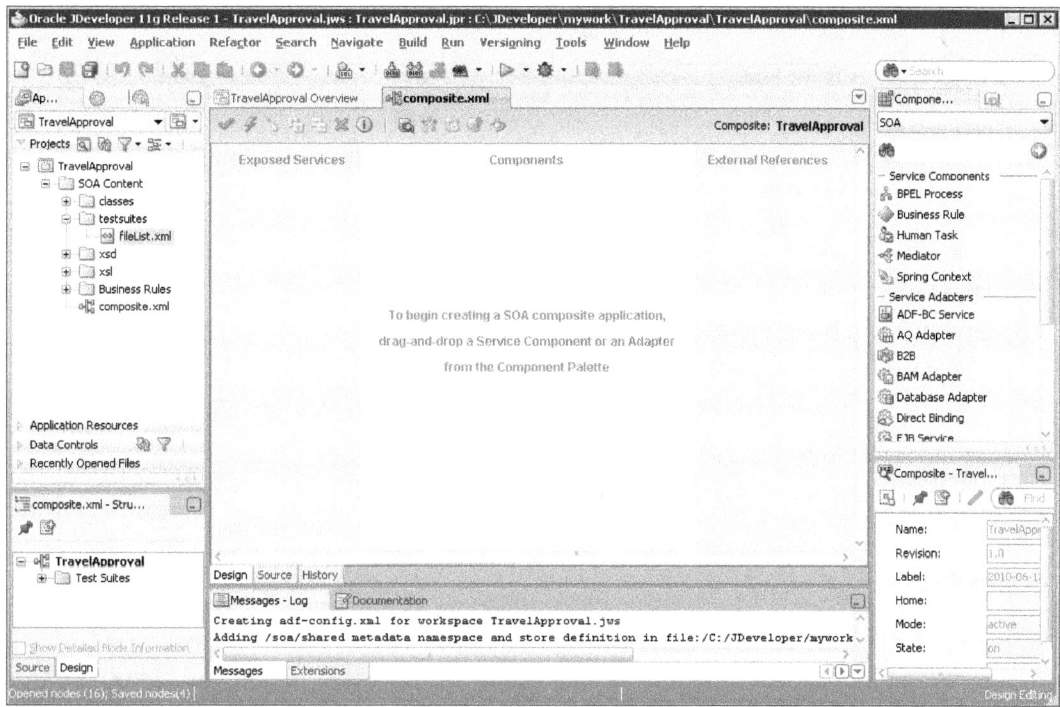

Adding the BPEL Process service component

To create the `TravelApproval` BPEL process, we have to add the BPEL Process service component to the **Components** lane of the composite application diagram. To do this, we drag-and-drop the **BPEL Process** from the **Component Palette** to the diagram.

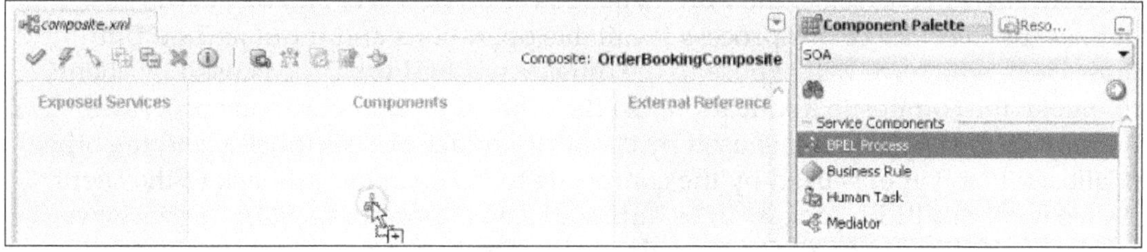

The **Create BPEL Process** dialog opens.

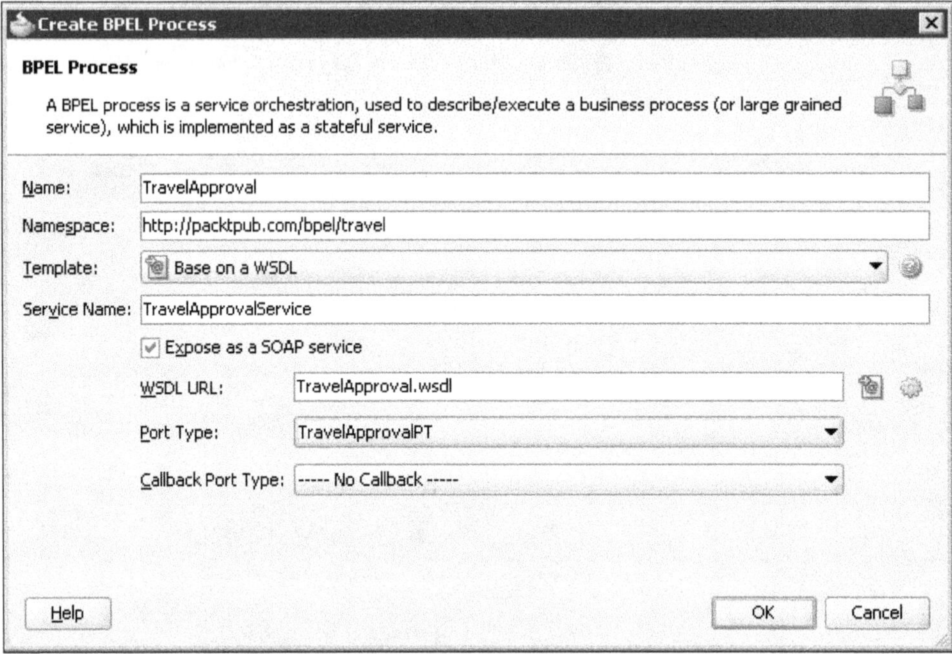

We set the name of the process to `TravelApproval` and the namespace to `http://packtpub.com/bpel/travel/`. We select the **Base on a WSDL** template. Then we click the **Find existing WSDLs** icon next to the WSDL URL field. The **SOA Resource Browser** dialog opens. We select **File System** as a source and browse to the `TravelApproval.wsdl` document. As our process is synchronous, we only also have to select the **Port Type** (`TravelApprovalPT`). The Port Type defines the interface of our process (available operations and input and output messages), which we will expose to the outside world. Port Type is used by clients to invoke the composite application. On the other side, asynchronous processes define two Port Types: one is used by clients to invoke the composite, and the other (Callback Port Type) is used by the composite to perform the callback to the client. As we want our BPEL process to be automatically exposed as a SOAP service, we can leave the **Expose as a SOAP service** value checked. This automatically creates the Web Service binding component and connects it with the BPEL process. Otherwise, we would have to add the service manually.

Service components can have more service bindings. For example, we could expose our BPEL process with the Web Service and Direct Service bindings.

Our composite application diagram now looks like this:

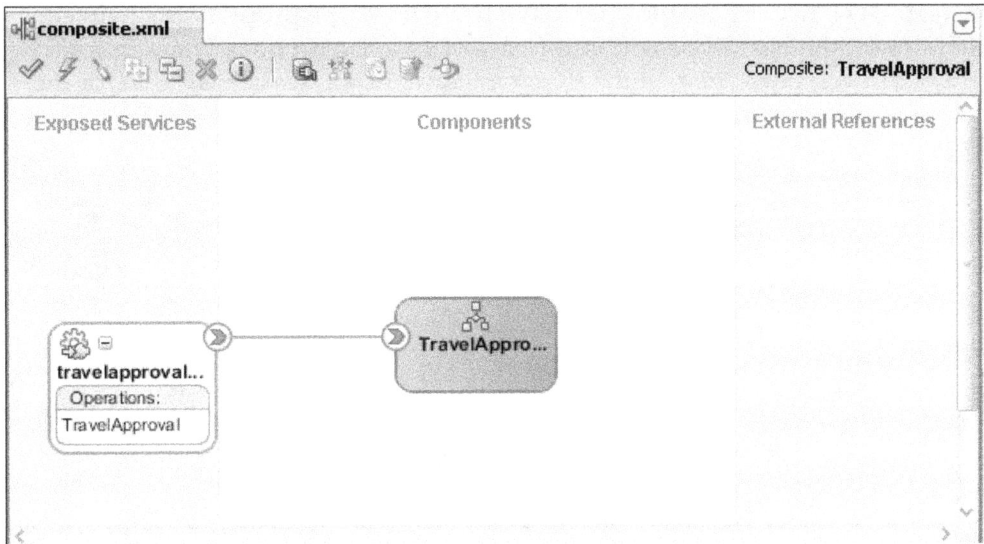

We can see that the TravelApproval BPEL process is the only service component that implements the composite application and that the process is exposed as a web service; therefore, the only way to invoke the composite application is through the use of the SOAP protocol.

Adding references

Next, we have to add partner services to our composite application. The TravelApproval BPEL process uses three external services: `AmericanAirlines` ticket service, `DeltaAirlines` ticket service, and `EmployeeTravelStatus` service. As all three services are simple web services, we will drag three **Web Service** binding components to the **External References** lane of the composite diagram. The **Create Web Service** dialog opens. We leave the **Type** property unchanged. We have to set the **Port Type** and in the case of an asynchronous web service, also the **Callback Port Type**. In the following screenshot, we can see that for the `AmericanAirlines` service, we select `FlightAvailabilityPT` for the **Port Type** and `FlightCallbackPT` for the **Callback Port Type**.

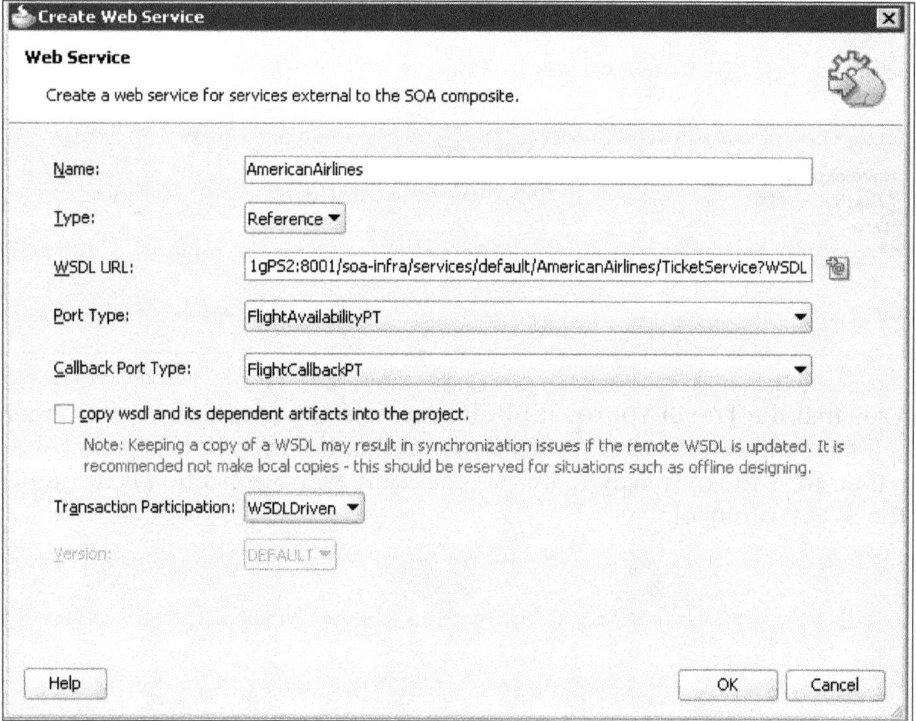

If we do not know the exact location of the WSDL, we can use **SOA Resource Lookup** by clicking on the **Find existing WSDLs** icon (next to the **WSDL URL** field). The **SOA Resource Browser** dialog window opens:

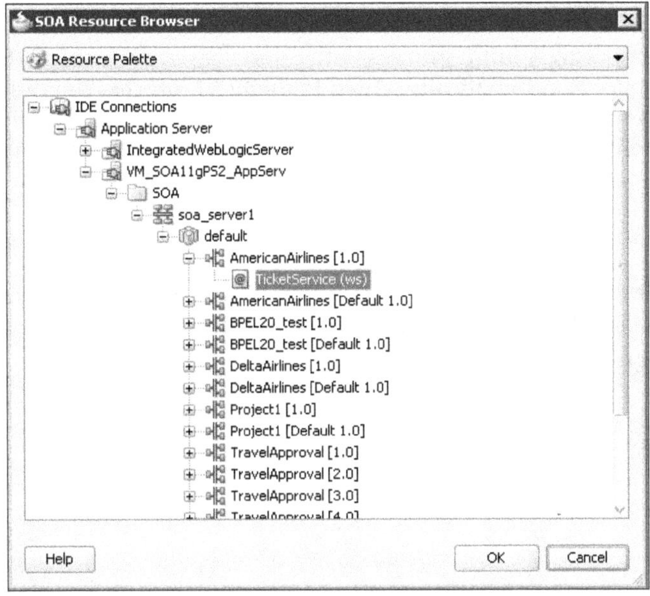

Here we can select the source for choosing the WSDL resource: **File System**, **Resource Palette**, or **Application**. Using the **Resource Palette** we can browse for resources from application servers, MDS repositories, UDDI registries, and Oracle Enterprise Repository (first we need to create connections to those sources on the **Resource Palette** tab).

After adding all three references, we have to wire them to the BPEL process. This can be done by simply dragging a wire from the BPEL process service component to each reference.

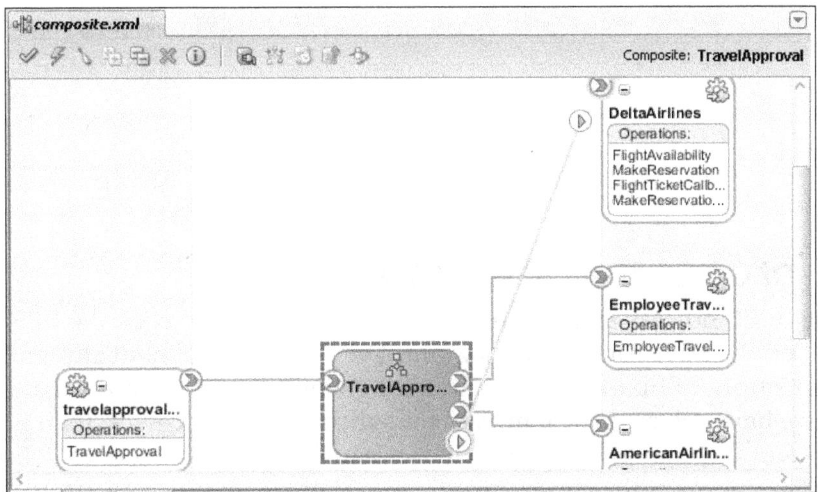

> When wiring a BPEL process with references, a partner link for each reference is automatically added to the BPEL process definition, as we will see later in this chapter. In fact, instead of adding references to the composite diagram, we could also create partner links in the BPEL Component Designer, which would automatically create references and wire them with the BPEL process.

The following screenshot shows the completed SOA composite diagram. The next step is to implement the TravelApproval BPEL process using the BPEL Component Designer.

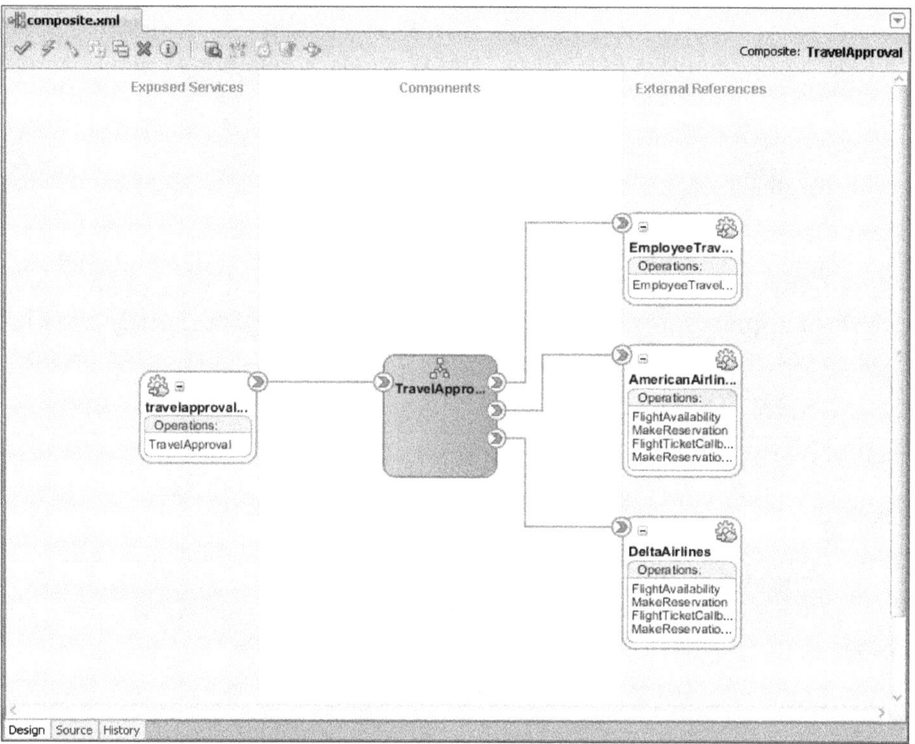

BPEL process implementation

To start the BPEL process implementation, we simply double-click the BPEL service component on the SOA composite diagram. The BPEL Component Designer opens with almost empty BPEL implementation. It depends on the template that we have chosen. If we have selected the template for synchronous processes, then the initial `<receive>` and the final `<reply>` activities are included. If we were to define an asynchronous interface, the process would end with an `<invoke>` activity.

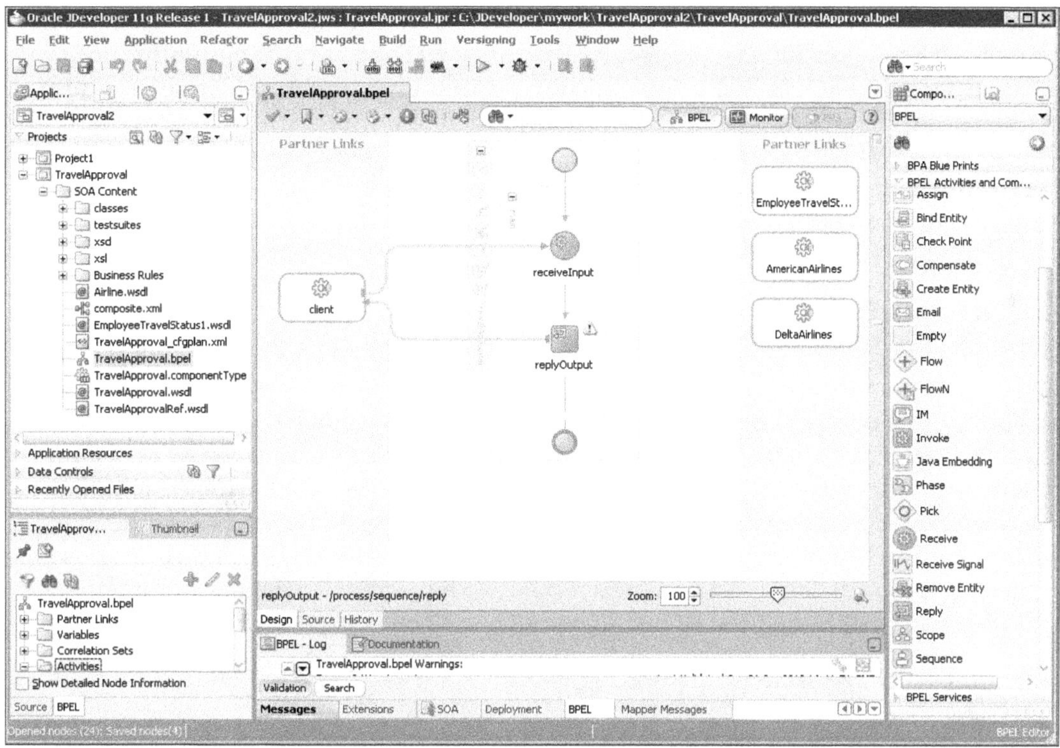

The BPEL Component Designer is a visual editor for implementing BPEL processes. BPEL Component Designer provides three views. In this chapter, we will only use **BPEL view**, which is used to implement the BPEL process. If we were to generate our BPEL from BPMN using Oracle BPA Suite, we would also use **BPA view**. **Monitor view** is used to add sensors and monitoring objects to process activities in order to implement business process monitoring. We will discuss monitoring of BPEL processes in Chapter 8.

Using the BPEL view, we can simply add activities by dragging them from the **Component Palette**. In the previous screenshot, we can see that the editor consists of three vertical swim-lanes. The left lane contains the client partner link that represents the interface through which clients can invoke the process. The middle lane contains the sequence of activities that implement the BPEL process. In the right lane, we add partner links to external services.

BPEL Component Designer also provides the source-code view where we can edit the BPEL code directly. Changes made in the source view are reflected immediately in the BPEL Component Designer visual representation, and vice versa.

Please note that it is not the intention of this section to provide in-depth instructions on using JDeveloper BPEL Component Designer. Rather, we will highlight the most important features, including, adding partner links, creating variables, adding activities, copying variables, entering XPath functions, using XSLT Mapper, and Validation Browser. For detailed instructions on using JDeveloper, please refer to the Oracle documentation, which is accessible at `http://www.oracle.com/technetwork/developer-tools/jdev/ documentation/index.html`.

Adding partner links

When developing BPEL processes, the first step is usually to create partner links. Note that in our example all three partner links have already been generated, as we wired our BPEL process to the references on the composite diagram. However, if we want to add a new partner link, we have to expand the **BPEL Services** in the **Component Palette** (upper-right side of the screen). From there we select the **Partner Link/Adapter/Web Service** and drag-and-drop it to the **Partner Links** section of the main design window. Alternatively, we can right-click in a main design window and use the context menu. A dialog window opens where we have to enter the partner link name and the details, including the WSDL location, partner link type, and both roles:

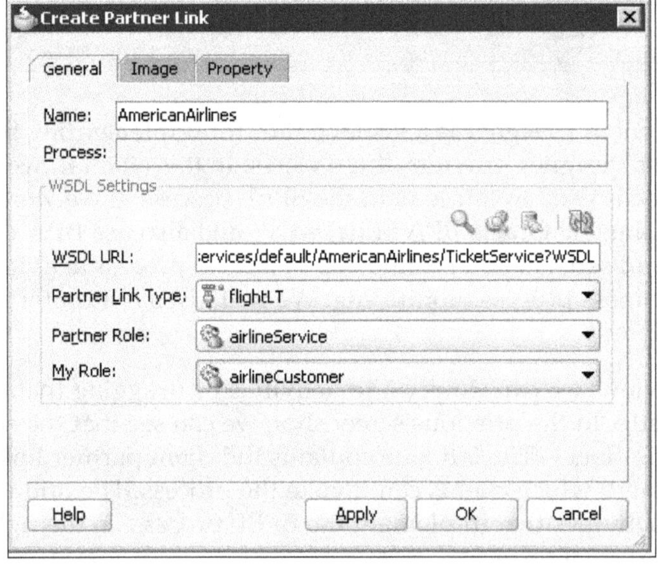

If we do not know the exact location of the WSDL, we can use **SOA Resource Browser** by clicking on the magnifying glass icon. Notice, that when we create a BPEL partner link, a corresponding reference is automatically added to the composite diagram and wired to the BPEL process.

Adding variables

To add variables to the BPEL process we have two choices. We can add them manually, as we will show in this section, or we can use automatic variable creation, as we will see in the next section. Let us first have a look at how we can add variables manually or edit existing variables. In the **BPEL Structure** navigator window (lower left side of the screen), we navigate to the variables. We can see that two variables (named `inputVariable` and `outputvariable`) were automatically created. Then we either click an existing variable or right-click to create a new one. A dialog window opens where we have to specify the variable name and type:

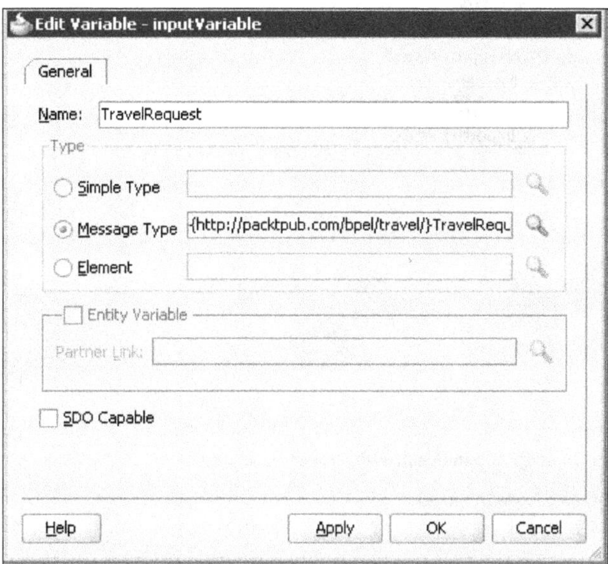

In addition to standard BPEL variables, Oracle SOA Suite 11*g* also supports Entity variables. Entity variables are not like regular XML DOM variables. They use an SDO-based in-memory data structure and are able to detect changes to underlying data in the data source. We will discuss entity variables in Chapter 6.

We select Message Type and click on the magnifying glass icon to open the **Type Chooser**. Here, we can navigate through message types in partner links or project WSDL files and select the appropriate type:

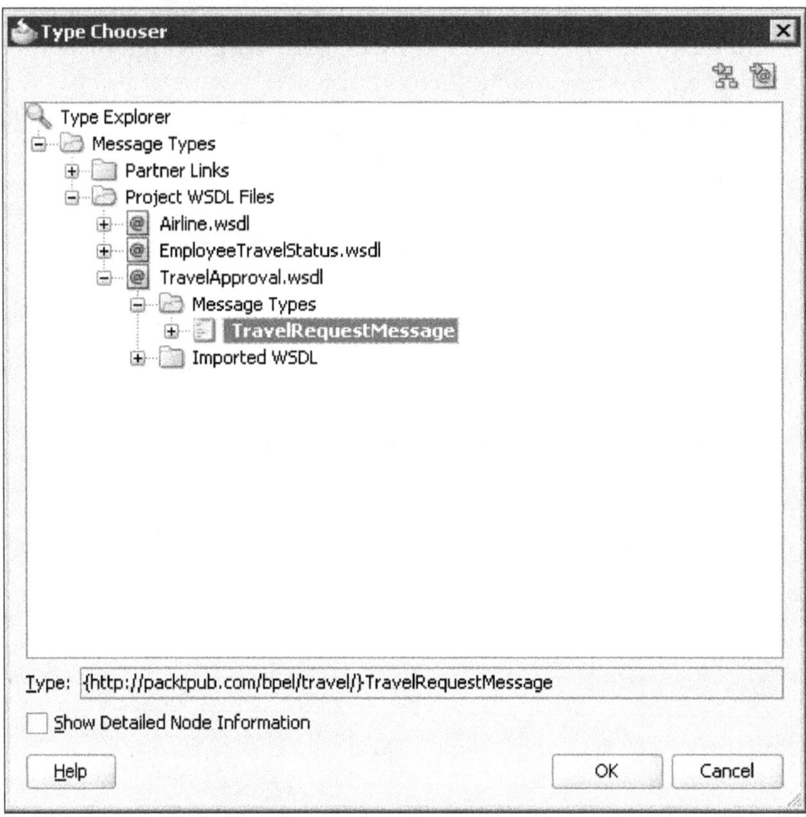

If we have selected a simple type, we can choose from the predefined XML types:

In our TravelApproval process, we will rename `inputVariable` to `TravelRequest` and `outputVariable` to `TravelResponse`.

Adding process activities

Adding process activities is straightforward. We select an activity from the **BPEL Activities and Components** list of the **Component Palette** and drag-and-drop it to the process. After double-clicking the activity, a dialog window opens, where we enter the activity parameters. The **Component Palette** provides access to standard BPEL activities, such as `<assign>`, `<compensate>`, `<empty>`, and so on. In addition to the BPEL activities that we have covered in the previous chapters, we can also choose the following:

- **`<flowN>` activity**: Provides support for parallel execution
- **Java Embedding:** Enables inclusion of Java code into BPEL
- **User Notification**: A wizard for using the Notification service
- **Transform**: Enables access to the XSLT engine and XSLT Mapper through an XPath function
- **User Task**: A wizard for using the Workflow service
- **Business Rule:** Enables inclusion of business rules into BPEL

We will explain these and other Oracle specific activities in Chapter 5.

Now, let's implement our TravelApproval process. First, we select the `<scope>` activity from the **Component Palette** and drag-and-drop it to the process. We name the scope `RetrieveEmployeeTravelStatus`. Inside the scope, we add the `<invoke>` activity, which will be used for invoking the `EmployeeTravelStatus` service. Now we have to open the **Invoke** activity editor, shown in the following screenshot. This can be done either by double-clicking the activity, or by visually connecting it to the selected partner link. We set the name of the activity and connect it to the `EmployeeTravelStatus` partner link. We also have to select the operation and create (or select if they already exist) input and output variables.

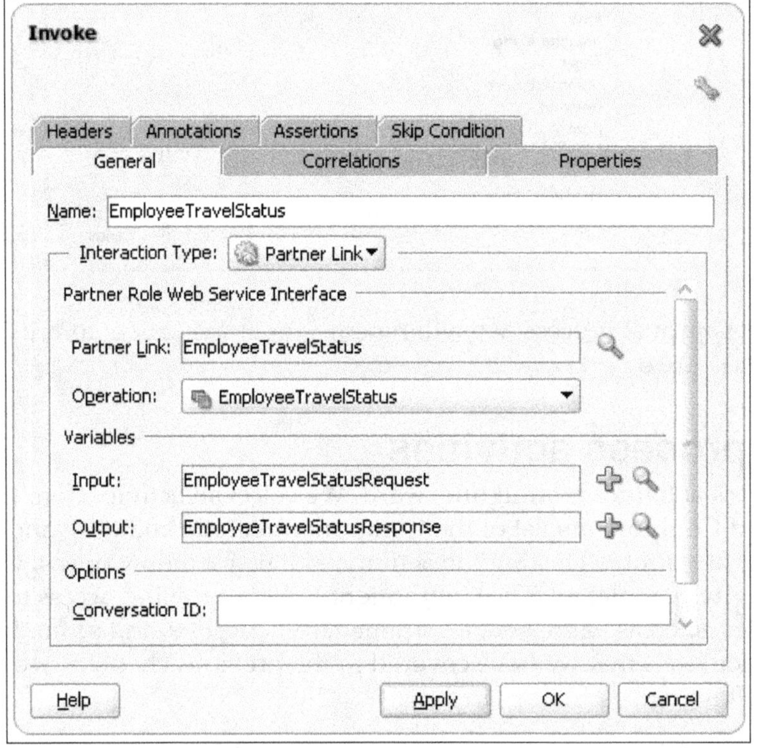

Variables can be automatically created by clicking the plus sign. The **Create Variable** dialog opens. We name the input variable `EmployeeTravelStatusRequest` and the output variable `EmployeeTravelStatusResponse`.

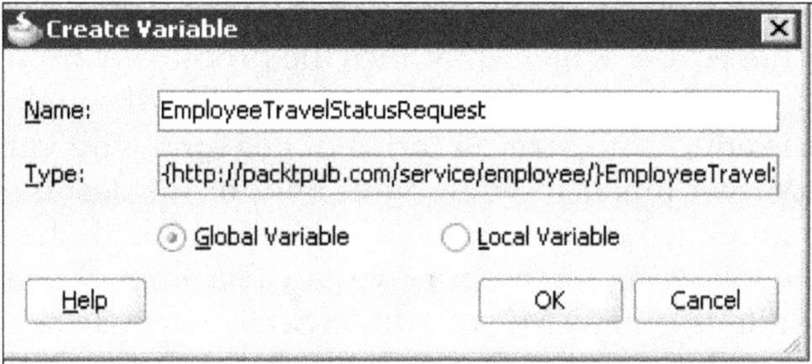

Now, we have to add an `<assign>` activity that will be used to assign the value to the `EmployeeTravelStatusRequest` variable. A dialog window opens, where we have to specify the copy rules, as shown in the following screenshot:

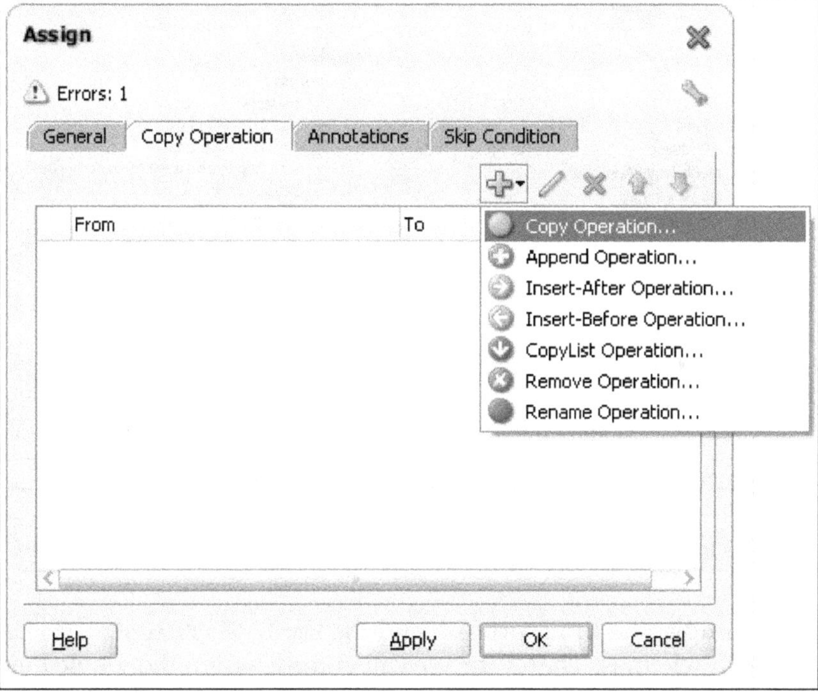

For adding new copy rules in the `<assign>` activities or editing existing rules, we can use the **Copy Rule** editor, which simplifies the procedure. Using the editor, we can create the `<from>` and `<to>` expressions by navigating through the variables trees. The **Copy Rule** editor supports all forms of `assigns` with variable, expression, XML fragment, or partner link being the source and/or the destination of the assignment. When copying variables, we can navigate through the variables tree, as shown in the following screenshot. We can also enter expressions using XPath Expression Builder, enter XML, or edit/create a new partner link. In our example, we have to assign an employee from the `TravelRequest` variable to the `EmployeeTravelStatusRequest` variable.

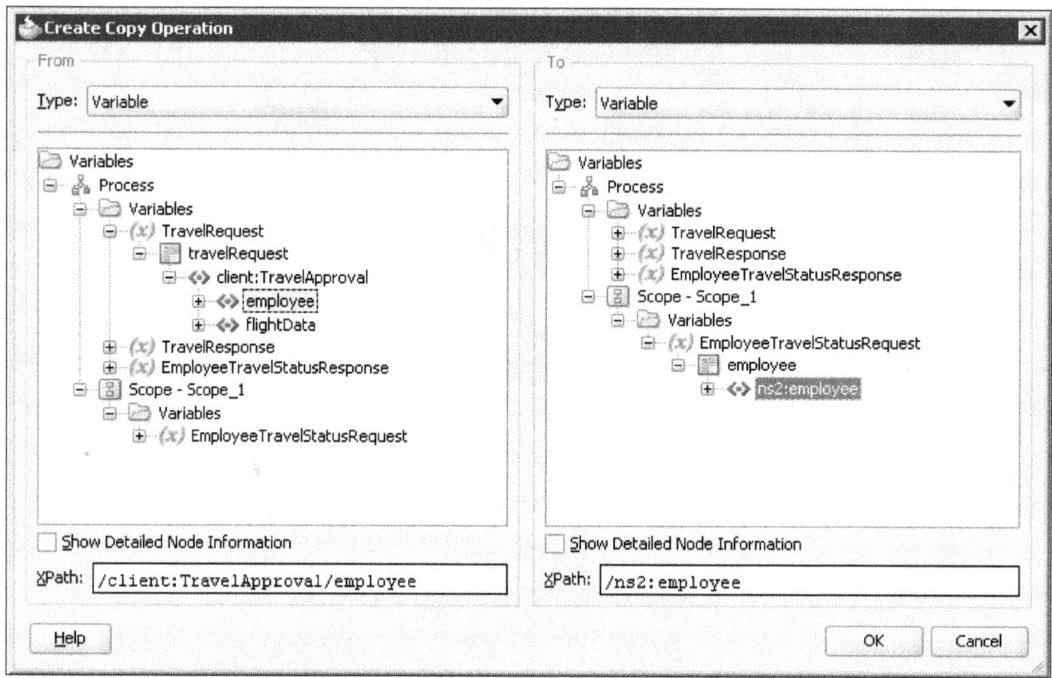

In our simple example, the BPEL process and the `EmployeeTravelStatus` service use the same XML schemas. Therefore, we can simply assign the whole employee from one variable to another. However, in reality this might not be the case. In BPEL processes, we often need to transform XML (stored in variables). For example, we have to modify the vocabulary to adapt the output of one service to the input of the other. We might also want to transform XML to other markup languages. Instead of using XPath, Oracle SOA Suite 11*g* provides a built-in XSLT engine. To compose XSLT stylesheets JDeveloper BPEL Component Designer provides a build in **XSLT Mapper**, which simplifies the mapping definition considerably.

To activate the XSLT engine from a BPEL process we need to add the transformation activity to the process. We do this by dragging-and-dropping the **Transform** activity from the **Component Palette** to the process. This activity simply calls the built-in XSLT engine.

After double-clicking the activity, a **Transform** window appears. Here we have to select the source and the target variable name, and the corresponding parts. Then we have to enter the XSLT filename:

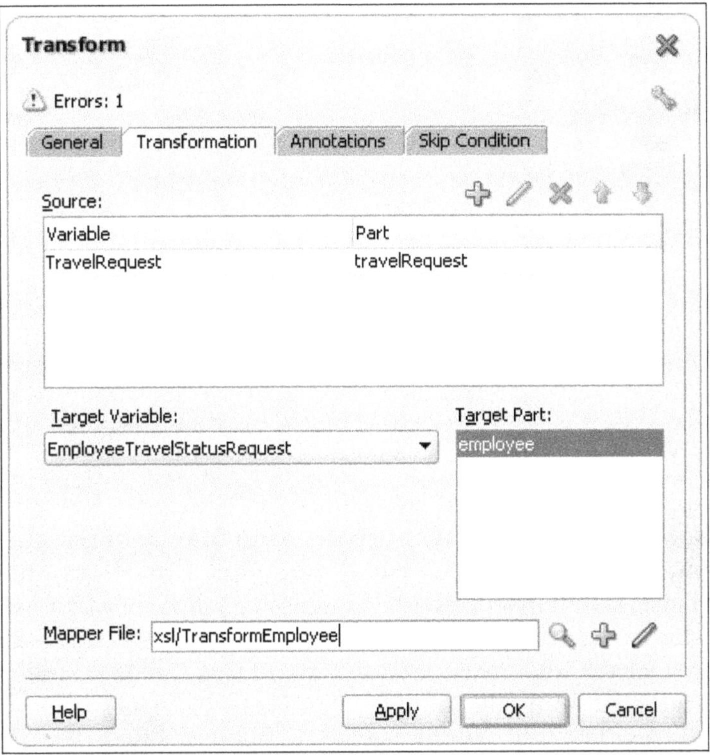

After clicking the *plus* icon to create a mapping, the **XSLT Mapper** window opens. We can drag-and-drop the elements from the left side to the right side. We can also use XPath functions, which we can select from the **Component Palette** in the upper-right side of the window (Oracle provides support for XPath 1.0, some XPath 2.0, and Oracle-specific functions). As a result, an XSLT stylesheet is generated, which takes care of the transformation:

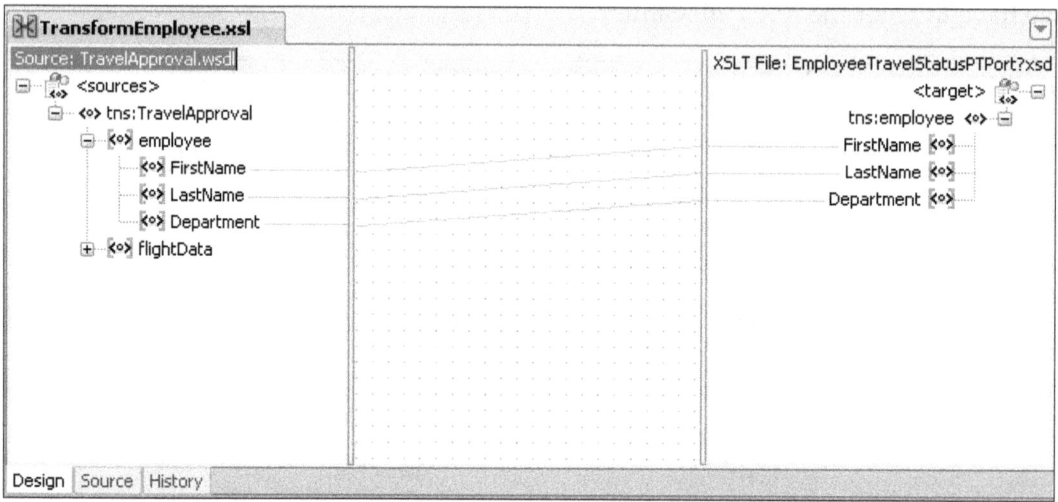

With **XSLT Mapper**, we use several functions which influence the mapping and transform the source data. We can also use the **Auto Map** feature, which tries to map attributes automatically. This way we can develop XSLT transformations relatively easily without being familiar with the XSLT language. For more information on XSLT, please refer to `http://www.w3.org/TR/xslt`. For more information on **XSLT Mapper**, please refer to Oracle Fusion Middleware Developer's Guide for Oracle SOA Suite 11*g*, which is accessible at `http://download.oracle.com/docs/cd/E12839_01/integration.1111/e10224/title.htm`.

Next, we have to create a variable which will be used as an input when invoking both airlines services. We can use the same variable, as both services have identical interfaces. We name the variable `FlightDetails`. Now, we create a new `<assign>` activity to assign flight request data to the newly created variable. We name it `AssignFlightDetails`. Our example now looks like this:

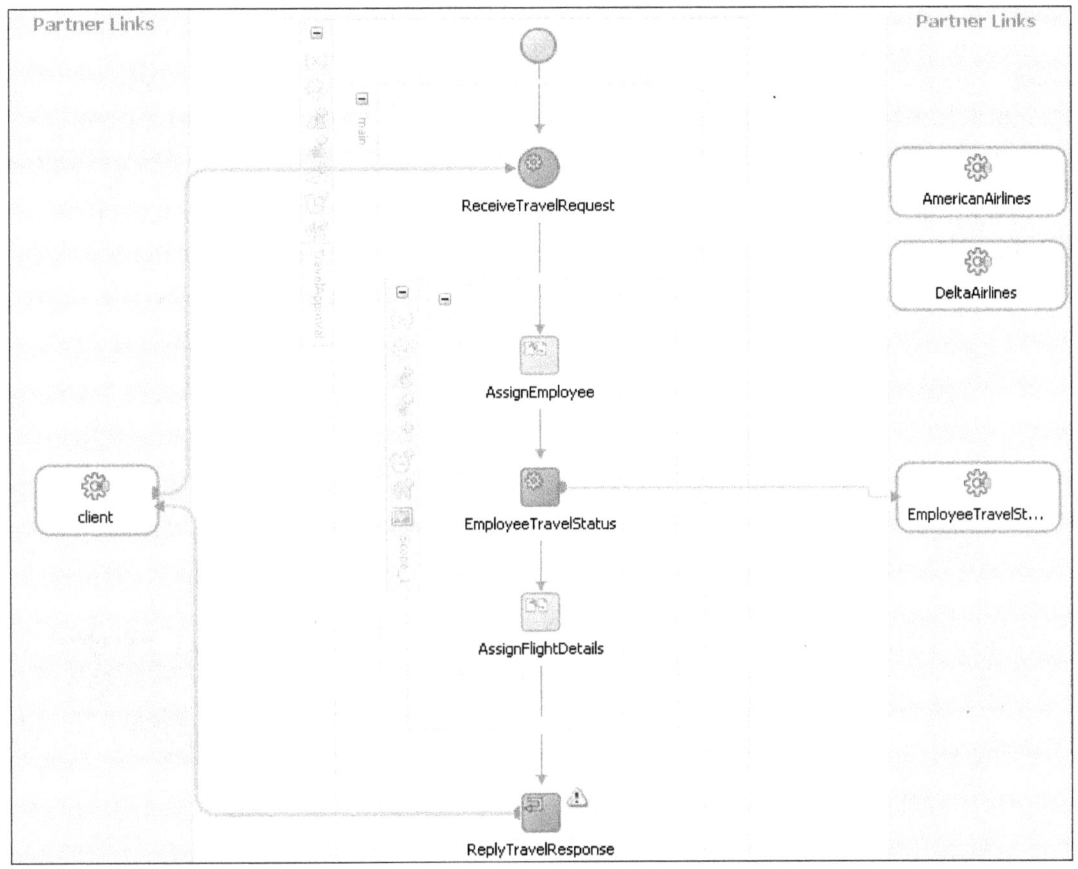
Partner Links
Partner Links
ReceiveTravelRequest
AmericanAirlines
DeltaAirlines
AssignEmployee
client
EmployeeTravelStatus
EmployeeTravelSt...
AssignFlightDetails
ReplyTravelResponse

Next, we will add the `<flow>` activity, as we want to invoke both airline services in parallel to retrieve ticket offers. For invoking airline services, we need `<invoke>` (operation `FlightAvailability`) and `<receive>` (operation `FlightTicketCallback`) activities, as services are asynchronous. Input for both service calls will be the `FlightDetails` variable. We also have to create two output variables (`FlightResponseDA` and `FlightResponseAA`) that contain ticket offers. After adding two `<invoke>` and two `<receive>` activities, our example looks like this (scope `RetrieveEmployeeTravelStatus` is collapsed to improve readability):

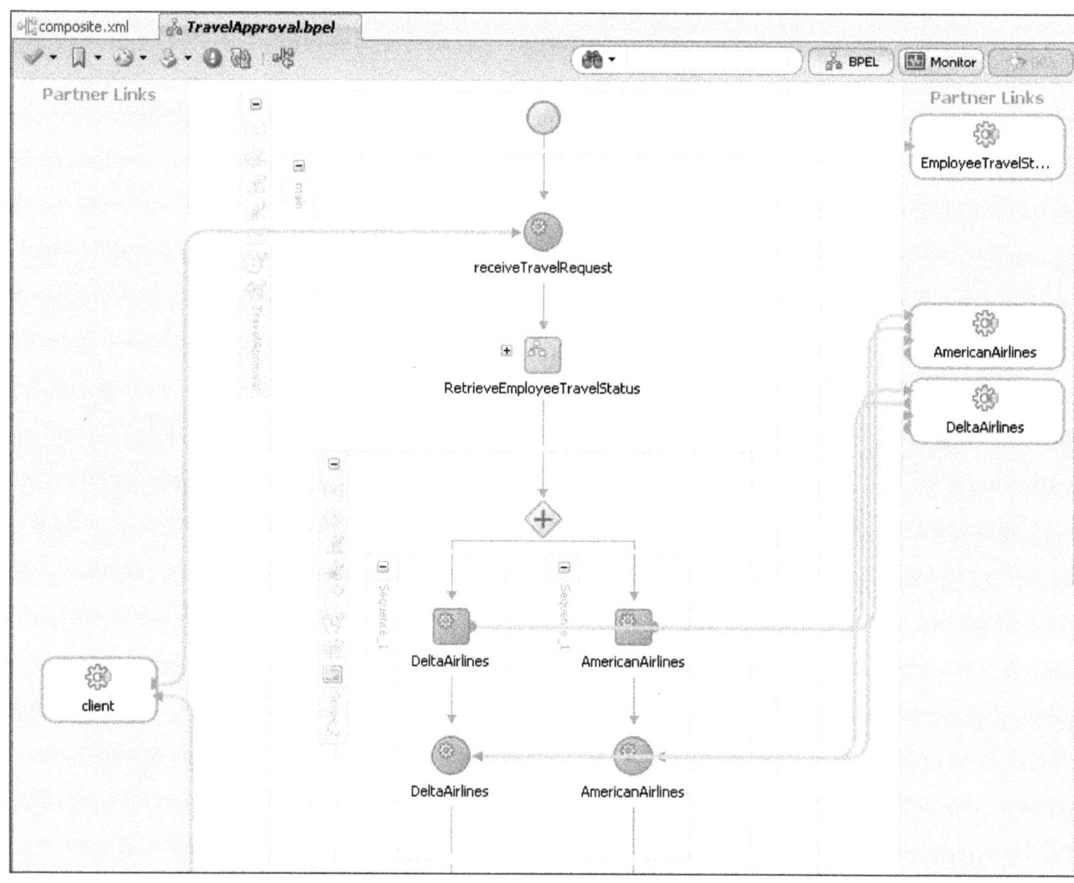

Next, we have to compare both prices and make a reservation of a cheaper flight ticket. We drag-and-drop the `<switch>` activity. A `case` and `otherwise` elements are generated automatically. Now, we will specify the condition for the case. To do that, we need to click on the **condition** to launch the **Expression Builder** editor. This editor is accessible from all dialogs where an XPath expression needs to be entered by pressing on the **Expression Builder** icon. In the left side, we can navigate through BPEL variables. In the right side, we can select various functions. XPath Expression Builder supports XPath 1.0, but also XPath 2.0 and Oracle-specific XPath extensions functions, which are covered in Chapter 5. Pressing *Ctrl+Space* in the **Expression Body** window, we get context-sensitive help. The following screenshot shows how we can create a condition for selecting the cheapest ticket:

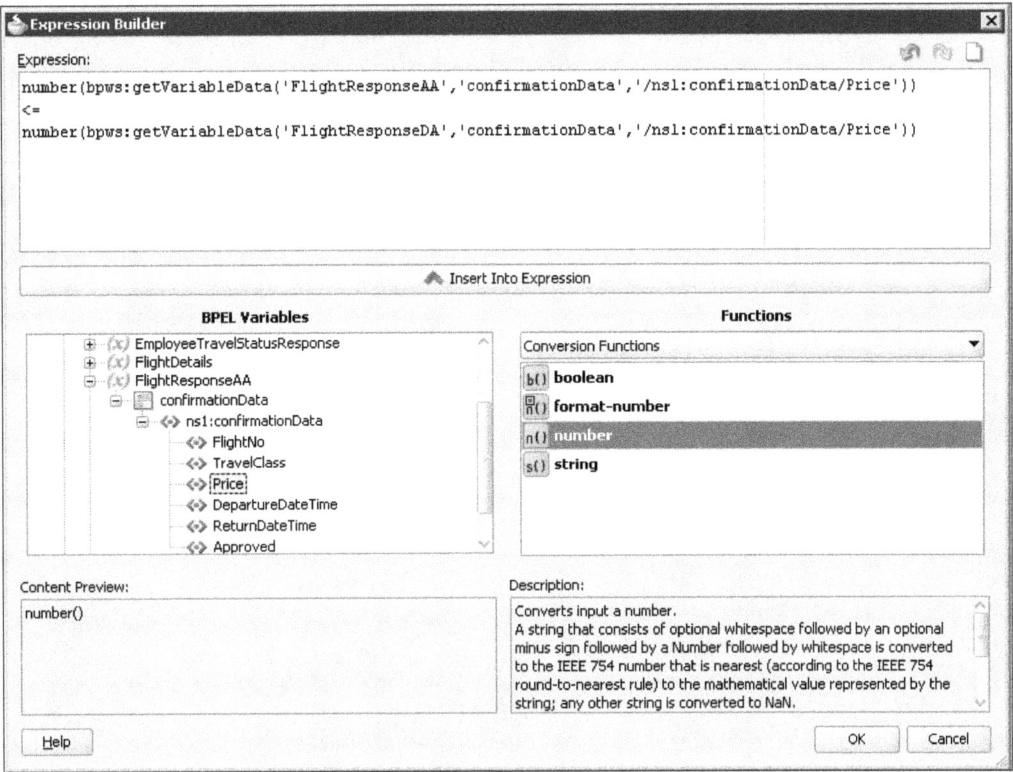

Based on the selected flight ticket, we make a reservation by invoking the appropriate airline service (we use the `MakeReservation` operation). As an input we use either the `FlightResponseDA` or the `FlightResponseAA` variable (depending on which airline was selected). For the output, we use the `TravelResponse` variable, which is also the output variable of the process. This brings us to the following completed process (the first two scopes are collapsed to improve readability):

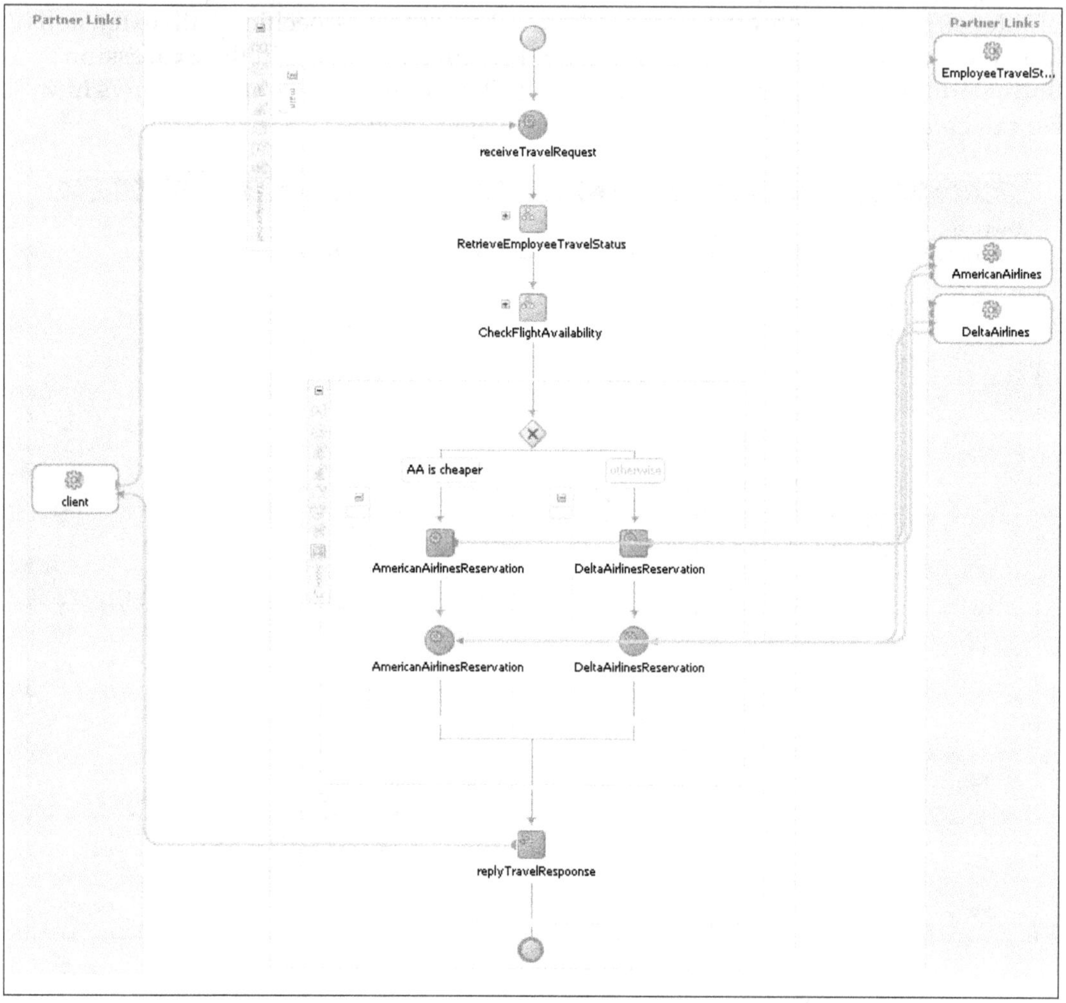

The example can be downloaded from the Packt Publishing website.

Validating BPEL processes

To simplify finding and correcting errors and warnings, JDeveloper provides BPEL validation. A triangle icon is used to indicate that we have to correct the settings of the activity.

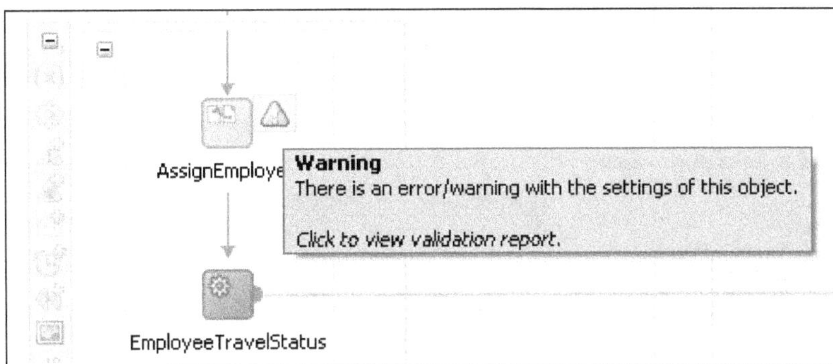

By clicking the triangle icon, the BPEL Validation Browser opens. We can also access it by clicking the check icon in the main design window:

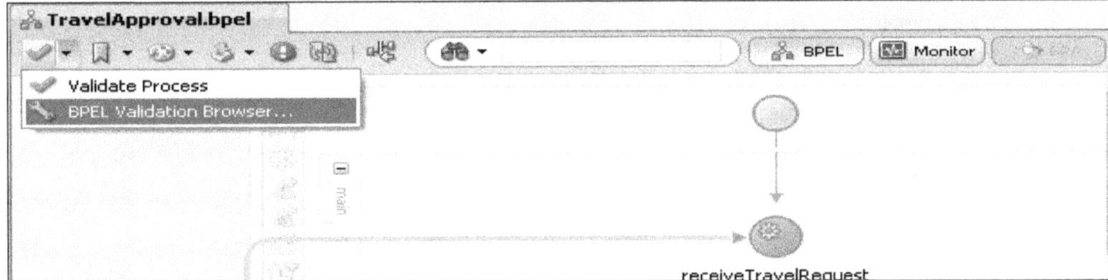

The **BPEL Validation Browser** window opens. In the following screenshot, we can see that there is an error in the BPEL process related to the `assign` activity, as no copy rules are specified. The browser also suggests the solution:

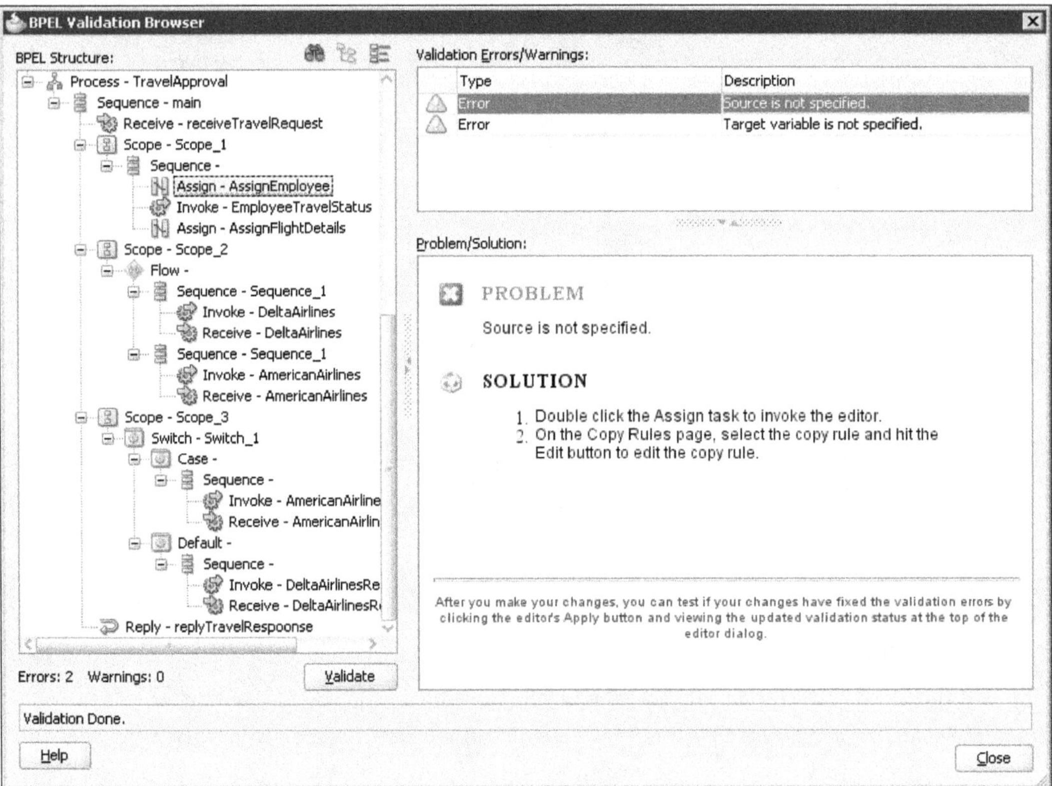

Testing SOA composite applications

Oracle SOA Suite 11*g* enables us to simulate the interaction between an SOA composite application and external web services it uses, by providing an automated test suite framework for creating, deploying, and running repeatable tests on SOA composite applications. This way we are able to test composite applications before deploying them to a production environment. With the use of the test suite framework, we can simulate interactions with partner web services, validate process steps, and create test reports.

A test suite is used to group one or more test cases, where each test case defines a set of actions that have to be executed during the test run. By using emulations, we are able to simulate the behavior of services and service binding components. Assertions enable us to specify the expected value of data or process flow to be able to verify the result. When performing the test run, if actual values are the same as the expected values, we say the test run was successful. To create a new **test suite** in JDeveloper, we have to right-click the **testsuites** folder in the **Application Navigator** and select **Create Test Suite**:

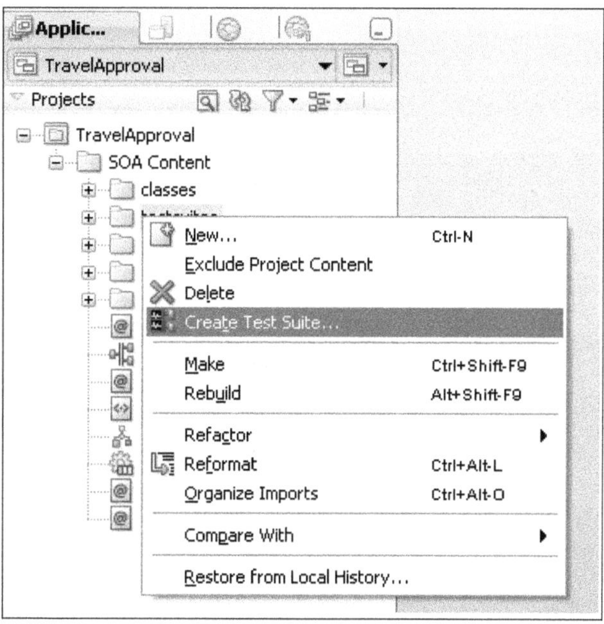

We enter test suite name and click **OK**. The **Create Composite Test** dialog appears. We type a test name and optional description and click **OK.**

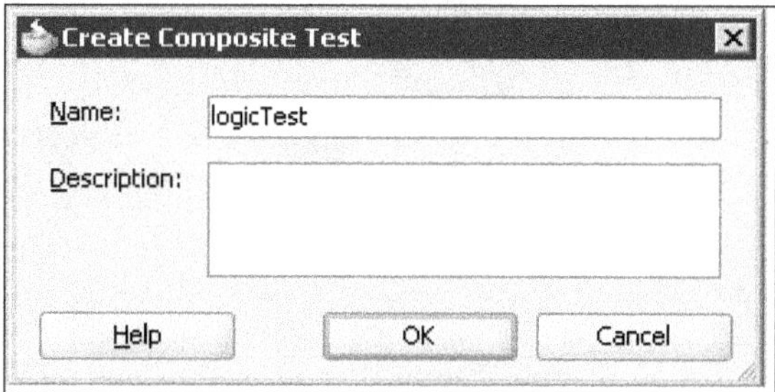

This creates a test file named `logicTest.xml` and SOA Composite editor opens in test mode. We can always switch back to design mode by clicking the **Return to SOA Composite Diagram** icon.

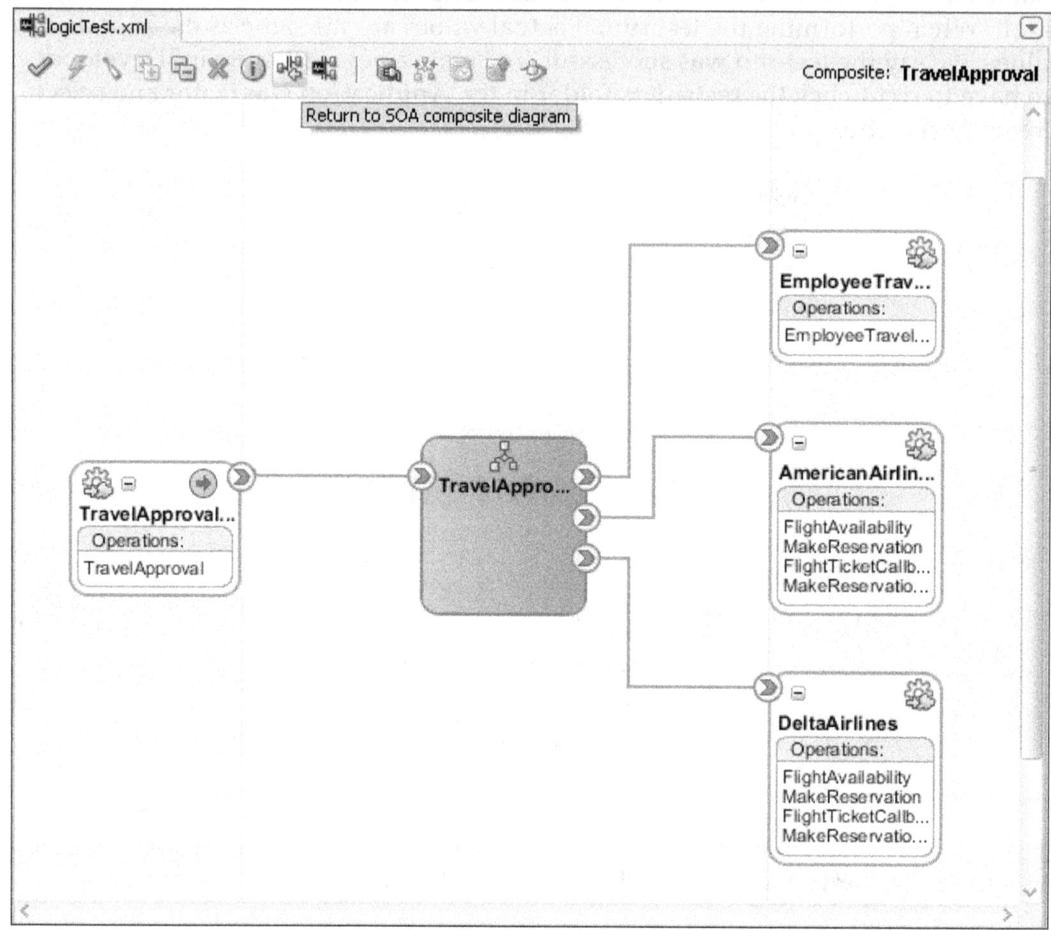

Here we can create test initiations, assertions, and emulations. First, we will create the initiate message used to invoke the SOA composite application test. To do that, we have to double-click the service binding component. The **Initiate Messages** dialog appears:

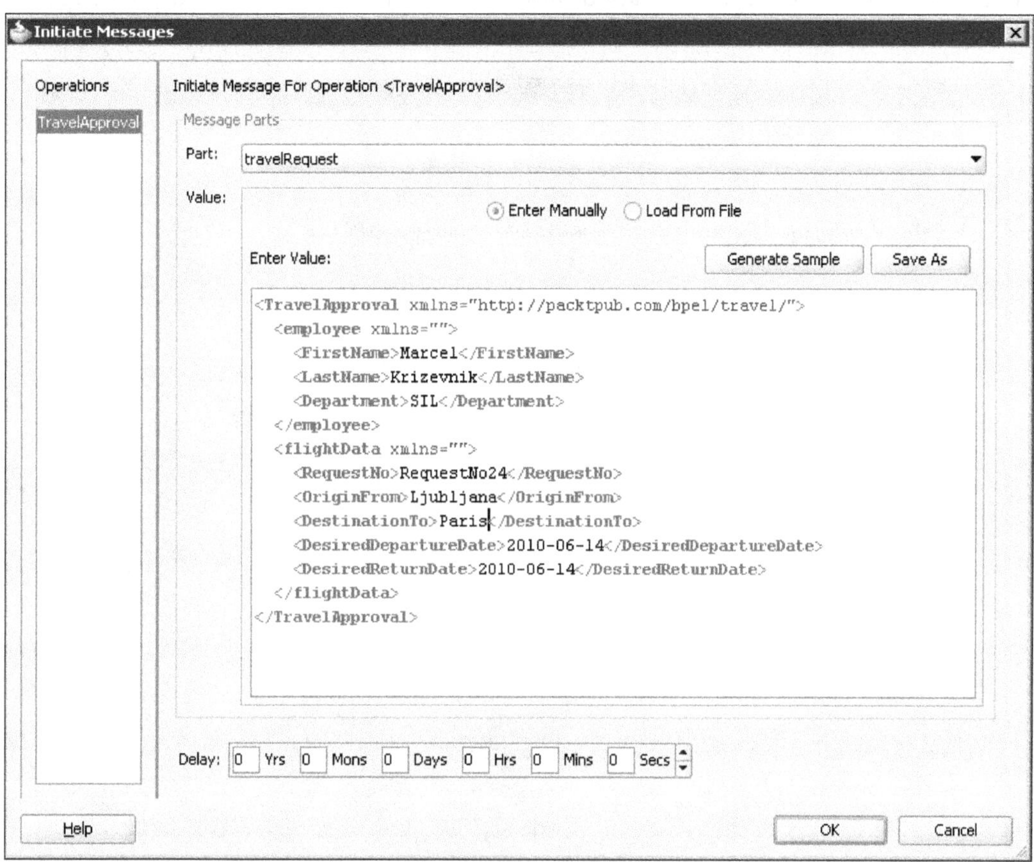
Initiate Messages
Operations
TravelApproval
Initiate Message For Operation <TravelApproval>
Message Parts
Part:
travelRequest
Value:
Enter Manually
Load From File
Enter Value:
Generate Sample
Save As
<TravelApproval xmlns="http://packtpub.com/bpel/travel/">
<employee xmlns="">
<FirstName>Marcel</FirstName>
<LastName>Krizevnik</LastName>
<Department>SIL</Department>
</employee>
<flightData xmlns="">
<RequestNo>RequestNo24</RequestNo>
<OriginFrom>Ljubljana</OriginFrom>
<DestinationTo>Paris</DestinationTo>
<DesiredDepartureDate>2010-06-14</DesiredDepartureDate>
<DesiredReturnDate>2010-06-14</DesiredReturnDate>
</flightData>
</TravelApproval>
Delay: 0 Yrs 0 Mons 0 Days 0 Hrs 0 Mins 0 Secs
Help
OK
Cancel

Here we generate a message to initiate the SOA composite application. We close the dialog by clicking **OK**. Now, we will emulate messages, returned from three partner services. We have to double-click each wire connecting a partner service and the BPEL process and open the **Emulates** tab. Here we click the *plus* sign to create a new emulation. The **Create Emulate** dialog appears. We generate a sample output message and confirm by clicking **OK**:

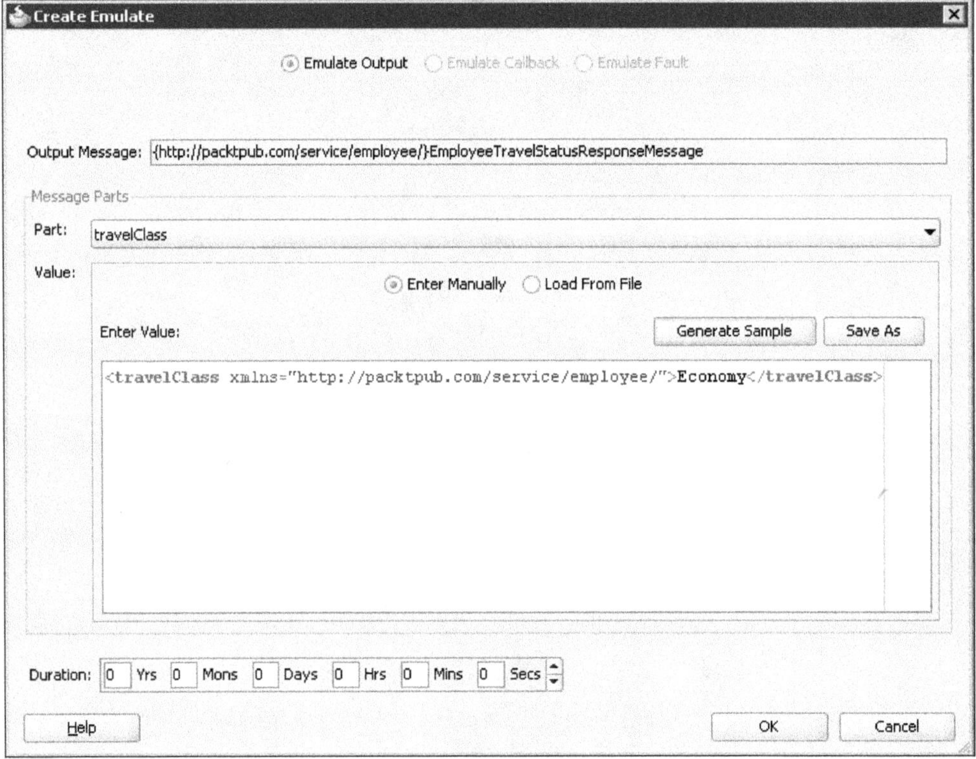

Now we have to emulate both airline services. We will emulate both Callback operations (`FlightTicketCallback` and `MakeReservationCallback`). The following screenshot shows the emulation of the `FlightTicketCallback` operation for the American Airlines partner service.

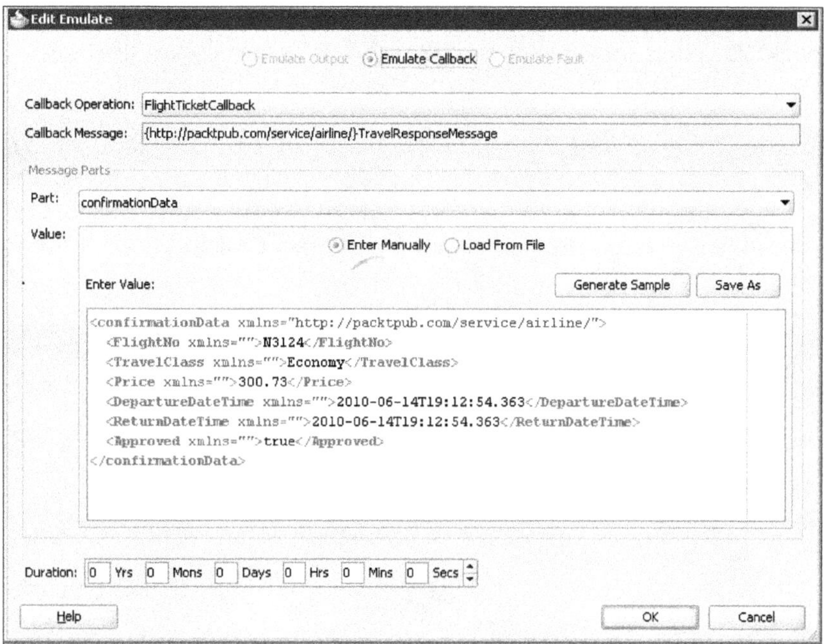

The emulation of the `MakeReservationCallback` operation:

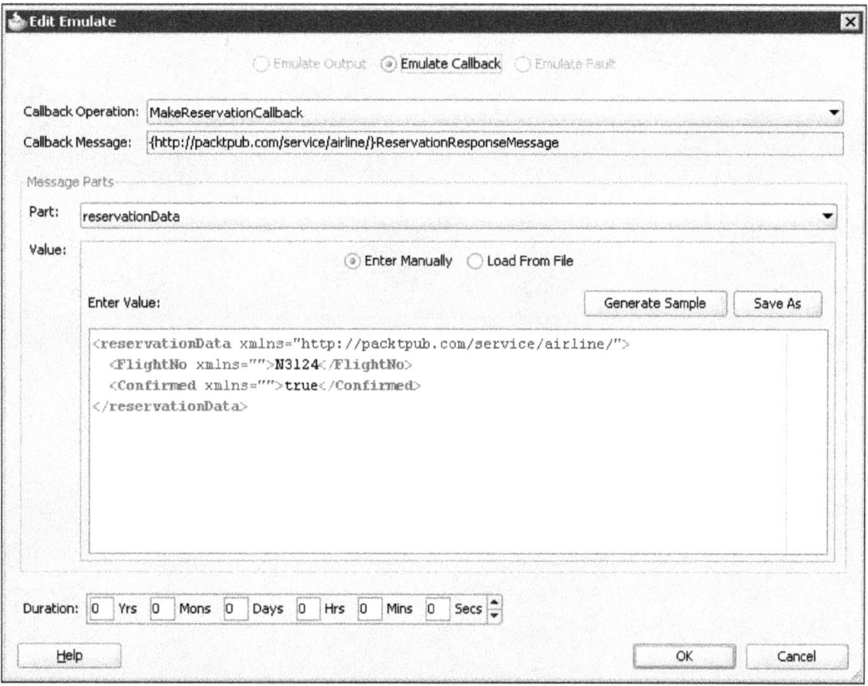

We repeat the upper step for the Delta Airlines partner service; however, we will set the price to 330.72. Therefore, we expect that the BPEL process will choose the ticket from American Airlines.

Now we have to create an assertion to verify the BPEL process response. We create an assertion by double-clicking the wire that connects the BPEL process and the service binding component. On the **Asserts** tab, we create a new **Assert Output**, which specifies the expected process result (we expect that the ticket number `N3124` was selected and confirmed):

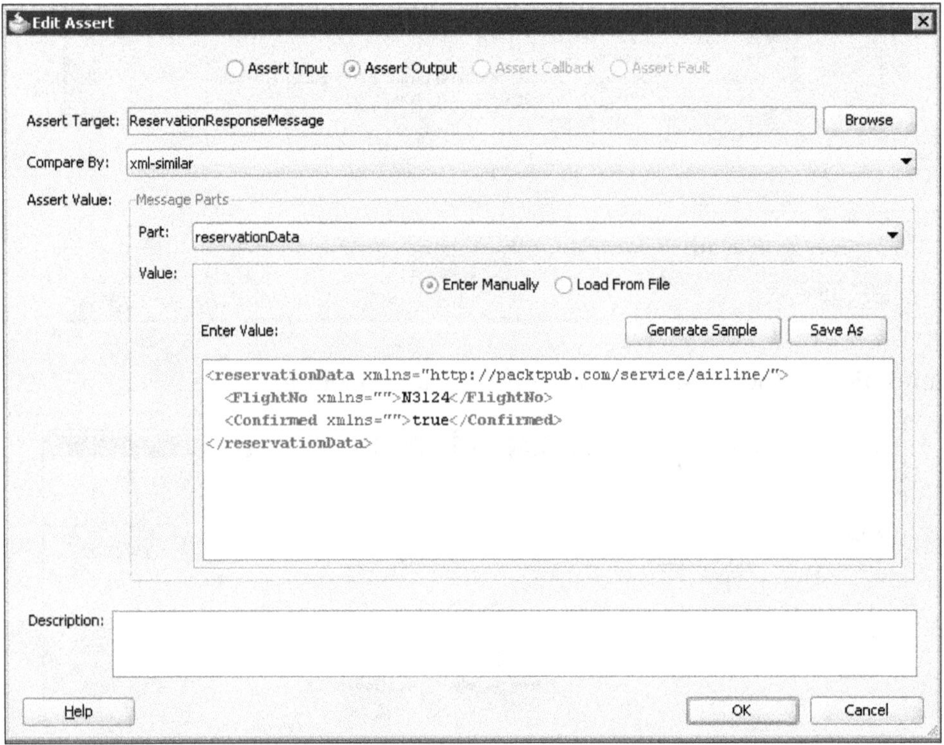

We click **OK** twice to close the dialogs. Our SOA composite application opened in test mode now looks like this:

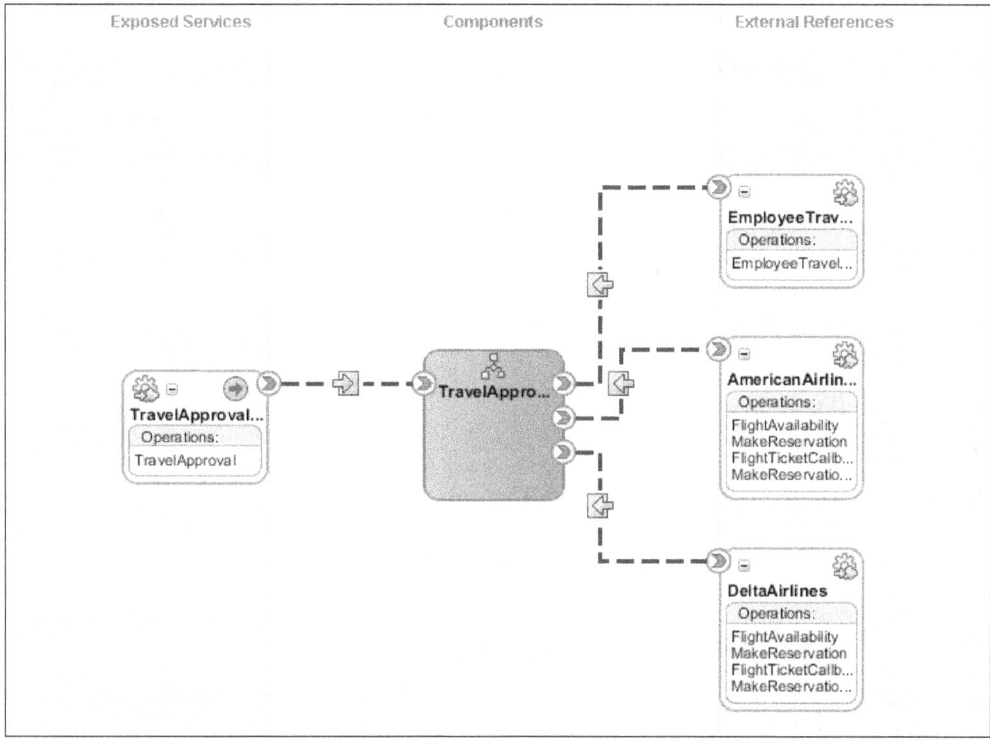

After creating the test suite and test cases, we can deploy them as part of the SOA composite application. Then we can run test cases using the Oracle EM Console. We will demonstrate this in the *Managing SOA composite applications* section.

Deploying SOA composite applications

Let us now show how we deploy a BPEL process to the Oracle SOA Server. We will assume that Oracle SOA Suite 11*g* has been successfully installed according to the installation instructions and that it uses the default port 8001. As every BPEL process is part of a SOA composite application, we deploy it as every other composite. The first step of deployment is to package the SOA composite application into an SOA archive (SAR) JAR file. A SAR file is a special JAR file that requires a prefix of `sca_` (for example, `sca_HelloWorld_rev1.0.jar`).

> The SAR file is analogous to the BPEL suitcase archive of the previous releases, but at the higher composite level and it can contain additional service components of other types (Mediator, Business Rule, Spring, and Human Task).

The packaged SAR can include the following:

- Services, references, and service components.
- **Oracle Web Service Manager** (**OWSM**) policies and human workflow tasks flows.
- Metadata, such as WSDL, XSD, and XSLT files. These metadata are deployed to an SOA Infrastructure partition on the server. We can access these artifacts from JDeveloper using an SOA-MDS connection.

We can create SAR files and deploy them to the server using one of the following tools:

- Oracle JDeveloper
- Ant scripts
- **WebLogic Scripting Tool** (**WLST**) commands

Generated SAR files can also be deployed using EM Console.

Deploying from JDeveloper

First, we have to create a connection to the Oracle WebLogic Server to which we want to deploy an SOA composite application. From the **File** main menu we select **New**. In the **General** list we select **Connections**. Then we select **Application Server Connection** and click **OK**. We enter the connection name. For the connection type, we select **WebLogic 10.3**. Then, we click **Next.**

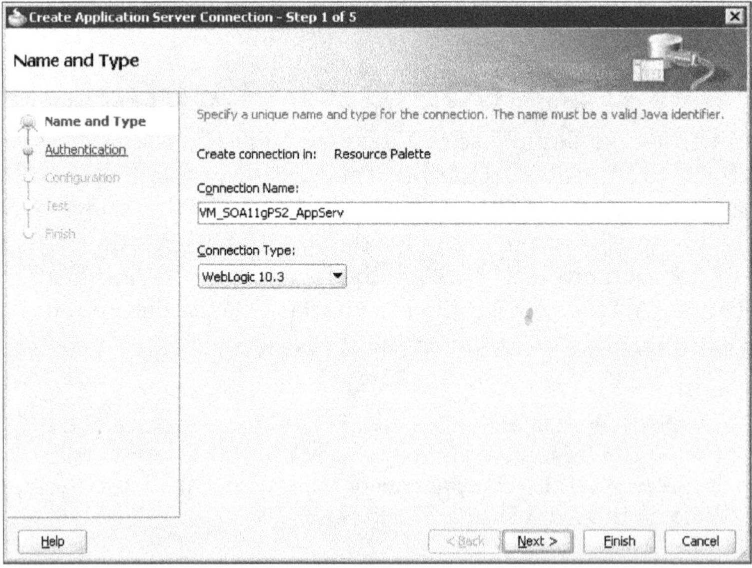

We enter username and password and click **Next** again. Now, we enter a WebLogic server hostname, port, and domain:

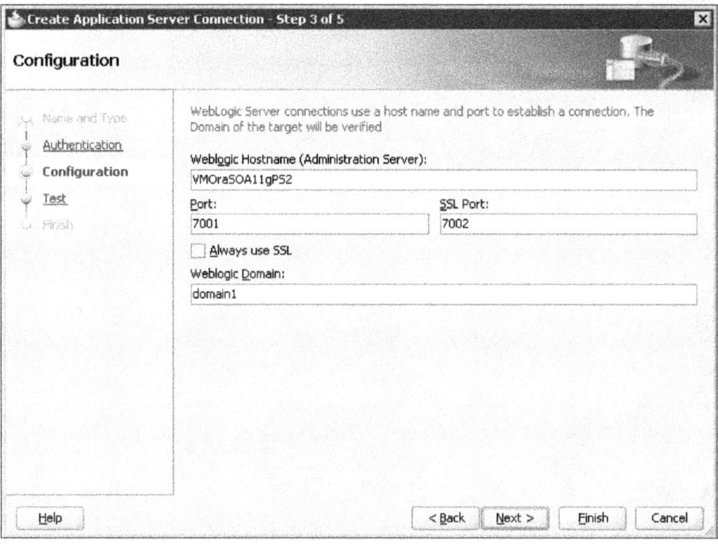

Then we click **Finish.** The connection to the application server is now created.

In order to deploy an SOA composite application, we have to right-click the SOA project and select **Deploy | Project_name**.

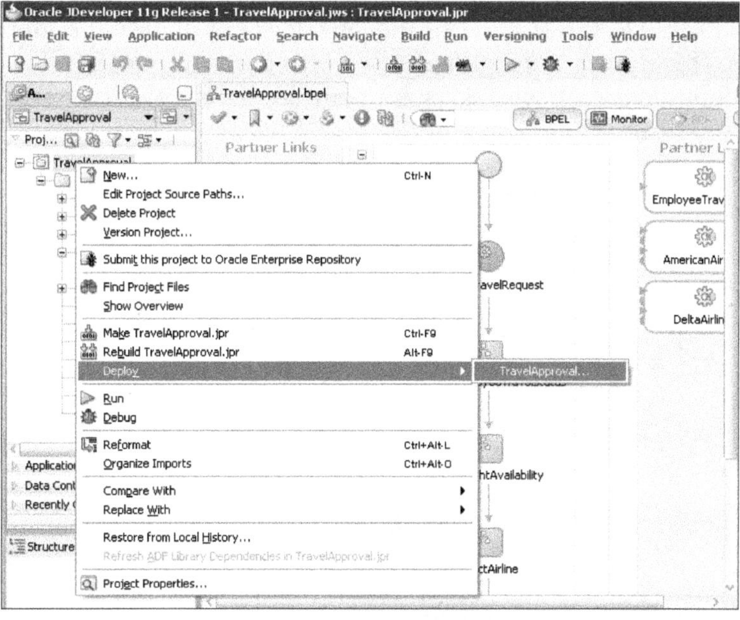

The deploy project wizard appears.

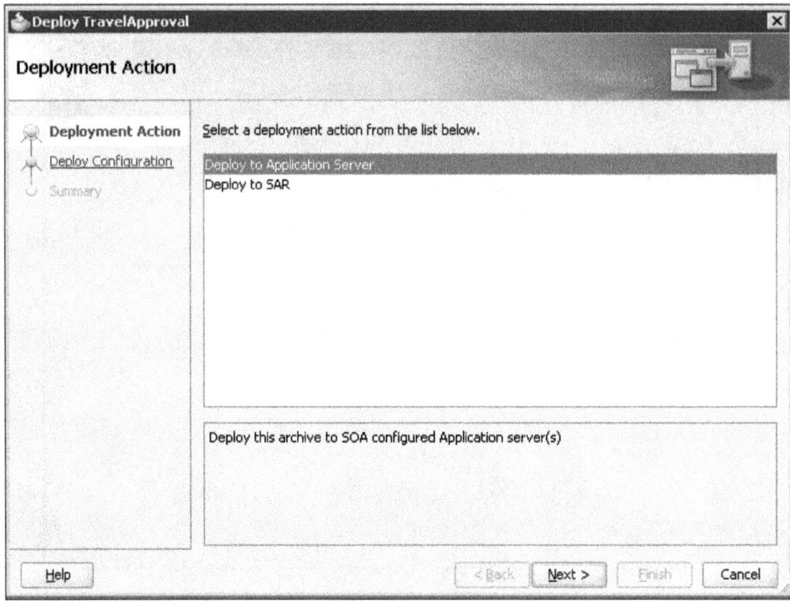

We have to select one of the following deployment options:

- **Deploy to Application Server**: Creates a SAR file for the selected project and deploys it to the Oracle WebLogic server.
- **Deploy to SAR**: Creates a SAR file, but does not deploy it to the application server. This option is useful if the server is currently not running, we do not have deployment privileges, or we want to deploy multiple SAR files using a batch script.

If we select the first option, the **Deploy Configuration** display appears:

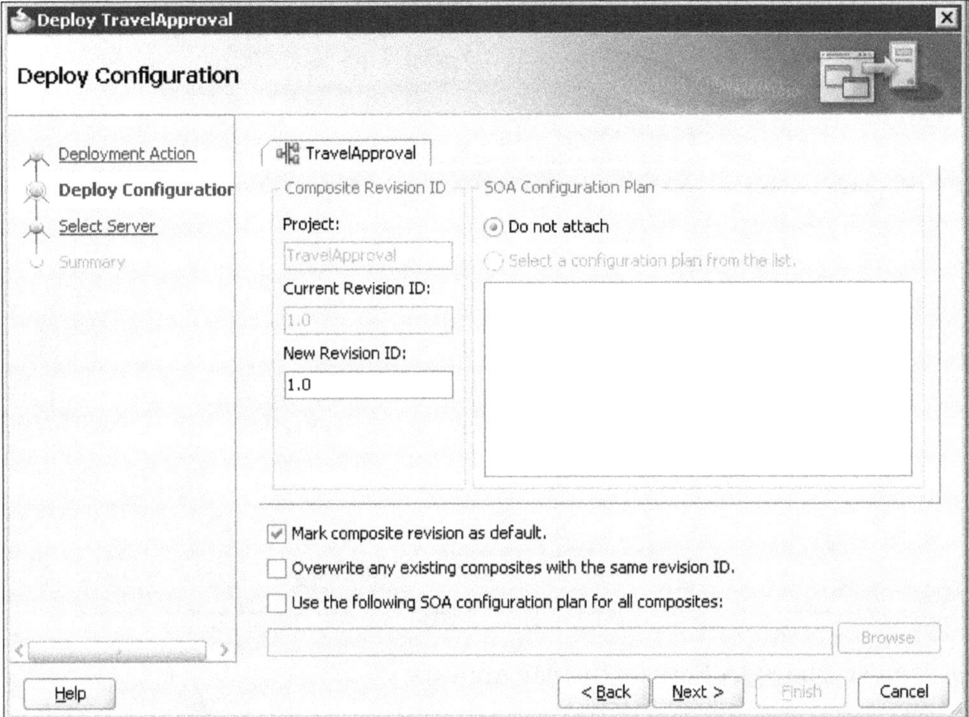

Here, we can change the revision (**Revision ID)**, mark the composite revision as default, and select whether we want to overwrite existing composites with the same **Revision ID**. Revision numbers are used to deploy different versions of the same composite and run them simultaneously.

Optionally, we can also attach a configuration plan. Then we click **Next.**

> Configuration plans are simple XML configuration files, used to search-and-replace environment-specific values (JDBC connection string, hostnames, ports) when moving or deploying projects to different environments (typically development, test, and production).

Now, we have to select the application server connection:

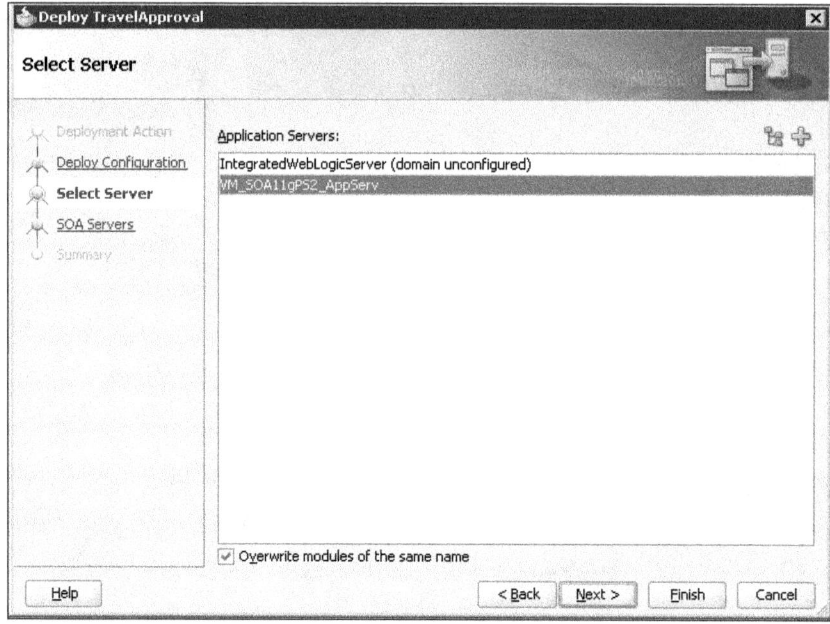

We click **Next**. The **SOA Servers** display appears:

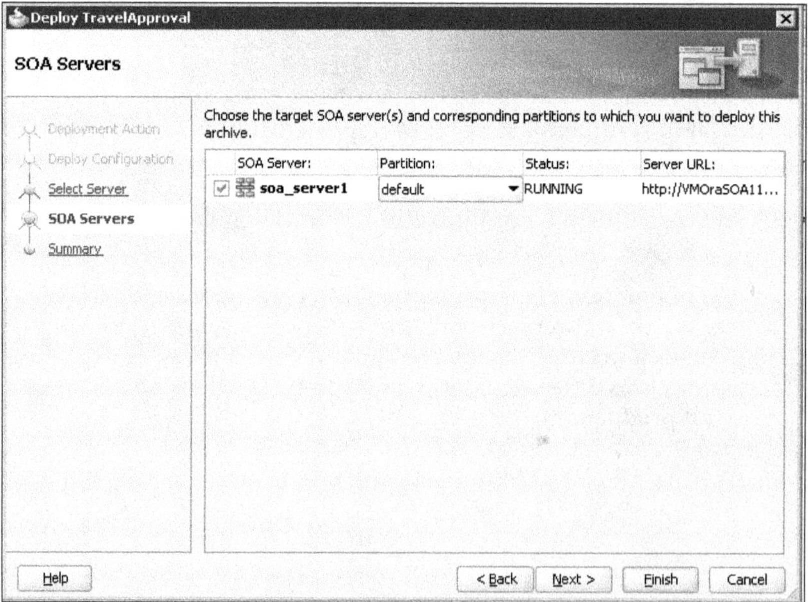

Here we have to select the SOA server and partition to which we want to deploy our SOA composite application.

> Oracle SOA Server is logically divided into partitions. The default partition (named `default`) is created automatically during the installation. In fact, partition is a new name for BPEL domains from Oracle SOA Suite 10*g*. The name has changed, as it could be easily confused with WebLogic Server domains.

By clicking **Next**, the **Summary** display appears:

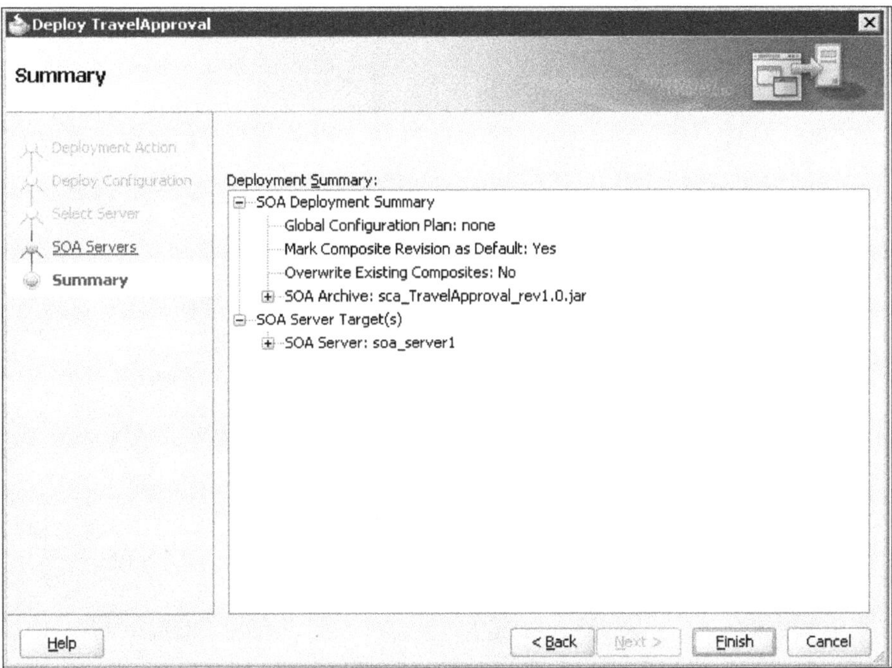

After clicking **Finish**, we can view the messages that display in the **Deployment** log window at the bottom of JDeveloper. If the deployment was successful, the SAR file is created under the **deploy** folder with a naming convention of `sca_compositename_revrevision_number.jar`. Now, we can test and manage our deployed application using EM Console.

Creating configuration plans in JDeveloper

As already explained, a configuration plan is an XML file that can be attached to the SAR file during the deployment of an SOA composite application. It allows us to define search-and-replace operations that have to be performed when deploying to a specific environment. We usually create one deployment plan for each environment. In JDeveloper, we can create a configuration plan by right-clicking the **composite.xml** file and selecting **Generate Config Plan**:

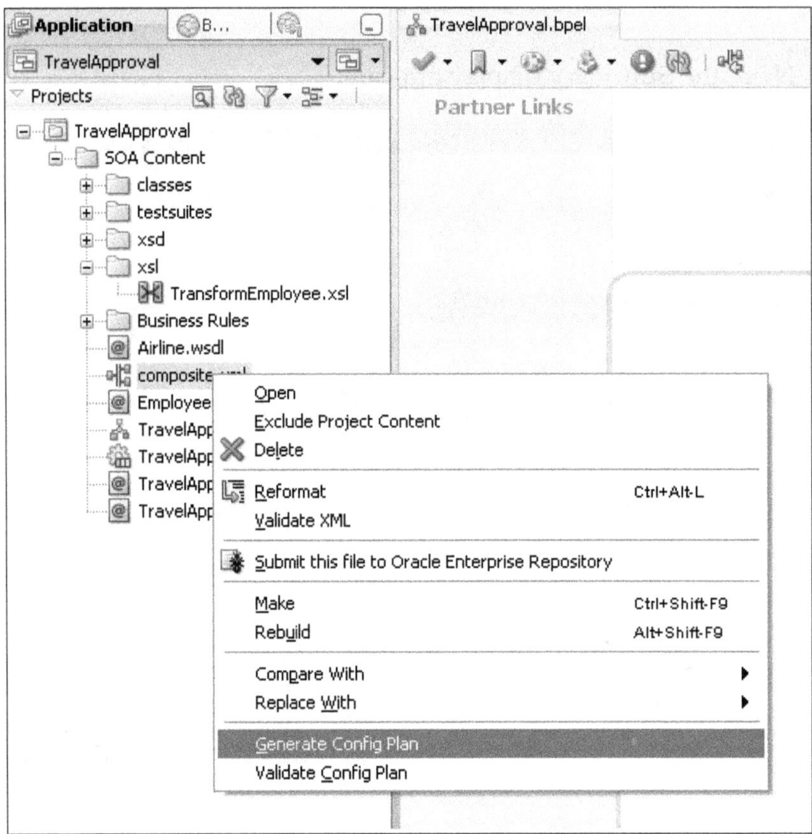

The **Composite Configuration Plan Generator** dialog appears as follows:

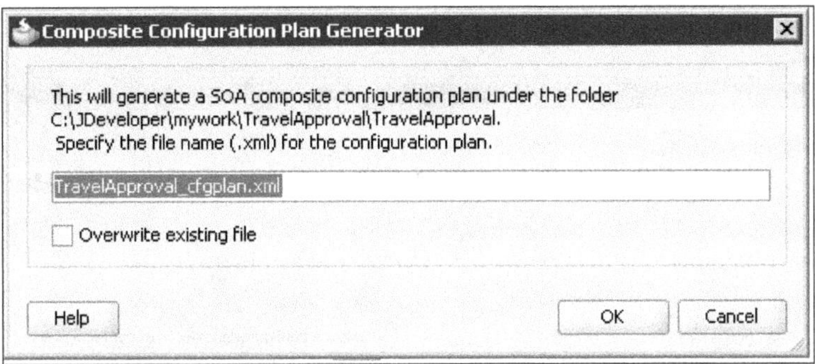

We can change the name of the configuration plan and specify whether we want to overwrite existing file with the same name. We click **OK**. This creates and opens a configuration plan file for editing. Here, we can modify environment-specific properties, like hostnames, port numbers, JDBC connection string, and so on. In the following example, we change the server hostname from `VMOraSOA11gPS2` to `OraSOA11g_Test`, and the port number from `8001` to `8011`.

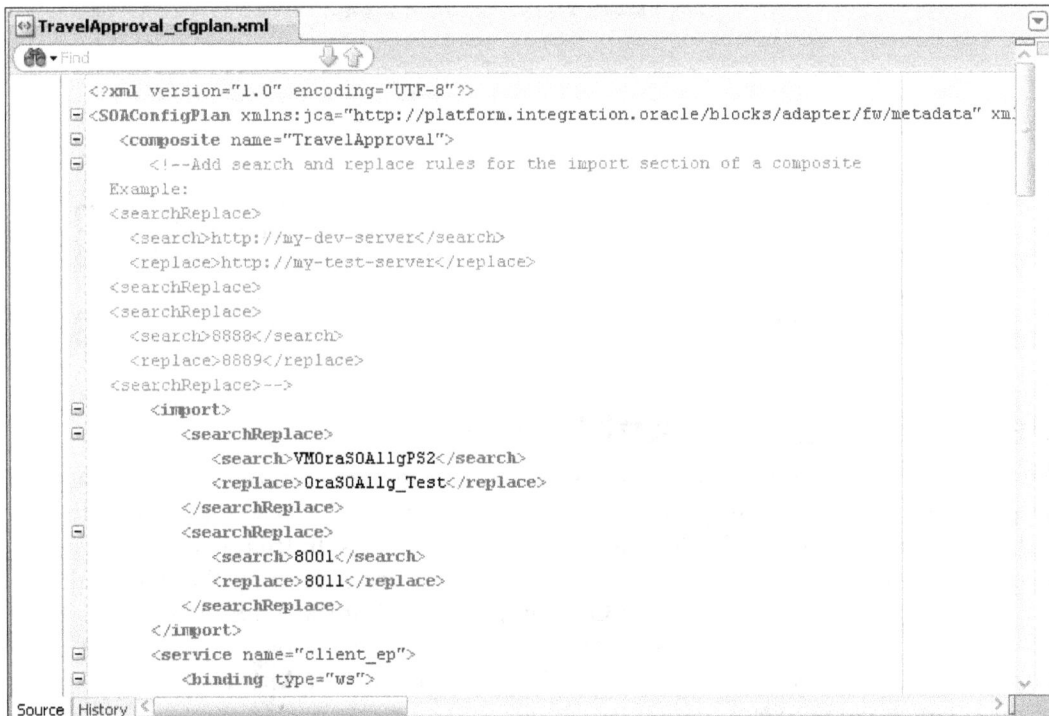

```
TravelApproval_cfgplan.xml
<?xml version="1.0" encoding="UTF-8"?>
<SOAConfigPlan xmlns:jca="http://platform.integration.oracle/blocks/adapter/fw/metadata" xm
  <composite name="TravelApproval">
    <!--Add search and replace rules for the import section of a composite
 Example:
 <searchReplace>
   <search>http://my-dev-server</search>
   <replace>http://my-test-server</replace>
 <searchReplace>
 <searchReplace>
   <search>8888</search>
   <replace>8889</replace>
 <searchReplace>-->
    <import>
      <searchReplace>
        <search>VMOraSOA11gPS2</search>
        <replace>OraSOA11g_Test</replace>
      </searchReplace>
      <searchReplace>
        <search>8001</search>
        <replace>8011</replace>
      </searchReplace>
    </import>
    <service name="client_ep">
      <binding type="ws">
Source | History
```

We can validate the configuration plan by right-clicking the file and selecting **Validate Config Plan.** Now we can attach the created configuration plan during the deployment:

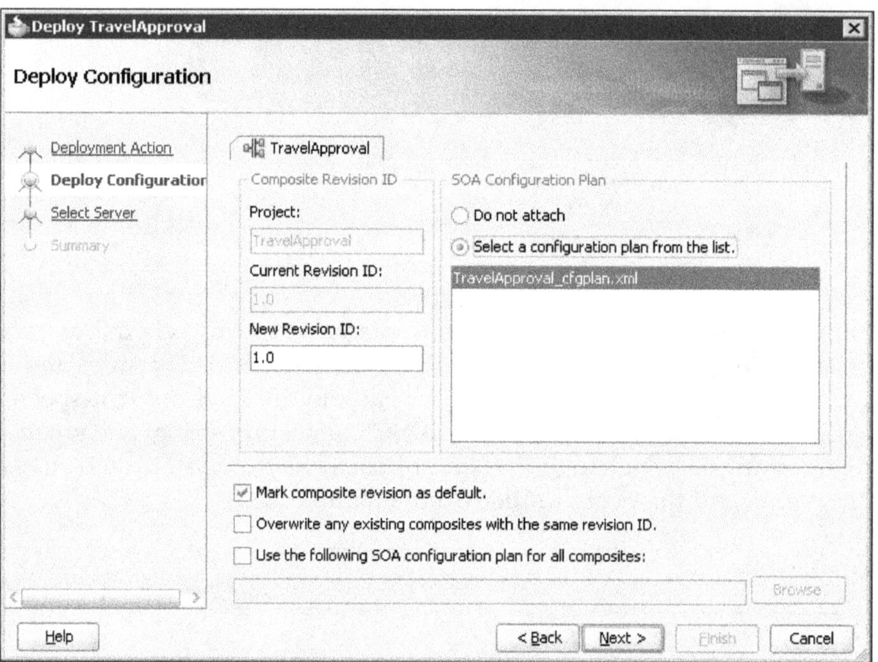

Creating and attaching the configuration plan does not modify the source **composite.xml** and related WSDL and XSD files. Replacement occurs only when the SOA composite application is deployed.

Deploying using Ant Scripts

We can also manage SOA composite applications from a command line using **Ant** scripts or the WLST scripting utility. These options are well suited for automation and can be easily integrated into existing release processes. In this section, we will take a quick look at how to compile and deploy SOA projects using the **Ant** utility. For instructions on how to manage SOA composites using the WLST utility, please refer to Oracle Documentation. **Ant** scripts reside in the `Middleware_Home\SOA_Suite_Home\bin` directory. For additional information about **Ant**, visit `http://ant.apache.org`.

ANT_HOME and JAVA_HOME environment variables have to be set to be able to deploy composite applications using the **Ant** utility.

This is an example of compiling an SOA composite application:

```
ant -f ant-sca-compile.xml
-Dscac.input=c:\mywork\TravelApproval\TravelApproval\composite.xml
```

This is an example of packaging an SOA composite application into a SAR file:

```
ant -f ant-sca-package.xml
-DcompositeDir=C:\mywork\TravelApproval\TravelApproval
-DcompositeName=TravelApproval
-Drevision=2.0
```

This is an example of deploying an SOA composite application:

```
ant -f ant-sca-deploy.xml
-DserverURL=http://VMOraSOA11gPS2:8001
-DsarLocation=C:\compiled_packages\sca_TravelApproval_rev2.0.jar
-Doverwrite=true
-Duser=weblogic
-DforceDefault=true
-Dconfigplan=C:\compiled_packages\config_plans\TravelApproval_cfgplan.
xml
```

Managing SOA composite applications

We can manage deployed SOA composite application a using a combination of Oracle JDeveloper and Oracle Enterprise Manager Console (EM Console).

Managing SOA composites using JDeveloper

Using JDeveloper, we are able to deploy, undeploy, activate, and retire SOA composite application revisions. First, we have to create a connection to an Oracle WebLogic Administration Server on which the SOA Infrastructure is deployed. Then we open the **Application Server Navigator**. We expand the connection name. By expanding the **SOA** folder, all deployed SOA composite applications and services appear:

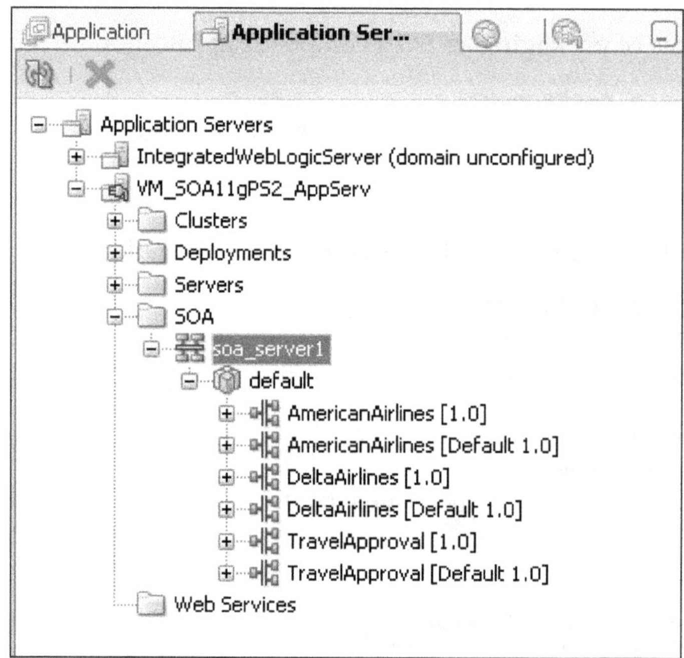

If we right-click a deployed SOA composite application, we can perform one of the following actions (the actions that display are based upon the current state of the application):

Option	Description
`Retire`	Allows us to retire the selected composite revision. This means that we are no longer able to creates new instance of the retired revision. However, existing instances are able to complete normally. Every retired composite revision can be activated again.
`Activate`	This action activates a retired composite revision.

Option	Description
`Undeploy`	We use this action if we want to undeploy a composite application revision. The consequence of this action is that we are no longer able to initiate a new instance of this revision and the state of all running instances is changed to stale.
`Set Default Revision`	We use this action if we want to set the selected composite revision to be the default.

If we right-click the **SOA** folder and select **Deploy SOA Archive**, we are able to deploy a pre-built SOA composite application archive.

Managing SOA composites using Enterprise Manager Console

With the use of Oracle EM Console we can deploy, undeploy, initiate, debug, test and manage SOA composite applications. To log into the Oracle EM console, we have to open a web browser and access the following URL: `http://host_name:port/em`, where `host_name` is the name of the host on which Oracle EM Console is installed and `port` is a number that is set during the installation process (default is 7001). We enter a username (`weblogic` is the default EM Console administrator username) and password and click **Login**. The EM Console opens, displaying the status of servers and deployed applications.

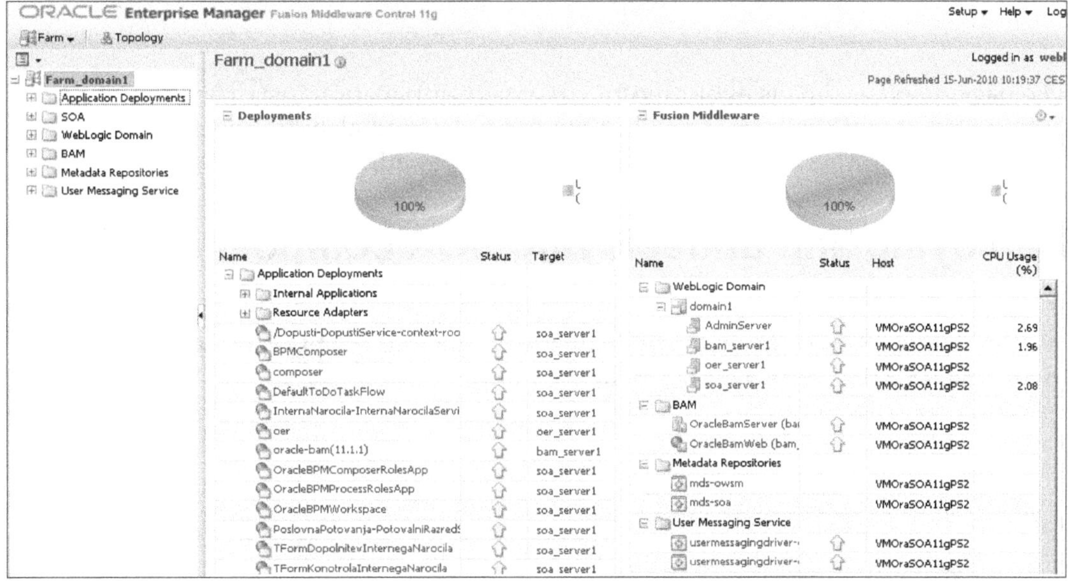

Now, we will navigate to Oracle SOA Suite administration tasks through the **SOA Infrastructure** home page. There we can access and manage all deployed SOA composite applications, service engines, service components, and so on. To navigate to the **SOA Infrastructure** home page, we have to expand the **SOA | soa-infra** in the navigator. This displays all SOA composite applications running in the **SOA Infrastructure**. If we click **soa-infra**, the **Dashboard** page of the **SOA Infrastructure** opens:

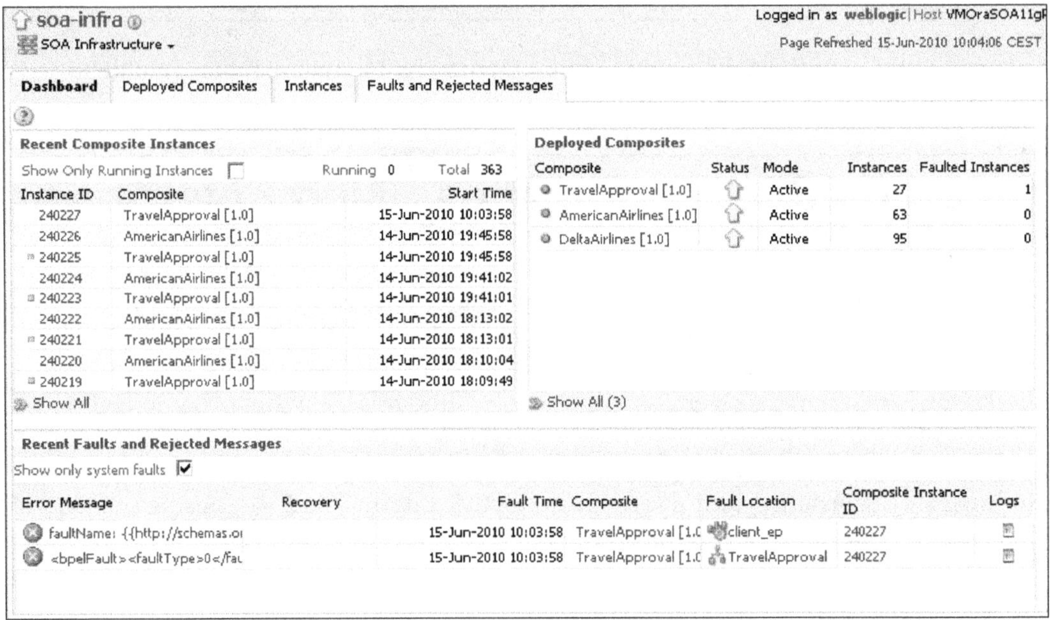

The page displays details about recent composite application instances, deployed composites, recent faults, and rejected messages. We can also click a specific SOA composite application name or **Instance ID** to access additional information.

Deploying and undeploying SOA composite applications

We can deploy SOA composite applications by opening the **SOA Infrastructure** menu and selecting **SOA Deployment | Deploy**.

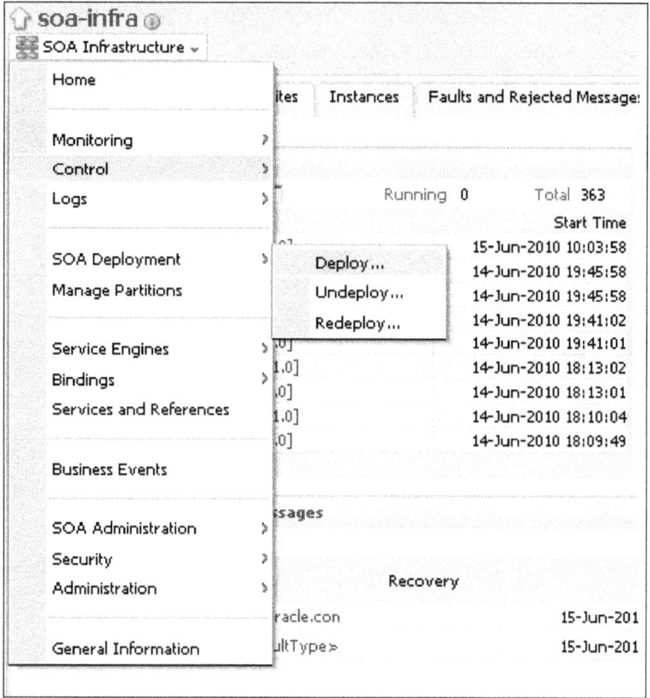

The following display appears:

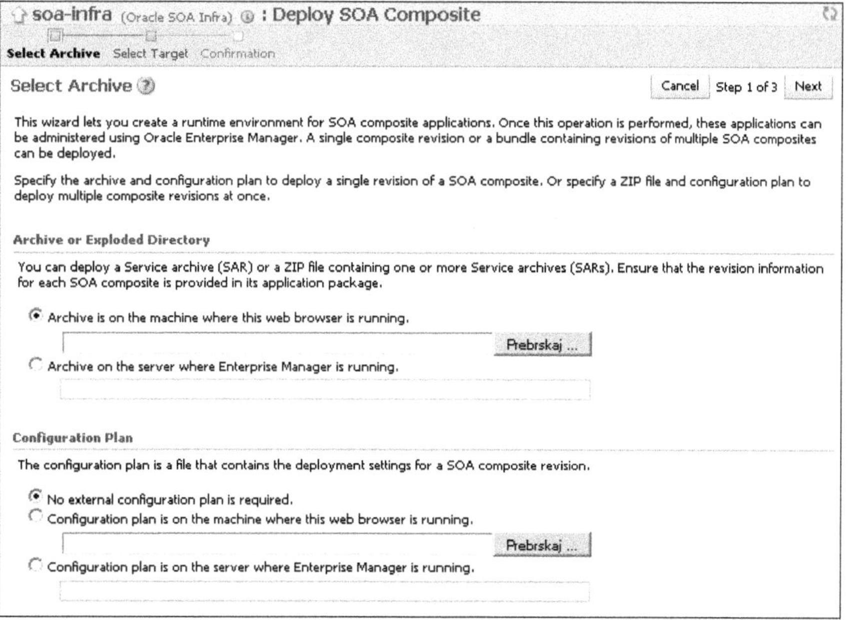

Here we can browse for an **SOA Archive** (**SAR**) file or a ZIP file containing multiple SAR files. We can also attach a configuration plan. Then we click **Next**. We have to select the **SOA Partition** where to deploy the composite application.

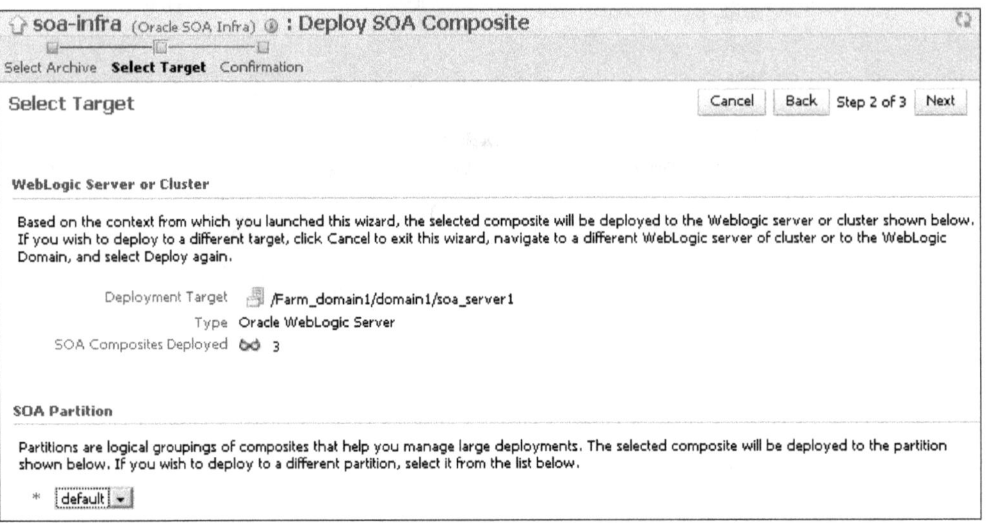

We click **Next**. On the **Confirmation** screen, we can select whether we want to deploy as a default revision or not.

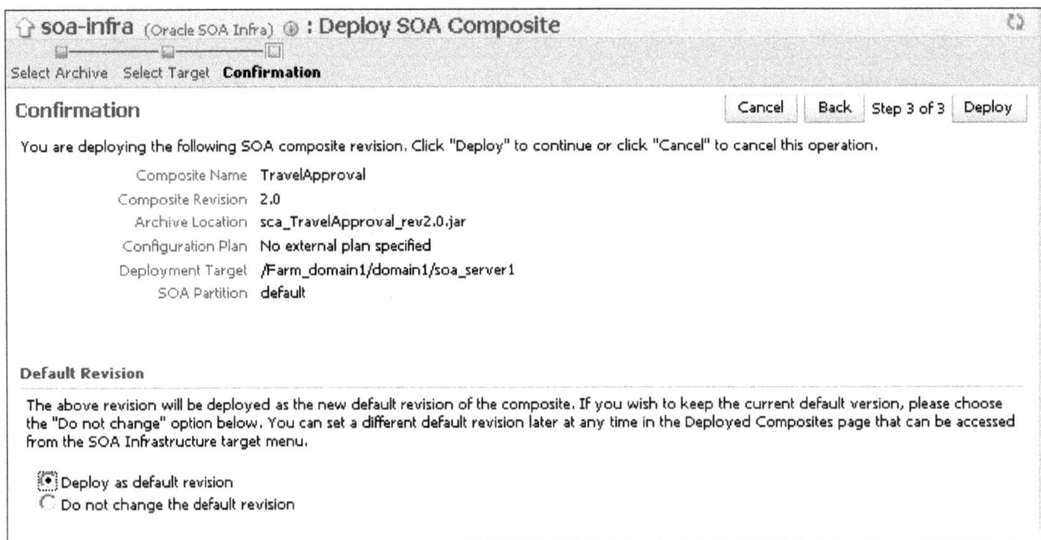

Finally, we deploy the composite application by clicking **Deploy**.

If we want to undeploy the composite application, we open the **SOA Infrastructure** menu and select **SOA Deployment | Undeploy**. In the next step, we have to choose the application:

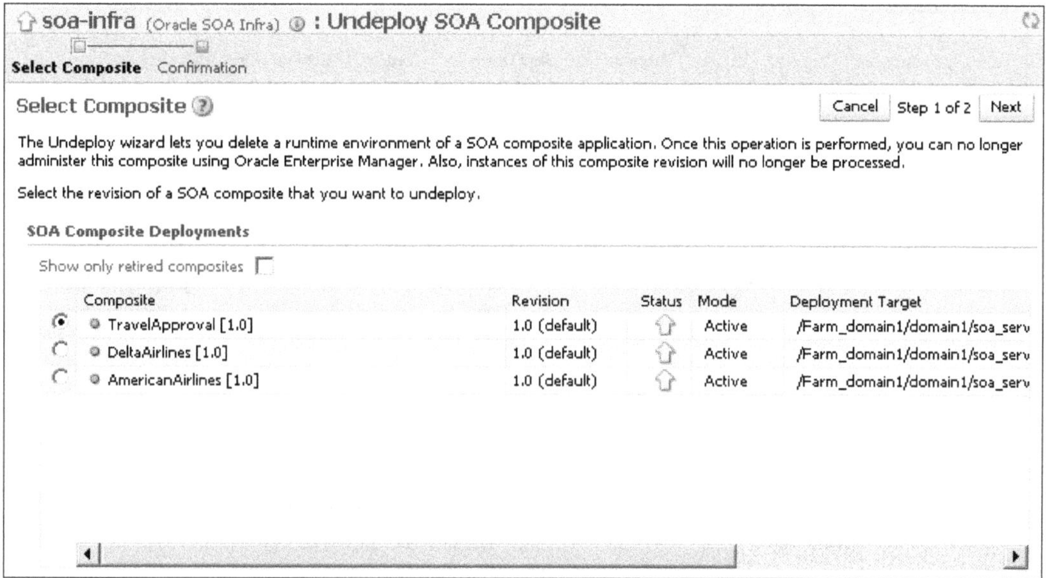

We click **Next** and finish with undeployment by clicking **Undeploy** on the **Confirmation** screen.

Initiating an SOA composite application test instance

Under **soa-infra**, we select a specific SOA composite application. A page showing detailed information about a composite application appears:

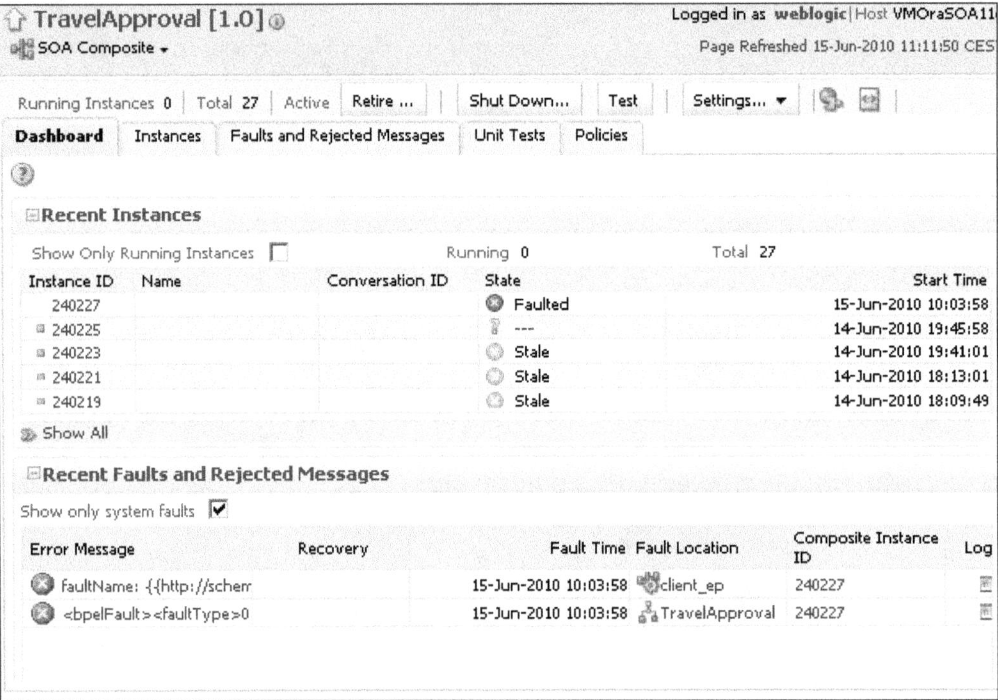

To initiate a new composite instance, we click the **Test** button on the toolbar.

The **Test** button is enabled only if the composite application is exposed as a Web Service.

The **Test Web Service** web page for initiating an instance appears:

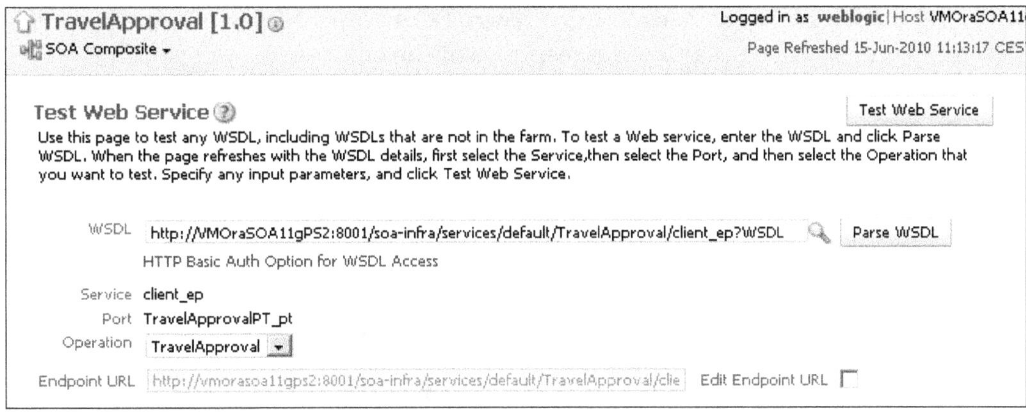

We have to select the operation we want to invoke and enter the input values in the input fields on the bottom of the **Request** tab:

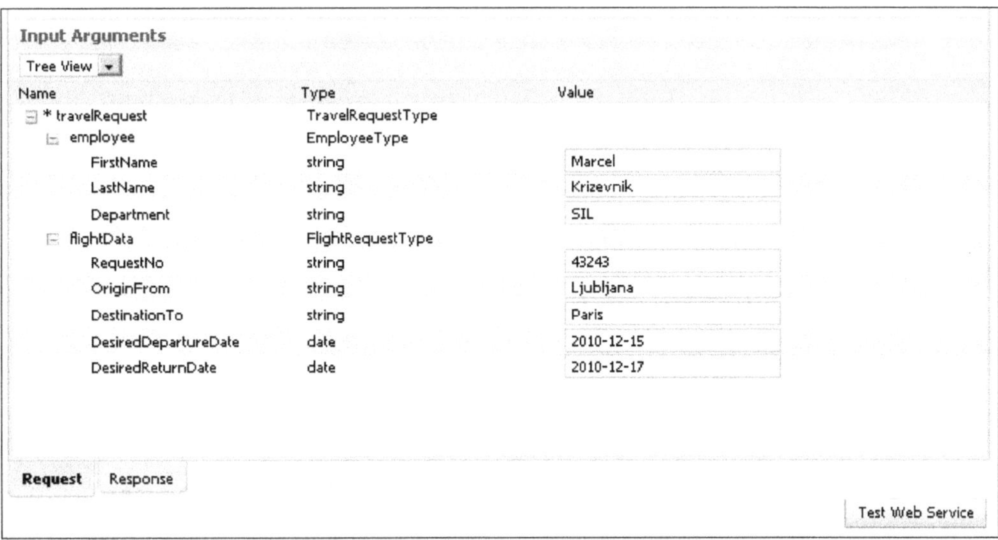

Notice that this tab also enables you to specify security, quality of service, HTTP transport, stress testing options, and so on. However, we will only enter the input arguments.

We can also switch to the **XML View** to see and set the SOAP request in XML form.

By clicking **Test Web Service**, we initiate a new SOA composite instance. The following page opens, displaying the response of the composite application:

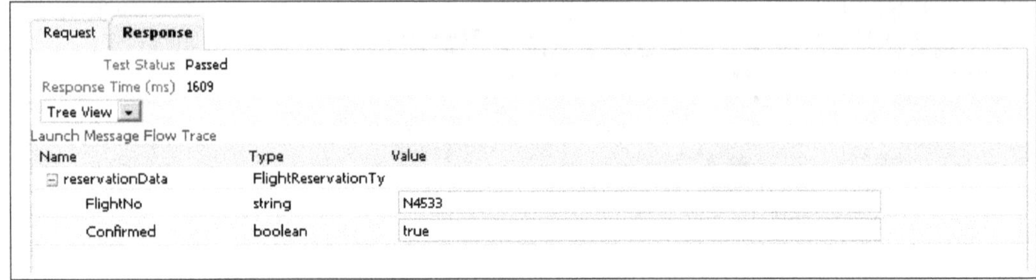

Viewing the SOA composite instances flow trace

After initiating a new composite instance, we can see the instance flow trace by clicking the **Launch Message Flow Trace** link. The **Flow Trace** page appears:

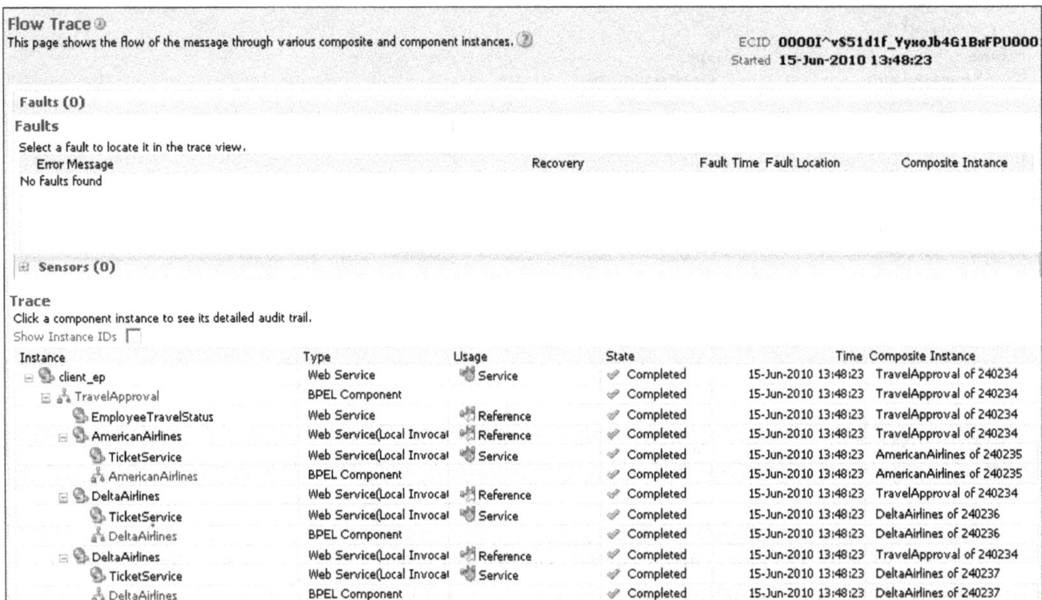

We can also access the instance flow trace using the **Instances** tab of the **SOA Infrastructure** home page, which also offers rich search functionality.

In the previous screenshot, we can see that the instance has completed successfully (state **Completed**). We can also see the state of all service components and binding components and the time when a particular service component or binding component has been completed. If we click on the `TravelApproval` BPEL Component link, a page displaying the BPEL process instance details appears. On the **Audit Trail** tab, we can see the trace of the BPEL process and all received and sent messages.

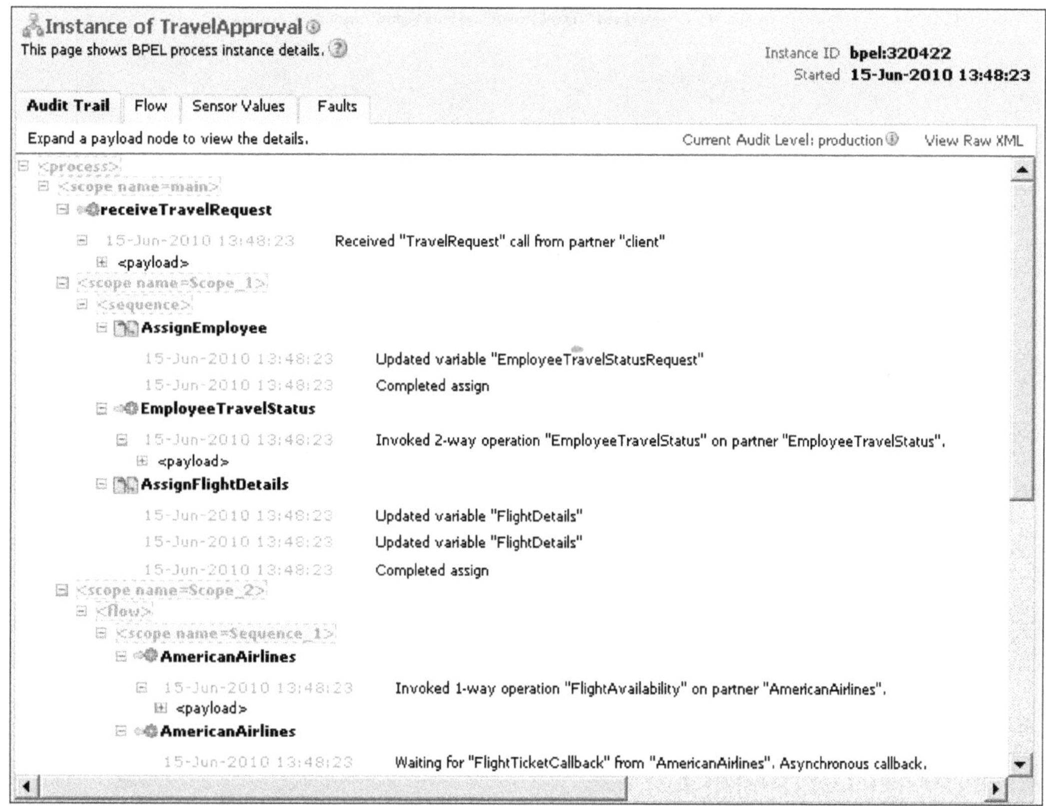

If we want to see the complete XML message, we have to click the *plus* sign in front of the **<payload>**:

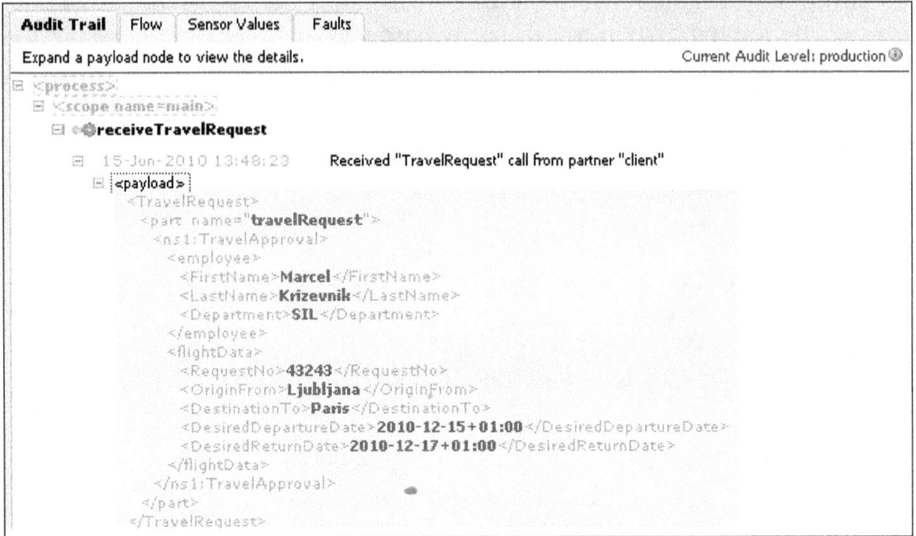
Audit Trail
Flow
Sensor Values
Faults
Expand a payload node to view the details.
Current Audit Level: production
<process>
<scope name=main>
receiveTravelRequest
15-Jun-2010 13:48:23
Received "TravelRequest" call from partner "client"
<payload>
<TravelRequest>
<part name="travelRequest">
<ns1:TravelApproval>
<employee>
<FirstName>Marcel</FirstName>
<LastName>Krizevnik</LastName>
<Department>SIL</Department>
</employee>
<flightData>
<RequestNo>43243</RequestNo>
<OriginFrom>Ljubljana</OriginFrom>
<DestinationTo>Paris</DestinationTo>
<DesiredDepartureDate>2010-12-15+01:00</DesiredDepartureDate>
<DesiredReturnDate>2010-12-17+01:00</DesiredReturnDate>
</flightData>
</ns1:TravelApproval>
</part>
</TravelRequest>

If we want to see the visual flow of the BPEL process instance, we have to switch to the **Flow** tab:

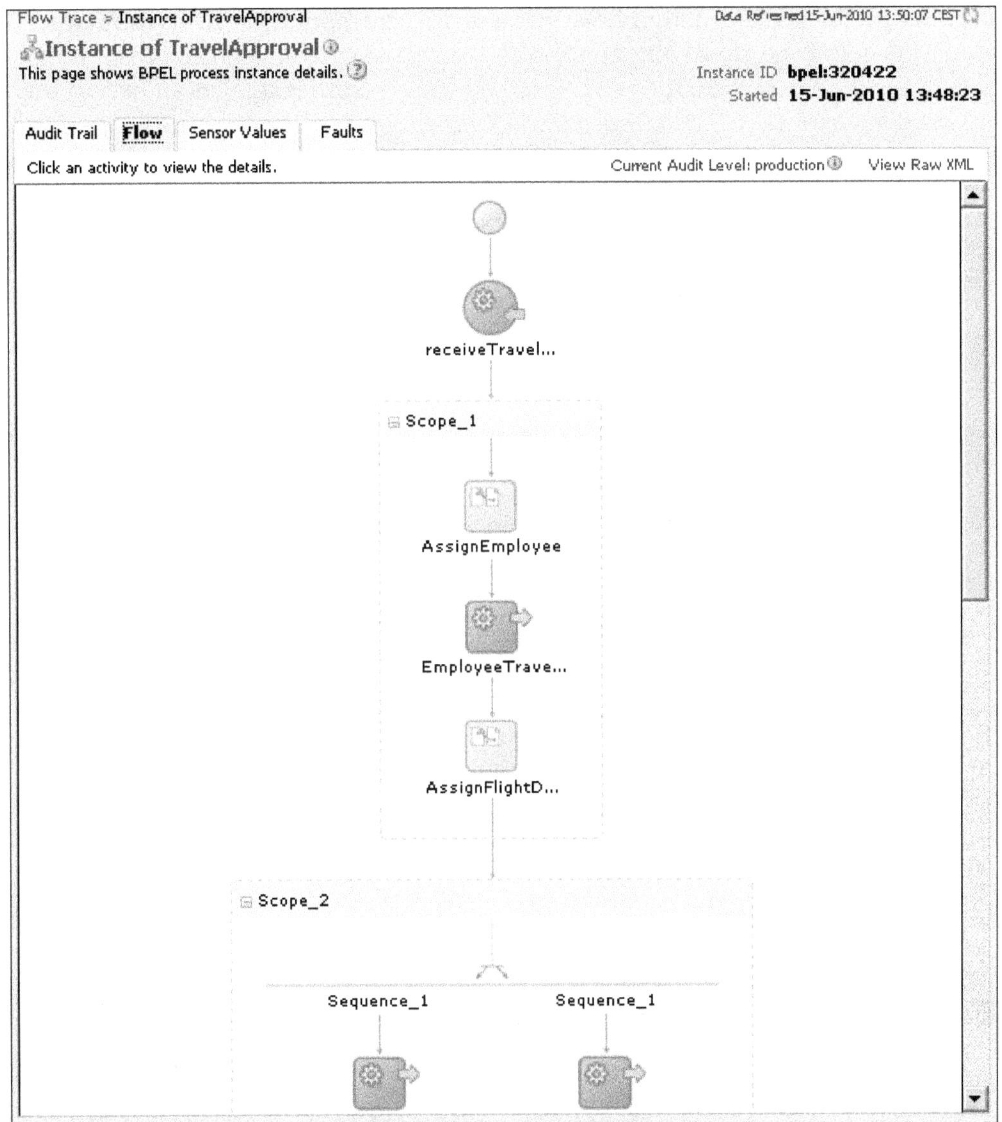
Flow Trace > Instance of TravelApproval
Instance of TravelApproval
This page shows BPEL process instance details.
Instance ID bpel:320422
Started 15-Jun-2010 13:48:23
Audit Trail
Flow
Sensor Values
Faults
Click an activity to view the details.
Current Audit Level: production
View Raw XML
receiveTravel...
Scope_1
AssignEmployee
EmployeeTrave...
AssignFlightD...
Scope_2
Sequence_1
Sequence_1

By clicking on the specific activity, we can see the corresponding XML input and output. This enables us to debug and verify the processing of each activity. If we click on the `<receive>` activity, we can see the received message, as shown in the following screenshot:

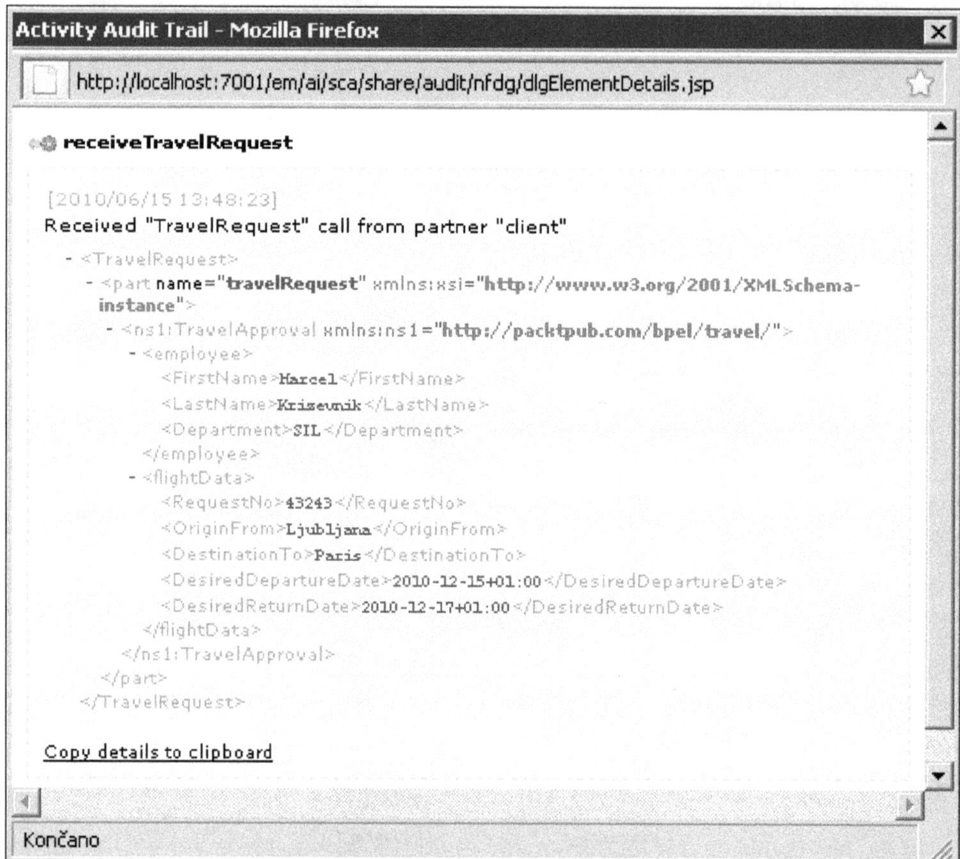
Activity Audit Trail - Mozilla Firefox
http://localhost:7001/em/ai/sca/share/audit/nfdg/dlgElementDetails.jsp
receiveTravelRequest
[2010/06/15 13:48:23]
Received "TravelRequest" call from partner "client"
- <TravelRequest>
- <part name="travelRequest" xmlns:xsi="http://www.w3.org/2001/XMLSchema-instance">
- <ns1:TravelApproval xmlns:ns1="http://packtpub.com/bpel/travel/">
- <employee>
<FirstName>Marcel</FirstName>
<LastName>Krizevnik</LastName>
<Department>SIL</Department>
</employee>
- <flightData>
<RequestNo>43243</RequestNo>
<OriginFrom>Ljubljana</OriginFrom>
<DestinationTo>Paris</DestinationTo>
<DesiredDepartureDate>2010-12-15+01:00</DesiredDepartureDate>
<DesiredReturnDate>2010-12-17+01:00</DesiredReturnDate>
</flightData>
</ns1:TravelApproval>
</part>
</TravelRequest>
Copy details to clipboard
Končano

Automatic testing of SOA composite instances

Using EM Console, we can run test cases that were created in JDeveloper and deployed as part of the composite application. This enables us to test SOA composite application before deploying it to the production environment. To test SOA composite application, we first have to select the SOA composite application under **soa-infra** in the navigator. Then we click on the **Unit Test** tab. The test cases that were deployed as part of the SOA composite application appear as follows:

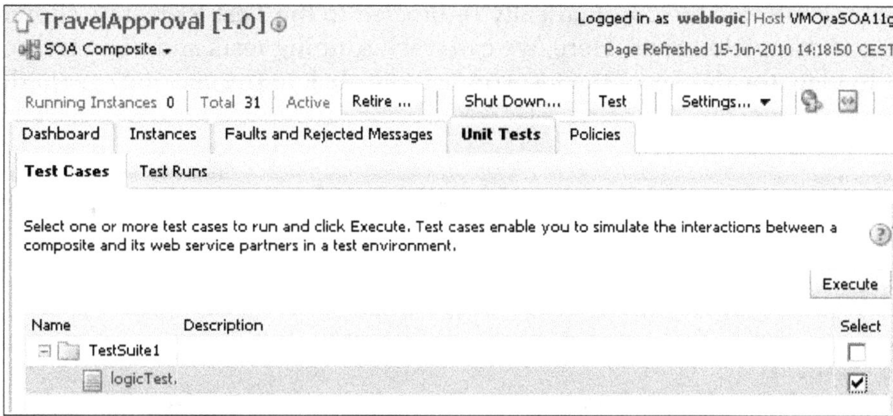

We can select the entire test suite or individual test cases and click **Execute**. We are prompted to create a test. We have to specify a test run name. We can also define the timeout and number of concurrent test instances:

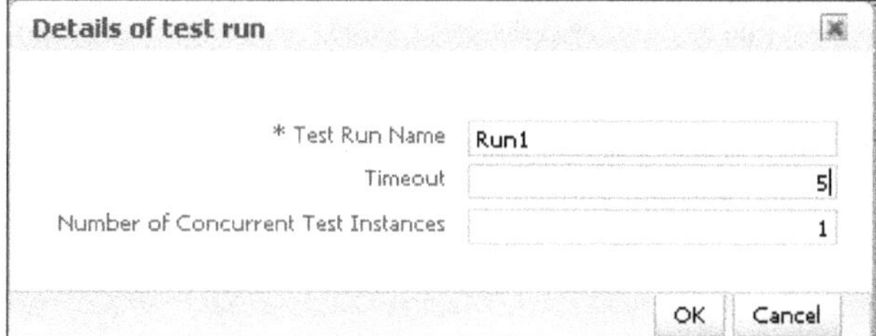

After clicking **OK,** we are automatically redirected to the **Test Runs** tab, showing the running and completed tests. Here, we can track running tests and view test results. In order to view the details of the test run, we can click to the specific row in the **Test Run Name** column.

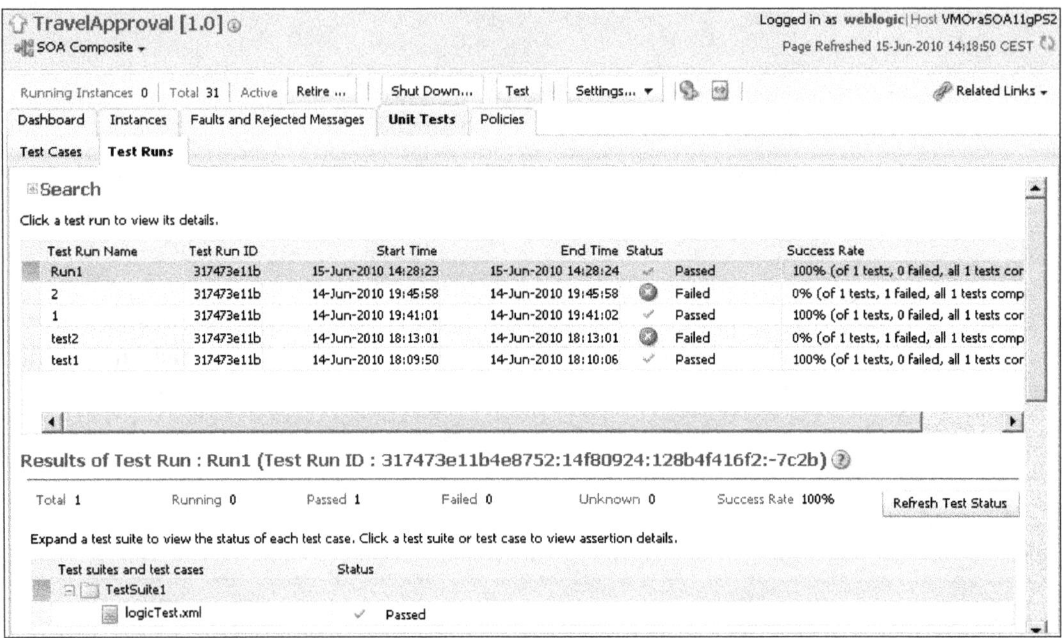

Assertion details are displayed at the bottom of the page. In the following screenshot, we can see that the actual result of the BPEL process equals the expected value; therefore, the test case was successful. (We can see the expected value and actual value by clicking the **[XML]** link.)

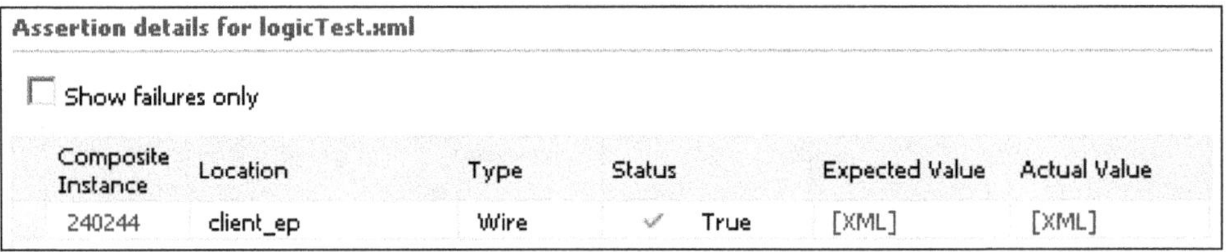

Developing and deploying BPEL 2.0 processes

As we already mentioned, Oracle SOA Suite 11*g* PS 2 supports BPEL 2.0; however, this version is not yet production ready, so by default BPEL version 1.1 is used. If we want to develop and deploy BPEL 2.0 processes, we have to use the **Source** view of the BPEL Component Designer. In this section, we will convert our TravelApproval BPEL process to BPEL 2.0 and deploy it to the SOA Server.

First, we have to change the BPEL namespace which specifies the BPEL version to `http://docs.oasis-open.org/wsbpel/2.0/process/executable`.

```
process name="TravelApproval"
     targetNamespace="http://packtpub.com/bpel/travel/"
     xmlns="http://docs.oasis-open.org/wsbpel/2.0/process/executable"
     xmlns:client="http://packtpub.com/bpel/travel/"
     xmlns:ora="http://schemas.oracle.com/xpath/extension"
     xmlns:bpelx="http://schemas.oracle.com/bpel/extension"
   ...
</process>
```

Next, we will modify all **<from>** and **<to>** elements inside **<assign>** activities, as BPEL 2.0 introduces an improved data access mechanism, where we can access variable data using simple XPath expressions (without requiring usage of `bpws:getVariableData`). For example, the `AssignEmployee` **<assign>** activity has to be modified as shown:

BPEL 1.1 code:

```
<assign name="AssignEmployee">
   <copy>
      <from variable="TravelRequest" part="travelRequest"
            query="/client:TravelApproval/employee"/>
      <to variable="EmployeeTravelStatusRequest" part="employee"
            query="/ns2:employee"/>
   </copy>
</assign>
```

BPEL 2.0 code:

```
<assign name="AssignEmployee">
   <copy>
      <from>$TravelRequest.travelRequest/employee</from>
      <to>$EmployeeTravelStatusRequest.employee</to>
   </copy>
</assign>
```

Next, we have to replace the BPEL 1.1 **<switch>** activity with **<if>** activity, which was introduced in BPEL 2.0.

BPEL 1.1 code:

```
<switch>
   <case condition="number(bpws:getVariableData('FlightResponseAA',
                  'confirmationData','/ns1:confirmationData/Price'))
         &lt;= number(bpws:getVariableData('FlightResponseDA',
                 'confirmationData','/ns1:confirmationData/Price'))">
  ...
   </case
   <otherwise>
  ...
   </otherwise>
</switch>
```

BPEL 2.0 code:

```
<if>
  <condition>number($FlightResponseAA.confirmationData/Price) &lt;=
                 number($FlightResponseDA.confirmationData/Price)

  </condition>
  ...
  <else>
  ...
  </else>
</if>
```

When finished, we can deploy the BPEL 2.0 process in the same way as any BPEL 1.1 process (as part of the SOA composite application). We can initiate a process instance using the EM Console. If we look at the visual flow of the BPEL process instance, we can see that the instance has been executed successfully:

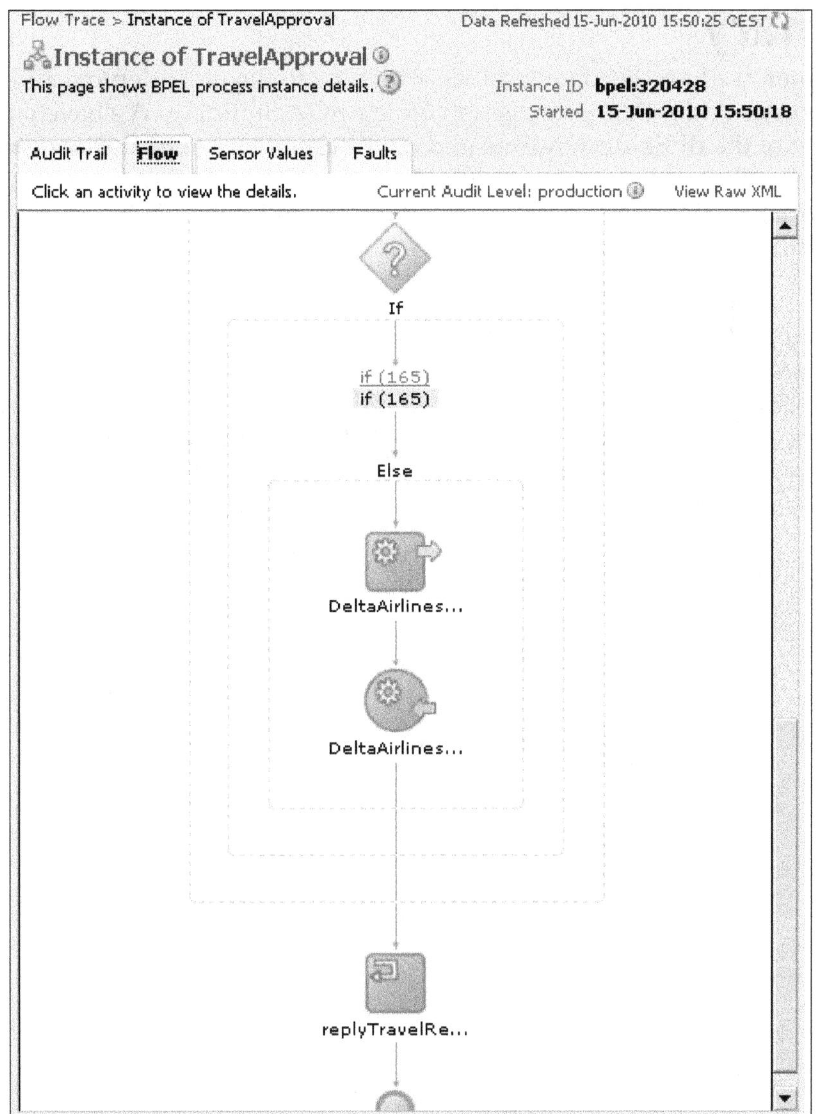
Flow Trace > Instance of TravelApproval
Data Refreshed 15-Jun-2010 15:50:25 CEST
Instance of TravelApproval
This page shows BPEL process instance details.
Instance ID bpel:320428
Started 15-Jun-2010 15:50:18
Audit Trail
Flow
Sensor Values
Faults
Click an activity to view the details.
Current Audit Level: production
View Raw XML
If
if (165)
if (165)
Else
DeltaAirlines...
DeltaAirlines...
replyTravelRe...

Summary

In this chapter, we have become familiar with how to develop, deploy, and manage SOA composites with BPEL processes in Oracle SOA Suite 11*g*. We have completed an overview of the BPEL design-time and runtime environment and reviewed the major features. We have also become familiar with Oracle Enterprise Manager Console, which enables us to deploy, test, manage, and debug BPEL processes within SOA composite applications.

For BPEL development, Oracle provides an integrated graphical development environment in JDeveloper. JDeveloper simplifies the development considerably and offers several tools that simplify the development, such as Copy Rule editor, XPath Expression builder, XSLT Mapper, and the BPEL Validation browser. We have become familiar with the SOA Composite Editor. We have demonstrated how to develop an SOA composite with a BPEL process in JDeveloper, how to test it, and deploy it. We have also shown how to manage SOA composite applications.

In the next chapter, we will look at the advanced BPEL features of Oracle SOA Suite 11*g*.

5

BPEL Extensions, Dynamic Parallel Flow, Dynamic Partner Links, Notification Service, Java Embedding, and Fault Management Framework

In this chapter, we will discuss the advanced BPEL features provided by Oracle SOA Suite 11*g*. We will overview the extension functions and activities. We will take a detailed look at the dynamic parallel flows and dynamic partner links. Then we will overview the Notification Service for sending and receiving asynchronous notifications using e-mail and other channels. We will also look at Java embedding. Next, we will explain how to implement advanced fault management through the use of fault policies. We will demonstrate the use of presented features on the asynchronous `TravelApproval` BPEL process that we have already developed in *Chapter 2*.

Human Workflow extension and support for BAM (Business Activity Monitoring) are be covered in Chapters 7 and 8.

In this chapter, we will discuss the following:

- Extension functions and activities, provided by Oracle SOA Suite 11*g*
- Dynamic parallel flow and dynamic partner links
- Notification Service
- Java embedding
- Fault management framework

Extension functions and activities

In chapters 2 and 3, we saw that BPEL is very flexible with respect to the expression and query language used. By default, XPath 1.0 is used; however, any other language supported by the BPEL server can also be used. The idea behind this flexibility is to open up BPEL for future versions of XPath and XQuery. XPath 1.0 does not provide all functions necessary to develop BPEL processes. Therefore, the BPEL specification defines additional functions such as `getVariableData()`, `getVariableProperty`, and `getLinkStatus()`.

Remember that when BPEL 2.0 is used, we do not need the `getVariableData()` extension function in order to access variable data.

Oracle SOA Suite 11*g* provides several additional BPEL extension functions and activities to simplify development of business processes. However, using functions and activities described in this section limits the portability of BPEL processes because these will not be available on other BPEL servers.

Oracle SOA Suite 11*g* provides the following BPEL extension functions and activities:

- **Oracle-specific BPEL activities**: These include activities for data/array manipulation, Java embedding, parallel dynamic flows, sending notifications, and so on. They are defined in the `http://schemas.oracle.com/bpel/extension` namespace, for which the `bpelx` prefix is used. Examples not only include `<bpelx:append>`, `<bpelx:remove>`, `<bpelx:insertBefore>`, `<bpelx:copyList>`, but also `<bpelx:exec>` and `<bpelx:flowN>`. These activities will be explained later in this chapter.

- **XPath 2.0 functions**: These functions are not Oracle specific, and taken strictly are not part of XPath 1.0, which is the default query language. They are used for data manipulation and are defined in the `http://www.oracle.com/XSL/Transform/java/oracle.tip.pc.services.functions.Xpath20` namespace, for which the prefix `xp20` is used. Examples include `xp20:compare()`, `xp20:current-date()`, `xp20:lower-case()`, and so on. For more information on XPath 2.0 please visit `http://www.w3.org/TR/xpath20/`.
- **Oracle-specific XPath extension functions**: These are used primarily for data manipulation and are defined in the `http://schemas.oracle.com/xpath/extension` namespace. Usually the `ora` prefix is used. These functions are described later in this section.
- **XPath extension function for LDAP access and user authentication**: These functions are defined in the `http://schemas.oracle.com/xpath/extension/ldap` namespace with `ldap` prefix. Examples include `ldap:listUsers()` and `ldap:search()`.
- **Oracle-specific XSLT transformation extension functions**: These are helpful in stylesheet transformations. The namespace is `http://www.oracle.com/XSL/Transform/java/oracle.tip.pc.services.functions.ExtFunc`, for which the `oraext` prefix is usually used. Example functions are `oraext:square-root()` and `oraext:right-trim()`.

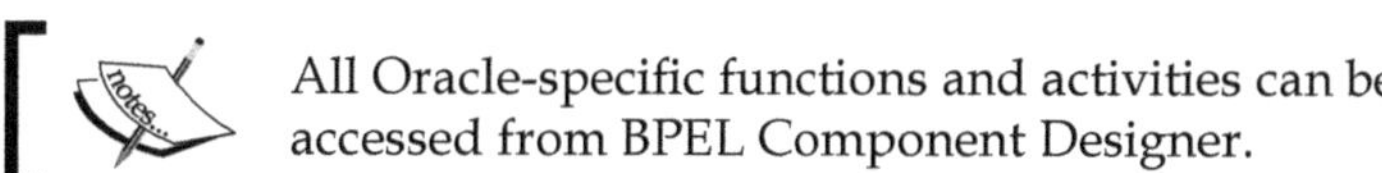

All Oracle-specific functions and activities can be accessed from BPEL Component Designer.

We will look at the most important extension functions and activities based on their functionality:

- Transformation and query support
- Data and array manipulation
- XML manipulation
- Date and time expressions
- Process identifications
- LDAP access and user management

Later in this chapter, we will also take a detailed look at the important extension activities, such as `<flowN>` and `<exec>`.

Transformation and query support

In real-world business processes we often have to match the schema of our XML document to the schema required by the partner web service. Consider our TravelApproval process example. Here we designed both the process and the partner web services, so we only had to perform minimal transformations for calling the Employee or Airlines Web Services. In real-world scenarios this will often not be the case and we will have to make more complex transformations. To perform the transformations, we can use the BPEL `<assign>` activity. As this can be time consuming, Oracle provides an XSLT engine and an extension function through which we can activate the XSLT engine. This enables us to use XSLT to perform complex data transformations. Using XSLT is more appropriate than using `<assign>` because XSLT is the standard transformation language for XML. Also, sometimes we already have the stylesheets for the transformations. This way we can easily integrate them into BPEL processes. To activate the XSLT engine we use the `ora:processXSLT()` function. The function requires two parameters—the XSLT stylesheet and the XML input on which the transformation should be made. The result of the function is the transformed XML. The syntax is `ora:processXSLT('stlyesheet','XML_input')`. Note that the same function is defined in the `http://schemas.oracle.com/bpel/extension/xpath/function/xdk` namespace as well. We can use either. Usually we use this function within the `<assign>` activity, in the `<from>` clause. For example, to modify our TravelApproval process and make a more complex transformation to prepare the input for the Employee web service, we could use the XSLT engine, as shown in the following code excerpt:

```
<assign>
  <copy>
    <from expression="ora:processXSLT('employee.xslt',
      bpws:getVariableData('TravelRequest','employee'))"/>
    <to variable="EmployeeTravelStatusRequest" part="employee"/>
  </copy>
</assign>
```

For this code to work, we must create the `employee.xslt` stylesheet and deploy it with the process. For more information on XSLT, please refer to `http://www.w3.org/TR/xslt`.

> The `ora:processXSLT()` function can be accessed from BPEL Component Designer, which provides a graphical tool for creating stylesheets.

In addition to the XSLT engine, Oracle SOA Suite 11*g* also provides an xSQL engine, which can be used in a similar way to the XSLT engine. It can be activated using the `ora:processXSQL()` function. We have to provide the xSQL template and the input XML on which the query should be performed as `ora:processXSQL('query_template','XML_input')`.

Data and array manipulation

Data manipulation in BPEL is done with the `<assign>` activity, where we can use XPath and BPEL functions in the `<from>` and `<to>` clauses. In addition, Oracle provides several custom functions that ease data manipulation considerably. A very important aspect in data manipulation is arrays. In *Chapter 3*, we mentioned that arrays in BPEL are realized with XML elements that can occur more than once. In XML schema they are identified with the `maxOccurs` attribute, which can be set to a specific value or can be unbounded (`maxOccurs="unbounded"`). The items are addressed with the XPath, as shown in the following example:

```
<assign>
  <copy>
    <from variable="TicketOffer"
          part="ticket"
          query="/item[1]"/>
    <to variable="FirstOffer" part="ticket"/>
  </copy>
</assign>
```

Often we need to dynamically address the items. Instead of hardcoding the index, we can use a variable, such as:

```
<variable name="position" type="xs:int"/>
```

We could then create the XPath query expression, store it in a variable, and then use this variable to address the desired item, as shown in the following example:

```
<assign>
  <copy>
    <from expression="concat('/item[',
                      bpws:getVariableData('position'), ']')"/>
    <to variable="itemAddress"/>
  </copy>
  <copy>
    <from expression="bpws:getVariableData('TicketOffer', 'ticket',
                      bpws:getVariableData('itemAddress'))"/>
    <to variable="SelectedOffer" part="ticket"/>
  </copy>
</assign>
```

Alternatively, we can use an Oracle-specific function called `ora:getElement()`. The function takes four parameters—variable name, part name, query path, and element index:

```
ora:getElement('variable_name', 'part_name', 'query', index)
```

Using this function, the previous example would look as follows:

```
<assign>
  <copy>
    <from expression="ora:getElement('TicketOffer', 'ticket',
                       '/item', bpws:getVariableData('position'))"/>
    <to variable="SelectedOffer" part="ticket"/>
  </copy>
</assign>
```

We usually dynamically address items in loops using the `<while>` activity. To determine the number of items (array size), we can use the Oracle-specific function `ora:countNodes()`. The function returns the number of items as an integer and takes three parameters—variable name, part name, and query path (the last two parameters are optional):

```
ora:countNodes('variable_name', 'part_name', 'query')
```

To count the number of ticket offers in our example, we could use the following code:

```
<assign>
  <copy>
    <from expression="ora:countNodes('TicketOffer',
                       'ticket', '/item')"/>
    <to variable="NoOfOffers"/>
  </copy>
</assign>
```

To append a variable to the existing variable (array), we can use the Oracle-specific activity `<bpelx:append>`. This activity can be used within the `<assign>` activity. To add a new ticket offer to the existing offers, we can use the following code:

```
<assign>
  <bpelx:append>

    <bpelx:from variable="NewOffer" part="ticket" />
    <bpelx:to variable="TicketOffer" part="ticket" />

  </bpelx:append>
</assign>
```

In a similar way, we can use other extension activities, including `<bpelx:insertBefore>` and `<bpelx:copyList>`.

In addition to standard DOM-based variables, Oracle also supports the use of SDO-based variables in the same process. The Oracle BPEL Service Engine automatically converts back and forth between DOM and SDO forms. However, when using SDO-based variables, there are some limitations, as SDO specifications do not support some advanced XPath features (for example, there is no support for `and`, `or`, and `not`).

We have seen that Oracle-specific functions and activities simplify data and array management considerably. Next, we look at functions related to XML manipulation.

XML manipulation

In some cases, our BPEL processes will invoke Web Services that return strings. The content of these strings is XML. This approach is used by some developers, particularly on the .NET platform. Using such Web Services with BPEL is problematic because no function exists to parse string content to XML. In programming languages such as Java and C# we use XML parser functions or XML serialization (JAXB in Java).

Oracle therefore provides a custom function called `ora:parseEscapedXML()`. The following function takes a string as a parameter and returns structured XML data:

```
ora:parseEscapedXML(string)
```

Let us suppose that the Employee web service returns a string instead of XML. We can parse it using the `ora:parseEscapedXML()` function:

```
<!-- Synchronously invoke the Employee Travel Status Web Service -->
<invoke partnerLink="employeeTravelStatus"
  portType="emp:EmployeeTravelStatusPT"
  operation="EmployeeTravelStatus"
  inputVariable="EmployeeTravelStatusRequest"
  outputVariable="EmployeeTravelStatusResponseString" />
<assign>
  <copy>
    <from expression="ora:parseEscapedXML(
      bpws:getVariableData('EmployeeTravelStatusResponseString'))"/>
    <to variable="EmployeeTravelStatusRespose" part="employee"/>
  </copy>
</assign>
```

To perform an inverse operation, convert structured XML to a string; we can use the `ora:getContentAsString()` function. It takes structured XML data as a parameter and returns a string:

```
ora:getContentAsString(XMLElement)
```

To get the node value as an integer instead of a string we can use the `ora:integer()` function:

```
ora:integer(node)
```

To add single quotes to a string we can use the `ora:addQuotes()` function:

```
ora:addQuotes(string)
```

Oracle even provides a function to read the content of a file. The function is called `ora:readFile()` and is often used together with the `ora:parseEscapedXML()` function, which converts the file content to structured XML (if the file content is XML). The syntax of the `ora:readFile()` function is:

```
ora:readFile('file_name')
```

Next, we look at the expressions related to date and time.

Date and time expressions

Sometimes in our BPEL processes we need the current date and/or time, for example, to time-stamp certain data. For this, we can use the Oracle-specific functions. The most important are:

- `ora:getCurrentDate()`: Get current date
- `ora:getCurrentTime()`: Get current time
- `ora:getCurrentDateTime()`: Get current date and time

Note that all three functions return strings (and not the date or date/time types). All three functions also take an optional parameter that specifies the date/time format. The format is specified according to `java.text.SimpleDateFormat`. For details, refer to Java API documentation at `http://java.sun.com/j2se/1.4.2/docs/api/java/text/SimpleDateFormat.html`.

To format an XML Schema `date` or `dateTime` to a string representation, which is more suitable for output, Oracle provides the `ora:formatDate()` function. The syntax of the function that returns a string is as follows:

```
ora:formatDate('dateTime', 'format')
```

Once again, the format is specified according to `java.text.SimpleDateFormat` format.

A similar function is provided in the `xp20` namespace as:

```
xp20:format-dateTime('dateTime', 'format')
```

Next, let us look at functions related to process identification.

Process identification

Oracle provides several functions related to process identification. With these functions we can get process IDs, instance creator, and more. These functions are:

- `ora:getProcessId()`: Returns the ID of the current BPEL process
- `ora:getInstanceId()`: Returns the process instance ID
- `ora:getConversationId()`: Returns the conversation ID used in asynchronous conversations
- `ora:getCreator()`: Returns the process instance creator
- `ora:generateGUID()`: Generates a unique **GUID (Globally Unique ID)**

LDAP access and user management

XPath extension functions for LDAP access and user authentication are defined in the `http://schemas.oracle.com/xpath/extension/ldap` namespace with `ldap` prefix. These functions are:

- `ldap:listUsers('properties','filter')`
- `ldap:search('properties','filter','scope'?)`
- `ldap:authenticate('properties','userId','password')`

With this, we have concluded the overview of BPEL extension functions provided by Oracle SOA Suite 11*g*. In the next section, we will take a look at the dynamic parallel flow activity.

Dynamic parallel flow

In Chapter 2 we became familiar with the `<flow>` activity, which enables us to start several parallel activities. In our TravelApproval process example, we have used `<flow>` activity to start two parallel sequences that acquired plane ticket offers from American and Delta Airline web services. As the operation invocation for the ticket offer has been asynchronous, we had to use a `<receive>` activity to wait for the callbacks.

The problem with the `<flow>` activity is that we need to know in advance how many parallel activities are required. The number of parallel activities is specified by the BPEL code. In several real-world use cases this is limiting because the number of required parallel branches can depend on the information stored in a variable or received from the partner web service. In such cases, `<flow>` activity is inadequate.

Oracle SOA Suite 11*g* therefore provides `<flowN>` activity, which can create multiple parallel activities at runtime. The number of parallel activities is specified by a variable. The parallel branches created by `<flowN>` perform the same operations but use different data (variables). Each branch gets a unique index number, which can be used to acquire the data (for example using XPath expressions and XML sequences that mimic arrays).

`<flowN>` functionality is very similar to the BPEL 2.0 parallel `<forEach>` activity.

The `<flowN>` activity is defined in the `http://schemas.oracle.com/bpel/extension` namespace, for which `bpelx` prefix is used. The syntax is shown as follows:

```
<bpelx:flowN N="number-of-parallel-flows"
             indexVariable="variable-name-for-index">

   activity

</bpelx:flowN>
```

We have to specify the number of parallel flows that need to be created; for this, the attribute `N` is used. Usually, we will use an expression to get the number of parallel flows from a variable (using `bpws:getVariableData()` function) or to count the number of parameters of array items (using `ora:countNodes()` for example). We also have to specify the variable name used for the index—this is the number of the parallel flow that has been created. Such variable should be of type `xs:int` or similar. We will use the variable to extract the appropriate data, for example from an array. The parallel branches created by `<flowN>` execute the same activities, but they usually use different data, for which the index variable is used.

To some the `<flowN>` activity might look similar to the `<while>` activity. Notice, however, that there is a huge difference between them. The `<while>` activity creates a loop that is executed several times in sequence. The `<flowN>` activity creates several branches that are executed in parallel.

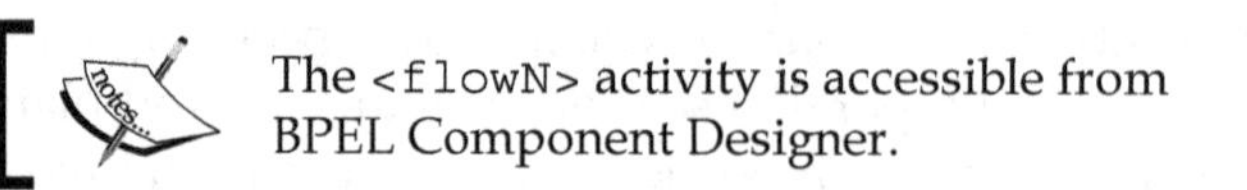

The `<flowN>` activity is accessible from BPEL Component Designer.

The code within the <flowN> activity is executed in parallel; therefore, we have to take care about parallel access to variables and other resources (for example, partner links). If variables are updated within <flowN>, we should make sure that we do not use the same variable instance in multiple branches. We should also not use the same partner link in parallel branches. Usually, it is appropriate to include the activities within <flowN> in a scope. For more information on scopes and serializable access to variables, please refer to Chapter 3.

Within <flowN>, we might want to use different data for each parallel branch, or store several responses from partner links. The most appropriate way to achieve this is to use arrays or XML sequences where the maximal occurrence of an element is unbounded. Therefore, we should be familiar with XPath and also with Oracle-specific functions for management of data and arrays. We have covered these earlier in this chapter.

Finally, we will often want that different parallel branches invoke operations of different partner Web Services. To achieve this, we will have to use dynamic partner links. We have explained dynamic partner links in Chapter 3.

Dynamic flow example

To demonstrate how we can use the <flowN> activity, let us modify our TravelApproval process example. So far, our example has invoked two airline Web Services in parallel using the <flow> activity (American and Delta Airlines). We will extend the example so that it will invoke several Web Services. The list of Web Services (actually their addresses) will be provided as the input parameter. In real-world use cases, this information could be retrieved from a service, database, or somewhere else.

The output from the airline Web Services will be stored in an array. We will also modify how the best offer is selected. So far, we have used a simple <switch> activity that had to select between two offers. Now we will write a <while> loop which will select the lowest offer from all offers stored in the array.

This example will demonstrate beside the <flowN> activity how to use dynamic partner links, array, and loops. Our TravelApproval process will require several modifications:

- First, we will have to supplement the input message from the client, which will have to include the list of partner links (Airline Web Services) our process should invoke to get an airline ticket offer. We will have to modify the process WSDL to achieve this.
- Then, we will need to modify the part of the process that makes parallel invocations to Airline Web Services. Here we will use the <flowN> activity and use an array to store the results.

- Next, we will use dynamic partner links to invoke airline web services in parallel.
- Finally, we will modify the code, which selects the best offer. We will use a `<while>` loop to make the selection and access the results from Airline Web Services to compare the prices.

Please notice that the example assumes that all Airline Web Services provide the same WSDL interface. Let us start with modifying the WSDL.

Providing a list of partner links

To provide a list of Airline Web Services that our process should invoke to get airline ticket offers, we will modify the WSDL of the process. In Chapter 3 we explained that the partner link endpoint references in BPEL are stored as `wsa:EndpointReferences` as defined by WS-Addressing. We will use this XML element in the client message to specify the addresses of Airline Web Services.

To achieve this we will add a part to `TravelRequestMessage`. The part `airlineData` will be of type `AirlineDataType`:

```
<message name="TravelRequestMessage">
  <part name="employee" type="emp:EmployeeType" />
  <part name="flightData" type="aln:FlightRequestType" />
  <part name="airlineData" type="tns:AirlineDataType" />
</message>
```

We will define the `AirlineDataType` as a sequence of `wsa:EndpointReferences`. To use the `wsa:EndpointReference` element in our schema, we will have to import the WS-Addressing schema. It can be found in the SOA **Metadata Store** (**MDS**) using the `oramds:///soa/shared/common/ws-addressing.xsd` path. (In order to access SOA-MDS from JDeveloper, we have to create a SOA-MDS connection). We will write the following schema:

```
<xs:schema elementFormDefault="qualified"
  targetNamespace="http://packtpub.com/bpel/travel/"
  xmlns:xs="http://www.w3.org/2001/XMLSchema"
  xmlns:wsa="http://schemas.xmlsoap.org/ws/2003/03/addressing">
  <xs:import
    namespace="http://schemas.xmlsoap.org/ws/2003/03/addressing"
    schemaLocation="oramds:///soa/shared/common/ws-addressing.xsd"/>
  <xs:complexType name="AirlineDataType">
    <xs:sequence>
        <xs:element name="AirlineLink" maxOccurs="unbounded">
```

```
            <xs:complexType>

                <xs:sequence>
                    <xs:element ref="wsa:EndpointReference" />
                </xs:sequence>

            </xs:complexType>
        </xs:element>
    </xs:sequence>

  </xs:complexType>
</xs:schema>
```

Dynamic parallel invocation of airline services

Next, we will modify the part of the TravelApproval process that makes parallel invocations to Airline Web Services. We will use the `<flowN>` activity to make as many parallel invocations as there are addresses provided in the input message from the client. We will also store the results of each airline web service in an array.

We will modify the `CheckFlightAvailability` scope. First, we will declare the variables. We will need the index variable that we will call `index` and will be of type `xs:int`. We will also declare a `CombinedFlightResponse` variable, where we will store the output of each Airline Web Service:

```
<variables>

  <!-- output from all Airlines -->
  <variable name="CombinedFlightResponse"
    messageType="aln:TravelResponseMessage"/>

  <!-- counter for flowN -->
  <variable name="index" type="xsd:int"/>
</variables>
```

Next, we will replace the `<flow>` activity with `<flowN>`. We will use the index as the `indexVariable`. The `<flowN>` should start as many parallel branches, as there are addresses in the input message from the client. We will use the `ora:countNodes()` function to count the number of Airline Web Service addresses:

```
<bpelx:flowN N="ora:countNodes('TravelRequest',
                               'airlineData',
                               '/airlineData/trv:AirlineLink')"
                               indexVariable="index">
```

Dynamic partner links

We have already mentioned that we will invoke Airline Web Services in parallel branches, created by `<flowN>`. As the addresses of Web Services are provided in the message from the client, we will need to create a dynamic partner link in each branch. The parallel branches will execute the same activities (including the `<invoke>` for operation invocation and `<receive>` for callback). This means that the same variable will be used to store the result from the callback. To shield the parallel branches, we will use a local scope for each branch.

In the scope we will declare a partner link, called `Airline`. We will also declare a variable used to store the result from the callback (`FlightResponse`):

```
<scope name="LocalScopeFlowN">
  <partnerLinks>

    <partnerLink name="Airline"
      partnerLinkType="aln:flightLT"
      myRole="airlineCustomer"
      partnerRole="airlineService"/>

  </partnerLinks>

  <variables>

    <!-- output from Airline -->
    <variable name="FlightResponse"
      messageType="aln:TravelResponseMessage"/>

  </variables>
```

Next we will define a sequence (remember that it will be started in parallel branches). Within the sequence, we will first copy the Airline Web Service endpoint reference (address) to the partner link. Then we will invoke the web service and wait for the callback:

```
<sequence>
  <!-- Create the partner link  -->
  <assign>
    <copy>
        <from expression="bpws:getVariableData('TravelRequest',
                          'airlineData',
                          concat('/airlineData/trv:AirlineLink[',
                          bpws:getVariableData('index'),
                          ']/wsa:EndpointReference'))"/>
        <to partnerLink="Airline"/>
   </copy>
  </assign>

  <!-- Invoke the airline web service -->
```

```
<invoke partnerLink="Airline"
                    portType="aln:FlightAvailabilityPT"
                    operation="FlightAvailability"
                    inputVariable="FlightDetails" />

<receive partnerLink="Airline"
                     portType="aln:FlightCallbackPT"
                     operation="FlightTicketCallback"
                     variable="FlightResponse" />
```

Finally, we will store the result in the array called `CombinedFlightResponse`. We will use the Oracle-specific `<bpelx:append>` activity to achieve this, as follows:

```
        <!-- Store the result -->
        <assign>
           <bpelx:append>
               <bpelx:from variable="FlightResponse"
                 part="confirmationData" />
               <bpelx:to variable="CombinedFlightResponse"
                 part="confirmationData" />
           </bpelx:append>
         </assign>
     </sequence>
  </scope>
</bpelx:flowN>
```

Offer selection loop

The final step is to modify the code, which selects the best offer. We will replace the simple `<switch>` activity with a `<while>` loop, where we will iterate through all offers and compare them by price. We will store the final result in the `TravelResponse` variable. We will also need a variable where we will store the temporary result from the airline that we compare to the best offer. We will name this variable `TempResponse`:

```
<variables>
  <variable name="TempResponse"
    messageType="aln:TravelResponseMessage"/>
</variables>
```

The `<while>` loop will make as many iterations as there are Airline Web Services that have been invoked. We will get this number by counting the Airline Web Service addresses using `ora:countNodes()` function. To access the array data, we will use the `ora:getElement()` function. The code is shown below:

```
<assign>
  <copy>
    <from expression="0"/>
    <to variable="index"/>
  </copy>
  <copy>
    <from expression="ora:getElement('CombinedFlightResponse',
                      'confirmationData',
                      '/confirmationData/confirmationData','1')" />
    <to variable="TravelResponse" part="confirmationData" />
  </copy>
</assign>
<while condition="bpws:getVariableData('index') &lt;
                 ora:countNodes('TravelRequest',
                 'airlineData','/airlineData/trv:AirlineLink')">
  <sequence>
    <assign>
        <copy>
            <from expression="bpws:getVariableData('index') + 1"/>
            <to variable="index"/>
        </copy>
        <copy>
            <from
              expression="ora:getElement('CombinedFlightResponse',
                          'confirmationData',
                          '/confirmationData/confirmationData',
                          bpws:getVariableData('index'))" />
            <to variable="TempResponse" part="confirmationData" />
        </copy>
    </assign>

    <switch>
       <case condition="bpws:getVariableData('TempResponse',
                       'confirmationData',
                       '/confirmationData/aln:Price')
                       &lt; bpws:getVariableData('TravelResponse',
                       'confirmationData',
                       '/confirmationData/aln:Price')">
            <assign>
                <copy>
```

```
                    <from variable="TempResponse" />
                    <to variable="TravelResponse" />
                </copy>
            </assign>
        </case>

    </switch>
  </sequence>

</while>
```

Testing the example

We are now ready to deploy the example to the BPEL server and test it. We deploy the process following the steps described in Chapter 4. Then we initiate a process instance using EM Console.

In the visual flow representation, we can observe how many parallel branches have been started and how many times the loop has executed:

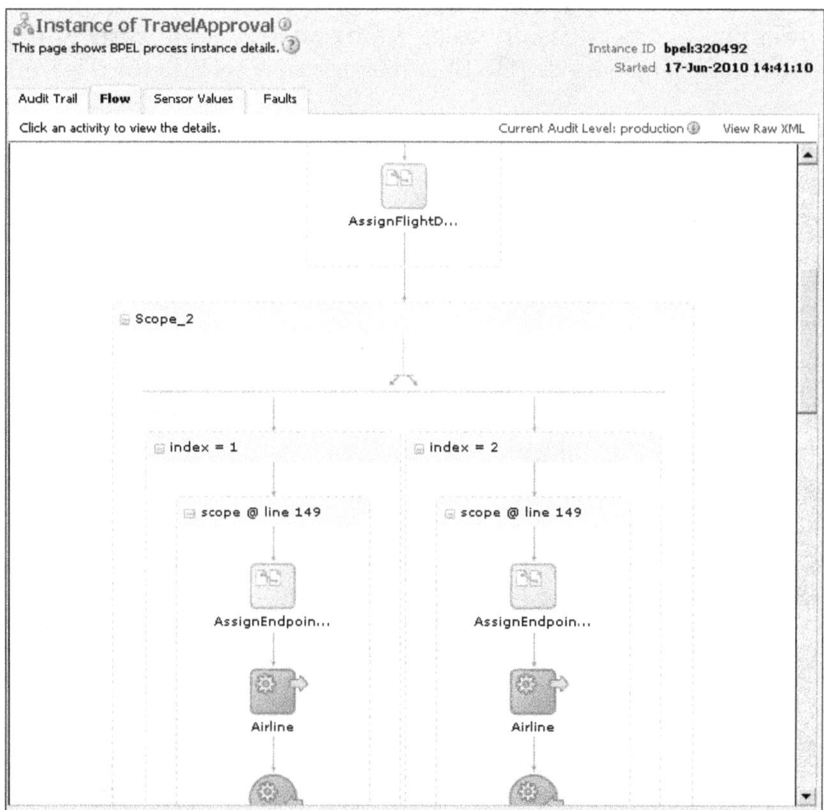

With this, we have concluded our example in which we have demonstrated dynamic parallel flows, dynamic partner links, arrays, and loops. In the next section, we will show how to send user notifications using Oracle extension activities.

Notification Service

Business processes sometimes require that notifications are sent to the users or participants. For example, our TravelApproval process might want to notify the employee by e-mail about which flight ticket has been selected. Another use case is when an exception occurs in a business process. Then we can use notifications by e-mail or by other channels to notify the responsible person and require intervention.

BPEL specification does not provide a mechanism for sending e-mails or other notifications. Therefore, we would need to create a web service (partner link) which is capable of sending and/or receiving notifications. This web service would provide port types with operations for sending and receiving notifications and we would use `<invoke>` and `<receive>` activities to invoke them—the same as for any other service.

Fortunately, Oracle SOA Suite 11*g* already provides such a service—it is called Notification Service. Notification Service uses the underlying infrastructure, provided by Oracle User Messaging Service (UMS), which is a new feature for release 11*g*.

It provides support for the following channels:

- E-mail
- Voice messages
- IM
- SMS

> The fax and pager notification channels are not supported in 11*g* Release 1 (11.1.1).

Notification Service exposes its operations like any other web service through WSDL, and also through Java interfaces. The overall architecture of the User Messaging Service is shown in the following figure:

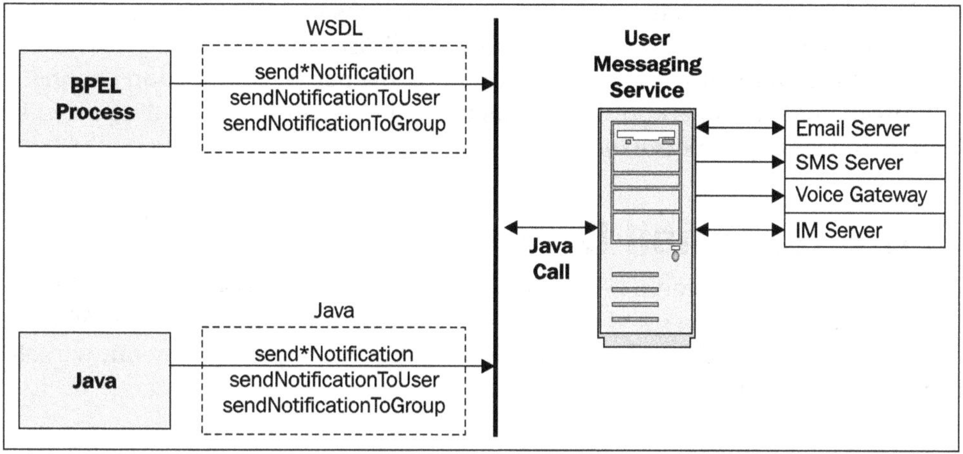

To use Notification Service in our process we have to create a partner link and invoke the provided operations. Through WSDL interface Notification Service exposes the `NotificationService` port type. It provides the following operations:

- `send*Notification`, where `*` can be `Email`, `SMS`, `Voice`, or `IM` (Instant Messaging)
- `sendNotificationToUser`, used to send notification to a specific user
- `sendNotificationToGroup`, used to send notifications to a group of users

The operations take various input messages. The `sendEmailNotification` operation, for example, takes the `EmailNotificationRequest` input message, which is of `EmailPayloadType`. The latter is defined in the corresponding `NotificationService` XML Schema and basically consists of elements, such as from address, to address, subject, body, and so on.

In addition, Notification Service also provides a Java interface (API). It is implemented as the Java class `oracle.tip.pc.services.notification.NotificationService`, which provides methods with the same name as the WSDL interface. Notification Service uses a WSIF binding to expose the operations through WSDL.

In JDeveloper BPEL Component Designer, we can implement sending of notifications to users or groups by simply dragging one of the following extension activities from the **Component Palette**:

- **E-mail**: Enables sending text notifications over the E-mail channel
- **Voice**: Enables sending voice notifications over the Voice channel
- **SMS**: Enables sending short messages over the SMS channel
- **IM**: Enables sending instant messages over the IM channel

- **User Notification**: This generic activity enables sending notifications over all supported channels. When designing the BPEL process, we do not have to select the channel we want to use. In fact, the actual notification channel is resolved at runtime and it depends on end user preferences, defined in UMS (User Messaging Service).

Setting the Email Driver

If we want to send and receive e-mail notifications, we have to set the Email Driver first. To do this, we have to go to the EM Console and then open the **User Messaging Service** node. From the **User Messaging Email Driver** drop-down menu, we select **Email Driver Properties**.

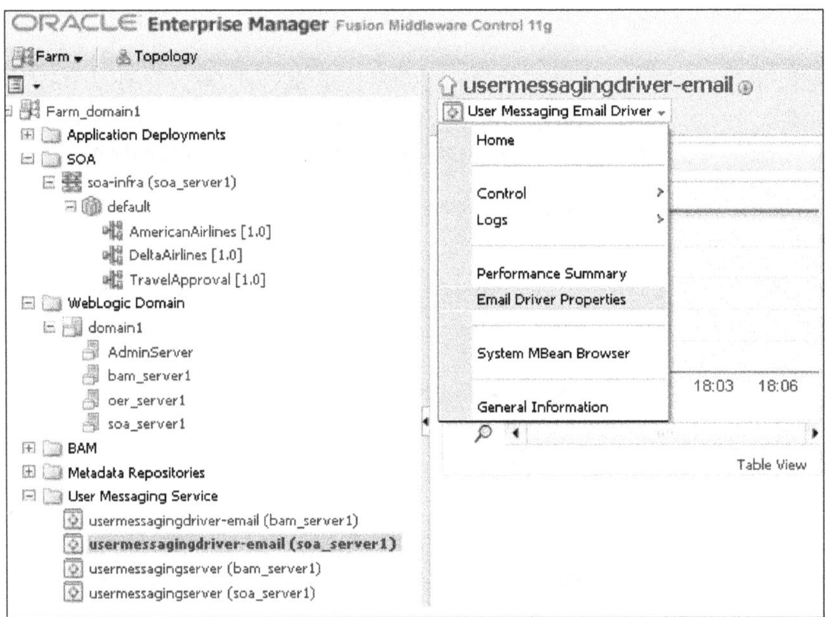

Here we have to set the set various properties on the Email Driver, including the details about the e-mail server like **OutgoingMailServer**, **OutgoingMailServerPort**, **OutgoingMailServerSecurity** (optional), **OutgoingUsername** and **OutgoingPassword**.

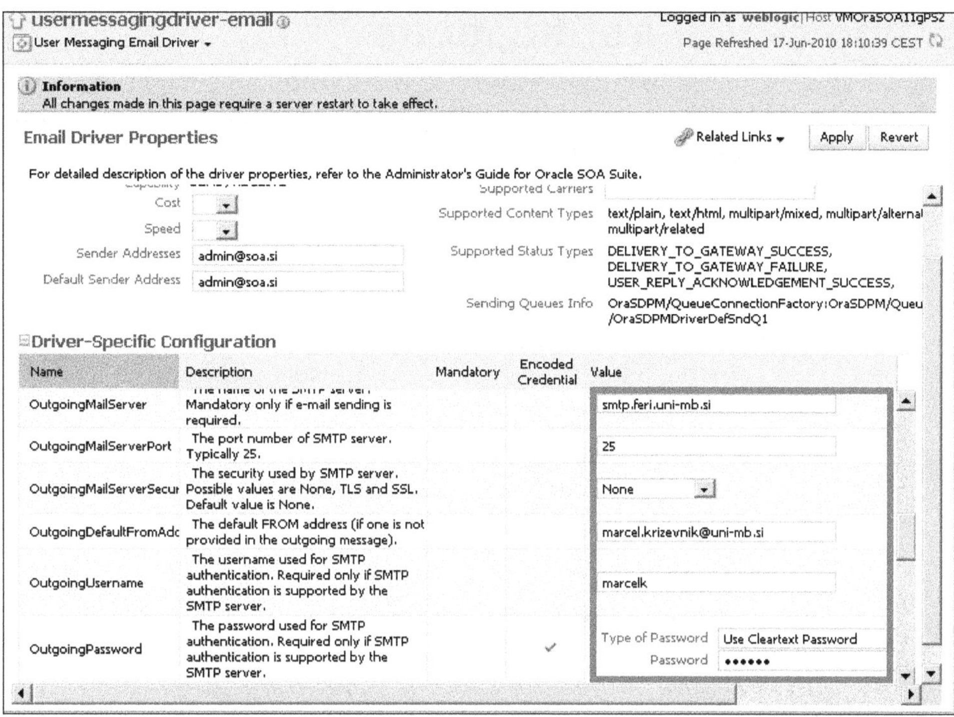

Then we click **Apply**. Next, we have to adjust the settings for the **Workflow Notification**. From the **SOA Infrastructure** drop-down menu, we select the **SOA Administration | Workflow Notification Properties**. Here we have to set the **Notification Mode** to either **All** or **Email**.

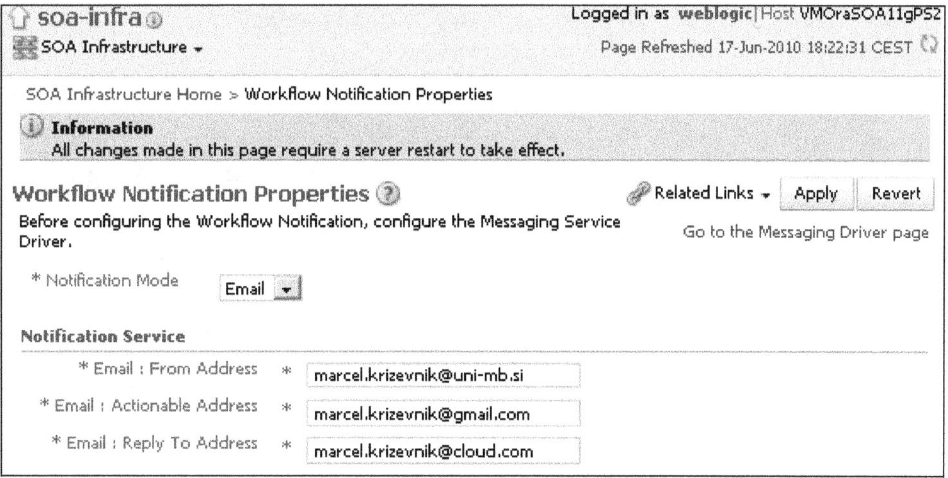

Finally, we confirm the changes by clicking **Apply** and restart the SOA Server.

Sending e-mail notifications

To demonstrate how to use Notification Service we will add an e-mail notification to our TravelApproval process example. Originally, our process selected the best ticket offer by comparing offers from American and Delta Airlines' web services and invoked a callback to the client. We will add the e-mail notification just before the client callback.

Before we start modifying the BPEL code, we need to make modifications to the `TravelRequest` message in the TravelApproval process WSDL. We must add the e-mail address to which our process will send the confirmation. Therefore, we first define an `EmailType` (in the `TravelApproval.wsdl` file) as follows:

```
<types>
  <xs:schema elementFormDefault="qualified"
    targetNamespace="http://packtpub.com/bpel/travel/">

    <xs:complexType name="EmailType">
        <xs:sequence>
            <xs:element name="Address" type="xs:string" />
        </xs:sequence>
    </xs:complexType>
  </xs:schema>
</types>
```

Next, we add a new `email` part to the `TravelRequestMessage`:

```
<message name="TravelRequestMessage">
  <part name="employee" type="emp:EmployeeType" />
  <part name="flightData" type="aln:FlightRequestType" />
  <part name="email" type="tns:EmailType" />
</message>
```

Now we are ready to modify the BPEL source code (`TravelApproval.bpel)` file. We will add a scope and within it, we will create the e-mail variable, assign the values, and invoke Notification Service to send the e-mail.

The easiest way to add Notification Service to the BPEL process is to use the JDeveloper BPEL Component Designer, which provides a convenient wizard. We will drag-and-drop the **Email** activity from the **Component Palette** to the process after the `CheckFlightAvailability` scope, as shown in the following screenshot:

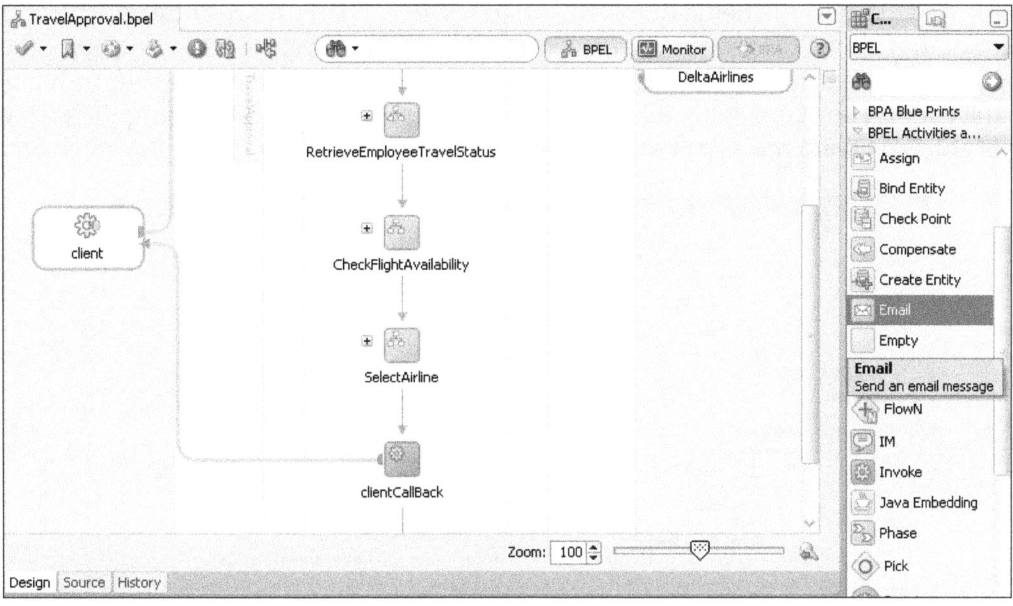

The **Email** editor opens. Now we have to specify the e-mail details, including the e-mail account used for sending the mail (**From Account**), **To** address, **Cc** and **Bcc**, **Reply to** address, **Subject**, and message **Body**. We could use static values for all these fields (and just type them in), but this would make little sense. Rather, we will use the values from BPEL variables, which we will access with functions, such as `getVariableData()`. We can also use other available XPath and extension functions.

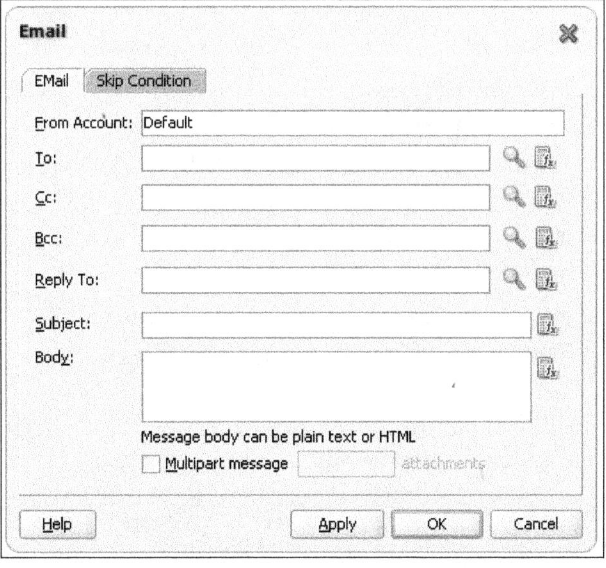

Let us now discuss the fields that we have to specify. The **From Account** specifies the account that the BPEL process will use to send e-mails. Next, we have to specify the addresses the mail will be sent to. For the **To** address we will use the input provided by the client. Therefore, we will start the XPath **Expression Builder** using the icon on the right and create the XPath expression.

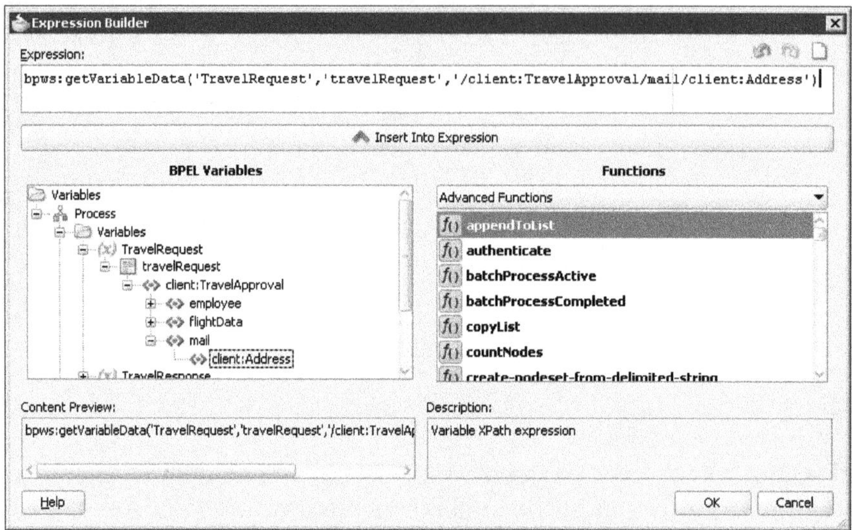

Alternatively, we could use the e-mail address from a BPEL user account. In the same way, we will set values for **Subject** and **Body**, and finish the wizard, as shown in the next screenshot:

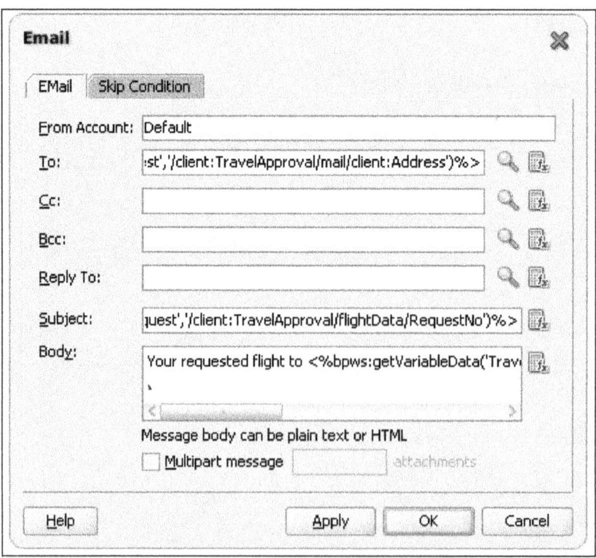

By clicking **OK** we return back to the BPEL Component Designer. We can see that the **Notification Service** partner link was added automatically. Our SOA Composite application now looks as follows:

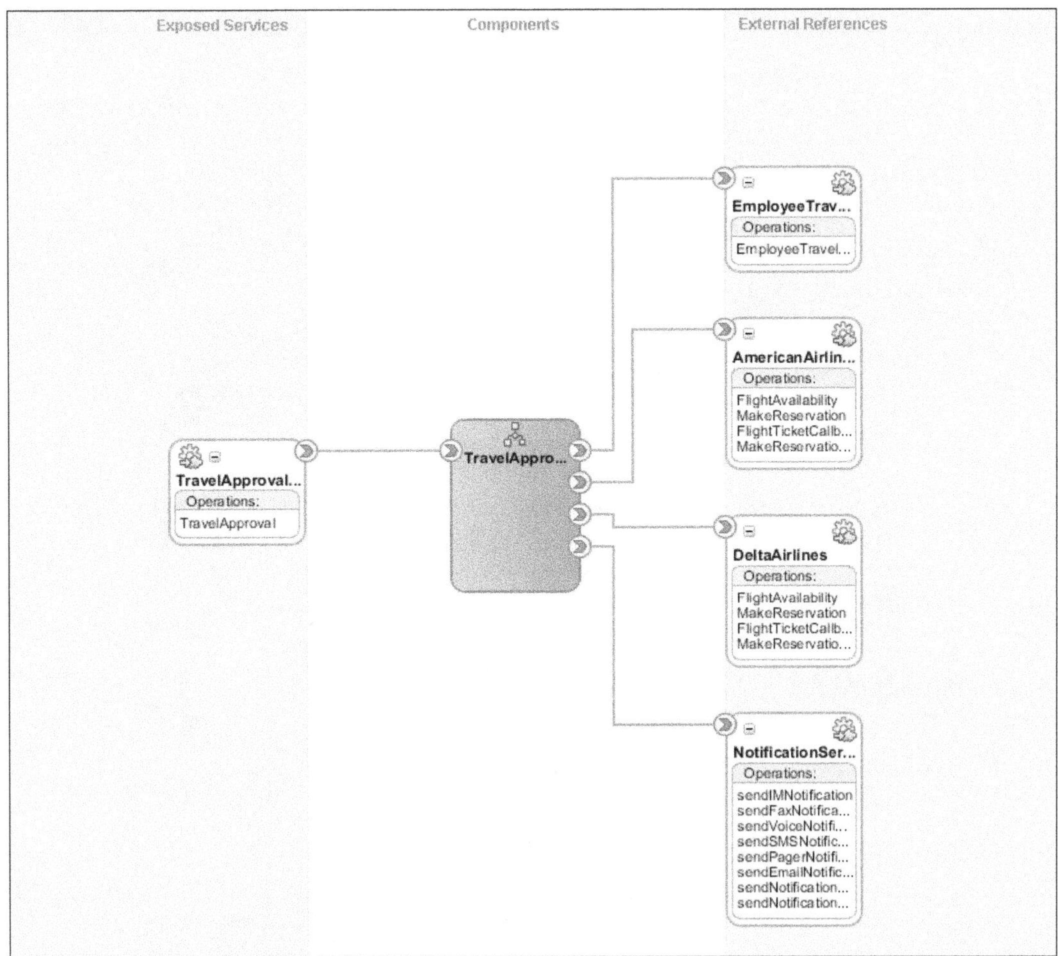

Review of code

The wizard has generated a new scope. Within the scope, three variables have been generated—the input variable `varNotificationReq` containing the e-mail payload, the `varNotificationResponse` containing the response from Notification Service, and the fault variable `NotificationServiceFaultVariable`:

```
<scope name="NotificationService">
  <variables>
    <variable name="varNotificationReq"
```

```
          messageType="ns5:EmailNotificationRequest"/>
        <variable name="varNotificationResponse"
          messageType="ns5:ArrayOfResponse"/>
        <variable name="NotificationServiceFaultVariable"
          messageType="ns5:NotificationServiceErrorMessage"/>
      </variables>
```

Then, the <assign> activity is generated, which is used to assign the values to the e-mail message payload. We have created the <copy> statements using the XPath **Expression Builder**. Alternatively, we can edit the source code directly. In the following code excerpt, we show the part used to assign the subject:

```
    <sequence>
      <assign name="Assign">
      ...
        <copy>
            <from expression="concat('Travel confirmation for
                              ',bpws:getVariableData('TravelRequest',
                              'employee','/employee/emp:FirstName'),'
                              ',bpws:getVariableData('TravelRequest',
                              'employee','/employee/emp:LastName'))"/>
            <to variable="varNotificationReq" part="EmailPayload"
                           query="/EmailPayload/ns5:Subject"/>
        </copy>
      ...
```

Finally, the wizard has generated the <invoke> activity for the sendEmailNotification operation:

```
        <invoke name="InvokeNotificationService"
                      partnerLink="NotificationService"
                      portType="ns5:NotificationService"
                      operation="sendEmailNotification"
                      inputVariable="varNotificationReq"
                      outputVariable="varNotificationResponse"/>
      </sequence>
    </scope>
```

Testing the example

We can deploy this example directly from JDeveloper. After starting the process using EM Console, we can verify that the e-mail has arrived.

The source code of this and all examples can be downloaded from `http://www.packtpub.com/`.

Java code embedding

Java code embedding is a method for integrating Java code and resources into BPEL processes. It allows us to embed Java code snippets directly into BPEL process code. This provides the opportunity to use Java for certain aspects where BPEL does not provide an appropriate activity. It also provides a possibility to use Java code to call other Java resources (EJBs, JCA, JMS, and so on).

To embed Java code snippets into BPEL, Oracle provides a custom BPEL activity called `<exec>`, defined in the `http://schemas.oracle.com/bpel/extension` namespace. This namespace is usually declared with the `bpelx` prefix, so we write the activity as `<bpelx:exec>`.

The BPEL server will execute the Java code, embedded in the `<exec>` activity, within its **JTA (Java Transaction API)** transaction context. If the embedded Java code calls EJBs (session or entity beans), the transactional context will be automatically propagated. If an exception occurs during the execution of the embedded Java code, the exception will automatically be converted to a BPEL fault and thrown to the BPEL process.

The `<exec>` activity supports three attributes (in addition to the BPEL standard attributes):

- `import`: Used to import Java packages.
- `language`: Denotes the used language. Currently the only supported language is Java, but support for other languages such as C# may be added.
- `version`: Denotes the version of the language. The supported versions of Java are 1.3, 1.4, and 1.5.

The `<exec>` activity also provides built-in methods we can use in the embedded Java code. They allow us to access and update BPEL variables, get JNDI access, update the audit trail, and set priorities, and other parameters. These built-in methods are explained in the following table.

Method	Description
`Object getVariableData(String name)`	Access BPEL variables
`Object getVariableData(String name, String partOrQuery)`	
`Object getVariableData(String name, String part, String query)`	
`void setVariableData(String name, Object value)`	Update BPEL variables
`void setVariableData(String name, String part, Object value)`	
`void setVariableData(String name, String part, String query, Object value)`	
`void addAuditTrailEntry(String message, Object detail)` `void addAuditTrailEntry(Throwable t)`	Add an entry or an exception to the audit trail
`Object lookup(String name)`	JNDI lookup
`Locator getLocator()`	Access to BPEL Process Manager Locator service
`long getInstanceId()`	Returns the process instance unique ID
`void setTitle(String title)` `String getTitle()`	Set/get the title of the process instance
`void setStatus(String status)` `String getStatus()`	Set/get the status of the process instance
`void setPriority(int priority)` `int getPriority()`	Set/get the priority of the process instance
`void setCreator(String creator)` `String getCreator()`	Set/get the creator of the process instance

Method	Description
`void setCustomKey(String customKey)` `String getCustomKey()`	Get/set the custom key for the process instance
`void setMetadata(String metadata)` `String getMetadata()`	Get/set the metadata of the process instance
`void setIndex(int i, String value )` `String getIndex(int i)`	Get/set the search index, `i` can range from 1 to 6
`File getContentFile(String rPath)`	Access to the files stored in the BPEL suitcase (JAR)
`String getPreference(String key)`	Access to the preferences defined in the `bpel.xml` deployment descriptor

Invoking a Java class from embedded code

Now we will modify our `TravelApproval` BPEL process code. Instead of invoking the `EmployeeTravelStatus` service, we will use the `<exec>` activity, which will return the employee travel status and set the `EmployeeTravelStatusResponse` variable. First we will drag-and-drop the **Java Embedding** activity from the **Component Palette** to the process. If we double-click it, the **Java Embedding** editor opens. Here we can enter the name and choose the Java version. In the **Code Snippet** text area, we can write the Java code as shown in the following screenshot:

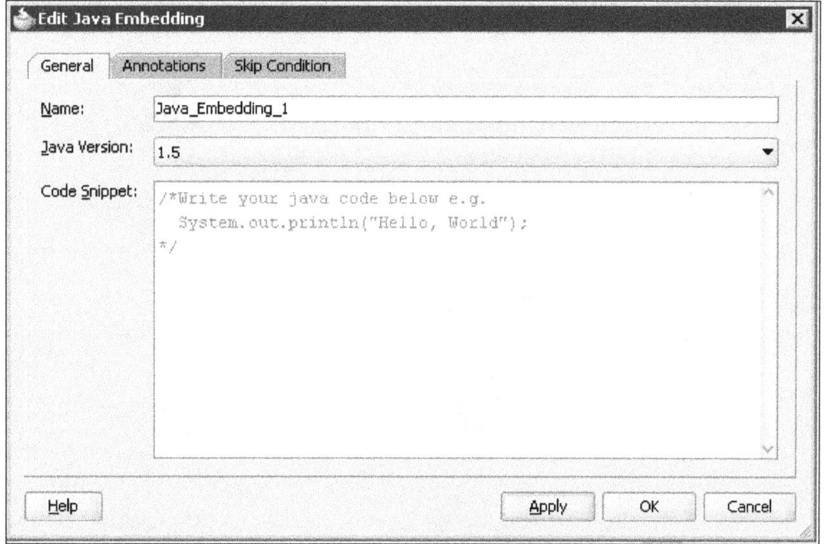

In case we want to use custom Java classes, we have to create JAR files and add them to the `application_name/project/SCA-INF/lib` directory. In our example, we will use the same Java classes, which are used to implement the `EmployeeTravelStatus` service—`EmployeeTravelStatusImpl`, `EmployeeType`, and `TravelClassType`. In order to use those classes, we have to import the DOM Element and our classes using the **Source** code view.

```
<process...>
...
  <sequence>
    <receive.../>
    ...
    <bpelx:exec import="com.packtpub.service.employee.*"/>
    <bpelx:exec import="org.w3c.dom.Element"/>
    <bpelx:exec name="Java_Embedding_1" version="1.5"
      language="java"><![CDATA[...]]></bpelx:exec>
    ...
    <invoke.../>
  </sequence>
</process>
```

Now we will write the Java code. First we have to retrieve the employee data from the `TravelRequest` BPEL variable using the `getVariableData()` function. Then we invoke the `employeeTravelStatus()` method to get employee travel status. We then add an entry to the trail. Finally, we set the `EmployeeTravelStatusResponse` BPEL variable using the `setVariableData()` function. Our Java code now looks as follows:

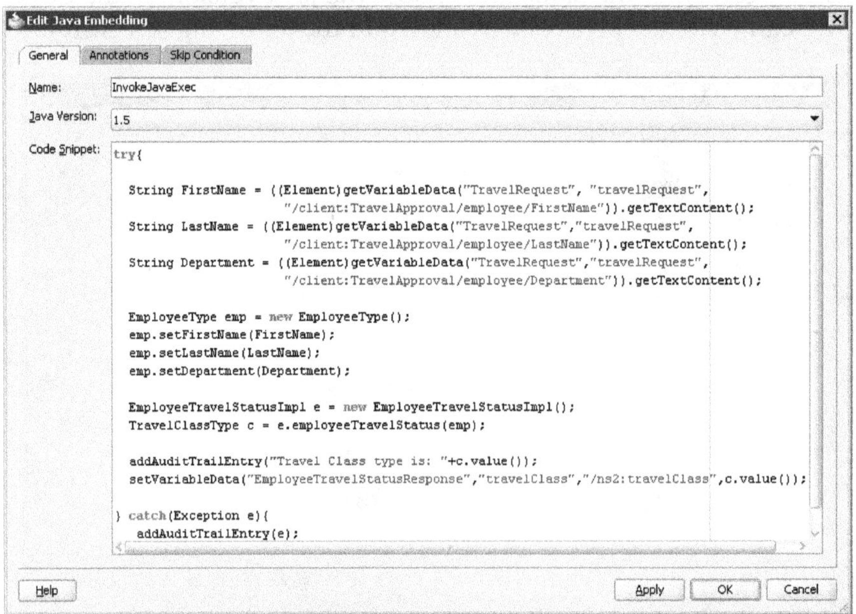

The next figure shows the changed `RetrieveEmployeeTravelStatus` scope:

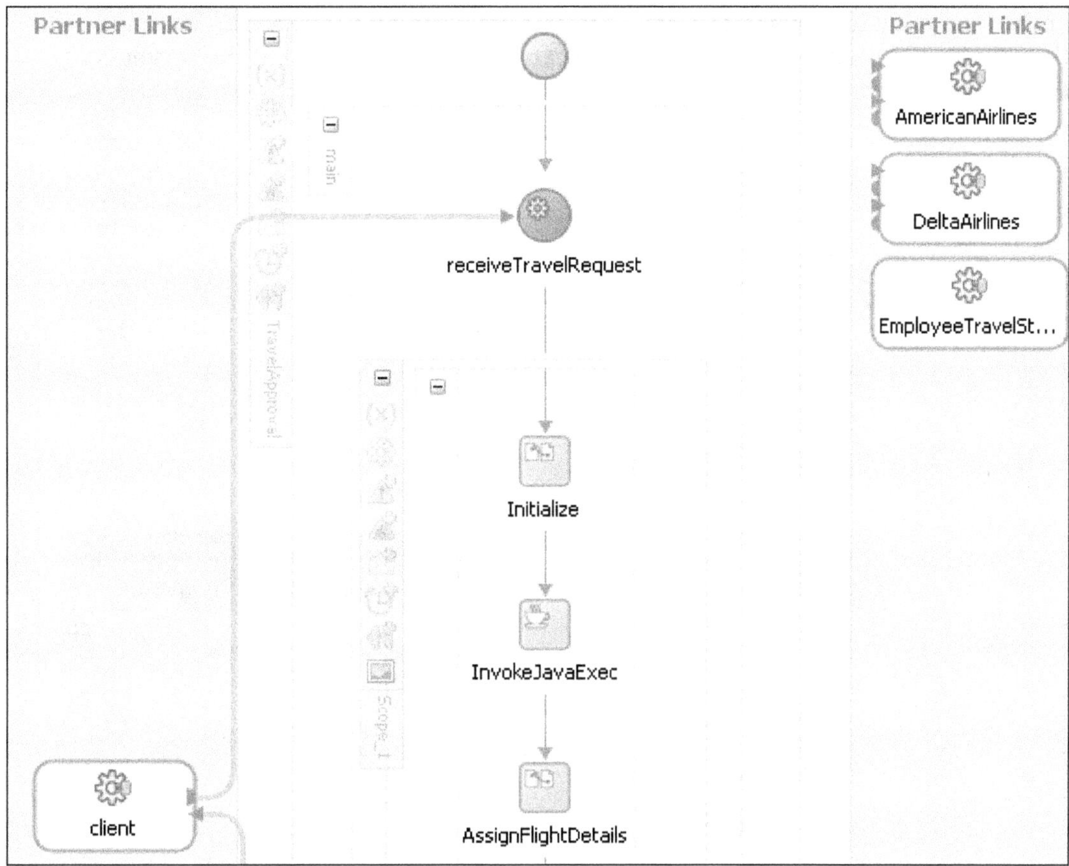

Now we are ready to deploy the process using JDeveloper. We will use EM Console to start the process and observe the visual flow, where we can see that the Java embedded code has been executed, as shown in the next screenshot. To ensure that the Java class has been invoked, we can observe the output at the server console window.

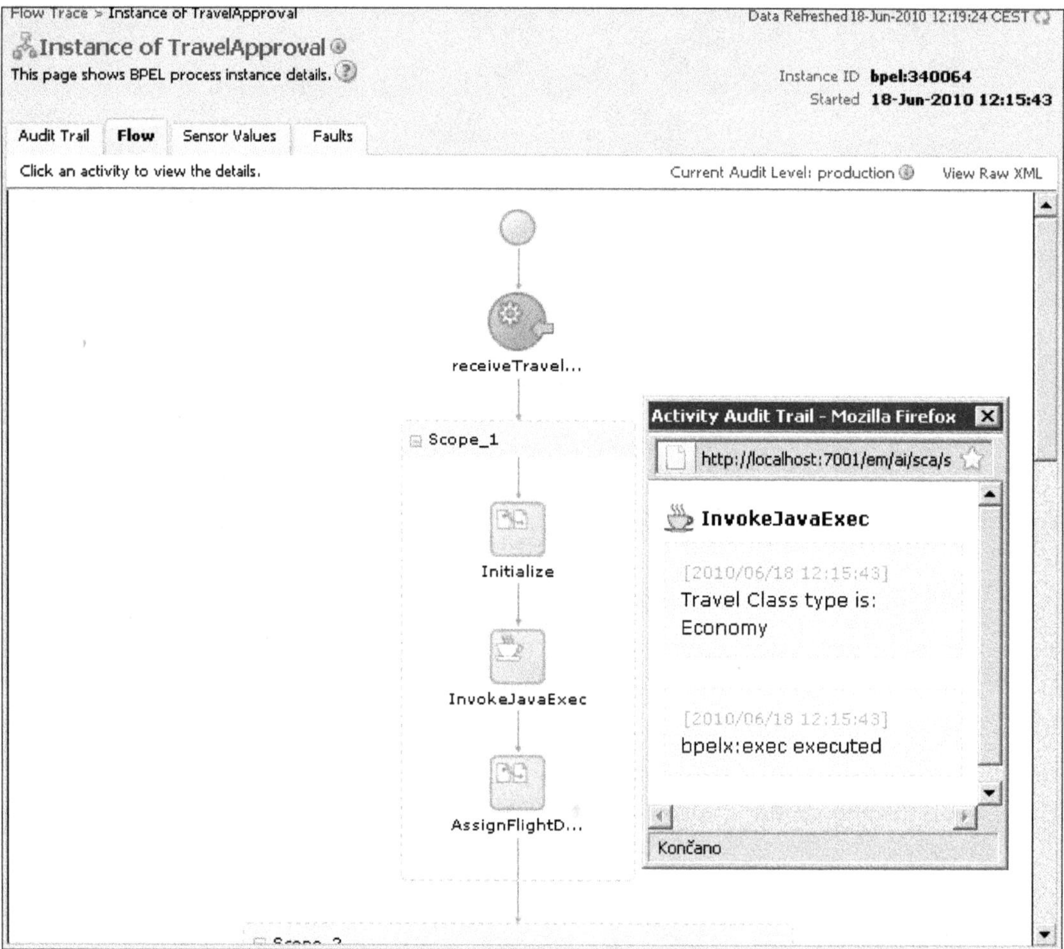

In the next section, we will look at the fault management framework.

Fault management framework

In addition to standard BPEL fault handling mechanism, Oracle SOA Suite 11*g* provides a generic fault management framework for handling faults in BPEL processes. This framework presents an alternative to designing BPEL processes with `<catch>` activities and allows us to externalize fault handling in a separate file, which makes the BPEL code more readable. Using the fault management framework, we are able to catch both business and runtime faults for an `<invoke>` activity.
We use the fault policy file (`fault-policies.xml`) to define fault conditions and corresponding recovery actions. Each fault condition specifies a particular fault or groups of faults, which it attempts to handle, and the corresponding action for it.
We can choose between the following supported recovery actions:

- **Retry**: When we want to retry the failed `<invoke>` activity. We can set the number of retries and the interval between retries (static, exponential).
- **Human intervention**: The activity stops processing. We can manually perform recovery actions using the EM Console.
- **Terminate process**: Terminates the process.
- **Java code**: We can execute an external Java class. The Java class must implement a method that returns a string (`REPLAY`, `RETHROW`, `ABORT`, `RETRY`, `MANUAL`).
- **Rethrow fault**: The fault management framework rethrows the fault to the BPEL fault handlers.
- **Replay Scope**: Replays a scope in which the fault has occurred.

As fault policy is not specific to a composite, we also need a fault policy binding file (`fault-bindings.xml`) file, which is used to associate the policies from the policy file with specific SOA composite applications, service components, or reference-binding components. A fault policy file and fault policy bindings files are usually placed in the same directory as the `composite.xml` file. However, they can also be stored in different locations, allowing us to reuse policy definitions across multiple components, composites, and projects.

Fault policies defined with the fault management framework override any fault handling defined in the BPEL process. However, using the fault management framework, we can rethrow faults back to the `<catch>` activities.

In this chapter, we will demonstrate the use of fault policies by shutting-down the `EmployeeTravelStatus` service, which will result in a remote fault. We will define the fault-handling policy to handle this exception using the human intervention recovery action.

Creating a fault policy

First we will create a `fault-policies.xml` file and save it to the same directory as `composite.xml`. We can use the following template:

```
<?xml version="1.0" encoding="UTF-8" ?>
<faultPolicies xmlns="http://schemas.oracle.com/bpel/faultpolicy">
  <faultPolicy version="2.0.1" id=""
    xmlns:env="http://schemas.xmlsoap.org/ soap/envelope/"
    xmlns:xs="http://www.w3.org/2001/XMLSchema"
    xmlns="http://schemas.oracle.com/bpel/faultpolicy"
    xmlns:xsi="http://www.w3.org/2001/ XMLSchema-instance">
    <Conditions>
        <!-- Add your fault handlers here -->
    </Conditions>
    <Actions>
        <Action id="my-java-handler">
        <javaAction className=
          "soatraining.faulthandling. MyFaultHandler"
          defaultAction="ora-terminate" propertySet="myProps">
            <returnValue value="OK" ref="ora-rethrow-fault"/>
        </javaAction>
        </Action>
        <!-- Retry -->
        <Action id="ora-retry">
            <retry>
                <retryCount>4</retryCount>
                <retryInterval>2</retryInterval>
                <exponentialBackoff/>
            </retry>
        </Action>
        <!-- Rethrow action -->
        <Action id="ora-rethrow-fault">
            <rethrowFault/>
        </Action>
        <!-- Human Intervention -->
        <Action id="ora-human-intervention">
            <humanIntervention/>
        </Action>
        <!-- Terminate -->
        <Action id="ora-terminate">
            <abort/>
        </Action>
    </Actions>
    <Properties>
```

```
        <propertySet name="myProps">
            <property name="logFileName">myfaulthandler.log</property>
            <property name="logFileDir">c:\temp</property>
        </propertySet>
    </Properties>
  </faultPolicy>
</faultPolicies>
```

Now we have to edit the created file. First we specify the ID of the policy file (for example `TravelApprovalFaults`). Then we add a new entry to the `<Conditions>` and specify the type of the fault we want to handle (in our case `bpelx:remoteFault`) and the recovery action (in our case `ora-human-intervention`). Under `<Actions>`, we can see all supported types of recovery actions:

```
<?xml version="1.0" encoding="UTF-8" ?>
<faultPolicies xmlns="http://schemas.oracle.com/bpel/faultpolicy">
  <faultPolicy version="2.0.1" id="TravelApprovalFaults"
    xmlns:env="http://schemas.xmlsoap.org/ soap/envelope/"
    xmlns:xs="http://www.w3.org/2001/XMLSchema"
    xmlns="http://schemas.oracle.com/bpel/faultpolicy"
    xmlns:xsi="http://www.w3.org/2001/ XMLSchema-instance">
    <Conditions>
        <faultName
          xmlns:bpelx="http://schemas.oracle.com/bpel/extension"
            name="bpelx:remoteFault">
        <condition>
            <action ref="ora-human-intervention"/>
        </condition>
        </faultName>
    </Conditions>
    <Actions>
        <Action id="my-java-handler">
            <javaAction
              className="soatraining.faulthandling. MyFaultHandler"
              defaultAction="ora-terminate" propertySet="myProps">
                <returnValue value="OK" ref="ora-rethrow-fault"/>
            </javaAction>
        </Action>
        <!-- Retry -->
        <Action id="ora-retry">
            <retry>
                <retryCount>4</retryCount>
                <retryInterval>2</retryInterval>
                <exponentialBackoff/>
            </retry>
        </Action>
```

```
            <!-- Rethrow action -->
            <Action id="ora-rethrow-fault">
                <rethrowFault/>
            </Action>
            <!-- Human Intervention -->
            <Action id="ora-human-intervention">
                <humanIntervention/>
            </Action>
            <!-- Terminate -->
            <Action id="ora-terminate">
                <abort/>
            </Action>
        </Actions>
        <Properties>
            <propertySet name="myProps">
               <property name="logFileName">myfaulthandler.log</property>
               <property name="logFileDir">c:\temp</property>
            </propertySet>
        </Properties>
      </faultPolicy>
    </faultPolicies>
```

We save the file. Now we will create the `fault-bindings.xml` file and save it in the same directory. We will use this file to associate the `fault-policies.xml` file to our SOA composite application. We have to specify the ID of the previously created `fault-policies.xml` file. The content of the file is as follows:

```
<?xml version="1.0" encoding="UTF-8" ?>
<faultPolicyBindings version="2.0.1"
  xmlns="http://schemas.oracle.com/bpel/faultpolicy"
  xmlns:xsi="http://www.w3.org/2001/XMLSchemainstance">
  <composite faultPolicy="TravelApprovalFaults"/>
</faultPolicyBindings>
```

Next we will deploy our SOA composite application. In order to test the defined fault policy, we will shutdown the `EmployeeTravelStatus` service. We can do this in the EM Console by clicking the service and opening the **Application Deployment** menu and then selecting **Control | Shut Down**, as shown in the following screenshot:

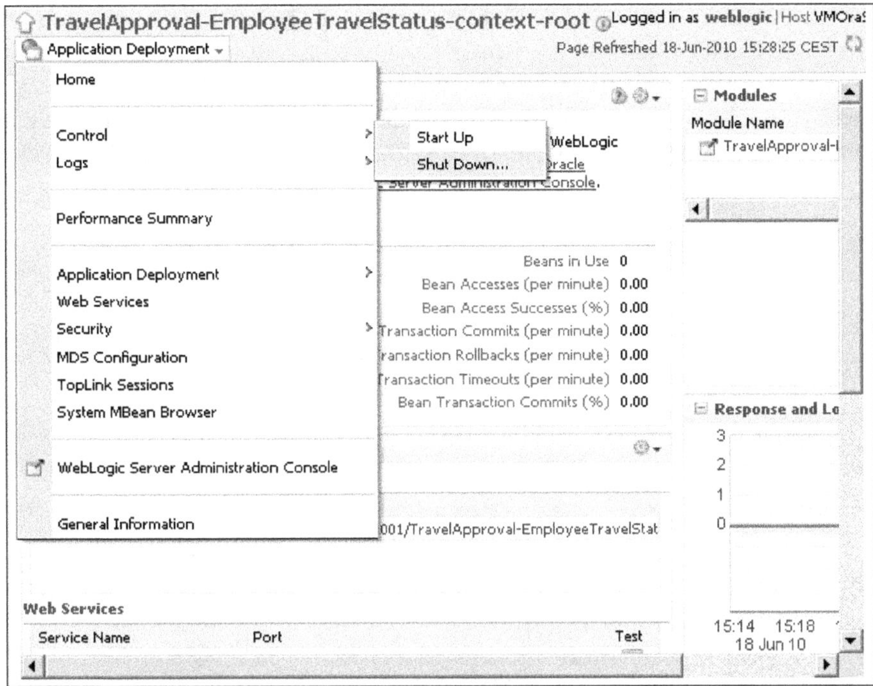

Now we will initiate a new process instance. If we view the audit trail of the created instance, we can see that the invocation of the `EmployeeTravelStatus` service has faulted, but it is waiting for manual recovery.

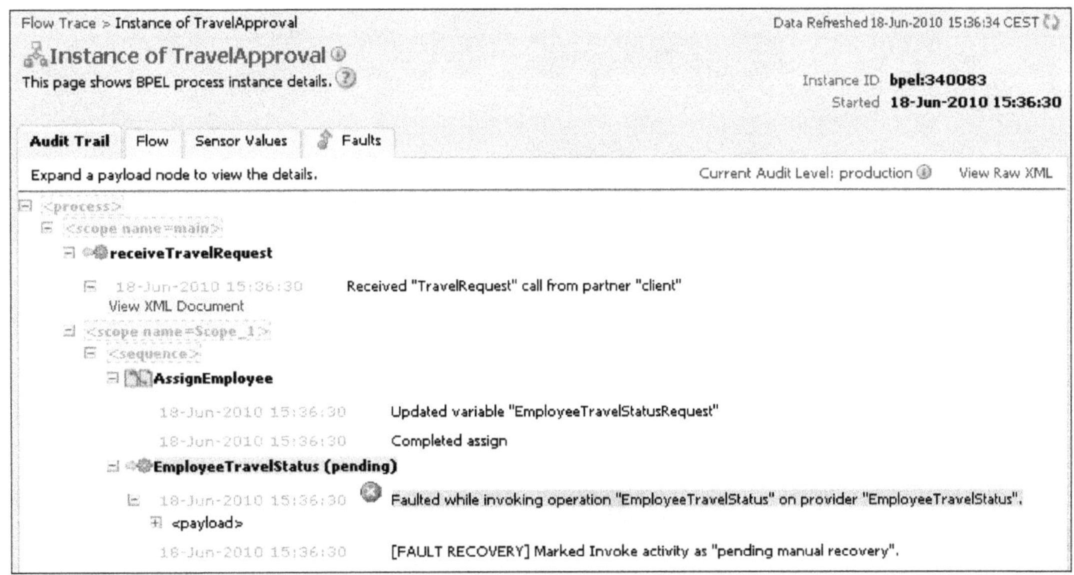

Before attempting to recover, we will startup the `EmployeeTravelStatus` service. If we want to go back to the instance audit trail, we can switch to the **Faults** tab. Here we can select the fault and try to recover the instance. We can choose between recover actions such as **Retry**, **Abort**, **Replay**, **Rethrow**, and **Continue**. We can also change the values of process variables. We will select **Retry** and click **Recover**.

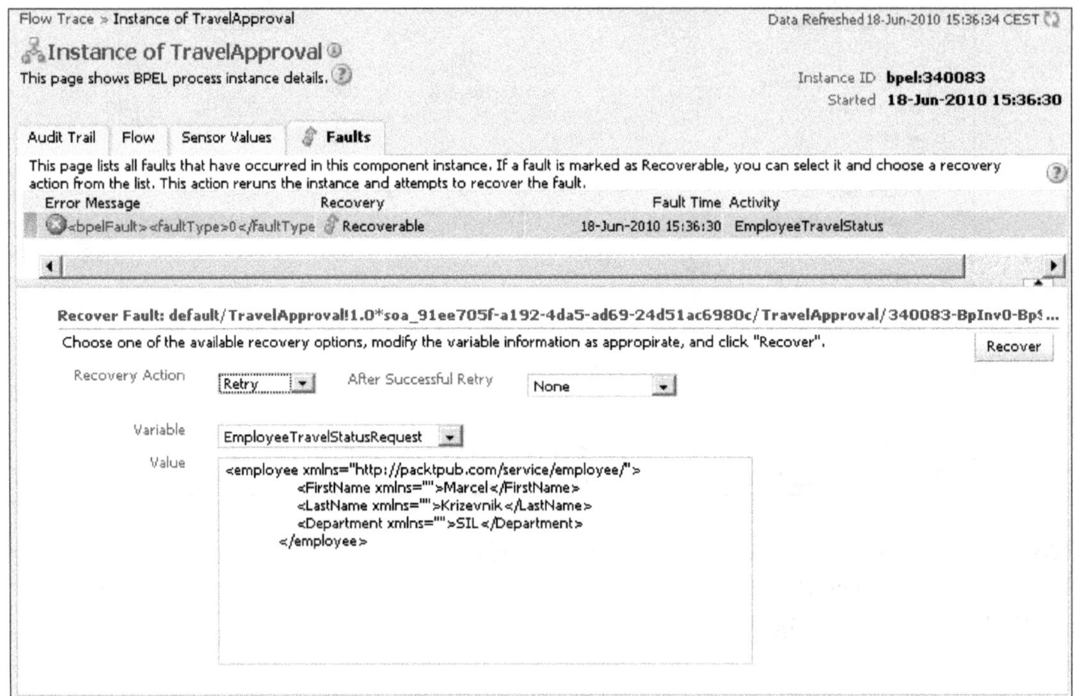

If we switch back to the **Audit Trail** tab, we can see that the instance was successfully recovered and has completed successfully.

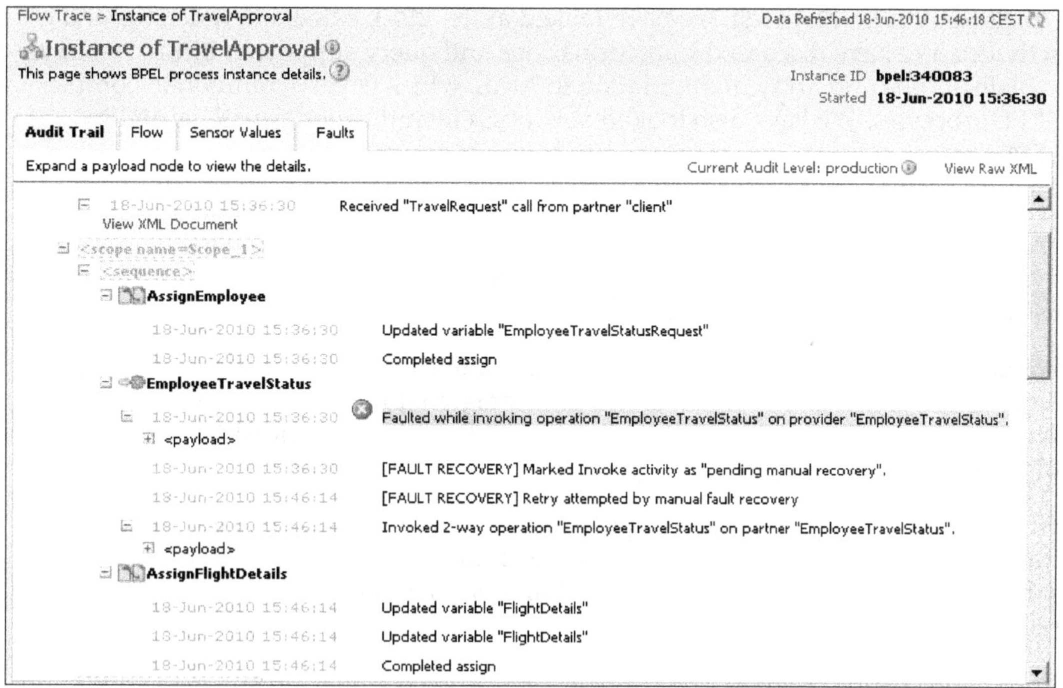
Flow Trace > Instance of TravelApproval
Data Refreshed 18-Jun-2010 15:46:18 CEST
Instance of TravelApproval
This page shows BPEL process instance details.
Instance ID bpel:340083
Started 18-Jun-2010 15:36:30
Audit Trail
Flow
Sensor Values
Faults
Expand a payload node to view the details.
Current Audit Level: production
View Raw XML
18-Jun-2010 15:36:30 Received "TravelRequest" call from partner "client"
View XML Document
<scope name=Scope_1>
<sequence>
AssignEmployee
18-Jun-2010 15:36:30 Updated variable "EmployeeTravelStatusRequest"
18-Jun-2010 15:36:30 Completed assign
EmployeeTravelStatus
18-Jun-2010 15:36:30 Faulted while invoking operation "EmployeeTravelStatus" on provider "EmployeeTravelStatus".
<payload>
18-Jun-2010 15:36:30 [FAULT RECOVERY] Marked Invoke activity as "pending manual recovery".
18-Jun-2010 15:46:14 [FAULT RECOVERY] Retry attempted by manual fault recovery
18-Jun-2010 15:46:14 Invoked 2-way operation "EmployeeTravelStatus" on partner "EmployeeTravelStatus".
<payload>
AssignFlightDetails
18-Jun-2010 15:46:14 Updated variable "FlightDetails"
18-Jun-2010 15:46:14 Updated variable "FlightDetails"
18-Jun-2010 15:46:14 Completed assign

Summary

In this chapter, we have become familiar with several advanced BPEL features of Oracle SOA Suite 11*g*. First, we have looked at the BPEL extension functions and activities. We have discussed transformations and query support in BPEL. We have explained data and array manipulation in XML, which is very common in complex BPEL processes. We have also looked at process identification functions and LDAP access.

We have looked at dynamic parallel flows, which enable us to develop BPEL processes that have a flexible number of parallel flows. Related to parallel flows are dynamic partner links, which allow us to define partner links at runtime. This allows us to build flexible BPEL processes.

We have also looked at Notification Service. Notification Service allows us to send e-mails, text messages, voice mail and thus integrate BPEL processes with messaging. We have also looked at Java embedding in BPEL. Although embedding Java into BPEL is not a sound practice, it is good to know that it is possible.

Finally, we have looked at the fault management framework. The fault management framework allows us to control and manage faults in BPEL processes in a more sophisticated way than with BPEL fault handlers. This way we can achieve higher reliability of BPEL process instances.

In the next chapter, we will look at additional advanced BPEL features of Oracle SOA Suite 11*g*.

6
Entity Variables, Master and Detail Processes, Security, and Business Events in BPEL

In this chapter, we will continue the discussion of the advanced BPEL features provided by the Oracle SOA Suite 11*g* PS2. We will discuss the Oracle's extension to standard BPEL variables—Entity variables. As it is a very important feature, we will also show how to secure SOA Composite applications by attaching security policies. Finally, we will overview two new BPEL extensions that Oracle introduced in SOA Suite 11*g*—the support for Maser-Detail processes and the ability to publish and subscribe to business events from a BPEL process. We will demonstrate the use of presented features on the asynchronous `TravelApproval` BPEL process that we have already developed in *Chapter 2*.

In this chapter, we will discuss the following:

- Entity variables
- Master and Detail processes
- Securing SOA Composite applications
- Using Business Events in BPEL

Entity variables

Support for entity variables is an Oracle extension that has been introduced in Oracle SOA Suite 11*g*. Entity variables are not like regular DOM variables which are disconnected message payload. In fact, entity variables use SDO-based in-memory data structure and are able to detect changes to underlying data in the data source. When using entity variables, only a reference (key) to the data is stored to the BPEL dehydration store (as part of process instance state) when the instance is dehydrated, while the actual data is stored in a remote data source (database table). During every instance rehydration, the infrastructure automatically loads fresh data, as other applications may change the data while the process instance is dehydrated. Therefore, we do not have to be concerned about refreshing our local copy of data. Entity variables can be especially useful in long-running BPEL processes, when we want to avoid using stale data.

In order to use entity variables, we first have to create the Oracle **Application Development Framework Business Component** (**ADF-BC**) backend data access service. The ADF-BC service is responsible for updating remote data every time the BPEL process is dehydrated to the database (when entering the `<wait>` activity or during the asynchronous call) and for loading fresh data during instance rehydration. Then we add the ADF-BC service as a reference to the SOA composite diagram and wire it to the BPEL process. Finally, we can create the entity variable and connect it with the ADF-BC partner link.

In order to enable the use of entity variables in BPEL processes, Oracle introduced the following BPEL extension activities (activities are defined in the `http://schemas.oracle.com/bpel/extension` namespace, usually declared with the `bpelx` prefix):

- `<bpelx:bindEntity>`: Used to set the key of the entity variable. This action connects the entity variable to a row in a database.
- `<bpelx:createEntity>`: Used to create a new entity variable. This action inserts a new row in the table.
- `<bpelx:removeEntity>`: Used to remove the entity variable. This action removes a row from the table.

In BPEL processes, entity variables can be used in the same way as standard DOM-based variables. However, when using SDO-based variables, there are some limitations when using advanced XPath features (for example, there is no support for `and`, `or`, and `not`).

To demonstrate the use of entity variables, we will modify our `TravelApproval process`. Instead of calling the `EmployeeTravelStatus` service, we will use the entity variable to get the employee travel class information directly from the database. During the execution of the BPEL process instance (we will insert a `<wait>` activity, so that the process instance will dehydrate), we will change the travel status of an employee and see that the value is automatically updated when the instance rehydrates.

If we want to demonstrate the use of the entity variable, we first need a database table to store the employee travel class information. We will use the `HR` sample schema (schema is automatically created during the Oracle database installation), which already contains an `EMPLOYEES` table. The table already contains columns, such as `EMPLOYEE_ID`, `FIRST_NAME`, `LAST_NAME`, and so on. However, we will alter the table by adding two new columns (`DEPARTMENT_NAME` and `TRAVEL_CLASS`). Now all employee-related data will be accessible through the entity variable; therefore, we will also change the input to the BPEL process. Instead of passing employee data, we will just pass the unique identifier (`employeeId`). After modifying the `EMPLOYEES` table, we will create new ADF-BC service, which will provide access to remote data. Then we will remove the `EmployeeTravelStatus` reference from our composite application and add a new reference (newly created ADF-BC service). Finally, we will create a new entity variable (`EmployeeEV`) and bind it to the `employeeId` identifier from the `TravelRequest` input message.

Altering the EMPLOYEES table

First, we have to connect to the HR sample schema as a user `HR` (if the account is locked we have to unlock it first). Then, we alter the `EMPLOYEES` table by adding two new columns—`DEPARTMENT_NAME` and `TRAVEL_CLASS`. The `EMPLOYEES` table now looks as follows:

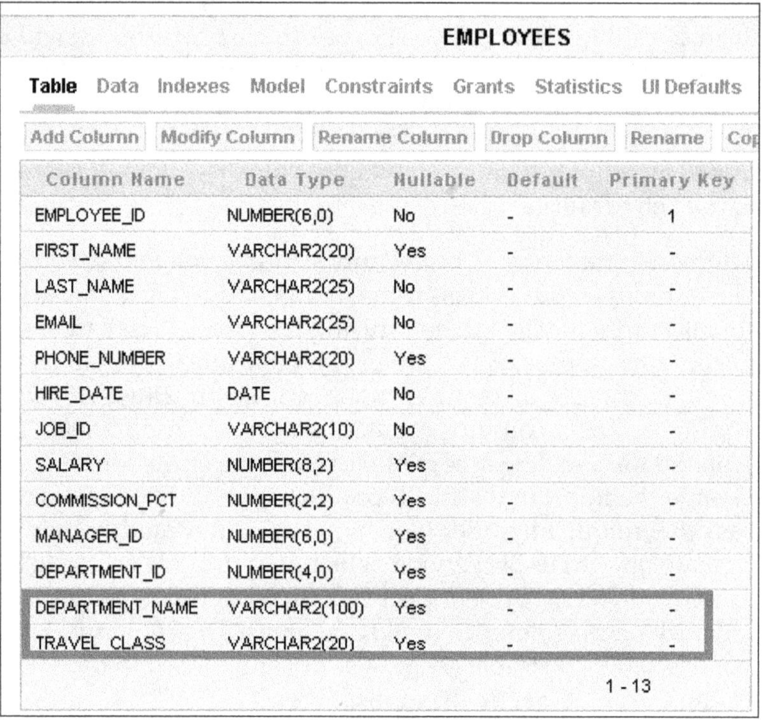

EMPLOYEES

Table Data Indexes Model Constraints Grants Statistics UI Defaults

Add Column Modify Column Rename Column Drop Column Rename Co

Column Name	Data Type	Nullable	Default	Primary Key
EMPLOYEE_ID	NUMBER(6,0)	No	-	1
FIRST_NAME	VARCHAR2(20)	Yes	-	-
LAST_NAME	VARCHAR2(25)	No	-	-
EMAIL	VARCHAR2(25)	No	-	-
PHONE_NUMBER	VARCHAR2(20)	Yes	-	-
HIRE_DATE	DATE	No	-	-
JOB_ID	VARCHAR2(10)	No	-	-
SALARY	NUMBER(8,2)	Yes	-	-
COMMISSION_PCT	NUMBER(2,2)	Yes	-	-
MANAGER_ID	NUMBER(6,0)	Yes	-	-
DEPARTMENT_ID	NUMBER(4,0)	Yes	-	-
DEPARTMENT_NAME	VARCHAR2(100)	Yes	-	-
TRAVEL_CLASS	VARCHAR2(20)	Yes	-	-

1 - 13

We can also enter some test data, which will be used later for testing.

Creating the data source

Next, we have to create a data source on the WebLogic admin server, through which the ADF-BC service will connect to the database. We open the WebLogic Server Administration Console, using the URL `http://host_name:port/console`, where `host_name` is the name of the host on which the Administration Console is installed and `port` is a number that is set during the installation process (default is `7001`). Under the **Domain Structure**, we select **Services** | **JDBC** | **Data Sources**. We click **New** to create a new data source. The following page opens:

We enter the **JNDI Name** (`jdbc/HRDataSource`) and **Name** of the data source. We click **Next** three times. Then we have to enter the connection details as shown in the following screenshot:

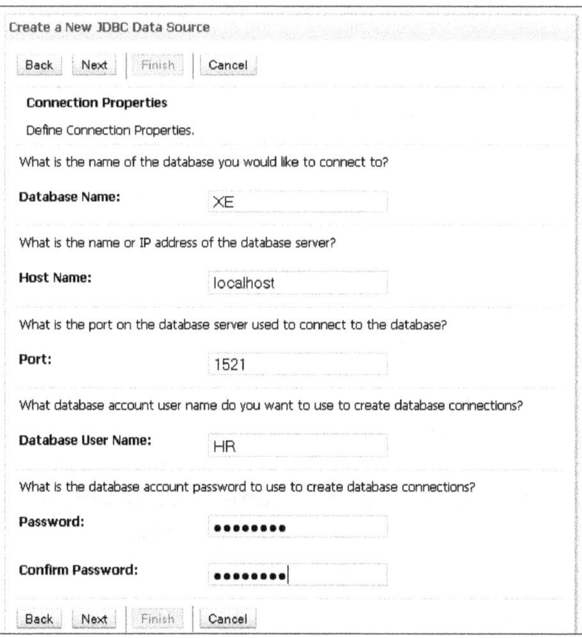

We click **Next** again. Here we can test the connection. By clicking **Next**, the final screen opens, where we select the target server.

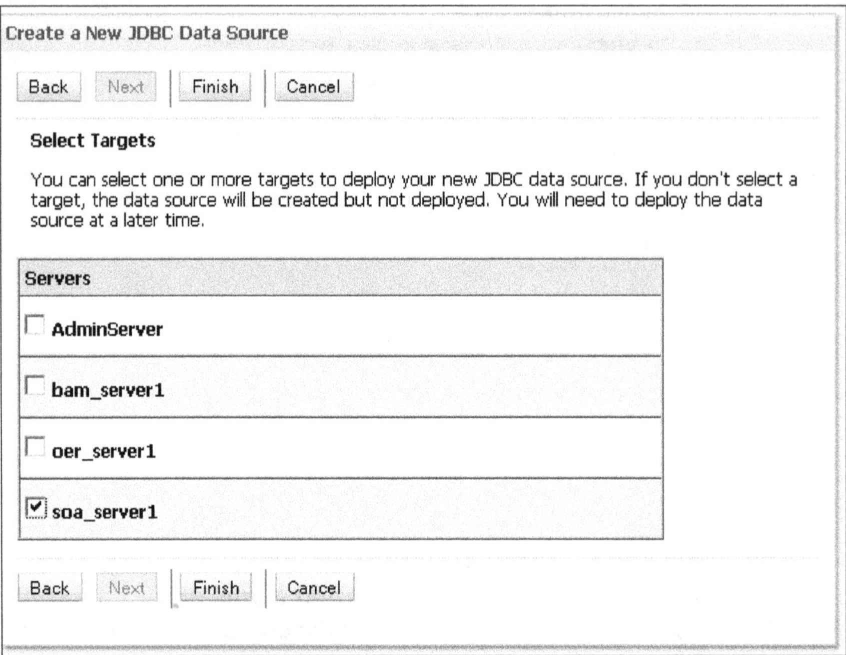
Create a New JDBC Data Source
Back
Next
Finish
Cancel
Select Targets
You can select one or more targets to deploy your new JDBC data source. If you don't select a target, the data source will be created but not deployed. You will need to deploy the data source at a later time.
Servers
AdminServer
bam_server1
oer_server1
soa_server1
Back
Next
Finish
Cancel

We click **Finish** to confirm all previous steps.

Creating the ADF-BC service

In this section, we first create a new generic application and project for the ADF-BC service.

> As ADF is out of the scope of this book, we will not discuss the details and will just provide the basic steps for creating an ADF-BC service.

We set the name of the project to `EmployeeSDO` and select **ADF Business Components** from **Available Project Technologies**. Then we click **Finish** to close the empty project. Next, we right-click the created project and select **New**. In the **New Gallery** window, we select **ADF Business Components**. On the **Items** list on the right side, we select **Business Components from Tables**.

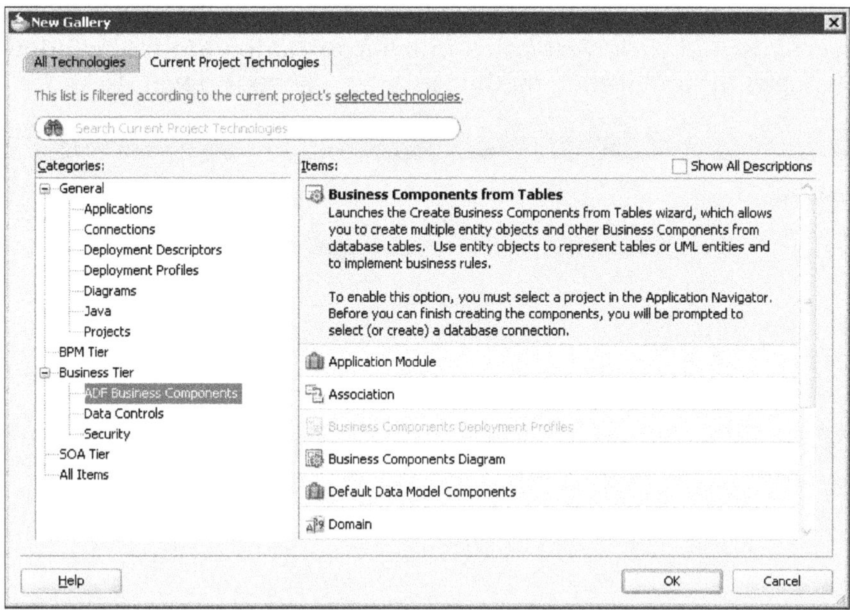

In the next step, we have to create a connection to the `HR` database. After entering the connection parameters, we click **OK**. The **Entity Objects** screen opens. We click the **Query** button to retrieve tables. We select the `EMPLOYEES` table and move it to the **Selected** list on the right.

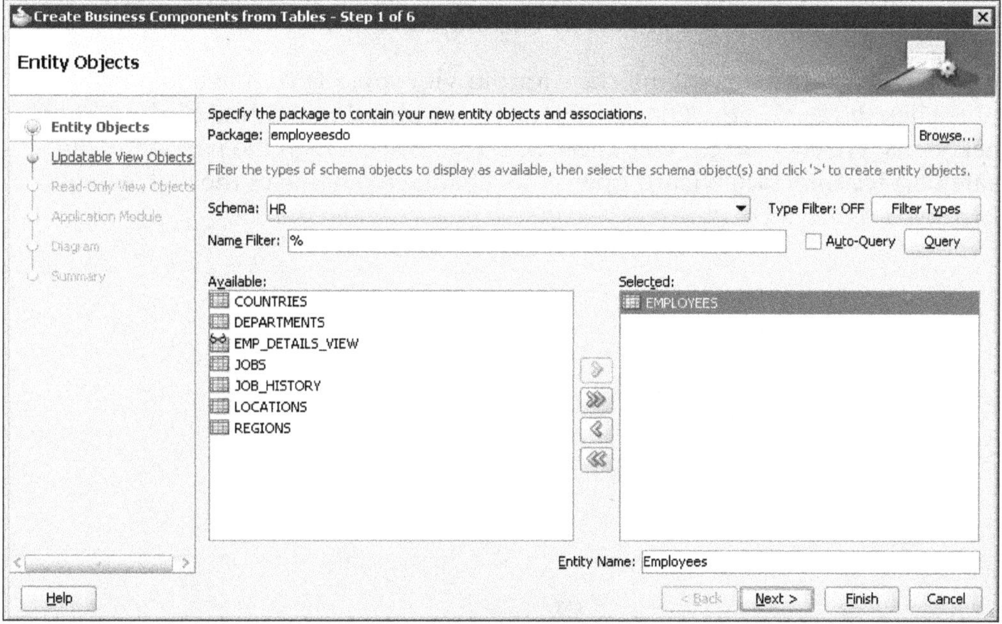

We click **Next**. The **Updatable View Object** window opens. We move the `Employees` to the **Selected** list and click **Next** twice. In the **Application Module** window we enter the name of the application module as `EmployeeSDOAppModule`.

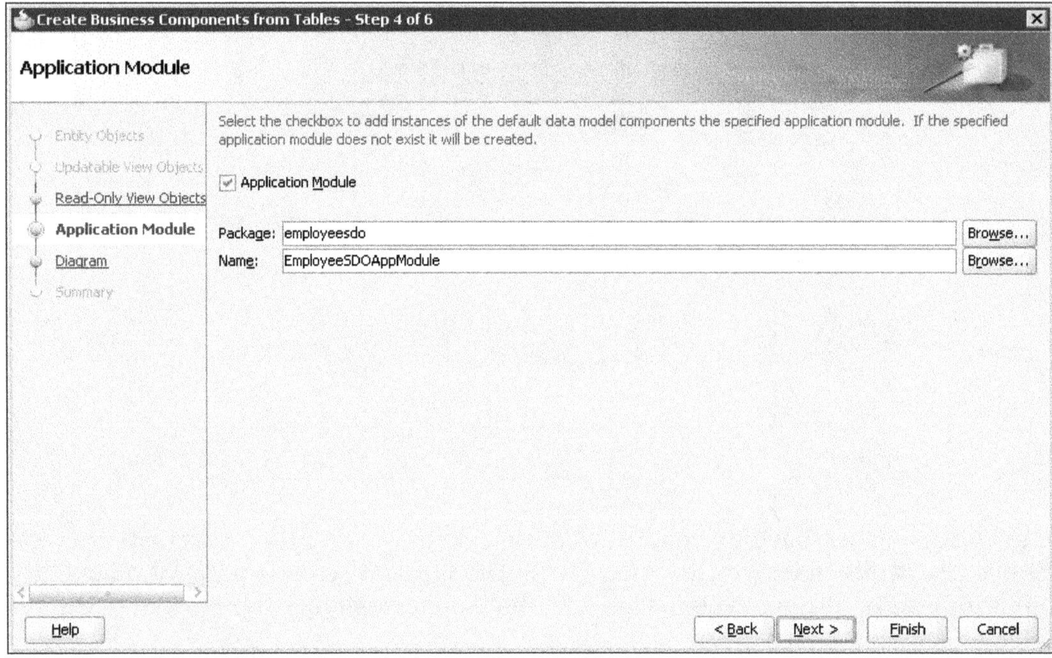

We click **Finish** and save the project by clicking **Save all**.

Next, we will create a service interface for our view object. We have to double-click the `EmployeeSDOAppModule`. The application module configuration panel opens. We click on **Service Interface**. Then we click on the *plus* sign. The **Create Service Interface** wizard opens. We change the name of the web service to `EmployeeSDOService`.

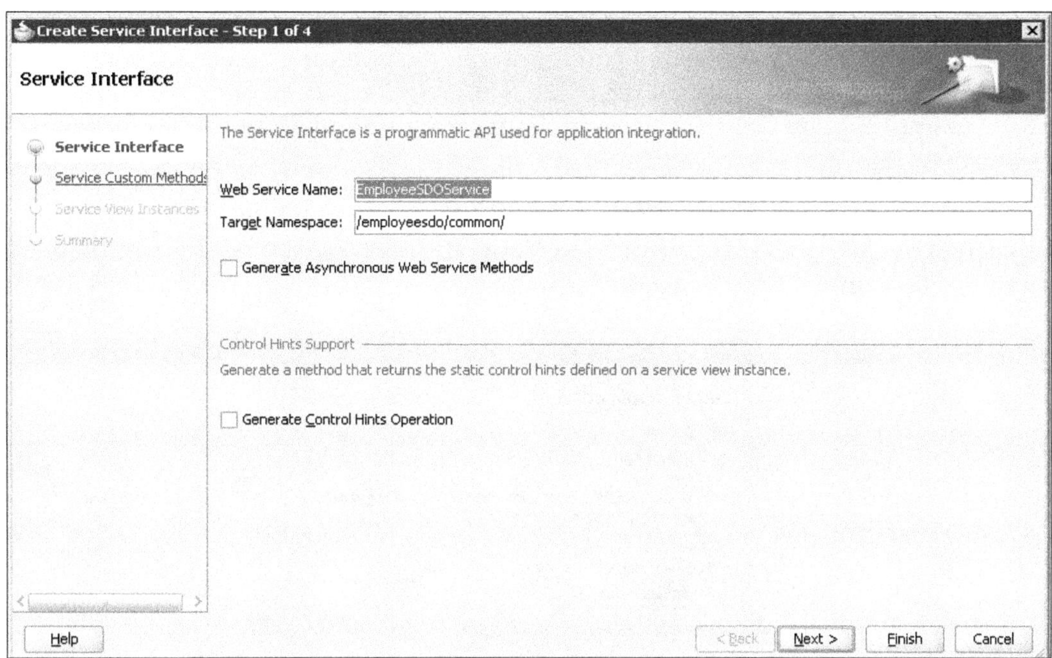

We click **Next** twice. On the **Service View Instances** screen, we move the `EmployeesView1` to the **Selected** list. On the bottom of the screen, we check all available operations.

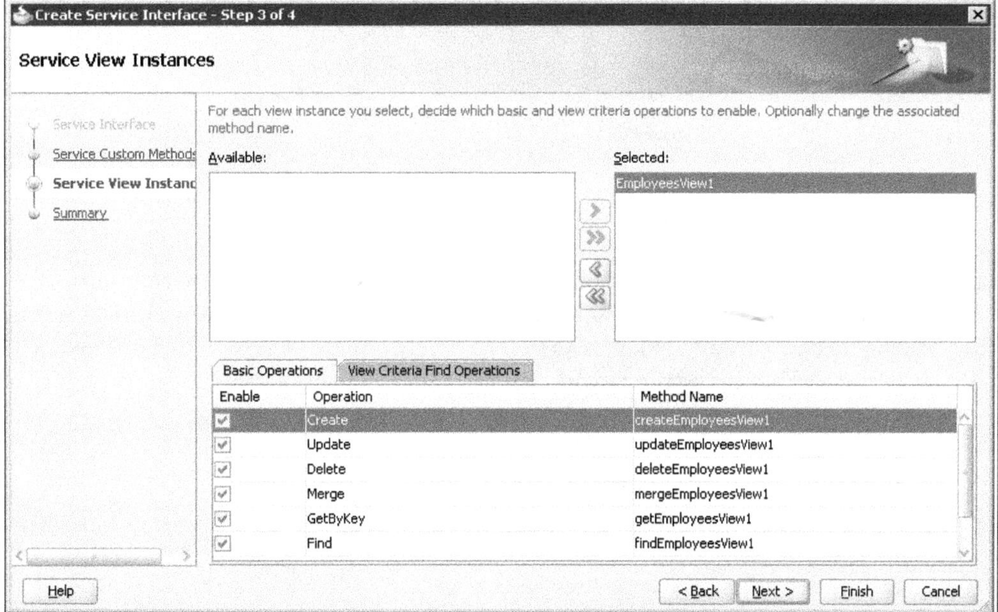

We click **Finish**. Then we open the **Configurations** on the `EmployeeSDOAppModule` and edit the `EmployeeSDOService` configuration. We enter the name of the previously created JDBC data source (`jdbc/HRDataSource`) and click **OK**. Then we select the `EmployeeSDOService` as the default configuration.

Next, we will create a new deployment profile. First, we have to right-click the `EmployeeSDO` project and select **Project Properties**. Under the **Java EE Application** we change the **Java EE Web Application Name** to `EmployeeSDO-webapp` and the **Java EE Web Context Root** to `employee-app`.

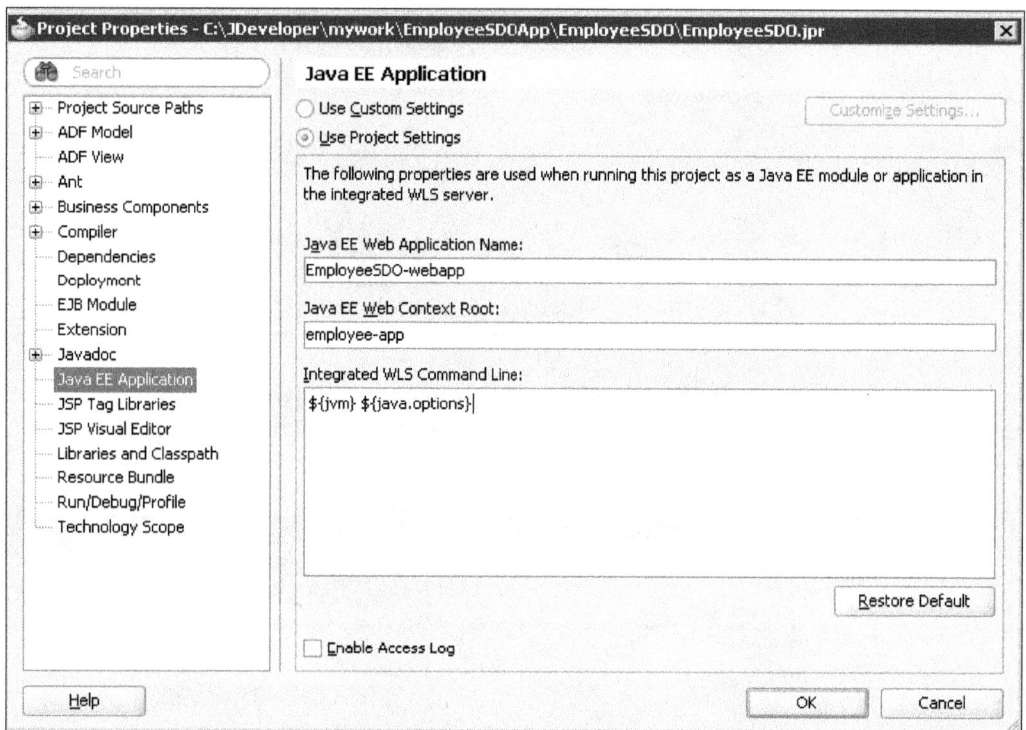

We click **OK** to close the window. Then we open the **Project Properties** again. We select **Deployment** and then click the **New** button to create a new deployment profile. As **Archive Type** we select `Business Components Service Interface`. We also change the **Name** of the profile to `employeeSDOProfile`.

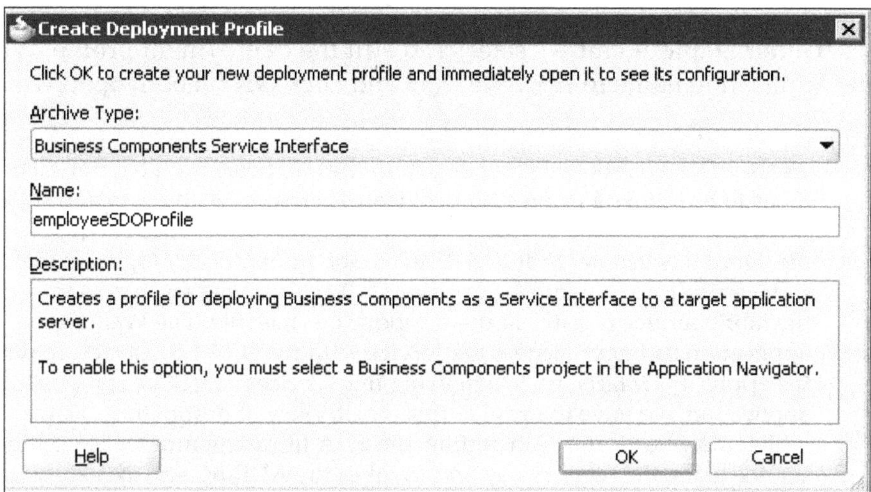

We click **OK** to close the window. Then we expand the `employeeSDOProfile` and edit the `MiddleTier`. As **Enterprise Application Name** we enter `EmployeeSDO`. We also change the name of the EAR file to `employee-app.ear`.

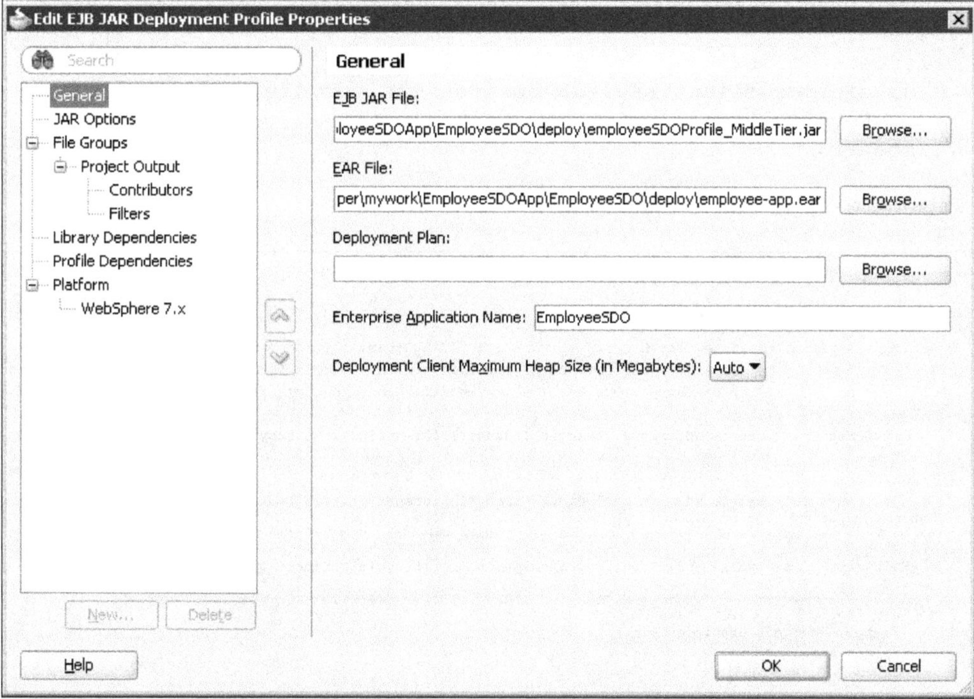

We close the window by clicking **OK** and save the project.

Next, we click on the **Application** menu in the toolbar and select **Application Properties**. Under **Deployment** we select and edit the deployment profile. We change the application name to `EmployeeApp` and click **OK** on both open windows.

> As the SDO ADF-BC service has to join the composite's global transaction, it has to be invoked using RMI protocol. Therefore, we have to add the WebLogic application listener to the `weblogic-application.xml` file. Once this listener is added, JDeveloper automatically registers the service application name (`<appname>_JBOServiceRegistry`) into the fabric service registry in the `composite.xml` file. The WebLogic application listener registers the service with the SOA Infrastructure when the application starts up. When using this service in an SOA composite application, we have to provide this registry key at design time, as we will demonstrate later. At runtime, the SOA Infrastructure looks up the service using the registry key and invokes the ADF-BC service using RMI protocol.

We open the `weblogic-application.xml` file, which can be found under **Application Resources | Descriptors | META-INF**. We switch to the source code view and paste the following code:

```
<listener>
  <listener-class>
    oracle.jbo.client.svc.ADFApplicationLifecycleListener
  </listener-class>
</listener>
```

The `weblogic-application.xml` file will now look as:

Finally, we can deploy our ADF-BC service by opening the **Application** menu and selecting **Deploy | CustomerSDO_customerSDOProfile | MyAppServerConnection**.

Modifying the SOA composite application

First, we have to modify the input of the `TravelApproval` process. Instead of passing the whole employee data (complex type `EmployeeType`), we will just pass the unique identifier (`employeeId`), which is of type `int`. Then, we will delete the `EmployeeTravelStatus` reference binding component and the BPEL activities for its invocation (in scope `RetrieveEmployeeTravelStatus`). Next, we will drag the **ADF-BC Service** component from the **Component Palette** to the **External References** swim-lane of our composite application. The **Create ADF-BC Service** window opens. We have to enter the **Name** (`EmployeeSDOService`), the **WSDL URL**, the **Registry** (`EmployeeApp_JBOServiceRegistry`), and select the **Port Type** (`EmployeeSDOService`).

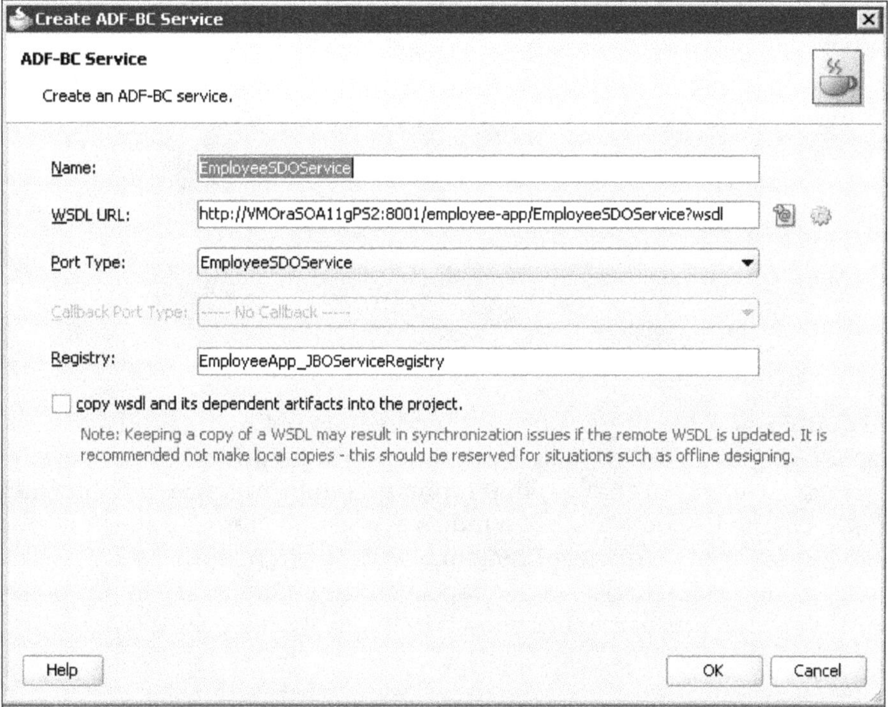

We close the window by clicking **OK**. Then we wire the `EmployeeSDOService` reference with the BPEL process. Our composite application now looks as shown in the following figure:

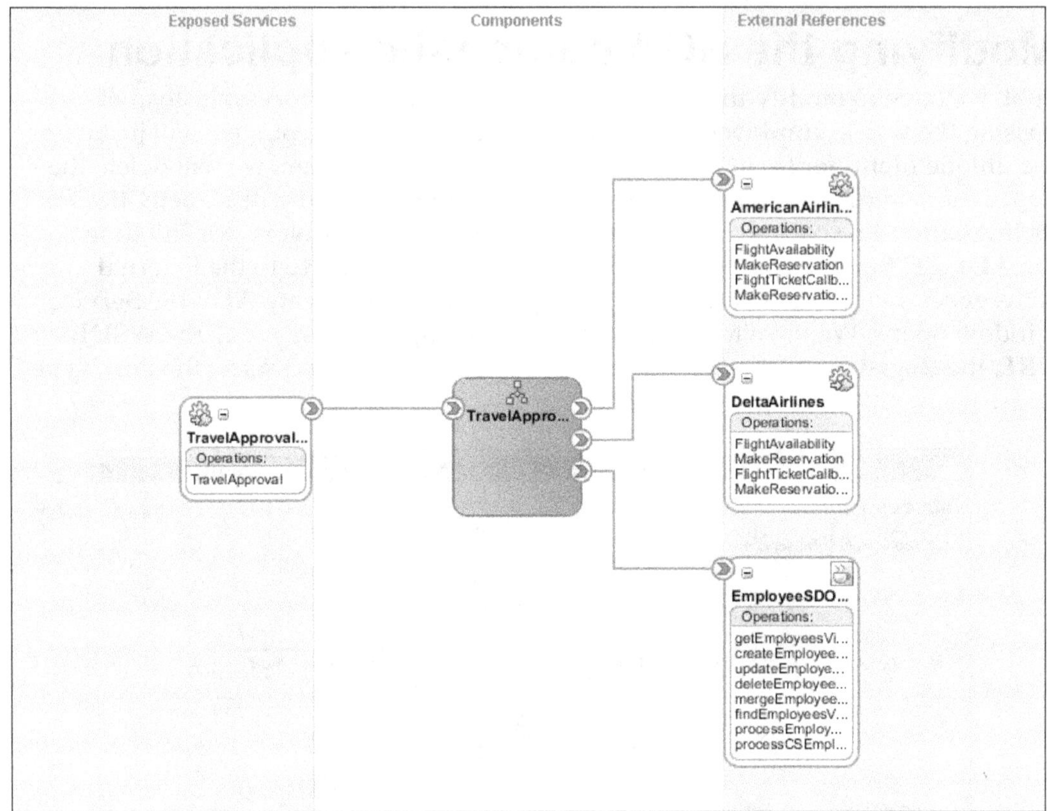

Next, we double-click the BPEL service component to get to the BPEL Component Designer. Now we will create a new entity variable (in scope `RetrieveEmployeeTravelStatus`) that represents the employee data (including travel class). On the **Create Variable** window we set the **Name** of the new entity variable to `EmployeeEV`. We select **Element** and click on the browse icon to select an element. In the **Type Chooser** we expand `Project WSDL Files` and browse to the `EmployeeViewSDO` element as shown in the next screenshot:

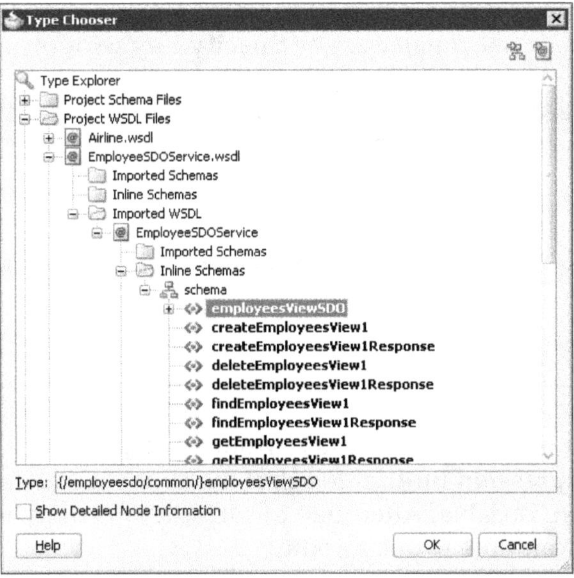

We click **OK** to close the **Type Chooser.** Back in the **Create Variable** window, we select the **Entity Variable** and choose the `EmployeeSDOService` for the partner link.

Next, we will drag the `<bindEntity>` activity from the **Component Palette** and drop it to the `RetrieveEmployeeTravelStatus` scope. After double-clicking the activity, the **Bind Entity** window opens. We set the **Name** of the activity to `BindEmployeeId` and select the **Entity Variable** (in our case `EmployeeEV`).

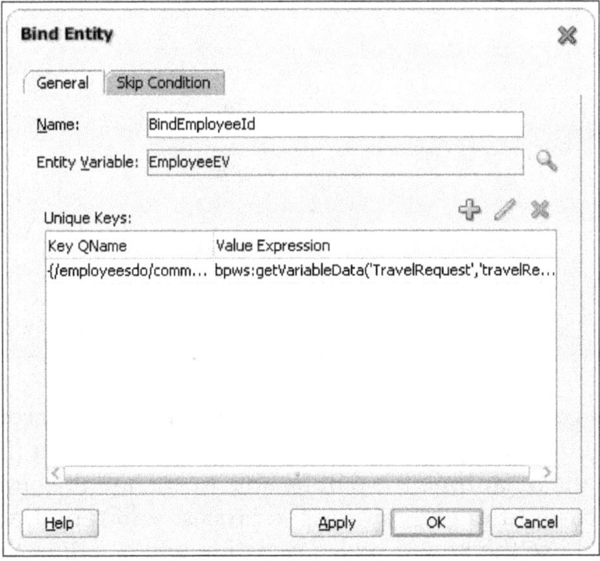

By clicking the plus sign, we have to add a unique key which will be used to bind the Entity variable to a row in a database. The **Specify Key** window opens.

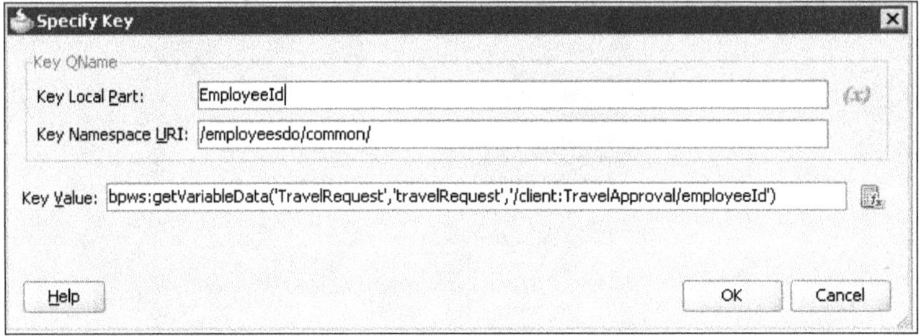

For a **Key Local Part** we select `EmployeeId` from the `EmployeeEV` variable. For **Key Value** we use the **Expression builder** to select the `employeeId` element from the input `TravelRequest` variable. After the `<bindEntity>` activity we add a `<wait>` activity and set the wait time to one minute.

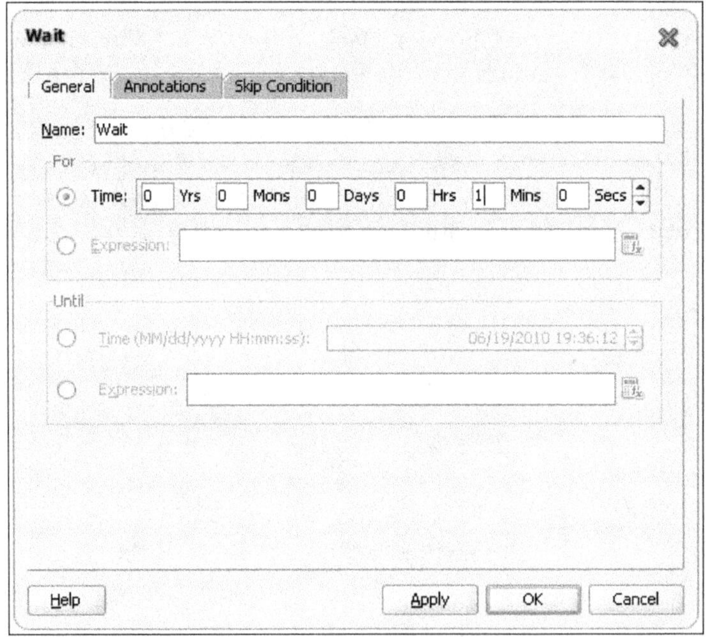

We will use `<wait>` activity just for testing purpose. When the process instance will enter the `<wait>` activity, it will dehydrate for a specified period (in our example, one minute) and in the meantime we will be able to change the employee travel class directly in the database. After one minute the process will rehydrate and we will see that the instance will use the new travel class value when calling the airline services.

We also have to add a new `<assign>` activity to set the value of the `FlightDetails` variable. We can ignore the **Variable is not initialized warning** on this `<assign>` activity, as we do not need to initialize entity variables.

Our BPEL process now looks as shown in the next screenshot (only the first part of the process that has been changed is shown to improve readability):

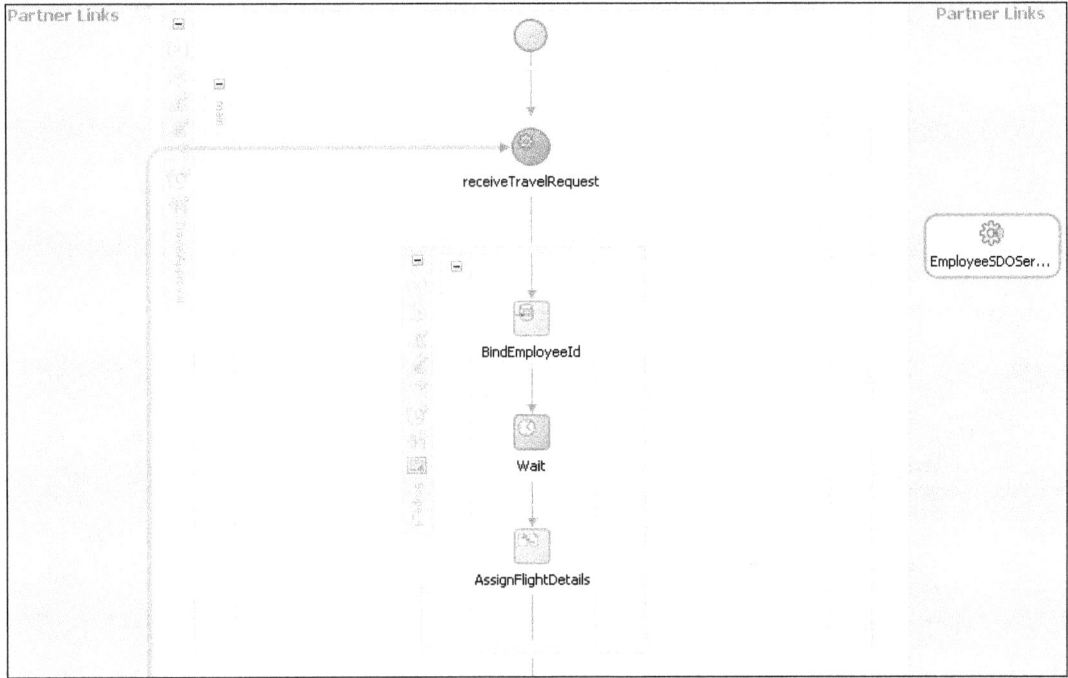

Finally, we can deploy and test our process.

Testing the entity variable

We will first go to the database and set the travel class of an employee that we will use in our test (for example, `EMPLOYEE_ID=100`) to value `Economy`.

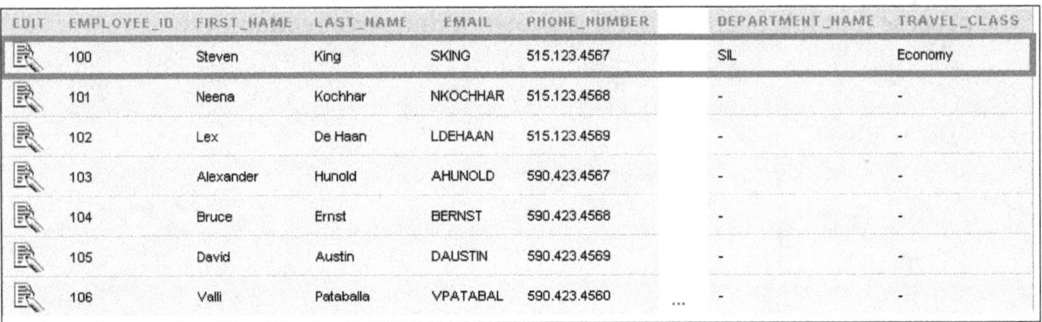

EDIT	EMPLOYEE_ID	FIRST_NAME	LAST_NAME	EMAIL	PHONE_NUMBER	DEPARTMENT_NAME	TRAVEL_CLASS
	100	Steven	King	SKING	515.123.4567	SIL	Economy
	101	Neena	Kochhar	NKOCHHAR	515.123.4568	-	-
	102	Lex	De Haan	LDEHAAN	515.123.4569	-	-
	103	Alexander	Hunold	AHUNOLD	590.423.4567	-	-
	104	Bruce	Ernst	BERNST	590.423.4568	-	-
	105	David	Austin	DAUSTIN	590.423.4569	-	-
	106	Valli	Pataballa	VPATABAL	590.423.4560 ...	-	-

We go to the EM Console and initiate a new instance of the process.

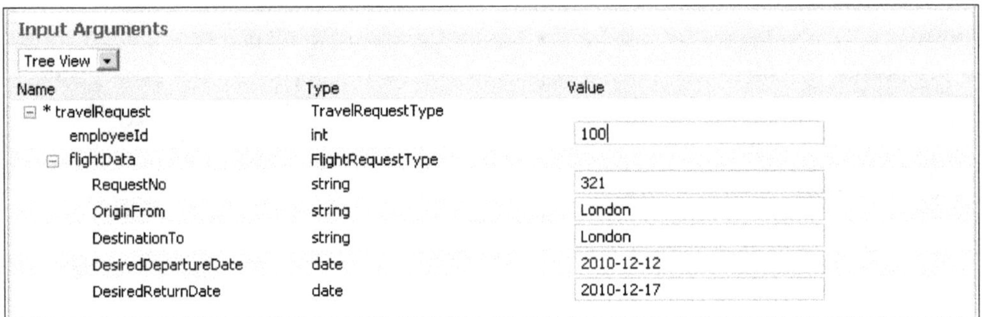

We click **Test Web Service**. Next, we open the visual **Flow** of the instance. We can see that the execution of the process instance was temporarily stopped and it is waiting for the expiry time. We can also see that during the dehydration, the `EmployeeEV` variable has been saved through the backend ADF-BC service.

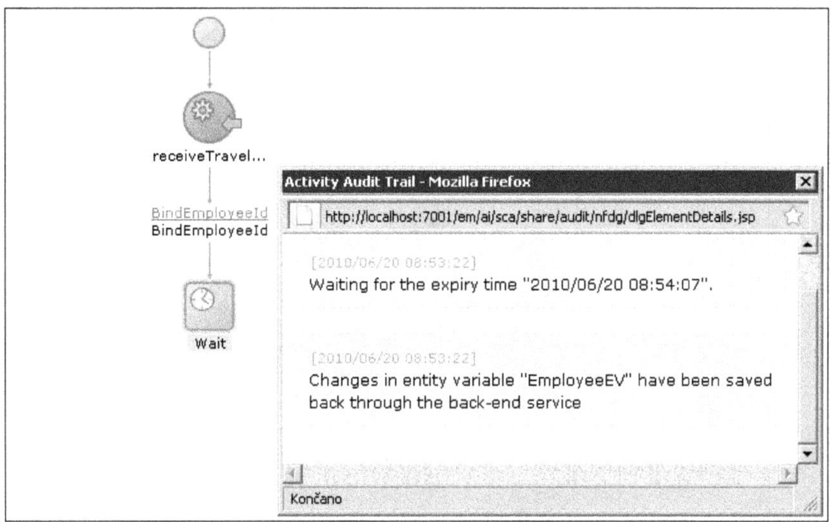

While the instance is dehydrated, we will change the travel class of the employee in the database to `First`.

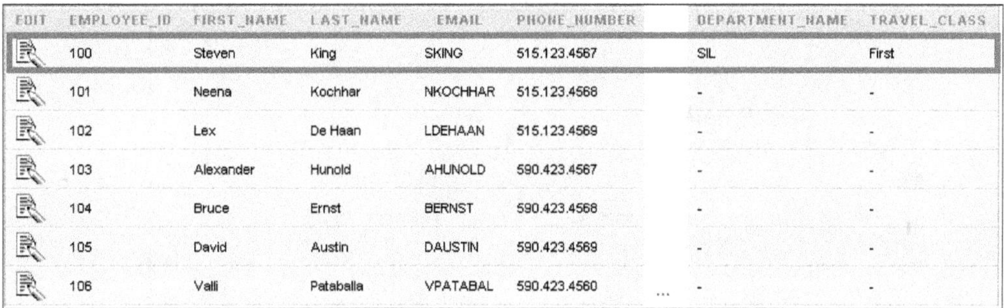

EDIT	EMPLOYEE_ID	FIRST_NAME	LAST_NAME	EMAIL	PHONE_NUMBER		DEPARTMENT_NAME	TRAVEL_CLASS
	100	Steven	King	SKING	515.123.4567		SIL	First
	101	Neena	Kochhar	NKOCHHAR	515.123.4568		-	-
	102	Lex	De Haan	LDEHAAN	515.123.4569		-	-
	103	Alexander	Hunold	AHUNOLD	590.423.4567		-	-
	104	Bruce	Ernst	BERNST	590.423.4568		-	-
	105	David	Austin	DAUSTIN	590.423.4569		-	-
	106	Valli	Pataballa	VPATABAL	590.423.4560	...	-	-

If we go back to see the visual **Flow** of the instance again, we can see that the instance was rehydrated (if one minute has already passed) and has completed.

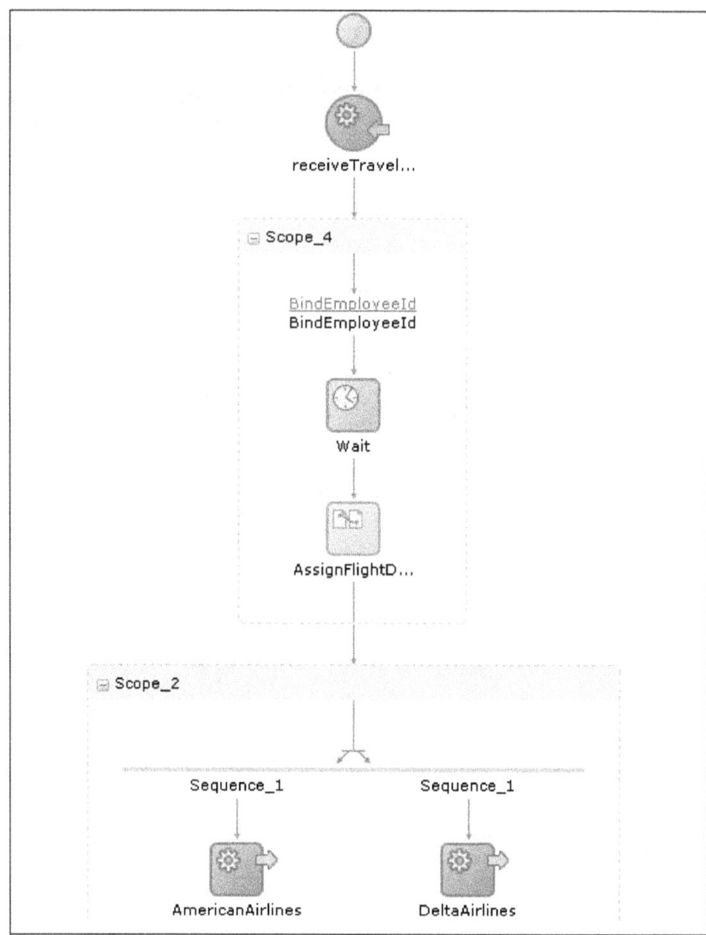

Now we will check if the instance used the new value of the employee travel class (`First`) when invoking the airline services. If we click on the `AmericanAirlines` `<invoke>` activity, we can see that the value has been refreshed.

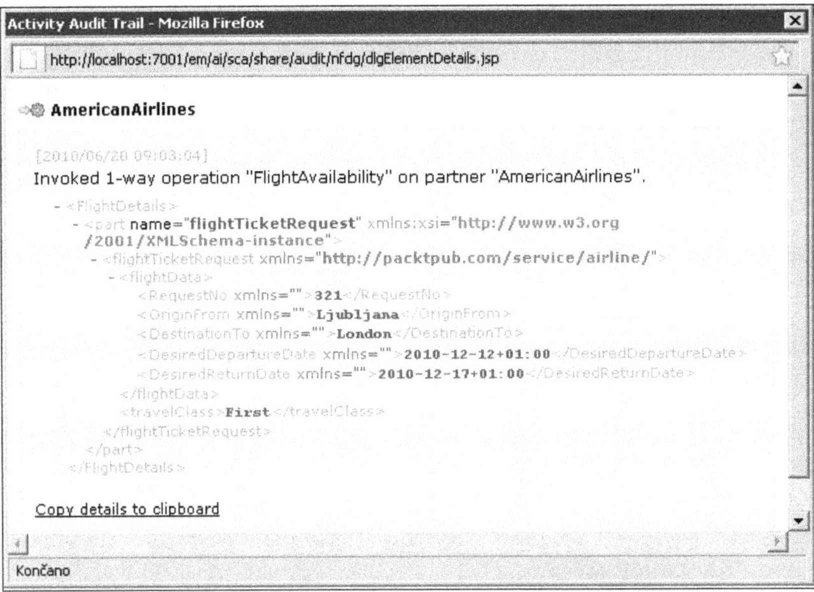

In the next section, we will look at the Master and Detail processes.

Master and Detail processes

By defining Master and Detail processes, we are able to coordinate a one-to-many relationship between a single Master process and multiple Detail processes. This pattern is useful in asynchronous communication, when a Master process invokes one or many Detail processes and then continues with processing. However, at a certain stage it needs to stop and wait to receive a signal from Detail processes to know whether all Detail processes have reached a certain stage. After receiving a signal from all Detail processes, the Master process can continue with processing. This means that the Master process does not need to wait for all Detail processes to finish (Detail process can send a signal to Master process before it actually finishes with its execution). This coordination is especially useful when the Master process invokes one-way operation of the detail and the Detail process does not return any message. A common use case is when a Master process delegates the processing to one or more Detail processes. However, before sending a final notification that processing is complete (or reached a certain stage), it needs to receive a signal from client processes.

In order to enable the coordination between Master and Detail processes, Oracle introduced the following BPEL extension activities (activities are defined in the `http://schemas.oracle.com/bpel/extension` namespace, usually declared with the `bpelx` prefix):

- `<bpelx:signal>`: Used to send a signal to the other processes (Master or Detail) to continue processing
- `<bpelx:receiveSignal>`: Used to temporarily stop processing and wait until it receives a signal from the other process (Master or Detail)

Both activities are coordinated using the `label` attributes. The following figure shows the overview of the Master-Detail coordination:

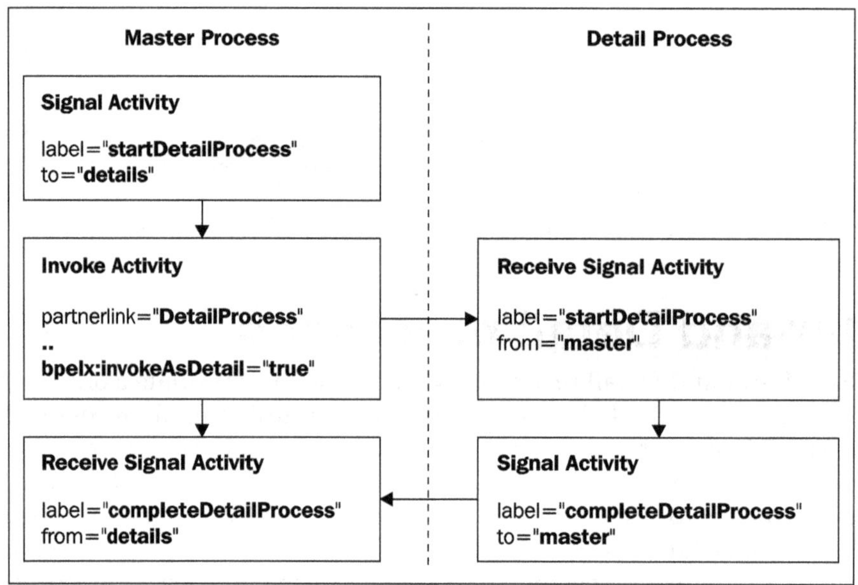

To demonstrate the use of Master-Detail coordination, we will modify our `TravelApproval process`. We will move the BPEL code for ticket reservation from `TravelApproval` (Master) BPEL process to a new BPEL process (we will name it `TicketReservationDetail`), which will represent a Detail process. The Master process will get the ticket offers and compare both prices. Then it will invoke the Detail process (using one-way operation), which will make the reservation of the selected flight ticket. The Master process will end with sending an e-mail notification to the requestor; therefore, it will need to know when (and if) the Detail process has successfully completed the reservation. To coordinate the control flow between the Master and Detail process, we will use `<signal>` and `<receiveSignal>` BPEL extension activities.

Creating the Detail process

First, we have to create a new XML schema, which will be used to define the input of the detail BPEL process. We do not need to define the output, as we will create a one way BPEL process. We use `http://packtpub.com/bpel/travel/reservation` as the target namespace. We create a new element (`flightReservation`) and a corresponding complex type (`FlightReservationRequestType`), which includes information about the selected airline (element `airline`) and the selected flight (element `confirmationData`).

```
<xs:schema xmlns:xs="http://www.w3.org/2001/XMLSchema"
  targetNamespace="http://packtpub.com/bpel/travel/reservation"
  xmlns:tns="http://packtpub.com/bpel/travel/reservation"
  xmlns:aln="http://packtpub.com/service/airline/"
  elementFormDefault="qualified">

  <xs:import namespace="http://packtpub.com/service/airline/"
    schemaLocation="FlightConfirmationType.xsd"/>

  <xs:element name="flightReservation"
    type="tns:FlightReservationRequestType"/>

  <xs:complexType name="FlightReservationRequestType">
    <xs:sequence>
        <xs:element name="confirmationData"
          type="aln:FlightConfirmationType"/>
        <xs:element name="airline" type="xs:string"/>
    </xs:sequence>
  </xs:complexType>
</xs:schema>
```

Next, we drag-and-drop a new **BPEL Process** Service Component to our SOA Composite diagram. The **Create BPEL Process** window opens. We enter the **Name** of the BPEL process (`TicketReservationDetail`), the **Namespace** (`http://packtpub.com/bpel/travel/reservation`), and select `One Way BPEL Process` as a **Template**. We uncheck the **Expose as a SOAP service** checkbox. Then, we define the **Input** of the BPEL process. We import the XML schema using the **Type Chooser** (we click on the magnifying glass icon) and select the `flightReservation` element. We click **OK** to close the window.

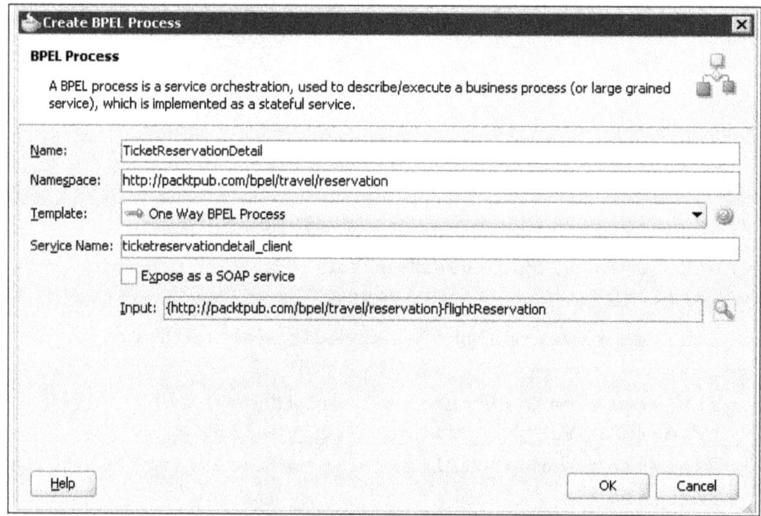

Now we wire the `TicketReservationDetail` BPEL process and both airline services. We also have to wire both BPEL processes. Our SOA composite diagram now looks as follows:

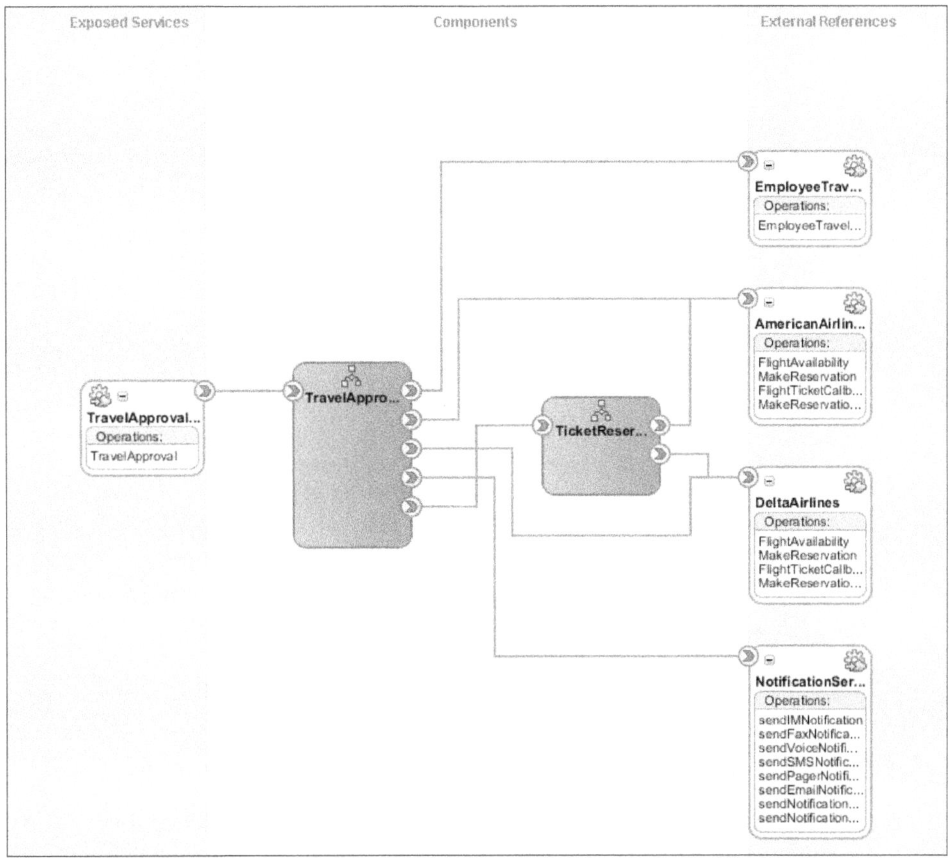

Now we will move the BPEL code for ticket reservation from `TravelApproval` to `TicketReservationDetail` BPEL process. In the `TicketReservationDetail` BPEL process, we also have to create input and output variables for invoking the airline services. The detail process now looks like shown on the following screenshot:

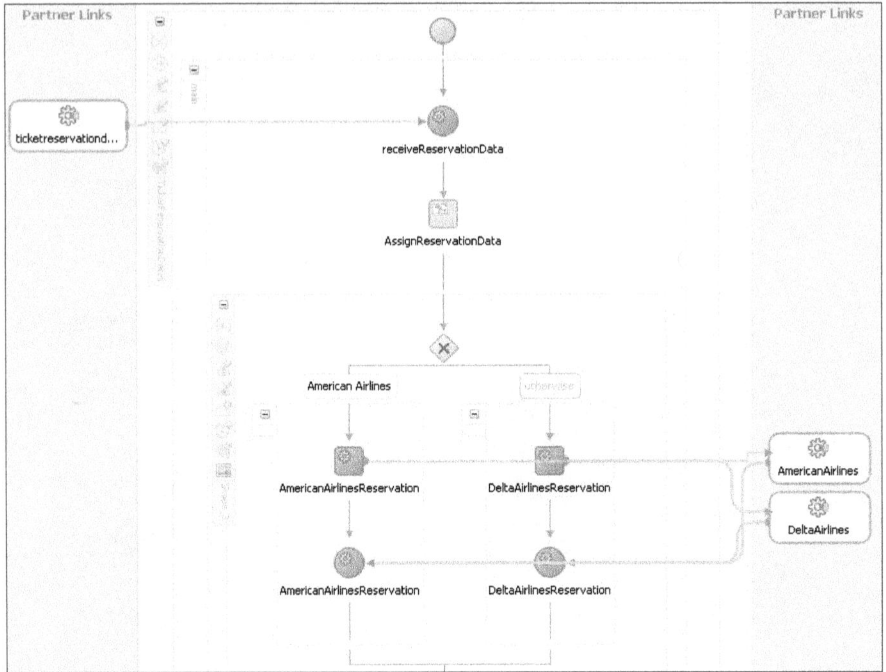

Modifying the Master process

As we already mentioned, we have to delete the BPEL code for ticket reservation and replace it with an `<invoke>` activity, which will be used to invoke the detail BPEL process. We rename the activity to `InvokeDetailProcess`. In front of the new `<invoke>` activity we also have to add a `<switch>` activity to compare both offers, and corresponding `<assign>` activities to set the input for the detail BPEL process. After the `<invoke>` activity we add a notification which will be used for sending an e-mail to the requestor to confirm the reservation. Our `TravelApproval` (Master) BPEL process now looks as shown in the next figure (only the last part of the process that has been changed is shown):

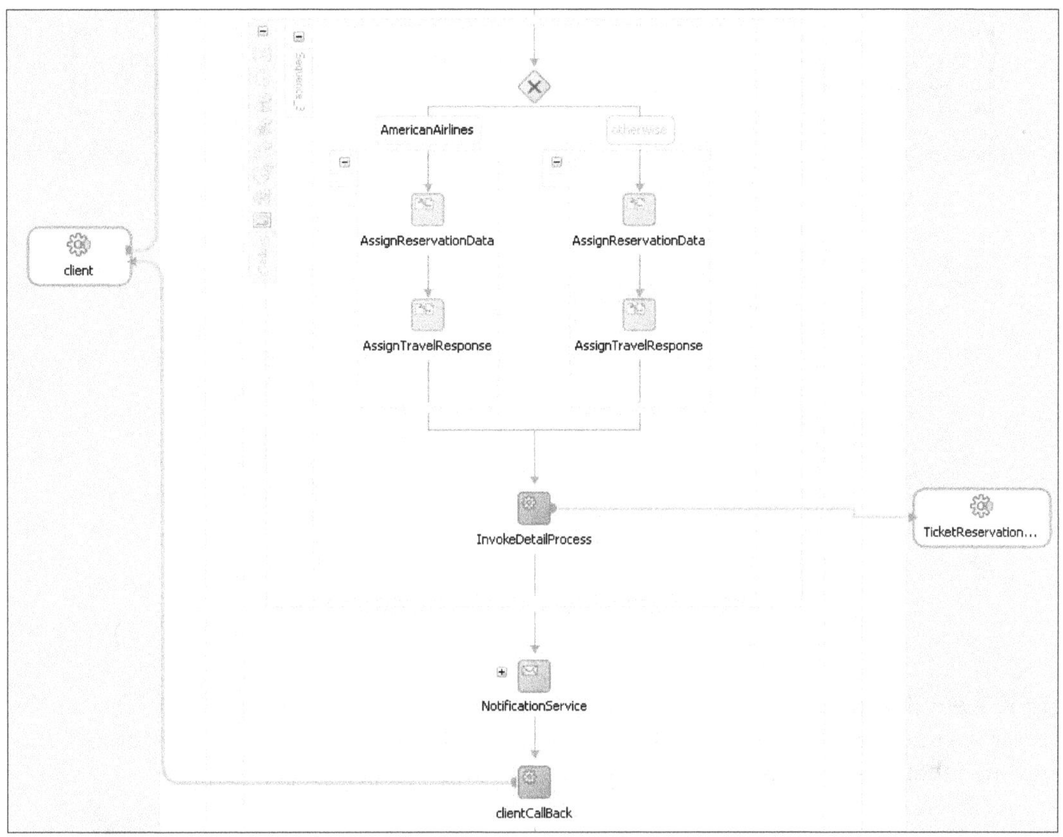

Adding <signal> and <receiveSignal> activities

As we want to coordinate the control flow of processes, we have to add `<signal>` and `<receiveSignal>` activities. First, we modify Master (`TravelApproval`) BPEL process. We drag-and-drop the `<signal>` activity in front of the `InvokeDetailProcess <invoke>` activity. We set the **Name** to `StartDetailProcess`. We also have to set the **Label** (`makeReservationDetail`) and specify that the signal will be sent to the `detail` process.

We will use the same label in the <receiveSignal> activity in the Detail process.

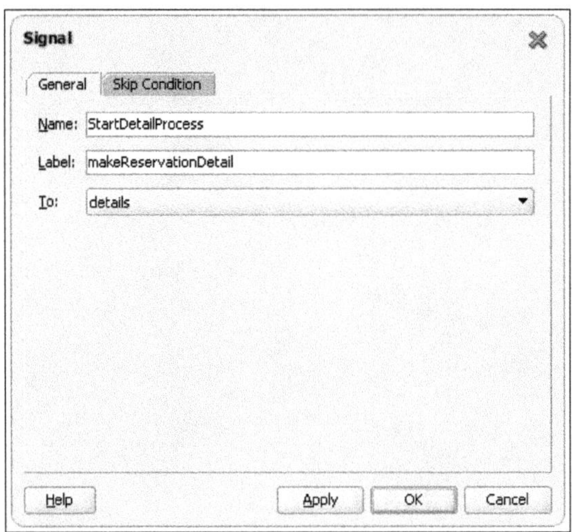

Now, we will add the `<receiveSignal>` activity in front of the `NotificationService` activity. We set the name to `ReceiveSignalFromDetail` and the label to `reservationCompleted`.

We will use the same label in the `<signal>` activity in the `details` process.

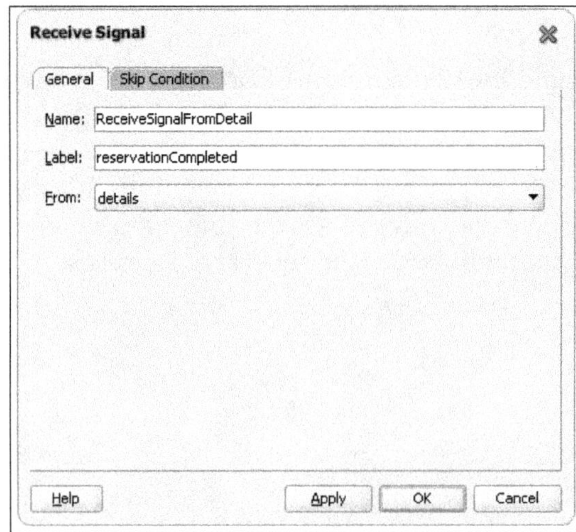

We also have to modify the `InvokeDetailProcess` `<invoke>` activity in the source code view by adding the `invokeAsDetail` argument:

```
<invoke name="InvokeDetailProcess"
        inputVariable="ReservationDataInput"
        partnerLink="ticketReservationDetailLT"
        portType="ns4:TicketReservationDetail"
        operation="process"
        bpelx:invokeAsDetail="true"/>
```

Our `TravelApproval` BPEL process now looks as follows (only the last part of the process that has been changed is shown):

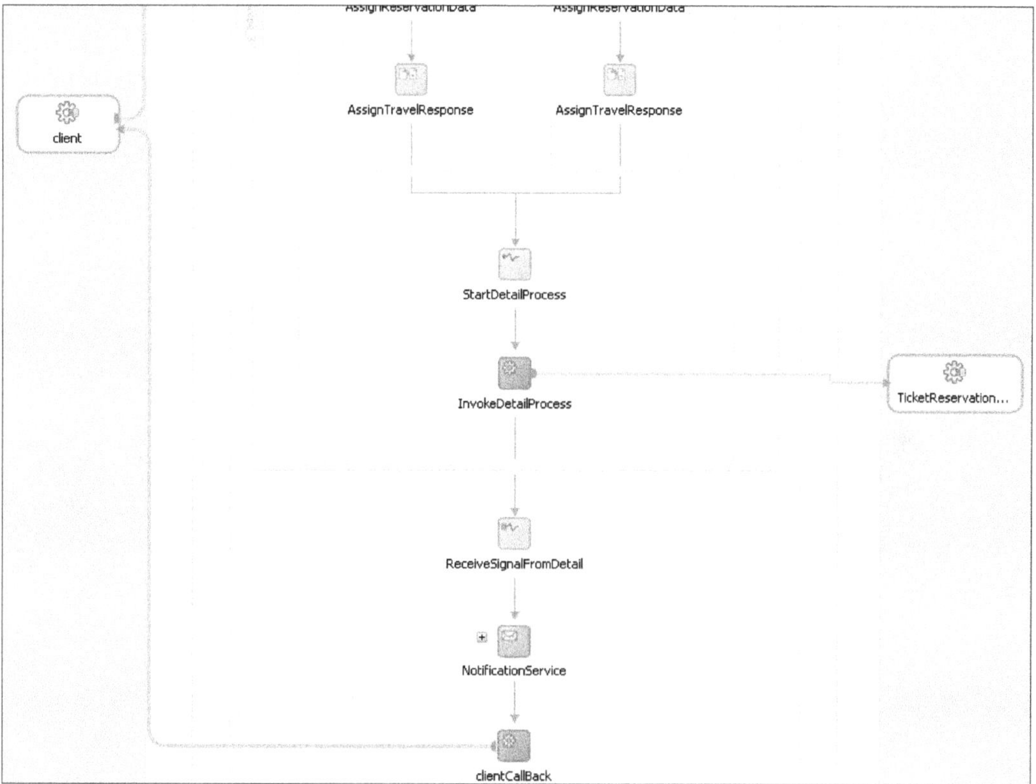

Next, we will modify the `detail` process. First, we will add a `<receiveSignal>` activity. We set the **Name** to `ReceiveSignalFromMaster`. For the **Label** we use the same value as in the `<signal>` activity of the Master process (`makeReservationDetail`). We also specify that the signal will be sent from the `master` process.

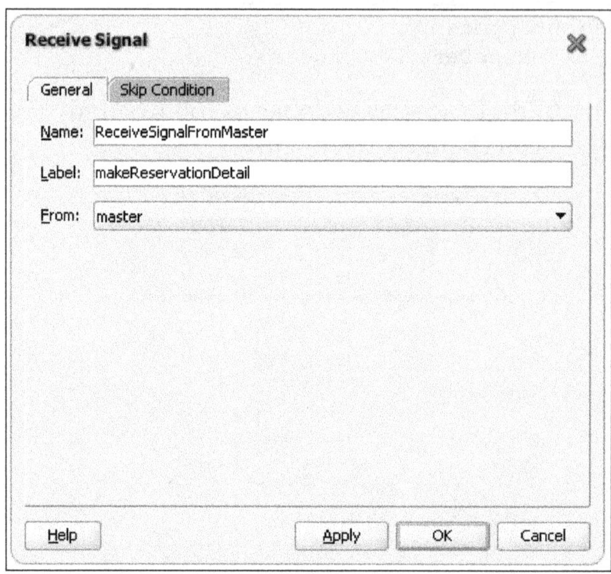

Next, we will add the `<signal>` activity at the end of the process to notify the Master that the reservation is complete. We enter the data as shown in the next screenshot:

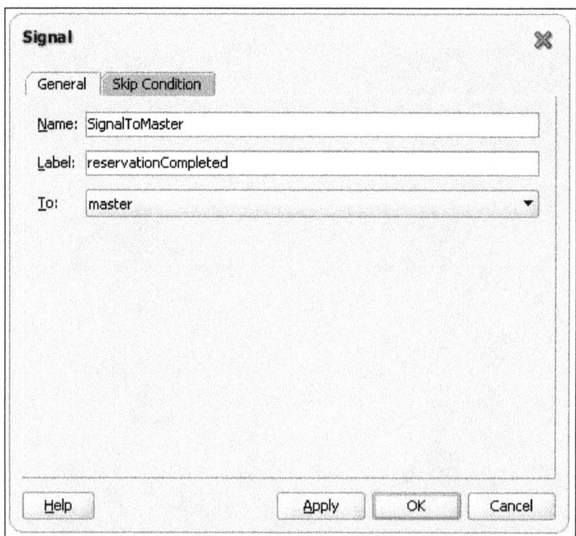

To be able to test if the `master` process really waits for the signal from the `detail` before sending the notification, we will add a `<wait>` activity in front of the `<signal>` activity and set the wait time to one minute. The `TicketReservationDetail` BPEL process now looks as follows (the `MakeReservation` scope is collapsed to improve readability):

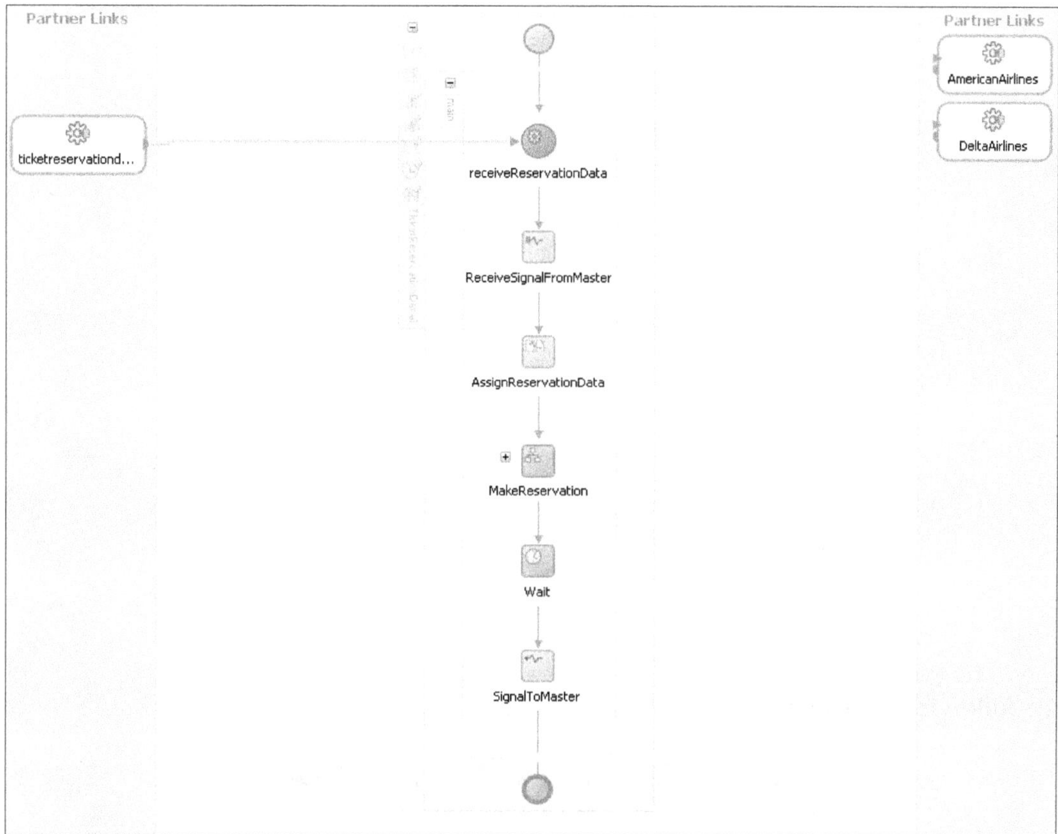

Now we can deploy and test our process.

Testing the Master-Detail coordination

To test the composite application we initiate a new process instance. Now we will look at the visual flow of the instance. As we can see on the following figure, the instance of the master process is waiting for the signal from the detail process.

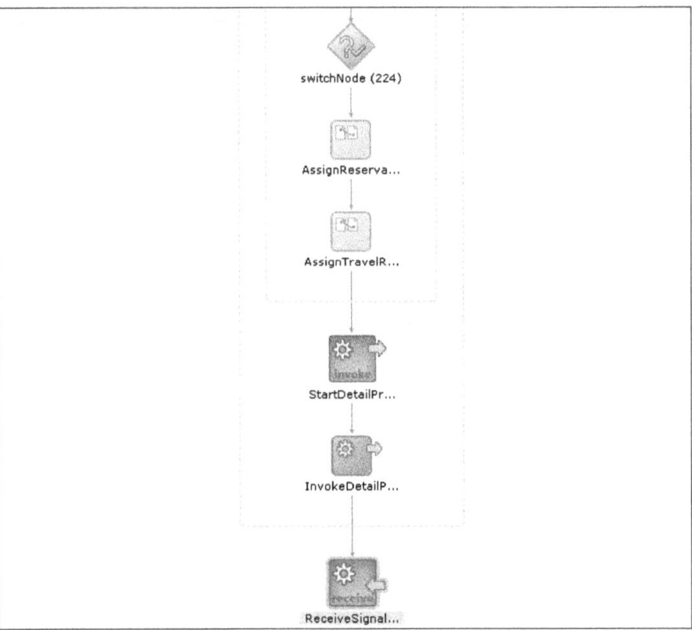

If we click on the `ReceiveSignalFromDetail` activity icon, we can see the following message:

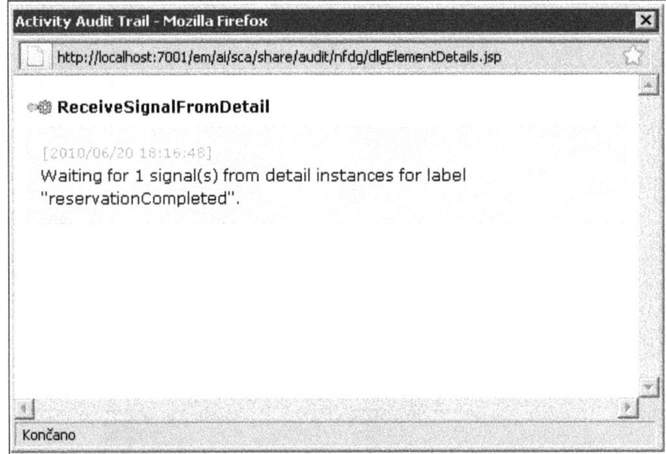

After one minute, the Detail process sends a signal and the Master process instance completes by sending notification to the requestor.

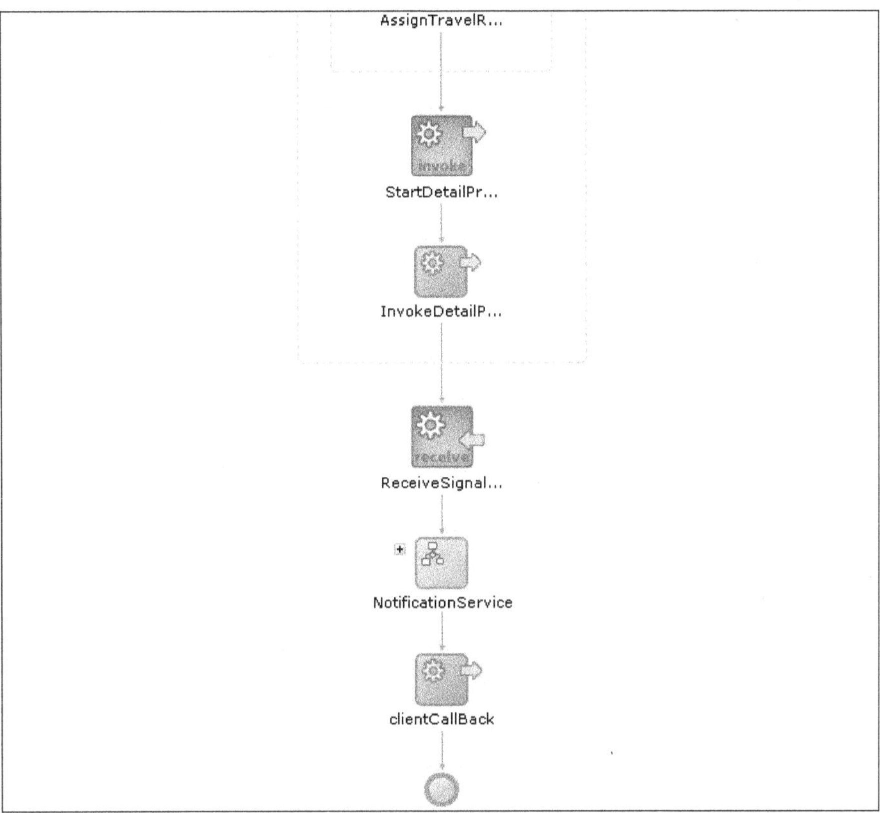

In the next section, we will look at how to secure SOA composite applications by attaching policies.

Securing SOA composite applications

Oracle SOA Suite 11*g* uses a policy-based model to centrally manage and secure Web Services across an organization. This functionality is provided by the Oracle Web Services Manager (OWSM), which is integrated into the SOA Infrastructure and implements an interceptor-based framework for enforcing security policies. It also enables end-to-end identity propagation inside composite applications. Policies can be declaratively managed (attached or detached) by developers in a design-time environment (using JDeveloper) and system administrators in a runtime environment (using EM Console). Policies can be attached to binding components (services and references) and service components.

Each policy consists of one or more assertions. The assertions are executed in the same order in which they appear in the policy. We can use one of many predefined policies, modify these policies, or create our own policies.

The following policy categories are supported:

- **Security policies**: WS-Security 1.0 and 1.1 standards are supported. Security policies enforce authentication and authorization of users, identity propagation, and message protection (integrity and confidentiality).
- **MTOM Attachments policies**: Provide optimal handling of large binary data.
- **Reliable Messaging policies**: Provide support for the WS-Reliable Messaging protocol for reliable end-to-end message delivery.
- **WS-Addressing policies**: Provide support for the WS-Addressing specification for addressing of SOAP messages.
- **Management policies**: Logging of requests, responses, and fault messages. Custom management policies can also be created.

Each category provides one or more policies we can attach. For example, the security category provides 27 pre-defined policies. Some of them are:

- `oracle/wss10_saml_token_service_policy`
- `oracle/wss10_message_protection_service_policy`
- `oracle/wss11_kerberos_token_service_policy`
- `oracle/wss11_kerberos_token_with_message_protection_service_policy`
- `oracle/wss11_message_protection_service_policy`
- `oracle/wss_http_token_service_policy`
- `oracle/wss_http_token_over_ssl_service_policy`
- `oracle/wss11_username_token_with_message_protection_service_policy`
- `oracle/wss_username_token_service_policy`

Attaching and detaching policies in JDeveloper

We usually use JDeveloper to attach policies for testing security in a design-time environment. We can attach policies to a binding component in SOA Composite Editor by right-clicking it and selecting **Configure WS-Policies**. The **Configure SOA WS Policies** window opens. We can add policies by clicking the plus sign under each category. When attaching policies to a binding component with an asynchronous interface, the policies must be configured separately for request and response messages.

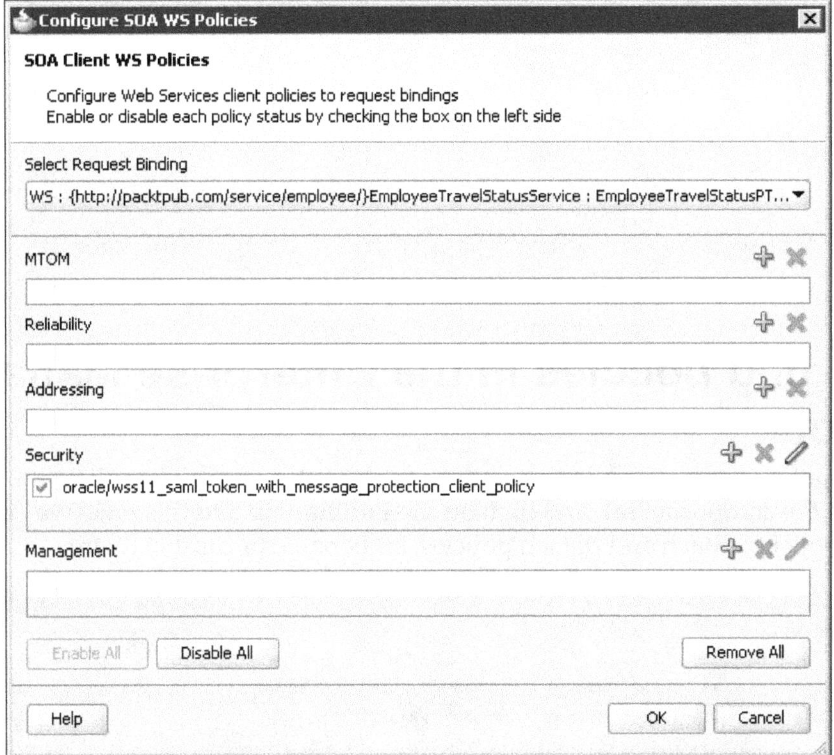

When we attach a policy to a service, we use service policy. If we want to attach policy to a reference, we have to use client policy.

We can also attach policies to service components. However, in that case we can only add **Security** and **Management** policies.

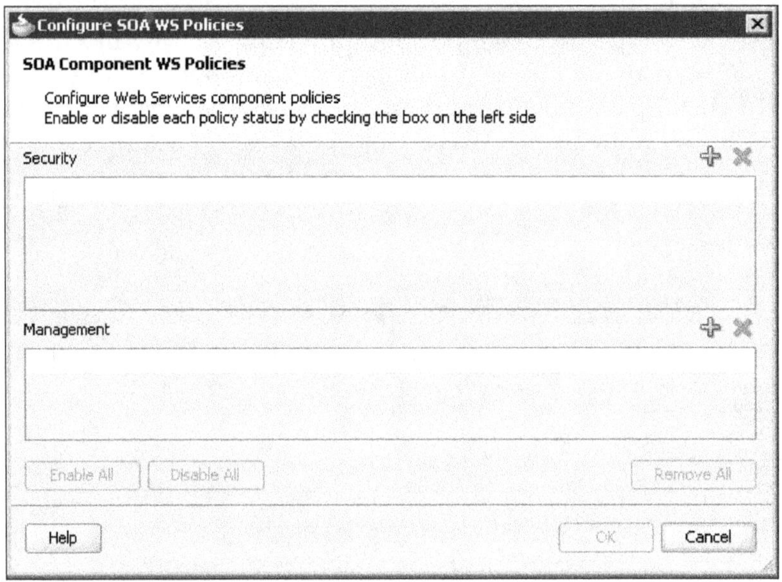

Managing policies in the Enterprise Manager console

To attach policies to secure our `TravelApproval` SOA composite application, we have to click on the composite link and then on the **Policies** tab. On this page we can see attached policies, attach and detach policies, and enable or disable them:

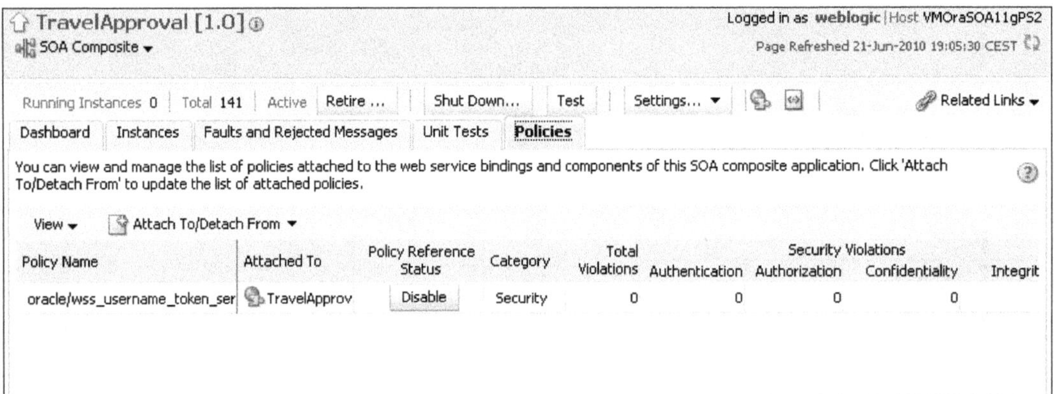

We select `TravelApprovalService` from the **Attach To/Detach From** drop-down. The **Attach/Detach Policies** page opens. We select the `oracle/wss_username_token_service_policy` policy from the **Security** category and attach it to the service. In this way, we secured our SOA composite application. Now if a client wants to invoke our application, it has to authenticate itself by providing a username and password (`UsernameToken` in the SOAP header).

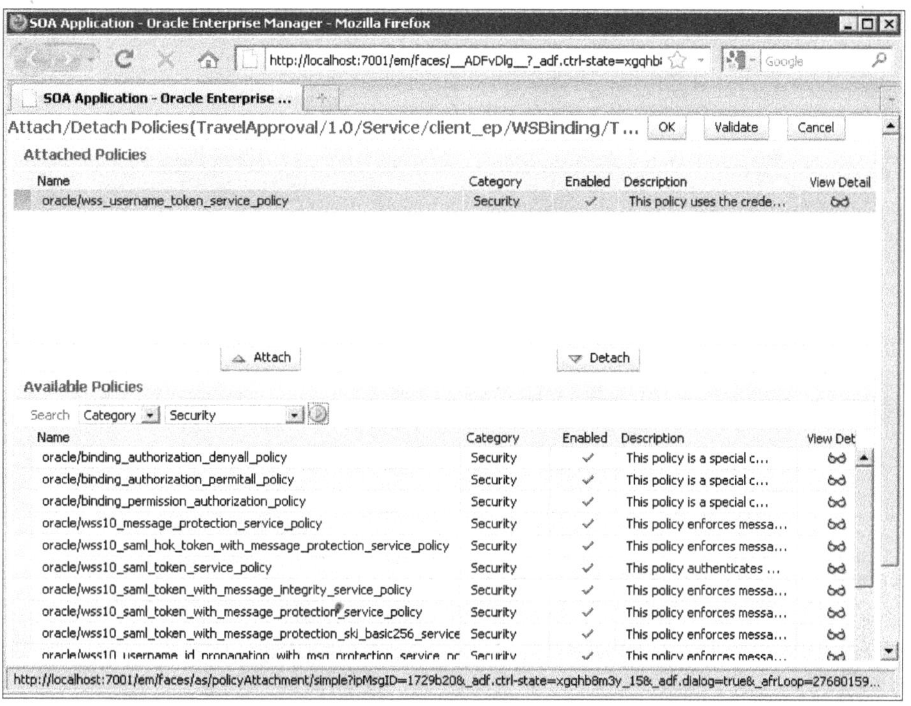

If we want to implement end-to-end security, we also have to secure all services (web services or SOA composite applications) that we invoke in our composite application, by attaching a service policy. In order to invoke secured services, we also need to attach corresponding client policies to our reference binding components in our composite application.

> Client identity is securely propagated throughout the composite. Therefore, we do not need to repeat the authentication process for every secured service we invoke. We just add a client security policy.

Testing security

We will first try to invoke our `TravelApproval` composite without the username and password. The **Webservice invocation failed** message appears, due to authentication failure.

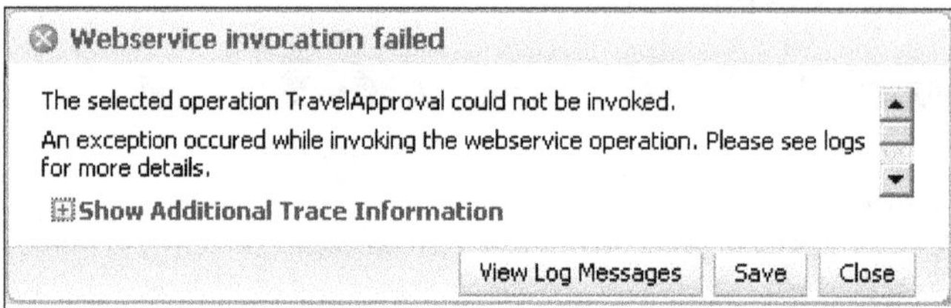

Now we repeat the test, but this time we will set the **WSS Username Token** on the top of the **Test Web Service** page.

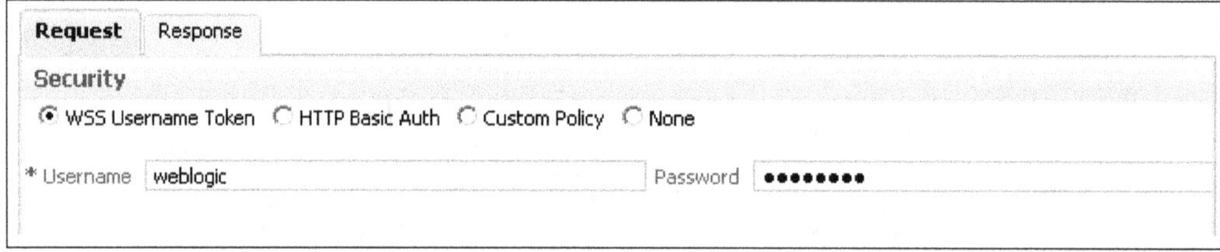

We can see that the invocation was successful.

Using business events in BPEL

Oracle SOA Suite 11*g* introduces support for **Event-Driven Architecture** (**EDA**) through the Event Delivery Network (EDN). EDN runs within every SOA instance and provides support for a publish/subscribe interaction pattern that allows us to implement loosely coupled interaction between different components in the architecture. Business events are typically a one-way (fire-and-forget) asynchronous way to send a notification. The main difference between direct service invocation and events-driven communication is that the author of the event does not have to know how many (if any) other components are interested in this event. It also does not care if subscribed components successfully received the business event. Therefore, in case the author of the message depends on the receiver, it is better to use the direct service invocation rather than business events.

For this release, there are two service components that can be used to publish or subscribe to business events—Mediator and BPEL process. However, EDN also provides the ability to publish and subscribe to events using other programming environments, such as Java, PL/SQL, and an ADF-BC application.

Business events can be defined using the Event Definition Language (EDL). EDL is an XML schema used to build business event definitions. EDL consists of the following:

- **Global name**: Typically a Java package name
- **Payload definition**: The payload is defined using an XML schema

Business definitions (EDL file and related artifacts) are deployed (or published) to the EDN. After an EDL is published, other applications can use it to subscribe to the defined business event. Raised events are delivered by EDN to the subscribed service components.

To demonstrate the use of business events in a BPEL service component, we will modify our `TravelApproval process`. First, we will create a new business event and name it `NewTravelRequest`. Then we will modify our `TravelApproval` BPEL code so that we will be able to initiate a process instance by publishing an event. At the end of the process, we will add an e-mail notification activity and modify the final `clientCallback` activity. Instead of a callback to the client, we will raise a new business event, called `ReservationSuccessful`. We have to remove the callback to the client, as if a BPEL process is initiated by a business event it does not have information about the client and the callback fails.

Defining the business event

We open the SOA Composite Editor and click on the **Event Definition Creation** icon.

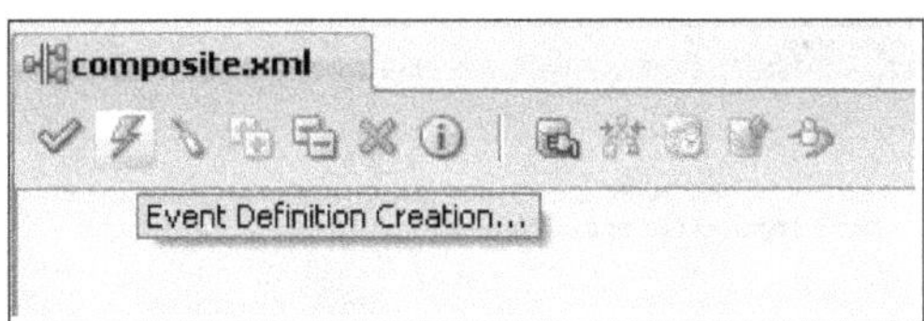

The **Create Event Definition File** window opens. We enter the **EDL File Name** (`TravelEvents`) and the **Namespace** (`http://packtpub.com/events/travel/`). Then, we add a new event by clicking the *plus* icon. We set the name of the event to `NewTravelRequest` and select the input element that contains information about the travel request. Then we create another event that will be used to publish the result of the BPEL process. We name it `ReservationSuccessful`. We click on **OK** to close the window.

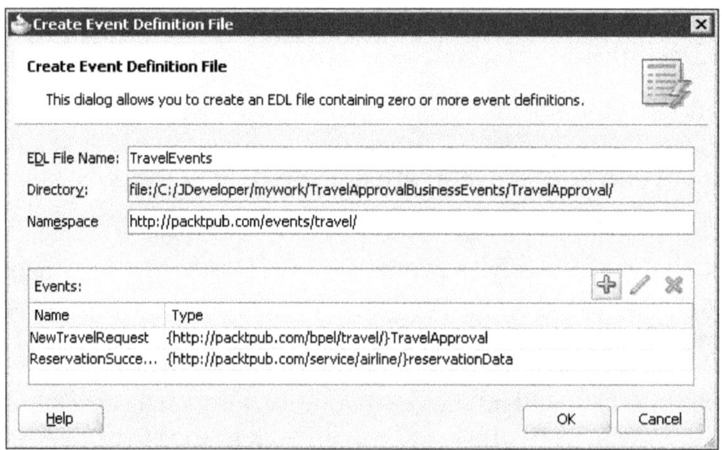

Modifying the BPEL process

As we already mentioned, BPEL process service components can be used to publish or subscribe to business events. If we want a BPEL process to be subscribed to an event, we can specify this when creating a new BPEL process by choosing the **Subscribe To Events** template.

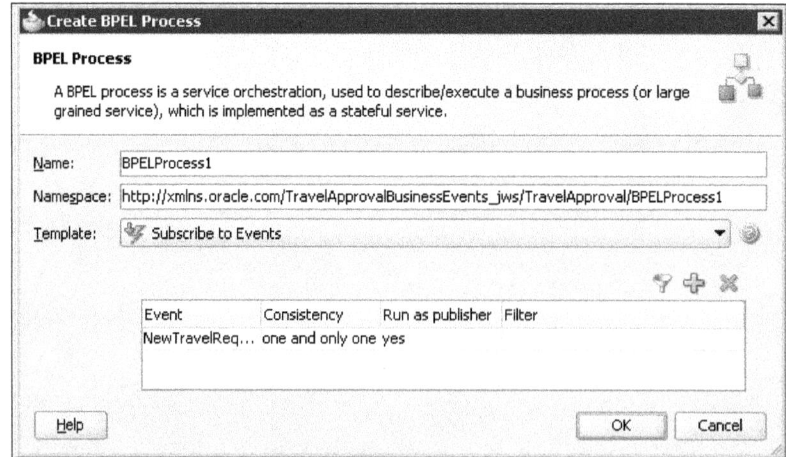

However, we can do the same using the BPEL Component Designer. If we double-click the initial `receiveTravelRequest` `<receive>` activity, we can change the **Interaction Type** from `Partner Link` to `Event` and choose the event we want to subscribe to (we also have to create a new input variable).

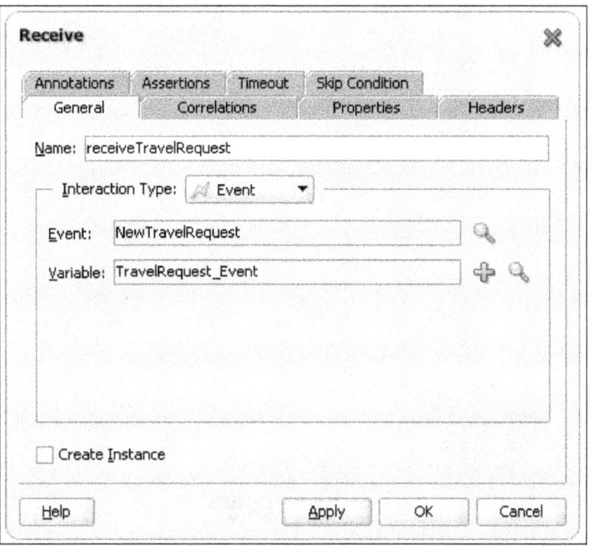

As we want our BPEL process to still be accessible through the Web Service interface, we will replace the `receiveTravelRequest` `<receive>` activity with a `<pick>` activity that defines two `<onMessage>` elements—one for receiving a SOAP message from a client, and one for receiving a business event (refer to the following screenshots).

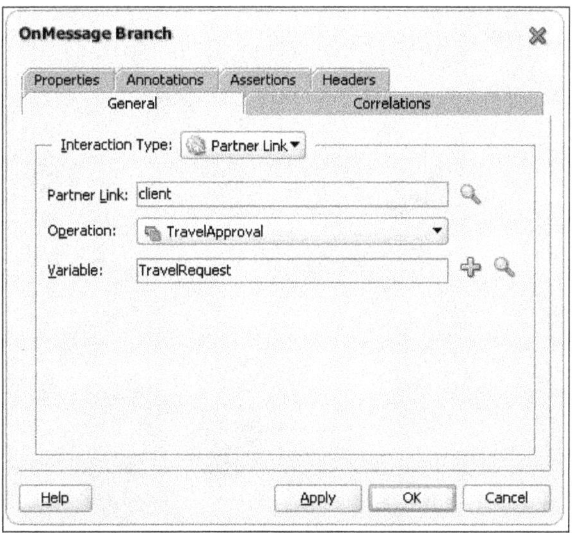

When configuring the `<onMessage>` element for receiving the business event, we set the **Interaction Type** to `Event`, as shown in the next screenshot:

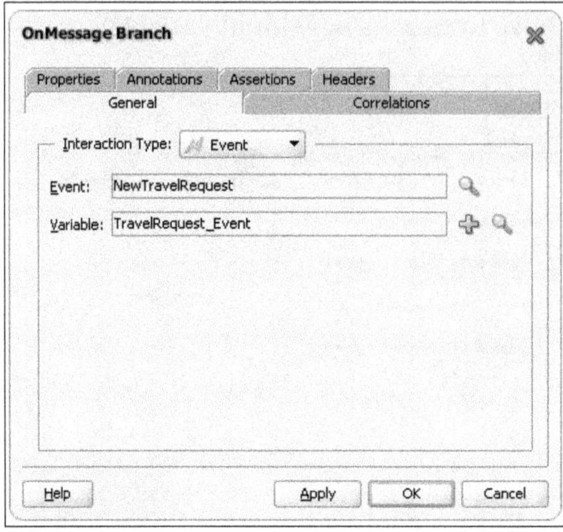

The next figure shows the modified BPEL process. Note that we had to create a new input variable for storing the received event (`TravelRequest_Event`). We use the `AssignTravelRequestEvent` `<assign>` activity to assign data from the `TravelRequest_Event` variable to the `TravelRequest` variable, which is used throughout the process.

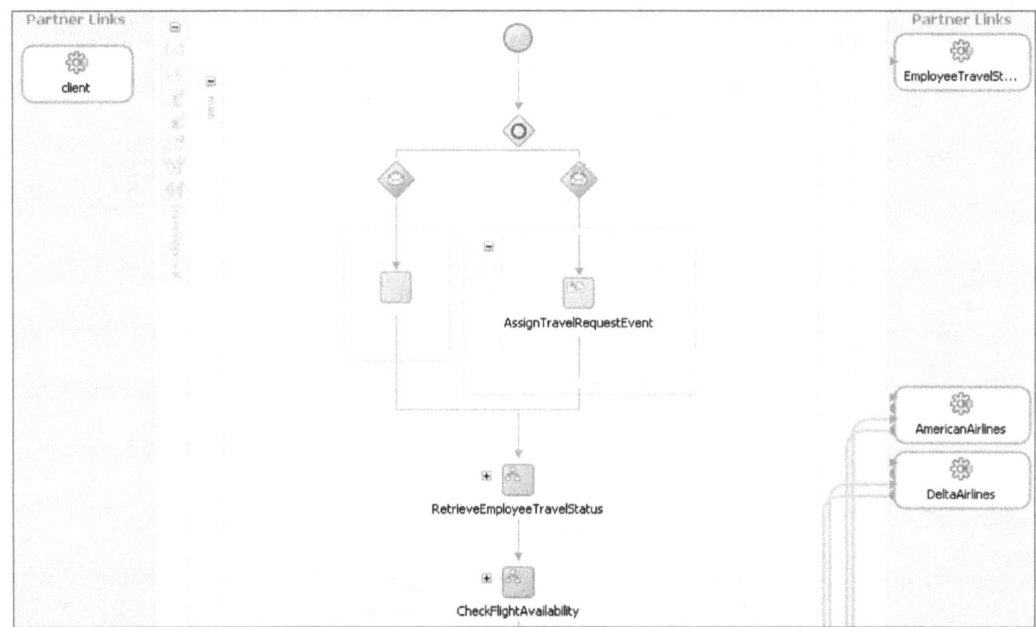

Next, we will add an e-mail notification at the end of the process to inform the requestor about the result. We will also modify the final `clientCallback` activity. Instead of invoking the client (when the instance is initiated by a business event, the BPEL process does not have information about the client), we will raise a new business event (`ReservationSuccessful`). We rename the activity to `publishReservationSuccessfulEvent`. We also need to create a new variable (`TravelResponse_Event`).

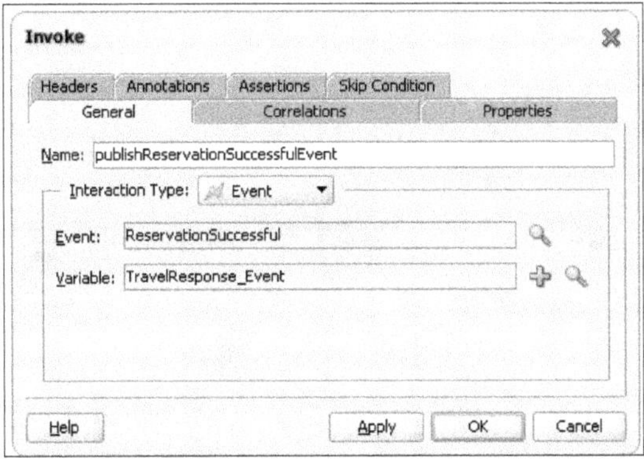

We also need an `<assign>` activity (`AssignTravelResponseEvent`) to copy the data from the `TravelResponse` variable (which is used throughout the process) to `TravelResponse_Event`. Our BPEL process (the final part) now looks as follows:

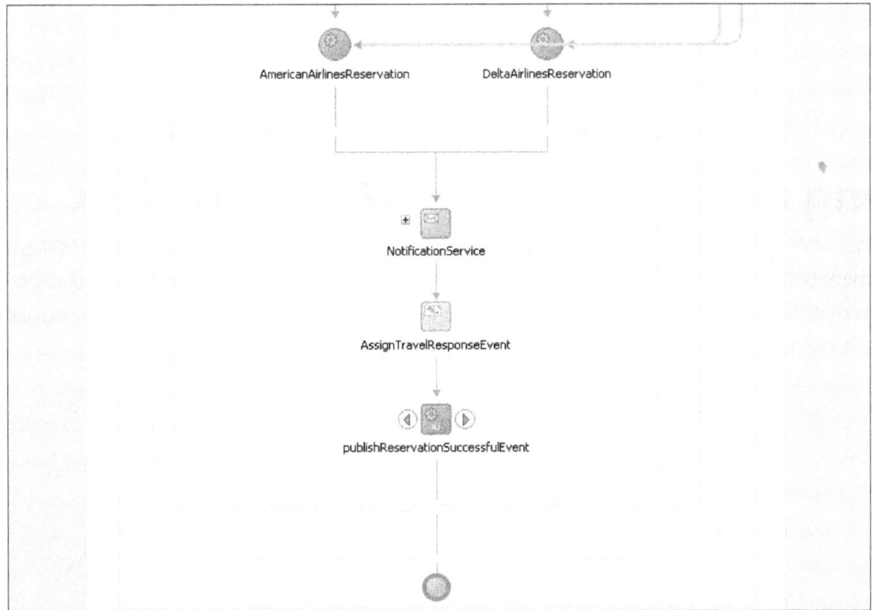

The next figure shows our modified SOA composite application. Pay attention to the lightning icons on the BPEL service component, indicating that the BPEL publishes (yellow lightning icon) and is subscribed to (blue lightning icon) a business event.

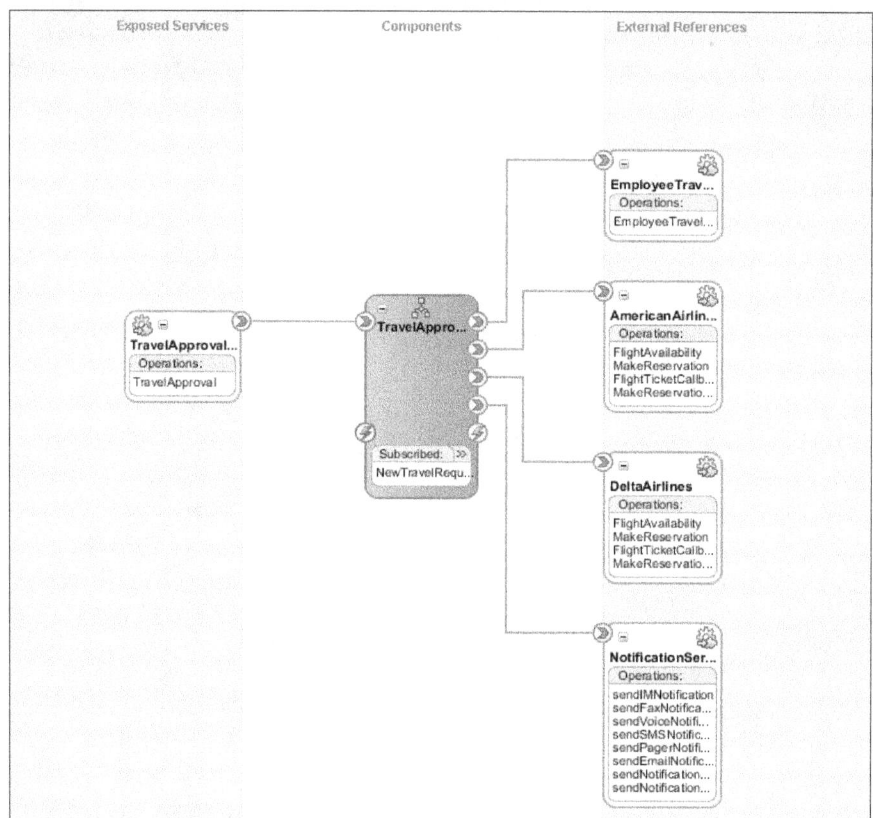

Testing the SOA composite application

To test the modified composite application, we will publish a `NewTravelRequest` event using the EM console. In a real-world scenario, events are published by other SOA composite applications or from other programming environments, such as Java, PL/SQL, and an ADF-BC application.

To be able to publish an event in the EM console, we have to right-click `soa-infra (soa_server1)` and select **Business Events**.

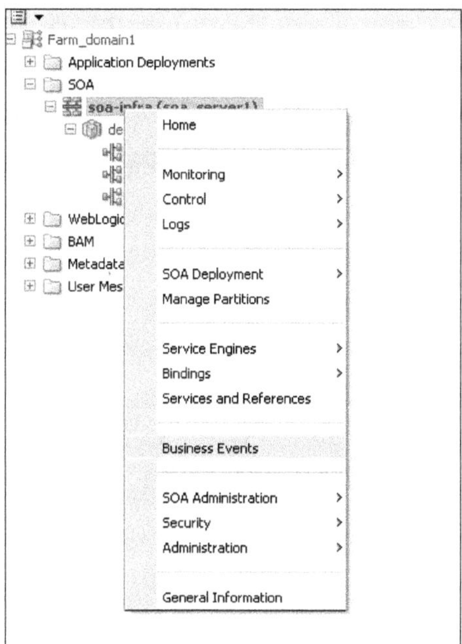

A **Business Events** page showing all published events opens. On the **Events** tab we can see all events and publish a new event by selecting it and clicking **Test**. On the **Subscriptions** tab we can see which components are subscribed to which events. The **faults** tab shows all faults.

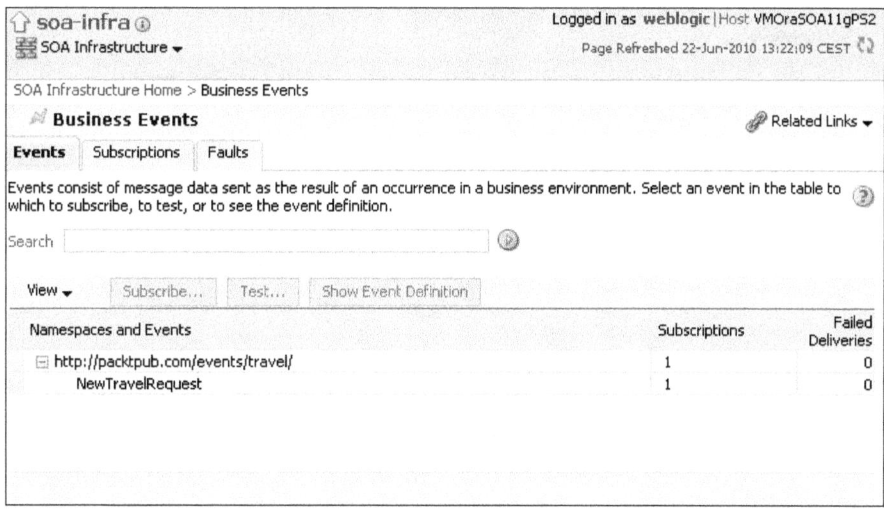

Now we click on the **Test** button. The test window opens. We enter the payload and publish the event by clicking **Publish**.

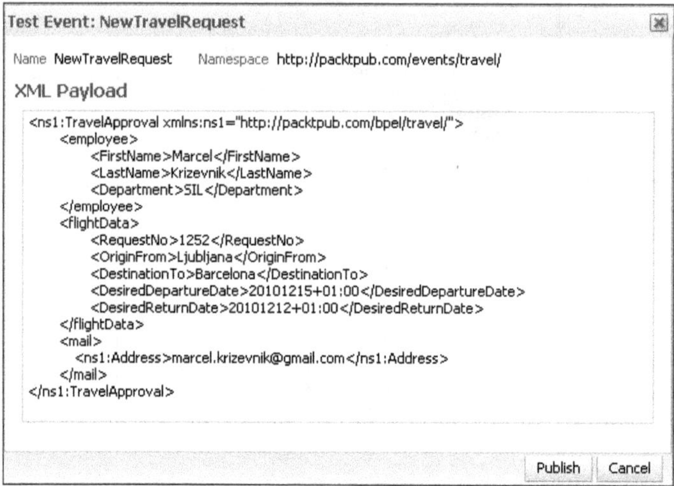
Test Event: NewTravelRequest
Name NewTravelRequest Namespace http://packtpub.com/events/travel/
XML Payload
<ns1:TravelApproval xmlns:ns1="http://packtpub.com/bpel/travel/">
<employee>
<FirstName>Marcel</FirstName>
<LastName>Krizevnik</LastName>
<Department>SIL</Department>
</employee>
<flightData>
<RequestNo>1252</RequestNo>
<OriginFrom>Ljubljana</OriginFrom>
<DestinationTo>Barcelona</DestinationTo>
<DesiredDepartureDate>20101215+01:00</DesiredDepartureDate>
<DesiredReturnDate>20101212+01:00</DesiredReturnDate>
</flightData>
<mail>
<ns1:Address>marcel.krizevnik@gmail.com</ns1:Address>
</mail>
</ns1:TravelApproval>
Publish
Cancel

We open the Flow Trace of the initiated instance. We can see that the instance was successfully completed (pay attention to the first row, indicating that the instance was initiated by the `NewTravelRequest` business event):

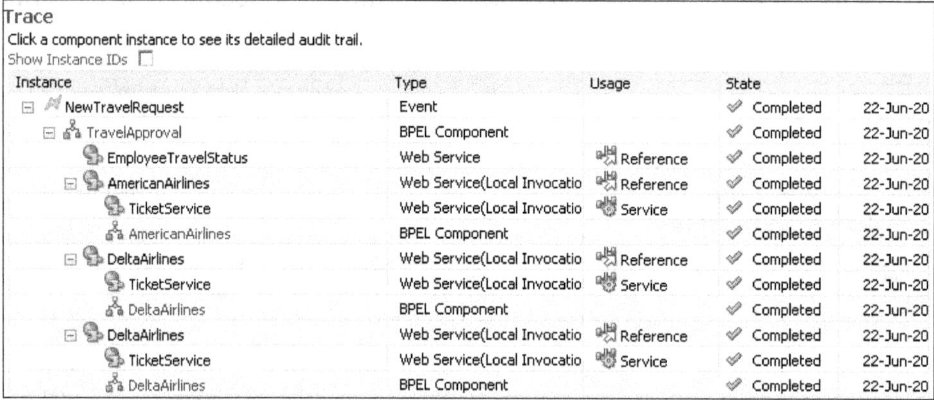

Trace

Click a component instance to see its detailed audit trail.

Show Instance IDs

Instance	Type	Usage	State	
NewTravelRequest	Event		Completed	22-Jun-20
TravelApproval	BPEL Component		Completed	22-Jun-20
EmployeeTravelStatus	Web Service	Reference	Completed	22-Jun-20
AmericanAirlines	Web Service(Local Invocatio	Reference	Completed	22-Jun-20
TicketService	Web Service(Local Invocatio	Service	Completed	22-Jun-20
AmericanAirlines	BPEL Component		Completed	22-Jun-20
DeltaAirlines	Web Service(Local Invocatio	Reference	Completed	22-Jun-20
TicketService	Web Service(Local Invocatio	Service	Completed	22-Jun-20
DeltaAirlines	BPEL Component		Completed	22-Jun-20
DeltaAirlines	Web Service(Local Invocatio	Reference	Completed	22-Jun-20
TicketService	Web Service(Local Invocatio	Service	Completed	22-Jun-20
DeltaAirlines	BPEL Component		Completed	22-Jun-20

As our BPEL process is still exposed as a SOAP Web Service, we can still invoke it using its web service interface.

Summary

In this chapter, we became familiar with advanced BPEL features of Oracle SOA Suite 11*g*. We overviewed entity variables and presented an example for using them. Entity variables can be very useful in long-running BPEL processes. We also looked at the Master and Detail processes and explained how to use signals to coordinate them.

We have explained how to secure BPEL processes and SOA composites using WS-Security. This is important, as we will in most cases need to use security. Finally, we have shown how to use events in BPEL processes.

In the next chapter, we will look at human interactions in BPEL.

7
Human Interactions in BPEL

Real-world business processes often require human interactions. For example, we might want to extend the TravelApproval business process so that a person approves (or rejects) the final ticket selection before making the reservation. Other examples include confirming stock prices, choosing loan offers, and so on. The BPEL specification does not provide a standard way to include human interaction in BPEL processes. However, Oracle SOA Suite 11*g* provides the **Oracle Human Workflow** component, which enables users to participate in SOA composite applications. Workflow is a set of services that enable human interaction in BPEL processes in a relatively easy way. Similar to the Notification service, the Workflow service exposes the interfaces through WSDL, and BPEL processes invoke it just like any other service.

In this chapter, we will first get familiar with the basic human workflow concepts, features, and architecture. Then we'll discuss the **Human Task** service component and how it can be used to enable human interaction in BPEL processes. Next, we will look at how to design a human task. Then we will show how to create ADF-based human task web forms. As a very important part of the Oracle Human Workflow, we will present the Oracle BPM Worklist Application, which can be used by users to access and act on the tasks assigned to them. We will demonstrate the use of presented components and features on our TravelApproval BPEL process that we have already used in previous chapters. We will add a human task, which will be used to approve or reject selected airline tickets, before making the ticket reservation.

In this chapter, we will discuss the following topics:

- Oracle Human Workflow concepts, features, and architecture
- Creating Human Tasks definitions
- Using Human Tasks in BPEL processes
- Creating Human Task forms
- Using the Oracle BPM Worklist Application

Human interactions in business processes

The main objective of BPEL has been to standardize the process automation. BPEL business processes make use of services and externalize their functionality as services. BPEL processes are defined as a collection of activities through which services are invoked. BPEL does not make a distinction between services provided by applications and other interactions, such as human interactions, which are particularly important. Real-world business processes namely often integrate not only systems and services, but also humans.

Human interactions in business processes can be very simple, such as approval of certain tasks or decisions, or complex, such as delegation, renewal, escalation, nomination, chained execution, and so on. Human interactions are not limited to approvals and can include data entries, process monitoring and management, process initiation, exception handling, and so on.

Task approval is the simplest and probably the most common human interaction. In a business process for opening a new account, a human interaction might be required to decide whether the user is allowed to open the account. In a travel approval process, a human might approve the decision from which airline to buy the ticket (as shown in the following figure).

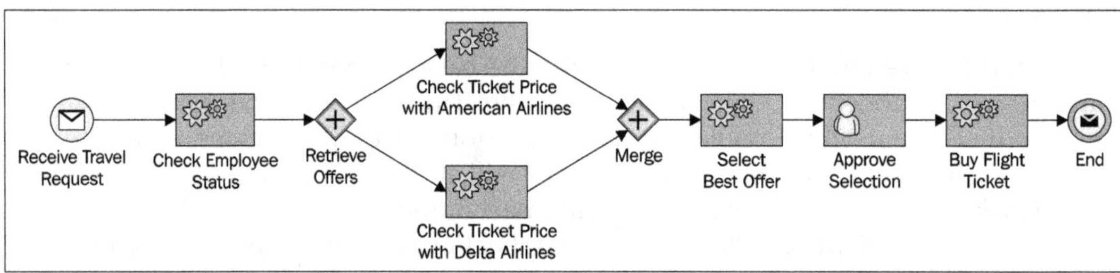

If the situation is more complex, a business process might require several users to make approvals, either in sequence or in parallel. In sequential scenarios, the next user often wants to see the decision made by the previous user. Sometimes, particularly in parallel human interactions, users are not allowed to see the decisions taken by other users. This improves the decision potential. Sometimes one user does not even know which other users are involved, or whether any other users are involved at all.

A common scenario for involving more than one user is workflow with escalation. Escalation is typically used in situations where an activity does not fulfill a time constraint. In such a case, a notification is sent to one or more users. Escalations can be chained, going first to the first-line employees and advancing to senior staff if the activity is not fulfilled.

Sometimes it is difficult or impossible to define in advance which user should perform an interaction. In this case, a supervisor might manually nominate the task to other employees; the nomination can also be made by a group of users or by a decision-support system.

In other scenarios, a business process may require a single user to perform several steps that can be defined in advance or during the execution of the process instance. Even more complex processes might require that one workflow is continued with another workflow.

Human interactions are not limited to only approvals; they may also include data entries or process management issues, such as process initiation, suspension, and exception management. This is particularly true for long-running business processes, where, for example, user exception handling can prevent costly process termination and related compensation for those activities that have already been successfully completed.

As a best practice for human workflows, it is usually not wise to associate human interactions directly to specific users; it is better to connect tasks to roles and then associate those roles with individual users. This gives business processes greater flexibility, allowing any user with a certain role to interact with the process and enabling changes to users and roles to be made dynamically. To achieve this, the process has to gain access to users and roles, stored in the enterprise directory, such as **LDAP** (**Lightweight Directory Access Protocol**).

Workflow theory has defined several workflow patterns, which specify the above-described scenarios in detail. Examples of workflow patterns include sequential workflow, parallel workflow, workflow with escalation, workflow with nomination, ad-hoc workflow, workflow continuation, and so on.

Human Tasks in BPEL

So far we have seen that human interaction in business processes can get quite complex. Although BPEL specification does not specifically cover human interactions, BPEL is appropriate for human workflows. BPEL business processes are defined as collections of activities that invoke services. BPEL does not make a distinction between services provided by applications and other interactions, such as human interactions.

There are mainly two approaches to support human interactions in BPEL. The first approach is to use a human workflow service. Several vendors today have created workflow services that leverage the rich BPEL support for asynchronous services. In this fashion, people and manual tasks become just another asynchronous service from the perspective of the orchestrating process and the BPEL processes stay 100% standard.

The other approach has been to standardize the human interactions and go beyond the service invocations. This approach resulted in the workflow specifications emerging around BPEL with the objective to standardize the explicit inclusion of human tasks in BPEL processes. The BPEL4People specification has emerged, which was originally put forth by IBM and SAP in July 2005. Other companies, such as Oracle, Active Endpoints, and Adobe joined later. Finally, this specification is now being advanced within the OASIS BPEL4People Technical Committee. The BPEL4People specification contains two parts:

- BPEL4People version 1.0, which introduces BPEL extensions to address human interactions in BPEL as a first-class citizen. It defines a new type of basic activity, which uses human tasks as an implementation, and allows specifying tasks local to a process or use tasks defined outside of the process definition. BPEL4People is based on the WS-HumanTask specification that it uses for the actual specification of human tasks.
- Web Services Human Task (WS-HumanTask) version 1.0 introduces the definition of human tasks, including their properties, behavior, and a set of operations used to manipulate human tasks. It also introduces a coordination protocol in order to control autonomy and lifecycle of service-enabled human tasks in an interoperable manner.

The most important extensions introduced in BPEL4People are people activities and people links. People activity is a new BPEL activity used to define user interactions; in other words, tasks that a user has to perform. For each people activity, the BPEL server must create work items and distribute them to users eligible to execute them. People activities can have input and output variables and can specify deadlines.

To specify the implementation of people activities, BPEL4People introduced tasks. Tasks specify actions that users must perform. Tasks can have descriptions, priorities, deadlines, and other properties. To represent tasks to users, we need a client application that provides a user interface and interacts with tasks. It can query available tasks, claim and revoke them, and complete or fail them.

To associate people activities and the related tasks with users or groups of users, BPEL4People introduced people links. People links are somewhat similar to partner links; they associate users with one or more people activities. People links are usually associated with generic human roles, such as process initiator, process stakeholders, owners, and administrators.

The actual users that are associated with people activities can be determined at design time, deployment time, or runtime. BPEL4People anticipates the use of directories such as LDAP to select users. However, it doesn't define the query language used to select users. Rather, it foresees the use of LDAP filters, SQL, XQuery, or other methods.

BPEL4People proposes complex extensions to the BPEL specification. However, so far it is still quite high level and doesn't yet specify the exact syntax of the new activities mentioned above. Until the specification becomes more concrete, we don't expect vendors to implement the proposed extensions. But while BPEL4People is early in the standardization process, it shows a great deal of promise.

The BPEL4People proposal raises an important question: Is it necessary to introduce such complex extensions to BPEL to cover user interactions? Some vendor solutions model user interactions as just another web service, with well-defined interfaces for both BPEL processes and client applications. This approach does not require any changes to BPEL. To become portable, it would only need an industry-wide agreement on the two interfaces. And, of course, both interfaces can be specified with WSDL, which gives developers great flexibility and lets them use practically any environment, language, or platform that supports Web Services.

Clearly, a single standard approach has not yet been adopted for extending BPEL to include Human Tasks and workflow services. However, this does not mean that developers cannot use BPEL to develop business processes with user interactions.

Human Task integration with BPEL

To interleave user interactions with service invocations in BPEL processes we can use a workflow service, which interacts with BPEL using standard WSDL interfaces. This way, the BPEL process can assign user tasks and wait for responses by invoking the workflow service using the same syntax as for any other service. The BPEL process can also perform more complex operations such as updating, completing, renewing, routing, and escalating tasks.

After the BPEL process has assigned tasks to users, users can act on the tasks by using the appropriate applications. The applications communicate with the workflow service by using WSDL interfaces or another API (such as Java) to acquire the list of tasks for selected users, render appropriate user interfaces, and return results to the workflow service, which forwards them to the BPEL process. User applications can also perform other tasks such as reassign, escalate, route, suspend, resume, and withdraw. Finally, the workflow service may allow other communication channels, such as e-mail and SMS, as shown in the following figure:

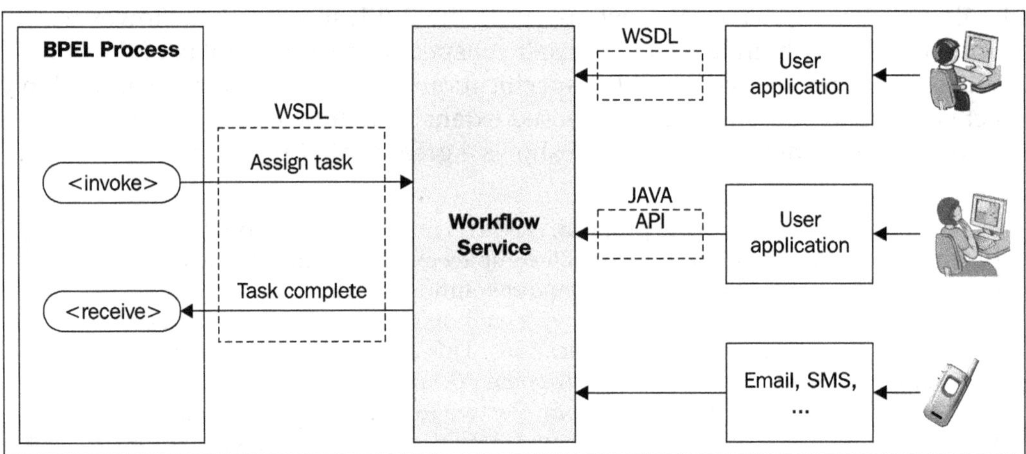

Oracle Human Workflow concepts

Oracle SOA Suite 11*g* provides the **Human Workflow** component, which enables including human interaction in BPEL processes in a relatively easy way. The Human Workflow component consists of different services that handle various aspects of human interaction with business process and expose their interfaces through WSDL; therefore, BPEL processes invoke them just like any other service. The following figure shows the overall architecture of the Oracle Workflow services:

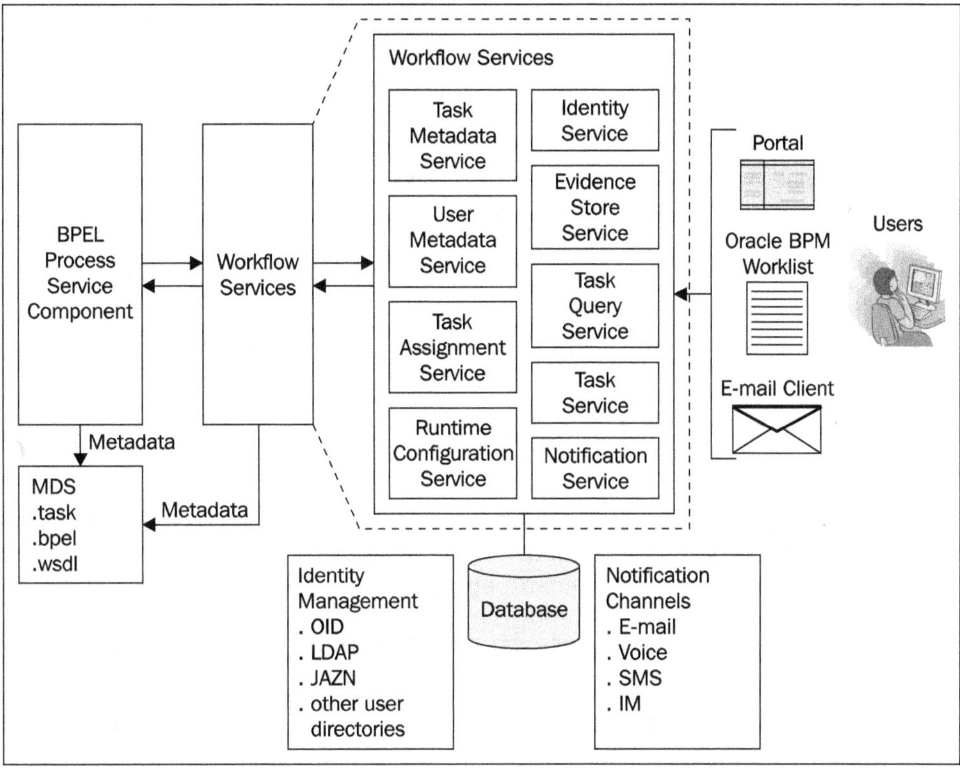

As we can see in the previous figure, the Workflow consists of the following services:

- **Task Service** exposes operations for task state management, such as operations to update a task, complete a task, escalate a task, reassign a task, and so on. When we add a human task to the BPEL process, the corresponding partner link for the Task Service is automatically created.
- **Task Assignment Service** provides functionality to route, escalate, reassign tasks, and more.
- **Task Query Service** enables retrieving the task list for a user based on a search criterion.
- **Task Metadata Service** enables retrieving the task metadata.
- **Identity Service** provides authentication and authorization of users and lookup of user properties and privileges.
- **Notification Service** enables sending of notifications to users using various channels (e-mail, voice message, IM, SMS, and so on).
- **User Metadata Service** manages metadata, related to workflow users, such as user work queues, preferences, and so on.

- **Runtime Configuration Service** provides functionality for managing metadata used in the task service runtime environment.
- **Evidence Store Service** supports management of digitally-signed workflow tasks.

BPEL processes use the Task Service to assign tasks to users. More specifically, tasks can be assigned to:

- **Users**: Users are defined in an identity store configured with the SOA infrastructure.
- **Groups**: Groups contain individual users, which can claim a task and act upon it.
- **Application roles**: Used to logically group users and other roles. These roles are application specific and are not stored in the identity store.

Assigning tasks to groups or roles is more flexible, as every user in a certain group (role) can review the task to complete it. Oracle SOA Suite 11*g* provides three methods for assigning users, groups, and application roles to tasks:

- **Static assignment**: Static users, groups, or application roles can be assigned at design time.
- **Dynamic assignment**: We can define an XPath expression to determine the task participant at runtime.
- **Rule-based assignment**: We can create a list of participants with complex expressions.

Once the user has completed the task, the BPEL process receives a callback from the Task Service with the result of the user action. The BPEL process continues to execute.

The Oracle Workflow component provides several possibilities regarding how users can review the tasks that have been assigned to them, and take the corresponding actions. The most straightforward approach is to use the **Oracle BPM Worklist** application. This application comes with Oracle SOA Suite 11*g* and allows users to review the tasks, to see the task details, and to select the decision to complete the task.

If the Oracle BPM Worklist application is not appropriate, we can develop our own user interface in Java (using JSP, JSF, Swing, and so on) or almost any other environment that supports Web Services (such as .NET for example). In this respect, the Workflow service is very flexible and we can use a portal, such as Oracle Portal, a web application, or almost any other application to review the tasks.

The third possibility is to use e-mail for task reviews. We use e-mails over the Notification service, which we have described earlier in this chapter.

Workflow patterns

To simplify the development of workflows, Oracle SOA Suite 11*g* provides a library of workflow patterns (participant types). Workflow patterns define typical scenarios of human interactions with BPEL processes. The following participant types are supported:

- **Single approver**: Used when a participant maps to a user, group, or role.
- **Parallel**: Used if multiple users have to act in parallel (for example, if multiple users have to provide their opinion or vote). The percentage of required user responses can be specified.
- **Serial**: Used if multiple users have to act in a sequence. A management chain or a list of users can be specified.
- **FYI (For Your Information)**: Used if a user only needs to be notified about a task, but a user response is not required.

With these, we can realize various workflow patterns, such as:

- **Simple workflow**: Used if a single user action is required, such as confirmation, decision, and so on. A timeout can also be specified. Simple workflow has two extension patterns:
    - **Escalation**: Provides the ability to escalate the task to another user or role if the original user does not complete the task in the specified amount of time.
    - **Renewal**: Provides the ability to extend the timeout if the user does not complete the task in the specified time.
- **Sequential workflow**: Used if multiple users have to act in a sequence. A management chain or a list of users can be specified. Sequential workflow has one extension pattern:
    - **Escalation**: Same functionality as above.
- **Parallel workflow**: Used if multiple users have to act in parallel (for example, if multiple users have to provide their opinion or vote). The percentage of required user responses can be specified. This pattern has an extension pattern:
    - **Final reviewer**: Is used when the final review has to act after parallel users have provided feedback.

- **Ad-hoc (dynamic) workflow**: Used to assign the task to one user, who can then route the task to other user. The task is completed when the user does not route it forward.
- **FYI workflow**: Used if a user only needs to be notified about a task, but a user response is not required.
- **Task continuation**: Used to build complex workflow patterns as a chain of simple patterns (those described above).

Creating Human Task definitions

In order to create new human task definition, we drag-and-drop the **Human Task** service component from the **Component Palette** to the composite application. The **Create Human Task** window opens. We set the name of the human task to `FlightTicketApproval` and leave the default namespace. We do not select the **Create Composite Service with SOAP Bindings**, as the human task does not have to be exposed through the web service interface, as we will use it from the BPEL process. If we would use the human task from an external client, we would expose it through the web service interface.

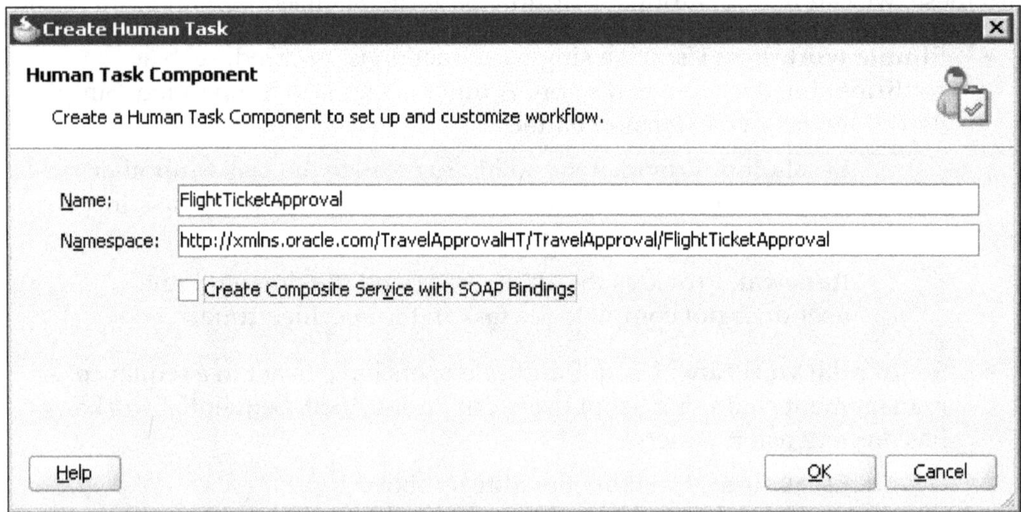

Then we wire the created human task and the BPEL process.

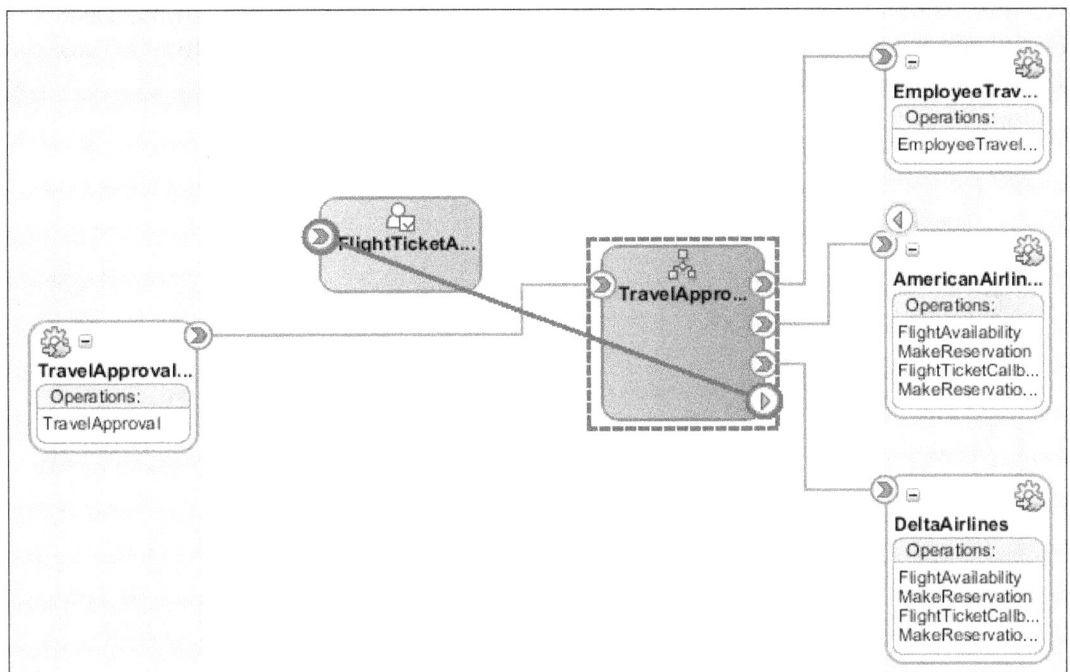

By wiring the human task and the BPEL process, a partner link for the `TaskService` is automatically created in the BPEL process.

Configuring a Human Task title and outcomes

We then double-click the `FlightTicketApproval` Human Task to open the **Task Definition Editor**. We enter `Flight ticket approval` as the **Task Title** (the **Task Title** displays on the BPM Worklist).

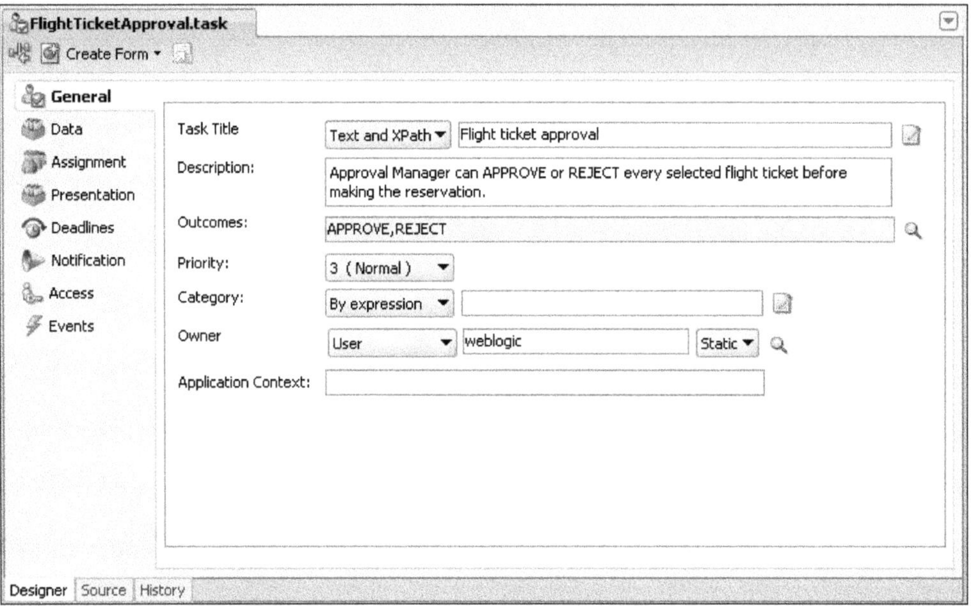

We can also optionally add a **Description** to the Human Task. We leave the default **Outcomes** (`APPROVE` and `REJECT`). When we want to define custom outcomes, we have to click on the magnifying glass icon to open the **Outcomes Dialog**, as shown in the following screenshot:

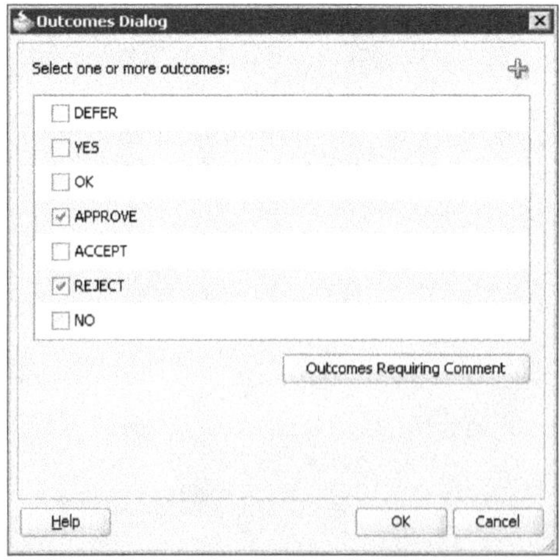

Here we can add new outcomes by clicking the green plus icon. We will not do this; therefore, we close the dialog by clicking **OK**. Back in the **Task Definition Editor** we could also set task **Priority** and **Category**. This can be useful for users of the BPM Worklist application, as they can easily group or filter their tasks based on the priority or category. However, we will not change these values.

We also select the task **Owner** (a person that has administrative privileges on the task). To select a person we click on the magnifying glass icon. The **Identity Lookup** dialog opens. Here we can browse users and select them. In our example, we select the `weblogic` user and click **OK** to close the dialog.

In order to be able to browse for users, we first have to create a connection to the SOA-managed server.

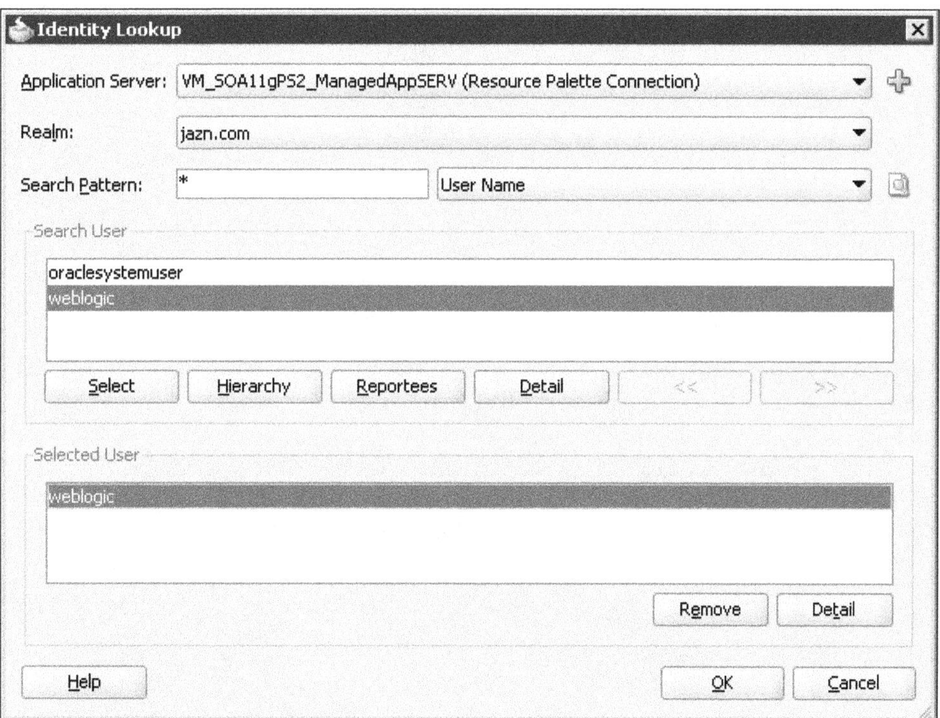

Configuring Human Task payload

Back in the **Task Definition Editor**, we click on the Data tab to set the task payload, as the approval manager will need data about an employee and the selected flight to decide whether to approve the flight ticket or not. Under the **Data** section we click on the plus icon and select **Add other payload**.

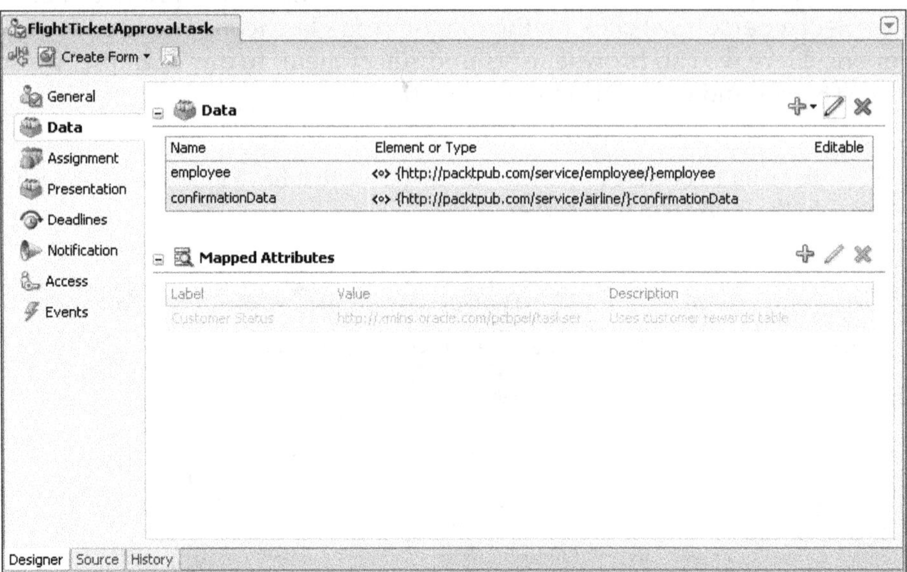

The **Add Task Parameter** dialog opens. We select **Element** and browse for the `employee` element, which is defined in the `EmployeeType.xsd` schema.

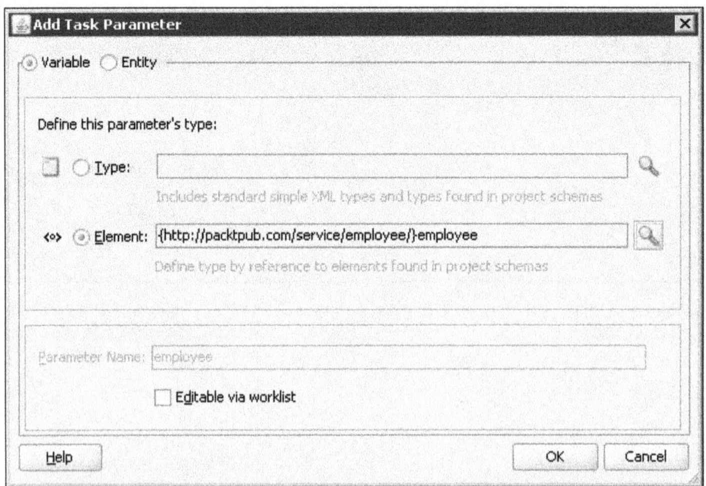

We leave the **Editable via worklist** unchecked, as the approval manager will not need to change the payload. We click **OK** to close the dialog. Then we add another element, which will contain information about the selected flight ticket (`confirmationData`).

Now we set the Human Task payload type. In the BPEL process, we will have to assign the actual data from BPEL variables to the payload.

Configuring Human Task assignments

Next, we open the **Assignment** tab, where we can assign the Human Task to a user, group, or an application role. We click on the **<Edit Participant>** and then on **Edit** to set the participant. The **Add Participant Type** dialog opens. We use the default **Type** (**Single**) and enter the **Label** of the participant (`Approval Manager`). Then we click on the plus icon to add a participant and select **Add User**. Again, we assign the task to user `weblogic`. However, the user could also be set dynamically by using the value from the task payload. In that case, we would have to change the **Data Type** to **By Expression** and use the **Expression Editor** to compose the XPath expression.

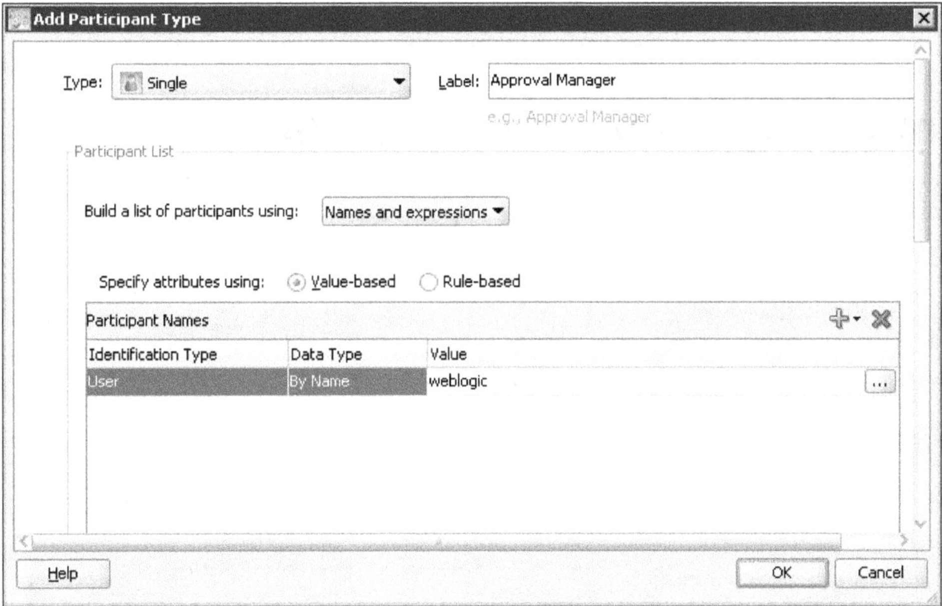

We click **OK** to close the dialog. Back in the **Task Definition Editor** we click on the edit icon in the upper-right corner. The **Configure Assignment** dialog opens. We switch to the **Assignment** tab and select the `weblogic` user to be an error assignee. The error assignee is responsible for performing corrective actions in case an error occurs.

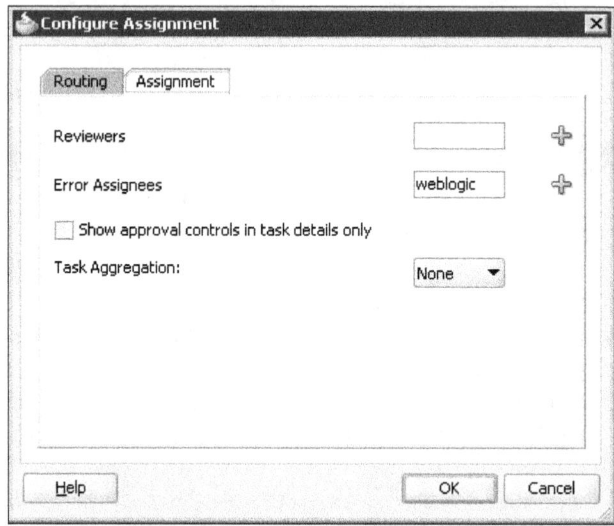

Configuring Human Task deadlines

Next, we switch to the **Deadlines** tab to set the task expiration. From the **Task Duration Settings** drop-down, we select **Expire after** and set the expiration time to `5` minutes (for testing purposes).

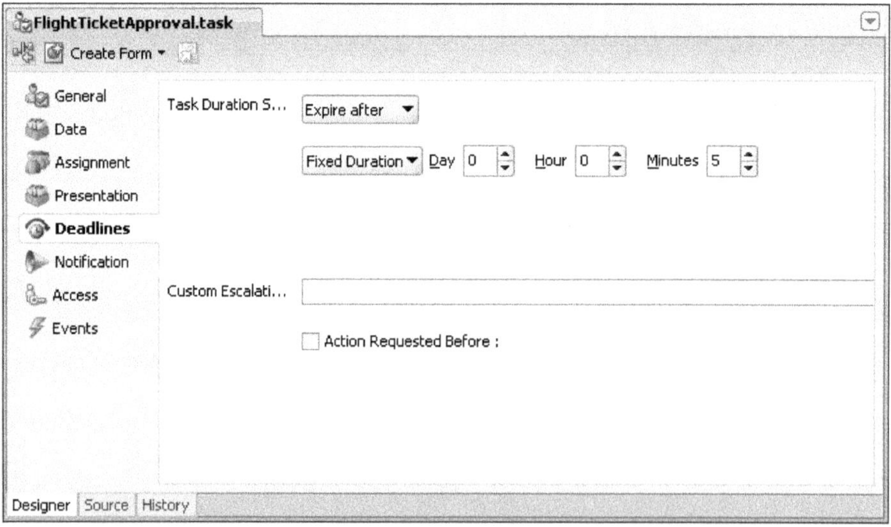

Configuring Human Task notifications

We then click on the **Notification** tab. We configure notifications, so that in case of task expiration or an error, a notification will be automatically send to task owner.

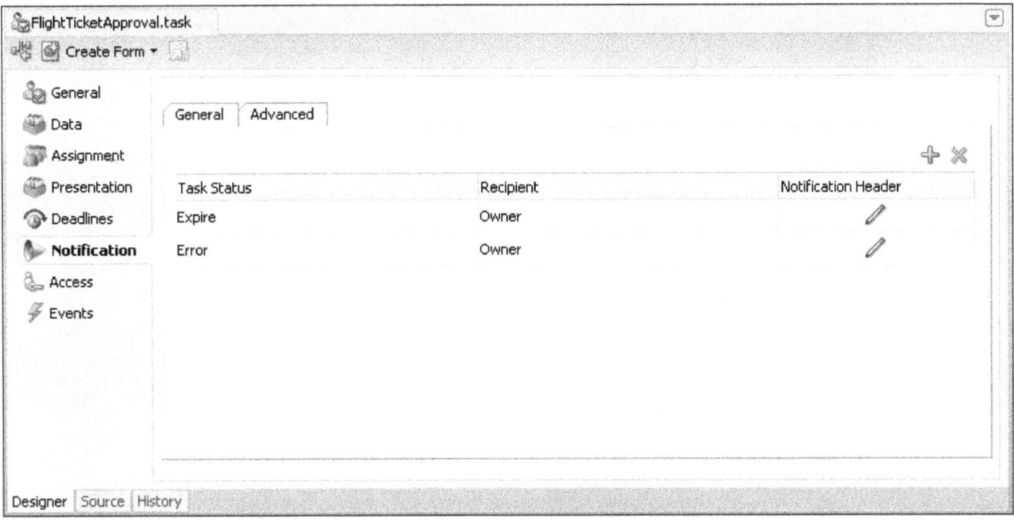

By clicking on the edit icon in the **Notification Header** column, we set the text of a notification message.

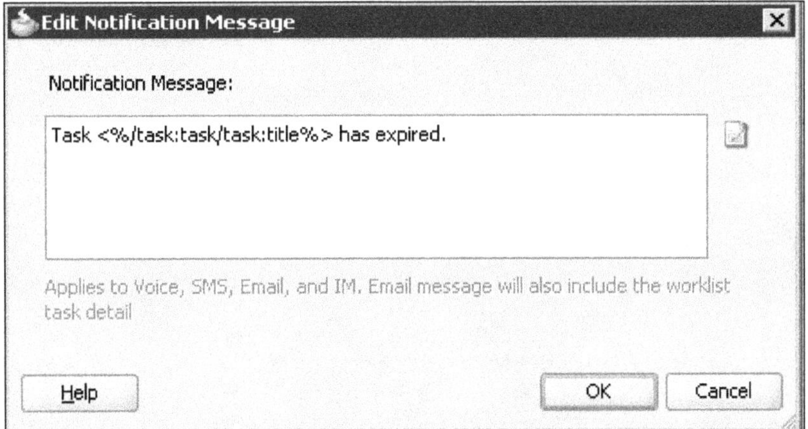

We click **OK** twice to close both dialogs and save the project.

Using Human Tasks in BPEL processes

We double-click the BPEL service component to open the BPEL Component Designer. We will add a human task after the `CheckFlightAvailability` scope. Now every ticket will have to be approved first before making the reservation. However, before adding the Human Task, we also have to create a new variable, which will contain the best offer. Data about the best offer and employee data will then be assigned to the Human Task payload. The decision of the Approval Manager will be based on this data.

Creating variable and adding <switch> activity

We name the new variable `FlightResponseBest`. The variable is of type `TravelResponseMessage` (same as `FlightResponseAA` and `FlightResponseDA`). We also add new **<switch>** activity to be able to compare both offers. Depending on the result, we copy the data from one of the variables containing the offer (`FlightResponseAA` or `FlightResponseDA`) to the `FlightResponseBest`. After creating the new variable and adding `<switch>` and corresponding `<assign>` activities, our BPEL process looks as follows:

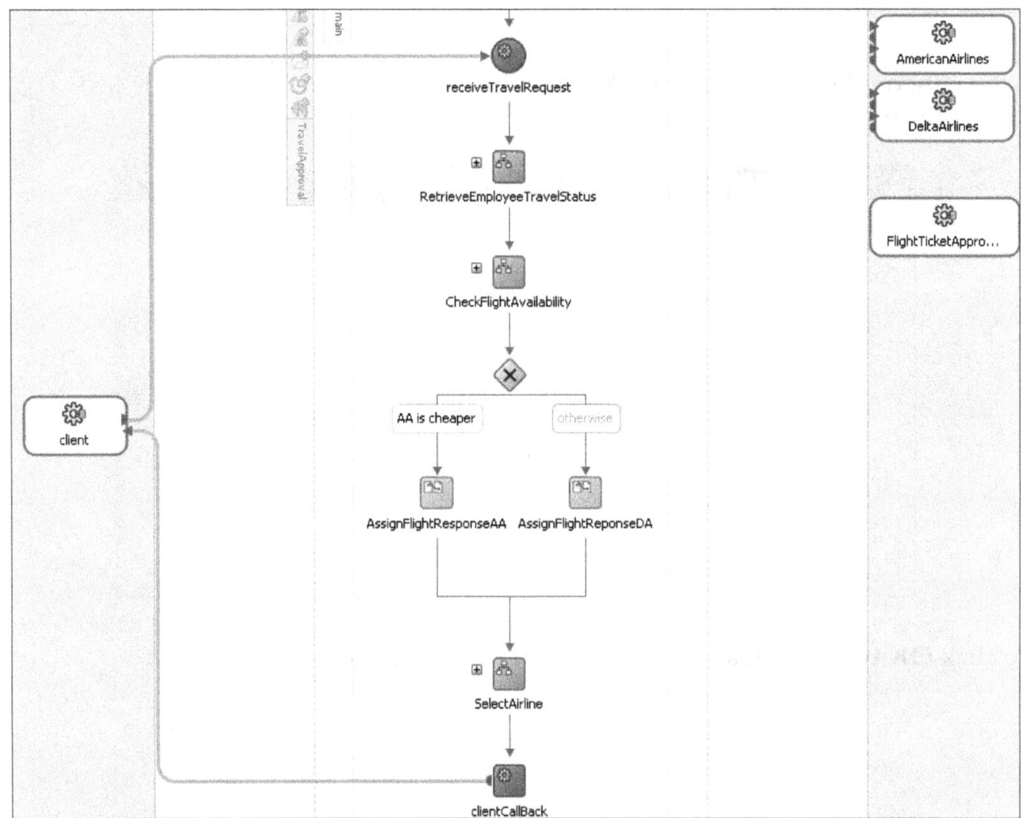

The next screenshot shows the condition expression, used for comparing the offers:

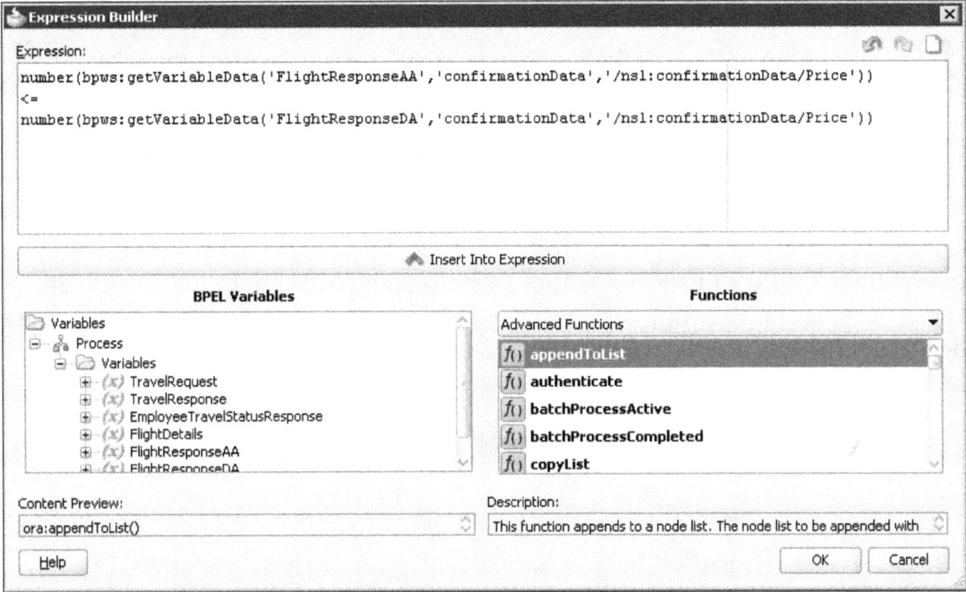

Adding a Human Task

Now, we can drag the **Human Task** service component from the **Component Palette** and drop it just after the new `<switch>` activity. The **Create Human Task** dialog opens.

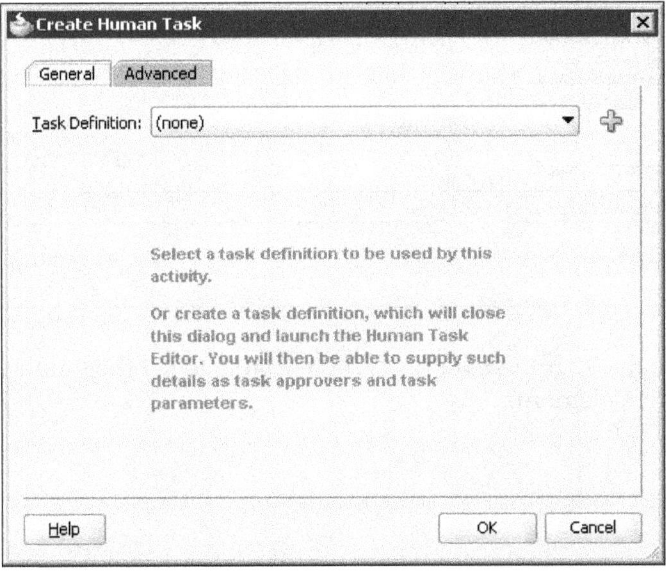

We can create a new Human Task definition by clicking on the plus icon. However, we can also select an existing task definition.

> Human Task definitions can be created either by using the SOA Composite Editor or directly in the BPEL Component Designer. If we create Human Task definition using the BPEL Component Designer, the BPEL process is automatically wired to the created human task on the SOA composite diagram.

We select `FlightTicketApproval` from the **Task Definition** drop-down. We can override task title and set the values of both task parameters (`employee` and `confirmationData`). We click on the three dots icon to open the **Task Parameters** dialog. To set the employee, we use the `TravelRequest` variable as shown in the following screenshot:

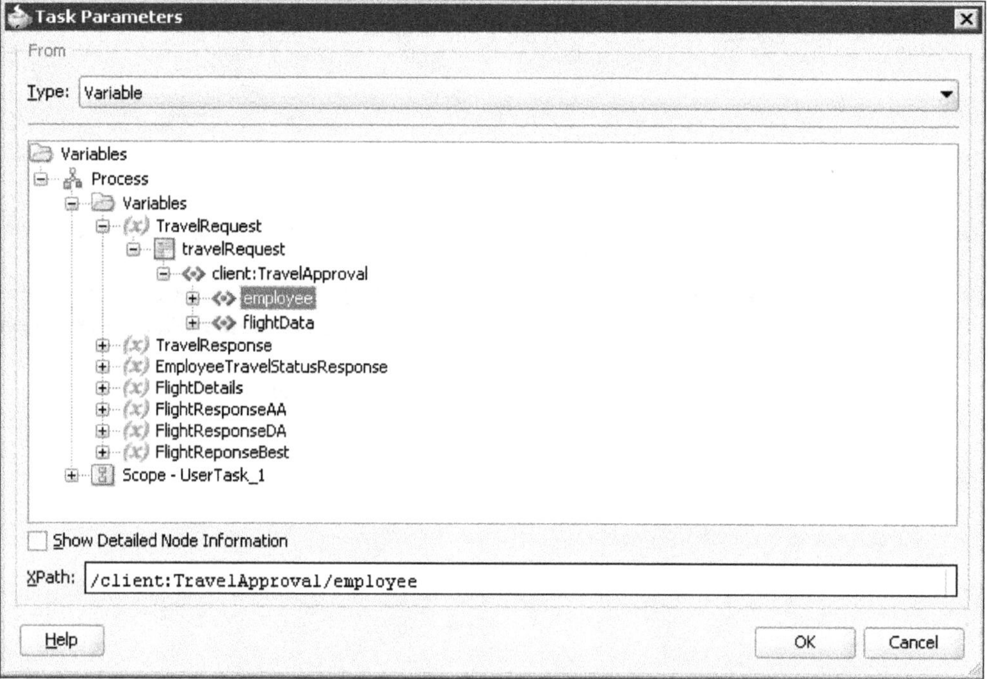

Similarly, we use the `FlightResponseBest` variable to set the value of the `confirmationData` element.

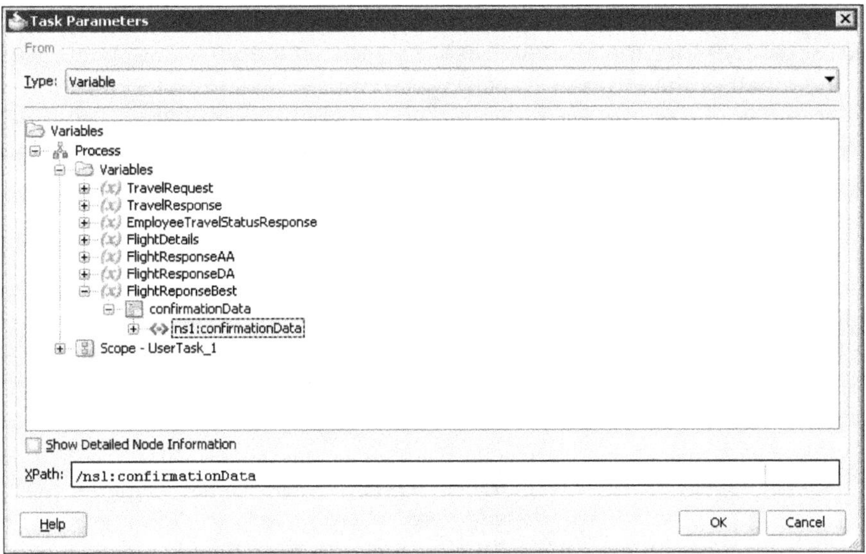

Our **Create Human Task** dialog now looks as follows:

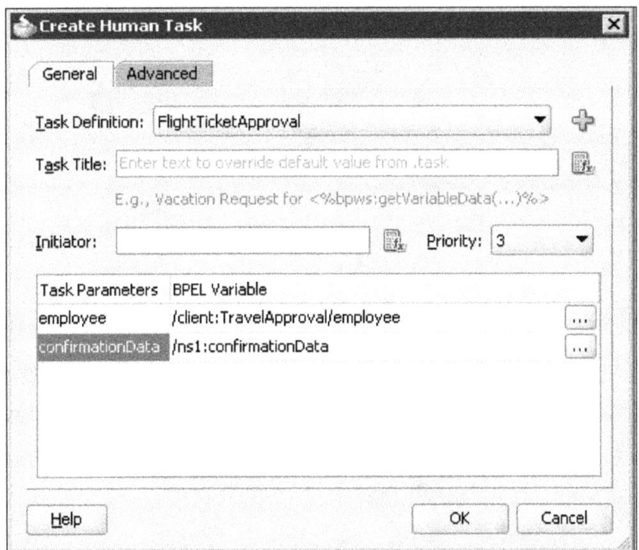

We click **OK** to close the dialog. We can see that a `<switch>` activity has been automatically added after the Human Task. The auto-generated `<switch>` is used to handle the result of the Human Task. As we specified in the task definition, the Approval Manager can either approve the flight ticket or reject it. For each possible task outcome there is a corresponding `<case>` element (condition expressions are automatically generated). Therefore, all activities that have to be executed if the flight ticket is approved have to be added to the `Task outcome is APPROVE` case branch. On the other hand, if the ticket is rejected, activities defined in the `Task outcome is REJECT` case branch will execute. Notice, that there is also the `<otherwise>` branch, which will execute in the case that the Human Task fails or expire. All case branches also have a `CopyPayloadFromTask` `<assign>` activity, which is used for copying the (potentially modified) task payload back to the BPEL variables so that they are refreshed.

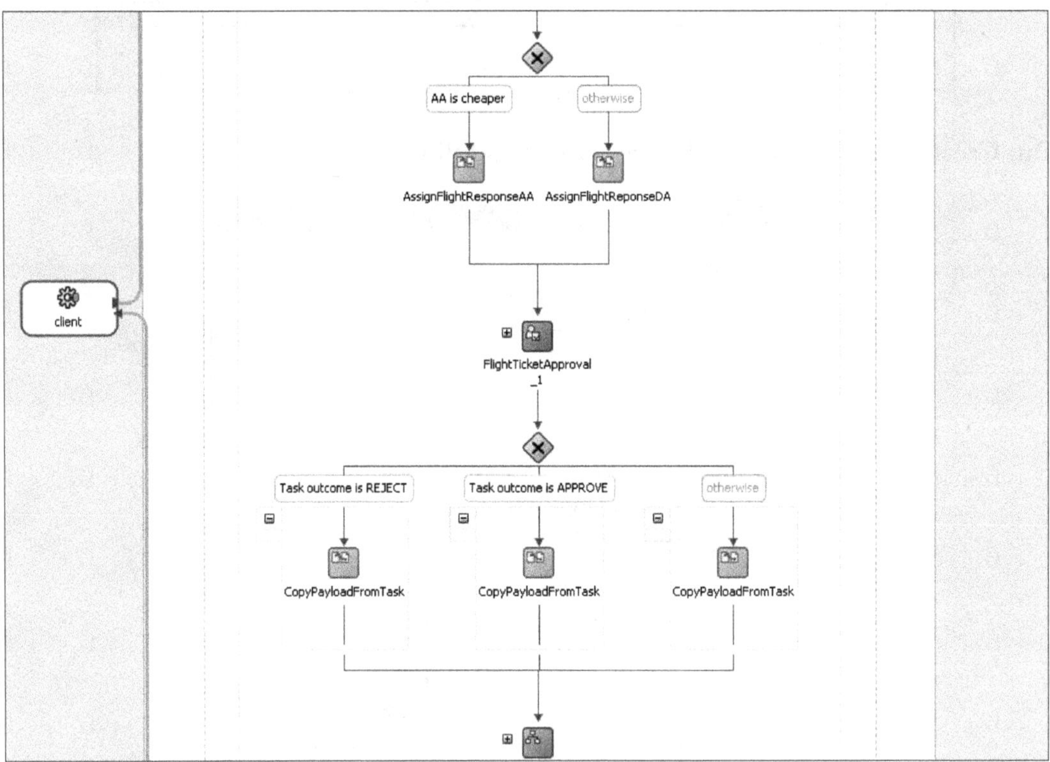

Configuring Human Task case branches

In our case, we do not need `CopyPayloadFromTask` activities, as the Approval Manager will not change the Human Task payload. However, we need to update the `TravelResponse` variable by setting `Confirmed` to `true` (in the case that the ticket is approved) or `false` (when the ticket is rejected or the task has failed or expired). Therefore, we rename those three `<assign>` activities to `UpdateTravelResponse`, delete all existing copy operations, and add a new copy operation to update the `TravelResponse` variable, as shown in the next screenshot:

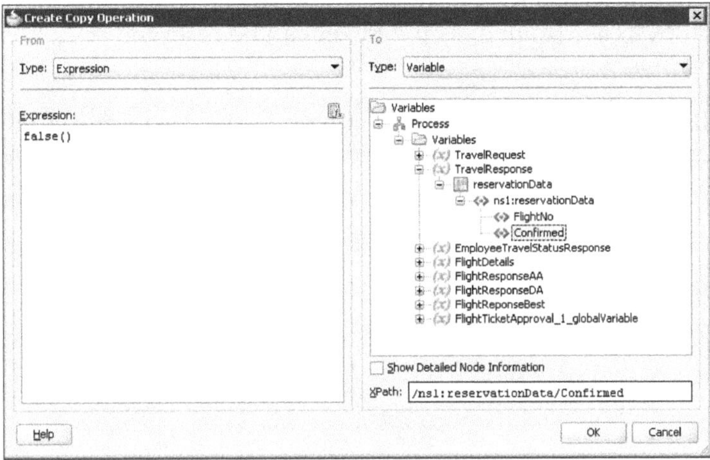

If we expand the `FlightTicketApproval_1` Human Task, we can see that it is actually a scope that contains `<assign>`, `<invoke>`, and `<receive>` activities for invoking the `TaskService`.

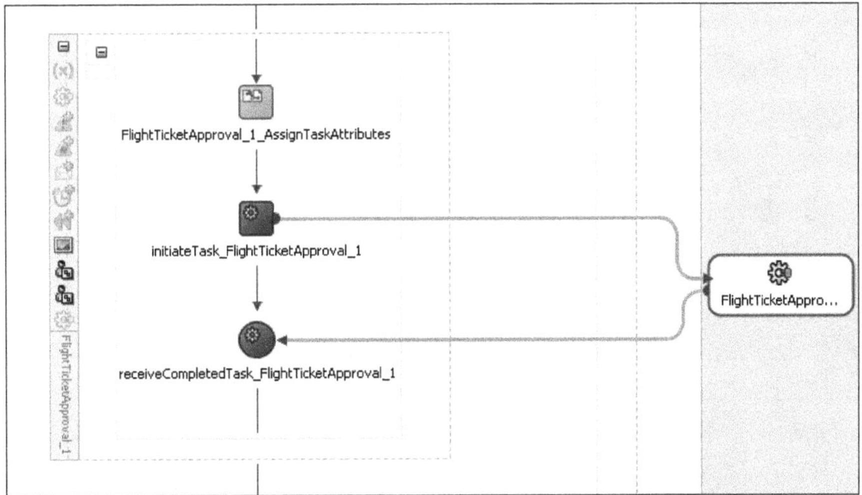

If we want to modify the human task definition, we can do this in three ways:

- In BPEL Component Designer by double-clicking the Human Task and clicking on the **Edit Task Definition** icon
- In BPEL Component Designer by double-clicking the `.task` file in **Application Navigator**
- In the SOA Composite Editor by double-clicking the Human Task service component

Now we will drag-and-drop the entire `SelectAirline` scope into the `Task outcome is APPROVE` case branch, as the ticket can be reserved only if the task outcome equals `APPROVE`.

Our modified BPEL process now looks as shown in the next figure (only the modified part of the process is shown):

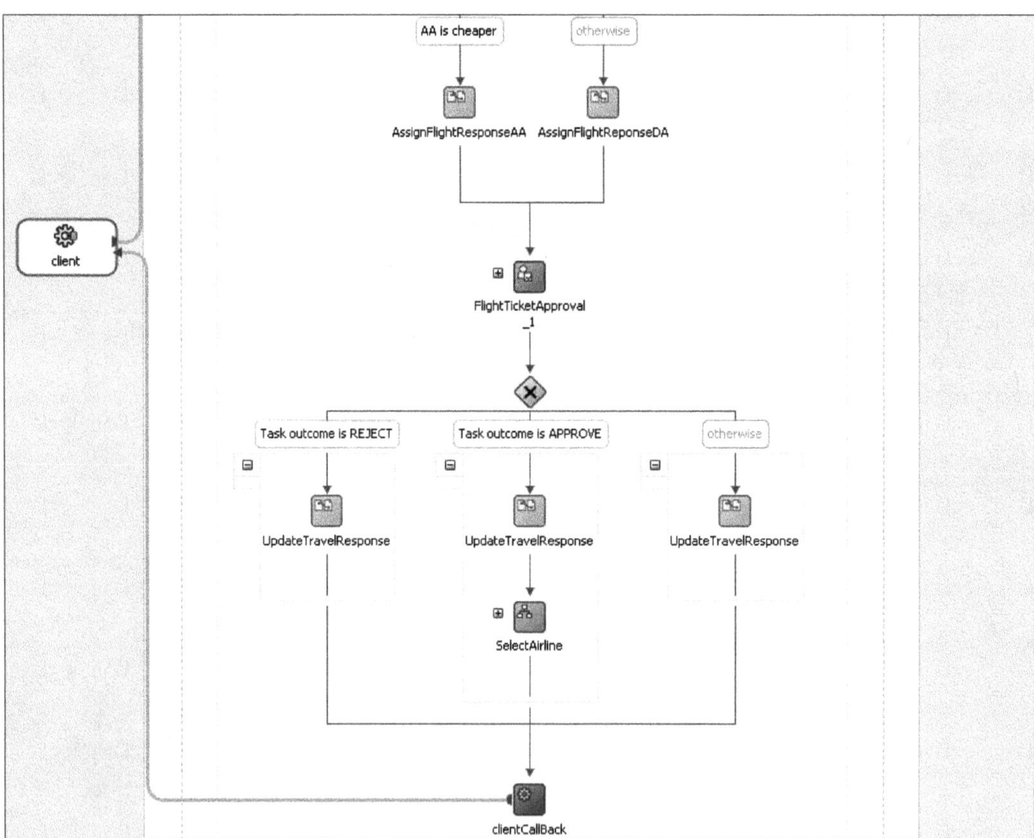

Creating Human Tasks forms

The task form is used to display the content of the task on the users worklist in the Oracle BPM Worklist application. In Oracle SOA Suite 11*g* we can create a task form using the Oracle Application Development Framework (Oracle ADF). When creating the task form, we have two options:

- We can use a wizard to auto-generate the task form
- We can create custom ADF task form in a separate project

As ADF is out of the scope of this book, we will just show how to auto-generate the task form by using a wizard.

Auto-generating a task form

We open the BPEL Component Designer. We right-click on the `FlightTicketApproval_1` Human Task and select **Auto-Generate Task Form**.

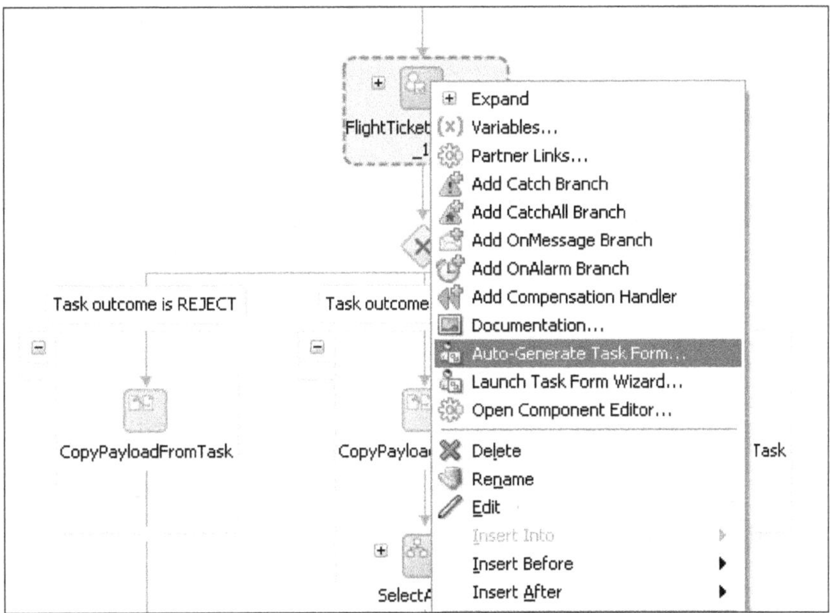

The **Create Project** dialog opens. We name the project `TFormFlightTicketApproval` and click **OK**.

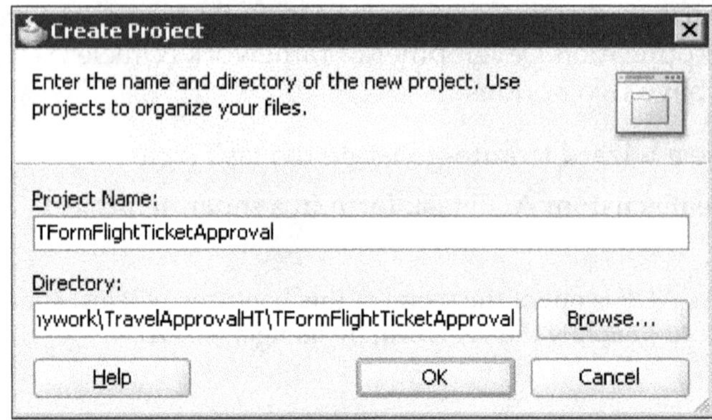

After clicking **OK**, we have to wait for a while as a new project is being generated in the background, until the `taskDetails1.jspx` page opens.

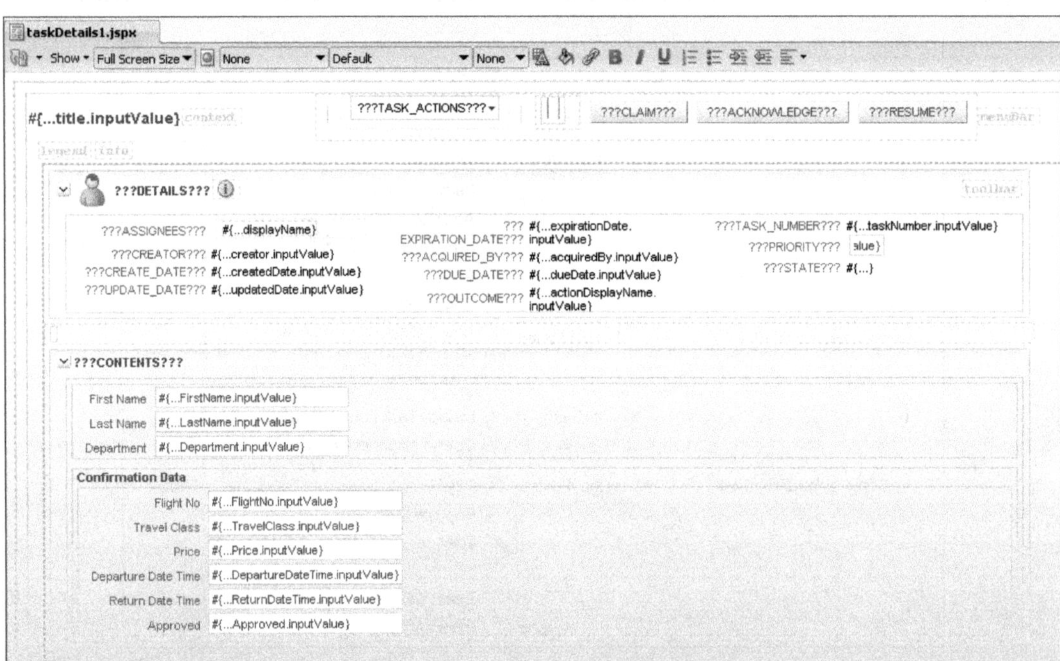

Modifying the task form

We can see that the task form has been successfully created and is ready to be deployed. However, we can also modify the form. We will do some minor changes. First, we remove the `Departure Date Time`, `Return Date Time`, and `Approved` components by selecting them and clicking on **Delete**. Then, we change the order of the rest of the fields and rename the `Confirmation Data` to `Flight Data`, as shown in the following screenshot:

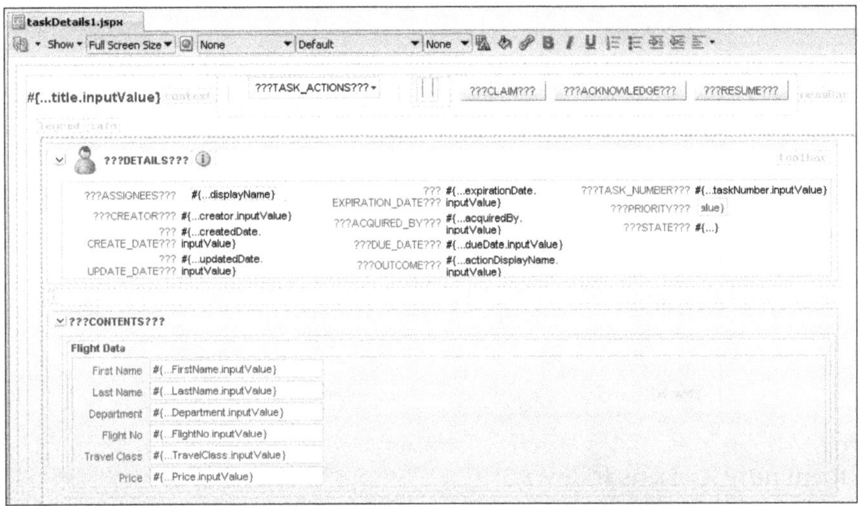

Finally, we modify all input textbox components to be read-only. We can do this by selecting the component and changing the **ReadOnly** property in the **Property Inspector** to `true`.

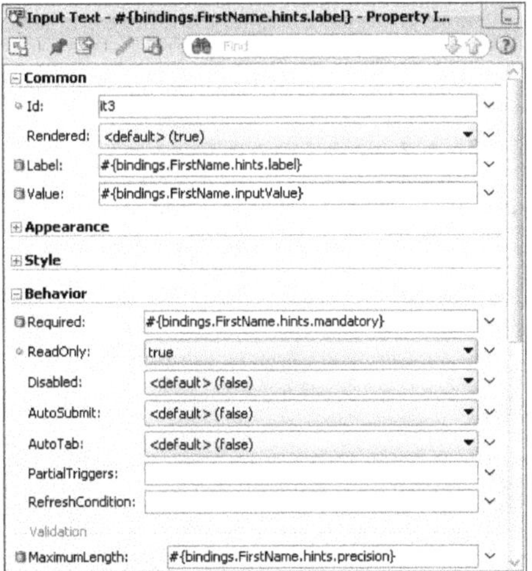

For the price, we also change the **Value** property by adding the € sign.

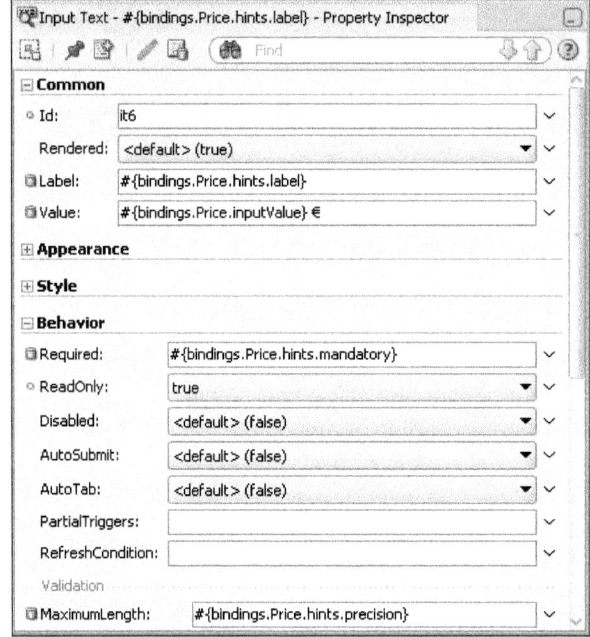

Our task form now looks as follows:

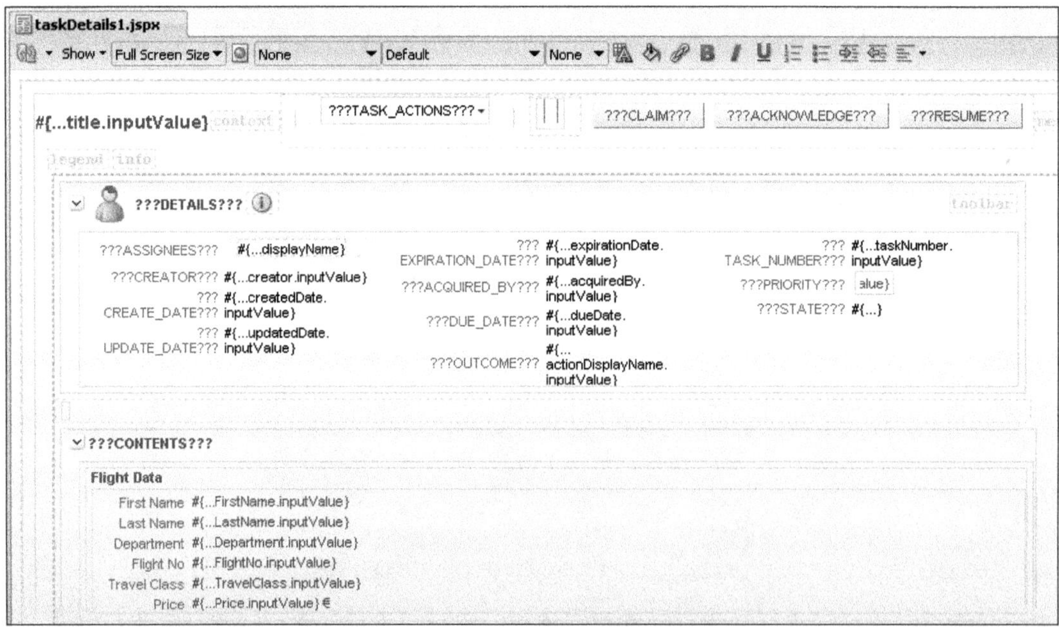

We save the project by clicking on the **Save All** icon in the toolbar and close the task form.

Deploying the SOA composite and task form

Now we will show how to deploy both projects. The easiest way is to deploy both projects at once. As the composite contains a Human Task which is connected to the task form ADF project, the **Task flow deployment** screen appears as part of the SOA composite deployment wizard, as shown in next screenshot. If we select the `TFormFlightTicketApproval` project, this project will be automatically deployed just after the SOA composite project.

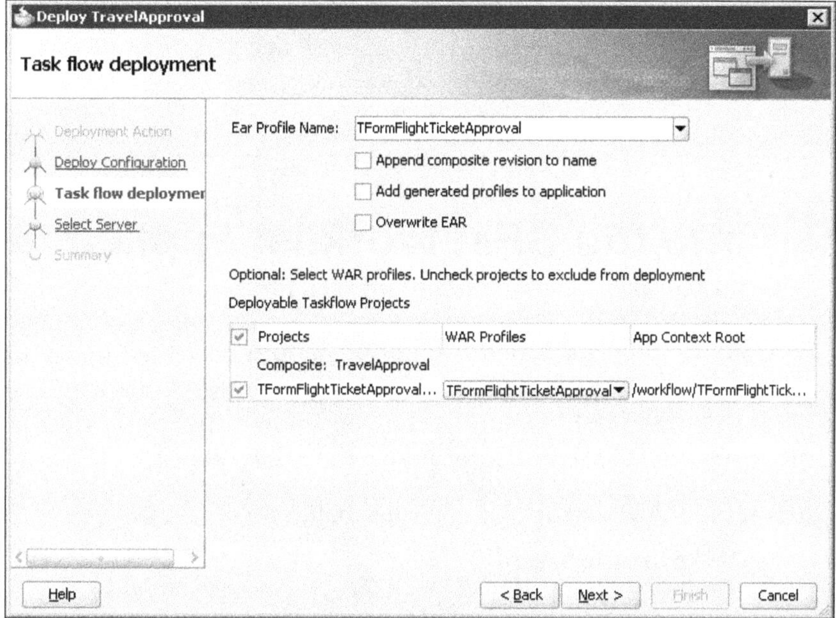

However, the task form ADF project can also be deployed separately. In that case, we have to be sure that the SOA composite project has already been deployed. To deploy the task form ADF project, we have to open the **Application** menu and select **Deploy | TFormFlightTicketApproval**.

Remember that task forms cannot be deployed by right-clicking the project and selecting **Deploy**.

Using the Oracle BPM Worklist application

To test the Human Task, we first need to initiate a new process instance. If we look at the trace of the instance, we can see that the instance is still running and is waiting for the `FlightTicketApproval` human task to complete.

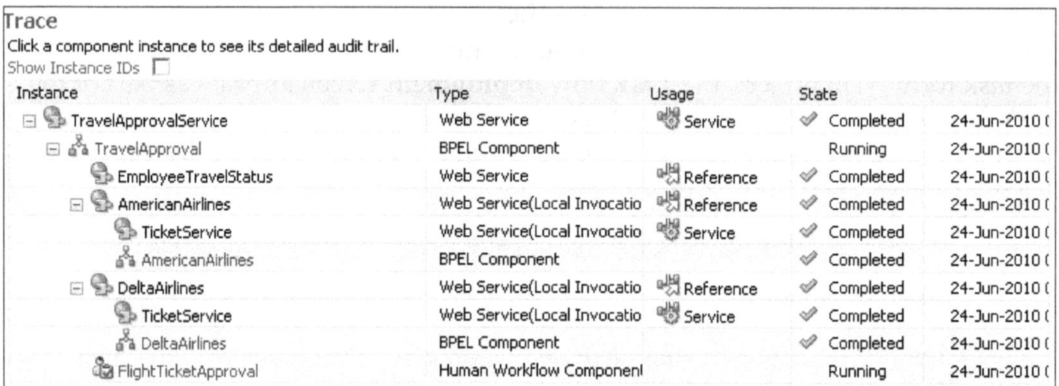

Trace
Click a component instance to see its detailed audit trail.
Show Instance IDs
Instance
Type
Usage
State
TravelApprovalService
Web Service
Service
Completed
24-Jun-2010
TravelApproval
BPEL Component
Running
EmployeeTravelStatus
Reference
AmericanAirlines
Web Service(Local Invocatio
TicketService
DeltaAirlines
FlightTicketApproval
Human Workflow Component

Logging into the BPM Worklist application

To complete the human task, we have to log into the Oracle BPM Worklist application using the following URL: `http://host_name:port/integration/worklistapp/`, where `host_name` is the name of the host on which the Worklist application is installed and `port` is the port number of the SOA-managed server (the default is `8001`). Oracle BPM Worklist is a very powerful application, allowing users not only to act on tasks, but also provides the following capabilities and more:

- Customizing the visual appearance and behavior
- Reassign tasks to other users
- Escalate, renew, withdraw, and suspend tasks
- Setting the vacation period to automatically reassign tasks during absence
- Creating reports on task productivity, time distribution, and so on
- Sending of notifications and alerts

However, we will not discuss advanced features in this section. Now, we log in to the BPM Worklist application as the user `weblogic`, as the task is assigned to this user. The BPM Worklist application opens as shown in next screenshot.

By default, the **Inbox** worklist view is selected and the user can see all tasks assigned to him in the **My Tasks** list. In our case, there is only one active task: `Flight ticket approval`. Remember that this is the name of the Human Task that we set during the creation of the Human Task definition.

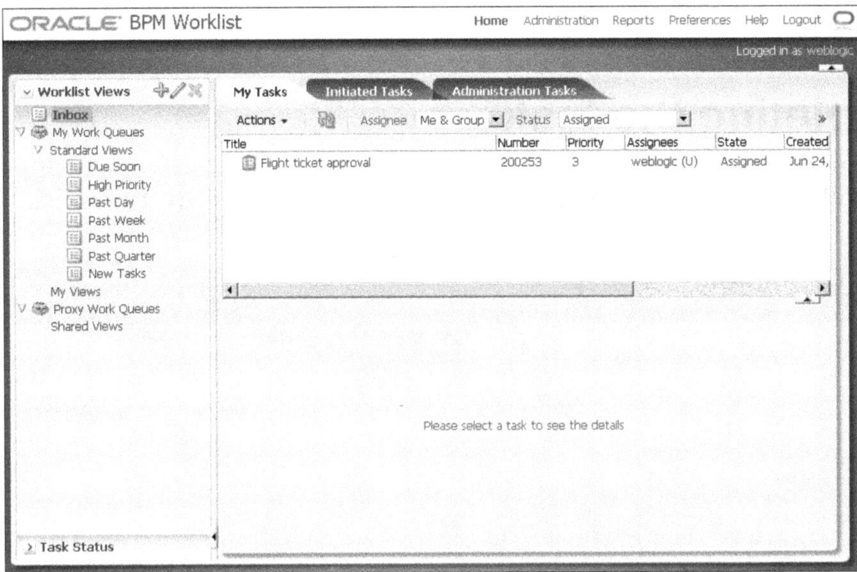

If we want to see the task details, we have to select the task. The ADF task form displaying task details opens at the bottom of the screen.

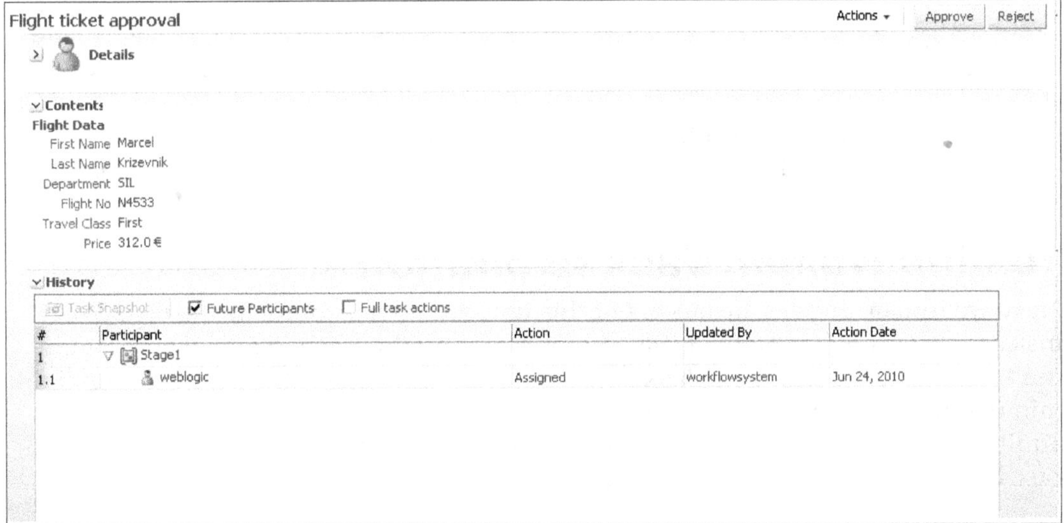

In the upper-left corner there is a task title. We can also see two buttons (**Approve** and **Reject**), that present possible task outcomes. In order to complete the task, we have to click on one of those two buttons. In the **Contents** section we can see the payload of the task, displaying information about the selected flight ticket. At the bottom of the task form we can also see the task history and add comments and attachments.

Completing the task

Now we will complete the task by clicking the **Approve** button (we will approve the flight ticket). The task is completed and is removed from the **My Tasks** list.

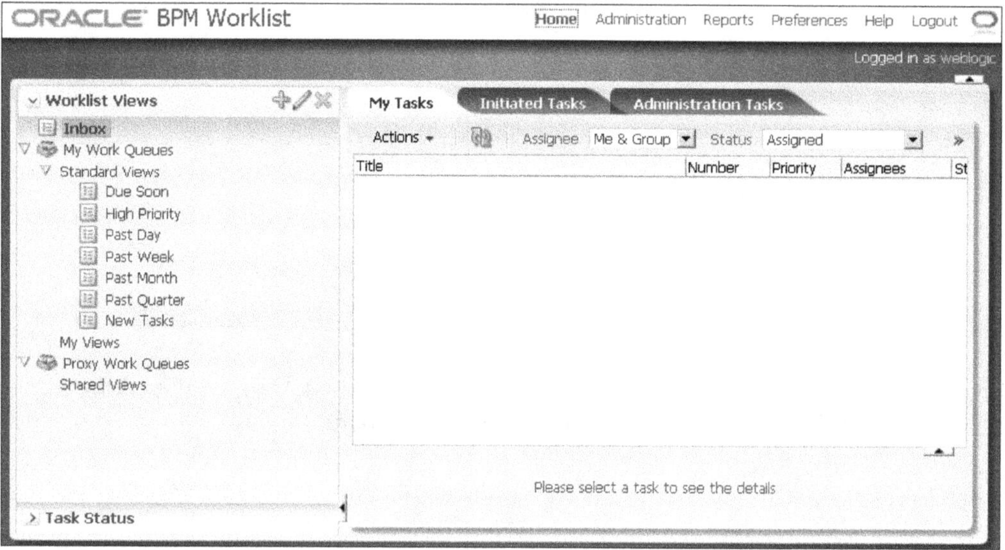

If we look at the flow trace of the instance, we can see that the instance has successfully completed and that the reservation of the flight ticket has been made.

Testing Human Task expiration

Next, we initiate another instance, but this time we do not complete the task. We instead let it expire (remember that we set the expiration time to 5 minutes). Again the `Flight ticket approval` task appears in the **My Tasks** list. However, after 5 minutes, the task expires and disappears from the list. If we look at the instance audit trail, we can see that the instance has completed by executing the otherwise case branch and that no ticket reservation has been made.

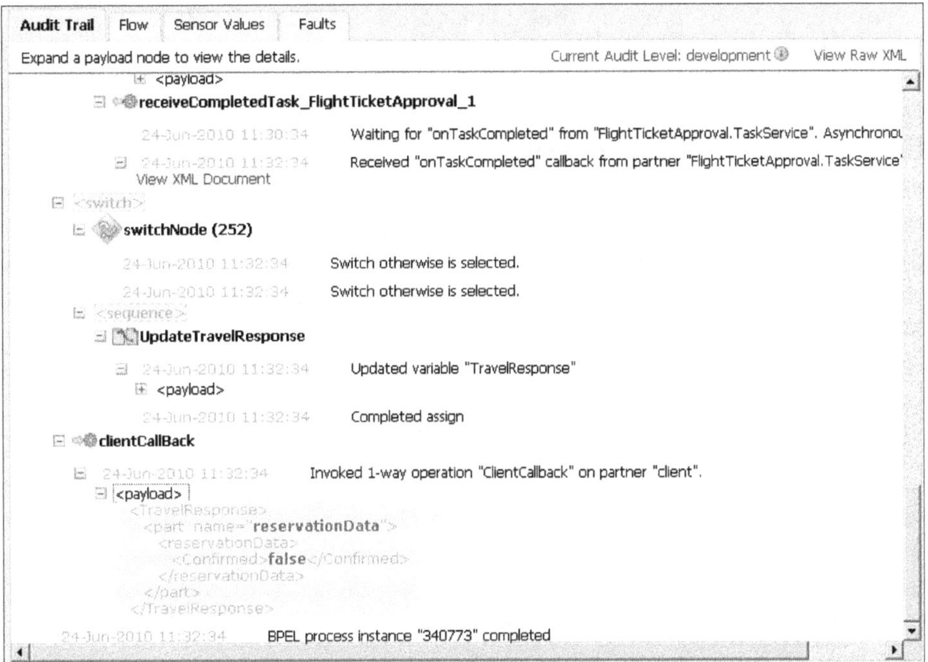

We do not need to use the Oracle BPM Worklist application. Instead, we can use the Workflow Service API and build our own worklist application by using ADF, Java, .NET, or other technology.

BPEL4People

BPEL4People has been developed to provide extensive support for human interactions in BPEL processes and to standardize the human interactions. Originally, the BPEL4People specification was defined by IBM and SAP. Other companies, such as Oracle, Active Endpoints, and Adobe have also joined. Today, this specification has being advanced within the OASIS BPEL4People Technical Committee. The BPEL4People specification contains two parts:

- BPEL4People version 1.0, which introduces BPEL extensions to address human interactions in BPEL
- Web Services Human Task (WS-HumanTask) version 1.0 introduces the definition of human tasks

BPEL4People is defined in a way that it is layered on top of the BPEL language. We will now have a brief look at the WS-HumanTask and then at the BPEL4People.

Brief look at WS-HumanTask

The WS-HumanTask specification introduces Human Tasks to BPEL. Human Tasks are *services*, implemented by humans. A Human Task has two interfaces. One interface exposes the service offered by the task, like a translation service or an approval service. The second interface allows people to deal with tasks, for example to query for human tasks waiting for them, and to work on these tasks. This is very similar to human tasks in WebSphere, with two main differences—WS-HumanTask standardizes tasks among different vendors, and WS-HumanTask introduces new activities for specifying the properties of human tasks. In WebSphere, we had to use the Integration Developer GUI instead.

WS-HumanTask makes a distinction between Human Tasks and notifications. Notifications are a special type of Human Task that allows the sending of information about noteworthy business events to users. Notifications are always delivered one-way. There is no response from notifications expected.

Overall structure

The overall structure of the human interactions definition is as follows:

```
<?xml version="1.0" encoding="UTF-8"?>
<htd:humanInteractions
  xmlns:htd="http://www.example.org/WS-HT"
  xmlns:xsd="http://www.w3.org/2001/XMLSchema"
  xmlns:tns="anyURI"
  targetNamespace="anyURI"
  expressionLanguage="anyURI"?
  queryLanguage="anyURI"?>

  <htd:extensions>?
    <htd:extension namespace="anyURI" mustUnderstand="yes|no"/>+
  </htd:extensions>
  <htd:import namespace="anyURI"?
    location="anyURI"?
    importType="anyURI" />*
  <htd:logicalPeopleGroups>?
    <htd:logicalPeopleGroup name="NCName" reference="QName"?>+
        <htd:parameter name="NCName" type="QName" />*
    </htd:logicalPeopleGroup>
  </htd:logicalPeopleGroups>

  <htd:tasks>?
```

```
    <htd:task name="NCName">+
        ...
    </htd:task>
  </htd:tasks>
  <htd:notifications>?
    <htd:notification name="NCName">+
        ...
    </htd:notification>
  </htd:notifications>
</htd:humanInteractions>
```

Human Tasks

The most important is the definition of the Human Task. The definition includes the following:

- Interface
- Priority
- People assignments
- Delegation
- Presentation elements
- Outcome
- Search priorities
- Renderings
- Deadlines (start and competition deadlines)

The WS-HumanTask specification foresees the following syntax to define a human task:

```
<htd:task name="NCName">
  <htd:interface portType="QName"
    operation="NCName"
    responsePortType="QName"?
    responseOperation="NCName"?/>
  <htd:priority expressionLanguage="anyURI"?>?
    integer-expression
  </htd:priority>
  <htd:peopleAssignments>
    ...
  </htd:peopleAssignments>
  <htd:delegation potentialDelegatees=
    "anybody|nobody|potentialOwners|other"/>?
```

```
      <htd:from>?
          ...
      </htd:from>
    </htd:delegation>
    <htd:presentationElements>
      ...
    </htd:presentationElements>
    <htd:outcome part="NCName" queryLanguage="anyURI">?
      queryContent
    </htd:outcome>
    <htd:searchBy expressionLanguage="anyURI"?>?
      expression
    </htd:searchBy>
    <htd:renderings>?
      <htd:rendering type="QName">+
          ...
      </htd:rendering>
    </htd:renderings>
    <htd:deadlines>?
      <htd:startDeadline>*
          ...
      </htd:startDeadline>
      <htd:completionDeadline>*
          ...
      </htd:completionDeadline>
    </htd:deadlines>
  </htd:task>
```

Escalations

Within the deadlines, escalations can be defined. An example of defining an escalation is shown as follows:

```
  <htd:escalation name="highPrio">
    <htd:condition>
      <![CDATA[
        (htd:getInput("OrderRequest")/amount < 1000
        && htd:getInput("OrderRequest")/prio <= 10) ]]>
    </htd:condition>

    <htd:notification name="ClaimApprovalOverdue">

      <htd:interface portType="tns:ClaimsHandlingPT"
        operation="escalate" />

      <htd:peopleAssignments>
          <htd:recipients>
```

```
            <htd:from logicalPeopleGroup="Manager">
                <htd:argument name="region">
                    htd:getInput("OrderRequest")/region
                </htd:argument>
            </htd:from>
        </htd:recipients>
    </htd:peopleAssignments>

    <htd:presentationElements>
        <htd:name>
            Order approval overdue.
        </htd:name>
    </htd:presentationElements>
  </htd:notification>
</htd:escalation>
```

In a similar way, a reassignment could be done.

Notifications

Notifications are defined with the following:

- Interface
- Priority
- People assignments
- Presentation elements
- Renderings

An example is shown as follows:

```
<htd:notification name="NCName">
  <htd:interface portType="QName" operation="NCName"/>
  <htd:priority expressionLanguage="anyURI"?>?
    integer-expression
  </htd:priority>
  <htd:peopleAssignments>
    <htd:recipients>
        ...
    </htd:recipients>
    <htd:businessAdministrators>?
        ...
    </htd:businessAdministrators>
  </htd:peopleAssignments>
  <htd:presentationElements>
```

```
    ...
  </htd:presentationElements>
  <htd:renderings>?
    ...
  </htd:renderings>
</htd:notification>
```

Programming interface

The WS-HumanTask specification also defines the API for applications that are involved with the life cycle of a human task or a notification. It provides several types of operations, including:

- Participant operations, such as operation for claiming tasks, starting, stopping, suspending tasks, completing tasks, setting priority, delegating, and so on
- Simple query operations, such as `getMyTasks` and `getMyTaskAbstracts`
- Advanced query operation, which provides several possibilities for retrieving the tasks
- Administrative operations for nominating and activating tasks, and setting generic human roles

The specification also defined XPath extension functions to retrieve Human Task properties.

Now that we are familiar with WS-HumanTask, let us have a brief look at the BPEL4People specification.

Brief look at BPEL4People

BPEL4People is a BPEL extension, which adds several activities to the BPEL language. The most important extensions introduced in BPEL4People are people activities and people links. People activities are used to define human interactions. For each people activity, the BPEL server must create work items and distribute them to users eligible to execute them. People activities can have input and output variables and can specify deadlines. This is very similar to what we have seen in the WebSphere support for human tasks.

To specify the implementation of people activities, BPEL4People introduces tasks. Tasks specify actions that users must perform. Tasks can have descriptions, priorities, deadlines, and other properties. Tasks can be represented in-line, or using WS-HumanTask.

To associate people activities and the related tasks with users or groups of users, BPEL4People introduces people links. They associate users with one or more people activities. People links are usually associated with generic human roles, such as process initiator, process stakeholders, owners, and administrators.

Overall structure

The overall structure of BPEL4People extensions is as follows:

```
<bpel:process ...
  xmlns:b4p="http://www.example.org/BPEL4People"
  xmlns:htd="http://www.example.org/WS-HT">
  ...
  <bpel:extensions>
    <bpel:extension namespace="http://www.example.org/BPEL4People"
      mustUnderstand="yes"/>
    <bpel:extension namespace="http://www.example.org/WS-HT"
      mustUnderstand="yes"/>
  </bpel:extensions>
  <bpel:import importType="http://www.example.org/WS-HT" .../>
  <b4p:humanInteractions>?
    <htd:logicalPeopleGroups>?
        <htd:logicalPeopleGroup name="NCName">+
            ...
        </htd:logicalPeopleGroup>
    </htd:logicalPeopleGroups>
    <htd:tasks>?
        <htd:task name="NCName">+
            ...
        </htd:task>
    </htd:tasks>
    <htd:notifications>?
        <htd:notification name="NCName">+
            ...
        </htd:notification>
    </htd:notifications>
  </b4p:humanInteractions>

  <b4p:peopleAssignments>
    ...
  </b4p:peopleAssignments>
  ...
  <bpel:extensionActivity>
    <b4p:peopleActivity name="NCName" ...>
```

```
        ...
      </b4p:peopleActivity>
    </bpel:extensionActivity>
    ...
</bpel:process>
```

Let us have a look at the new elements:

- The element `<b4p:humanInteractions>` contains declarations of elements from the WS-HumanTask namespace, such as `<htd:logicalPeopleGroups>`, `<htd:tasks>`, and `<htd:notifications>`. The element `<htd:logicalPeopleGroup>` specifies a logical people group used in an inline human task or a people activity. The `<htd:task>` element is used to provide the definition of an inline human task. The `<htd:notification>` element is used to provide the definition of an inline notification.
- The element `<b4p:peopleAssignments>` is used to assign people to process-related generic human roles.
- The new activity `<b4p:peopleActivity>` is used to model human interactions within BPEL processes.

People assignments

BPEL4People defines generic human roles. These roles define what a person or a group of people can do with the process instance. The specification defines three process-related generic human roles:

- **Process initiator**: Person that triggered the process instance
- **Process stakeholders**: People who can influence the progress of a process instance, for example, by adding ad-hoc attachments, forwarding a task, or simply observing the progress of the process instance
- **Business administrators**: People allowed to perform administrative actions on the business process instances

The syntax of people assignments looks like this:

```
<b4p:peopleAssignments>
  <b4p:processInitiator>?
    <htd:from ...>
        ...
    </htd:from>
  </b4p:processInitiator>
  <b4p:processStakeholders>?
    <htd:from ...>
```

```
      ...
    </htd:from>
  </b4p:processStakeholders>
  <b4p:businessAdministrators>?
    <htd:from ...>
      ...
    </htd:from>
  </b4p:businessAdministrators>
</b4p:peopleAssignments>
```

People activities

People activities are used to integrate human interactions within BPEL processes. A people activity can be integrated with an inline Human Task or with a standalone Human Task. An inline task can be defined as part of a people activity. A standalone Human Task is defined separately and can be used several times. To specify Human Tasks, we use the WS-HumanTask specification.

The overall syntax is as follows:

```
<b4p:peopleActivity name="NCName"
  inputVariable="NCName"?
  outputVariable="NCName"?
  isSkipable="xsd:boolean"?
  standard-attributes>
  standard-elements
    ( <htd:task>...</htd:task>
    | <b4p:localTask>...</b4p:localTask>
    | <b4p:remoteTask>...</b4p:remoteTask>
    | <htd:notification>...</htd:notification>
    | <b4p:localNotification>...</b4p:localNotification>
    | <b4p:remoteNotification>...</b4p:remoteNotification>
    )
  <b4p:scheduledActions>?
    ...
  </b4p:scheduledActions>
  <bpel:toParts>?
    <bpel:toPart part="NCName" fromVariable="BPELVariableName"/>+
  </bpel:toParts>
  <bpel:fromPart part="NCName" toVariable="BPELVariableName"/>+
  <bpel:fromPart>?

  </bpel:fromParts>
  <b4p:attachmentPropagation fromProcess="all|none"
    toProcess="all|newOnly|none"/>?
</b4p:peopleActivity>
```

Summary

In this chapter, we have looked at the human interactions in BPEL processes. Although BPEL has been initially designed for system-to-system interactions, it has quickly become obvious that business processes include human interactions.

The BPEL specification does not explicitly mention human interactions; therefore, two solutions have emerged over time. The first solution uses a dedicated Human Task service to handle human interactions. This way, a BPEL process can initiate a Human Task using the invoke activity in the same way as invoking any other service. The Human Task service exposes an API to the user interface application, which is responsible for showing the task list and the task details. This approach is common in all major SOA platforms, including Oracle.

The second approach has emerged with the BPEL4People and WS-HumanTask specifications. These specifications have standardized the approach to BPEL human interactions and made it portable through different SOA process servers. We have overviewed both specifications and have seen that there are no major conceptual differences between the current Oracle support and the approach taken in specifications. At the time of writing, it has not been clear how much support these specifications will get from SOA platform vendors.

In the next chapter, we will look at monitoring BPEL processes with BAM and will see how to add sensors to BPEL processes and how to develop BAM dashboards in order to monitor the **KPI** (**Key Performance Indicators**) and other process metrics.

8
Monitoring BPEL Processes with BAM

If we want to ensure high efficiency of our business processes, we need real-time information about the execution of business activities. We want to detect bottlenecks and other critical situations as soon as possible to be able to improve business operations and facilitates better business decisions. All this can be achieved using **Business Activity Monitoring** (**BAM**) systems. BAM enables us to monitor Key Performance Indicators (KPI) and other metrics and display the information in a BAM dashboard. We can also define alerts and notifications to be automatically notified when a critical situation occurs.

In this chapter, we will get familiar with Oracle BAM Server, which is an integral part of Oracle SOA Suite 11*g*. First, we will look at the Oracle BAM architecture and features. Then we will present possible ways to send business data from BPEL processes to Oracle BAM. We will also discuss data objects, sensors, sensor actions, monitoring objects, and BAM dashboards. Finally, we will demonstrate how to enable monitoring on our TravelApproval BPEL process that we have already used in previous chapters. The result will be a BAM dashboard, which will show real-time data about the execution of business processes by displaying a list of last process instances, the percentage of confirmed flight tickets, the effectiveness of the Approval Manager, and the number of reserved tickets by airline.

In this chapter, we will discuss the following:

- Oracle BAM architecture and features
- Sending data to Oracle BAM from BPEL process
- Creating data objects
- The use of monitoring objects
- The use of sensors and sensor actions
- Creating the BAM dashboard

Business Activity Monitoring

Business Activity Monitoring (BAM) provides a real-time operational view on the business processes and activities within an organization. This way business users and managers can get a real-time insight into business operations. This can help identify business problems, correct exceptions, and optimize processes. The objective of BAM is to ensure that business goals, such as time-to-market, customer response, profit, cost per order, order to cash, and so on are fulfilled.

BAM extends the scope of business intelligence beyond strategic and tactical business decision making to the management of day-to-day business operations. In contrast to traditional business intelligence that acts upon historical data, BAM uses real-time or near real-time data to provide operational insights into current business activities.

BAM helps us to identify how our business processes perform and where to optimize them. BAM gathers information about the Key Performance Indicators (KPIs) and other metrics derived from business processes, business activity data, and business events. It presents the KPIs and other metrics on dashboards, where business users and managers can monitor them and act upon them immediately. BAM also provides business users with alerts to potential business situations.

Business Activity Monitoring focuses on how your business is performing.

With BAM, we can gather data about process execution, such as how long does it take my process to execute on average, which activities are the most time consuming, how long does it take for human tasks to be claimed and completed, and so on. BAM can show us how many process instances are active at a specific time, and how long, on average, it takes to complete a process. They can also show us which users (employees) have started how many process instances, and so on.

We can also monitor more specific KPIs related to the process. For our TravelApproval business process example, we could monitor the following:

- The average price for the flight ticket for each travel class (economy, business, first)
- The percentage of flight tickets bought by each vendor
- The number of flight tickets that have/have not been approved
- The average duration of a business trip

- The time required for the user to get the ticket approval (through the human task)
- The average number of business travel requests per week/month

You can see that there can be several interesting indicators that we can monitor on a process. The more complex a process is, the more interesting indicators we can follow.

The added value of BAM in BPEL/SOA is that the BPEL process server provides means to monitor BPEL processes in a relatively simple way. This way, we can develop process monitor dashboards quickly and efficiently.

BAM is often overlooked by the development of SOA composite applications. Executives, however, often see the major added value, particularly in the ability to monitor business processes and observe the key indicators. Therefore, we should plan to develop BAM dashboards for each BPEL process composite application.

Oracle BAM architecture and features

The following figure shows the high-level architecture of Oracle BAM. The most important component is the Oracle BAM Server, which we will discuss in the next section. Oracle BAM Server is responsible for receiving, storing, and monitoring the data, and preparing it to be displayed in the reports. All data is stored in a BAM database in the form of data objects. However, Oracle BAM also enables us to use data from external data sources. Oracle BAM provides four mechanisms to update Oracle BAM Server with real-time data streaming: Oracle BAM Adapter, JMS Connector, Oracle Data Integrator, and Web Services API. Oracle BAM Adapter is the preferred and the fastest option; therefore, all SOA Suite components use it for sending data to BAM Server. BAM Adapter is a JCA-compliant adapter that can communicate with BAM Server through RMI, direct Java object invocations, or Web Services.

Another very important part of Oracle BAM is BAM Web Applications, which present the user interface for building the data model, alerts, creating and viewing reports, and managing users. We will look at the BAM Web Applications later in this chapter.

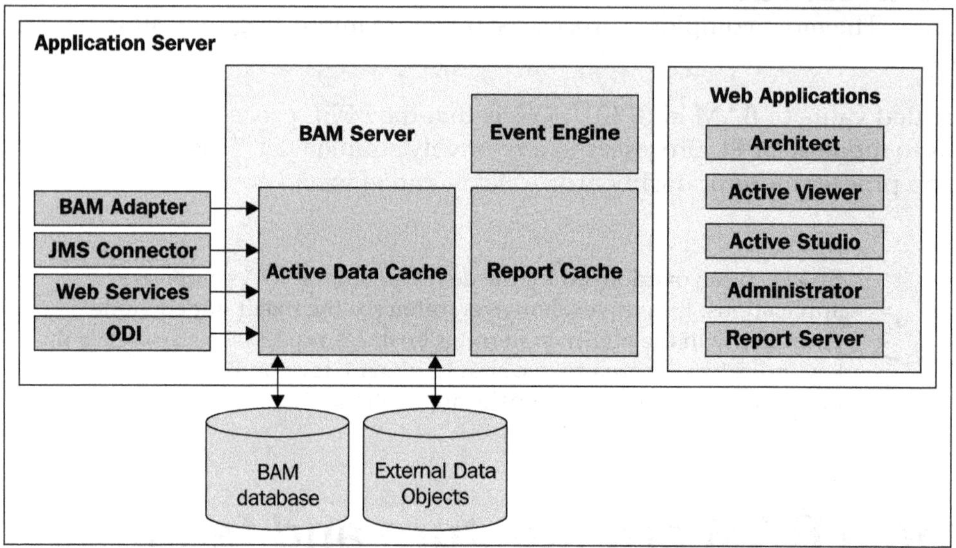

Oracle BAM Server

Oracle BAM Server is a J2EE application that runs as part of Oracle SOA Suite 11*g* and consists of three key components:

- Active Data Cache (ADC): It is a data storage system optimized for handling large amounts of data from various data sources in real time. All the data is stored in a BAM database in the form of data objects (data objects are actually database tables). However, to provide quick access to data, it also maintains in-memory, real-time views of business data in the form of view sets and active view sets. When ADC receives the request for changing the data in the data object (insert, update, upsert, delete), active data sets are notified of the changes and produce active data. ADC can receive data from various sources, such as SOA Composites, JMS, Web Service clients, Oracle Service Bus (OSB), Oracle Data Integrator (ODI), and so on.
- Event Engine: This continuously monitors the information in ADC for user-defined conditions and rules and executes actions (usually sending an e-mail notification).

- Report Cache: It maintains the view set snapshot memory from the ADC. When a user requests a report, it creates a snapshot of the active data and sends the data to the Report Server. The snapshot is used to create an initial display. If the data changes while the report is opened in the browser, Report Cache forwards these changes to the Report Server to refresh the report with the latest data. Report Cache allows the Report Server to be stateless.

Oracle BAM web applications

Oracle BAM web applications provide a user-friendly web-based interface for working with Oracle BAM. There are five BAM web applications:

- **Architect**: It enables us to create the data model (data objects), rules, and alerts and to connect to external data sources.
- **Active Studio**: It is used to create new and manage existing report definitions. We can also share reports with other users. When building the report we can use KPIs, charts, tables, spreadsheets, and more.
- **Active Viewer**: It is used by end-users to view the reports. When fresh information is available, users usually receive an e-mail containing the link to the report. By clicking on the link, the report is opened in Active Viewer.
- **Report Server**: It is a stateless engine for generating the reports by applying report definitions to the data sets retrieved from ADC. When the report is created, it is stored back in the ADC so that the process of report creation is not repeated every time the user wants to view the report.
- **Administrator**: It is used by the system administrator to create users and roles and to manage privileges.

Gathering BAM data from a BPEL process

To be able to monitor the process KPIs, we first need to make sure that the corresponding data is gathered during the BPEL process execution. Upon this data, we can develop a BAM dashboard, which business users and executives can use to monitor the process execution. In this section, we will focus on gathering the BAM data and will overview the possibilities that we have in Oracle BAM.

To gather the data for BAM, Oracle BAM uses the BAM data objects. Data objects are database tables that store data. Each data object has a specific layout, which can be a combination of data fields, lookup fields, and calculated fields. We have to make sure that the relevant data will be gathered during BPEL process execution, and stored to the data objects.

For gathering BPEL process execution data for the Oracle BAM data objects, we will use the Oracle BAM Adapter. It provides three mechanisms:

- We can define monitoring objects to transfer data to automatically generated Oracle BAM data objects.
- We can define sensors and corresponding sensor actions to publish data to manually created Oracle BAM data objects.
- Oracle BAM Adapter can be used as a partner link in a BPEL process. This allows us to transfer the data to BAM with an explicit activity of the BPEL process.

In our TravelApproval business process, we will demonstrate the use of all three approaches.

> To be able to send data to Oracle BAM from SOA composite applications, we need to configure the Oracle BAM Adapter using the WebLogic Administration Console. For instructions on how to configure Oracle BAM Adapter, please refer to *Oracle Fusion Middleware Administrator's Guide for Oracle SOA Suite.*

Monitoring objects

We can use monitoring objects to capture BPEL process execution data. This data is then sent to the BAM server and is available for analysis and display in BAM dashboards. We can define monitoring objects in JDeveloper, using the **Monitor** view.

The use of monitoring objects is the simplest way to enable BPEL process monitoring. If we use monitoring objects, the corresponding BAM data objects will be generated automatically. We can use the following three types of monitoring objects to gather information about the BPEL process:

- **Business Indicators** can be used to capture a snapshot of BPEL variables. A Business Indicator can contain several business metrics. Data gathered with Business Indicators is written to the `Business Indicator` data object. For every defined business metric, there is a corresponding column in the `Business Indicator` data object.
- **Intervals** are usually used to monitor effectiveness and to identify bottlenecks, as they allow us to monitor the time that is needed for a business process to go from one activity to the other. Data gathered with Interval monitoring objects is written to the `INTERVAL` data object.

- **Counters** are usually used to report how many times a particular BPEL activity is executed over a period of time. Data gathered with Counter monitoring objects is written to the `COUNTER` data object.

We have already mentioned that monitoring objects generate the corresponding data objects. In the previous paragraph, we have already mentioned three data objects, `COUNTER`, `INTERVAL`, and `Business Indicator`. Actually, not three but four data objects are created automatically. These are as follows:

- The `COMPONENT` data object is the main data object. It gathers much useful information about the specific SOA composite instance, such as how long a BPEL process instance takes to run, when did the instance start or end, were there any faults, and so on.
- The `COUNTER` data object contains data captured by the Counter monitoring object and is usually used to monitor how many times a particular business activity has been executed over a specified period of time.
- The `INTERVAL` data object contains information about the specific interval start time, end time, duration, and so on. This data object stores information captured by the Interval monitoring objects and when Activity monitoring is enabled.
- The `Business Indicator` data object contains data gathered by all Business Indicator metrics. Columns corresponding to defined business metrics are automatically added to this data object. The name of the data object is set depending on the partition name, composite name, and BPEL process name and follows the pattern: `BI_Partition_Name_Composite_Name_BPELPROCESS_Name`. A separate data object is created for every BPEL process in the composite.

We will need these data objects later when we create the BAM dashboard. At that time, we will need to know what data is stored in which data object in order to present it in the dashboard's graphs, charts, and other reports.

Sensors and sensor actions

The second possibility to monitor the execution of BPEL processes are sensors. However, when using sensors and sensor actions, we first have to create the data objects. We need to do this manually using the Oracle BAM Architect web application. We will show how we can define the data objects later in this chapter.

A sensor can be attached to an activity, variable, or fault. When the sensor is triggered, a corresponding sensor action is executed. A sensor action is connected to a specific data object and is responsible for writing the captured data to this data object.

BPEL Process Manager supports three types of sensors:

- **Activity sensors**: These are the most commonly used type of sensors. They can, for example, monitor the execution time of an activity or how long it takes to execute a scope. When creating an activity sensor, we can also specify a BPEL variable we want to monitor.
- **Variable sensors**: These enable us to monitor BPEL variables. They trigger every time the variable is changed.
- **Fault sensors**: These are used to monitor BPEL faults.

After defining sensors, we have to configure sensor actions, which are used to publish the sensor data to BAM data objects. For every sensor action, we have to specify the sensor, target data object, and operation (insert, upsert, delete, update) and create an XSL transformation which is used to map captured data to the data object. We will show how to do this on the TravelApproval business process example in the next section.

We can see that sensors provide a more sophisticated approach to gathering the BAM data than monitoring objects. With sensors, we can control the format of data objects. Sensors also provide more flexibility for gathering the BAM data. However, sensors also require more work than monitoring objects, as we have to define the data objects manually and configure sensor actions. For simpler BAM dashboards, monitoring objects might be adequate. In more complex scenarios, we will, however, in most cases need to use sensors. In this chapter, we will demonstrate both approaches. First, let us introduce the example that we will use for the demonstration.

Introduction to demonstration scenario

We will demonstrate how to enable the monitoring of a BPEL process on our TravelApproval business process example. We will use the version with a human task, which we have implemented in the previous chapter.

Before starting, we have to know what exactly we want to monitor with our BAM dashboard. Let's say that we want to create a dashboard that will show the following information:

- **A list of last process instances**: To be able to monitor this data, we have to capture a snapshot of BPEL variables during the instance execution. We will achieve this by defining the Business Indicator monitoring object. This data will then be written to an automatically created BAM data object. We will then use this data object when building the dashboard.

- **The percentage of confirmed flight tickets**: To calculate the percentage of confirmed flight tickets, we only need data about the number of instances and whether a specific instance was confirmed or not. We will use the same data object as for the list of last process instances. When building the dashboard, we will display this data using the pie chart diagram.
- **The number of reserved tickets by airline**: For every reserved ticket, we have to save the data about the airline to the corresponding BAM data object. The easiest way to do this would be to define the counter monitoring object. However, we will use this example to demonstrate how to create custom data objects and how to use sensors and a BAM Adapter partner link. When building the dashboard, we will display this data using the bar chart diagram.
- **The effectiveness of the Approval Manager person**: In our simple example, the Approval Manager has three hours to complete the human task. To be able to monitor his/her effectiveness, we have to save the data, about the duration of every task instance to a BAM data object. To capture this data we will simply enable activity monitoring and select that we want to monitor human tasks only. On the dashboard, we will display this KPI using the pie chart diagram.

To enable monitoring, we have to modify our BPEL process so that the data about the execution of business activities will be written to BAM data objects. In the next sections, we will demonstrate four scenarios:

- How to enable activity monitoring for all activities—which we will use to monitor the human tasks in the Travel Approval process, specifically the effectiveness of the Approval Manager person.
- How to use monitoring objects—which we will use to monitor the process instances and the percentage of confirmed flight tickets.
- How to use sensors and sensor actions—which we will use to monitor the number of reserved tickets by airline.
- How to use the BAM Adapter to explicitly transfer the monitor data to the BAM Server. We will show this scenario on the same example to monitor the number of reserved tickets by airline.

Finally, we will create a BAM dashboard using the Active Studio web application.

Enabling activity monitoring

To enable BAM in JDeveloper we switch to the **Monitor** view on the top-right corner of the BPEL Component Designer.

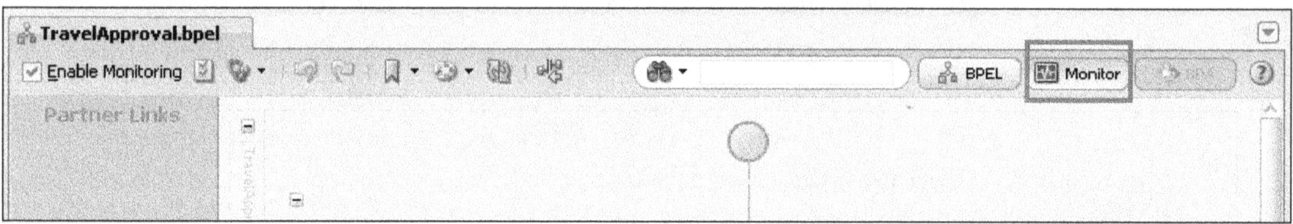

We have to make sure that the **Enable Monitoring** checkbox in the upper-left corner is selected. Using this checkbox, we can enable or disable all monitoring objects and sensors in a BPEL process.

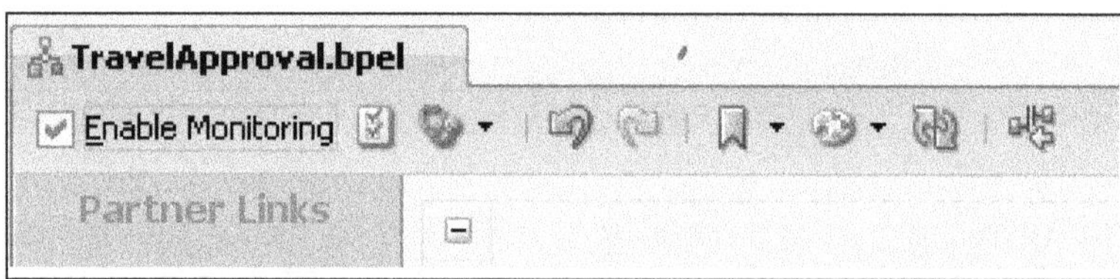

Now, if we look at the **Structure** pane, we can see that it contains three root folders: **Monitoring Objects**, **Sensors,** and **Sensor Actions**. This is a sign that we are in the monitoring view.

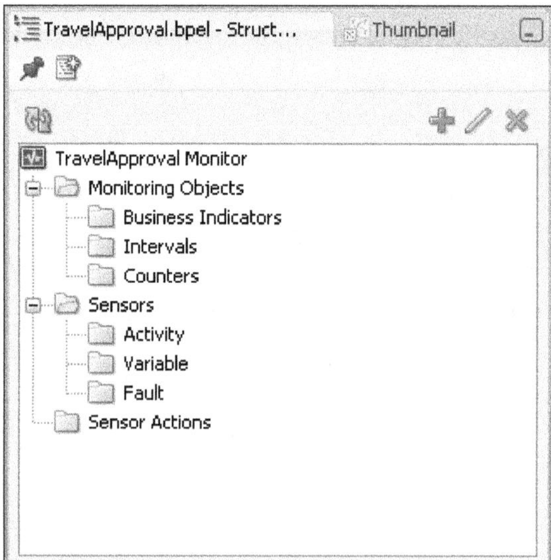

The easiest way to enable activity monitoring is to use a shortcut, which automatically captures execution information for all activities of the selected type. This shortcut is equal to manually adding Interval monitoring objects to all activities that we want to monitor. We will show how to manually add an Interval monitoring object in the next section.

We will enable activity monitoring for human tasks, specifically to monitor the effectiveness of the Approval Manager person. To achieve this, we need to gather data about the human task. To enable activity monitoring, we have to click the **Activity Monitoring Configuration** icon on the toolbar:

The **Activity Monitoring Configuration** dialog opens. For our example, we select the **Human Tasks Only** mode and select the **Enable Activity Monitoring** checkbox.

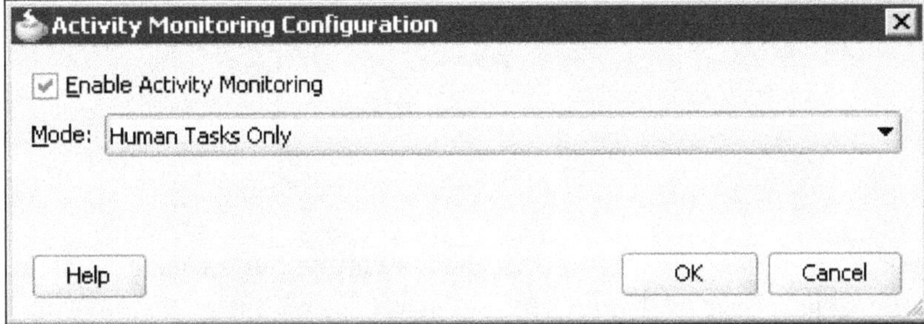

Now for every execution of the `FlightTicketApproval` human task, information about the activity duration, start time, and end time will be written to the `INTERVAL` data object. We need this information, as we want to monitor the effectiveness of the Approval Manager.

We click **OK** to close the dialog.

Using monitoring objects

Next, we will show how to use monitoring objects. Using the **Monitor** view in JDeveloper, we can create monitoring objects in three ways. First, we can right-click the activity, select **Create**, and then select the monitoring object type:

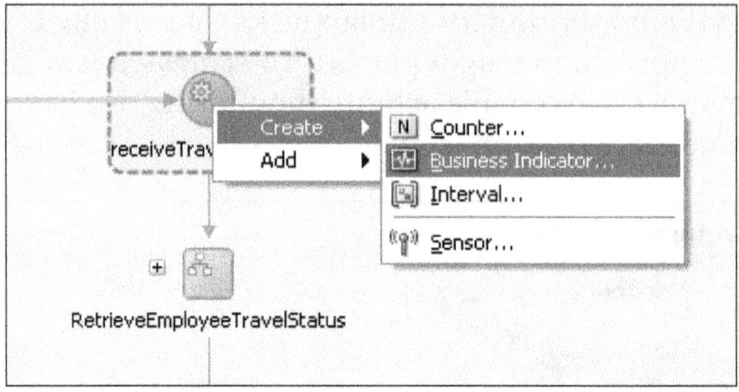

We can also create monitoring objects using the **Monitoring Objects** menu on the toolbar:

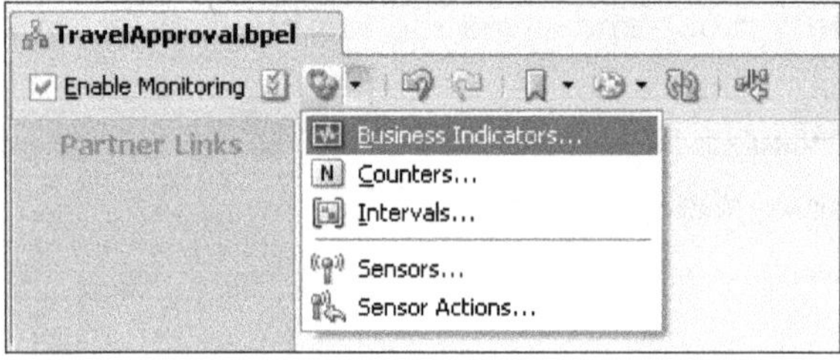

Monitoring objects can also be created in the **Structure** pane by right-clicking the monitoring object type and selecting **Create**:

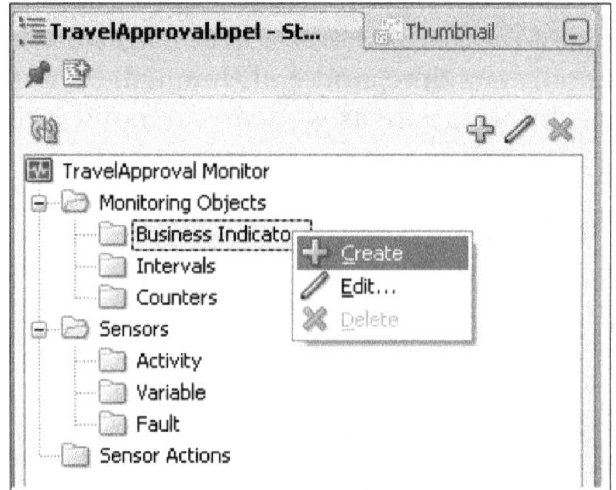

Creating a Business Indicator monitoring object

Now, we will create a monitoring object of type Business Indicator. We need this monitoring object to display the details of the last process instances and the percentage of confirmed flight tickets on our BAM dashboard. Remember that when using monitoring objects, only the Business Indicator can be used to capture variable data.

Instead of using the Business Indicator, we could also use sensors and sensor actions. However, in that case, we would have to create the BAM data object first. We will show how to use sensors later in this chapter.

To create the Business Indicator, we right-click the `clientCallBack` activity and select **Create** | **Business Indicator**. The **Business Indicator** dialog opens. We set the name to `TravelResponse_BI`.

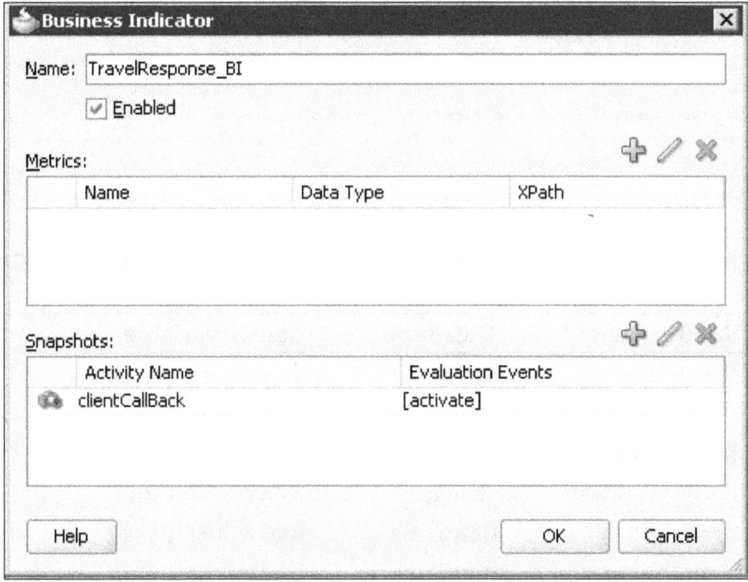

Notice that the `clientCallBack` snapshot is already on the **Snapshots** list. This means that during the activation of the `clientCallBack` activity, a snapshot of BPEL variables will be created. We want the snapshot to be created at the end of the process, as we need information on whether the flight ticket was approved or not. We will now add business metrics to specify the data that we want written to the `Business Indicator` data object.

To add a new business metric, we click the green *plus* icon. Then we have to set the name, the data type, and the XPath expression. We name the first metric `FirstName` and set the data type to `string`. Then we click on the *three dots* icon in the XPath column to open the **Expression Builder**.

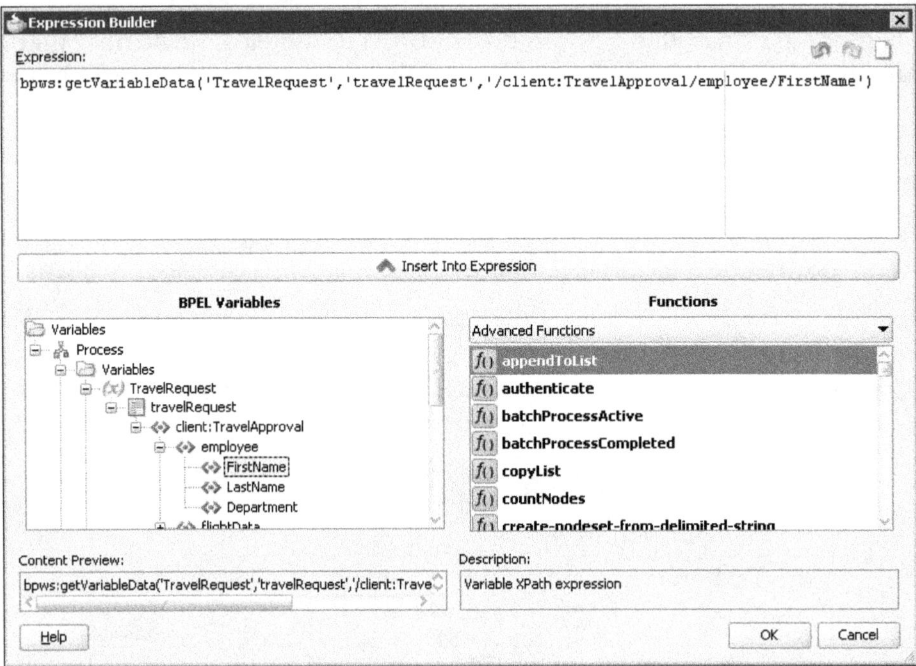

In a similar way, we add other business metrics as shown in the following table:

Metric name	Data type	Source variable
`FirstName`	string	`TravelRequest`
`LastName`	string	`TravelRequest`
`OriginFrom`	string	`TravelRequest`
`DestinationTo`	string	`TravelRequest`
`DepartureDate`	dateTime	`TravelRequest`
`ReturnDate`	dateTime	`TravelRequest`
`Price`	double	`FlightResponseBest`
`Confirmed`	string	`TravelResponse`

The **Business Indicator** dialog now looks like this:

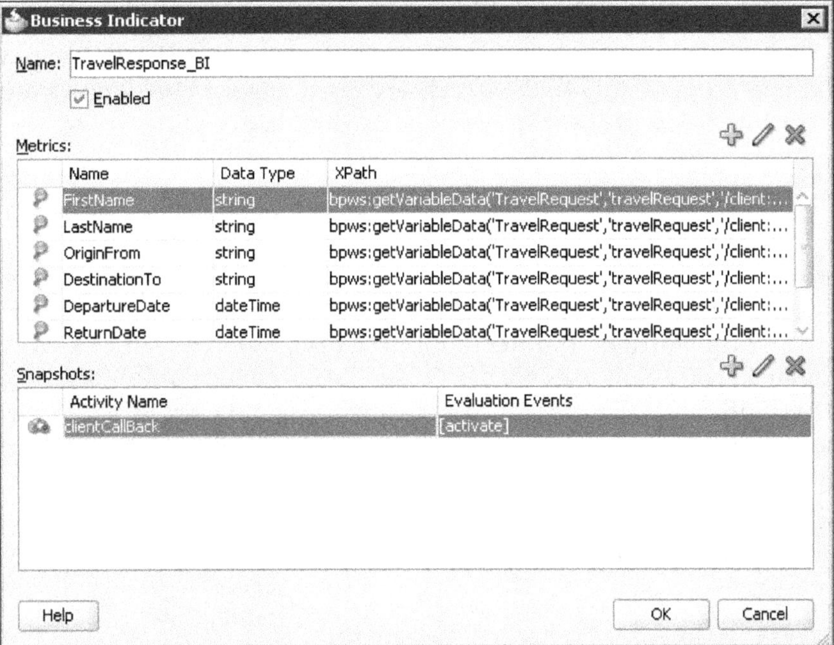

We click **OK** to close the dialog.

We can see that a Business Indicator icon is displayed in the top-right corner of the activity.

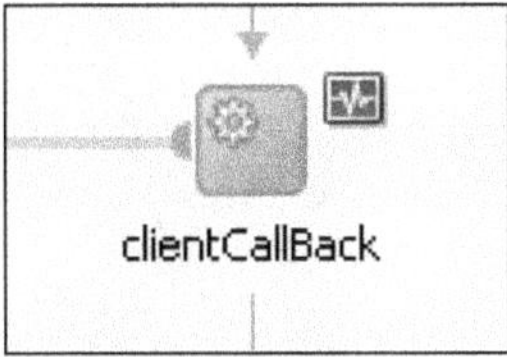

With the steps that we have done so far, we could already build three of four views on our BAM dashboard:

- A list of last process instances (`Business Indicator` data object)
- The percentage of confirmed flight tickets (`Business Indicator` data object)
- The effectiveness of the Approval Manager (`INTERVAL` data object)

We still do not have the information about the number of reserved flight tickets by airline. This can be done by adding Counter monitoring objects to the `AmericanAirlinesReservation` and `DeltaAirlinesReservation` activities. However, we will not use monitoring objects. Rather, we will show how to use sensors and how to send data to the BAM server using a BAM Adapter partner link. In the next section, we will show how to use BAM data objects.

Using sensors

In this section, we will show how to use sensors to count the number of reserved tickets by each airline. To achieve this, we will need to count the number of reserved tickets for American Airlines and the number of reserved tickets for Delta Airlines. To count the tickets we will use sensors. Sensors, however, require data objects. Therefore, we will first need to create a corresponding data object. Then we will establish a connection to the BAM server. Next, we will define the sensors and the corresponding sensor actions. Finally, we will also show how to use the BAM adapter as an alternative approach to the sensors. Let us start with creating a BAM data object.

Creating BAM data objects

We can create BAM data objects using the **Oracle BAM Architect** web application. To log into Oracle BAM Architect, we have to open a web browser and access the following URL: `http://host_name:port/OracleBAM/`, where `host_name` is the name of the host on which Oracle BAM is installed and `port` is a number that is set during the installation process (default is 9001).

Currently, the only supported browser is Internet Explorer 7.0 or higher.

We sign in as user `weblogic`. The Oracle BAM Start Page opens. From here, we can open other BAM web applications.

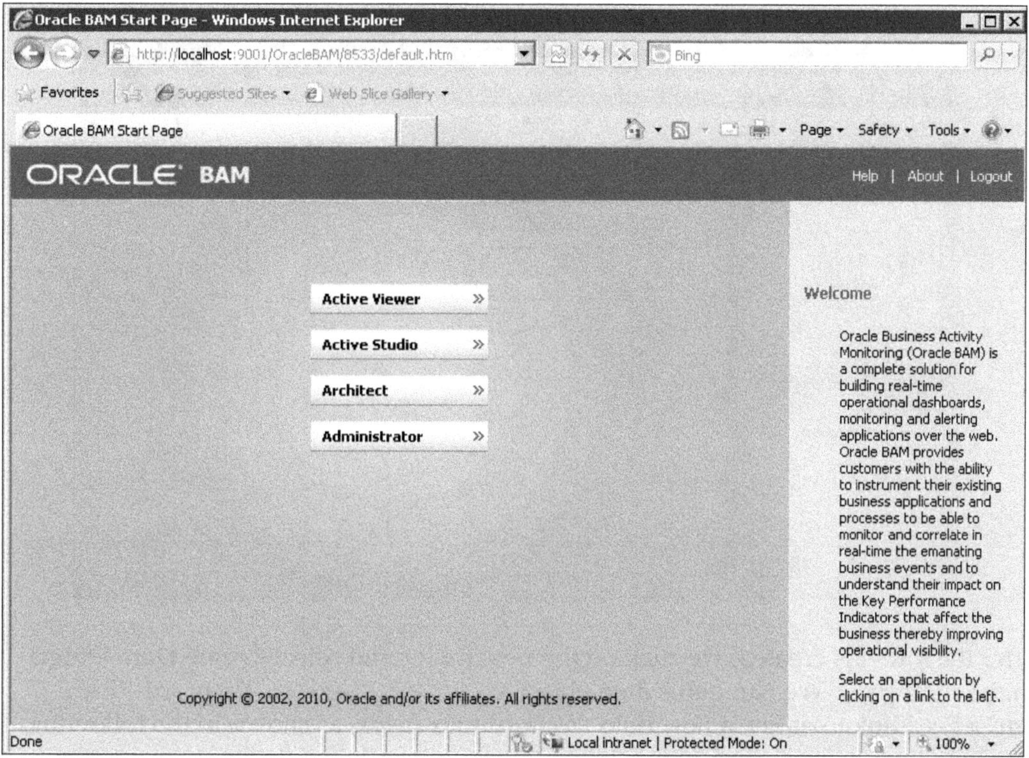

We open the Architect web application. We click on the **Data Objects** link and then on the **Create subfolder** link to create new subfolder. We name the folder `TravelApproval` and click **Create Folder**.

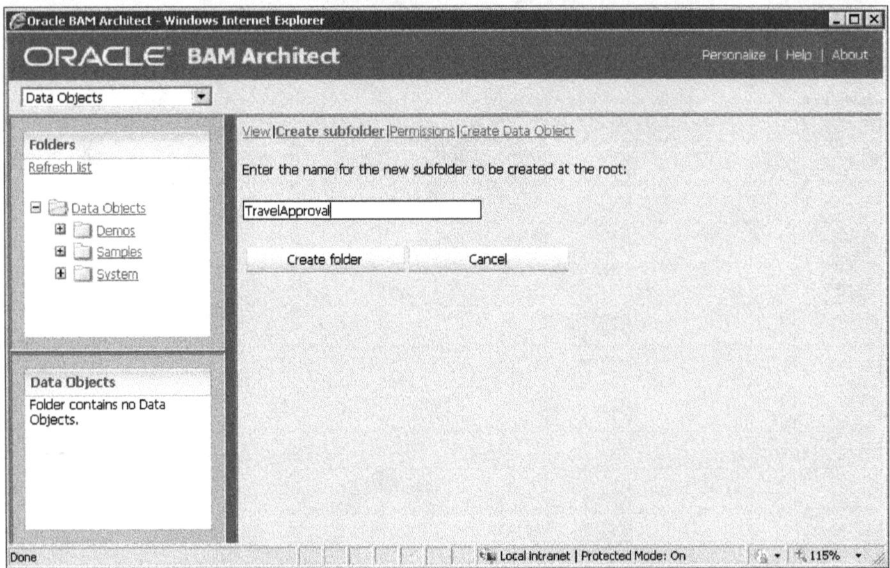

After the folder is created, we click on the new folder and select **Create Data Object** on the right pane. We name this data object `SELECTED_TICKETS`. Then, we click **Add a field** link to define a new field. We add four fields, as shown in the following screenshot:

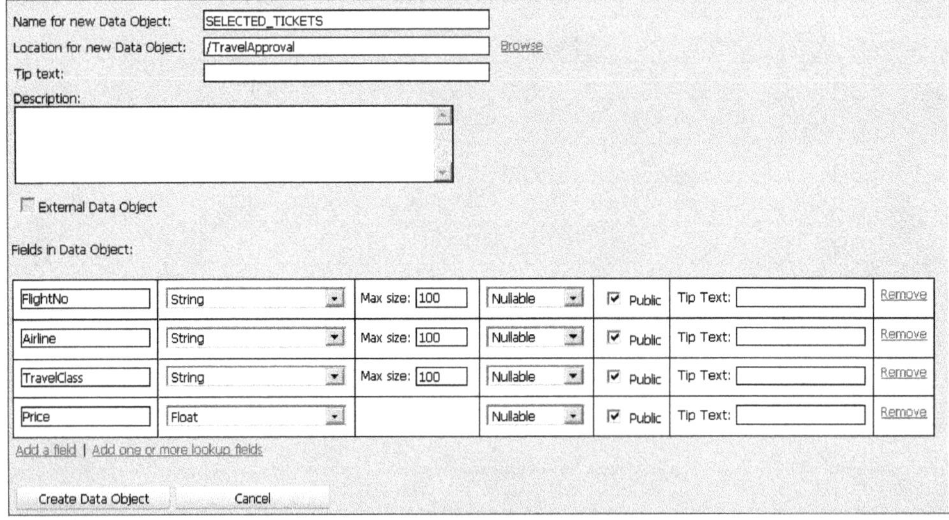

For our example, we only need the data about the selected airline. However, we will add more fields, as we want to show how to make XSL transformations when creating the sensor action.

We click **Create Data Object**. Now if we select the `TravelApproval` folder and look at the bottom of the left pane, we can see that it contains one data object.

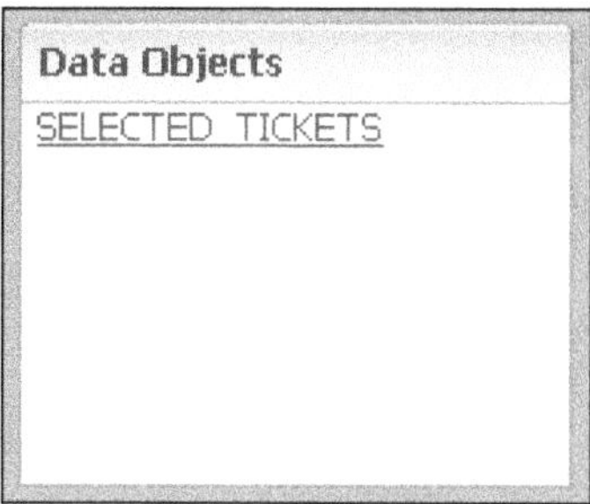

Creating a BAM server connection

Before we can create sensors and sensor actions, we have to create a connection to the BAM server. To do this, we have to go back to the JDeveloper again and open the BPEL process using the **Monitor** view. We right-click the **Connections** folder in **Application Resources** and select **New Connection | BAM**.

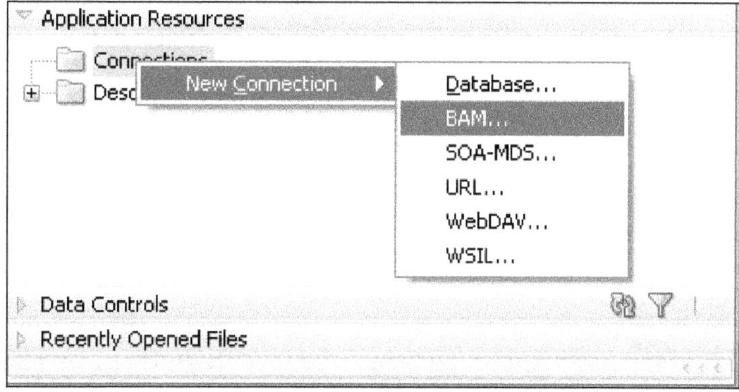

The **BAM Configuration Wizard** dialog opens. In step one, we enter the name of the connection and click **Next**.

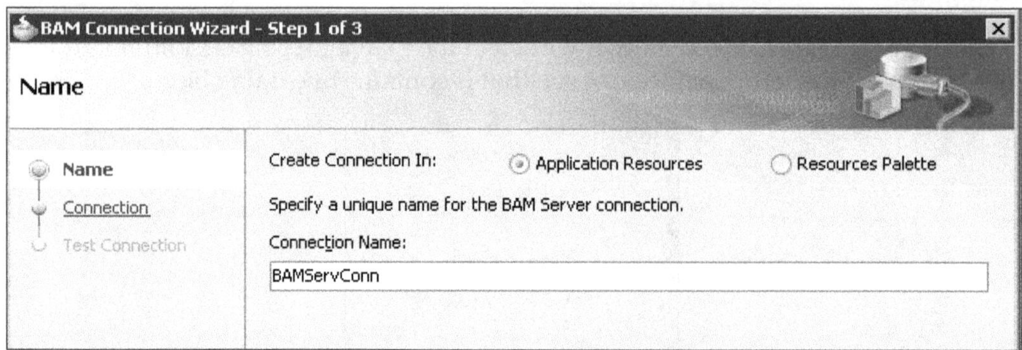

In step two, we enter the hostname for **BAM WebHost** and **BAM Server Host**. We also have to enter a username and password and provide the **HTTP Port** (default is **9001**).

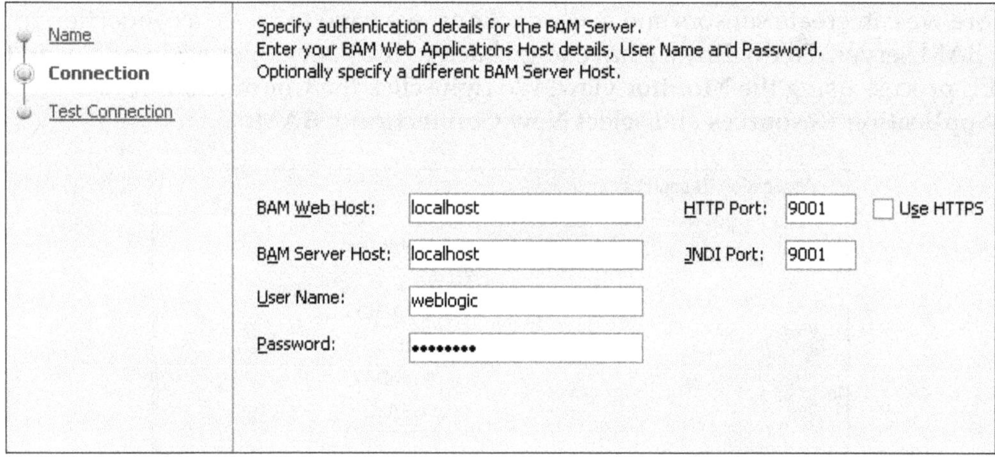

In the final step, we can test the connection and close the wizard by clicking **Finish**.

Creating sensors and sensor actions

To demonstrate the use of sensors, we will add a sensor to the `AmericanAirlinesReservation` activity. For every execution of the activity, the sensor will trigger the sensor action, which will send the data about the selected flight ticket (and selected airline) to the BAM server. This data will be written to the `SELECTED_TICKETS` data object.

We right-click the `AmericanAirlinesReservation` activity and select **Create | Sensor**. The **Create Activity Sensor** dialog opens. We set the name of the sensor to `AAReservationSensor`. From the **Evaluation Time** drop-down we select **Activation**, as we want the sensor to trigger only once, during the activation of the activity. Then we click the *plus* icon in the **Activity Variable Sensors** box to add a variable. The **Create Activity Variable Sensor** dialog opens. We click on the pencil icon to open the **Variable XPath Builder**. We select the `confirmationData` element from the `FlightResponseAA` variable, as shown in the following screenshot:

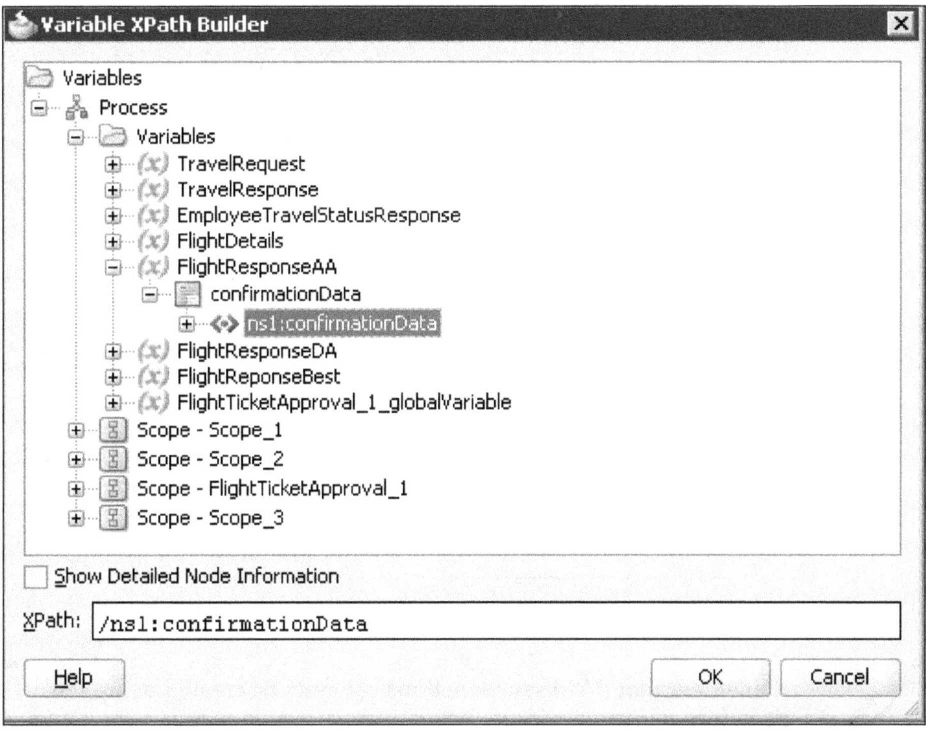

Then we click **OK** twice to close both dialogs and get back to the **Create Activity Sensor** dialog.

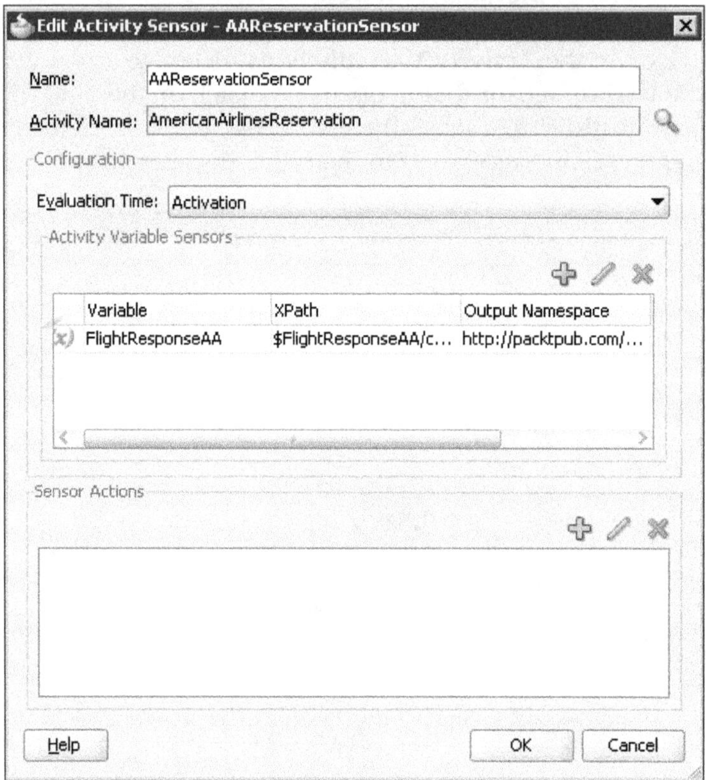

Remember that BAM sensor actions can only be created using the **Structure** pane.

We click **OK** to close the dialog. We can see that a Sensor icon is displayed in the top-right corner of the activity.

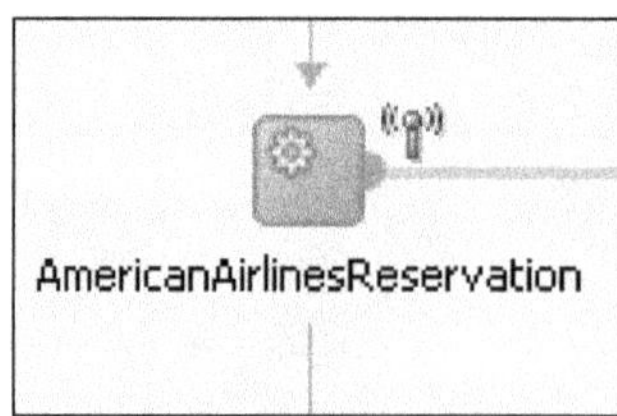

Next, we have to create BAM sensor action for the activity sensor we just created. We right-click **Sensor Actions** folder in the **Structure** pane and select **Create | BAM Sensor Action**. The **Create Sensor Action** dialog opens. We set the name of the action to `AAReservationSensorAction` and select the `AAReservationSensor`. Then we click on the *magnifying glass* icon to select the data object. The **BAM Data Object Chooser** dialog opens. We expand the BAM server connection and choose the `SELECTED_TICKETS` data object.

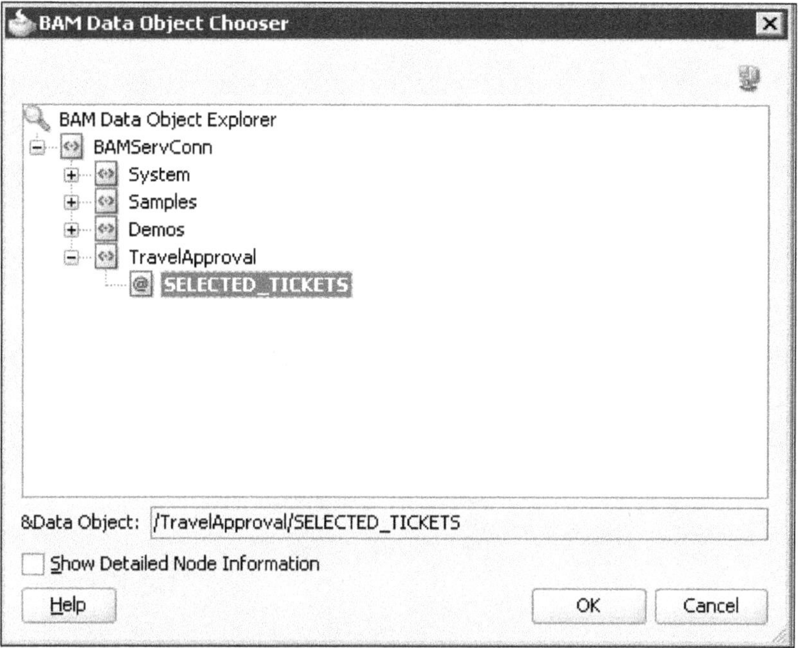

We click **OK** to close the dialog. Back on the **Create Sensor Action** dialog, we select **Insert** as the BAM operation. We keep the `Enable Batching` checkbox selected. Then we change the `BAM Connection Factory JNDI` setting if needed. However, in most cases we use the default value (`eis/bam/rmi`). This value is set when configuring the Oracle BAM Adapter. Now we have to create a mapping file to map the data from the variable to the selected data object. We can optionally change the name of the XSL file and click on the *plus* icon to create a mapping. We map the fields from the left side under **tns:actionData** | **tns:payload** | **tns:variableData** | **tns:data** | **sensor:confirmationData** to the corresponding fields on the right side.

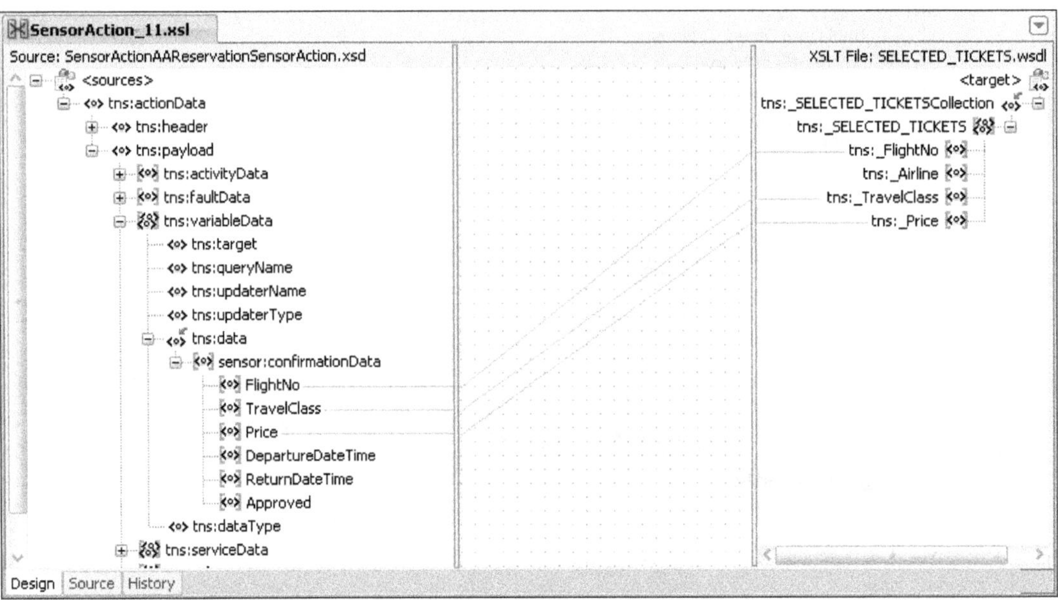

To set the `tns:_Airline` target field, we right-click on it and select **Set Text** | **Enter Text**. In the **Set Text** dialog, we set the name to `American`.

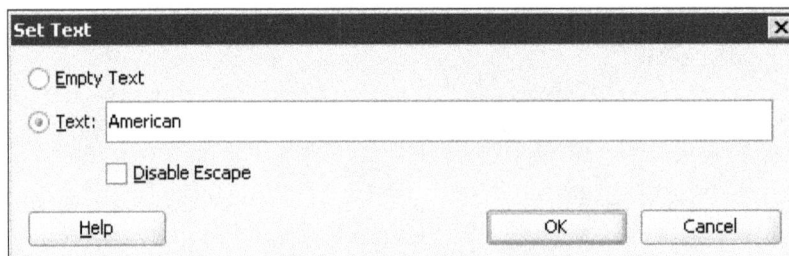

We will use this data to count the number of reserved tickets when building the BAM dashboard. We click **OK** to close the dialog. We also close the mapping file. Our sensor action is now configured as shown in the following screenshot:

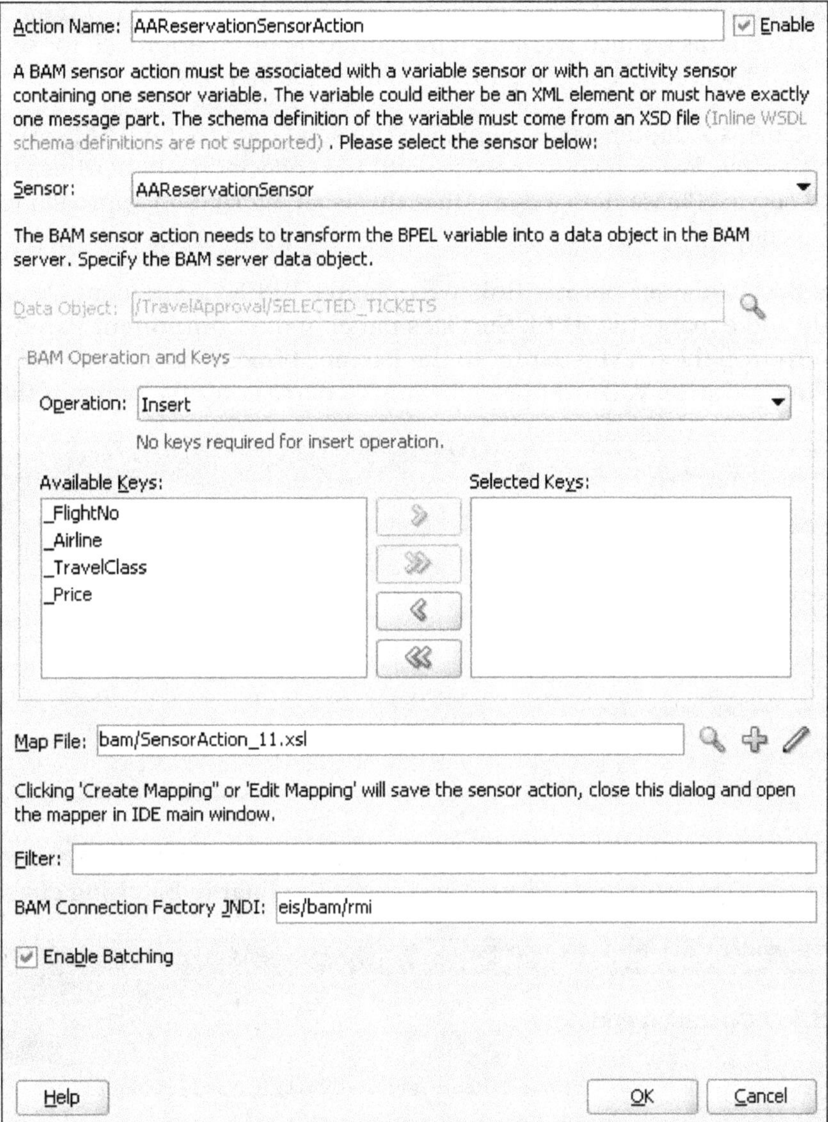
Action Name: AAReservationSensorAction
Enable
A BAM sensor action must be associated with a variable sensor or with an activity sensor containing one sensor variable. The variable could either be an XML element or must have exactly one message part. The schema definition of the variable must come from an XSD file (Inline WSDL schema definitions are not supported) . Please select the sensor below:
Sensor: AAReservationSensor
The BAM sensor action needs to transform the BPEL variable into a data object in the BAM server. Specify the BAM server data object.
Data Object: /TravelApproval/SELECTED_TICKETS
BAM Operation and Keys
Operation: Insert
No keys required for insert operation.
Available Keys:
_FlightNo
_Airline
_TravelClass
_Price
Selected Keys:
Map File: bam/SensorAction_11.xsl
Clicking 'Create Mapping" or 'Edit Mapping' will save the sensor action, close this dialog and open the mapper in IDE main window.
Filter:
BAM Connection Factory JNDI: eis/bam/rmi
Enable Batching
Help
OK
Cancel

Using the BAM Adapter partner link

Similar to `American Airlines`, we also have to monitor the number of tickets reserved by `Delta Airlines`. To do this, we could create another sensor and attach it to the to the `DeltaAirlinesReservation` activity as we did for `American Airlines`. However, we will not do this, as we also want to demonstrate the third approach for sending data to the BAM server by using the BAM Adapter partner link.

By using the BAM Adapter partner link, we can send data to the BAM server as a step in the process. We will show how to send the collected Delta Airlines ticket data to the BAM server. Please notice again that this is an alternative approach to sensors and sensor actions.

To add the BAM Adapter partner link, we open the BPEL Component Designer in **BPEL** mode and expand the **BPEL Services** panel in the **Component Palette**. Then, we drag-and-drop the BAM Adapter to the **Partner Link** swim-lane on the right. The **Adapter Configuration Wizard** opens. In step two, we enter the name of the service.

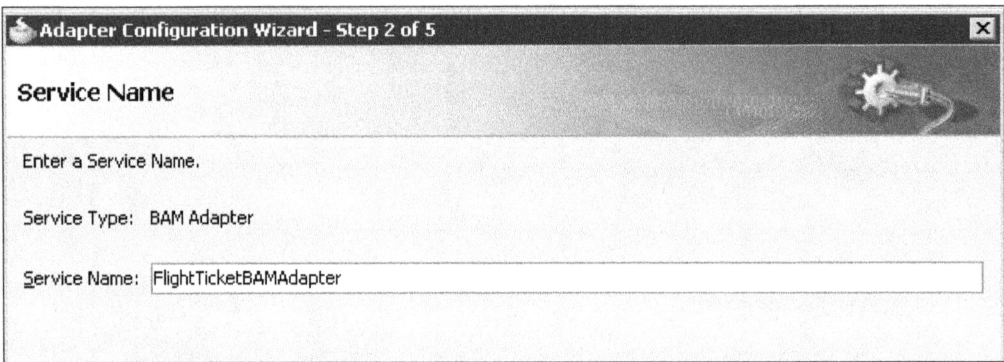

We click **Next**. In step three, we select the `SELECTED_TICKETS` data object, select **Insert** from the **Operation** drop-down, and select the **Enable Batching** checkbox.

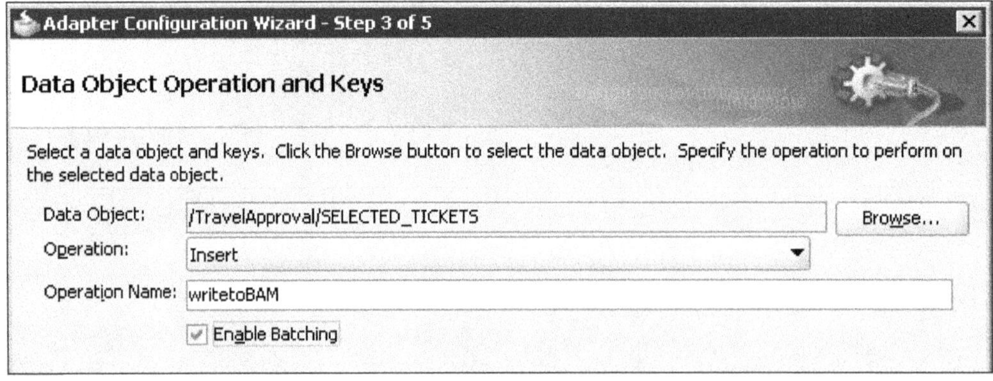

We click **Next**. In step four, we enter the **JNDI Name** for the BAM connection, set when configuring the Oracle BAM Adapter on the WebLogic Administration Console. Usually, the default value (`eis/bam/rmi`) is used.

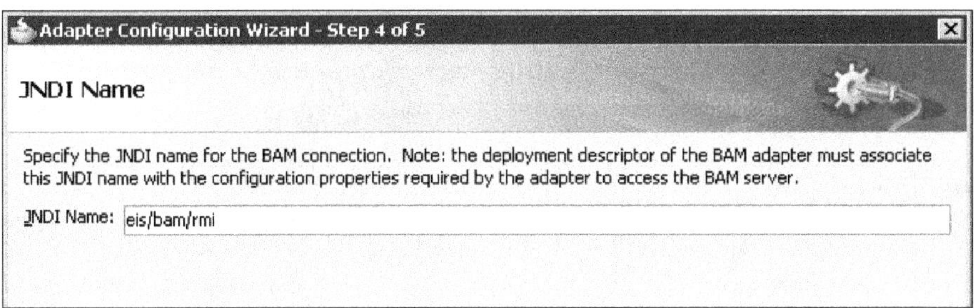

We click **Next** and then **Finish** to close the wizard.

Now, we add a new scope just in front of the `DeltaAirlinesReservation` **<invoke>** activity. We name the scope `sendTicketDataToBAM`. Then, we drag-and-drop an **<invoke>** activity into the new scope. We double-click the new activity to open the **Invoke** editor. We set the name of the activity to `sendDataToBAM`. For the partner link, we select `FlightTicketBAMAdapter`. We click on the *plus* icon next to the **Input** variable field to create a variable. We name the variable `sendDataToBAM_InputVariable`.

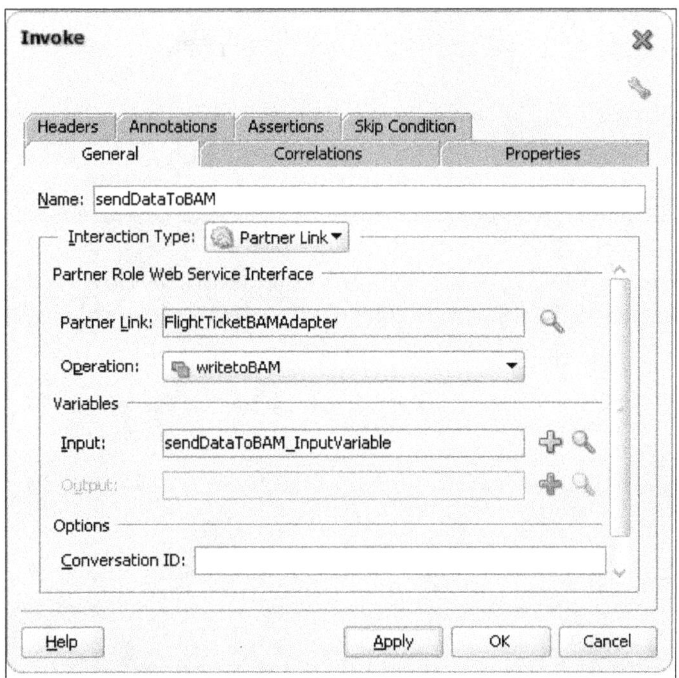

We click **OK** to close the dialog. Now we have to map the source data to the new variable. We drag-and-drop a Transform activity and name it `TransformTicketData`. We double-click the activity to open the **Transform** editor. We select the source variable (`FlightResponseDA`). For the target variable, we select `sendDataToBAM_InputVariable`. Then we click on the *plus* icon to create a mapping. We map the fields similar to what we did when creating the sensor action. However, this time we set the text of the `tns:_Airline` target field to `Delta`.

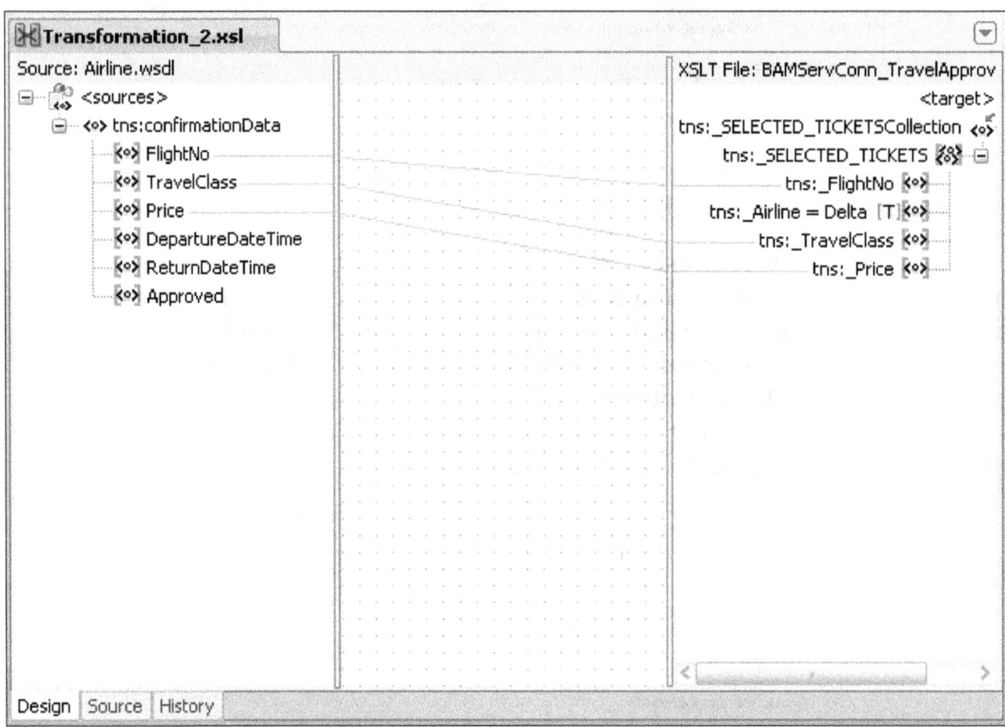

We close the mapping file. Now we switch to the **Monitor** view in the BPEL Component Designer and look at the part of the process for making ticket reservations, shown in the following screenshot:

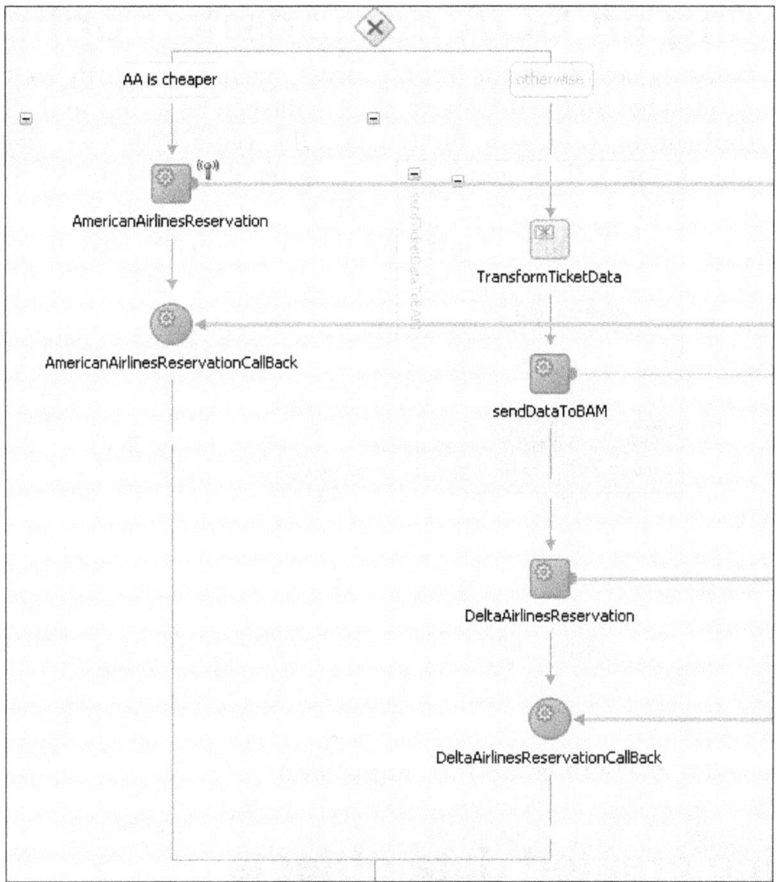

We can see the difference between the two approaches for monitoring the execution of an activity. The main advantage of using sensors is that we do not need to add new process activities and, therefore, the process is more readable. However, the result in both cases is the same: the ticket data is written to the `SELECTED_TICKETS` data object.

Deploying an SOA composite application

As we use monitoring objects in our BPEL process, we have to configure the `monitor.config` file before the deployment. The file can be found in the **Projects** panel in the **Application Navigator**. First, we set the folder where we want to save the data objects that will be generated during the deployment. We use the `TravelApproval` folder that we already created for the `SELECTED_TICKETS` data object. We also set the JNDI Name for the BAM connection and save the file.

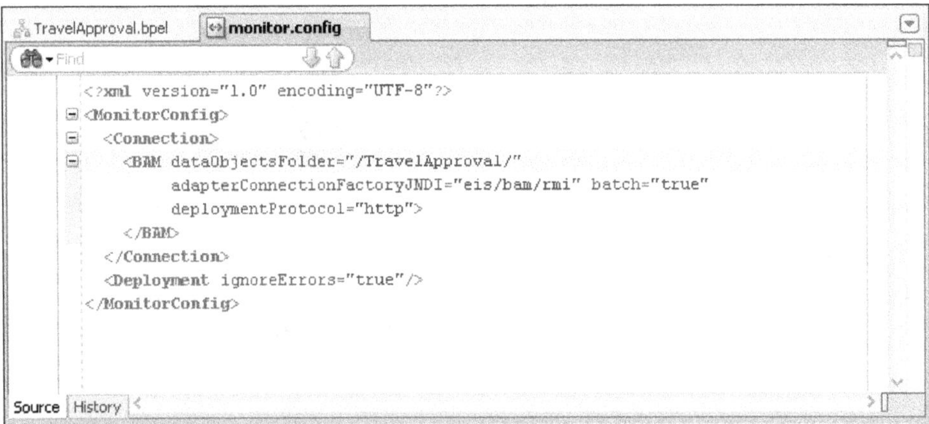

```
<?xml version="1.0" encoding="UTF-8"?>
<MonitorConfig>
  <Connection>
    <BAM dataObjectsFolder="/TravelApproval/"
         adapterConnectionFactoryJNDI="eis/bam/rmi" batch="true"
         deploymentProtocol="http">
    </BAM>
  </Connection>
  <Deployment ignoreErrors="true"/>
</MonitorConfig>
```

Now we can deploy the SOA composite application.

Checking created data objects

After deploying, we check if four data objects (`COMPONENT`, `COUNTER`, `INTERVAL` and `Business Indicator`) have been created during the deployment. We open the BAM Architect web application and click on the `TravelApproval` folder. We can see that the folder now contains five data objects, as we expected.

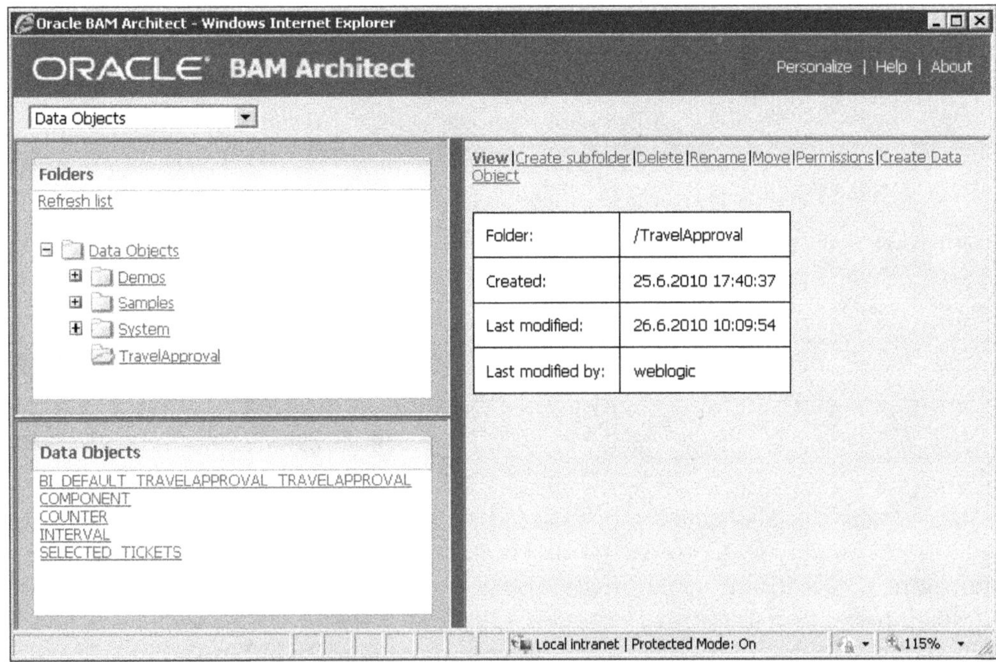

Testing data objects

Now we will initiate and complete a new instance of our composite application to test if the data is being written to the data objects. Then, we open the Oracle BAM Architect web application and click on the `TravelApproval` folder. To see the content of a specific data object, we click on it and select **Contents** on the right panel.

First, we look at the content of the Business Indicator data object (named `BI_DEFAULT_TRAVELAPPROVAL_TRAVELAPPROVAL`).

> The name of the Business Indicator data object can vary, depending on the partition name, composite name, and BPEL process name.

If we scroll to the right, we can see eight columns, which correspond to the defined business metrics. Columns are populated with the data from the BPEL process instance we just initiated.

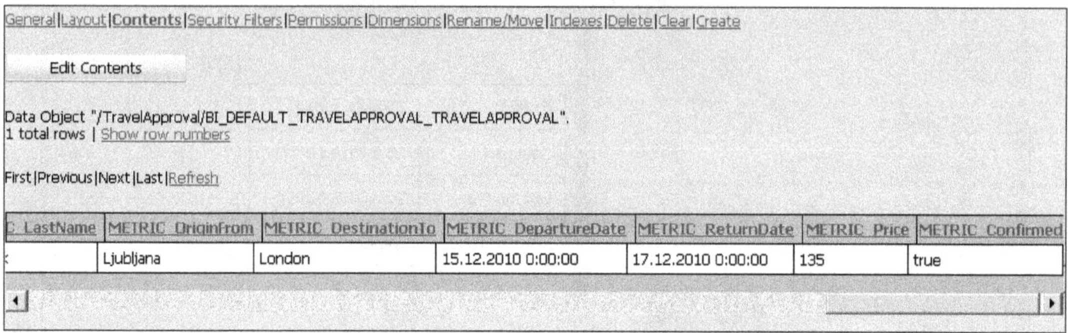

In a similar way can also check other data objects. The `COUNTER` data object is empty, as we did not create any Counter monitoring object. The `INTERVAL` data object contains one row with information about the duration of the human task. We will need this information (column `INTERVAL_RUNNING_TIME_IN_MIN`) when building the BAM dashboard to display the effectiveness of the a Approval Manager.

The data object `SELECTED_TICKETS` contains data about the selected flight ticket. We will need the data about the selected airline (column `Airline`) to display the number of reserved flight tickets by airline.

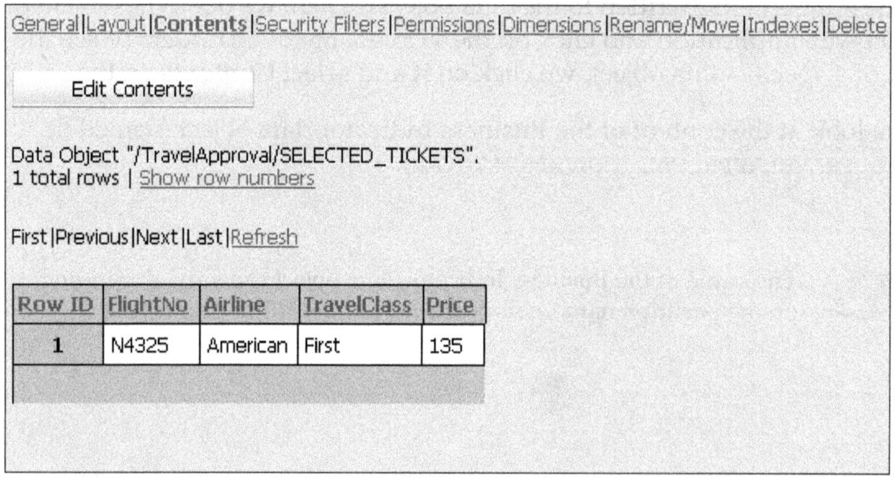

Now, we initiate some new composite instances to fill the data objects so that we will have some test data when building the BAM dashboard.

Building the BAM dashboard

To define the BAM dashboard, we have to open the Oracle BAM Active Studio web application (it can be accessed from the Oracle BAM Start Page).

Creating a report and choosing a report template

As we want to create a report that everyone can view, we click on to the **Shared Reports** tab.

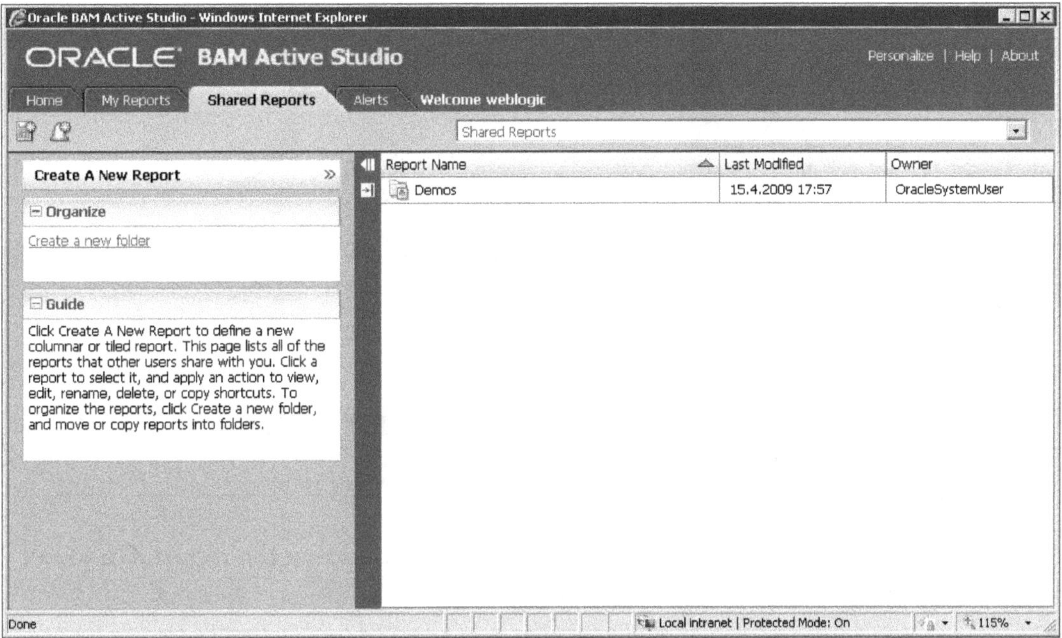

To keep reports organized, we click on the **Create a new folder** link to create a folder. We name the folder `TravelApproval`. Then we select the created folder and click **Create A New Report**. A page with predefined layout templates opens. We can choose between **Tiled Report** and **Columnar Report**. We select the template with four equal tiles and a thin separator.

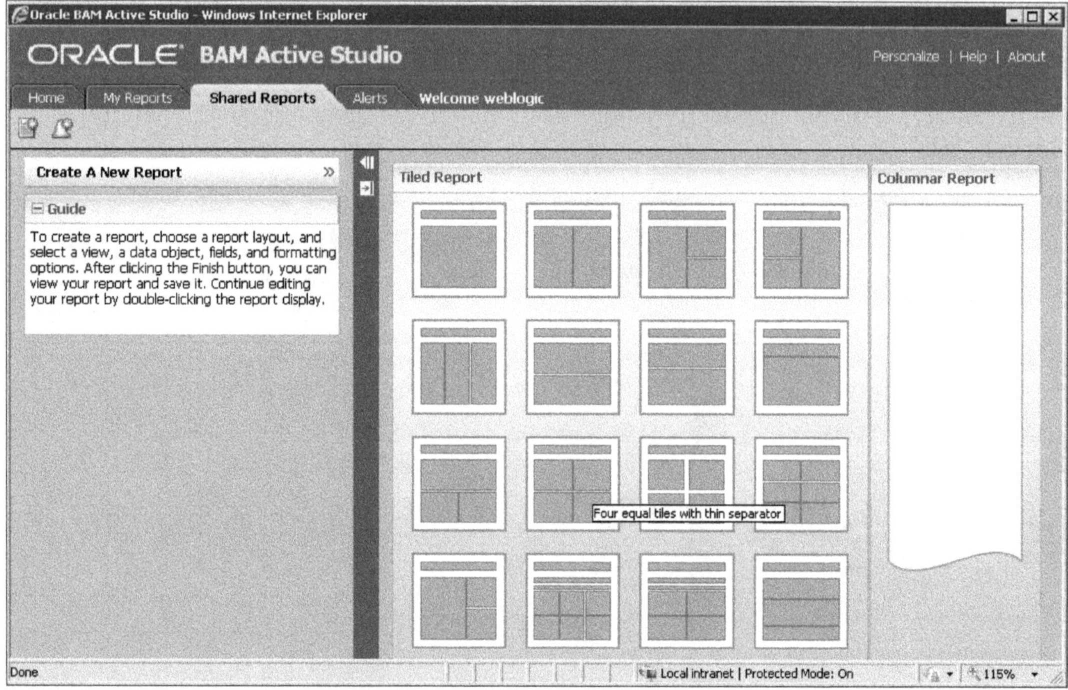

Now we can see various chart types we can use when building the report. On top of the page, we set the report title to `Travel Approval Report`.

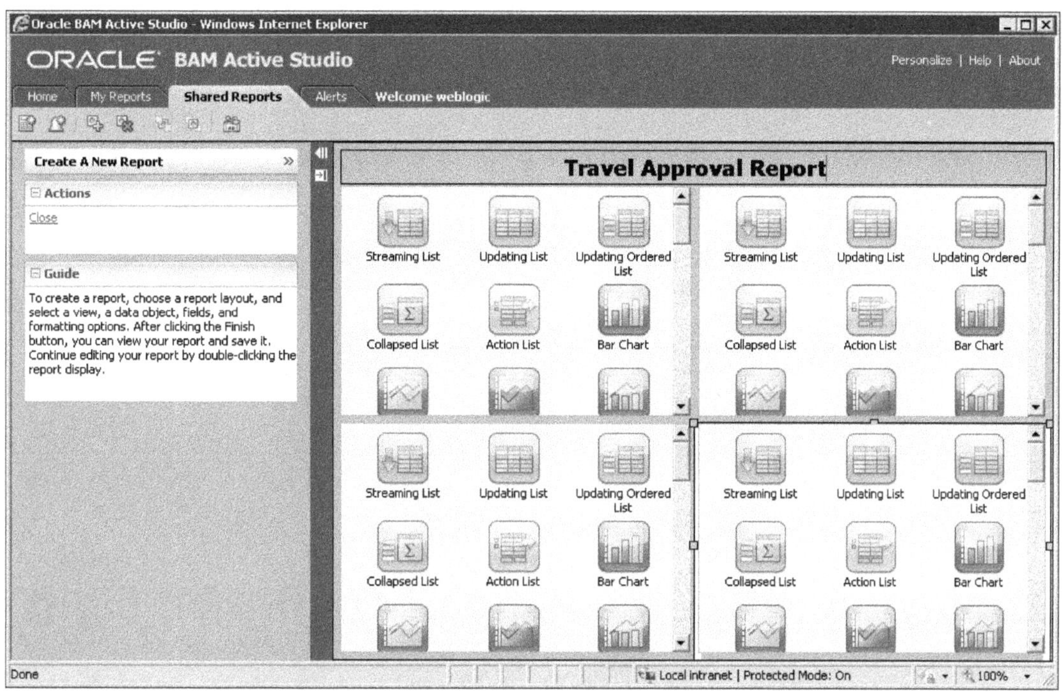

Displaying a list of process instances

First, we will define a view that will display the list of the last BPEL process instances. We select the **Streaming List** chart type in the upper-left view. Next, we have to specify the data object for this view. At the bottom of the screen, we double-click the `TravelApproval` folder and then select the `BI_DEFAULT_TRAVELAPPROVAL_TRAVELAPPROVAL` data object, which contains the data about the flight ticket.

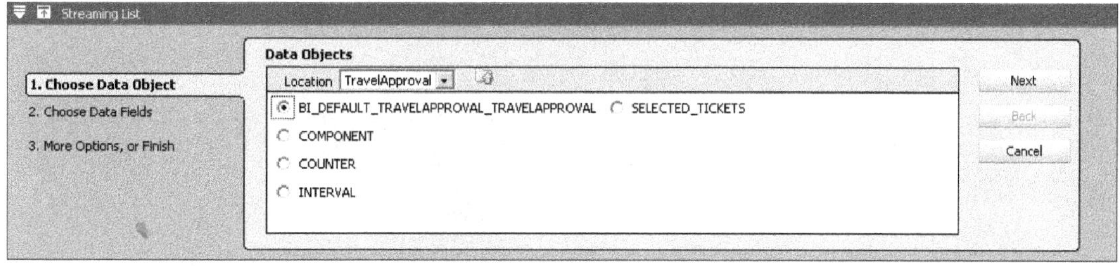

We click **Next**. Then, we have to select the data fields that we want to be displayed in the list. We select the following fields: `METRIC_FirstName`, `METRIC_LastName`, `METRIC_Price`, and `METRIC_Confirmed`. We can also change the order of the fields. We click **Next** again. Now we click on **Change View Properties**. Here, we set the **View Title** to **List of last process instances**.

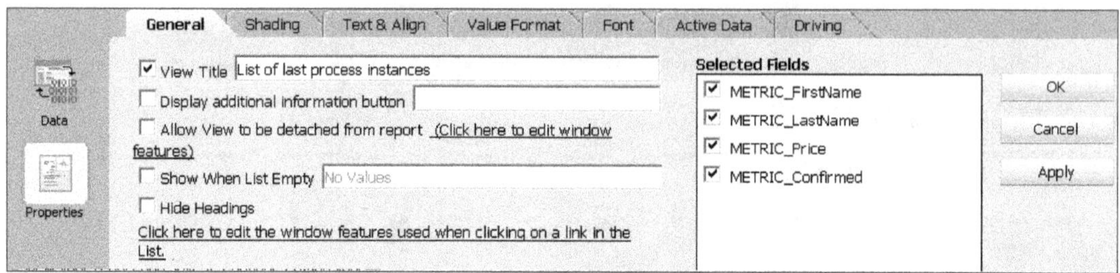

We click **OK**. Our first report view is now configured.

Displaying the percentage of confirmed flight tickets

Now, we will define a view that will contain a pie chart displaying the percentage of confirmed flight tickets. We select the **3D Pie Chart** in the upper-right view. Again, we select the `BI_DEFAULT_TRAVELAPPROVAL_TRAVELAPPROVAL` data object and click **Next**. On the **Choose Data Fields** screen we click **Next**, as we have to create a calculated field first. Then we click on the **Create a calculated field** link. We select an **if** expression and press the **Insert Express** button. We enter the calculation as shown in the following screenshot:

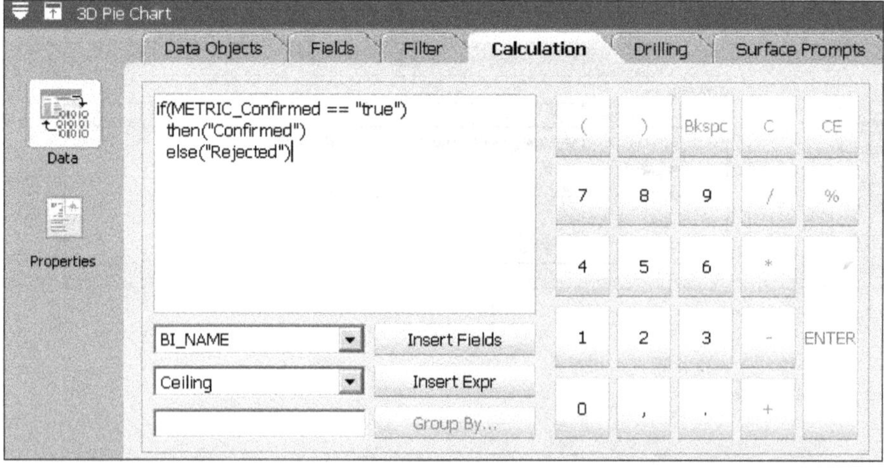

Then, we press the **ENTER** button and rename the calculated field to `Status`.

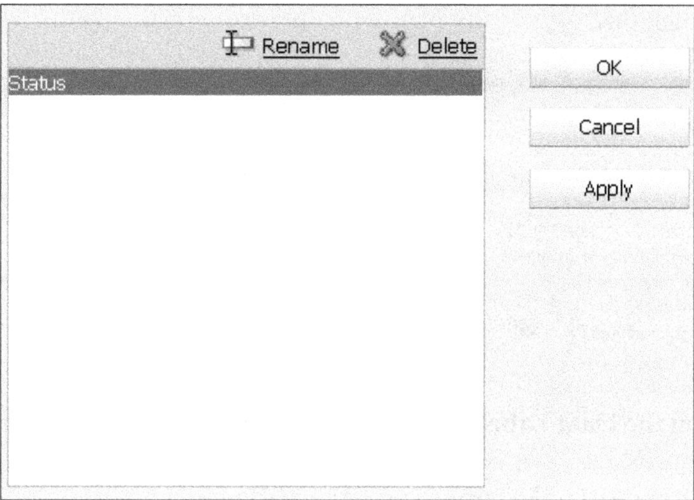

Then we click on the **Fields** tab. In the **Group by** list, we select the `Status` calculated field. Under **Chart Values**, we select `COMPONENT_INSTANCE_ID`. We select **Count Distinct** as the summary function.

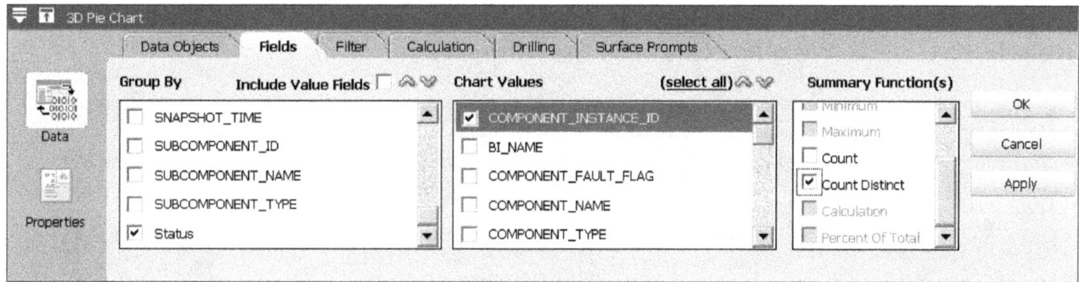

We click **Apply**. Then we click on the **Properties** icon on the left. We set the **View Title** to `Percentage of confirmed flight tickets` and select the **Display Legend** checkbox. We click **OK**.

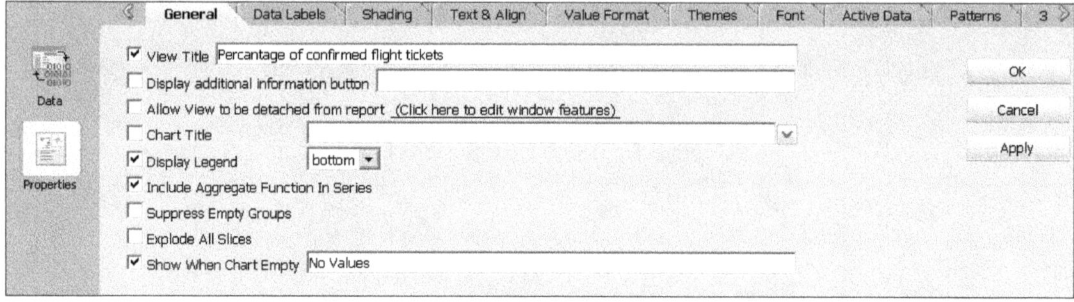

Then we click on the **Data Labels** tab. Here we deselect **Value** and select **Percent**. We click **OK**.

Displaying the number of reserved tickets by airline

We select the **3D Bar Chart** in the bottom-right view. We select the `SELECTED_TICKETS` data object and click **Next**. In the **Group by** and in the **Chart Values** list, we select `Airline`. We select **Count** as the summary function.

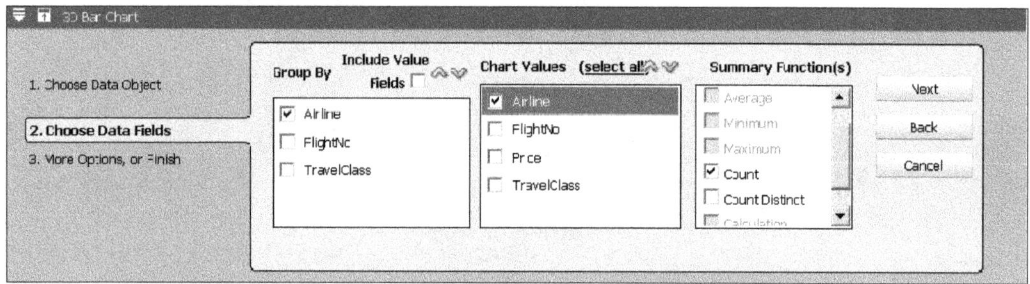

Then we click **Next.** We click on the **Change View Properties**. We change the **View Title** to **Number of reserved flight tickets by airline**. We also select the **Display Legend** checkbox.

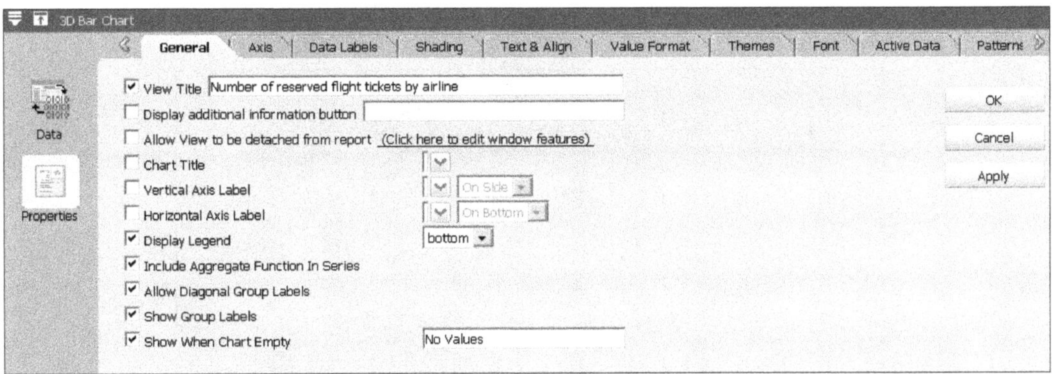

Then we click **OK**.

Displaying the effectiveness of the Approval Manager

In the last view, we want to display the effectiveness of the Approval Manager, who is responsible for reviewing the selected flight tickets. In our simplified example, the Approval Manager has three hours to complete the task by either confirming the flight ticket or rejecting it.

We select the **3D Pie Chart** in the bottom-left view. We select the `INTERVAL` data object and click **Next**. On the **Choose Data Fields** screen we click **Next**, as we have to create a calculated field first. Then we click on the **Create a calculated** field link. We select an **if** expression and press the **Insert Express** button. We enter the calculation as shown in the following screenshot:

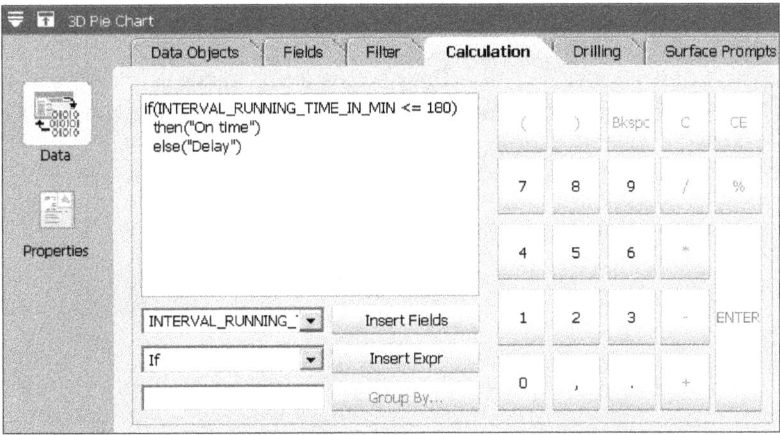

Then we press the **ENTER** button and rename the calculated field to `Effectiveness`.

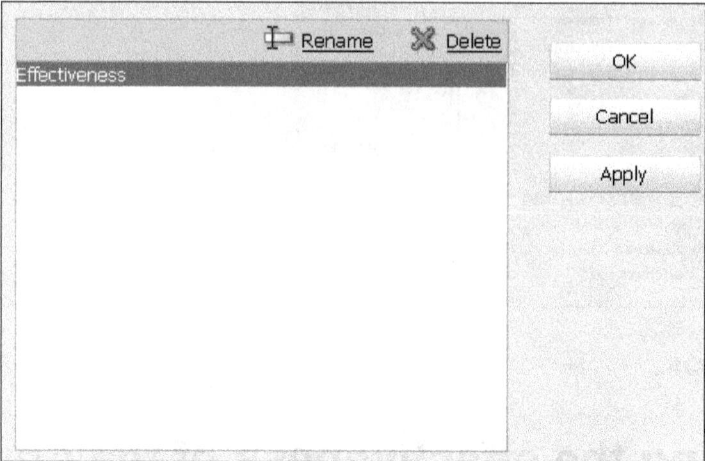

We click **OK**. Then, we click on the **Fields** tab. In the **Group by** list, we select the `Effectiveness` calculated field. Under **Chart Values** we select `COMPONENT_INSTANCE_ID`. We also select **Count Distinct** as the summary function.

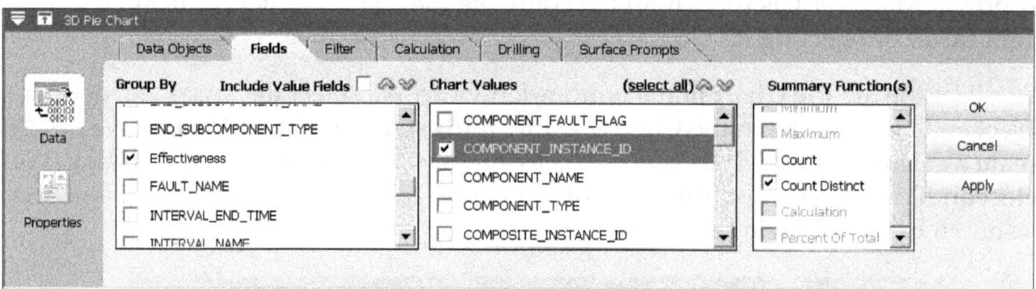

We click **Apply**. Then we click on the **Properties** icon on the left. We set the **View Title** to **Effectiveness of the Approval Manager** and select the **Display Legend** checkbox.

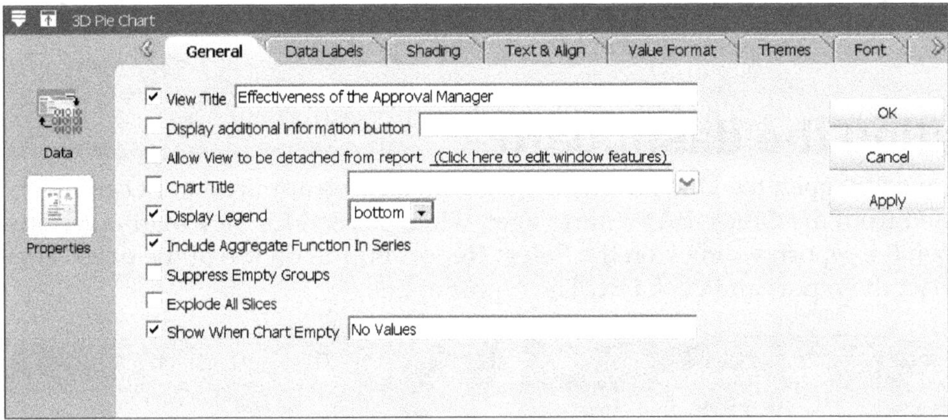

Then we click on the **Data Labels** tab. Here we deselect **Value** and select **Percent**. We click **OK**.

Our dashboard opened in Oracle BAM Active Studio now looks as shown in the following screenshot:

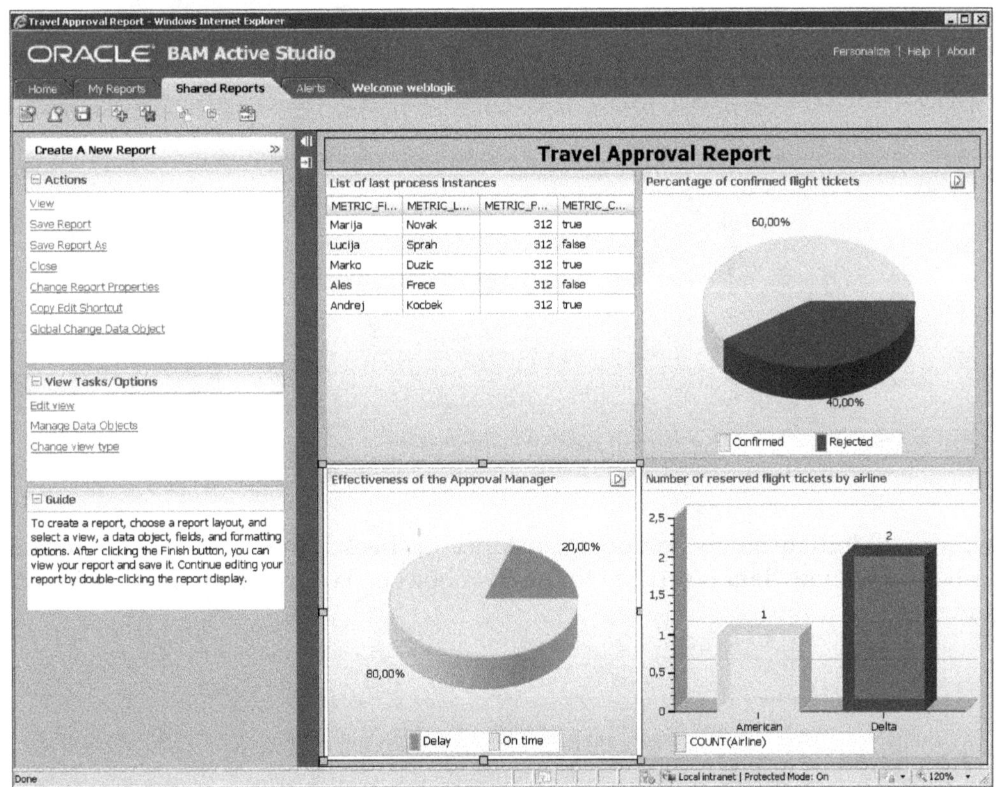

We save the report by clicking on the **Save Report As** link on the left. We select the `TravelApproval` folder and accept the default report name.

Testing the dashboard

Now, we will open the Oracle BAM Active Viewer web application (it can be accessed from the Oracle BAM Start Page), which is used for viewing the reports. To open the report, we click on the **Select Report** button on top of the page. Then we select the report and click **OK**. The report opens.

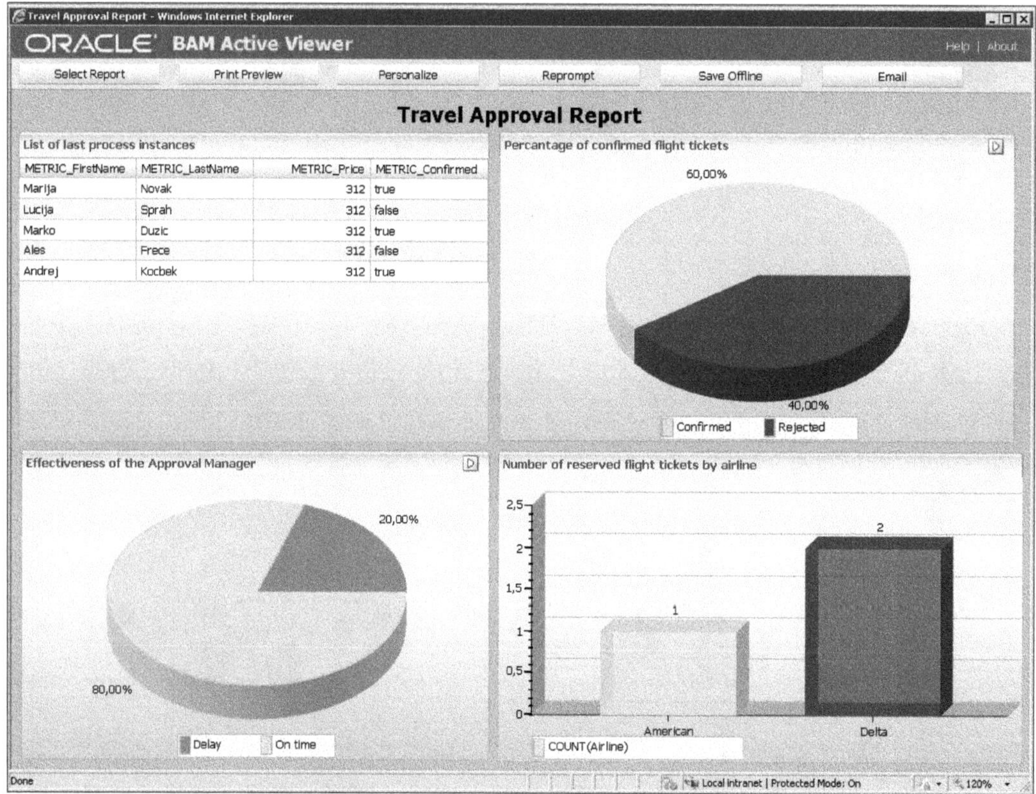

Now, we will initiate a new composite instance to check if the BAM dashboard really refreshes when new data is written to the data objects. We use the following input arguments:

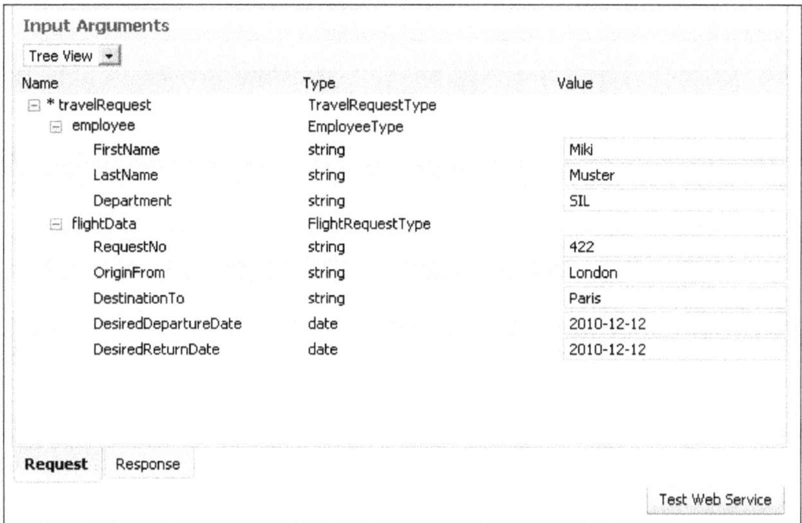

We approve the flight ticket using the Oracle BPM Worklist application. Then we open the BAM Active Viewer again. We can make sure that the BAM dashboard displays the latest data after just a few seconds.

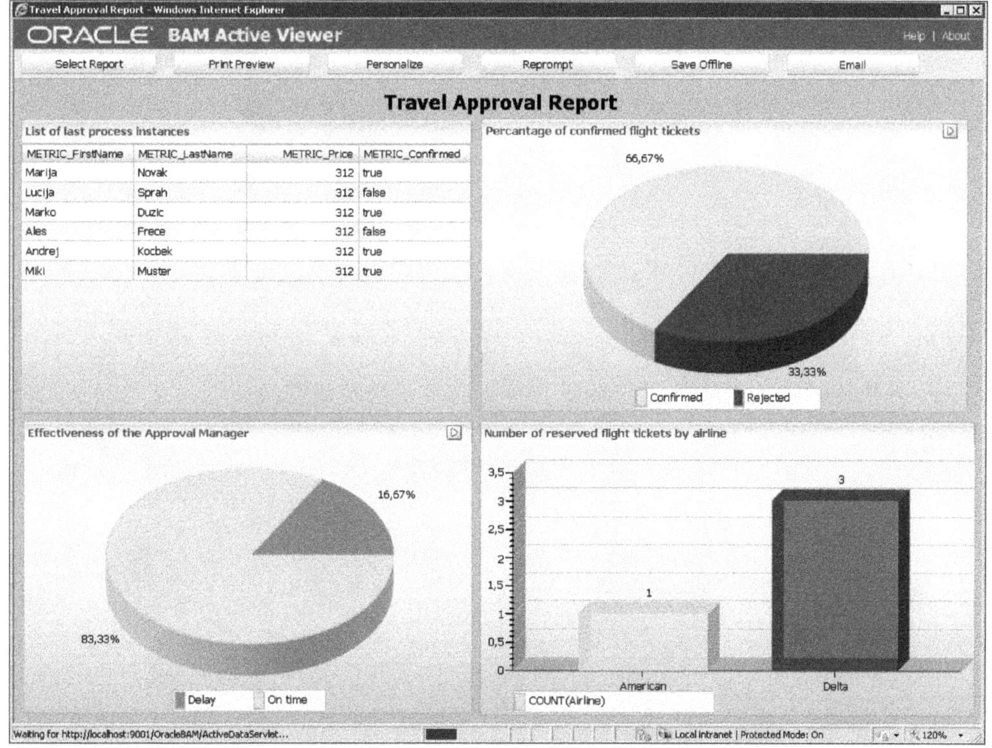

Summary

In this chapter, we have explained how to monitor BPEL processes with BAM. We have described the Oracle BAM architecture and features, including BAM Server and BAM Web Applications. We have explained how to use monitoring objects and how to use sensors and sensor actions.

With the use of an example, we have demonstrated how we can monitor a BPEL process. We have shown how to configure the monitoring objects and discussed various ways to create monitoring objects. We have shown how to create BAM data objects and establish BAM server connections.

We have shown how to create sensors and sensor actions, and how to use BAM Adapter partner links. Then we have explained how to build a BAM dashboard. We have explained how to create a report and how to choose the report template. We have also built a few reports. Finally, we have shown how to test a BAM dashboard.

In the next chapter, we will look at the Orace Service Bus and Oracle Service Registry and will show how to use BPEL processes with ESB and UDDI.

9

BPEL with Oracle Service Bus and Service Registry

If we want our SOA architecture to be highly flexible and agile, we have to ensure loose coupling between different components. As service interfaces and endpoint addresses change over time, we have to remove all point-to-point connections between service providers and service consumers by introducing an intermediate layer—Enterprise Service Bus (ESB). ESB is a key component of every mature SOA architecture and provides several important functionalities, such as message routing, transformation between message types and protocols, the use of adapters, and so on. Another important requirement for providing flexibility is service reuse. This can be achieved through the use of a **UDDI** (**Universal Description, Discovery and Integration**) compliant service registry, which enables us to publish and discover services. Using a service registry we can also implement dynamic endpoint lookup, so that service consumers retrieve actual service endpoint addresses from the registry at runtime.

In this chapter, we will get familiar with Oracle Service Bus (OSB), the Oracle strategic ESB. First, we will look at the OSB architecture and features. Then we will demonstrate the use of OSB on our Travel business process. We will show the combined use of OSB and Oracle Service Registry (OSR) to provide very high flexibility. Therefore, we will first publish the `EmployeeTravelStatus` service to the OSR. Then, we will open the Oracle Service Bus Console, create a new project, and import the service and all related artifacts from OSR. Next, we will create a proxy service for the `EmployeeTravelStatus` service. We will show how to define the proxy service message flow. We will also demonstrate some advanced features of OSB, such as service result caching. Then, we will deploy the new version of the `EmployeeTravelStatus` service with a slightly different interface and show how OSB can absorb these changes by simply adding an XSL transformation. Finally, we will publish the new proxy service to OSR and modify the corresponding reference binding component in our SOA composite, so that it will retrieve the proxy endpoint address from OSR at runtime.

In this chapter, we will discuss the following:

- Oracle Service Bus architecture and features
- Publishing services to OSR
- The use of Oracle Service Bus Console
- Importing resources from OSR to OSB
- Service Result Caching
- Creating a proxy service
- Adding XSL Transformations to the request pipeline
- Publishing a proxy service to OSR
- Dynamic endpoint lookup

Oracle Service Bus architecture and features

In Chapter 1, we discussed the importance of the ESB in SOA. We have identified that the ESB eliminates point-to-point connections between services and BPEL processes. ESB also provides a means to manage connections, control the communication between services, supervise the services and their **SLAs** (**Service Level Agreements**), and much more. The importance of the ESB often becomes visible after the first development iteration of an SOA composite application has taken place. For example, when a service requires a change in its interface or payload, the ESB can provide the transformation capabilities to mask the differences to existing service consumers. ESB can also mask the location of services, making it easy to migrate services to different servers. There are plenty other scenarios where ESB is important.

In this chapter, we will look at the **Oracle Service Bus** (**OSB**). OSB presents a communication backbone for transport and routing of messages across an enterprise. It is designed for high-throughput and reliable message delivery to a variety of service providers and consumers. It supports XML as a native data type; however, other data types are also supported. As an intermediary, it processes incoming service request messages, executes the routing logic, and transforms these messages if needed. It can also transform between different transport protocols (HTTP, JMS, File, FTP, and so on). Service response messages follow the inverse path. The message processing is specified in the message flow definition of a proxy service.

OSB provides some functionalities that are similar to the functionalities of the Mediator component within the SOA Composite, such as routing, validation, filtering, and transformation. The major difference is that the Mediator is a mediation component that is meant to work within the SOA Composite and is deployed within an SOA composite application. The OSB, on the other hand, is a standalone service bus. In addition to providing the communication backbone for all SOA (and non-SOA) applications, OSB's mission is to shield application developers from changes in the service endpoints and to prevent those systems from being overloaded with requests from upstream applications.

In addition to the Oracle Service Bus, we can also use the Mediator service component, which also provides mediation capabilities, but only within SOA composite applications. On the other hand, OSB is used for inter-application communication.

The following figure shows the functional architecture of Oracle Service Bus (OSB). We can see that OSB can be categorized into four functional layers:

- Messaging layer: Provides support to reliably connect any service by leveraging standards, such as HTTP/SOAP, WS-I, WS-Security, WS-Policy, WS-Addressing, SOAP v1.1, SOAP v1.2, EJB, RMI, and so on. It even supports the creation of custom transports using the Custom Transport Software Development Kit (SDK).
- Security layer: Provides security at all levels—Transport Security (SSL), Message Security (WS-Policy, WS-Security, and so on), Console Security (SSO and role-based access) and Policy (leverages WS-Security and WS-Policy).
- Composition layer: Provides a configuration-driven composition environment. We can use either the Eclipse plug-in environment or web-based Oracle Service Bus Console. We can model message flows that contain content-based routing, message validation, and exception handling. We can also use message transformations (XSLT, XQuery), service callouts (POJO, Web Services), and a test browser. Automatic synchronization with UDDI registries is also supported.

* Management layer: Provides a unified dashboard for service monitoring and management. We can define and monitor **Service Level Agreements (SLAs)**, alerts on operation metrics, and message pipelines, and view reports.

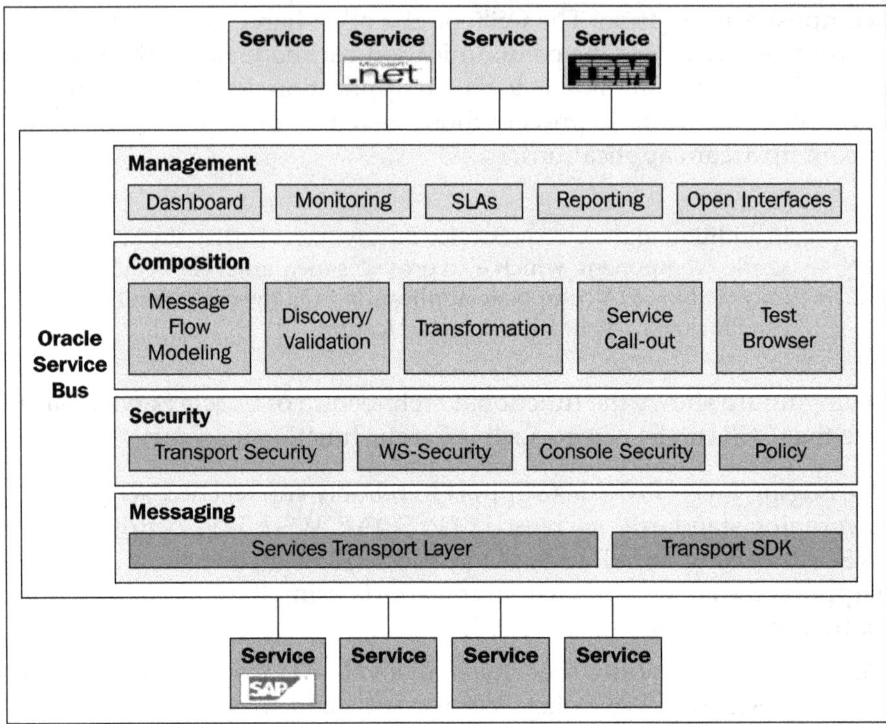

Proxy services and business services

OSB uses a specific terminology of proxy and business services. The objective of OSB is to route messages between business services and service consumers through proxy services.

Proxy services are generic intermediary web services that implement the mediation logic and are hosted locally on OSB. Proxy services route messages to business services and are exposed to service consumers. A proxy service is configured by specifying its interface, type of transport, and its associated message processing logic. Message flow definitions are used to define the proxy service message-handling capabilities.

Business services describe the enterprise services that exchange messages with business processes and which we want to virtualize using the OSB. The definition of a business service is similar to that of a proxy service; however, the business service does not have a message flow definition.

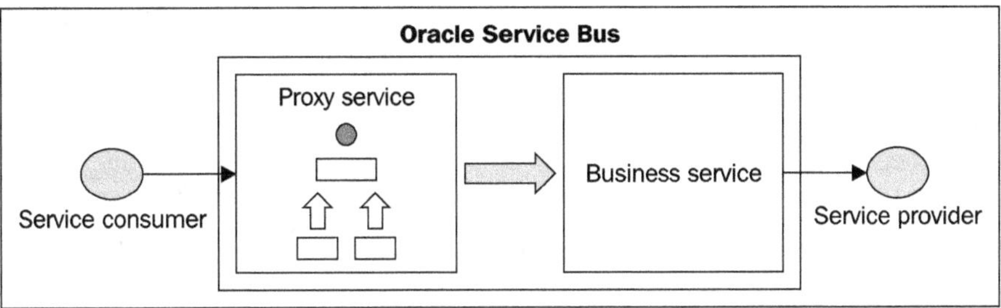

Message flow modeling

Message flows are used to define the message processing logic of proxy services. Message flow modeling includes defining a sequence of activities, where activities are individual actions, such as transformations, reporting, publishing, and exception management. Message flow modeling can be performed using a visual development environment (Eclipse or Oracle Service Bus Console).

Message flow definitions are defined using components, such as pipelines, branch nodes, and route nodes, as shown in the following figure:

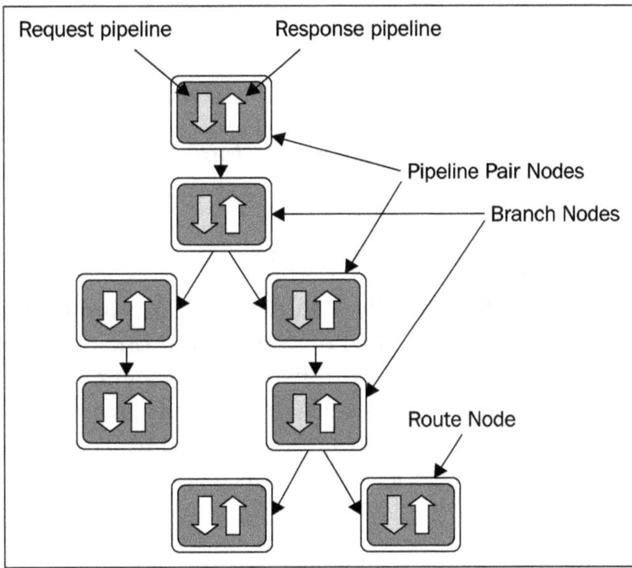

A pipeline is a sequence of stages, representing a one-way processing path. It is used to specify message flow for service requests and responses. If a service defines more operations, a pipeline might optionally branch into operational pipelines. There are three types of pipelines:

- Request pipelines are used to specify the request path of the message flow
- Response pipelines are used to specify the response path of a message flow
- Error pipelines are used as error handlers

Request and response pipelines are paired together as pipeline pairs.

Branch nodes are used as exclusive switches, where the processing can follow one of the branches. A variable in the message context is used as a lookup variable to determine which branch to follow.

Route nodes are used to communicate with another service (in most cases a business service). They cannot have any descendants in the message flow. When the route node sends the request message, the request processing is finished. On the other side, when it receives a response message, the response processing begins.

Each pipeline is a sequence of stages that contain user-defined message processing actions. We can choose between a variety of supported actions, such as Publish, Service Callout, For Each, If... Then..., Raise Error, Reply, Resume, Skip, Delete, Insert, Replace, Validate, Alert, Log, Report, and more. Later in this chapter, we will show you how to use a pipeline on the TravelApproval process. However, let us first look at the Oracle Service Registry, which we will use together with the OSB.

Oracle Service Registry

Oracle Service Registry (**OSR**) is a fully V3-compliant implementation of UDDI (Universal Description, Discovery and Integration), and one of the key components of Oracle SOA Suite 11*g*. It allows us to publish and discover services and service providers, and manage metadata about services (security, transport, or quality service) using taxonomies. Therefore, it plays an important role when trying to improve visibility and promote service reuse. It is also important in the scope of SOA governance.

A service registry is very important for various reasons. It provides a central place where all service definitions are stored. This becomes important when the number of services (including BPEL processes) grows. It helps to maintain an overview of services. A service registry also provides a central place where developers can search for existing services. This improves service reuse, which is one of the most important aspects of SOA. Of course, a service registry also provides means to publish a services for other developers to discover and reuse.

In addition to reuse, a service registry can also be helpful when we need to migrate services from one server to the other. This can happen because of various reasons, but one of the most common reasons is the migration between the development, test, and production environments. A service registry is also helpful when we need to version services and manage changes. With a service registry, we can also develop more loosely coupled composite applications, because we do not need to hard-code the service URLs. Rather, the application will resolve URLs at run time. In all cases, the service registry is often used together with the ESB.

We will not discuss all OSR details in this chapter. We will demonstrate how to publish a service, how to export/import resources between OSB and OSR, how to browse the OSR using JDeveloper, and how to enable dynamic endpoint lookup in an SOA composite application.

Logging into Oracle Service Registry

To log into Oracle Registry Control, we have to open a web browser and access the following URL: `http://host_name:port/application_name/uddi/web`, where `host_name` is the name of the host on which OSR is installed, `application_name` is name of the application (default name is `registry`), and `port` is a number that is set during the installation process.

OSR provides two web consoles: **Registry Control** and **Business service Control**. Registry Control provides an interface that is based on the UDDI specification and is useful for developers familiar with business entities and `tModels`. Business service Control, on the other hand, provides a simpler interface for less-technical users unfamiliar with `tModels` and other UDDI stuff. We can publish and discover services using both. In this chapter, we will show how to use Registry Control Console.

To log into the console, we click on the **Login** link in the upper-right corner and enter username and password. The Registry Control home page opens, as shown in the following screenshot:

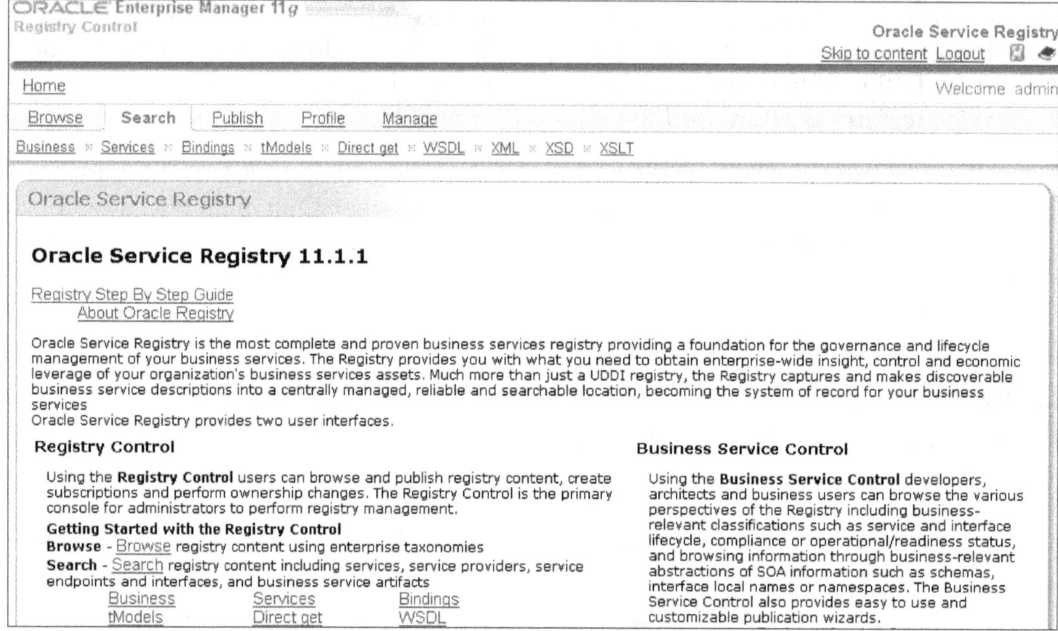

Publishing a business entity

Before publishing the `EmployeeTravelStatus` service, we have to publish a business entity (service provider). This is because the UDDI data model requires a business entity for each service, which is represented by a `tModel`. We click on the **Publish** link and then press the **Add business** button. We name the business entity **Packt Publishing**. We can also add a description and enter a custom business key.

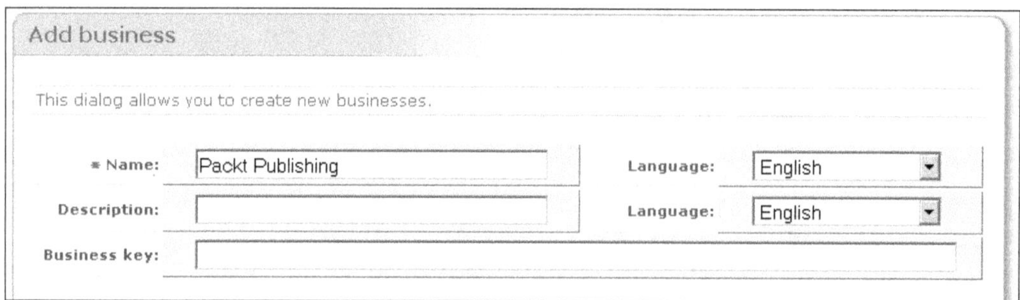

We click on the **Add business** button and then **Save changes**.

Publishing a business service

Back on the **Publish** page, we expand the **Businesses** folder, right-click the **Packt Publishing** business entity, and select **Publish WSDL**.

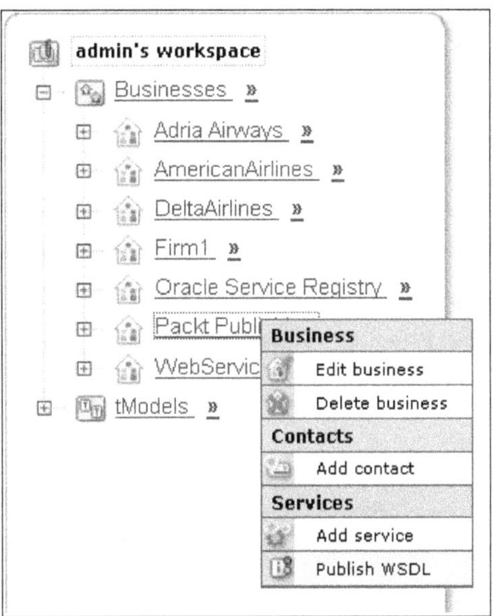

The **Publish WSDL document** page opens. We enter the **WSDL location** (**URI**) of the `EmployeeTravelStatus` service and click **Publish**.

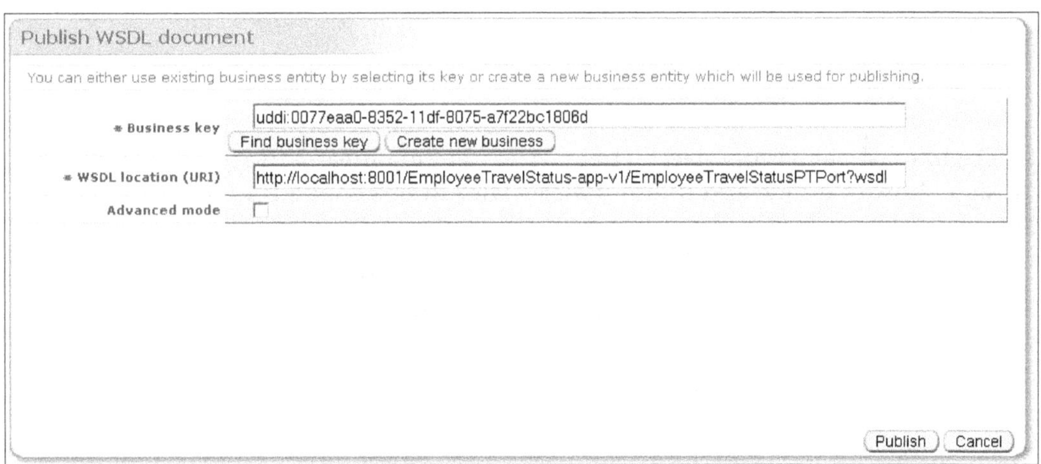

The **Publish summary** page opens. We can review the entities that have been published to the OSR. We click **OK**.

Using Oracle Service Bus Console

To log into Oracle Service Bus Console, we have to open a web browser and access the following URL: `http://host_name:port/sbconsole`, where `host_name` is the name of the host on which OSB is installed and `port` is a number that is set during the installation process. We log in as user `weblogic`. The Oracle Service Bus Console opens, as shown in the following screenshot:

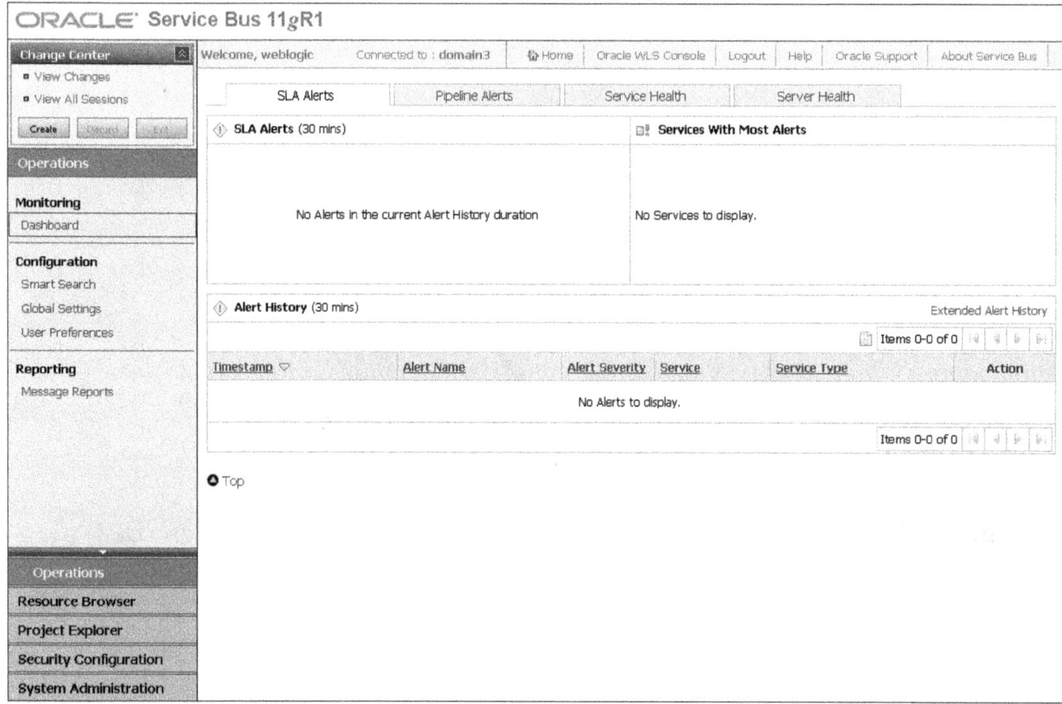

The **Dashboard** page is opened by default, displaying information about alerts. We will show how to define and monitor alerts later in this chapter. In the upper-left corner, we can see the **Change Center**.

Change Center is key to making configuration changes in OSB. Before making any changes, we have to create a new session by clicking the **Create** button. Then, we are able to make different changes without disrupting existing services. When finished, we activate all changes by clicking **Activate**. If we want to roll back the changes, we can click the **Discard** button. We can also view all changes before activating them and write a comment.

Creating a project and importing resources from OSR

First, we have to create a new session, by clicking the **Create** button in the **Change Center**. Next, we will create a new project. OSB uses projects to allow logical grouping of resources and to better organize related parts of large development projects. We click on the **Project Explorer** link in the main menu. In the **Projects** page, we enter the name of the project (`TravelApproval`) and click **Add Project**. The new project is now shown in the projects list on the left side in the **Project Explorer**. We click on the project.

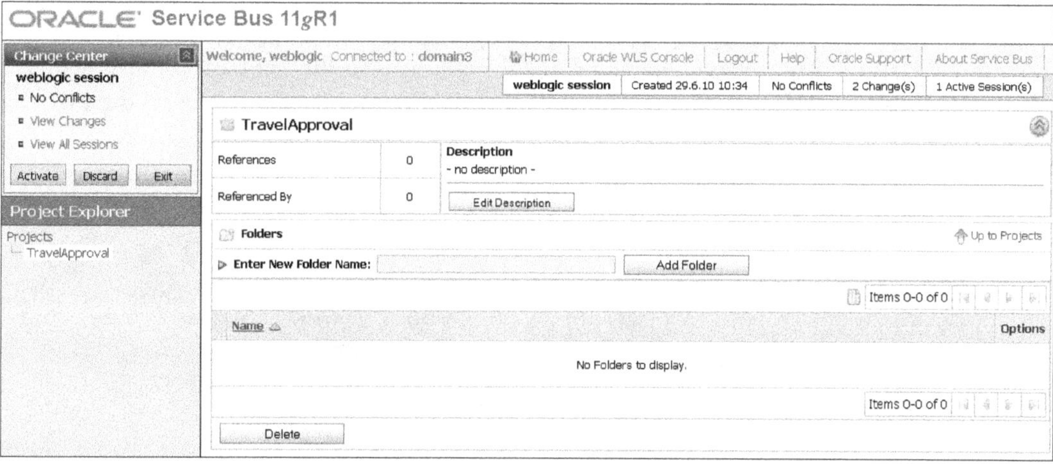

Next, we add folders to the project, as we want to group resources by type. To create a folder, we enter the folder name in the **Enter New Folder Name** field and click **Add folder**. We add six folders: `BusinessServices`, `ProxyServices`, `WSDL`, `XSD`, `XSLT`, and `AlertDestinations`.

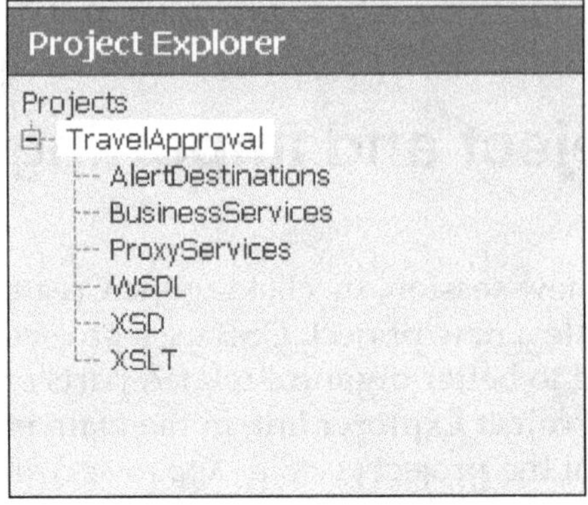

Next, we have to create resources. We will show how to import service and all related resources from the UDDI registry. Before creating a connection to the UDDI registry, we activate the current session. First, we review all changes. We click the **View Changes** link in the **Change Center**. We can see the list of all changes in the current session. We can also undo changes by clicking the *undo* link in the last column.

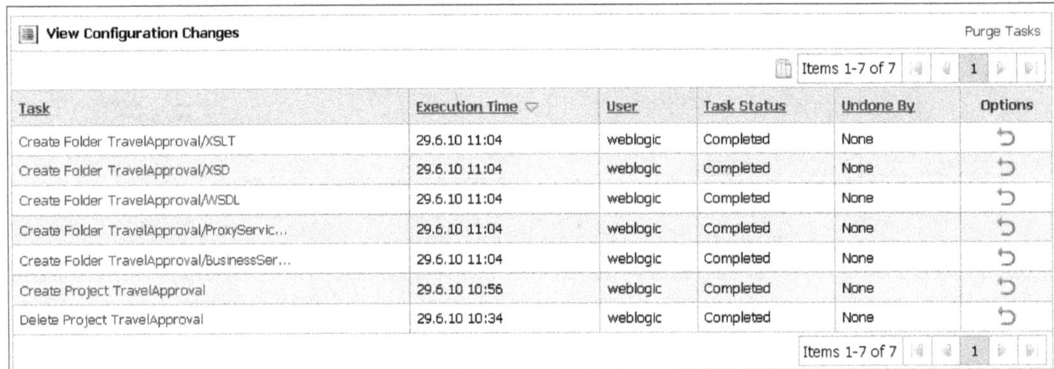

View Configuration Changes — Purge Tasks

Items 1-7 of 7

Task	Execution Time	User	Task Status	Undone By	Options
Create Folder TravelApproval/XSLT	29.6.10 11:04	weblogic	Completed	None	
Create Folder TravelApproval/XSD	29.6.10 11:04	weblogic	Completed	None	
Create Folder TravelApproval/WSDL	29.6.10 11:04	weblogic	Completed	None	
Create Folder TravelApproval/ProxyServic...	29.6.10 11:04	weblogic	Completed	None	
Create Folder TravelApproval/BusinessSer...	29.6.10 11:04	weblogic	Completed	None	
Create Project TravelApproval	29.6.10 10:56	weblogic	Completed	None	
Delete Project TravelApproval	29.6.10 10:34	weblogic	Completed	None	

Items 1-7 of 7

Now, we activate the session by clicking on the **Activate** button. The **Activate Session** page opens. We can add a description to the session and click **Submit**.

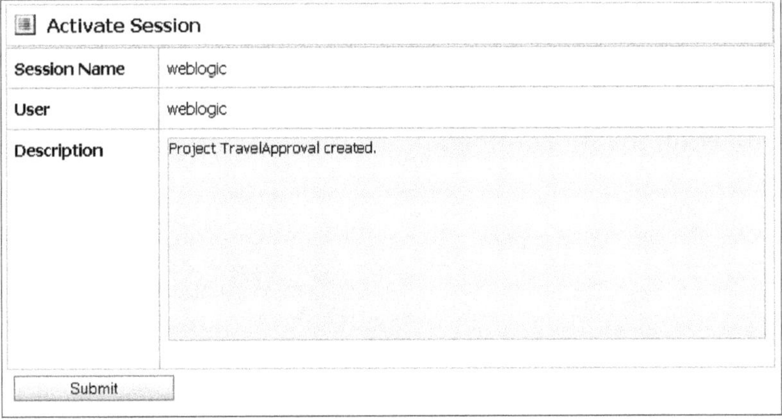

Activate Session

Session Name	weblogic
User	weblogic
Description	Project TravelApproval created.

Submit

Now, all changes made are activated.

Creating a connection to Oracle Service Registry

First, we start a new session in the **Change Center**. Then we click on the **System Administration** link in the main menu. We click on the **UDDI Registries** and then **Add registry** on the right side of the page. We enter connection parameters and click **Save**.

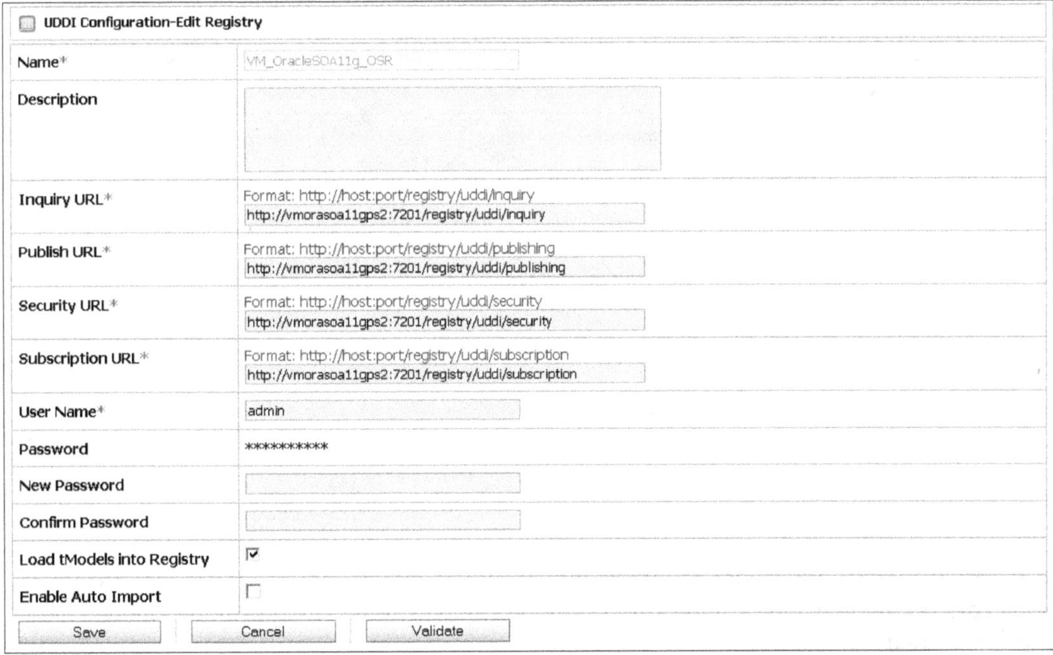

UDDI Configuration-Edit Registry

Name*	VM_OracleSOA11g_OSR
Description	
Inquiry URL*	Format: http://host:port/registry/uddi/inquiry http://vmorasoa11gps2:7201/registry/uddi/inquiry
Publish URL*	Format: http://host:port/registry/uddi/publishing http://vmorasoa11gps2:7201/registry/uddi/publishing
Security URL*	Format: http://host:port/registry/uddi/security http://vmorasoa11gps2:7201/registry/uddi/security
Subscription URL*	Format: http://host:port/registry/uddi/subscription http://vmorasoa11gps2:7201/registry/uddi/subscription
User Name*	admin
Password	***********
New Password	
Confirm Password	
Load tModels into Registry	☑
Enable Auto Import	☐

Save Cancel Validate

Now, the registry is listed in the **UDDI Registries** list, as shown next:

We can optionally activate a current session. In that case, we have to create a new session before importing resources from UDDI.

Importing resources from Oracle Service Registry

We click on the **Import from UDDI** link on the left-hand side. As there is only one connection to the registry, this connection is selected by default. First, we have to select the **Business Entity**. We select **Packt Publishing**. Then we click on the **Search** button to display all services of the selected business entity. In the next screenshot, we can see that currently there is only one service published. We select the service and click **Next**.

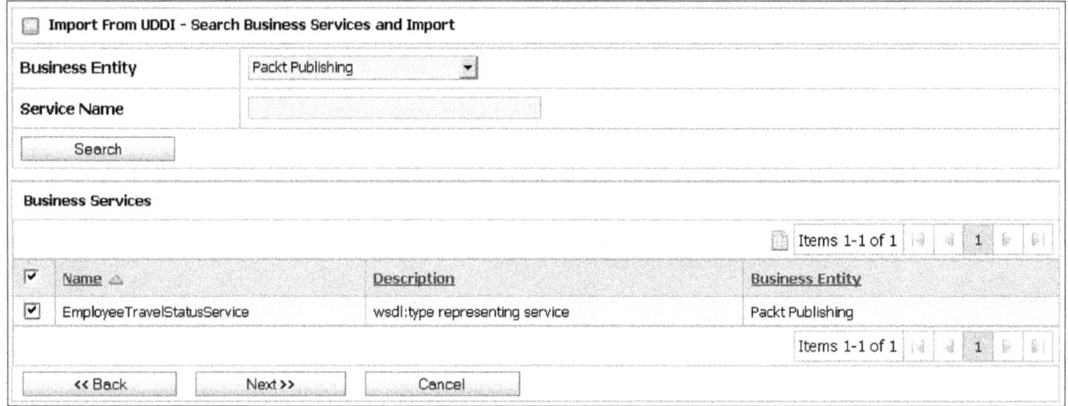

In the second step, we select the project and folder, where we want to save the resources. We select the `TravelApproval` project and the folder `BusinessServices` and click **Next**.

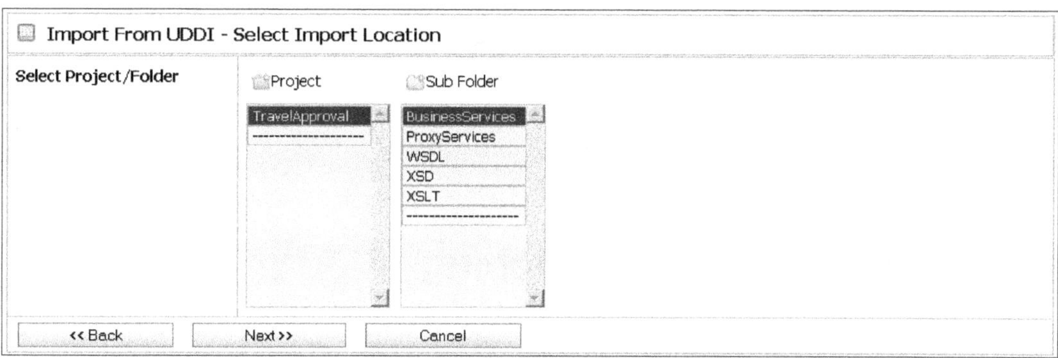

On the final screen, we just click the **Import** button. Now we can see that a business service, a WSDL, and three XSD resources have been created.

All resources have been created automatically, as we imported a service from the UDDI registry. If we create resources by hand, we first have to create an XML Schema in WSDL resources, and then the Business service.

As all resources have been saved to the `BusinessServices` folder, we have to move them to appropriate folders based on their type. We go back to the **Project Explorer** and click on the `BusinessServices` folder in the `TravelApproval` project. We can see all imported resources in the **Resources** list at the bottom of the page.

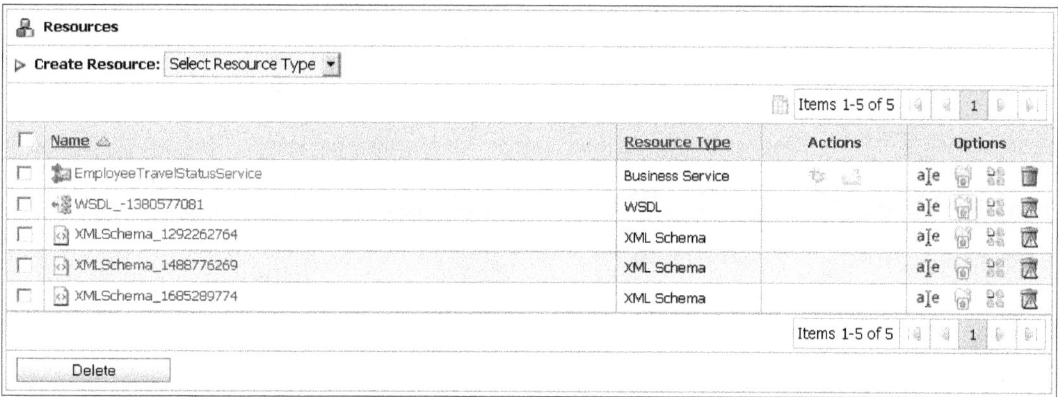

We can move resources by clicking on the *Move Resource* icon and then selecting the target folder. We move the WSDL resource to the `WSDL` folder and the XML Schemas to the `XSD` folder.

Configuring a business service

If we want to monitor service metrics, such as average response time, number of messages, and number of errors, we have to enable monitoring of the business service. We will also show how to improve performances by enabling service result caching, which is a new feature in OSB 11*g* PS2.

Enabling service result caching

OSB supports service result caching through the use of Oracle Coherence, which is an in-memory data grid solution. In this way, we can dramatically improve performances if the response of the business service is relatively static. To enable the use of service result caching globally, we have to open the **Operations** | **Global Settings** and set **Enable Result Caching** to `true`.

In the **Project Explorer**, we click on our Business service. On the **Configuration Details** tab, we will enable service result caching. We scroll-down and edit the **Message Handling Configuration**. Then we expand the **Advanced Settings**. We select the **Result Caching** checkbox. Next, we have to specify the cache token, which uniquely identifies a single cache result. This is usually an ID field. In our simplified example, we do not have an ID field; therefore, we will use the employee last name for testing purposes. We enter the following cache token expression: `$body/emp:employee/LastName`. Then we set the expiration time to **20** minutes.

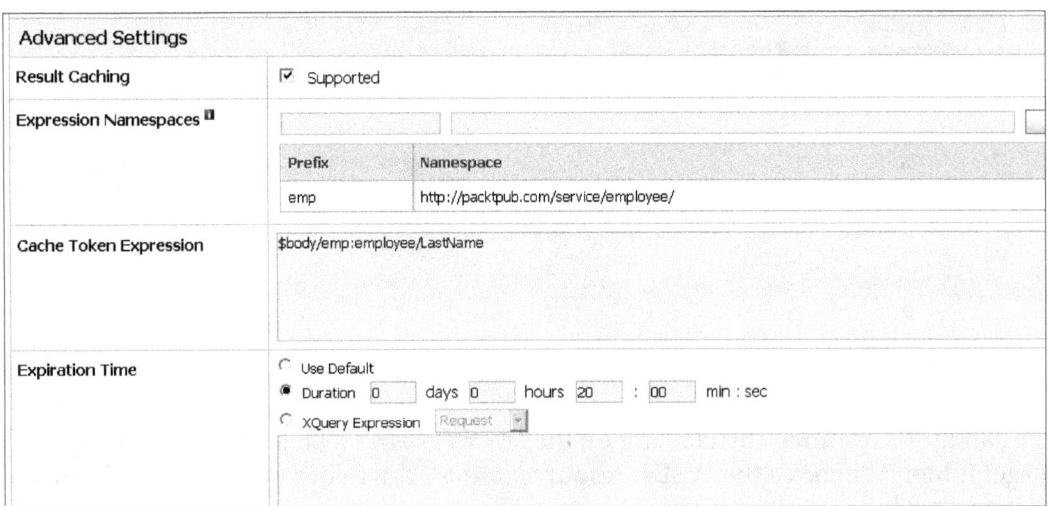

Then, we click **Next** and **Save**.

Now, if the business service locates cached results through a cache key, it returns those cached results to the client instead of invoking the external service. If the result is not cached, the business service invokes the external service, returns the result to the client, and stores the result in cache.

Service result caching works only when the business service is invoked from a proxy service.

Enabling service monitoring

Again, we click on our Business service and then click on the **Operational Settings** tab. We select the **Enabled** checkbox next to the **Monitoring** and set the **Aggregation Interval** to **20 minutes**. The aggregation interval is the sliding window of time over which metrics are computed. We can also define SLA alerts which are based on these metrics.

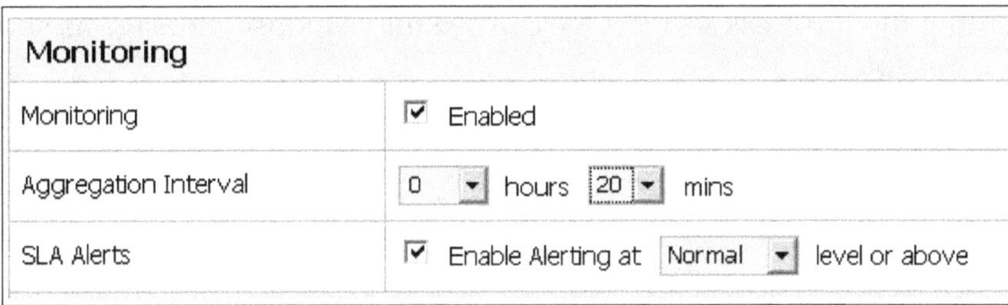

We click **Update** to save the changes. Then, we activate the changes by clicking on the **Activate** button in the **Change Center**.

Testing a business service

After activating the changes, we can test the business service using the **Test Console**. To open the console, we select the `BusinessServices` folder and then click on the *bug* icon next to the Business service.

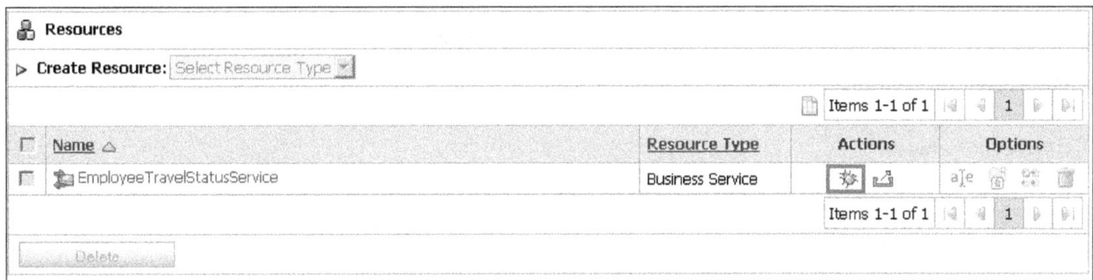

The **Test Console** opens. We set the XML payload and click the **Execute** button.

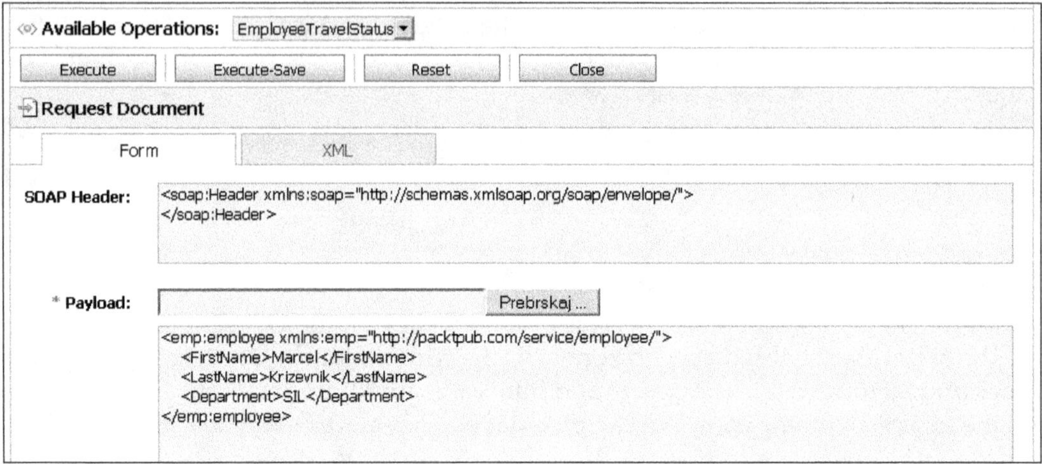
Available Operations: EmployeeTravelStatus
Execute
Execute-Save
Reset
Close
Request Document
Form
XML
SOAP Header:
<soap:Header xmlns:soap="http://schemas.xmlsoap.org/soap/envelope/">
</soap:Header>
* Payload:
Prebrskaj ...
<emp:employee xmlns:emp="http://packtpub.com/service/employee/">
<FirstName>Marcel</FirstName>
<LastName>Krizevnik</LastName>
<Department>SIL</Department>
</emp:employee>

After executing the Business service, we can see the response message as shown in the next screenshot:

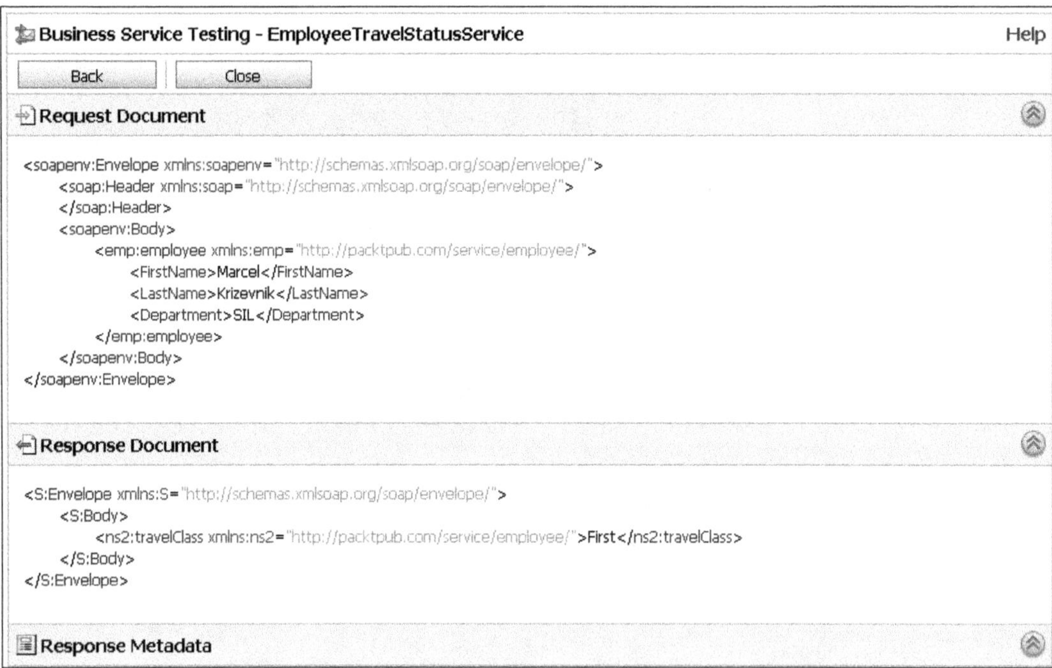
Business Service Testing - EmployeeTravelStatusService
Help
Back
Close
Request Document
<soapenv:Envelope xmlns:soapenv="http://schemas.xmlsoap.org/soap/envelope/">
<soap:Header xmlns:soap="http://schemas.xmlsoap.org/soap/envelope/">
</soap:Header>
<soapenv:Body>
<emp:employee xmlns:emp="http://packtpub.com/service/employee/">
<FirstName>Marcel</FirstName>
<LastName>Krizevnik</LastName>
<Department>SIL</Department>
</emp:employee>
</soapenv:Body>
</soapenv:Envelope>
Response Document
<S:Envelope xmlns:S="http://schemas.xmlsoap.org/soap/envelope/">
<S:Body>
<ns2:travelClass xmlns:ns2="http://packtpub.com/service/employee/">First</ns2:travelClass>
</S:Body>
</S:Envelope>
Response Metadata

Creating an Alert destination

Before creating a proxy service, we will create an Alert Destination resource, which will be later used for sending e-mail alerts to the administrator. Remember, that we have already created the `AlertDestinations` folder.

To be able to send e-mail alerts, we have to first configure the SMTP server on the **System Administration** page.

To create an Alert destination, we navigate to the `AlertDestinations` folder and then select the **Alert Destination** from the **Create Resource** drop-down. We set the name to `Administrator` and add an e-mail recipient by clicking the **Add** button. We enter the recipient e-mail address (we can add more recipients) and select the SMTP server.

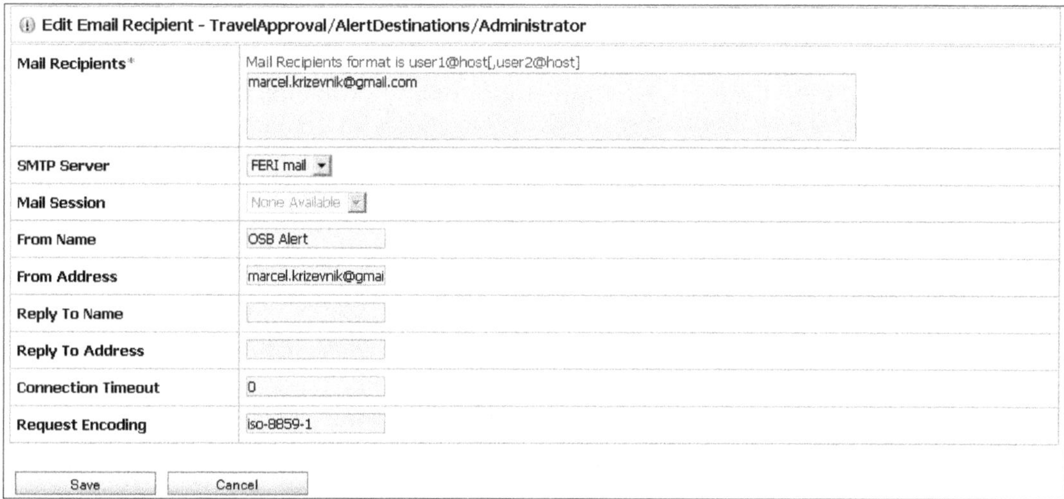

Then we click **Save** twice.

Creating a proxy service

Although at the first sight it might seem redundant, using a proxy service instead of calling the original business service directly has several advantages. If we add a proxy service between the service consumer and the original service, we gain transparency. Through OSB, we can monitor and supervise the service and control the inbound and outbound messages. This becomes important when changes happen. For example, when a service interface or the payload changes, the proxy service can mask the changes to all service consumers that have not yet been upgraded to use the new version. This is, however, not the only benefit. A proxy service can enable authentication and authorization when accessing a service. It can provide a means to monitor service SLAs, and much more. Therefore, it often makes sense to consider using proxy services.

We will show an example to demonstrate the capabilities of proxy services. We will create a proxy service, which will contain the message processing logic and will be used to decouple service clients from the service provider. Our proxy service will validate the request against the corresponding XML schema. It will also perform error handling and alert the service administrator of any problems with the service execution.

First, we start a new session (if there is no active session) by clicking the **Create** button in the **Change Center**. Then we navigate to the `ProxyServices` folder in the **Project Explorer**. We click on the **Create Resources** drop-down and select **Proxy Service**.

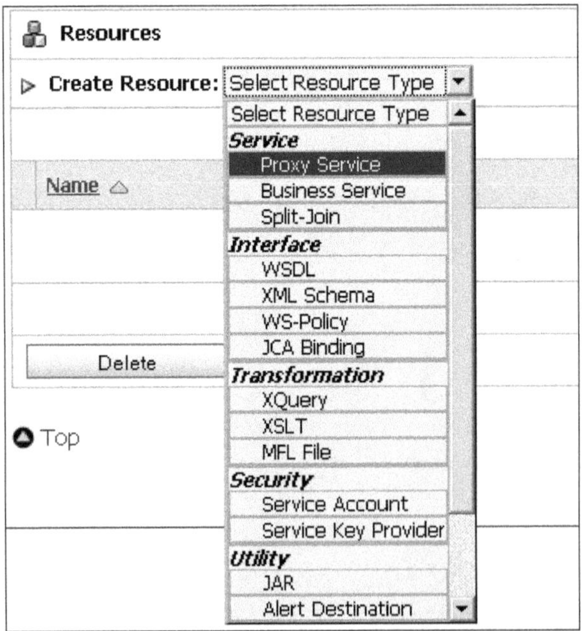

The **General Configuration** page opens. We set the name of the proxy service to `EmployeeTravelStatusServiceProxy`. We also have to define the interface of the service. We select the **Business service**, as we want the proxy service to use the same interface as the business service. We click the **Browse** button and select the `EmployeeTravelStatusService` business service.

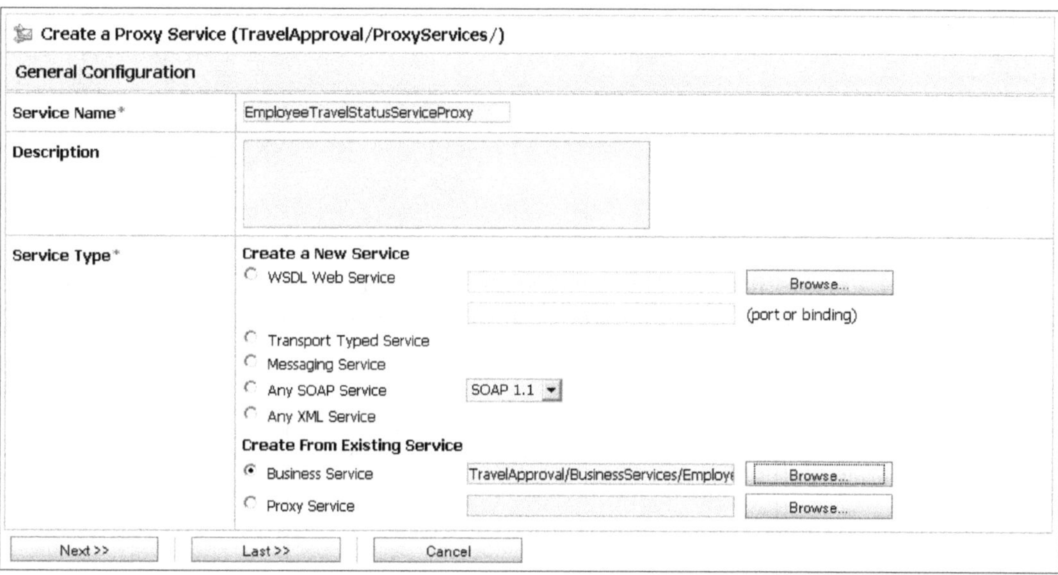

Then we click **Next**. On the **Transport Configuration** screen, we can change the transport **Protocol** and **Endpoint URI**.

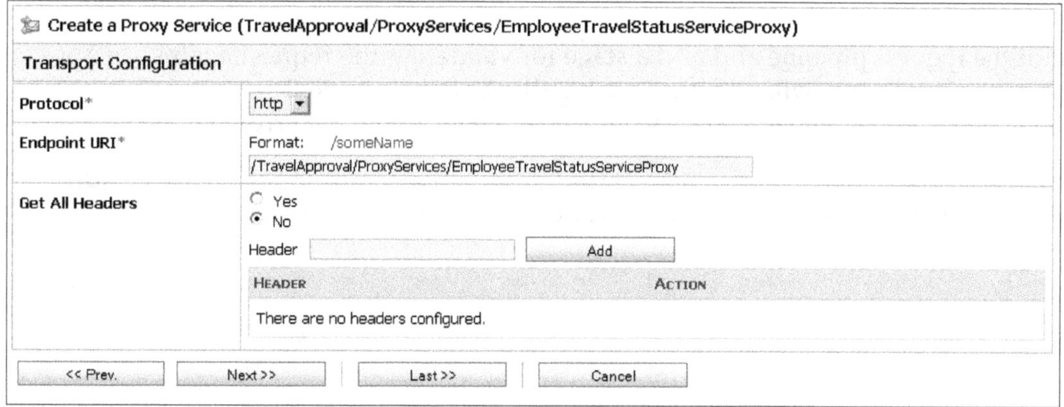

We use the defaults values and click **Next**. The **HTTP Transport Configuration** screen opens. We click **Next** on the remaining configuration screens. On the **Summary** page, we click the **Save** button at the bottom of the page.

Configuring Message Flow

We select the new proxy service. We then click on the **Edit Message Flow** icon in the **Resources** list to open the **Message Flow** editor.

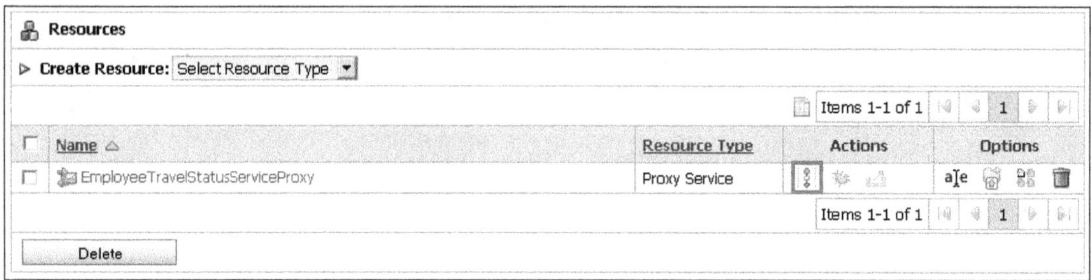

In the **Message Flow** editor, we can see that a route node for the `EmployeeTravelStatusService` business service already exists.

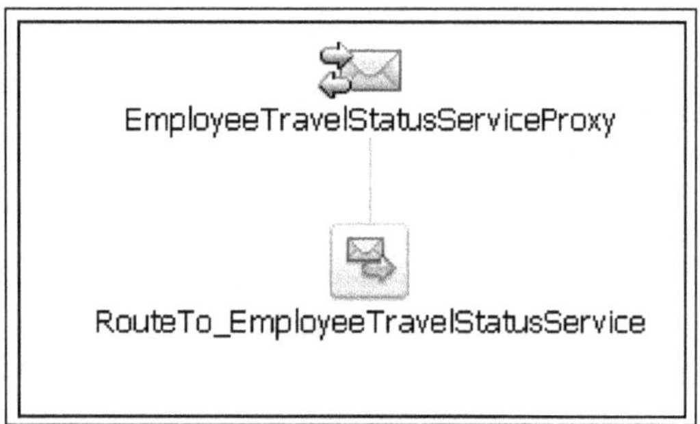

Now, we will modify the message flow by adding a pipeline pair. Then, we will edit the request pipeline and add a stage for validating the request against an XML Schema. Finally, we will add an error handler to the message flow and define a stage for sending an e-mail alert to an administrator every time the error occurs.

We click on the `EmployeeTravelStatusServiceProxy` envelope and select **Add Pipeline Pair**. A pipeline pair node is added to the message flow.

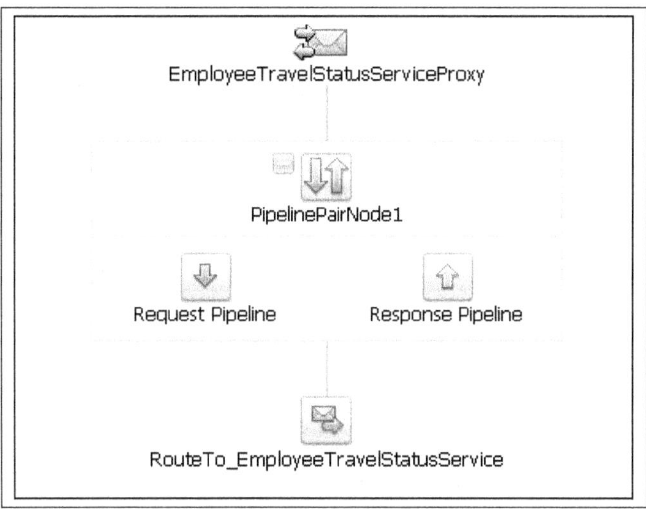

Now, we will edit the request pipeline. Remember that a pipeline contains a sequence of stages. We click on the `Request Pipeline` node and select **Add Stage**.

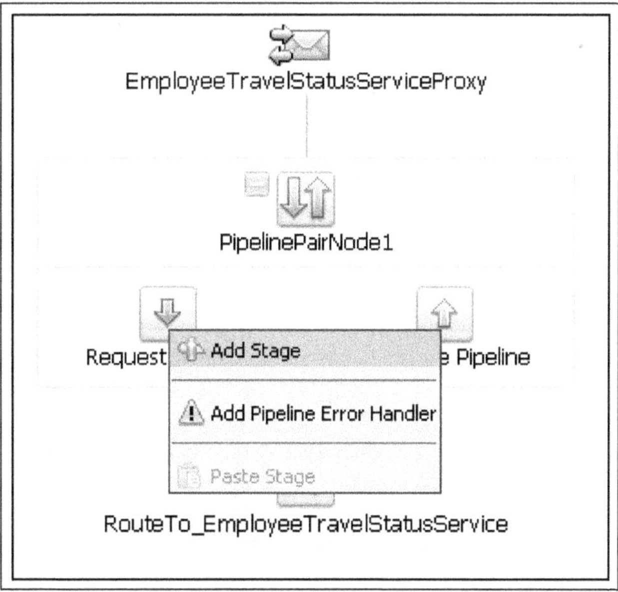

We click on the new stage and select **Edit Name and Comments**. We rename the stage to `Validate`. Next, we click on the stage and select **Edit Stage**. The **Edit Stage Configuration** screen appears. We click on **Add an Action** and select **Message Processing | Validate**.

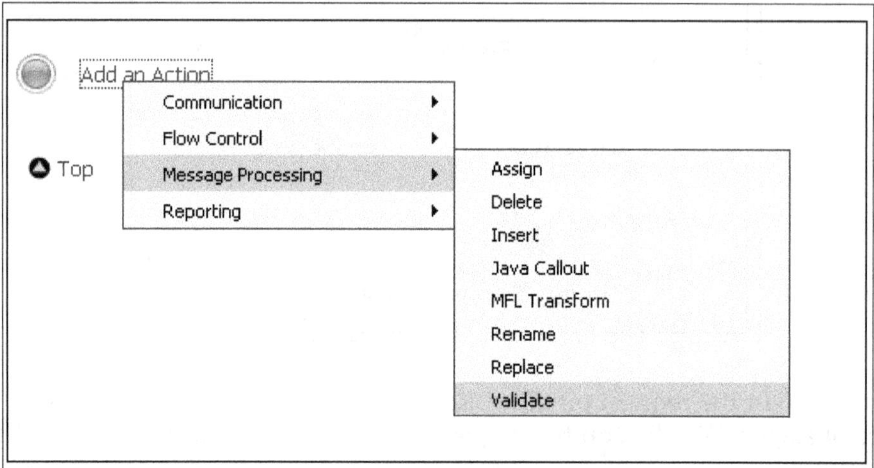

We specify that we want to validate `./emp:employee` in the variable `body` against the `EmployeeType` defined in the `XMLSchema_1488776269` XML Schema, as shown in the following screenshot:

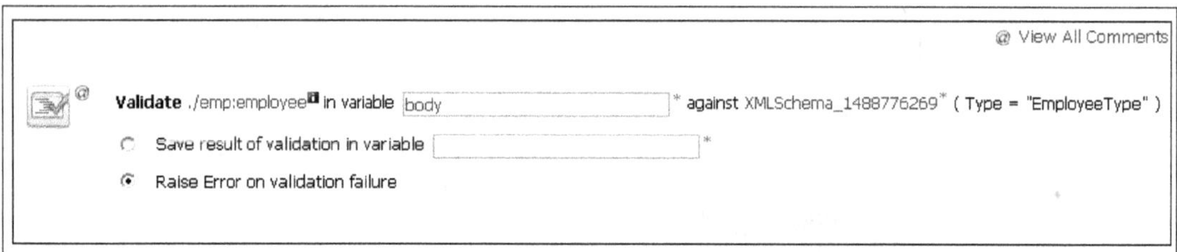

Then we click **Save** to save the changes and return to the **Message Flow** editor.

Now, we click on the envelope and select **Add Service Error Handler**. Then, we click on the **Error Handler** node and select **Add Stage**.

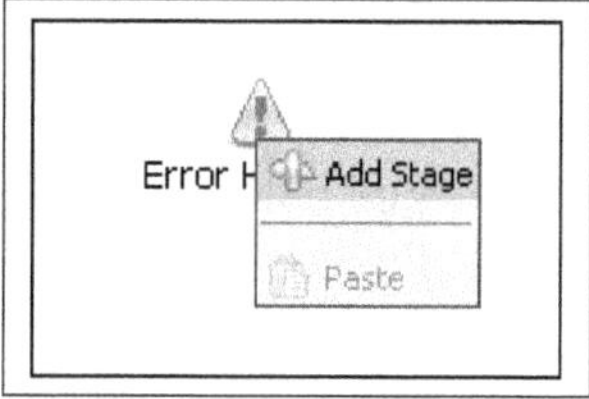

We rename the new stage to **Send Alert**. Next, we click on the stage and select **Edit Stage**. We add an **Alert** action as shown in the following screenshot:

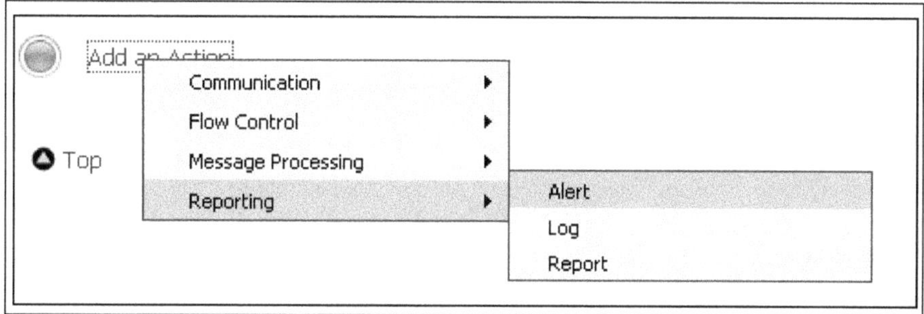

We configure the alert as shown in the following screenshot and click **Save All**.

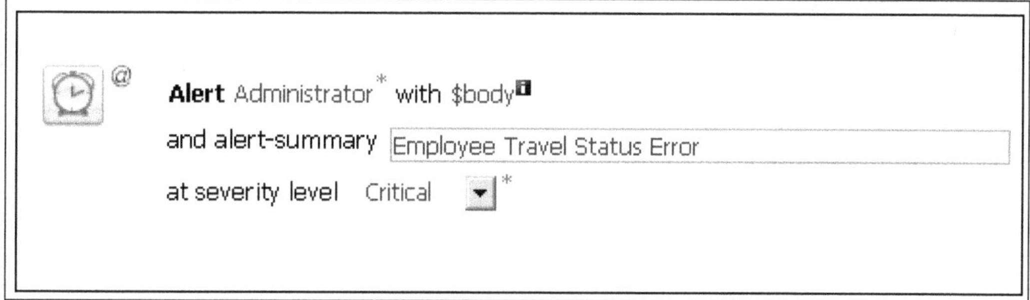

Then we activate the current session in **Change Center**.

Testing a proxy service

After activating the session, we can test the proxy service by selecting it and clicking on the *bug* icon in the **Resources** list. The **Test Console** window opens. We enter the XML payload and click **Execute**. We can see the service response and the invocation trace.

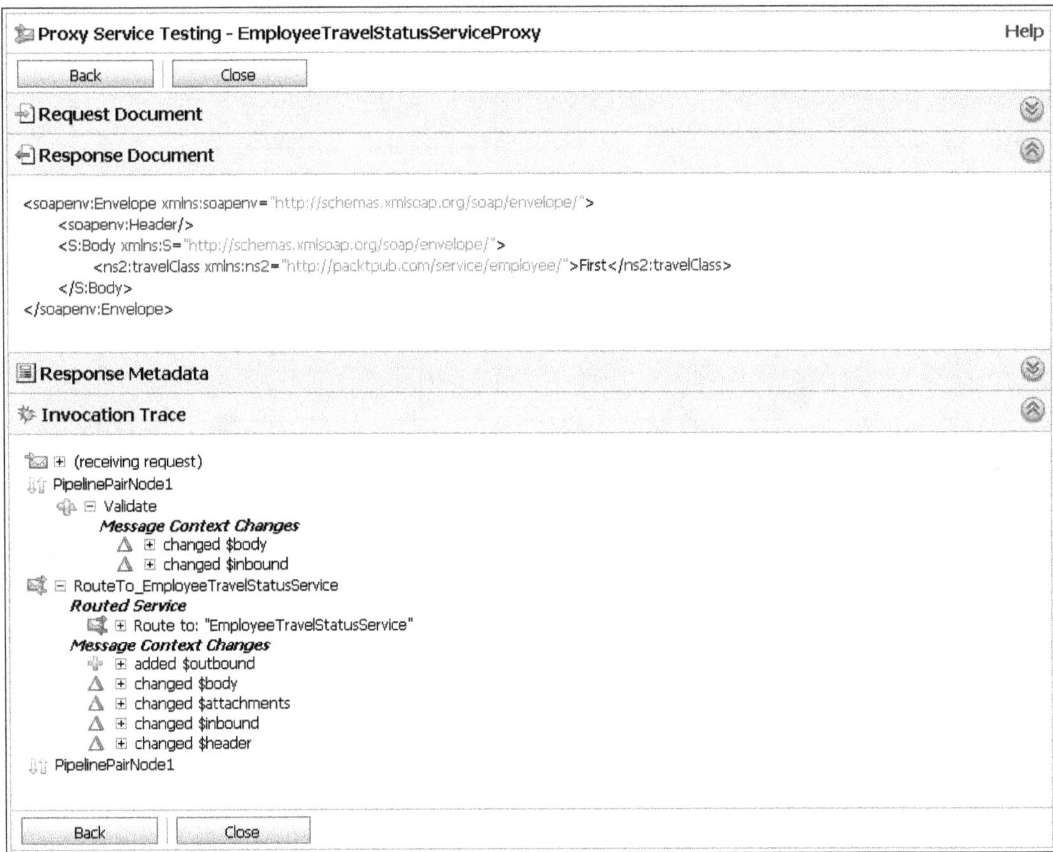

Now, we shut down the `EmployeeTravelStatus` service using the Oracle Enterprise Manager Console to test the service result caching and the error hander.

Then, we initiate the proxy service using the same input payload as before. We can see that the proxy service returns the same response although the `EmployeeTravelStatus` service is not running. This means that the service result caching works. Next, we initiate the proxy service using a different input payload. This time the invocation fails, as the response for this input is not cached.

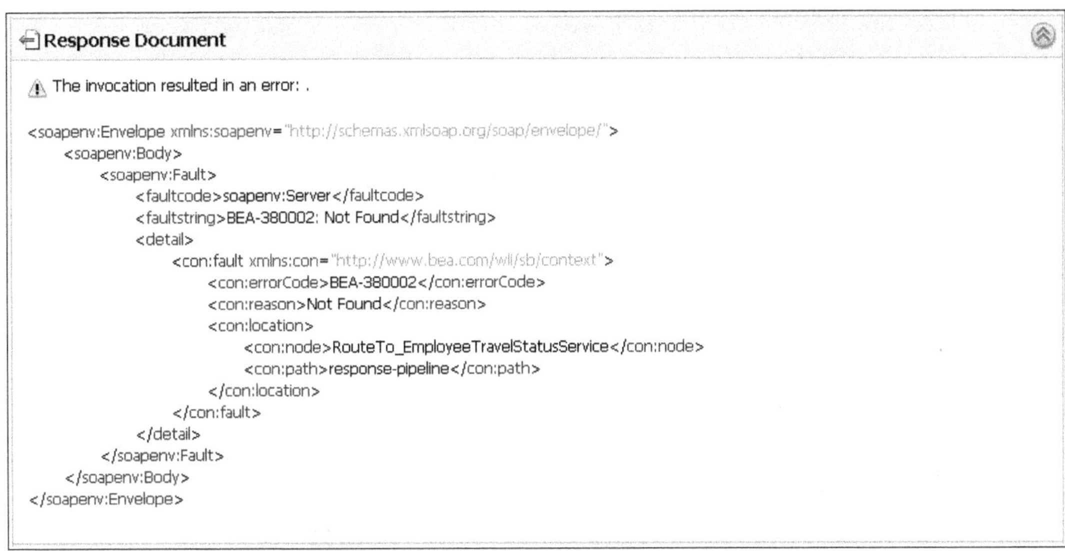
Response Document
The invocation resulted in an error: .
<soapenv:Envelope xmlns:soapenv="http://schemas.xmlsoap.org/soap/envelope/">
<soapenv:Body>
<soapenv:Fault>
<faultcode>soapenv:Server</faultcode>
<faultstring>BEA-380002: Not Found</faultstring>
<detail>
<con:fault xmlns:con="http://www.bea.com/wli/sb/context">
<con:errorCode>BEA-380002</con:errorCode>
<con:reason>Not Found</con:reason>
<con:location>
<con:node>RouteTo_EmployeeTravelStatusService</con:node>
<con:path>response-pipeline</con:path>
</con:location>
</con:fault>
</detail>
</soapenv:Fault>
</soapenv:Body>
</soapenv:Envelope>

If we click on the **Operations** link on the left-hand side and then select the **Pipeline Alerts** tab, we can see the pipeline alerts history and the details of alerts. As the proxy service execution failed, the error handler triggered an alert, as can be seen in the following screenshot:

SLA Alerts
Pipeline Alerts
Service Health
Server Health
Pipeline Alerts (30 mins)
Services With Most Alerts
TravelApproval/ProxyServices/EmployeeTravelStatusServiceProxy
100% Critical
Alert History (30 mins)
Extended Alert History
Items 1-1 of 1
Timestamp
Alert Summary
Alert Severity
Service
Service Type
Action
29.6.10 15:53
Employee Travel Status Error
Critical
TravelApproval/ProxyServices/EmployeeTra...
Proxy Service
Items 1-1 of 1

If we click on the **Service Health** tab, we can monitor metrics, such as average response time, number of messages, and number of errors for the current aggregation interval.

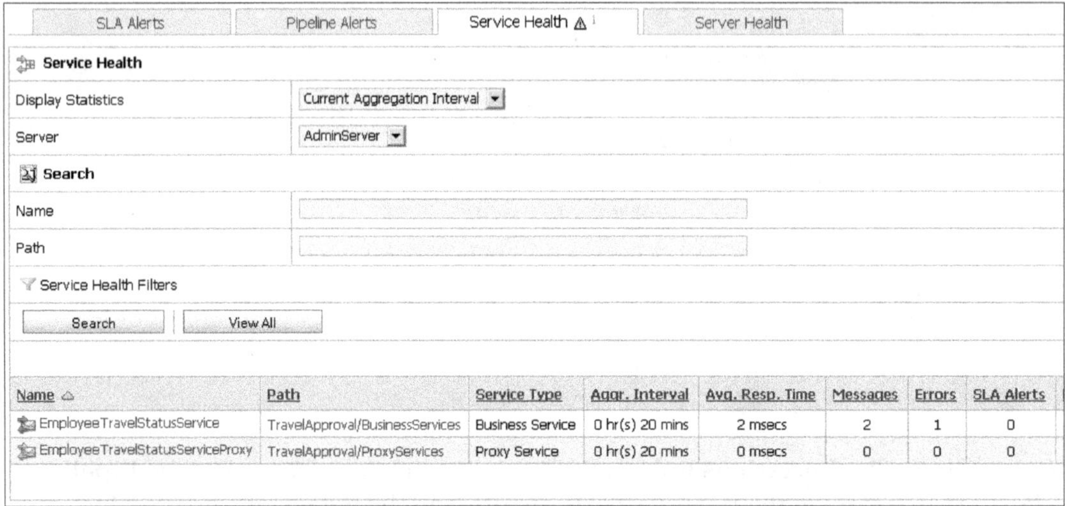

If we check an e-mail specified when configuring the Alert destination, we can make sure that an e-mail with the alert has been automatically sent. As we can see in the next screenshot, the alert contains data about the service, error severity, alert timestamp, and so on.

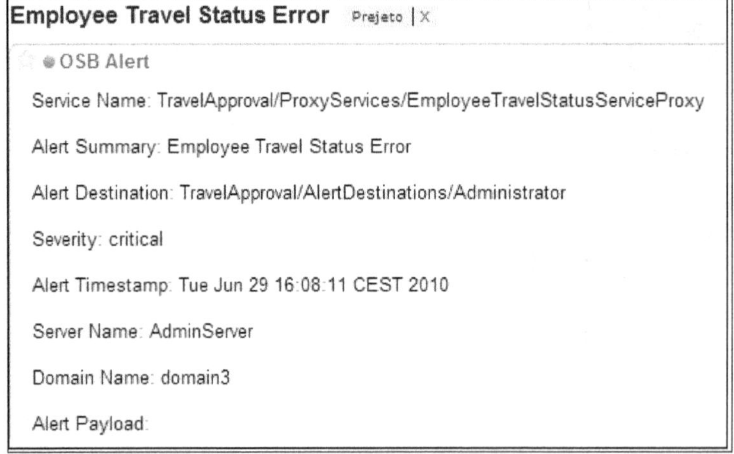

Employee Travel Status Error
Prejeto | X
OSB Alert
Service Name: TravelApproval/ProxyServices/EmployeeTravelStatusServiceProxy
Alert Summary: Employee Travel Status Error
Alert Destination: TravelApproval/AlertDestinations/Administrator
Severity: critical
Alert Timestamp: Tue Jun 29 16:08:11 CEST 2010
Server Name: AdminServer
Domain Name: domain3
Alert Payload:

Now we can start up the `EmployeeTravelStatus` service again.

Publishing a proxy service to the Oracle Service Registry

In a similar way as we imported the `EmployeeTravelStatus` service from the Oracle Service Registry, we can also publish our `EmployeeTravelStatusServiceProxy` proxy service in the opposite direction. This service will then be used from service consumers.

We click on the **System Administration** link in the main menu and then select **Publish to UDDI**. The **Publish to UDDI** screen appears, where we select the service we want to publish (`EmployeeTravelStatusServiceProxy`) and the Business entity (`Packt Publishing`).

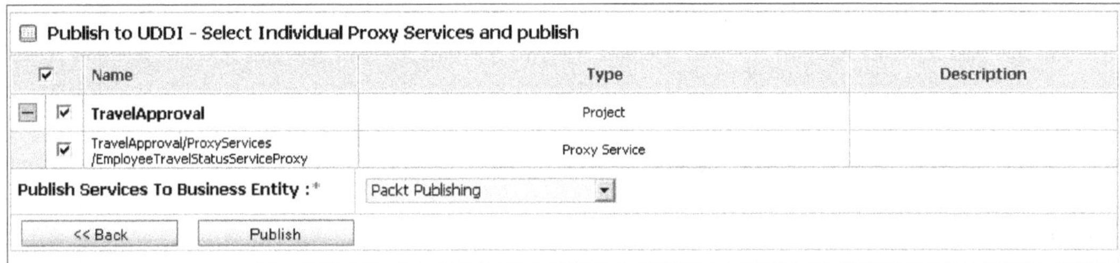

We publish the service by clicking on the **Publish** button.

Re-wiring an SOA composite application

Now we will re-wire the TravelApproval composite application to remove the direct connection to the service and replace it with the connection to the proxy service. We open our `TravelApproval` SOA composite application in JDeveloper again, and double-click the composite.xml to open the SOA Composite Editor. We will modify the `EmployeeTravelStatus` reference binding component, as we want to remove the direct connection to the service. Instead, we will use the proxy service we just created. We will find the Proxy service by browsing the Oracle Service Registry, therefore, we have to create a connection to the OSR on the **Resource Palette** first. To ensure even greater flexibility, we will enable dynamic endpoint lookup, so that the actual address of the proxy service will be retrieved from the OSR at runtime.

We double-click the `EmployeeTravelStatus` reference binding component. Then we click on the **Find existing WSDLs** icon next to the **WSDL URL** input field. The **SOA Resource Browser** dialog opens. We select **Resource Palette** as a source. Then we expand our UDDI connection and navigate to the `EmployeeTravelStatusServiceProxy` service, as shown in the following screenshot:

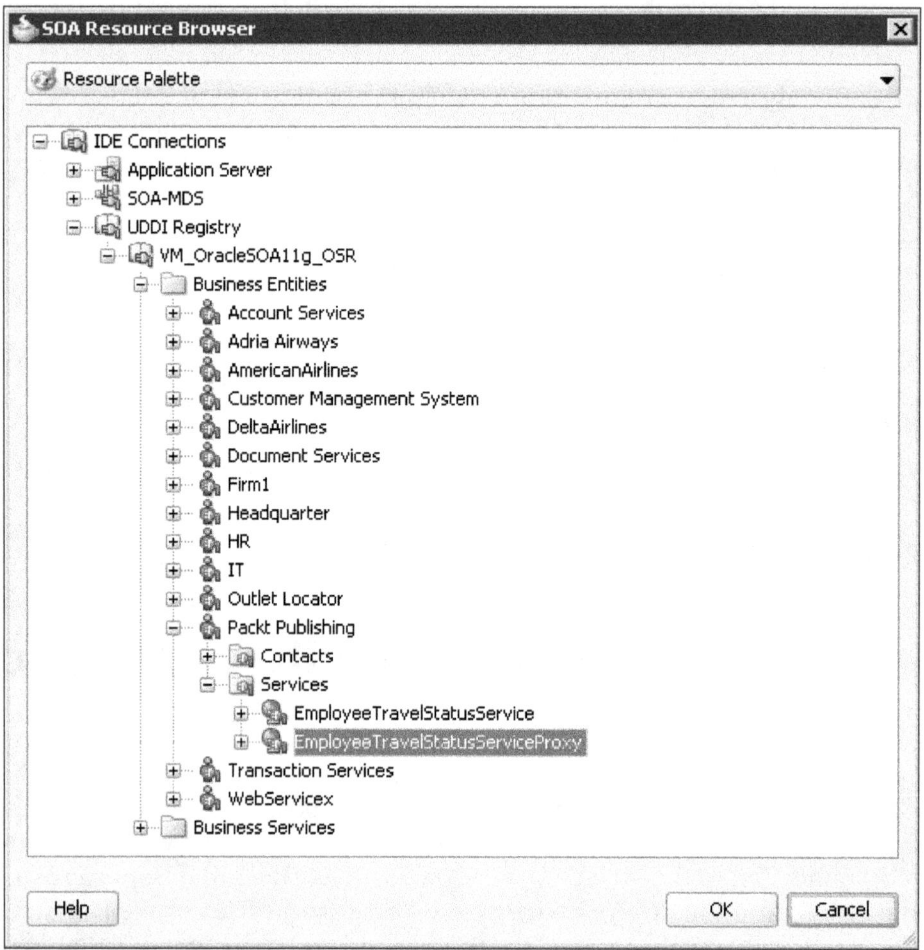

We click **OK**. The **UDDI Deployment Options** dialog opens.

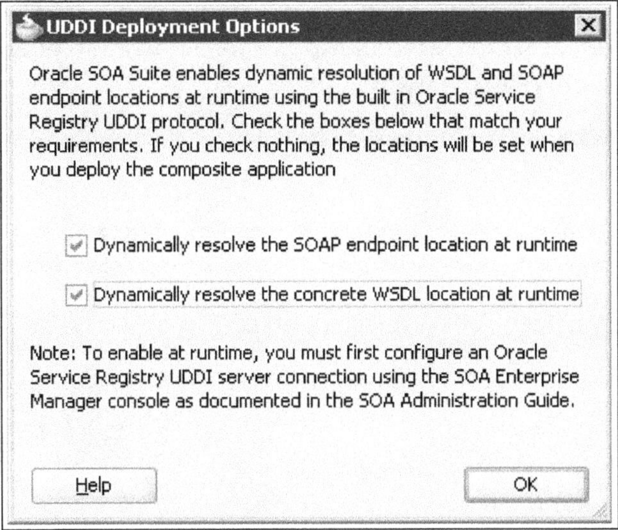

We select both checkboxes and click **OK**. Then we click **OK** again to close the **Update Reference** dialog and return to the SOA composite editor. We save the project by clicking **Save All**.

Notice that we were able to simply replace the `EmployeeTravelStatus` service with the proxy service, as the proxy service uses the same interface. If that was not the case, we would have to modify our `TravelApproval` BPEL process.

Now, we can re-deploy and test our composite application.

Oracle Service Bus use case

By decoupling the service provider from service consumers, we have achieved high flexibility. Now, let's have a look at what happens if we deploy a new version of `EmployeeTravelStatus` service which has a slightly different interface and different endpoint address. If we did not use mediation, we would have to modify and re-deploy all service consumers. In our case, there is no need to do that. Instead, we can simply modify the Proxy message flow and service consumers do not need to be aware of the change.

Now, we will demonstrate this scenario. Let's say that the new version of service uses the same namespace, but different input. The old version of service accepts the employee of the following type:

```
<xsd:complexType name="EmployeeType">
   <xsd:sequence>
      <xsd:element name="FirstName" type="xsd:string" minOccurs="0"/>
      <xsd:element name="LastName" type="xsd:string" minOccurs="0"/>
     <xsd:element name="Department" type="xsd:string" minOccurs="0"/>
   </xsd:sequence>
</xsd:complexType>
```

The new service version uses an extended version of the `EmployeeType` complex type.

```
<xsd:complexType name="EmployeeType">
   <xsd:sequence>
      <xsd:element name="Name" type="xsd:string" minOccurs="0"/>
      <xsd:element name="Surname" type="xsd:string" minOccurs="0"/>
      <xsd:element name="Department" type="xsd:string"minOccurs="0"/>
      <xsd:element name="Position" type="xsd:string" minOccurs="0"/>
      <xsd:element name="Age" type="xsd:int" minOccurs="0"/>
   </xsd:sequence>
</xsd:complexType>
```

The output of the service remains the same.

After deploying the new version, we publish it to the Oracle Service Registry. We also have to create an XSLT transformation, which will be used to transform the request message to the new type.

Modifying the Proxy message flow

We log into the Oracle Service Bus Console again and start a new session. Then we import the new version of the `EmployeeTravelStatus` service (`EmployeeTravelStatus-v2`) from the Oracle Service Registry, as we did before. We also have to import the XSLT transformation and save it to the `XSLT` folder.

Next, we have to edit the proxy service message flow. First, we will modify the route node, so that it will use the new version of the service. We click on the route node and select **Edit Route**. Then we click on the `EmployeeTravelStatusService` link. We select the new version of the service.

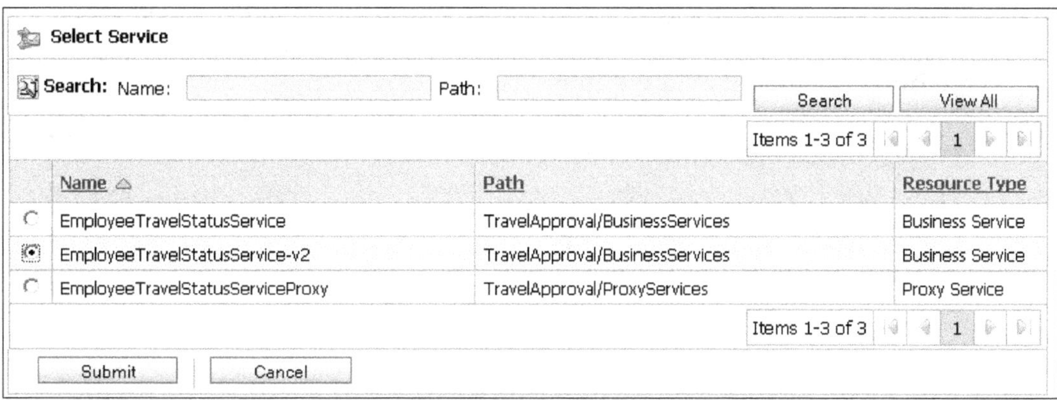

We click **Submit** and then **Save**. Then we click on the `Request Pipeline` and select **Add Stage**. We rename the stage to `TransformEmployee`. Then we edit the stage. We add a replace action.

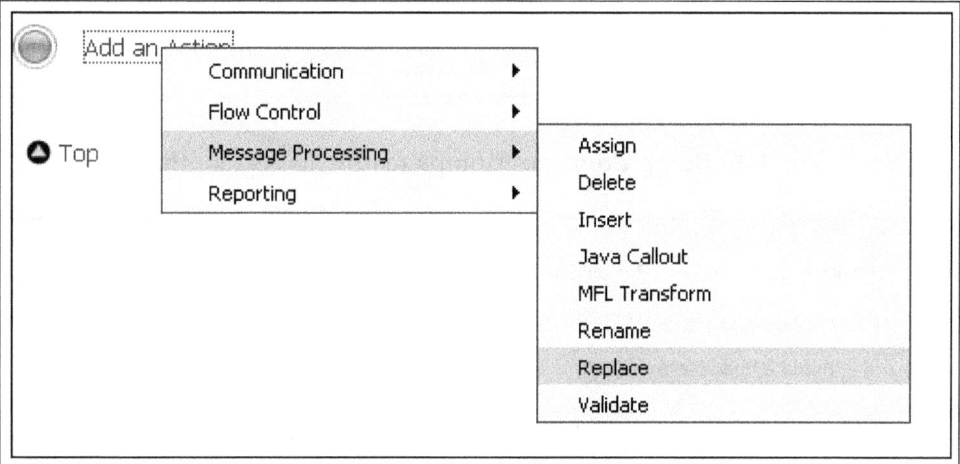

We specify that we want to replace `./emp:employee` in the variable `body`.

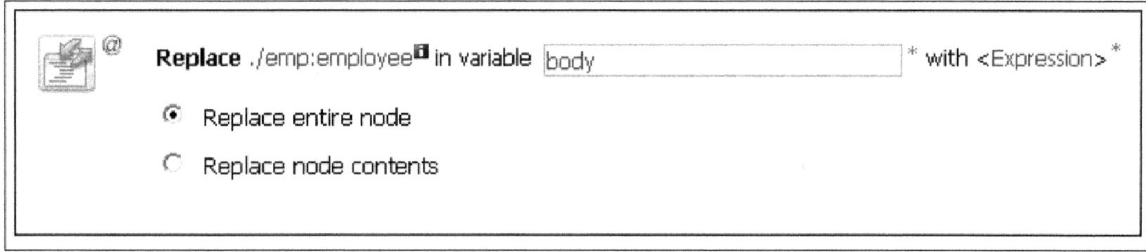

Now we have to select the XSLT transformation. We click on the **Expression** link. Then we click on **XSLT Resources** and select the XSLT transformation we want to use. In the **Input document** field we enter `$body/emp:employee`.

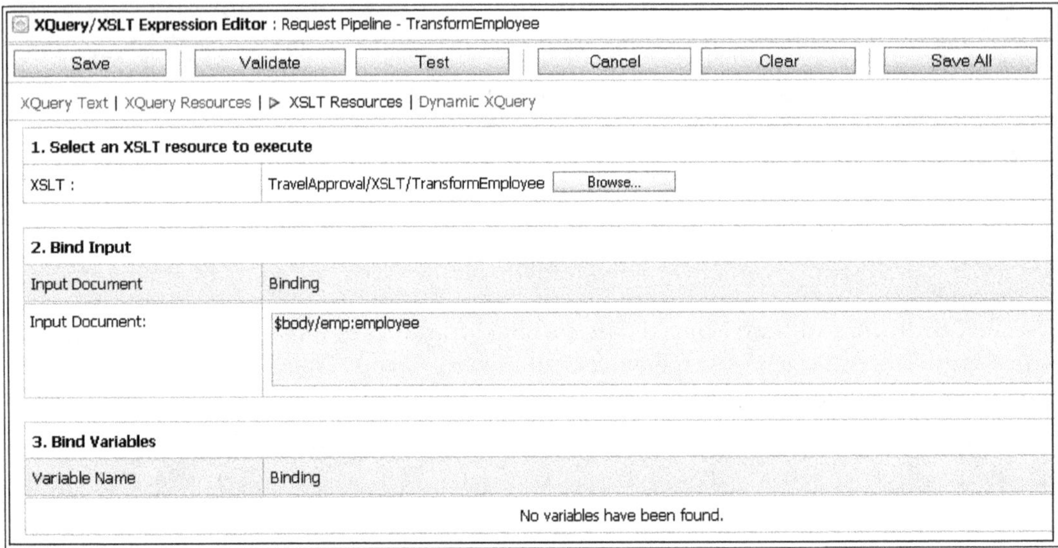

We click **Save**. The **Edit Stage Configuration** page now looks like this:

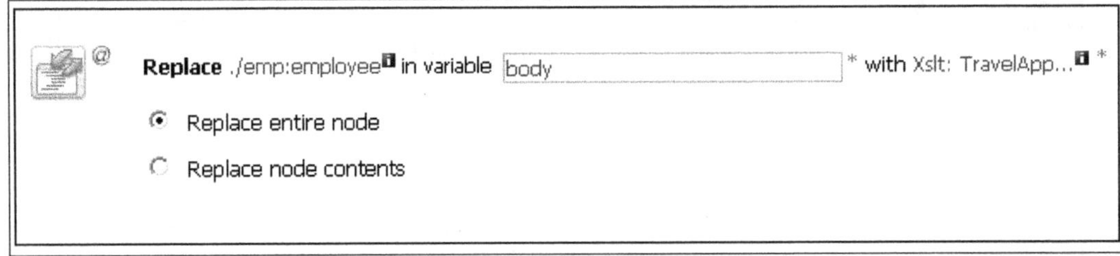

We click **Save**. Finally, we modify the `Validate` stage and specify that the input has to be validated against the new version of the XML Schema. We click **Save** to return to the message flow editor.

The following screenshot shows the modified Proxy message flow:

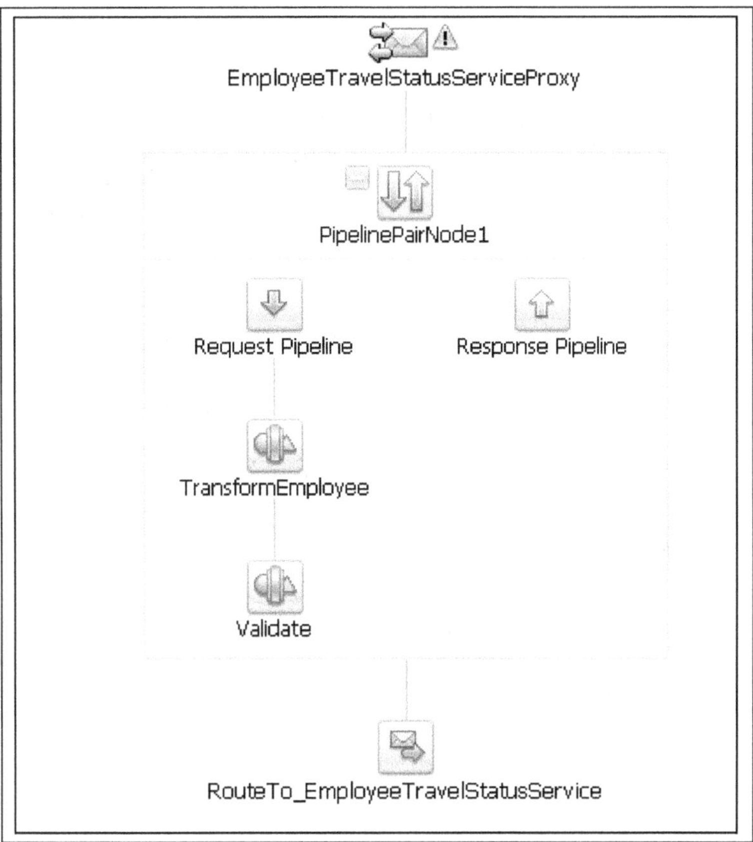

We click `Save` and then activate the session by clicking the **Activate** button in the **Change Center**.

Testing an SOA composite application

We open the Oracle Enterprise Manager Console. First, we shut down the old version of the `EmployeeTravelStatus` service. Then, we initiate a new instance of the `TravelApproval` composite application to test if the deployed composite application still works and uses the new version of the service. If we open the instance flow trace, we can make sure that the new version of the `EmployeeTravelStatus` service has been successfully invoked.

As we can see, when using Oracle Service Bus as an intermediate layer between service providers and consumers, there is no need to modify and redeploy our existing applications when changes occur. This gives us the much-needed flexibility, so that we are able to quickly adopt to business changes.

Summary

In this chapter, we have learned the use of Oracle Service Registry and Oracle Service Bus. Both products play an important role towards achieving a flexible SOA architecture. We have explained the architecture of Oracle Service Bus, including proxy services, business services, and message flow modeling. We have explained how to publish business entities and services to Oracle Service Registry.

We have shown how to use the service bus console, how to create a project, and import resources from the service registry. We have demonstrated how to configure business services, such as caching and monitoring. We have discussed alert destinations and shown how to create a proxy service, configure it, and publish it to the service registry. We have also shown how to re-wire the SOA composite to include the OSB proxy services. As these services are most usable when changes occur, we have demonstrated such a situation and concluded that the combined use of OSB and OSR can considerably improve the flexibility of SOA composite applications and their architecture.

In the next chapter, we will show how to implement the BPMN to BPEL round-tripping using Oracle BPA Suite and SOA Suite.

10

BPMN to BPEL Round-tripping with BPA Suite and SOA Suite

The first phase of the business process lifecycle is Business Process Modeling. During process modeling, business analysts, together with business owners, analyze the business process and define the activity flow. Usually BPMN (Business Process Modeling Notation) is used for modeling (for BPMN specifications please refer to `http://www.bpmn.org/`). One of the most important advantages of using BPMN is that BPMN models can be automatically converted to BPEL, and vice versa. In that case, we do not have to build BPEL processes from scratch. We can also propagate changes from BPEL back to BPMN. We call this round-tripping. Round-tripping is very important, as it eliminates the semantic gap between IT and process models, and allows us to keep the model (BPMN) and executable code (BPEL) in sync.

In this chapter, we will get familiar with Oracle BPA (Business Process Analysis) Suite.

> We use Oracle BPA Suite version 11.1.1.2, as version 11.1.1.3 is not yet available at the time of writing this book. As Oracle BPA Suite 11.1.1.2 currently supports BPMN 1.0, this version of the notation is used for describing BPMN-BPEL round-tripping throughout this chapter.

First, we will look at the Oracle BPA Suite architecture and features. Then, we will show how to model BPMN business processes using Oracle Business Process Architect. We will demonstrate the modeling on our v, which we have already used in previous chapters. Next, we will convert the BPMN model into a BPEL Blueprint. We will also discuss how various constructs map between BPMN and BPEL. Finally, we will open the BPEL Blueprint in JDeveloper and demonstrate the round-tripping between BPMN and BPEL.

Oracle SOA Suite 11*g* PS2 introduces the BPMN 2.0 service engine, which supports direct execution of BPMN 2.0 processes, meaning that there is no need to use the Oracle BPA Suite or to transform BPMN models to BPEL. We can model and implement BPMN processes using JDeveloper and then deploy them to the SOA platform using Oracle BPM suite 11*g*, which we will discuss in the next chapter.

In this chapter, we will discuss the following:

- Oracle BPA Suite architecture and features
- Mapping of constructs between BPMN and BPEL
- Modeling business processes using Oracle Business Process Architect
- Converting BPMN models to BPEL Blueprint
- Opening and implementing the process in JDeveloper
- Round-tripping between BPMN and BPEL

Oracle BPA Suite architecture and features

Oracle BPA Suite is a sophisticated tool for modeling and analysis of business processes. It is based on the market-leading IDS Scheer ARIS design platform. Using Oracle BPA Suite we are able to model, simulate, and optimize business processes. It enables us not only to model business processes, but also to define organizational models, IT architecture models, data models, and so on. The tool supports various business process modeling notations, such as BPMN, EPC (Event-driven Process Chain), eEPC (Extended Event-driven Process Chain), UML activity diagrams, and other less known notations. Oracle BPA Suite can also be integrated with Oracle SOA Suite as it supports round-tripping between business process models (BPMN) and the execution form (BPEL).

Oracle BPA Suite consists of four components:

- **Business Process Architect**: This is the most important component. It provides a user-friendly and intuitive interface for modeling, using standard techniques and methodologies. However, we are not limited to modeling only business processes. The tool also supports organizational modeling, data modeling, IT system landscapes, impact analysis, and report generation. We can also optimize business processes by performing simulations. Using Business Process Architect we can also translate EPC and BPMN business process models to BPEL Blueprint.

- **Business Process Publisher**: This component allows publishing business process models to the portal. Users can then view these models based on their role. This promotes collaboration and information sharing among various users in an enterprise.
- **Business Process Repository**: Enables storing of model metadata.
- **Business Process Repository Server**: Enables collaborative development with a shared repository. The server supports concurrent usage, check-in and check-out, role-based access, and so on.

Round-tripping between BPMN and BPEL

As business processes change over time, IT has to be able to react to these changes in a quick and efficient manner. This places a high responsibility on IT. However, in most cases IT is not flexible enough to follow these changes. The major problem with traditional approaches to software development is the huge semantic gap between IT and the process models. If we are able to automatically convert business requirements (business process model) to the executable form and perform a synchronization when changes occur, we can significantly improve flexibility.

BPMN-BPEL round-tripping follows the **MDA** (**Model-driven Architecture**) design approach, where business requirements first need to be modeled using a platform-independent modeling notation (BPMN) and then translated into executable form (BPEL). Also, changes to the BPEL can be propagated back to BPMN so that the model and the BPEL code are kept in synch. With BPMN-BPEL round-tripping, both business analysts and IT derive from one model, which allows us to align IT with business processes.

However, it often turns out that due to some important differences between BPMN and BPEL, the translation is not as straightforward as it may seem. BPEL is a typical block-structured language and does not support arbitrary cycles (the **While** activity can only capture structured cycles). There are also some other workflow patterns that cannot be translated to BPEL (for more information please refer to `http://www.workflowpatterns.com/`). In contrast, BPMN allows us to define process models in the form of graphs. We can look at BPMN as a super-set of BPEL. Therefore, not all BPMN processes can be directly translated to BPEL. In that case, we have to refactor the BPMN process model before the translation. This, however, can change the process model considerably, at least from the visual perspective (the process behavior is unchanged if the appropriate refactoring is performed). As a result, business people might have trouble understanding the converted model. The lack of support for arbitrary cycles usually arises if the process has many interleaved human tasks.

As already mentioned, Oracle supports BPMN-BPEL round-tripping through the use of Oracle BPA Suite and Oracle SOA Suite. It is worth mentioning that not only BPMN process models can be translated to BPEL. We can also translate between **EPC (Event-driven Process Chain)** and BPEL; however, BPMN is semantically much closer to BPEL and is therefore the preferred modeling notation.

Steps for BPMN-BPEL round-tripping

If we want to perform BPMN-BPEL round-tripping, we have to carry out the following steps:

1. **Model business process in Business Process Architect**: First, we model business process using BPMN notation. This is usually done by business analysts and business owners. They have to define the activity flow, information flow, roles, business rules, and business documents. During modeling, we can use all standard BPMN activities; however, Business Process Architect also introduces some extension activities—**Automated activity**, **Human Workflow activity**, **Notification activity**, and **Business Rule activity**. These activities are converted to corresponding BPEL activities upon BPEL transformation. If the process modeler has enough technical skills, it can also import XML schemas and concrete WSDL files of existing services, along with associating them with the automated activities. In that case, we get a more technical model, and corresponding BPEL Partner Links and Invoke activities are automatically generated upon transformation.
2. **Simulate business process**: This is an optional step. By performing process simulations, we can verify the process and identify possible bottlenecks, assess the average costs of a process instance, and so on. The result of running a simulation and optimizing the process is therefore called a to-be process model.
3. **Translate BPMN model into BPEL Blueprint**: When we finish with process modeling, we are ready to translate the BPMN model into BPEL Blueprint. BPEL Blueprint is actually an abstract-level BPEL process that is used to share common metadata between business users and IT. Before performing the translation, we can also validate the model. Then we enter the model description and select the BPEL process type (synchronous or asynchronous). After the translation, the BPEL Blueprint is saved to the BPA Repository and can be accessed by IT developers.
4. **Import BPEL Blueprint in JDeveloper**: First, the developer has to create a connection to the BPA server. Then, he creates a new SOA composite application and project, and selects the model the developer wants to import. Using the **BPA** view, the developer can also read the comments to business process and process activities to better understand the process.

5. **Implement BPEL process**: The developer has to add implementation details to BPEL Blueprint to make it concrete. He has to set the process input and output data, create variables, Partner Links (if the process modeler did not define concrete services), Assign activities, and so on. During the implementation, he can add new activities, however, he cannot delete activities defined by the business user. Using the SOA Composite Editor, he can always check if a new version of process model is available. If so, he can merge both models without losing his previous work. He can also update the BPMN model after adding new activities. In that case, the business process modeler is notified of the change and he has to confirm or decline the changes.
6. **Continuously synchronize BPMN model and BPEL code**: As business processes change over time, business analysts have to continuously update the process model. Also, developers have to synchronize BPEL code when changes occur and add appropriate implementation details, as we want to avoid the IT gap. Round-tripping is very important for real-world development, as it is the key to iterative SOA development which guarantees short development cycles and easy modifications to existing composite applications.

Mapping of BPMN constructs to BPEL

Before performing the BPMN-BPEL round-tripping, we have to understand how different BPMN 1.0 constructs (and Oracle extensions) translate to BPEL. The most important mapping rules for the translation of BPMN constructs to BPEL are as follow:

- Automated activities are translated to BPEL **Scopes**. If an automated activity is linked to a concrete business service, a corresponding **Invoke** and **Partner Link** are also created within the **Scope**, and the **Invoke** activity is linked to that **Partner Link**. If the automated activity has set input and output data, BPEL variables are also created. The activity metrics definition is converted into sensor variables within the scope.
- Human tasks translate to **Human Task** process activities. A **Partner Link** for `TaskService` and corresponding **Invoke**, **Receive**, and **Assign** activities are generated. **Human Task** properties are translated to business annotations.
- Notification activities translate to corresponding BPEL activities, based on the channel type (for example, notification activity of type e-mail translates to an **Email** extension activity). A **Partner Link** the for corresponding notification service is also created.

- Business rules are converted to **Business Rule** process activities with business annotation.
- Events translate to different BPEL activities, based on their type. Start events translate to **Receive** activity. A Timer intermediate event translates to a BPEL activity **Wait**. An Error intermediate event translates to a corresponding **Catch** element. An End event translates to either **Reply** (synchronous process) or **Invoke** (asynchronous process). An Error end event translates to **Throw**; a terminate end event translates to a **Terminate** BPEL activity.
- Services translate to **Partner Links.** However, services can be abstract or concrete. Concrete services (services that are associated with a concrete WSDL) translate to a concrete **Partner Link**, while abstract services translate to an abstract **Partner Link**.
- Business data translates to BPEL variables. When associated with an XSD, the XSD is also exported and the variable is set to the XSD type. Otherwise, variables are set to String type.
- Sub-processes map to an **Invoke** activity.
- **Structured cycles** (the loop has only one entry point and one exit point) translate to a BPEL **While** activity. Arbitrary (non-structured) cycles cannot be translated directly and have to be refactored before the translation.
- Data-based XOR Gateway translates to a BPEL **Switch** activity, as shown in the following figure (attributes of BPEL activities are not shown to improve readability).

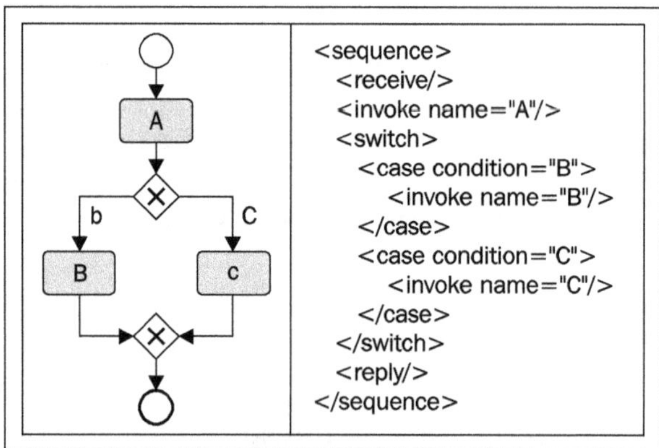

- An event-based XOR Gateway translates to a BPEL activity **Pick**, as shown in the following simple example.

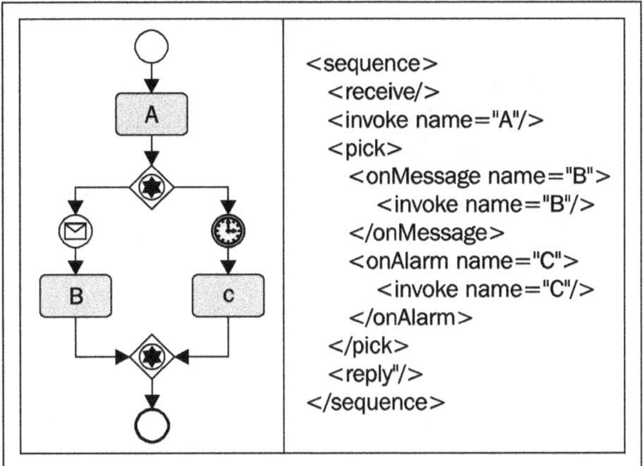

- An AND Gateway translates to an activity **Flow**.

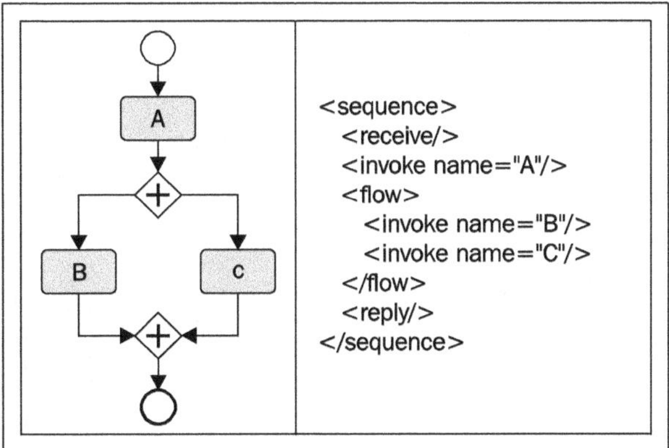

Mapping of BPEL constructs to BPMN

The mapping of BPEL code to BPMN 1.0 models follows the inverse rules as listed above. In general, mapping from BPEL to BPMN is straightforward, as we can look at BPEL as a sort of subset of BPMN. However, there are some BPEL constructs that do not map, such as **Event Handlers, Correlation Sets**, and some specific Oracle extension activities.

Demonstration scenario

We will now demonstrate how to model a business process using the Business Process Architect. We will use our TravelApproval business process example. First, we will show how to create a new project. Then we will get familiar with the **Designer** module and demonstrate how to add process activities and connect them into a process flow. We will also show how to validate the model and transform it into BPEL Blueprint. We will then open JDeveloper and import the generated BPEL Blueprint. In this chapter, we will not show how to implement BPEL, as this was already covered in previous chapters. However, we will demonstrate how the developer can synchronize his BPEL code with a new version of the process model. We will also show how the developer can propose changes to the model by adding new process steps and saving the changes to the BPA server. The business analyst has then to confirm or decline these changes.

Business process modeling in Business Process Architect

After opening Oracle Business Process Architect, the **Home** module opens, as shown in the next screenshot. On the left-hand side, we can see the **Modules** pane, showing all supported modules. We use the **Explorer** module for accessing the Business Repository (also known as BPA Repository), and creating new models and other related artifacts. The **Designer** module is used for business modeling. Using the **Administration** module, we are able to manage users, groups, privileges, and other system settings. We use the **Simulation** module for simulating business processes.

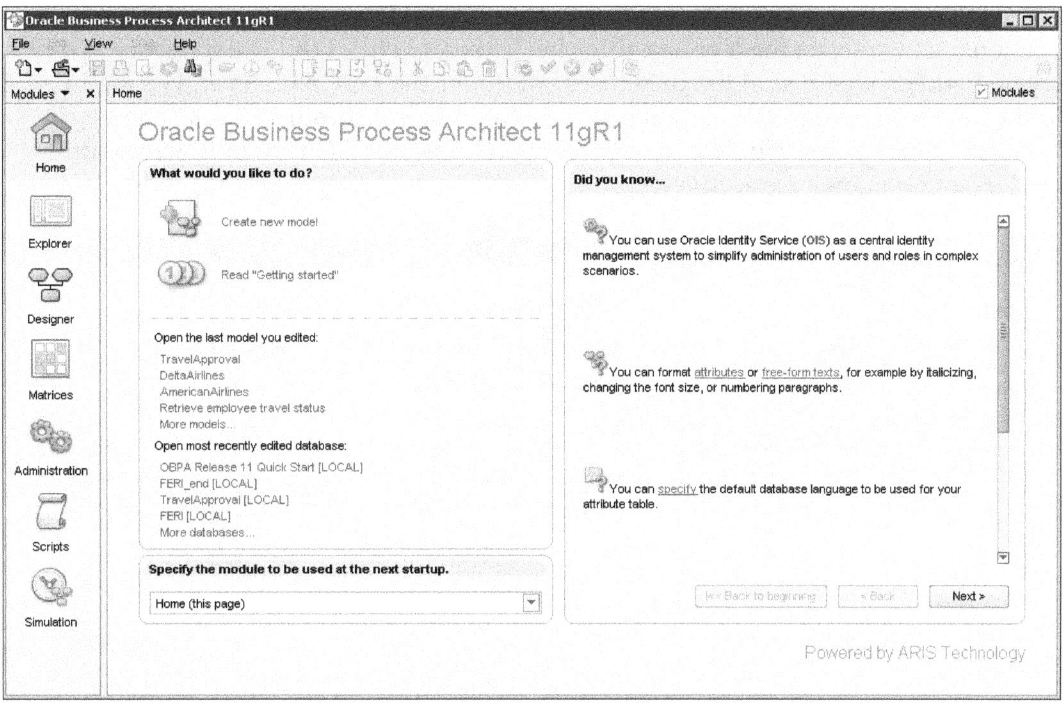

Creating the database

We open the **Explorer** module by clicking on the corresponding icon in the **Modules** pane. Remember that all process metadata is stored in the Business Repository (BPA Repository). BPA Repository is actually a database. In the case of local deployment, the Architect connects directly to the database. When using the Oracle BPA Repository Server, Architect connects to the server, which then connects to the database.

In our example, we will use local deployment. We expand the **LOCAL** server. Now the database is up and running. We can see all existing projects (called databases). We now create a new database by right-clicking the server and selecting **New | Database**. The **Create database** dialog opens.

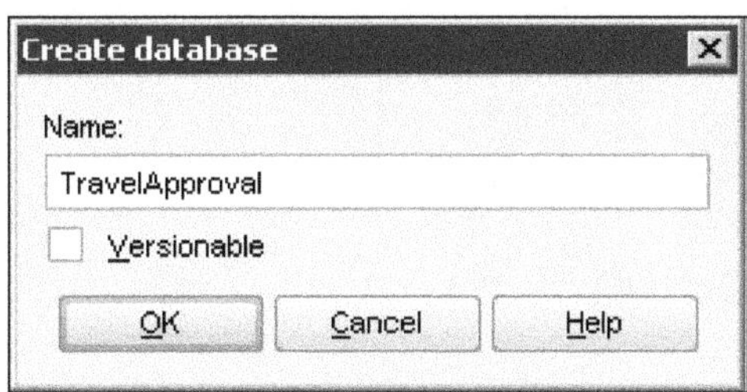

We set the name of the database to `TravelApproval`. If we want our database to be versionable, we select the **Versionable** checkbox and click **OK**. The database is now created and can be seen in the databases list under the **LOCAL** server. We log in to the database by right-clicking it and selecting **Log in** from the menu. The **Login Wizard** dialog opens. We enter a username and password (the default values are `system` and `manager` respectively).

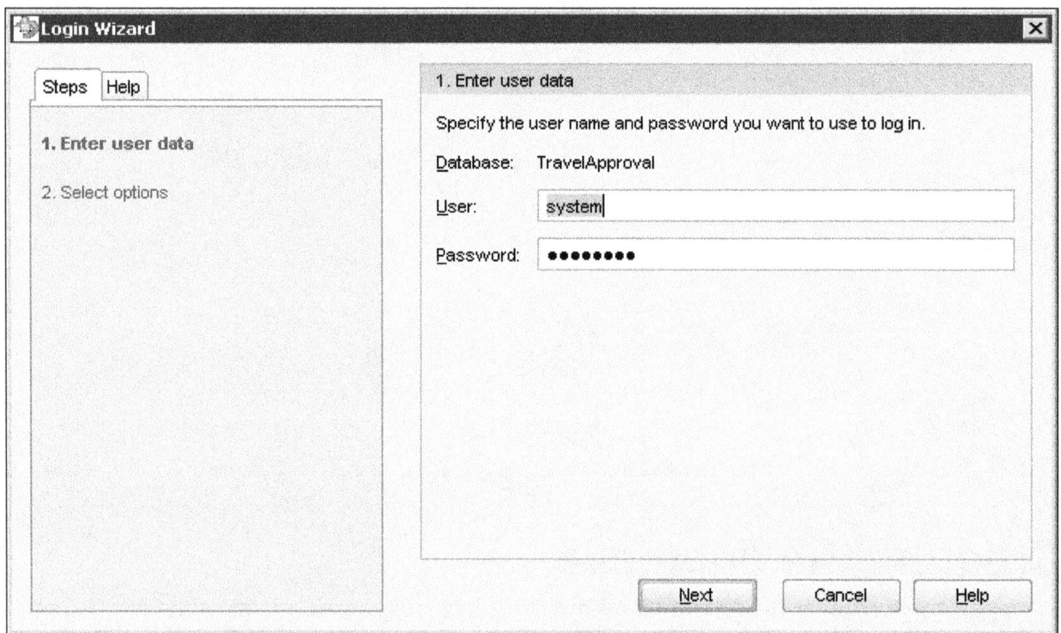

Then we click **Next**. On the next screen, we select the `Entire method` from the **Filter** list, as we want to see all the available information in our project.

By selecting the appropriate filter, we can filter the information we want to see. For example, if we select the `Business simulator` filter, we only see information related to performing business process simulations.

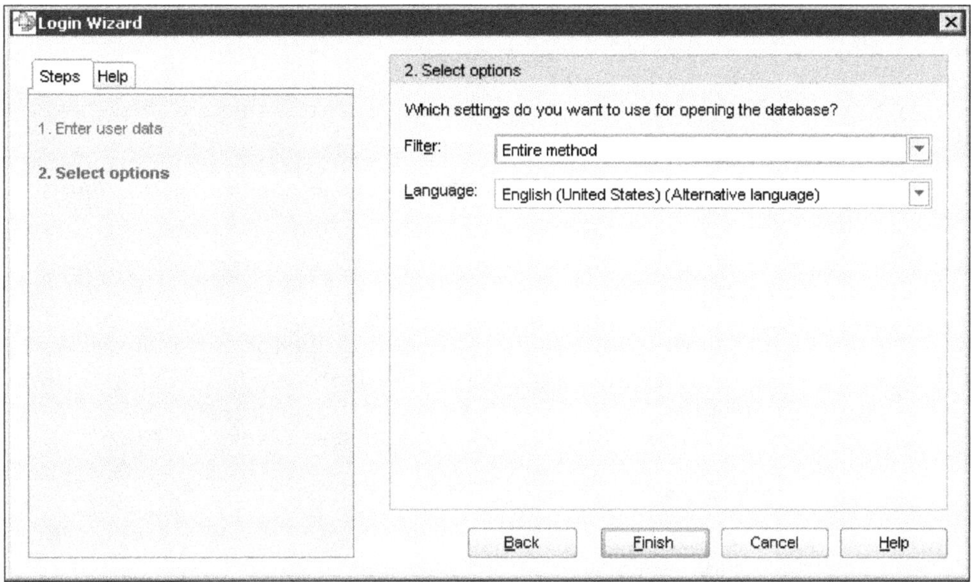

We click on **Finish**. Now, we are able to see the content of the database. In the next screenshot we can see that four folders (in Architect, folders are called **Groups**) were automatically created.

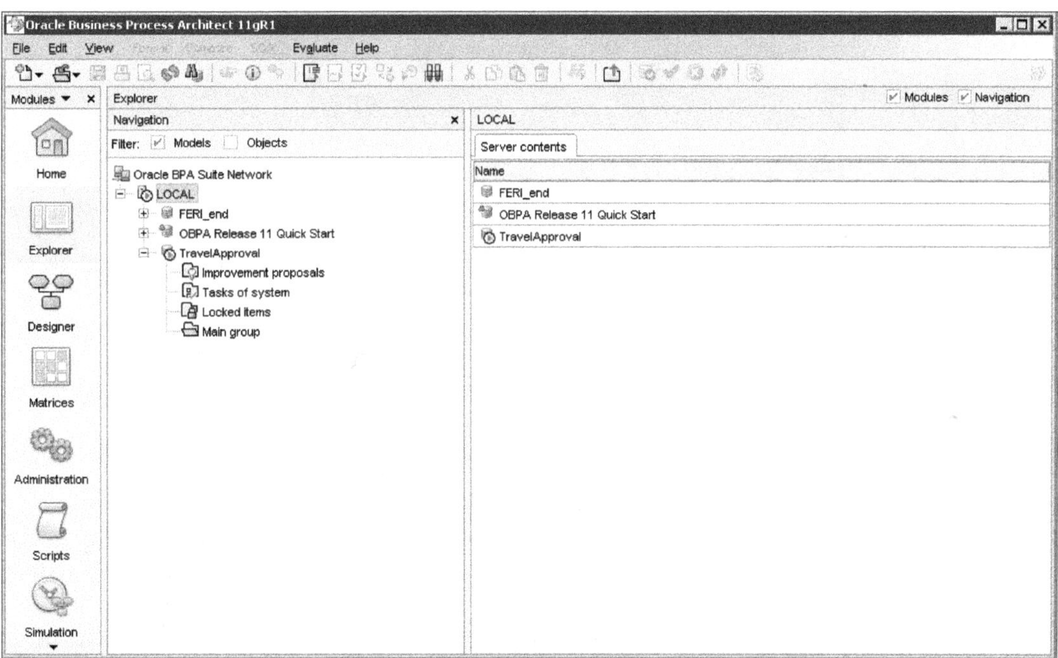

Next, we will create new groups, as we want to keep the content of the database organized. We will create the following groups:

- The **Business Processes** group will contain business process models and related artifacts.
- The **Services** group will contain business services, associated with automated activities.
- The **Participants** group will be used for storing roles that participate in the business process.
- The **SOA Profile** group will be used for storing the imported SOA Profiles, which are used when translating the business process to BPEL Blueprint.

To create a group, we right-click on **Main group** and select **New | Group**.

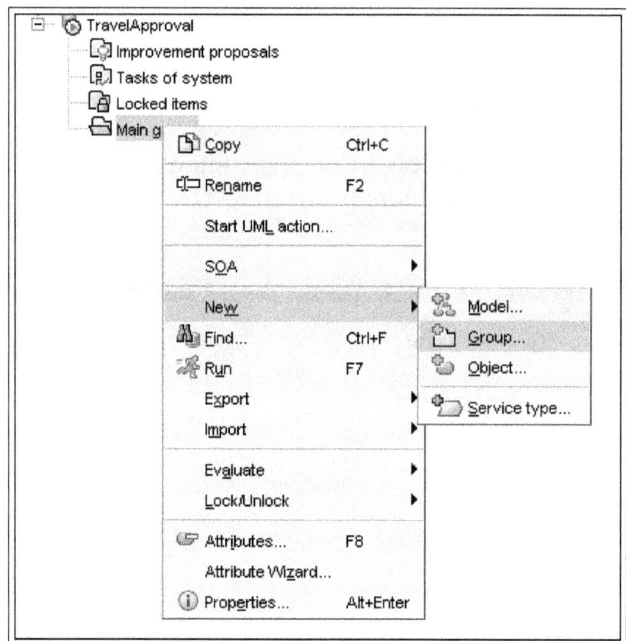

After the group is created, we can rename it. Next, we right-click the `SOA Profile` group and select **Import | SOA Profile**. In the dialog that appears we click **OK**. Notice, that five sub-groups (WSDL Profile, XML Profile, XSD Datatypes, XSD Profile, and XSD Structures) with stereotypes that are needed for performing the BPMN-BPEL round-tripping have been created. If we did not import the profile, it would be imported automatically during the translation of the model. However, we show how to do this by hand, as we want to import the SOA Profile into a separate group so that it is easier to manage.

The `TravelApproval` database opened in the **Explorer** module now looks as follows:

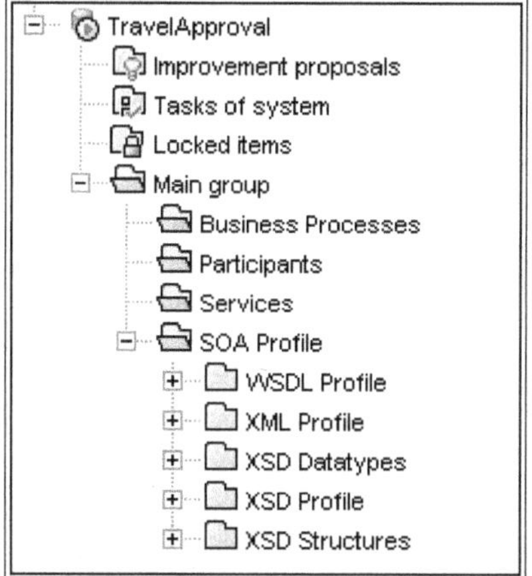

We save the database by clicking on the **Save** icon on the toolbar.

Modeling a business process

Now we will show how to create and model BPMN business processes using Oracle Business Process Architect.

Creating a new model

In the Explorer module, we right-click the `Business Processes` group and select **New** | **Model**.

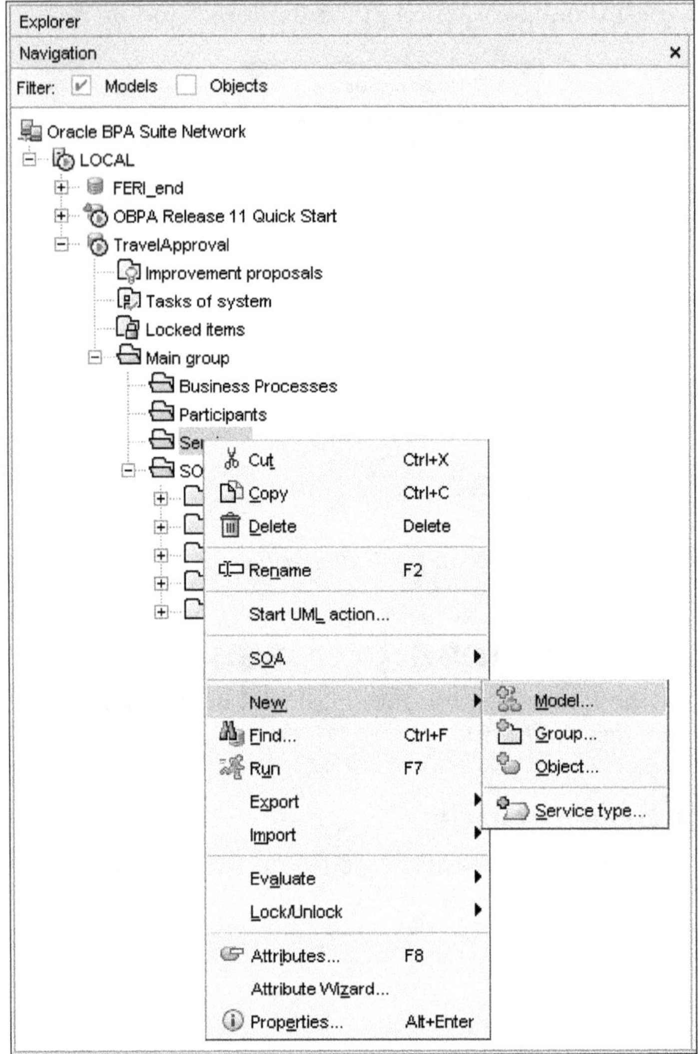

The **Create model** dialog opens. We select **Business process diagram (BPMN)** as the model type and name the model `TravelApproval`, as shown in the following screenshot.

Note that BPMN version 1.0 is supported in Oracle BPA Suite 11.1.1.2.

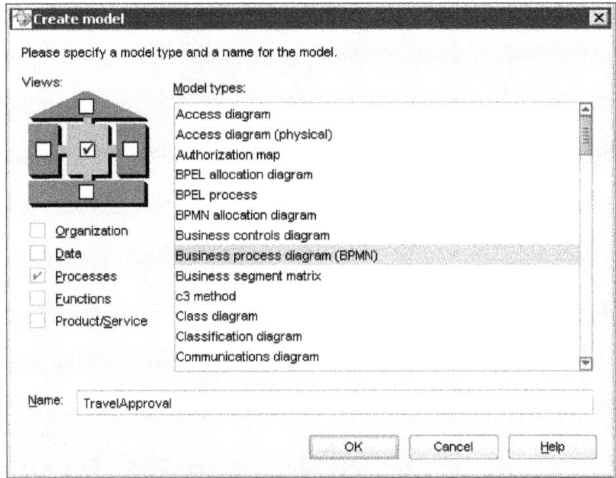

Then we click **OK**. We are automatically redirected to the **Designer** module.

Adding process activities and defining activity flow

In the **Designer** module, we can see an empty process diagram in the middle of the screen. On the right-hand side there is a **Symbols** palette displaying objects we can use during the modeling.

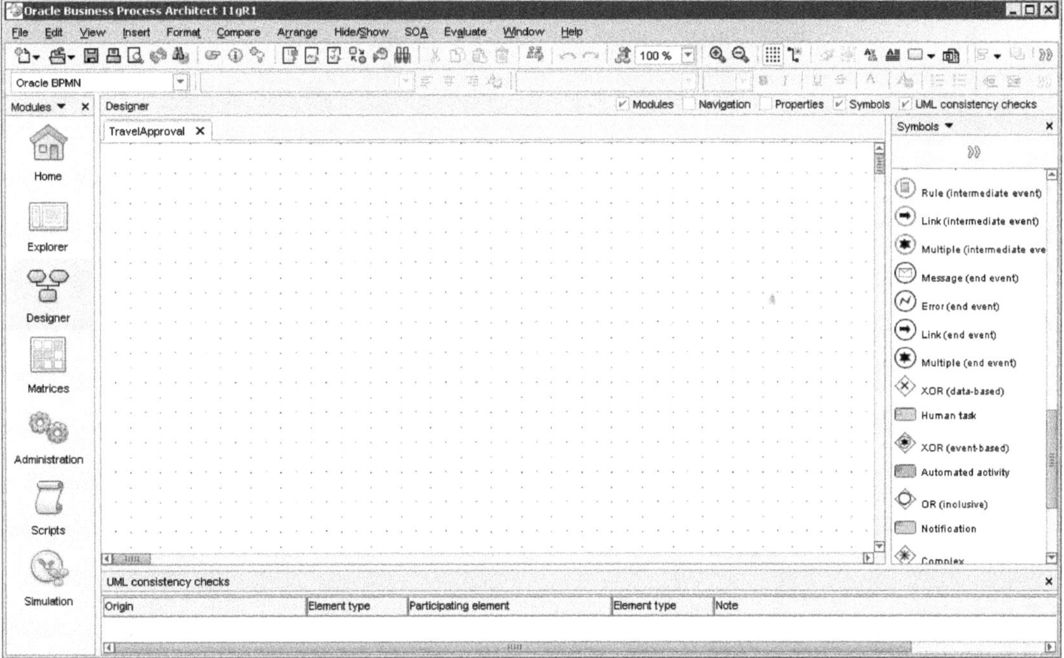

We can add objects from the **Symbols** palette to the canvas by clicking the object and then clicking the place on the canvas where we want to add it.

By default, not all objects are available in the **Symbols** palette. We can add additional objects by clicking the **Add symbols** icon on the top of the palette, or by pressing the *F12* key. By clicking on the **Symbols** drop-down, we can also switch between different views (**Small icons**, **Large icons**, and **Small icons with text**).

Now we will add the objects and define the activity flow. First, we add the **Lane** object to the business process diagram to create a swim-lane for the Approval Manager role. We set the name of the **Lane** to `Approval Manager`. We can resize the **Lane** by selecting it and dragging the corner. We can also change its name by clicking on the label next to the object and entering the text, or by editing the object properties.

Editing object properties

To edit object properties, we right-click the object and select **Properties**, or simply select the object and press *Alt+Enter*. In both cases, the **Object properties** dialog opens, as shown in the next screenshot. Here we can change various object properties. If we select **Attributes** on the left, we can change the name of the object.

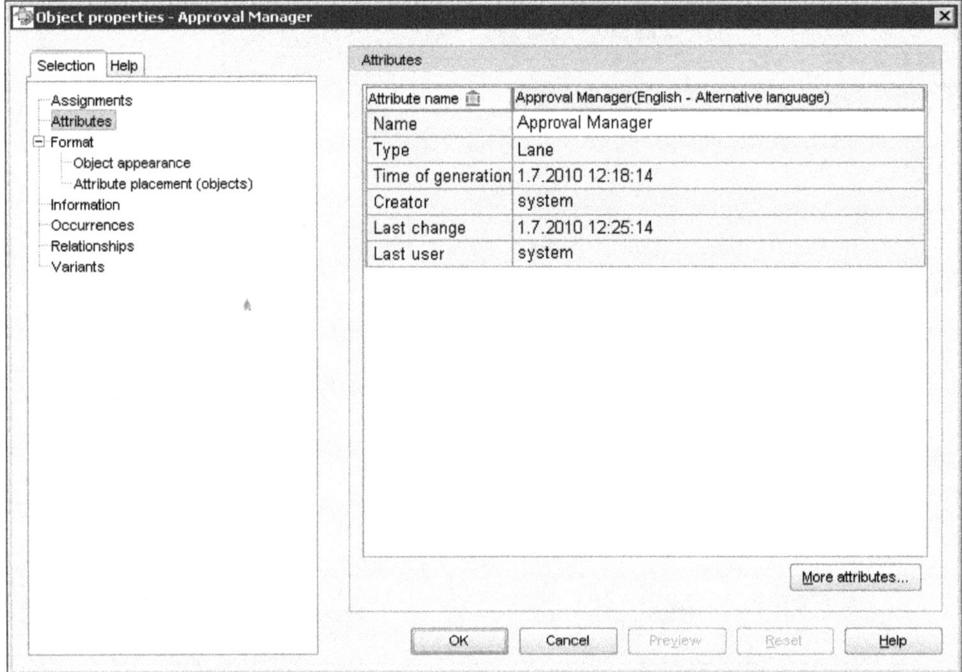

If we click on **Object appearance**, we can set the object background color, width, height, and so on. Then we switch to the **Attribute placement (objects)** screen, where we are able to set the attributes that we want to be displayed on the business process diagram, and their location. In the following screenshot, we can see that the attribute **Name** is displayed on the object's left side.

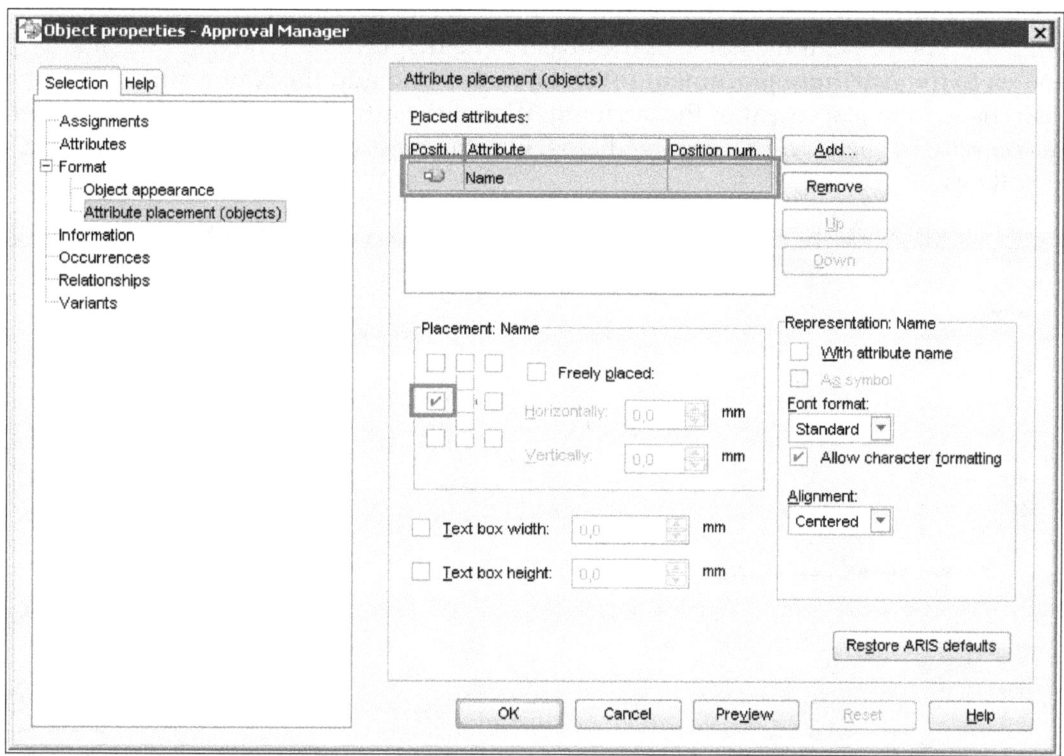

If we would like to replace the attribute, we remove the current attribute from the **Placed attributes** list and click on the **Add** button to open the **Add attributes** dialog. Then we select the attribute and click **OK** to close the dialog. After that, we can optionally change the attribute placement. We click **OK** to close the **Object properties** dialog.

Adding a start event

Next, we add the start event and place it into the **Lane**. As our process starts with receiving the message, we use the **Message (start event)** object. If the object is not listed in the **Symbols** palette, we have to add it by clicking the **Add symbols** icon on the top of the palette. By default, the object has no attributes displayed. Again, we open the **Object properties** dialog and set the name of the object to `Receive travel request`. As we want the name of the object to be displayed on the diagram, we switch to the **Attribute placement (objects)** screen and add the **Name** attribute. We also change the placement of the attribute. We set the attribute to be displayed under the object. We click **OK** to close the dialog. Our business process diagram now looks as follows:

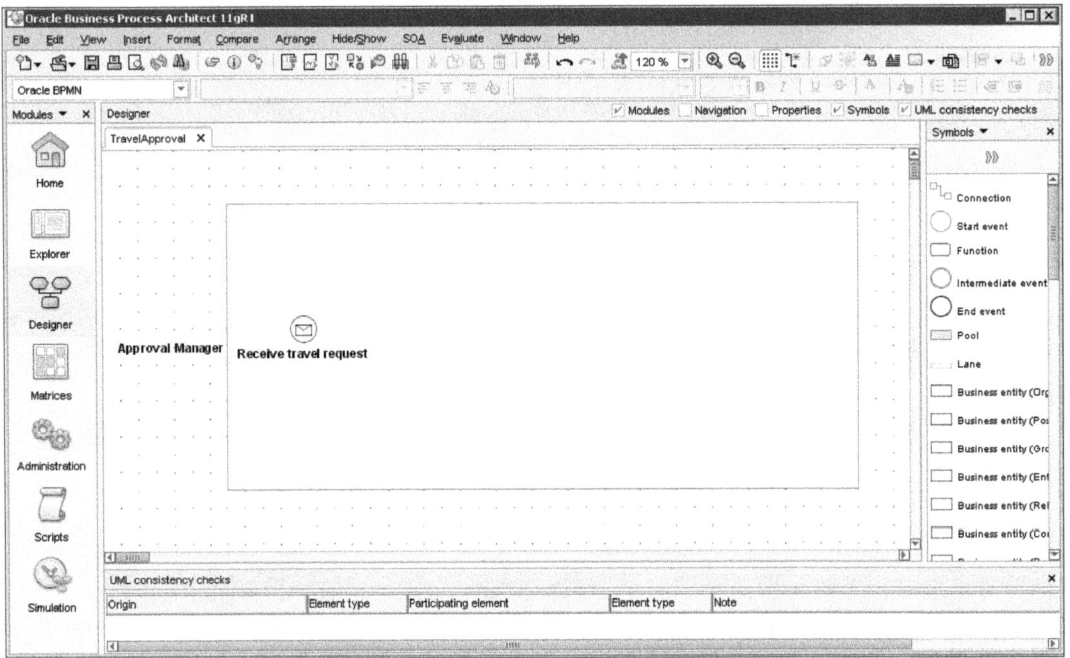

Adding automated activities

First, we will add automated activity for invoking the `EmployeeTravelStatus` service. In the **Symbols** palette, we select an **Automated activity** and place it next to the `Receive travel request` start event. The **Automated activity** dialog opens, as shown in the next screenshot. We set the name of the activity to `Retrieve employee travel status`. We also enter a **Description** of the activity. Descriptions are particularly useful for developers of a BPEL process to help them better understand the process.

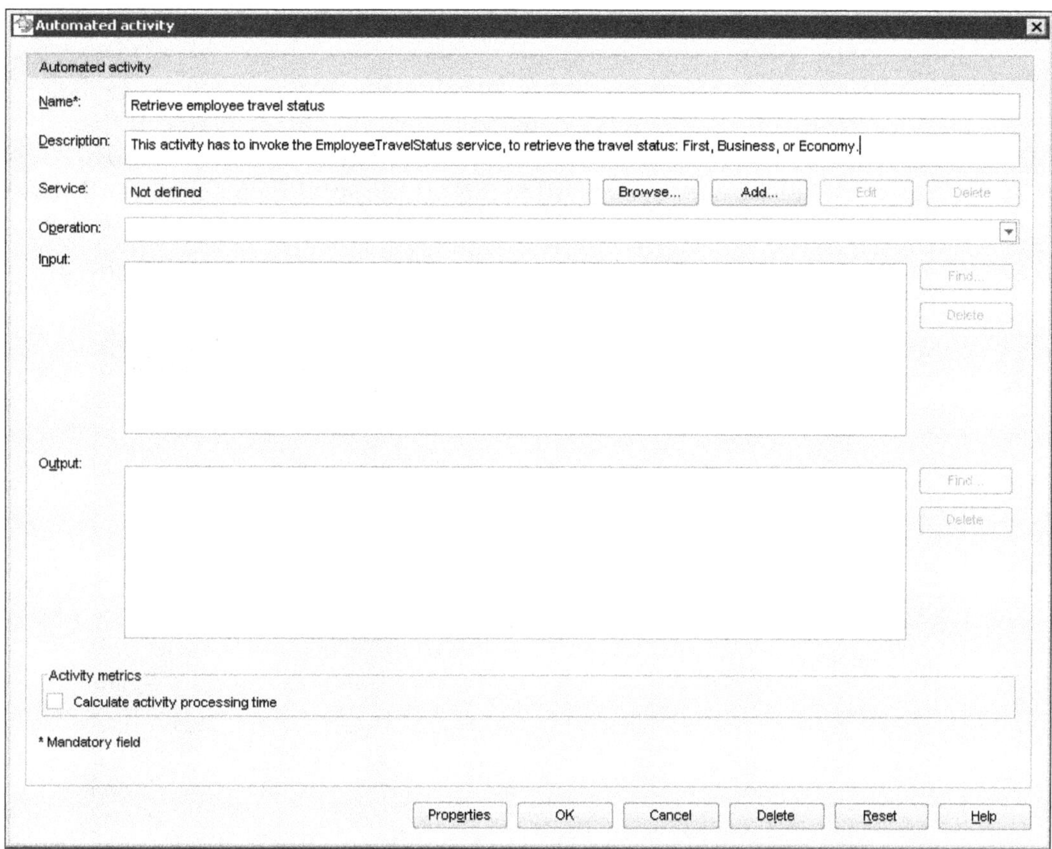

Next, we can specify the service we want to invoke. We have three options:

- We do not specify the service: In this case the activity will translate into an empty **Scope** upon BPEL translation, and the developer will have to add a corresponding **Partner Link** and **Invoke** activity. This option is useful when the business modeler does not have enough technical skills, or when the service does not yet exist.

- We import a concrete service by specifying the WSDL: Services can be imported using the **Explorer** module; however, we can also import a service from the **Automated activity** dialog. We click the **Add** button next to the **Service** field. The **Import service** dialog opens. We set the **Name** of the service to `EmployeeTravelStatus` and specify the WSDL URI. We also have to select the folder where we want to import the service. We click the **Browse** button to create a new group (we name it `EmployeeTravelStatus`) under the `Services` group. Optionally, we can also specify the service category, capabilities, and description.

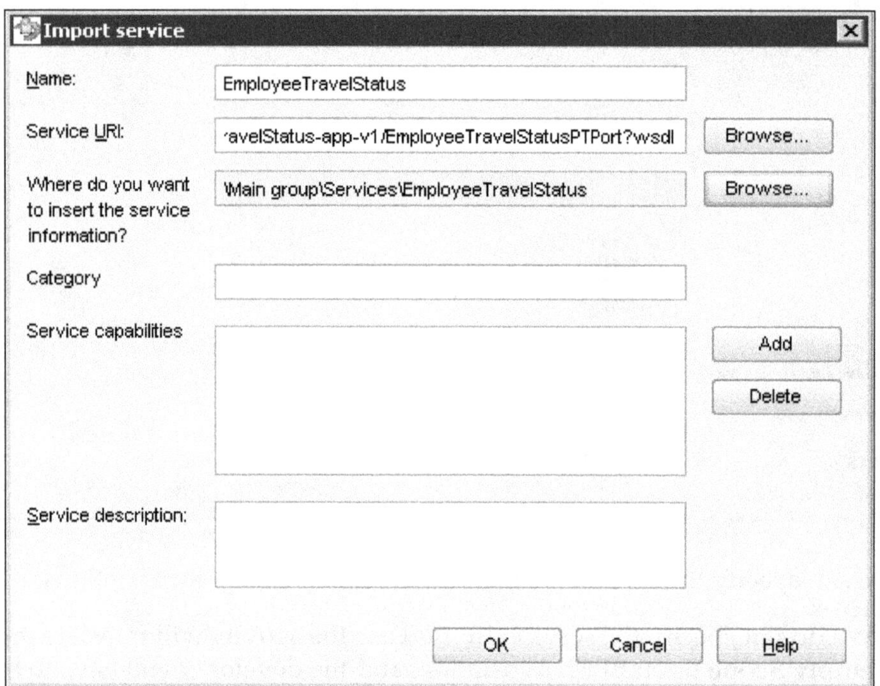

We click **OK** to import the service and close the dialog. Now we can also select the **Operation** we want to invoke.

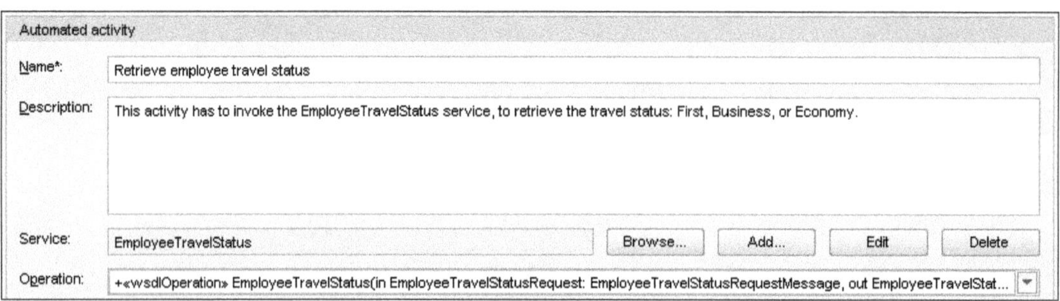

During the translation to BPEL, a corresponding concrete **Partner Link** and **Invoke** activity will be created.

* We can define an abstract service: The abstract service has a name, but it does not have the WSDL specified. During the translation, an abstract **Partner Link** and **Invoke** activity are created. To define an abstract service, we click on the **Browse** button, next to the **Service** field. The **Service browser** dialog opens. We then click on the **Abstract service** button. We set the service name to `EmployeeTravelStatus` and save it to a new group (we name it `EmployeeTravelStatus`) under the `Services` group. We click **OK** to get back to the **Service browser** dialog.

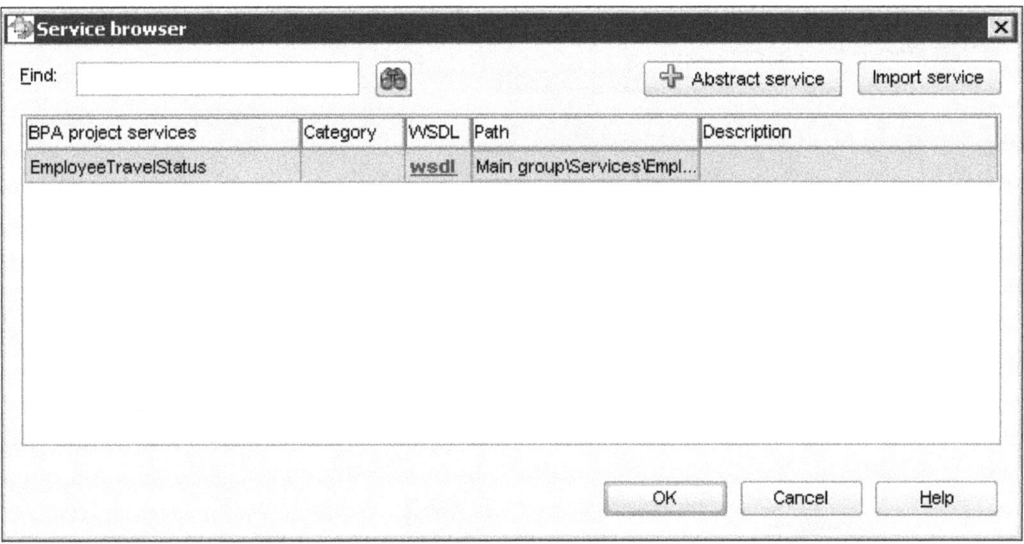

We select the new abstract service and click **OK** to close the dialog.

For our example, we will create abstract services for all services we need to invoke. We will specify concrete services later, during the BPEL implementation. In an **Automated activity** dialog we can also define input and output for the service. Similar as for services, we can also import concrete XSD files or define abstract data. However, we will leave these fields unchecked. At the bottom of the dialog, we can see the **Calculate activity processing time** checkbox. We select this checkbox if we want the activity sensors to be automatically created during the translation to BPEL. We leave this value unselected. Our `Retrieve employee travel status` automated activity is now set as shown in the following screenshot:

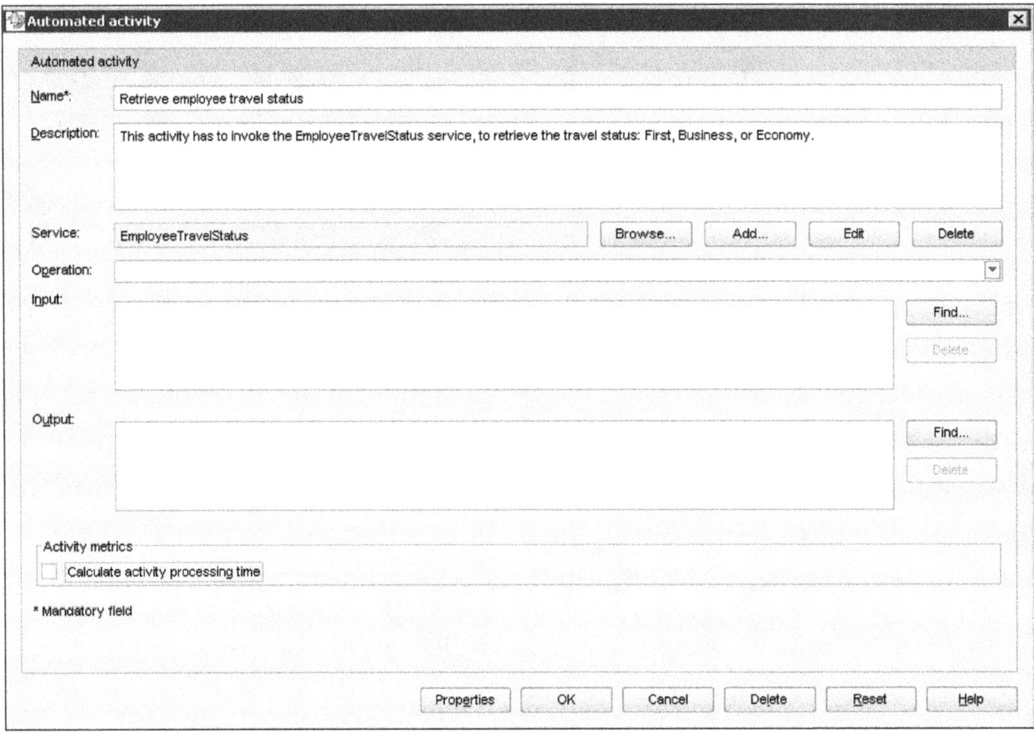

We click **OK** to close the dialog. Now, we have to connect the new automated activity to the `Receive travel request` start event. We select **Connection** in the **Symbols** palette and then first click on the start event and then the automated activity to connect them.

Next, we want to invoke both airline services to retrieve flight ticket offers. We add two new automated activities and name them `Get ticket offer Delta` and `Get ticket offer American`. We define them similar to the `Retrieve employee travel status` automated activity; therefore, we have to create two new abstract services—`DeltaAirlines` and `AmericanAirlines`. The next screenshot shows the current business process diagram.

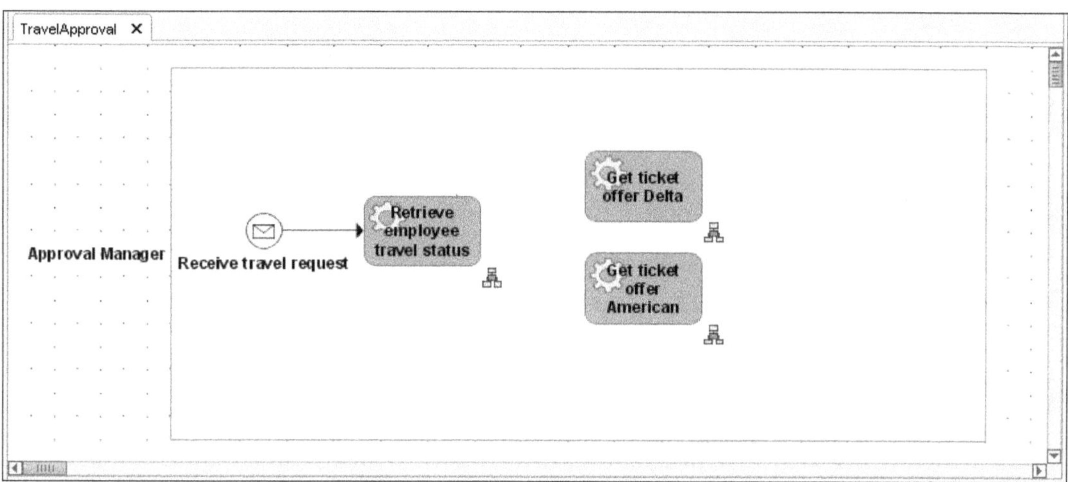

We add two **AND Gateway** objects and connect them with automated activities, as shown in the following screenshot:

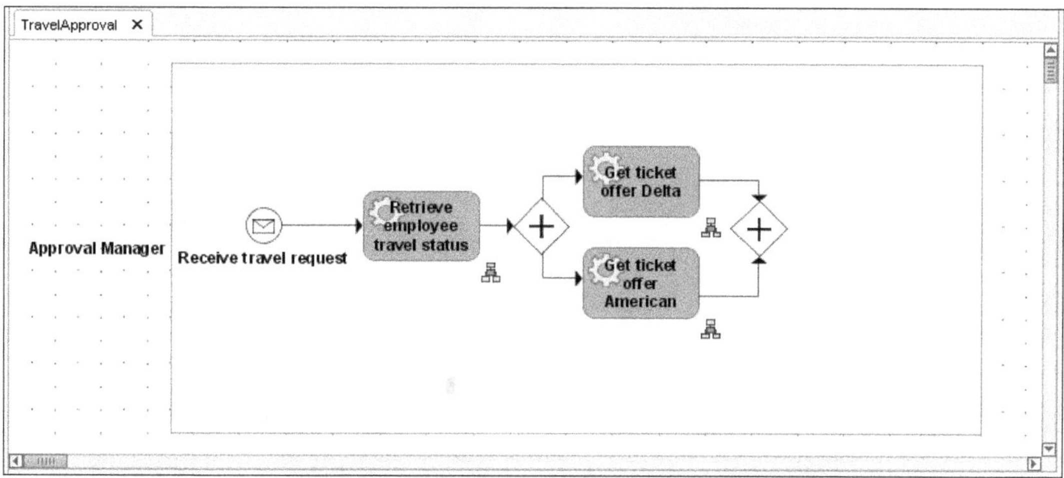

We save the project.

Adding a human task

The next step in the process requires human intervention. The Approval Manager has to review the offers and approve or reject the flight ticket. If he approves the ticket, the next step is to make a reservation. If he rejects the ticket, the process finishes.

In the **Symbols** palette, we select a **Human task** and place it on the process diagram. The **Human task** dialog opens, as shown in the next screenshot:

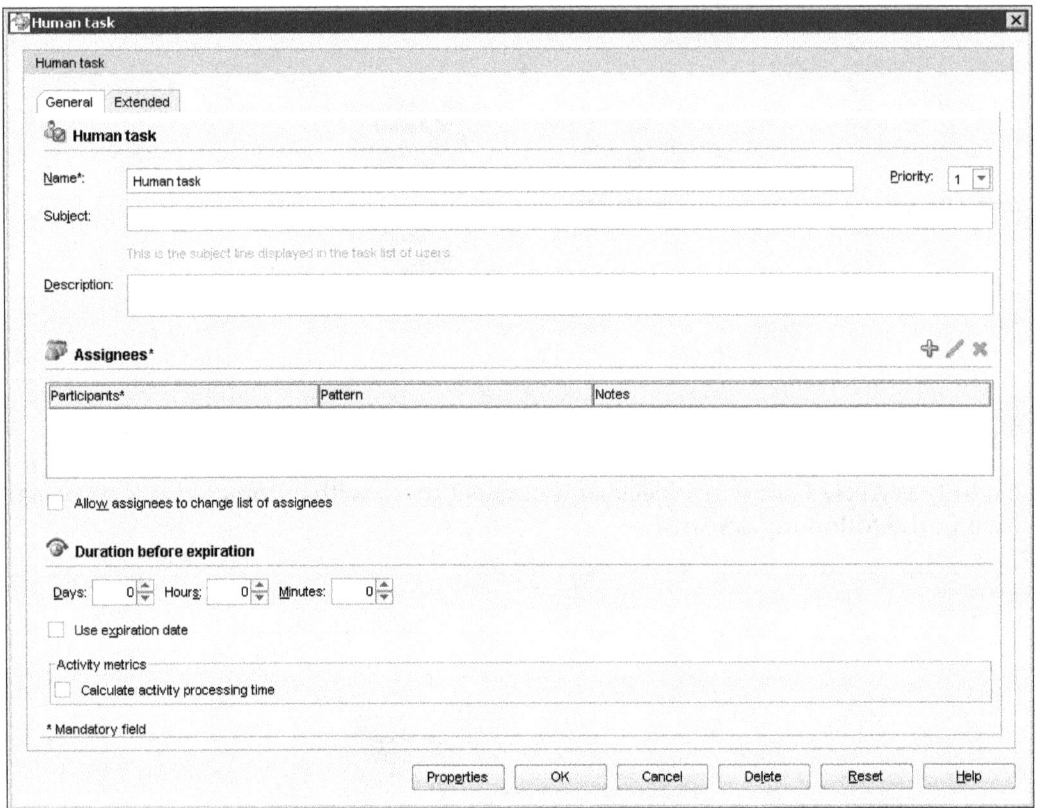

We set the **Name** and the **Subject** to `Flight ticket approval`. The **Subject** represents the title of the human task, which will be displayed in the Oracle Worklist Application at runtime. We also set the **Priority** to `3` and the expiration time to `2` days.

Then we set the assignments. We click on the green *plus* icon to add a participant, and the **Pattern** dialog opens. We select `Single approver` as the **Workflow pattern**. Then we click **Add** to create a new participant. We name the new participant `Approval Manager` and save it to the **Participants** group. We click on **OK**.

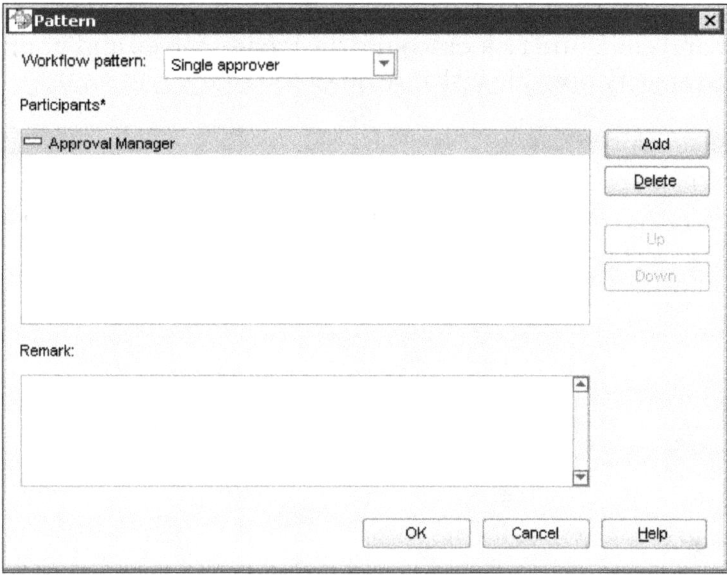

Back on the **Pattern** dialog, we click on **OK**. The `Flight ticket approval` human task is now set as follows:

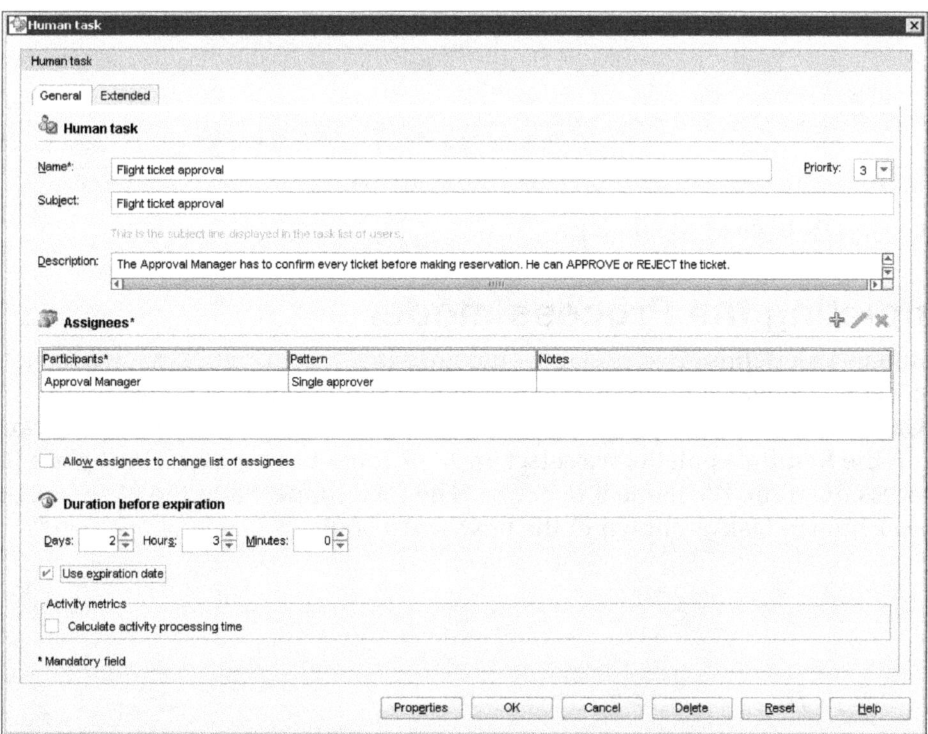

Next, we click on the **Extended** tab to see the advanced settings. Here we can specify the task owner and configure task outcomes, task parameters, and notification settings. We just specify possible task outcomes to `APPROVE,REJECT`.

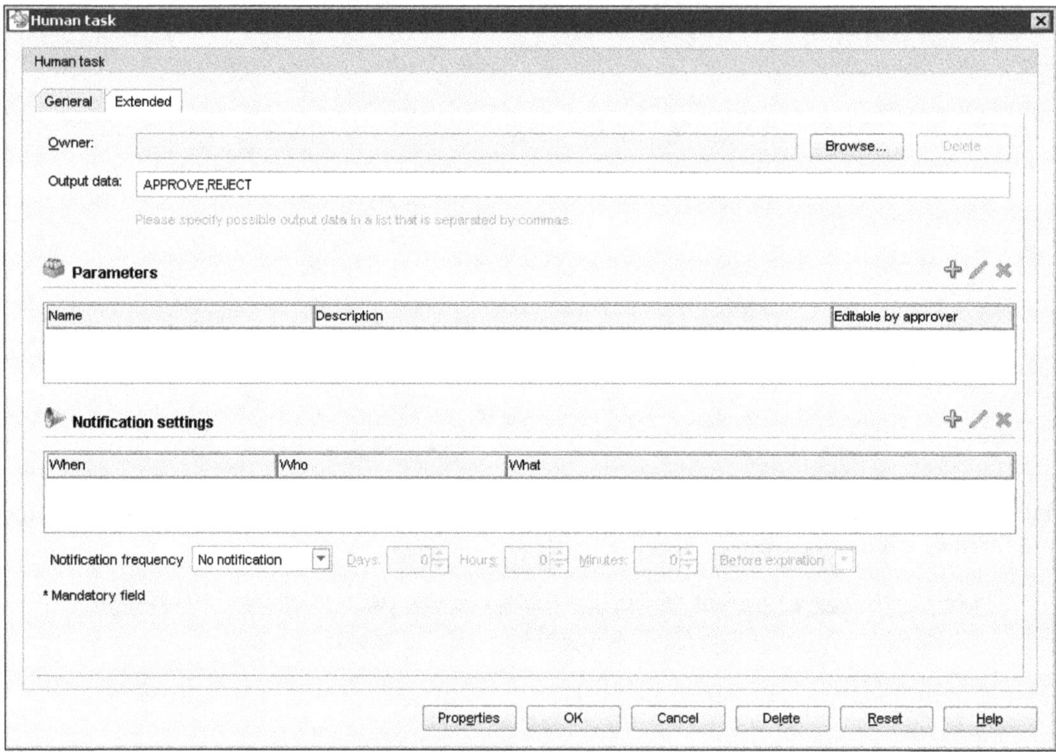

We click on **OK** to close the dialog.

Completing the Process model

As a human task defines two possible outcomes (`APPROVE` or `REJECT`), we have to add an **XOR Gateway** to handle the outcome by taking the appropriate path. An **XOR Gateway** is a mutually exclusive gateway, meaning that only one path can be taken. In the **Symbols** palette, we select an **XOR (data based)** object and place it on the process diagram. We name it `Outcome`. Then we connect it to the `Flight ticket approval` human task as shown in the next screenshot.

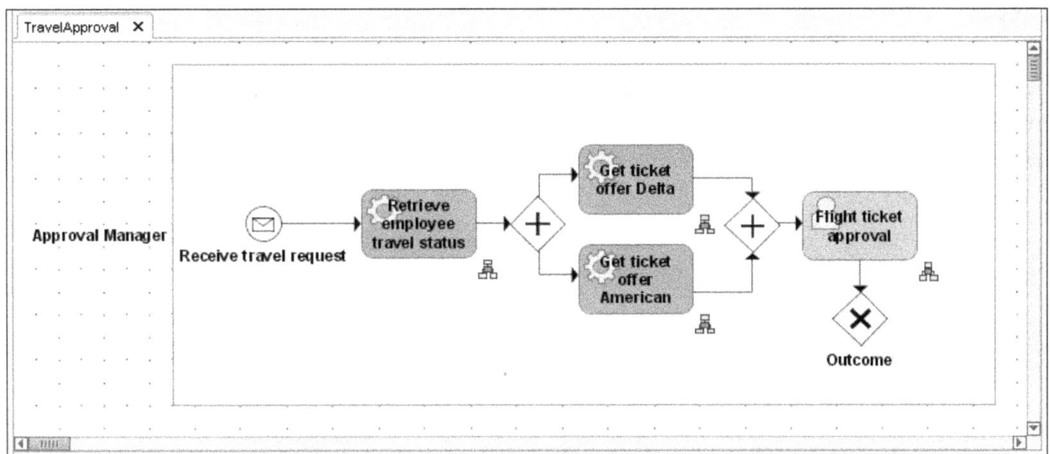

If the human task outcome is `APPROVE`, then the next step is to make a reservation of the selected ticket. We need another **XOR (data based)** object, as we need to check which airline was selected. We also need two new automated activities—`Delta reservation` and `American reservation`.

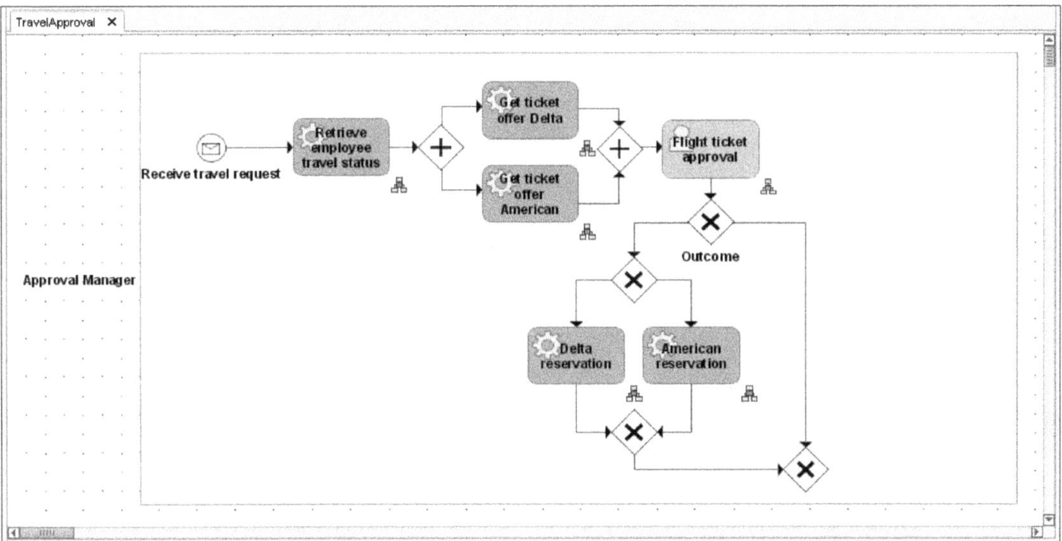

Next, we have to set the condition expressions for both exclusive gateways. To set a condition expression, we have to double-click the connection that represents a possible path to open the **Connection properties** dialog. Then we select **Attributes** on the left-hand side and set **Condition** to either `Expression` or `Default`. We can also specify a **Condition expression**, as shown in the next screenshot.

If the **Condition** and **Condition expression** attributes are not on the list, we have to add them by clicking the **More attributes** button.

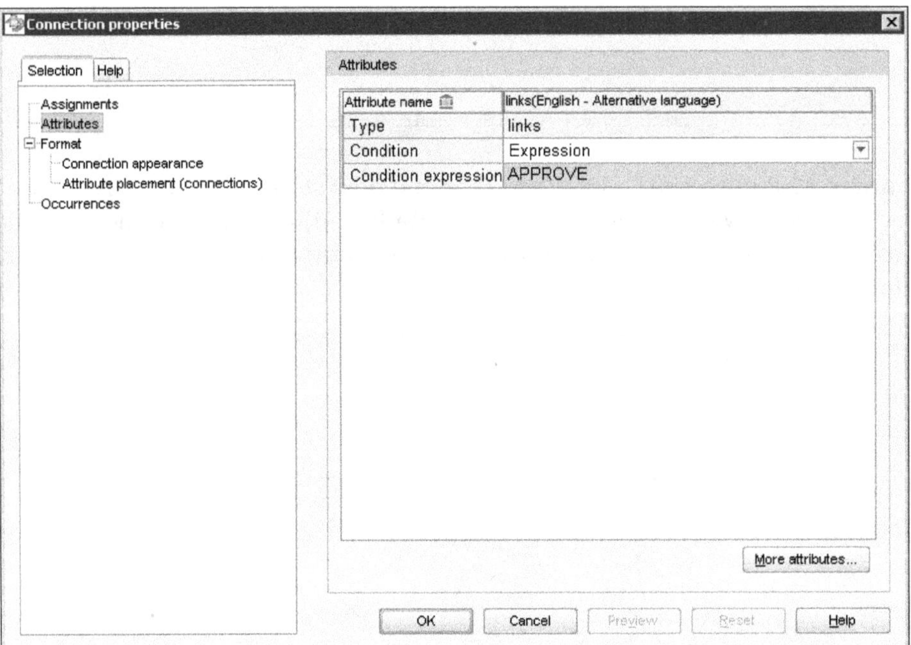

After specifying all condition expressions, we add the **End event** object and finish with modeling.

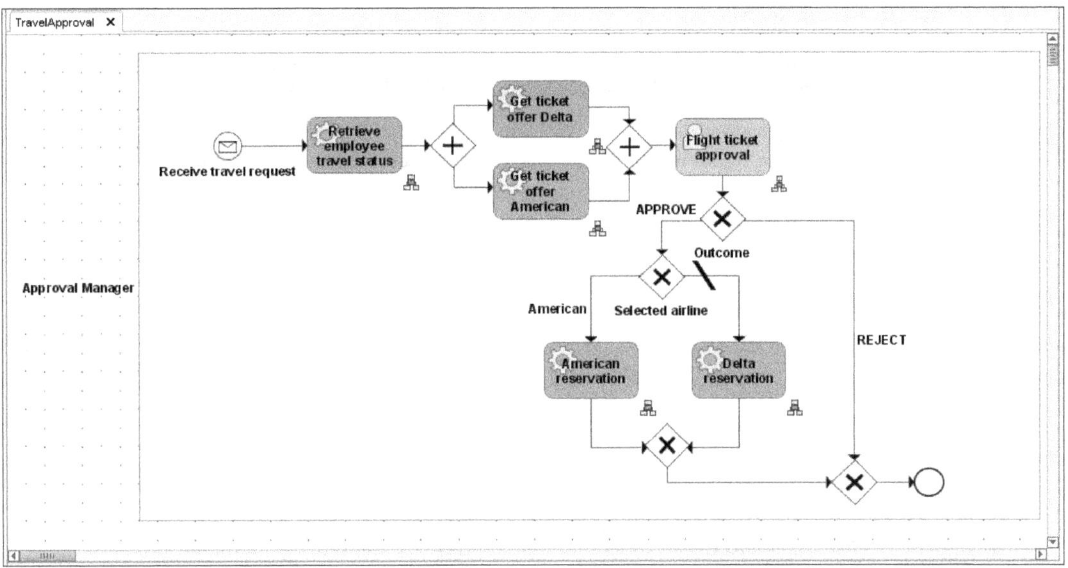

Transforming a business process into BPEL

We are now ready to translate the model into BPEL Blueprint and associated BPEL skeletal code. During the translation, the generated BPEL Blueprint is saved to the BPA Repository. IT developers have to open the process and add implementation details to make the process executable.

To start the transformation, we open the model in **Designer** module. From the **SOA** menu we select **Share Blueprint with IT**.

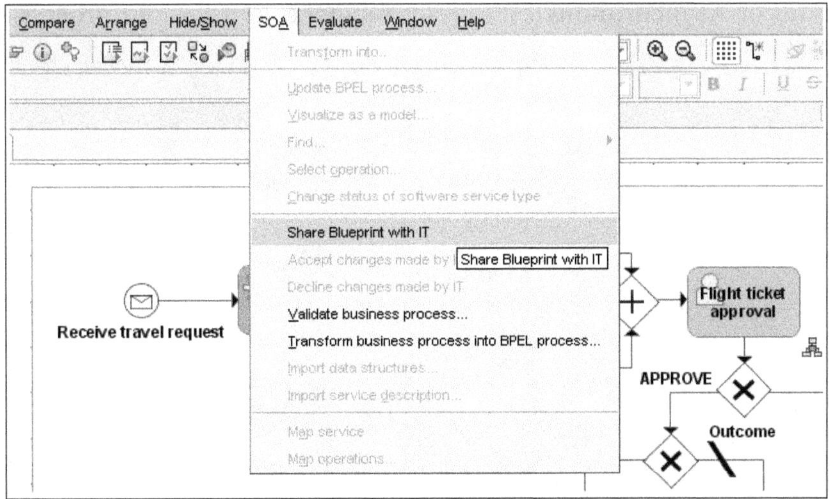

The **Information** dialog opens.

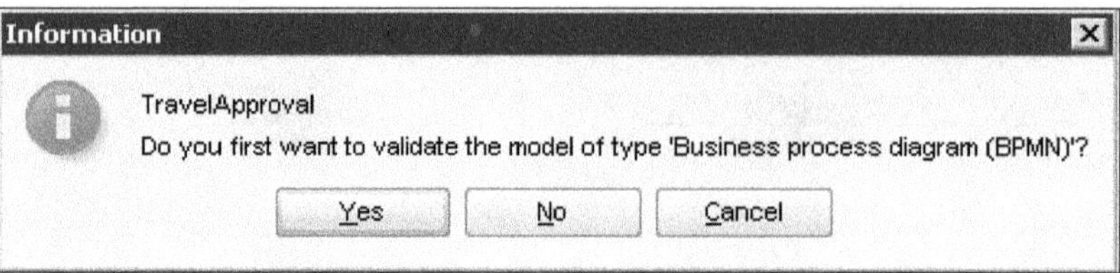
Information
TravelApproval
Do you first want to validate the model of type 'Business process diagram (BPMN)'?
Yes
No
Cancel

If we want to validate the model before the translation, we click **Yes**. The validation result is opened in the web browser, as shown in the next screenshot. We can see that our model contains no errors or warnings.

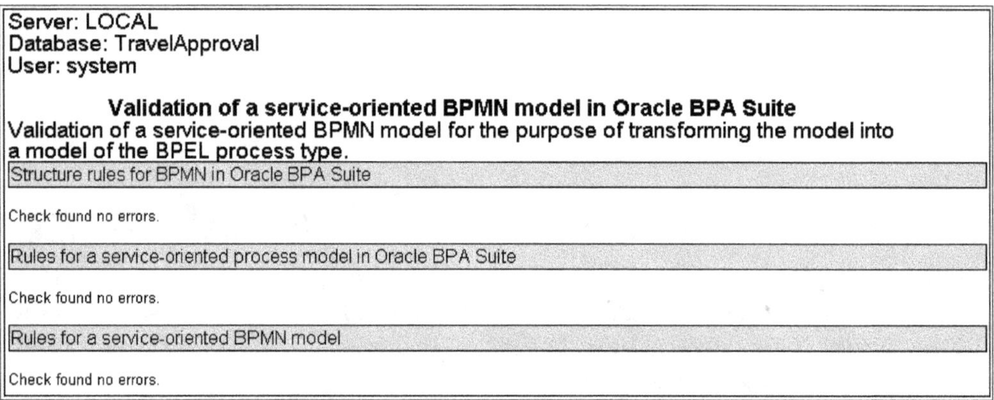
Server: LOCAL
Database: TravelApproval
User: system
Validation of a service-oriented BPMN model in Oracle BPA Suite
Validation of a service-oriented BPMN model for the purpose of transforming the model into a model of the BPEL process type.
Structure rules for BPMN in Oracle BPA Suite
Check found no errors.
Rules for a service-oriented process model in Oracle BPA Suite
Check found no errors.
Rules for a service-oriented BPMN model
Check found no errors.

At the same time, the **Transformation properties** dialog opens in Business Process Architect. Here we can enter a process description and select a process type (**Synchronous** or **Asynchronous**). We select **Asynchronous**, as our process contains a human task.

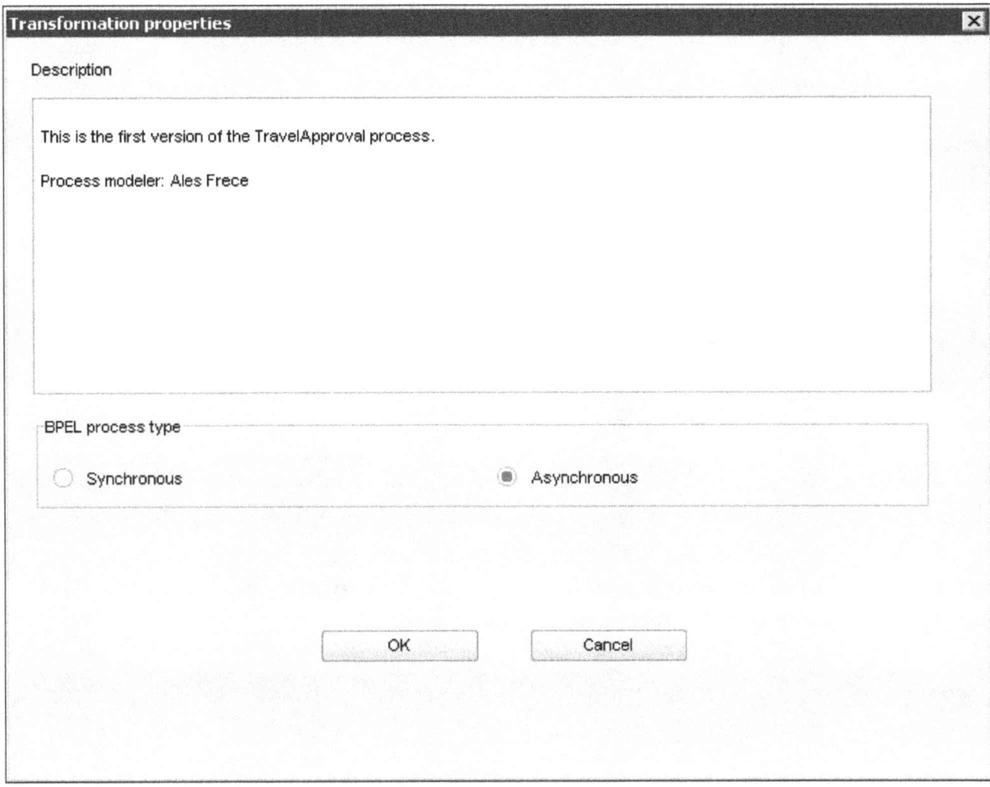

We click on **OK** to start the transformation. If the transformation was successful, the **Message** dialog is displayed.

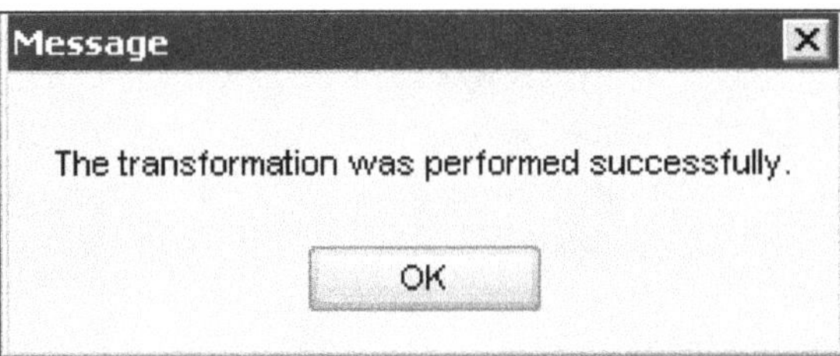

Not all BPMN process models can be converted into BPEL. For example, BPEL does not support arbitrary (unstructured) cycles. If a BPMN model contains arbitrary cycles, we have to refactor the model before the translation. This is usually done by an IT expert.

Now the BPEL Blueprint and associated skeletal BPEL code have been generated and saved to the BPA Repository.

Using BPEL Blueprints in Oracle JDeveloper

The business process model is used as a starting point to generate the BPEL executable code. To import the generated BPEL Blueprint, we first have to create a connection to the BPA Repository. Next, we create a new SOA project and select the model we want to import. Then we can start adding implementation details to make the BPEL code executable. When a new version of a process model is available in the BPA Repository, we have to synchronize our BPEL code with the new model version. We can also add new activities and try to update the BPMN model in the BPA Repository. However, these changes have to be accepted by a business analyst.

Creating a connection to the BPA Repository

First we have to make sure that the Business Process Architect is up and running. We open Oracle JDeveloper and select **New** in the **File** menu. The **New Gallery** dialog opens. In the **Categories** section on the left we select **Connections** and then **BPA Server Connection** from the **Items** list on the right.

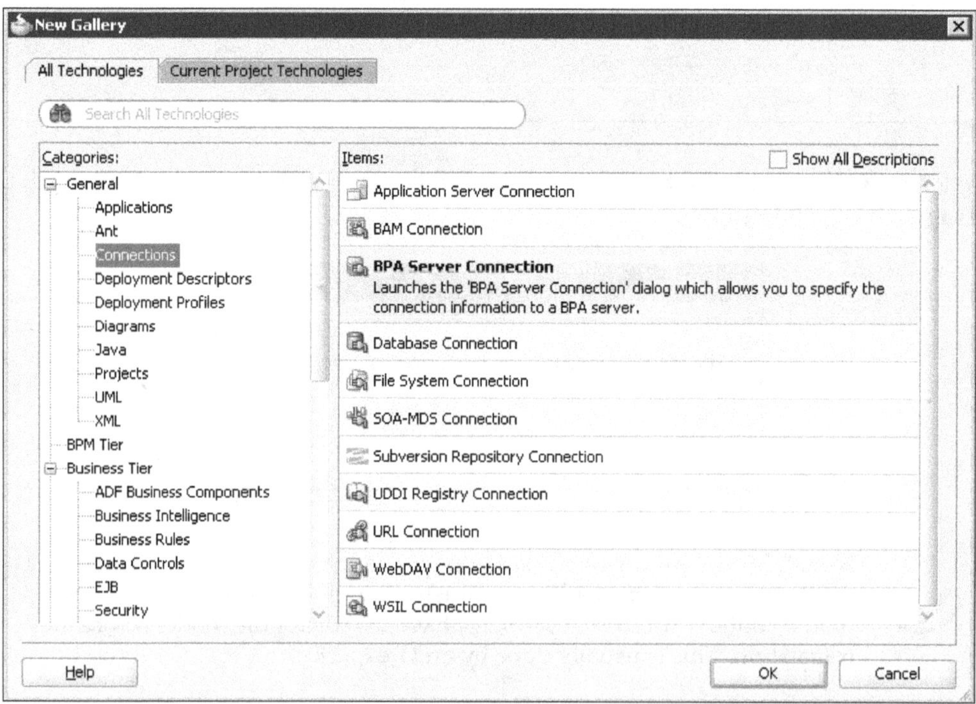

We click **OK**. In the **BPA Server Connection** dialog we enter the connection name, select `Local Server` for **Location**, select the database, and enter a **Username** and **Password**. If we open the **Test** tab, we can also test the connection.

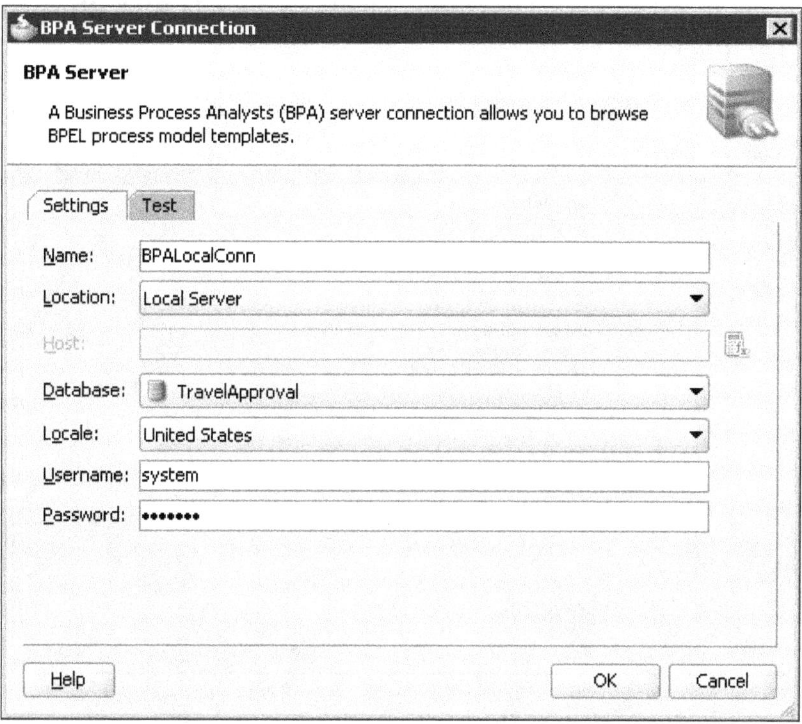

We click on **OK** to close the dialog.

Creating an application and an SOA Project

First we create a new SOA application and SOA project. We already described how to do this in previous chapters; therefore, we will not explain all the steps in detail. However, this time we select **Composite From Oracle BPA Blueprint** as a **Composite Template**.

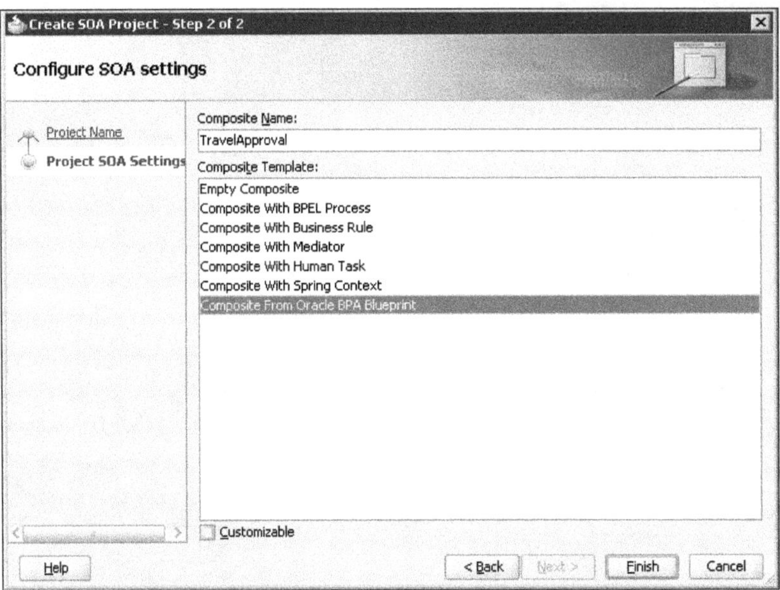

We click on **Finish**. The **Create BPA Blueprint Composite** dialog opens. We select the process model we want to implement and click on **OK**.

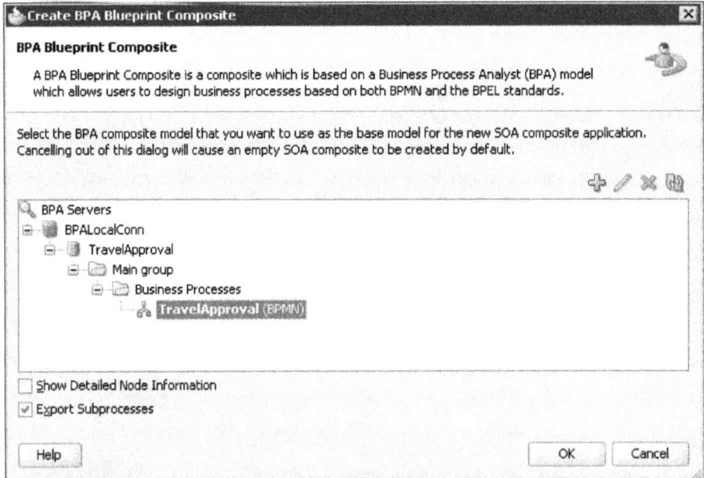

Understanding the generated BPEL code

When the project is created, the SOA Composite Editor opens, as shown in the following screenshot.

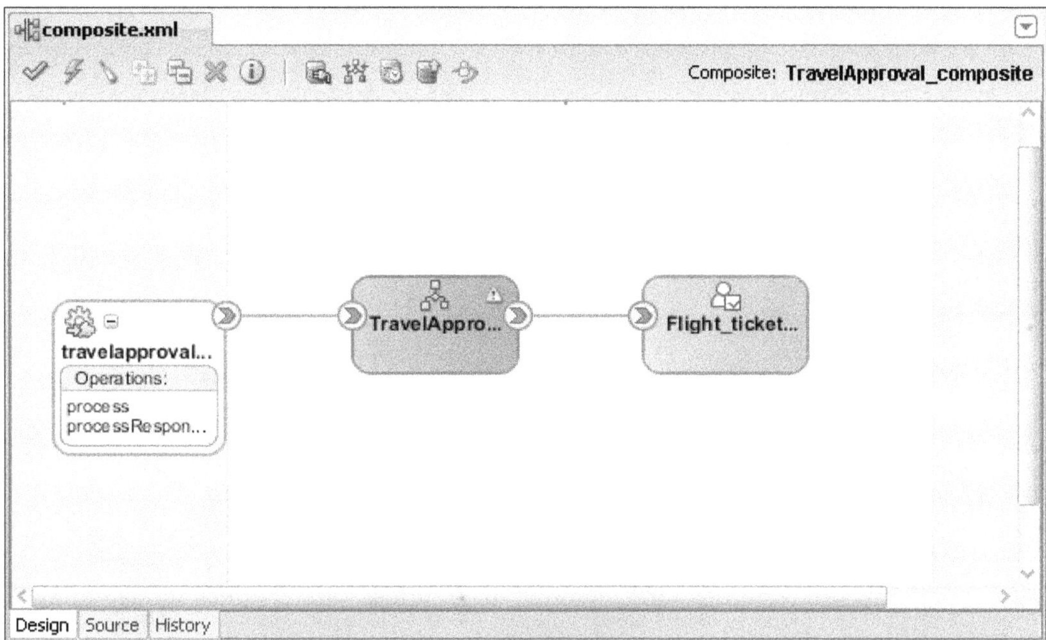

We can see that an SOA Composite application contains a BPEL process and Human Task service components. Now we double-click the `TravelApproval` BPEL process to open the BPEL Component Designer. The BPEL Component Designer opens in **BPA** view, where we can see the generated BPEL Blueprint.

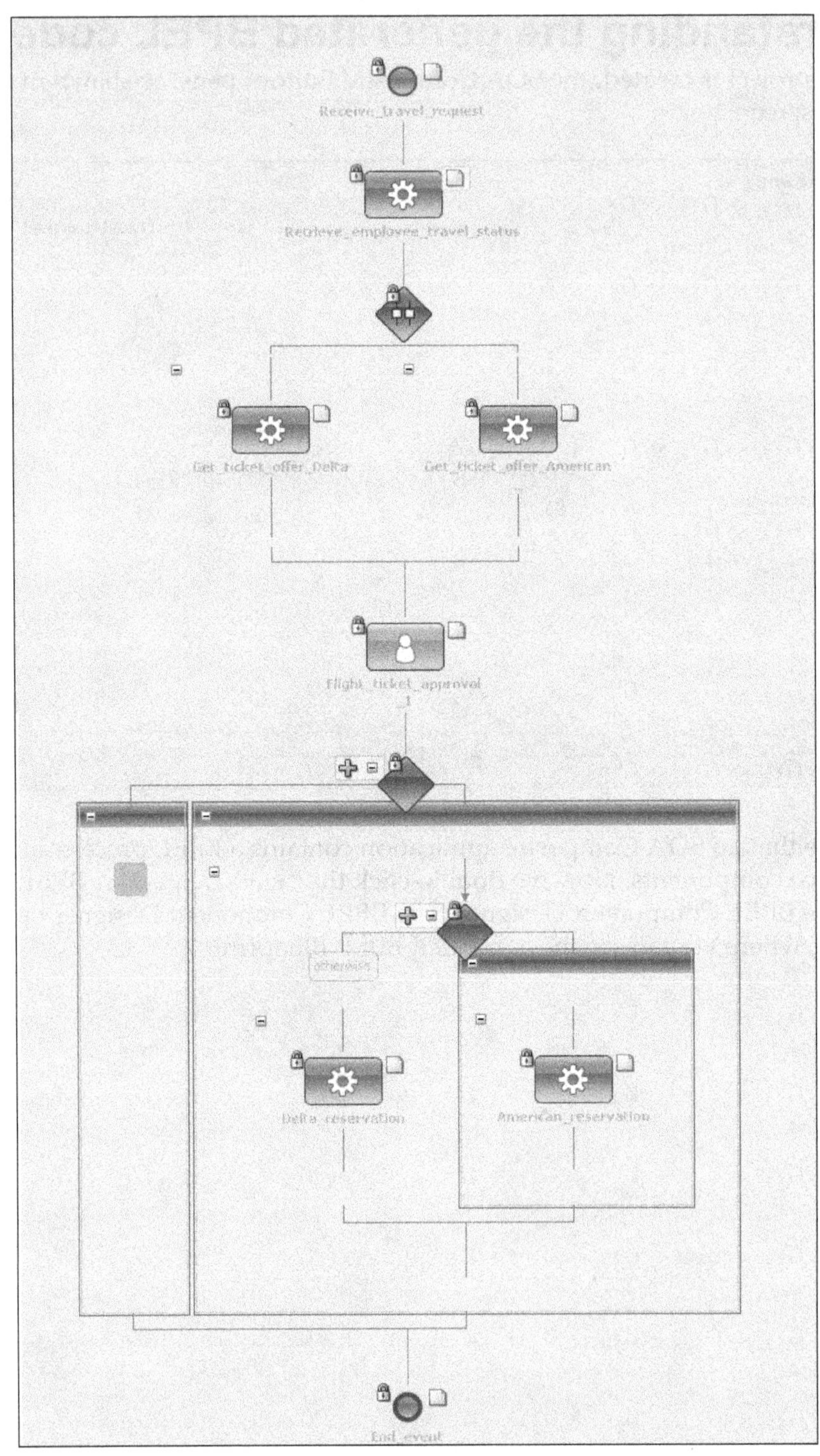
Receive_travel_request
Retrieve_employee_travel_status
Get_ticket_offer_Delta
Get_ticket_offer_American
Flight_ticket_approval
otherwise
Delta_reservation
American_reservation
End_event

Using the **BPA** view, we can read annotations to the process and process activities to better understand the process. To read annotations, we have to click on the *sticky notes* icon next to the activity. The annotation of the `Flight ticket approval` Human Task activity is shown as follows.

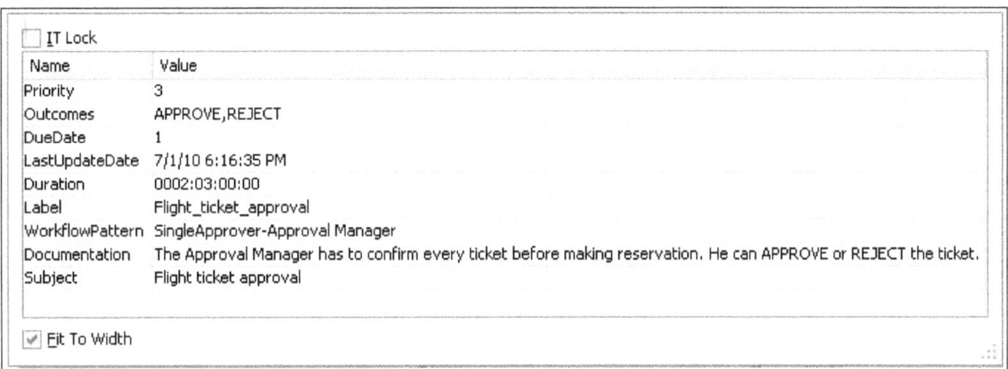

IT Lock
Name Value
Priority 3
Outcomes APPROVE,REJECT
DueDate 1
LastUpdateDate 7/1/10 6:16:35 PM
Duration 0002:03:00:00
Label Flight_ticket_approval
WorkflowPattern SingleApprover-Approval Manager
Documentation The Approval Manager has to confirm every ticket before making reservation. He can APPROVE or REJECT the ticket.
Subject Flight ticket approval
Fit To Width

Locks next to the activities indicate that the IT developer cannot delete these steps. Using the **BPA** view, the developer can also add process steps that he wants to be propagated back to the BPMN model. We will demonstrate this later in this chapter.

If we look at the BPEL source code, we can see how annotations are added to the process and process activities. In the following code snippet, we can see annotations to the scope `Retrieve_employee_travel_status`. Under `<bpelx:analysis>`, we can see several properties that include information about when the business activity was last updated (`LastUdpateDate`), the ID of the activity (`BusinessId`), and documentation (`Documentation`).

```
<scope name="Retrieve_employee_travel_status">
  <bpelx:annotation
    xmlns:bpelx="http://schemas.oracle.com/bpel/extension">
    <bpelx:pattern patternName="bpelx:automated"/>
    <bpelx:analysis>
        <bpelx:property name="LastUpdateDate">
          7/1/10 3:34:05 PM</bpelx:property>
        <bpelx:property name="Documentation">This activity has to
          invoke the EmployeeTravelStatus service, to
          retrieve the travel status: First, Business, or
          Economy.</bpelx:property>
        <bpelx:property name="BusinessId">
          Scope_69d341e5-84f9-11df-4948-000c29b1a451</bpelx:property>
    </bpelx:analysis>
  </bpelx:annotation>
  ...
</scope>
```

To implement the process, we have to switch to the **BPEL** view. In the next screenshot, we can see that automated activities were translated into **Scopes** with the same name. As we defined abstract services, abstract **Partner Links** and **Invoke** activities were also generated and the AND Gateway was translated into the **Flow** activity. A **Human Task** activity and corresponding **Partner Link** for the `TaskService` were also generated.

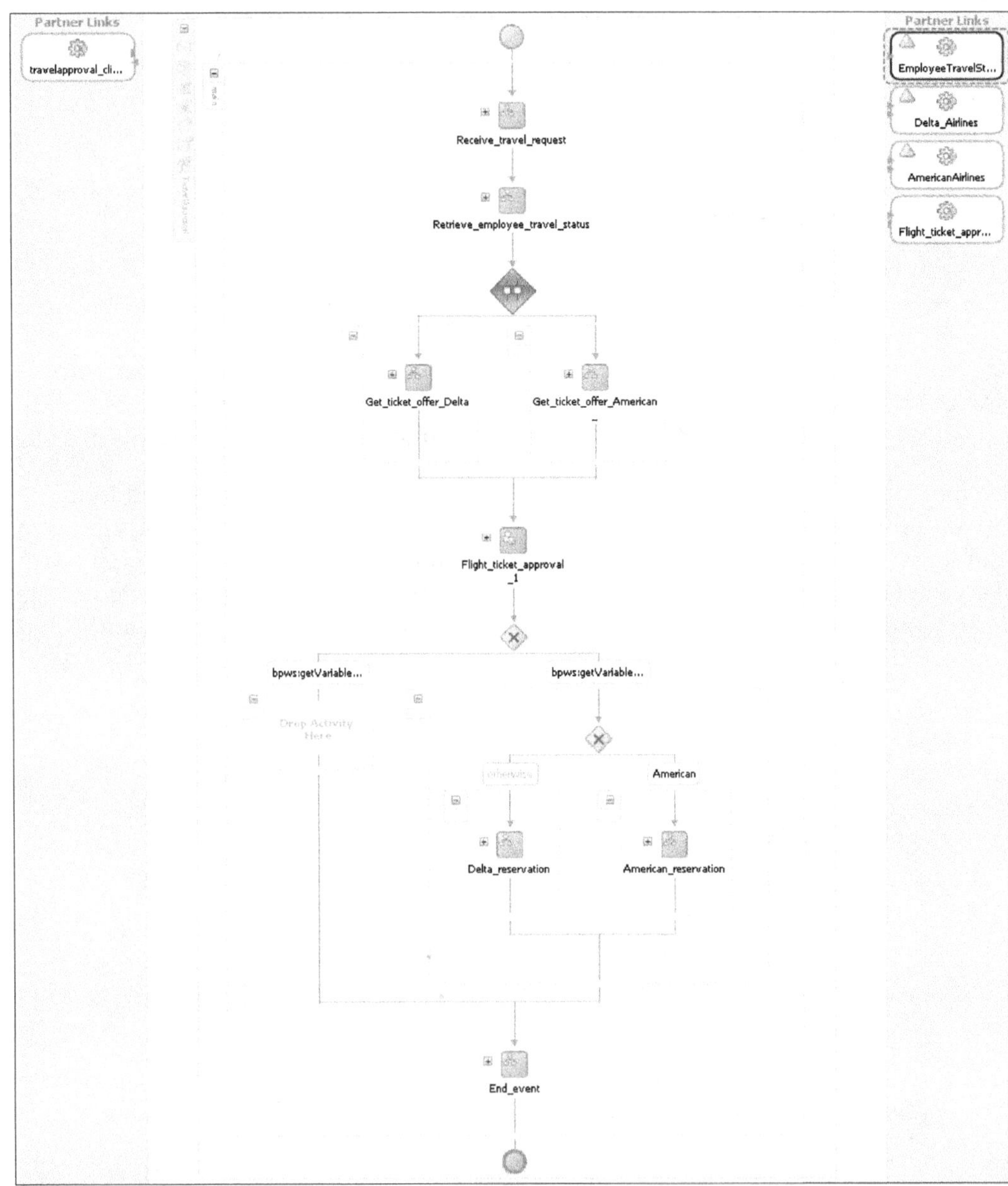

To make the BPEL process executable, we have to follow these steps:

1. Import XML Schemas and set the process input and output.
2. Link abstract Partner Links to a concrete service by providing WSDL.
3. Create BPEL variables.
4. Set **Invoke** activities by selecting an operation and input and output variables.
5. Add **Assign** activities to copy data between variables.
6. Set the **Human Task** assignment and payload.
7. Set **Condition expressions.**

In this chapter we will not demonstrate how to implement the BPEL process, as this was already covered in previous chapters.

BPMN-BPEL round-tripping

We have demonstrated how to model the first version of a business process and translate it into BPEL Blueprint. As business processes change over time, new process versions occur. Therefore, the BPMN model and BPEL code have to be continuously synchronized. We will demonstrate this BPMN-BPEL round-tripping in the following sections.

Propagating changes from BPMN to BPEL

First, we will demonstrate how changes to BPMN model can be propagated to BPEL. Then, we will show how changes made in BPEL code can be propagated back to the BPMN model to keep both models in sync.

Modifying the BPMN model

Let us open the Oracle Business Process Architect again. We open our `TravelApproval` business process in **Designer** module. We modify the process by adding a **Notification** activity at the end of the process flow. The modified model now looks like the following screenshot.

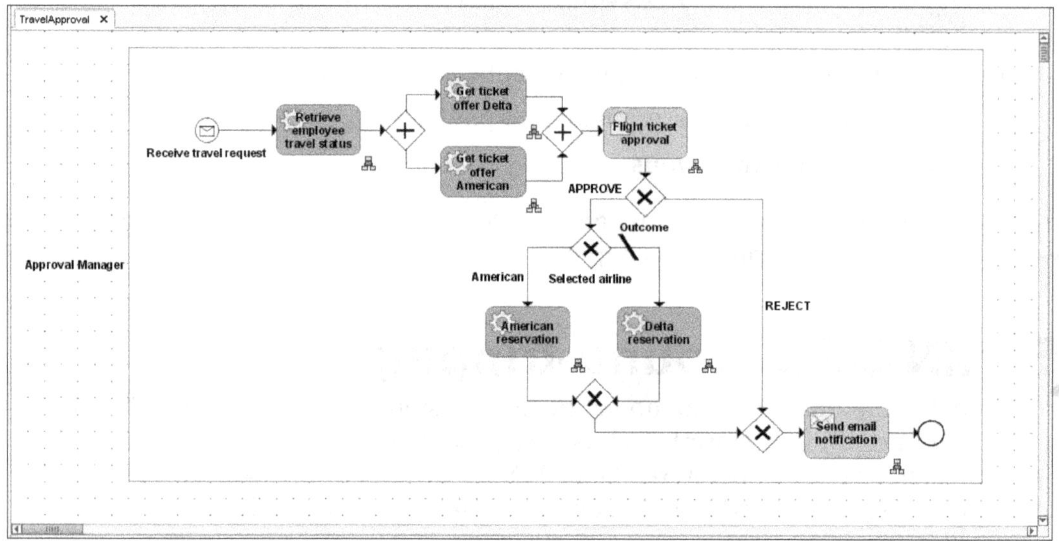

Then we translate the new version of the process into BPEL Blueprint again, by selecting **Transfer business process into BPEL process** from the **SOA** menu.

Refreshing BPEL Blueprint

Every time we open the SOA Composite Editor, the tool checks if a new version of the process is available in the BPA Repository. If so, the text **New version has been detected!** is displayed on the top of the page.

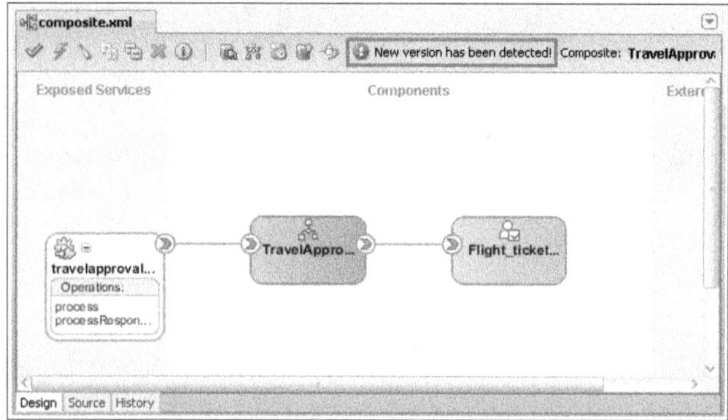

We can then refresh the BPEL process by clicking on the *Refresh from BPA Server* icon.

The **Refresh from BPA Server** dialog opens. We select a connection to the BPA server and click on the **Compute Model Differences** to analyze the differences between the local blueprint and the new version, available on the BPA server. The differences are displayed as shown.

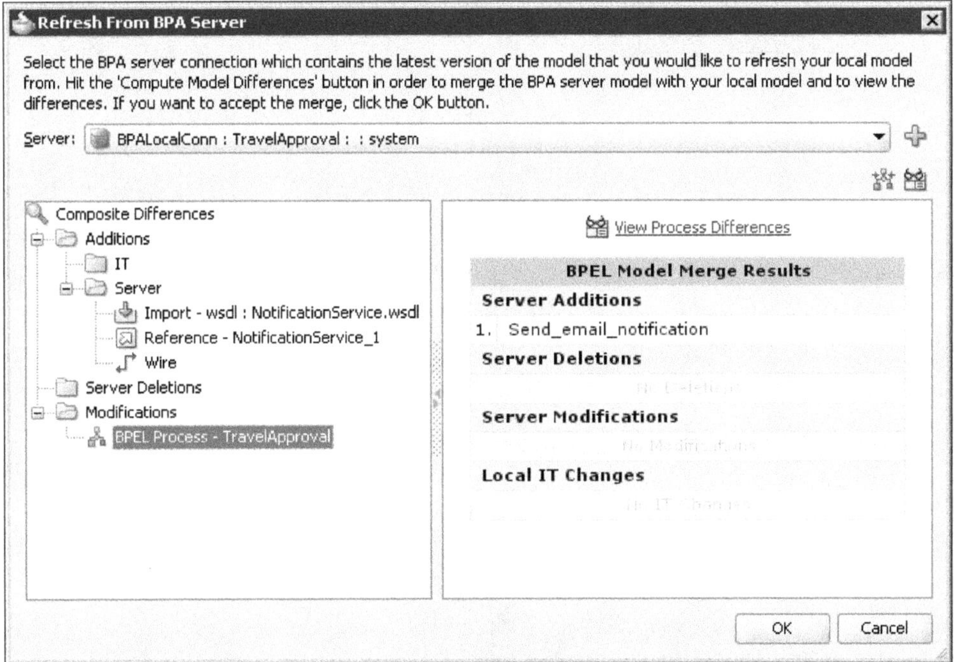

We click on the **View Process Differences** link to see the differences in visual mode. The **Process Differences** dialog opens. At the bottom of the page, we can see how the process will look, after the merging.

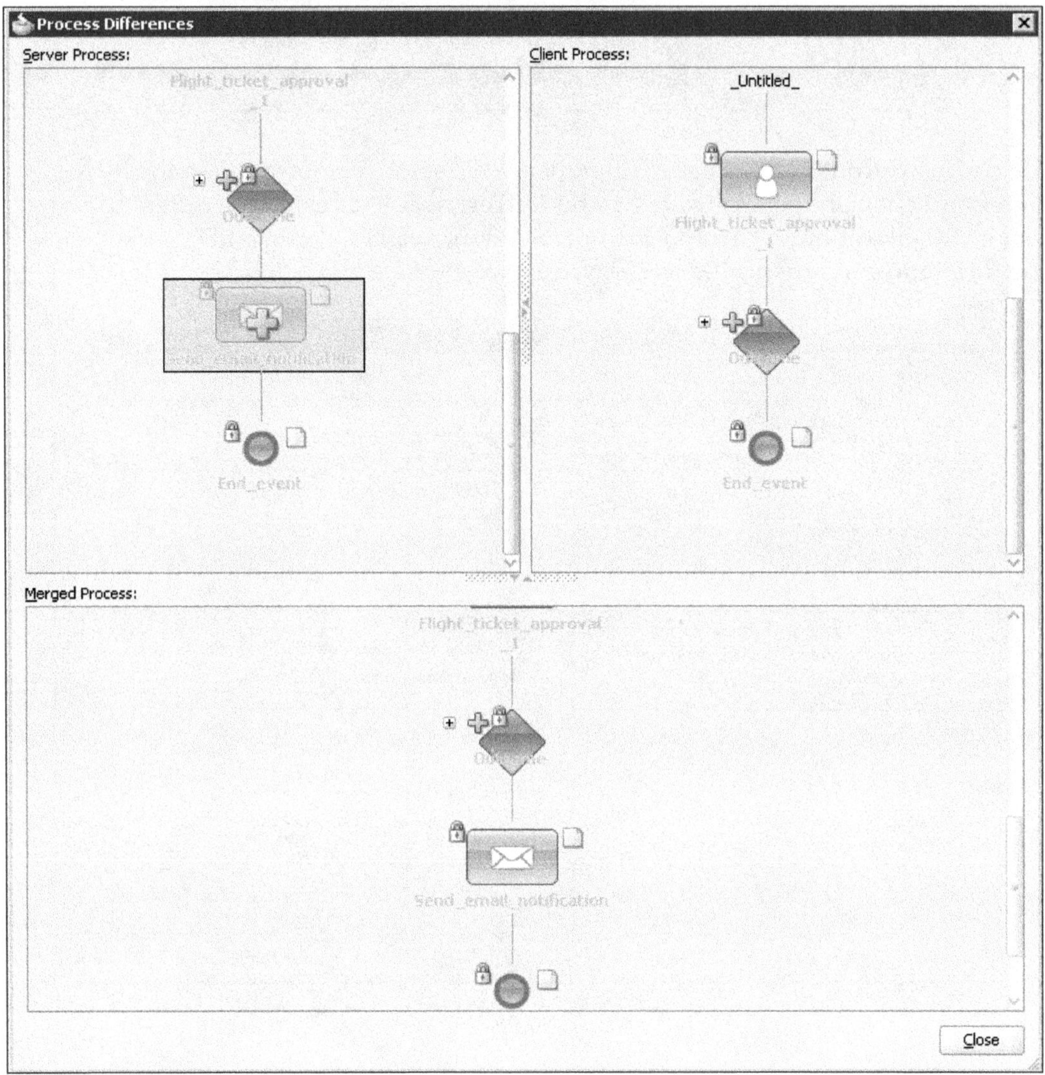

We click **Close** to close the dialog. Then we click **OK** to accept the changes and refresh the BPEL code.

If we look at the BPEL Blueprint, we can see that an **Email notification** activity has been added at the end of the process and that, corresponding **Partner Link** has been created.

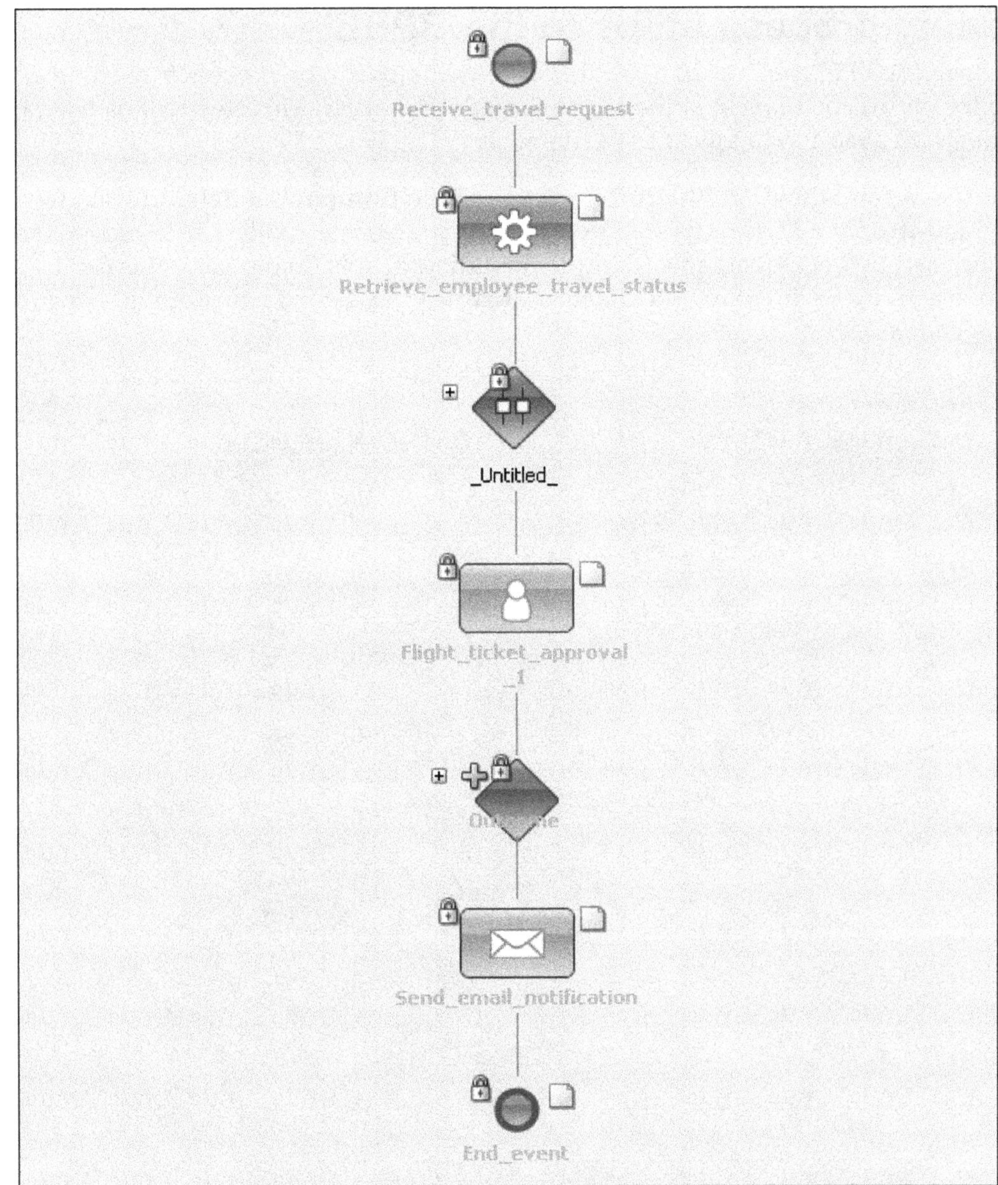

Propagating changes from BPEL to BPMN

If the developer adds some important steps to the process and wants to propagate those changes back to the BPMN model, he can save the new version of the model to the BPA server. A business analyst is automatically notified of the proposal and has to accept or decline the changes.

Adding process steps to the BPEL

We open the BPEL process in **BPA** view. We will modify the process by adding a step for saving the request at the beginning of the process. This step will be used for storing every received request to the database.

First, we expand the **BPA Blueprints** section in the **Component Palette**. Then we drag-and-drop the **IT Details** step to the process. This is actually a BPEL scope that can be used by developers to add implementation details. In our case, this can be an **Invoke** activity for invoking the database adapter. We set the name of the scope to `Save_request`.

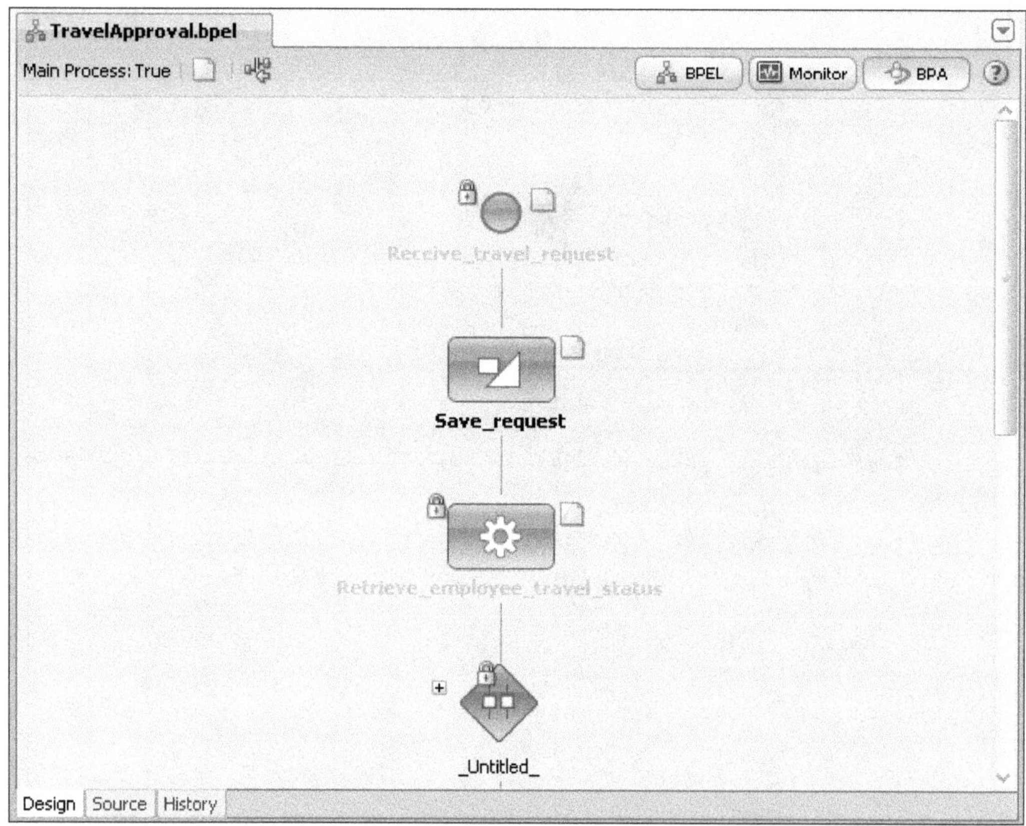

We open the SOA Composite Editor and click on the *Save to BPA Server* icon.

We select the connection to the server and click **Save**.

If the model is currently opened in the Business Process Architect, the operation will fail.

Now, the changes have been propagated to the BPA server.

Updating the BPMN model

When the process modeler tries to open the model in **Designer** module, the following message box is displayed.

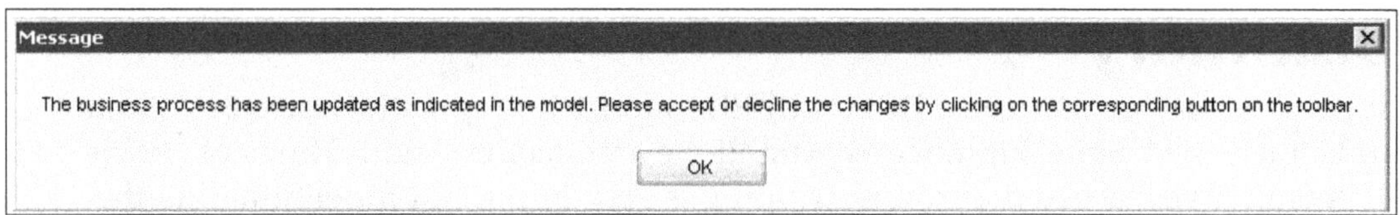

After clicking **OK**, the model is displayed and the new activity is highlighted.

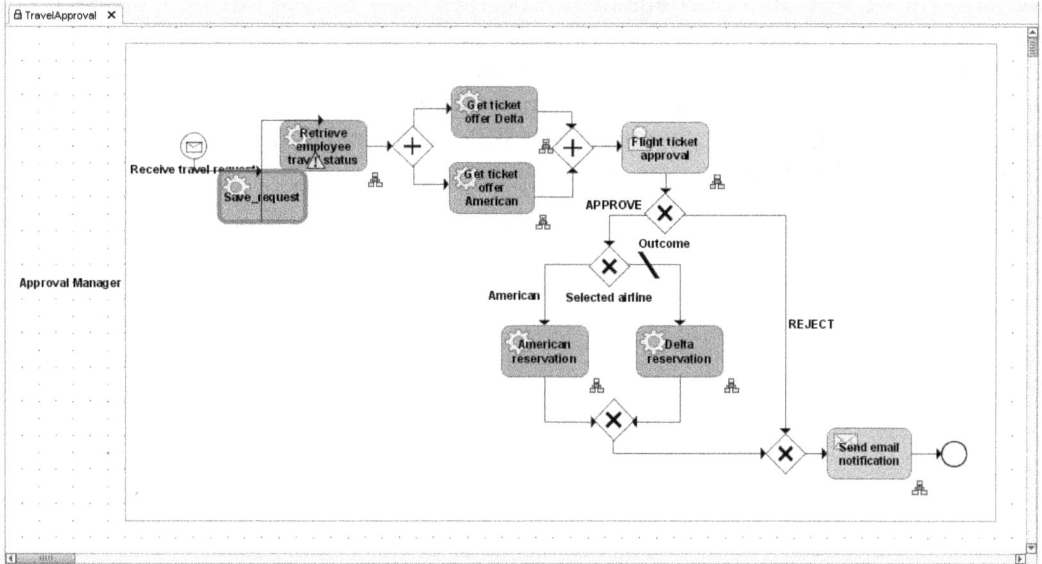

The modeler has to decide whether he will accept the changes or not. He confirms his decision by clicking on the appropriate icon on the toolbar (**Accept changes made by IT** or **Decline changes made by IT**).

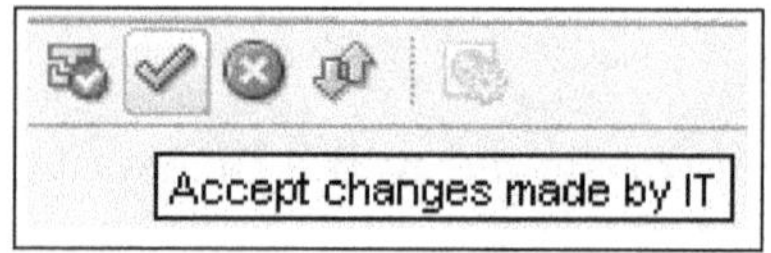

After taking a decision, the new model version is transformed into BPEL Blueprint and saved to the BPA Repository.

Summary

In this chapter, we discussed BPMN-BPEL round-tripping with Oracle BPA Suite and Oracle SOA Suite. First, we explained the architecture and features of Oracle BPA Suite. We learned that round-tripping is very important for eliminating the semantic gap between IT and process models. We have also discussed how various constructs map between BPMN and BPEL.

We have shown how to model business processes using Oracle Business Process Architect and how to translate those models to BPEL Blueprints. We also demonstrated how to open BPEL Blueprints in JDeveloper and how to merge BPEL code with a new model version when changes occur. At the end, we showed how IT developers can propose improvements to a BPMN model using JDeveloper and how a business analyst can approve or decline those changes.

11
Integrating BPEL with BPMN using BPM Suite

In the previous chapter, we got familiar with how BPMN process models modeled with Oracle BPA Suite have to be converted into BPEL skeletal code before we can implement them and deploy to the runtime environment. This approach has some drawbacks, as the resulting BPEL code can sometimes be very hard to understand. Oracle SOA Suite 11*g* PS2 introduces an interesting new feature—BPMN 2.0 execution engine. BPMN 2.0 engine is provided by the **Oracle BPM** (**Business Process Management**) **Suite 11*g***, which is layered on top of the Oracle SOA Suite. Oracle BPM Suite provides full support for all stages of the business process development lifecycle, including business process modeling, process simulations, business process implementation, deployment, and execution. As BPMN processes can be directly implemented and deployed, there is no need to transform them to BPEL. The result is a much shorter and simplified development cycle. However, in order to be executable, BPMN models have to be modeled with much more detail. With Oracle BPM Suite, BPMN Process is a new type of service component in SOA Composite Editor. This means that we can use it together with other service components (BPEL Process, Human Task, Business Rule, Mediator, and Spring Context) inside a single SOA composite application.

In this chapter, we will get familiar with the Oracle BPM Suite 11*g*. First, we will look at the Oracle BPM Suite architecture and features. Then we will demonstrate how to model and implement the BPMN business process using Oracle BPM Studio. The main focus of this chapter will be to show how both, BPMN and BPEL processes, can be used inside a single SOA composite application. We will demonstrate this on our TravelApproval process example. We will use a BPMN process for defining the top-level process flow, which will include human interaction and will invoke two BPEL processes: one for retrieving flight ticket offers and one for making the ticket reservation. Finally, we will deploy the composite and initiate a new instance to test the application and see the instance audit trail.

In general, BPMN processes are more appropriate for human-centric flows, while BPEL processes are well suited for automated service orchestrations.

In this chapter, we will discuss the following:

- Oracle BPM Suite architecture and features
- Modeling and implementing business processes using BPM Studio
- Integrating BPEL with BPMN inside a single composite application
- Deploying and testing BPMN processes

Oracle BPM Suite architecture and features

Oracle BPM Suite provides a unified environment for designing, implementing, executing, and monitoring processes. It provides full support for the **Business Process Modeling Notation** (**BPMN**) version 2.0. High-level architecture of BPM Suite is shown in the following figure:

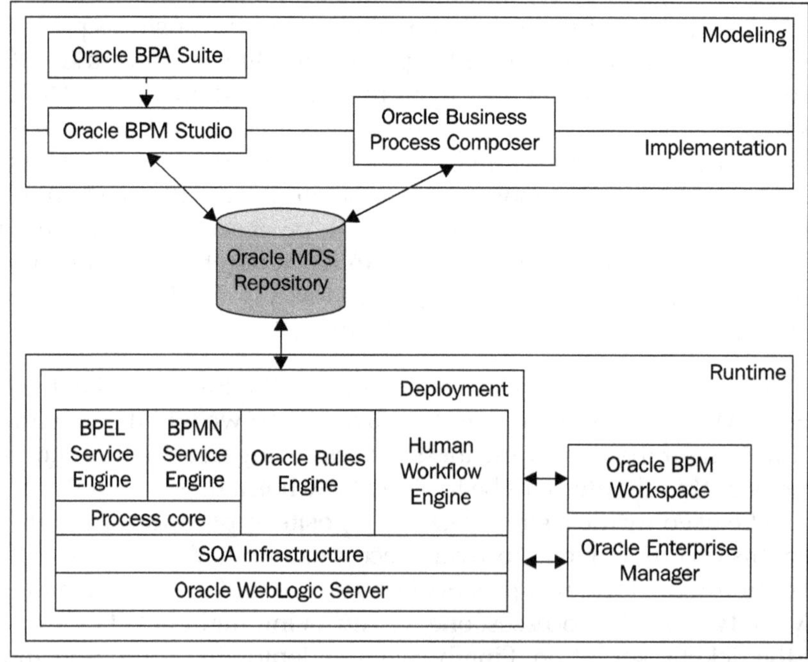

The first stage of every business process lifecycle is process modeling. Business analysts can model business processes using one of the following tools:

- Oracle BPM Studio runs in JDeveloper and provides a user-friendly environment for business process modeling and implementation. Business analysts can use a BPM role, which enables them to use a simplified version of JDeveloper by hiding all unnecessary technical functionality. Using BPM Studio, they can also perform process simulations.
- Oracle Business Process Composer is a web-based application for business analysts. They can model business processes and save the projects to the common metadata repository (MDS). They can also create projects based on predefined project templates, edit them, and deploy them directly to runtime. Using Business Process Composer, business analysts can also edit Oracle Business Rules at runtime.
- Oracle BPA Suite has been already presented in the previous chapter. Oracle BPM suite enables us to import business process models from Oracle BPA Suite and implement them using Oracle BPM Studio.

Before a business analyst can start with process modeling, they have to create a new Oracle BPM project. Projects are some sorts of containers for business processes and related data. When the business analyst finishes with modeling, they save the project into the common MDS (Meta Data Service) repository, which enables collaboration between business analysts and developers. Using BPM Studio, process developers are able to connect to the repository and open the project to add implementation details. During implementation, developers can also use other components, such as Adapters, Business Rules, Human Tasks, BPEL Processes, and so on. Oracle BPM projects are deployed at runtime as SOA composite applications. The most important component of BPM runtime is the Oracle BPM Engine. Oracle BPM Engine provides support for BPMN and BPEL processes. The engine consists of three separate components: a BPMN service engine, a BPEL service engine, and a common process core. Oracle BPM Suite also uses product components provided by Oracle SOA Suite, including Business Rules, Human Workflow, and so on.

When an SOA composite application created using Oracle BPM is deployed, it can be managed and configured with the use of Oracle Enterprise Manager Console, which we already got familiar with in Chapter 4. Another important runtime web-application is Oracle BPM Workspace, which embeds a lot of task list functionality and enables human interaction with SOA composite applications created using Oracle BPM. Using Oracle BPM Workspace, users can act on tasks assigned to them, view process instances, and monitor business processes using the dashboard. Oracle BPM also enables collaboration by providing integration with Oracle Process Spaces, which is a collaborative workspace built on top of WebCenter Spaces.

Demonstration scenario

We will demonstrate the use of Oracle BPM Suite on our TravelApproval business process example. To be able to show how BPMN and BPEL processes can be used inside a single composite application, we will restructure the process into two levels. We will use a BPMN process for defining the high-level process flow, which will include human interaction and will invoke two BPEL processes: one for retrieving ticket offers and one for making the ticket reservation. Finally, we will deploy the composite application to the BPM runtime and test it.

Business Process Modeling and implementation in Oracle BPM Studio

To be able to create and deploy BPM projects, we first have to install the Oracle BPM Studio 11*g* extension for JDeveloper, which is an extension on top of the Oracle SOA Composite Editor JDeveloper extension. It can be accessed at `http://www.oracle.com/technology/products/jdev/101/update/fmw_products.xml`.

Creating a BPM application and project

Let us open the Oracle BPM Studio using the **Default role**, so that we will be able to model and implement the process at the same time.

We create a new application and select **BPM Application** for **Application Template**.

We can also create an SOA Application and add the BPM technology scope later.

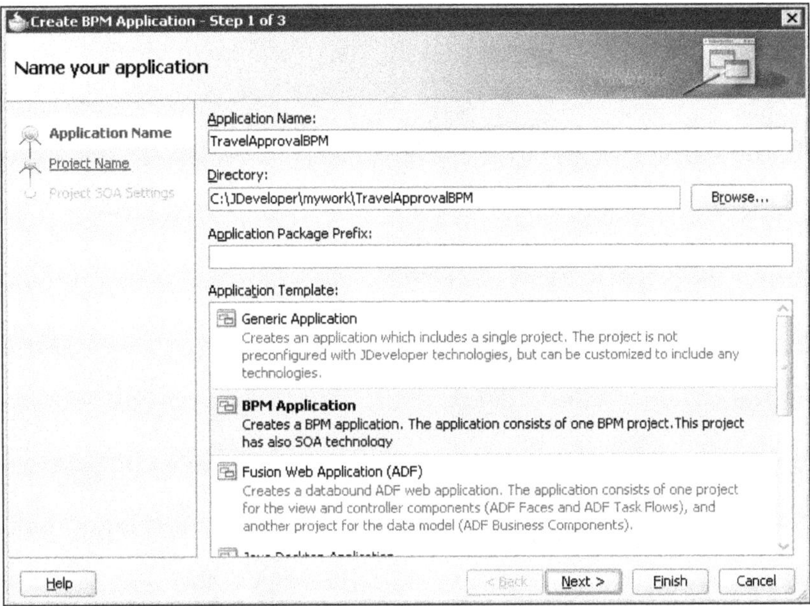

We click **Next**. On the next screen, we set the name of the project to `TravelApproval` and click **Next** again. On the **Configure SOA settings** screen, we select **Empty Composite** from the **Composite Template** list, as we want to show how to create a BPMN process using the SOA Composite Editor.

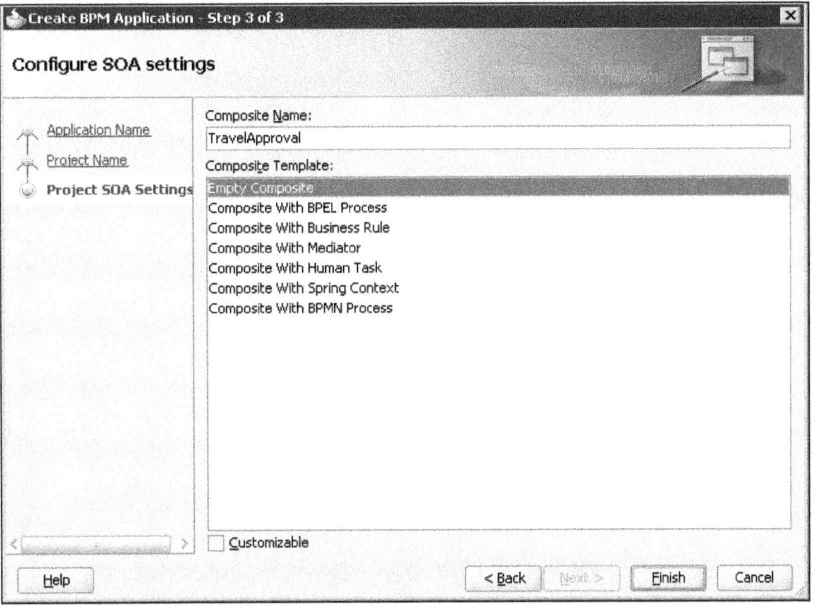

We click **Finish**. The SOA Composite Editor opens. If we look at the **Component Palette**, we can see the **BPMN Process** on the list of available service components.

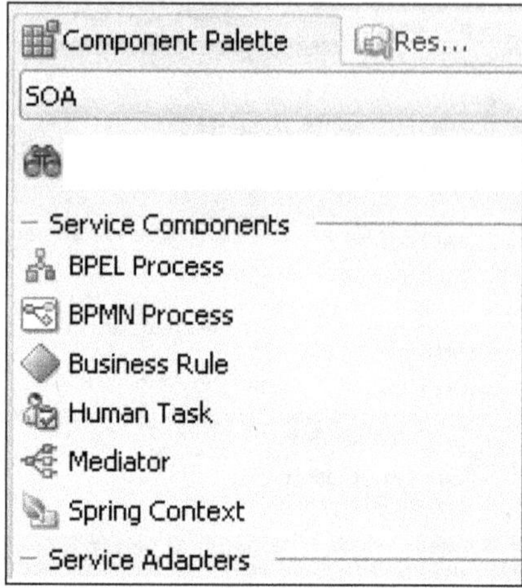

Creating a BPMN process

We drag-and-drop a **BPMN Process** service component from the **Component Palette** to the **Components** swim-lane of the composite diagram. The **Create BPMN Process** wizard opens.

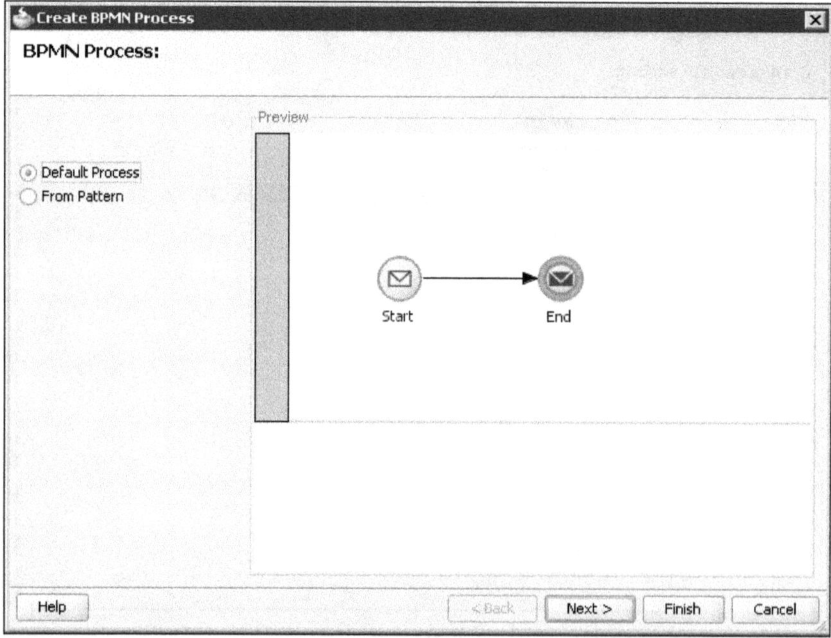

Here we have to select the process type. If we select **Default Process**, a BPMN process with a message start and end event is created. The process is also exposed as a service and can be invoked from other service components inside the same composite and from other composite applications. The exposed service is asynchronous, meaning that it defines two port types (interfaces): the request port type is used by the client to invoke the composite and the callback port type is used by the composite to perform the callback to the client. If we click on the **From Pattern**, we can choose between **Manual Process**, **Asynchronous Process**, and **Synchronous Process**. Manual process is a special type of process that requires human interaction. It starts and ends with one start and end event and is not exposed as a service; however, it can be invoked from other BPMN processes inside the same composite.

We select **Default Process** and click **Next**. On the next screen, we set the process name to `TravelApproval`. We can also enter a process description and an author here.

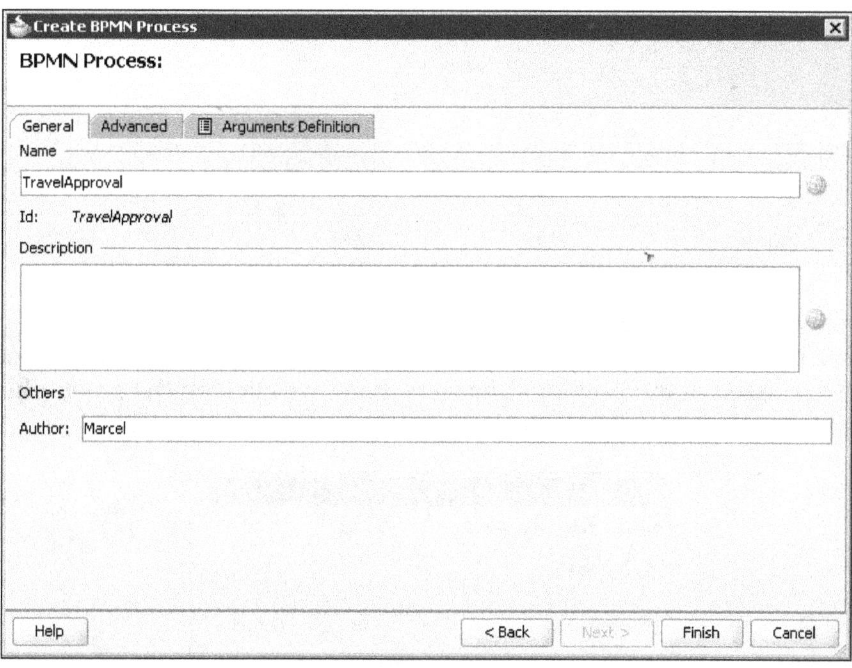

Then we click on the **Advanced** tab. Here we can set process sampling points and the namespace. Process sampling points are used for collecting information about the performance of flow objects. The generated data is stored into BPM, pre-defined cubes, which enable advanced process analytics. Using BPM we can also define Business Indicators and send data to Oracle BAM. Process analysts can then view these metrics using Oracle BPM Workspace Dashboards or Oracle BAM. We discussed Oracle BAM in Chapter 8.

We leave the **Inherit project default** option selected. We set the namespace of the BPMN process to `http://packtpub.com/bpmn/travel/`.

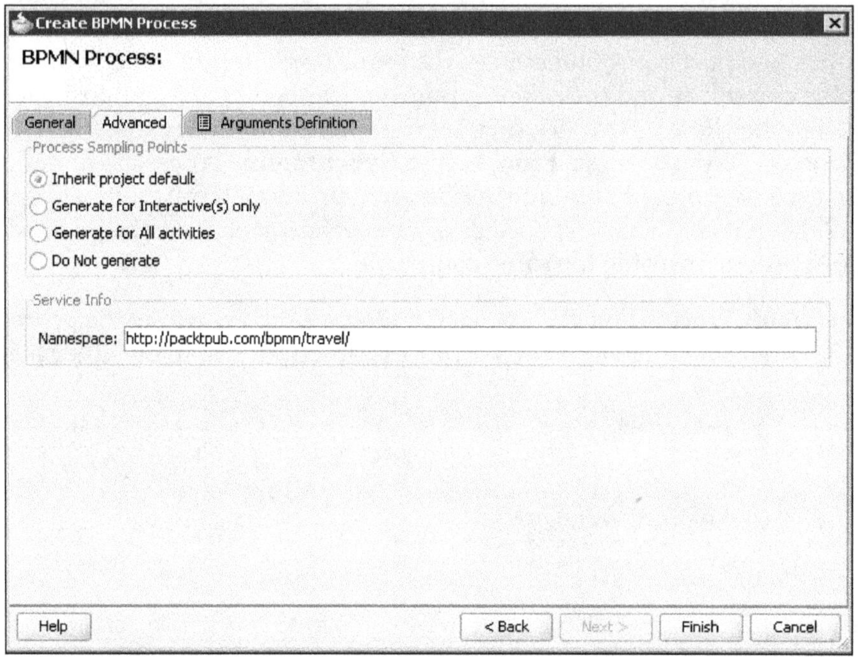

Then we click on the **Arguments Definition** tab to set the process input and output. We will use the same input and output as for the `TravelApproval` BPEL processes, which we discussed in the previous chapters. First, we click on the green plus icon to add an input argument. We name the argument `TravelRequest`.

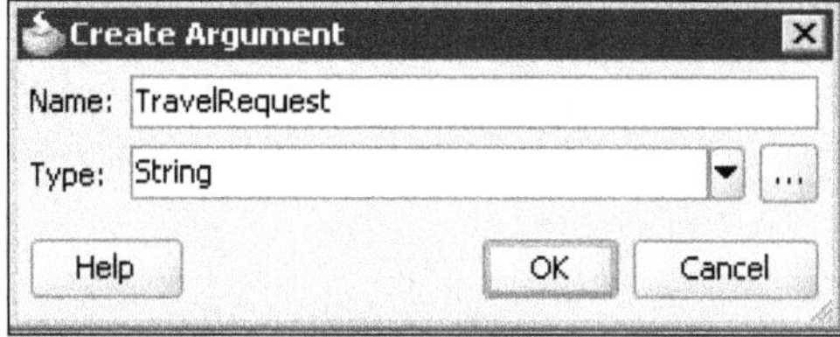

As the argument will be of complex type, we click on the three dots icon to open the **Browse Types** dialog. From the **Type** drop-down, we select **<Component>**.

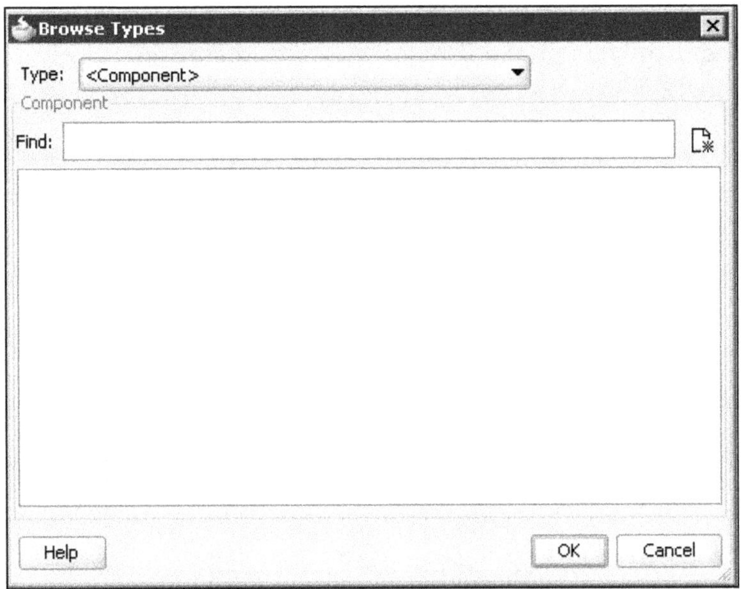

Then we click on the **New** icon next to the **Find** search field. The **Create Business Object** dialog opens, as shown in the following screenshot. We name the business object `TravelRequest`.

We also have to set the **Destination Module** in the catalog. We click on the magnifying glass icon to open the **Browse Modules** dialog. We create a new module and name it **Data**.

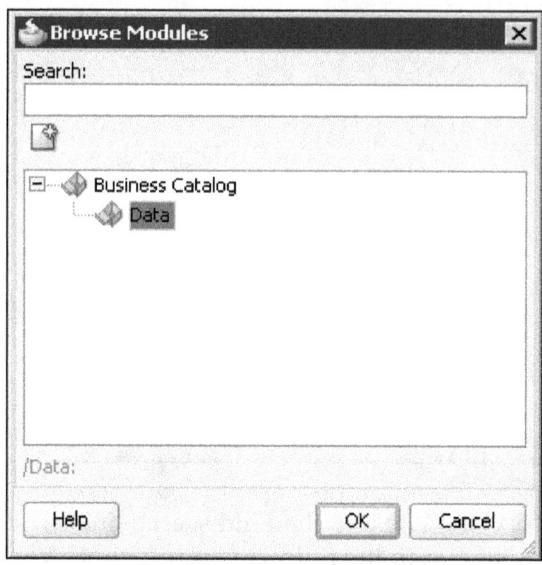

We click **OK** to close the dialog. As our new business object will be based on an XML Schema, we check the **Based on External Schema** checkbox and click on the magnifying glass icon on the right. We import the schema using the **Type Chooser** and select the type or element we want to use. The **Create Business Object** dialog now looks like shown on the following screenshot:

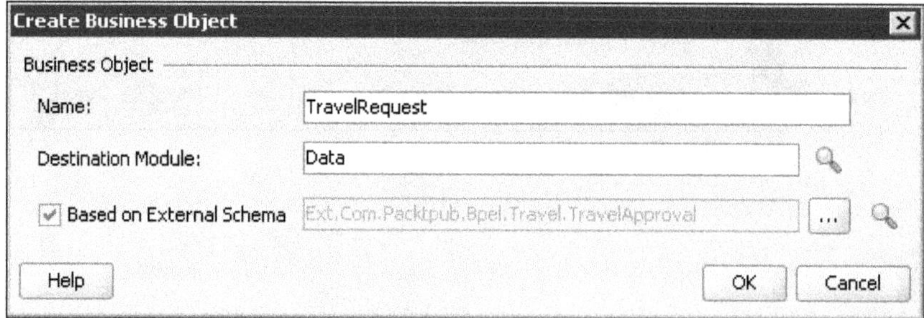

We click **OK**. Back in the **Browse Types** dialog, we select `TravelRequest` business object and click **OK**.

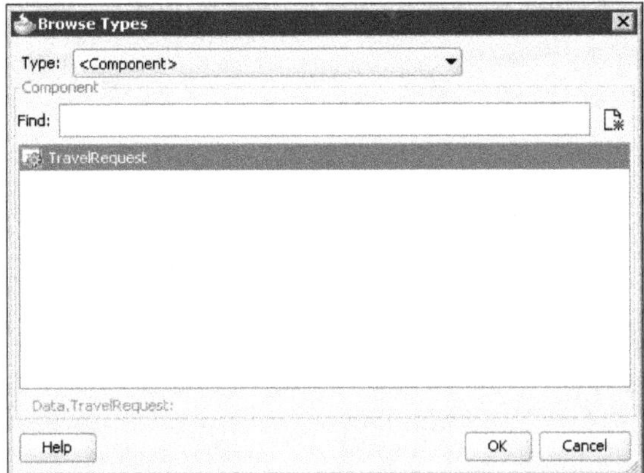

The **Create Argument** dialog now looks as shown on the following screenshot:

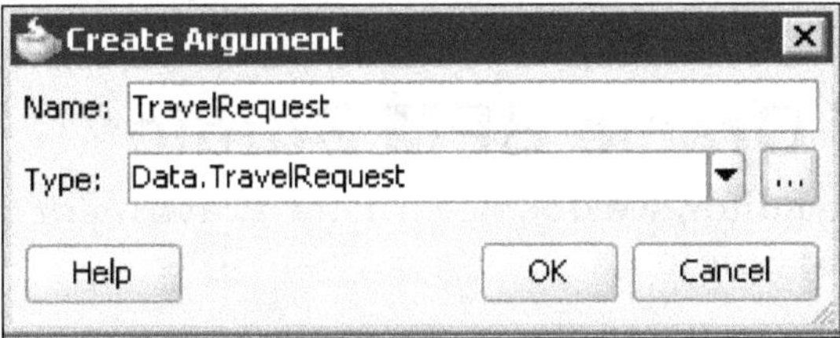

We click **OK** to return to the **Arguments Definition** tab of the **Create BPMN Process** wizard.

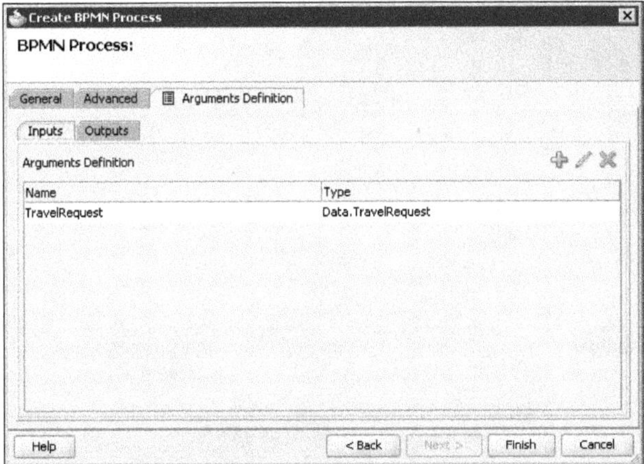

In the same way, we also set the process output and click **Finish**. Our composite application opened in SOA Composite Editor now looks like this:

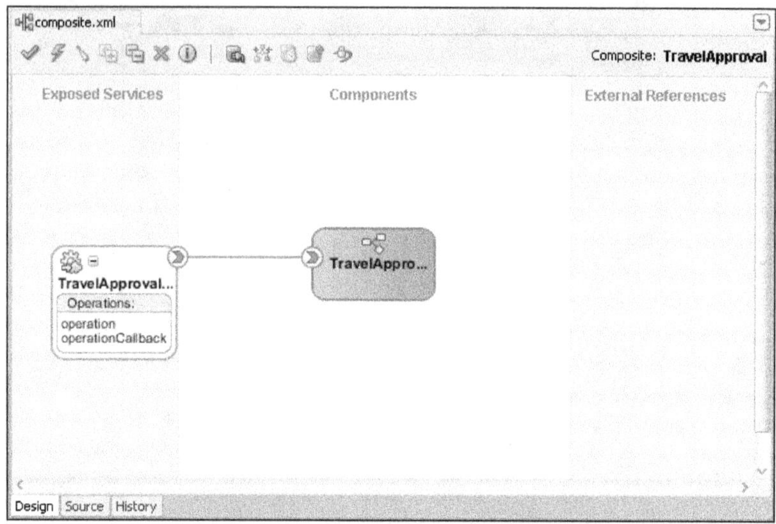

Overview of Oracle BPM Studio

In the SOA Composite Editor, we double-click the `TravelApproval` BPMN process to open the Oracle BPM Studio.

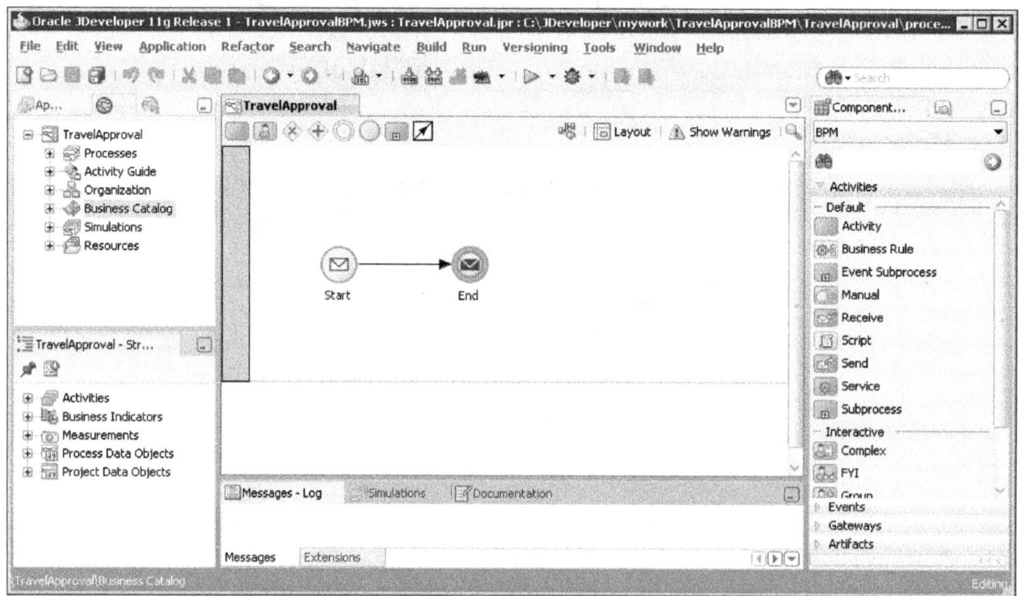

In the middle of the screen, we can see the BPMN Process Editor, which enables us to model business processes by dragging and dropping BPMN components (called flow objects) from the **Component Palette**. If we look at the **Component Palette** on the right-hand side, we can see the list of supported BPMN flow objects. Flow objects are divided into four groups: **Activities**, **Events**, **Gateways**, and **Artifacts**.

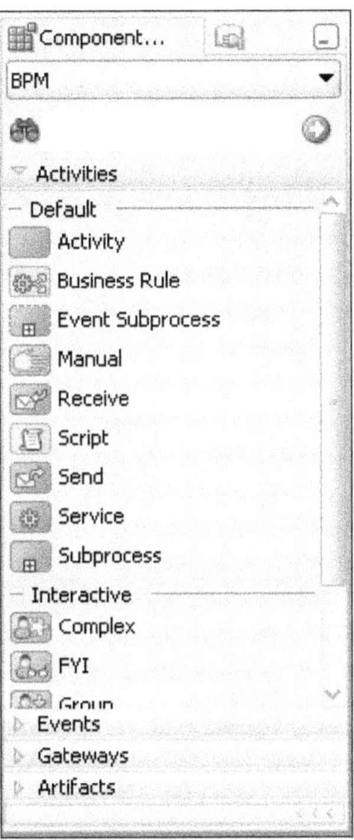

In the upper-left corner, we can see Oracle BPM Project Navigator, which shows the hierarchical content of the BPM project.

The **Processes** component contains all BPMN and BPEL processes inside the project. **Activity Guide** contains information about defined milestones for the project. **Organization** contains organizational elements, such as Roles, Organizational chart, Holidays, and Calendar. **Business Catalog** is a repository for storing components we use to implement a BPMN process, such as Errors, Events, Human Tasks, Business Rules, Business Objects, Business Exceptions, and so on. Business Catalog is organized using modules. It provides the following predefined modules: Errors, Events, HumanTasks, References, BusinessRules, Services, and Types. Predefined modules cannot be removed or renamed, because the components stored in them are dynamically generated, based on the SOA composite. These components are also called synthesized components. However, we are able to create custom modules. Modules can be also nested, which allows us to create a hierarchical structure. Organizing components using modules significantly improves the readability of the project and it makes it easier to locate a specific component. The **Simulations** component contains simulation models.

Oracle BPM MDS Browser allows us to access projects and project templates stored in the Oracle BPM MDS Repository. We can check out, lock, export, and delete projects.

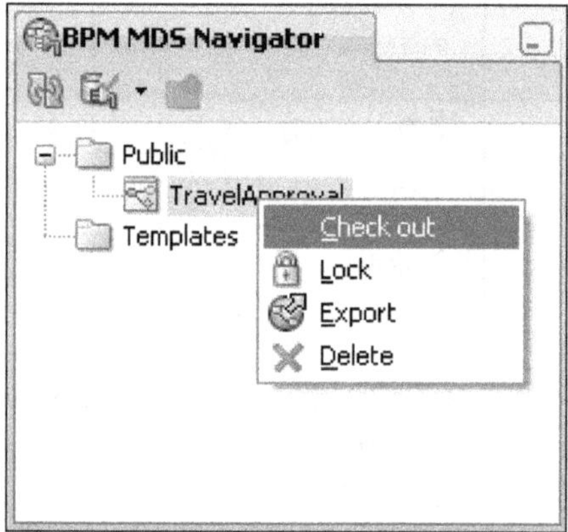

The **Structure** window displays a structural view of the components selected in the BPM Project or Application Navigator. Using the Structure window, we can edit process properties, create data objects, create simulations, convert BPMN process to BPEL, and so on.

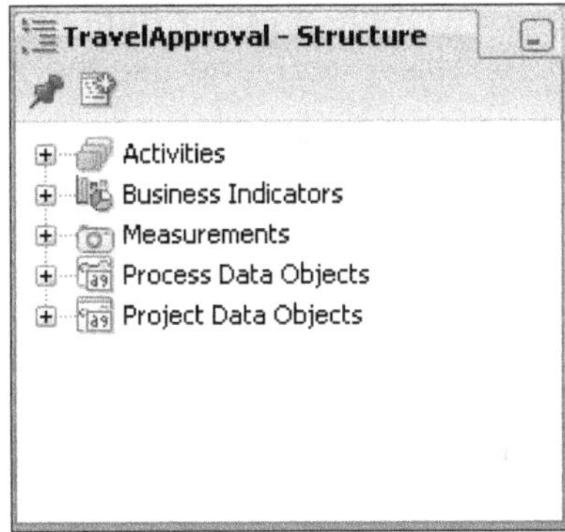

Implementing a BPMN process

Now we will demonstrate how to implement a simple BPMN business process using Oracle BPM Studio. First, we will create a variable (data object) which will store information about the received travel request.

Creating data objects

Oracle BPM supports two types of data objects: process data objects and project data objects. The difference between the two is that the scope of a process data object is limited to the process within which it is defined. On the other hand, the definition of project data object is shared across all processes within the same project (actual values of data objects may be different for every instance). The main benefit of using project data objects is that when changing the definition of the data object, we do not have to make those changes in all the processes that define the same data object. In our simple example, we will use only process data objects. We right-click on the **Process Data Objects** in the **Structure** window and select **New**. We name the data object `travelRequest` and use the previously created `TravelRequest` business object for the data type.

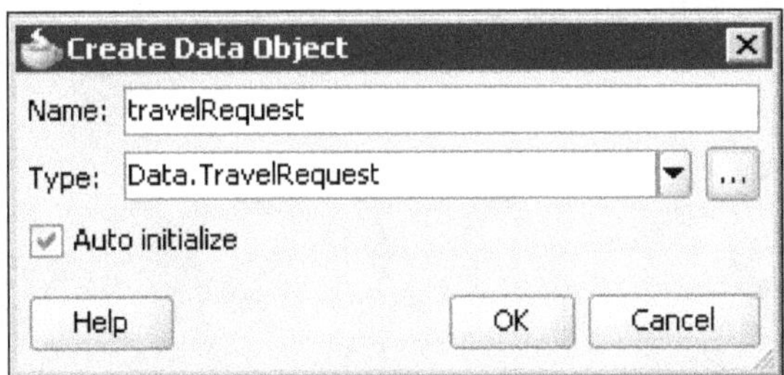

We click **OK**. In the same way, we create another data object for storing the result of the process. We name it `travelResponse` and use the `TravelResponse` business object for the data type.

Configuring start and end events

We double-click the start event. On the **Basic** tab, we change the name of the event to `Receive travel request`. Then we click on the **Implementation** tab.

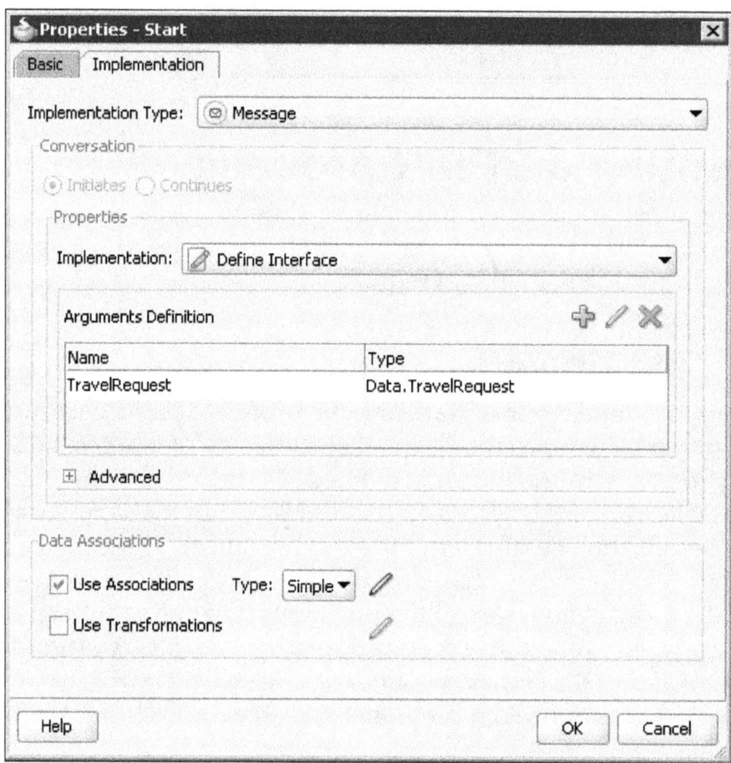

Here we have to configure the mapping between the received input and the `travelRequest` data object, which will be used throughout the process. Remember that in BPEL, we have to use **Assign** and **Transform** activities to define the mapping. In BPMN processes, this can be easily done using **Data Associations**. We can use data associations to define the input and output from a flow object to an external service or process. To define expressions, we use the **Data Association Editor**. To open the **Data Association Editor**, we select the **Use Associations** checkbox and then click on the edit icon on the right. Here we can simply drag-and-drop the `travelRequest` data object from the data objects list on the right-hand side to the **Outputs** field, as shown in the following screenshot:

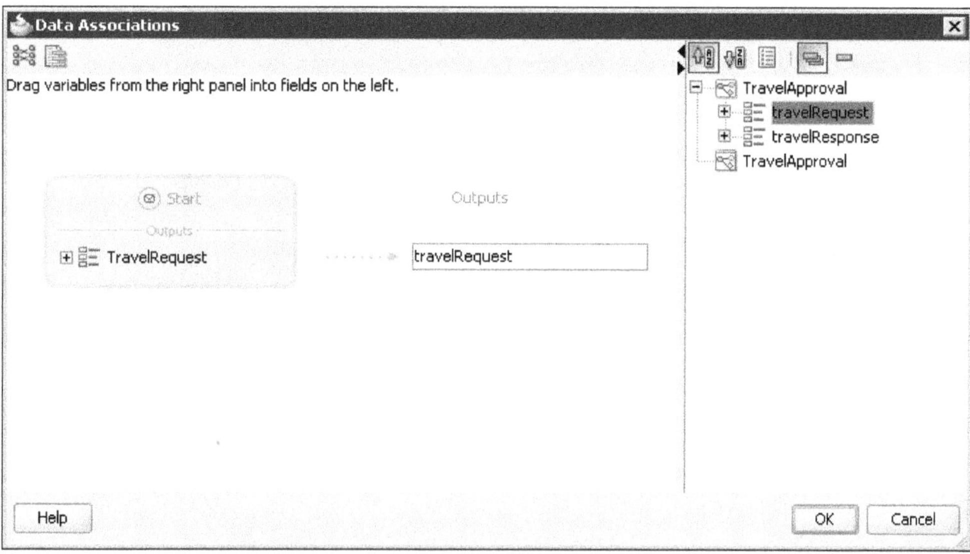

We click **OK** to close the **Data Associations** editor. In a similar way, we configure the end event. However, this time we have to map the data from the `travelRequest` data object to the process output.

Invoking synchronous service

The next step in the process requires invoking the `EmployeeTravelStatus` service to retrieve the employee travel class. Synchronous service can be invoked with the use of the **Service** task. However, before we are able to invoke an external service, we have to add it to the business catalog as a reference. To do that, we have to open SOA Composite Editor and add a reference binding component on the composite diagram. We drag-and-drop a **Web Service** from the **Component Palette** to the **External References** swim-lane. In the **Create Web Service** dialog, we name the reference `EmployeeTravelStatus`, enter WSDL URL, and select Port Type. Then we click **OK**. In the **Customize Adapter Settings** dialog, we click **Cancel**. Our SOA composite application now looks as shown in the following screenshot:

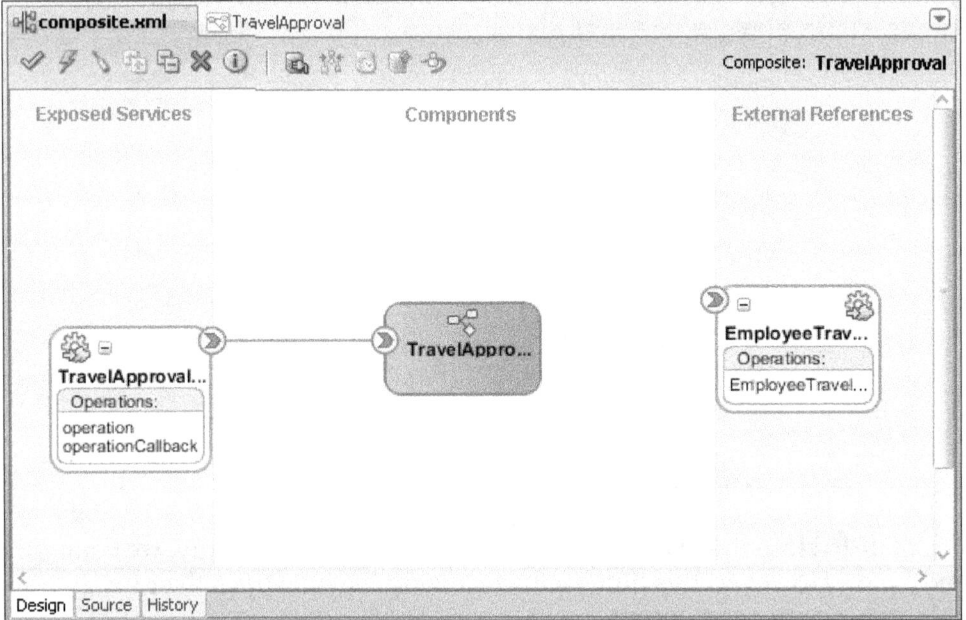

We cannot wire a BPMN process with other binding or service components using the SOA Composite Editor. However, when we add a new component, it is automatically available in the business catalog. The wire on the composite diagram is automatically added when we configure the BPMN flow object for invoking the component.

We double-click the `TravelApproval` BPMN process to open the Oracle BPM Studio. We drag-and-drop the **Service** flow object from the **Component Palette** to the process. The **Properties - Service Task** dialog opens. On the **Basic** tab, we set the name to `Retrieve employee travel class`. Then we open the **Implementation** tab. From the **Implementation** drop-down, we select **Service Call**. Then we click on the magnifying glass icon next to the **Name** field. In the **Type** dialog, we select `EmployeeTravelStatus` and click **OK**.

Now we have to define input and output for the service call. We select the **Use Associations** checkbox and click on the edit icon. In the **Data Associations** editor, we first set the input by dragging and dropping `employee` from the `travelRequest` data object to the **Inputs** field. Before setting the output, we have to create an appropriate data object for storing the returned travel class data. This can be done by simply right-clicking the `TravelApproval` process on the right and selecting **Add**.

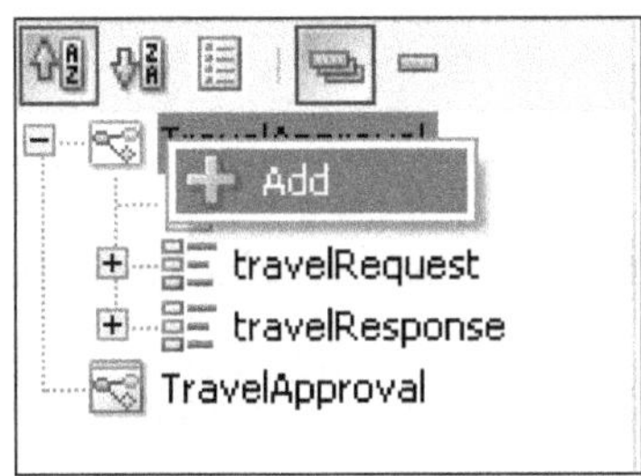

In the **Create Data Object** dialog, we name the data object `travelClass` and set the type to `TravelClass`.

The `TravelClass` business object has been automatically added to the catalog when we created the `EmployeeTravelStatus` reference binding component.

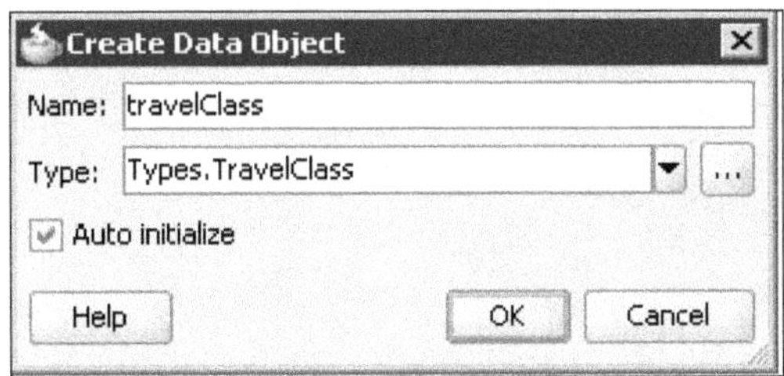

We click **OK** to close the dialog. Now we can drag-and-drop the `travelClass` data object to the **Outputs** field, as shown in the following screenshot:

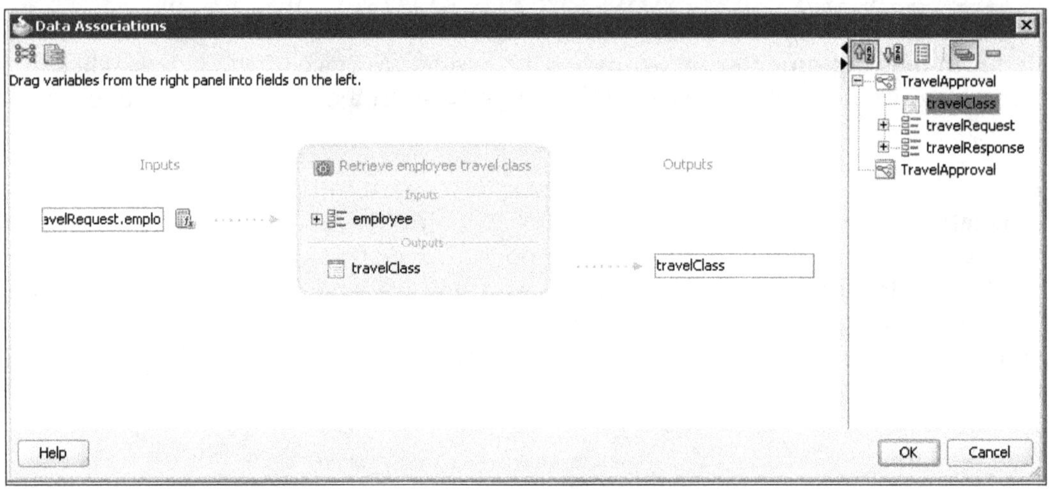

We click **OK** to return to the **Properties - ServiceTask** dialog.

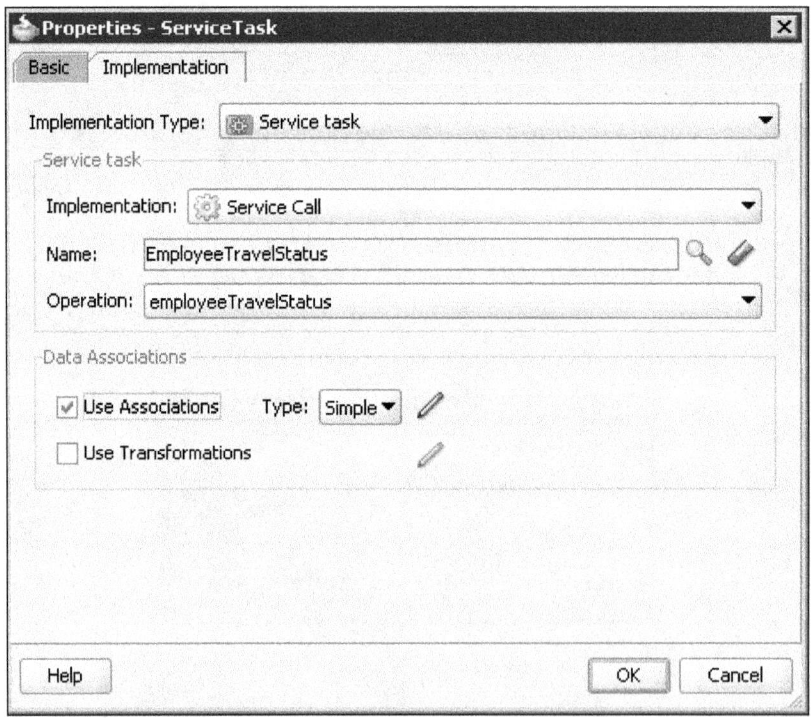

We click **OK** again to return to the BPMN process.

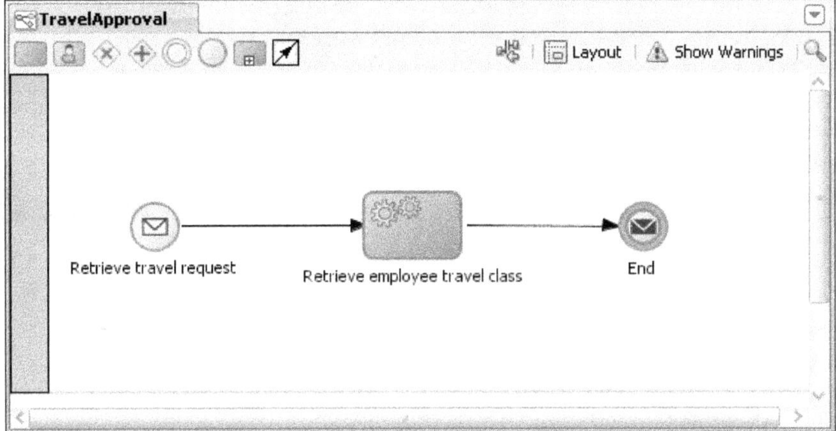

If we open the SOA Composite Editor, we can see that the wire between the `TravelApproval` BPMN process and `EmployeeTravelStatus` reference has been added automatically.

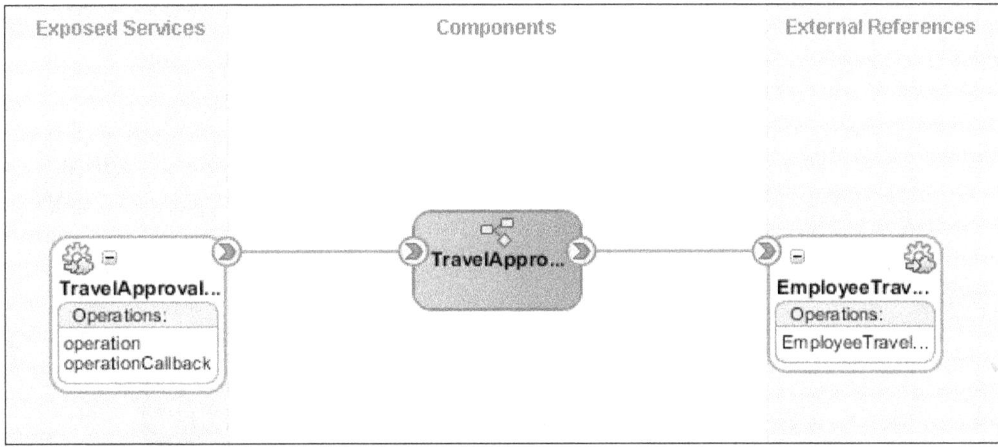

We save the project.

Adding the first BPEL process

Now we will create a BPEL process, which will be used for retrieving flight ticket offers. The process will also compare the offers and return data about the selected flight ticket and the selected airline. We open the SOA Composite Editor and drag-and-drop the **BPEL Process** service component to the **Components** swim-lane of the composite diagram. The **Create BPEL Process** dialog opens.

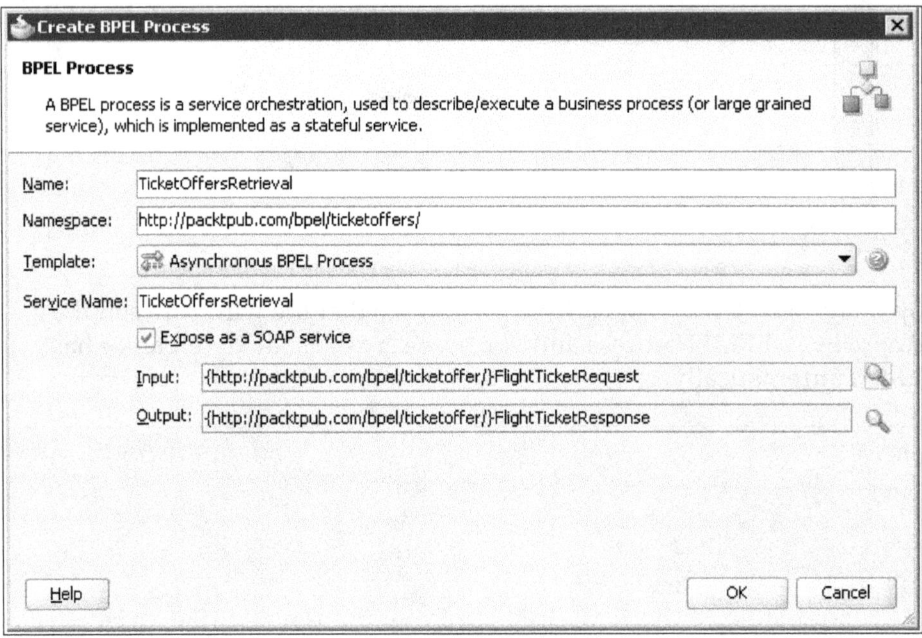

We set the name the process name to `TicketOffersRetrieval` and the namespace to `http://packtpub.com/bpel/ticketoffers/`.

A BPEL process has to be exposed as a service to be able to invoke it from a BPMN process.

We also set the process input and output. The process input is defined by the `FlightTicketRequestType`, which contains data about the desired flight and the employee travel class:

```
<xsd:schema xmlns:xsd="http://www.w3.org/2001/XMLSchema"
            targetNamespace="http://packtpub.com/bpel/ticketoffer/"
            xmlns:tns=" http://packtpub.com/bpel/ticketoffer/"
            xmlns:emp="http://packtpub.com/service/employee/"
            xmlns:aln="http://packtpub.com/service/airline/"
            elementFormDefault="qualified">
...

  <xsd:complexType name="FlightTicketRequestType">
    <xsd:sequence>
      <xsd:element name="flightData" type="aln:FlightRequestType"/>
      <xsd:element name="travelClass" type="emp:TravelClassType"/>
    </xsd:sequence>
  </xsd:complexType>
</xsd:schema>
```

The process output is defined by the `FlightTicketResponseType`, which contains data about the selected flight ticket and the airline:

```
<xsd:schema xmlns:xsd="http://www.w3.org/2001/XMLSchema"
            targetNamespace="http://packtpub.com/bpel/ticketoffer/"
            xmlns:tns=" http://packtpub.com/bpel/ticketoffer/"
            xmlns:aln="http://packtpub.com/service/airline/"
            elementFormDefault="qualified" >

...

<xsd:complexType name="FlightTicketResponseType">
    <xsd:sequence>
      <xsd:element name="flightData" type="aln:FlightConfirmationType
      "/>
      <xsd:element name="airline" type="xsd:string"/>
    </xsd:sequence>
  </xsd:complexType>
</xsd:schema>
```

Then we add references for two airline services and wire them with the BPEL process, as shown next.

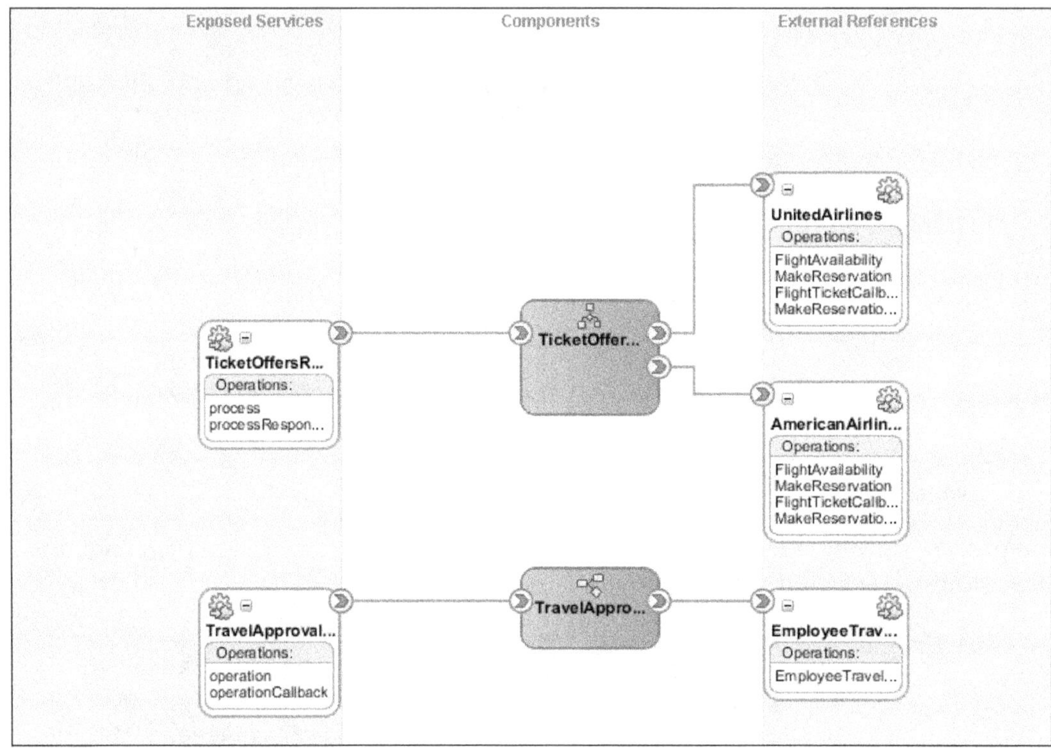

In this chapter, we will not explain how to implement the BPEL process. The following screenshot shows the implemented BPEL process.

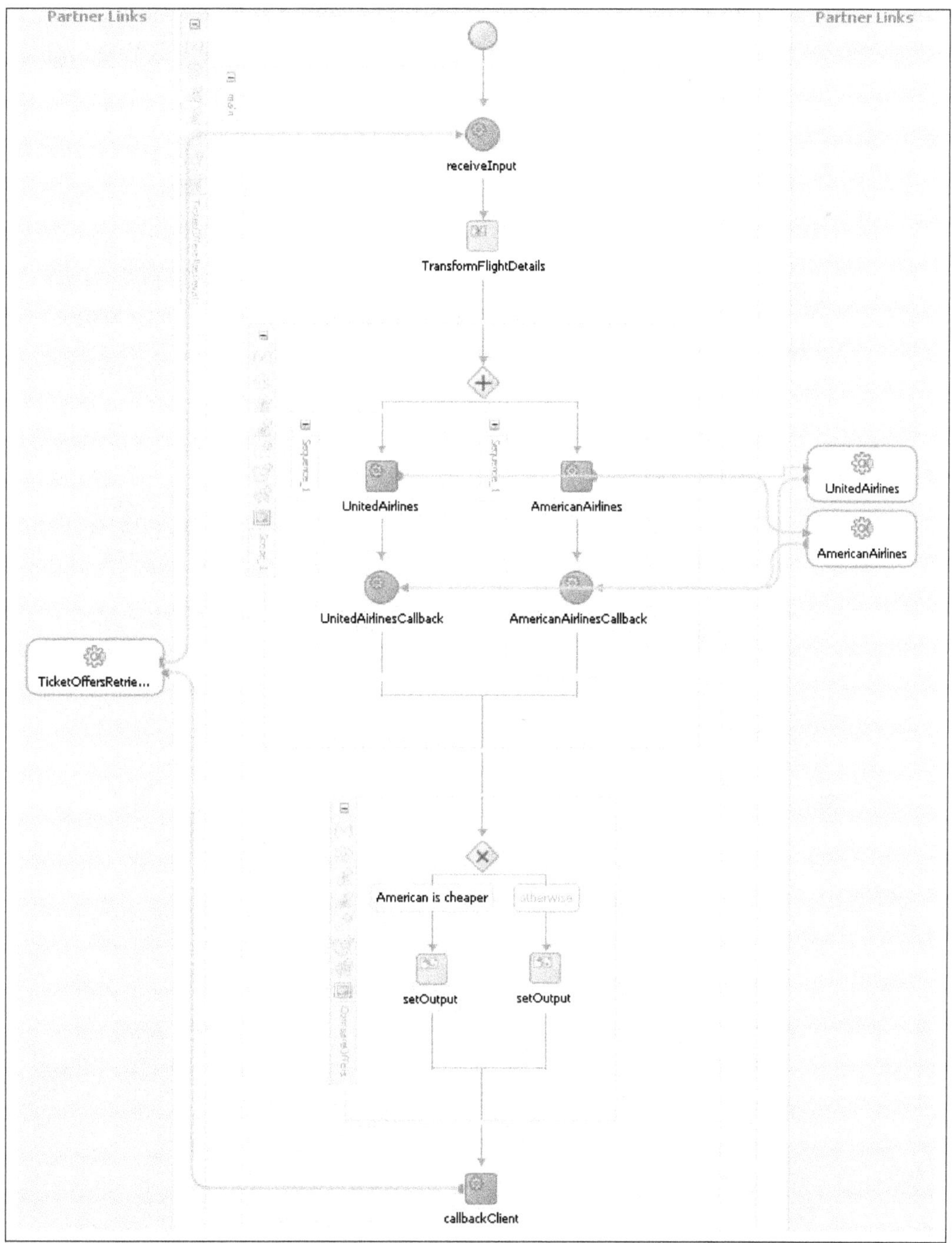

Invoking a BPEL process from BPMN

We open Oracle BPM Studio again. As the BPEL process is asynchronous, we need two flow objects to be able to invoke it (the first for invoking the process and the second for receiving the response). In general, we have two options when invoking asynchronous services or processes:

- We can use a **Message Throw** event to invoke the process or service and a **Message Catch** event to receive an asynchronous response
- We can use **Send Task** to invoke the process or service and **Receive Task** to receive an asynchronous response

Both approaches perform similar functionalities. However, we cannot use the message throw event to invoke a BPMN process that is initiated with a message receive task. Similarly, we cannot use the send task to invoke a BPMN process that is initiated with a message start event. When invoking an asynchronous BPEL process we can use both presented approaches. In our example, we will use the latter approach. First, we drag-and-drop a **Send Task** flow object to the process. The **Properties-SendTask** dialog opens. On the **Basic** tab, we set the name of the object to `Retrieve offers`. Then we open the **Implementation** tab. We select **Service Call** from the **Implementation** drop-down list and select the `TicketOffersRetrieval` BPEL process.

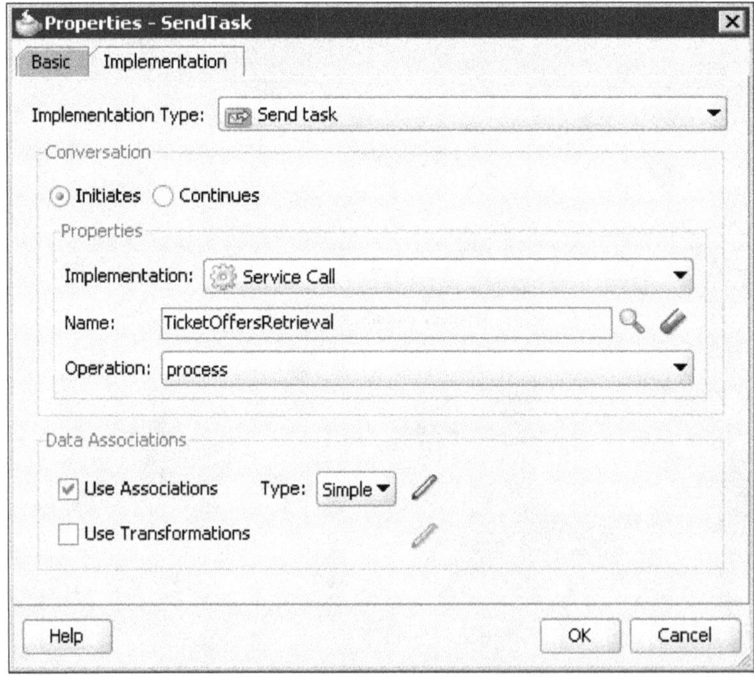

We also configure data associations.

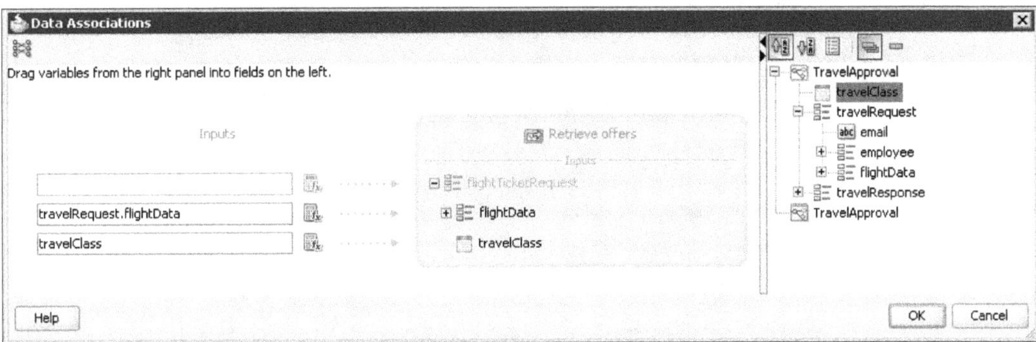

We click **OK** to close the close both dialogs.

Next, we drag-and-drop a **Receive Task** flow object and place it just after the **Send Task.** We name the object `Retrieve offers callback`. On the **Implementation** tab, we select **Continues** for the conversation type, and select `Retrieve offers` from the **Initiator Node** drop-down list. We also configure data associations. In the **Data Associations** dialog, we have to create a new data object to store the result from the BPEL process. We set the name of the new data object to `selectedTicket` and the type to `FlightTicketResponseType`.

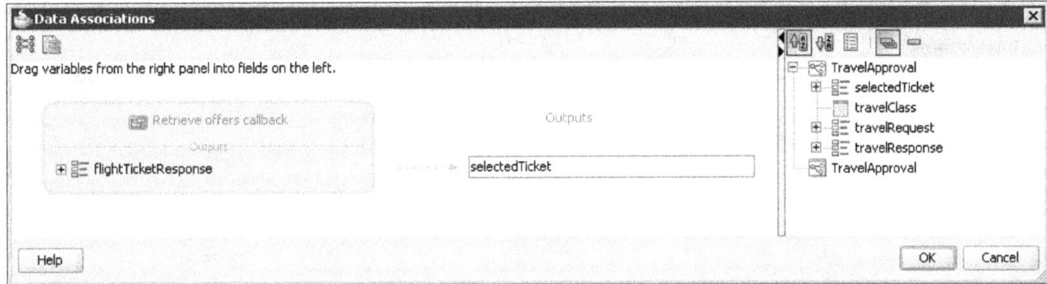

We click **OK**. The new **Receive Task** flow object is now configured as shown next.

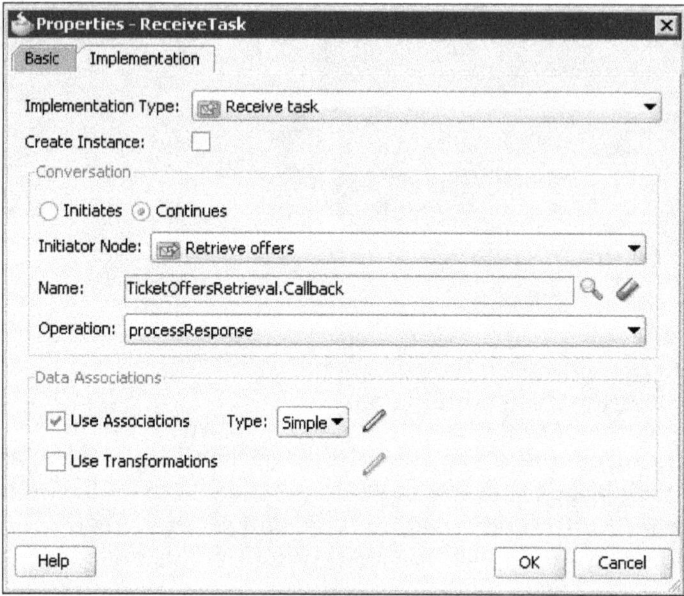

We click **OK** to close the dialog. Our `TravelApproval` BPMN process now looks like this:

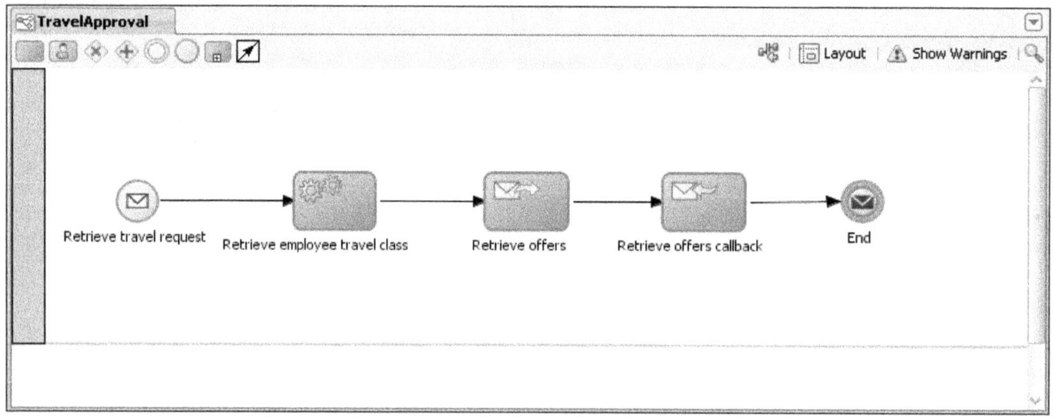

If we open the SOA Composite Editor, we can see that a wire between the `TravelApproval` BPMN process and the `TicketOffersRetrieval` BPEL process has been added automatically.

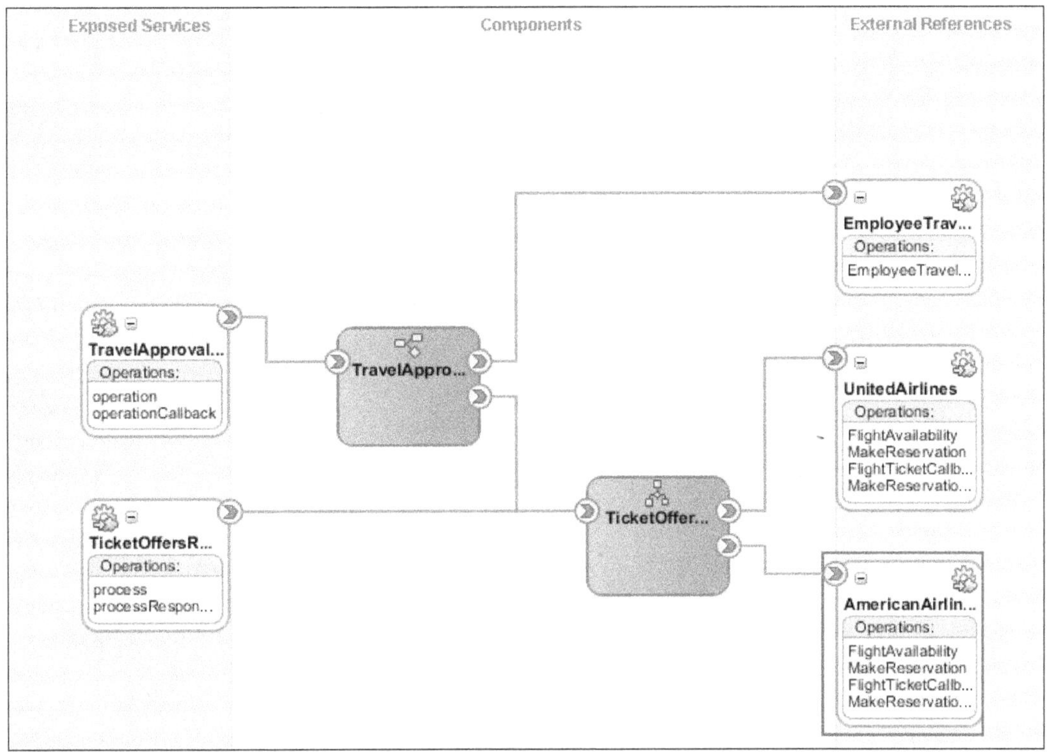

Adding a human task

The next step in the `TravelApproval` process requires human intervention, as the Approval Manager has to approve or reject the selected flight ticket. When creating human tasks in BPM project, we can follow two approaches:

- We can create a human task using the SOA Human Task Editor
- We can use the simplified interface that Oracle BPM provides

We will demonstrate the latter approach. We open Oracle BPM Studio and drag-and-drop a **User** interactive flow object from the **Component Palette** to the process diagram.

Oracle BPM Suite enables us to use interactive activities, which are shortcuts to different workflow patterns supported by the Oracle Human Workflow.

The **Properties - UserTask** dialog opens. On the **Basic** tab, we set the name of the object to `Flight ticket approval`. Then we open the **Implementation** tab.

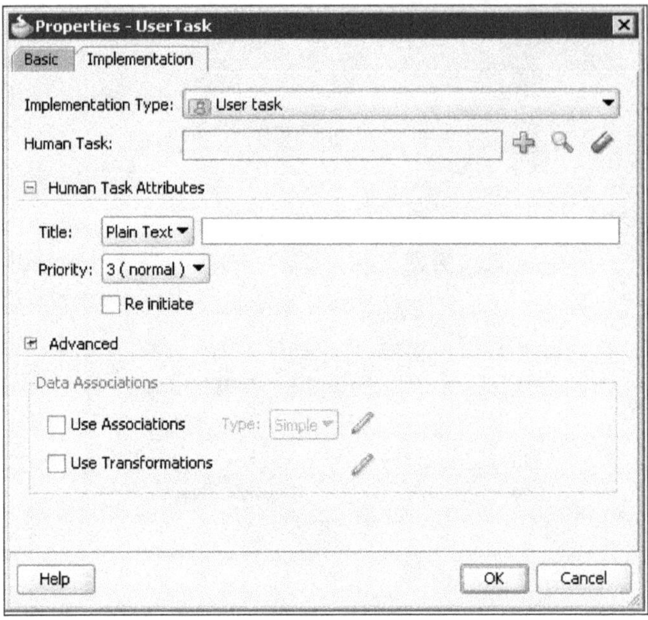

We click on the green plus icon to create a new human task definition. The **Create Human Task** dialog opens. This is a simplified version of the SOA Human Task Editor that we are already familiar with.

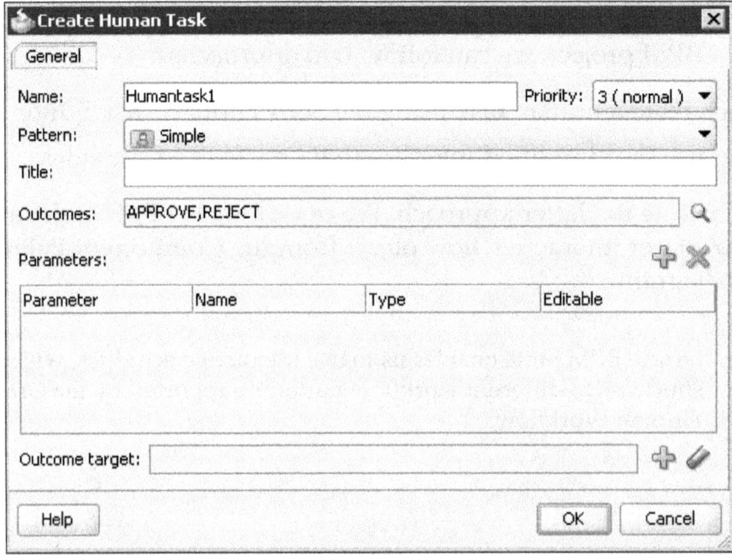

We name the human task `FlightTicketApproval`. We use the default workflow pattern. Then we set the title to `Flight ticket approval`. The title will be displayed in the Oracle BPM Workspace during runtime. We accept the default outcomes (`APPROVE` and `REJECT`). Next, we have to set human task parameters. To add a parameter, we click on the green plus icon. The **Data Objects** window appears on the right side. We simply drag-and-drop the `selectedTicket` data object to the **Parameters** list on the left. Now we have to create a data object to store the human task outcome. We right-click the `TravelApproval` process in the **Data Objects** window and select **Add**. We name the data object `taskOutcome` and select **String** from the **Type** drop-down menu. Then we drag-and-drop the new data object to the **Outcome target** field. The `FlightTicketApproval` human task is now configured as shown in the following screenshot:

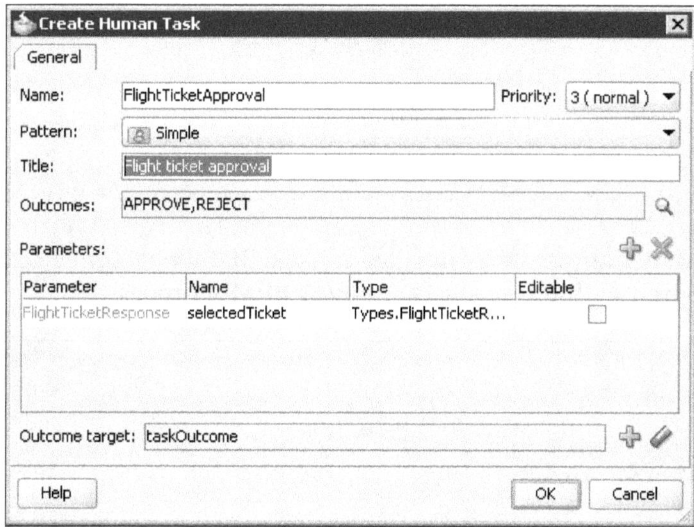

We click **OK** twice to close both dialogs. The **Role properties** dialog is displayed. We create a new logical role and name it **Approval Manager**.

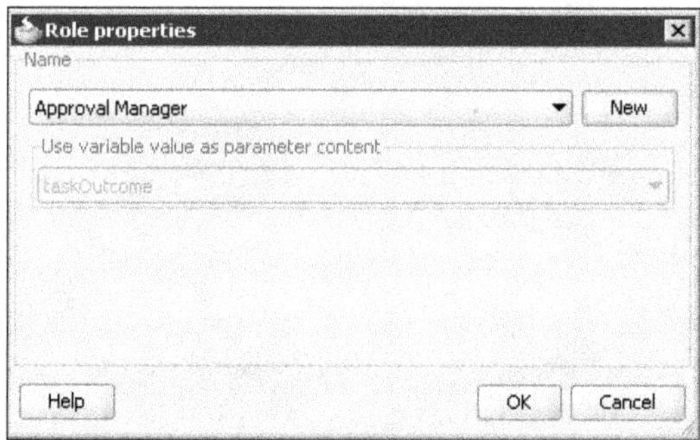

We use roles to model who is responsible for performing the human task. These roles are automatically mapped to the corresponding LDAP roles during runtime. We click **OK** to close the dialog. Notice that a swim-lane with a role name has been automatically created. Our `TravelApproval` BPMN process now looks like this:

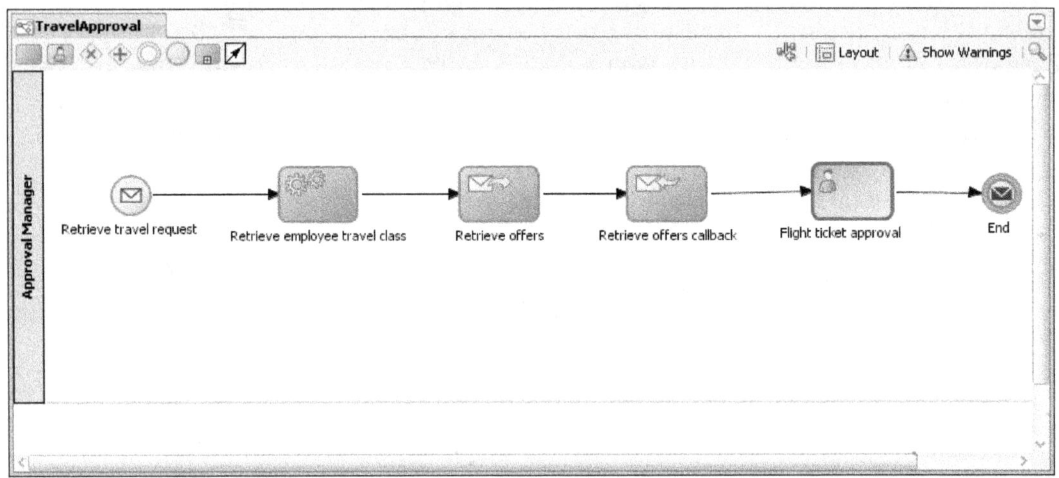

If we open the SOA Composite Editor, we can see that the `FlightTicketApproval` human task is wired with the `TravelApproval` BPMN process.

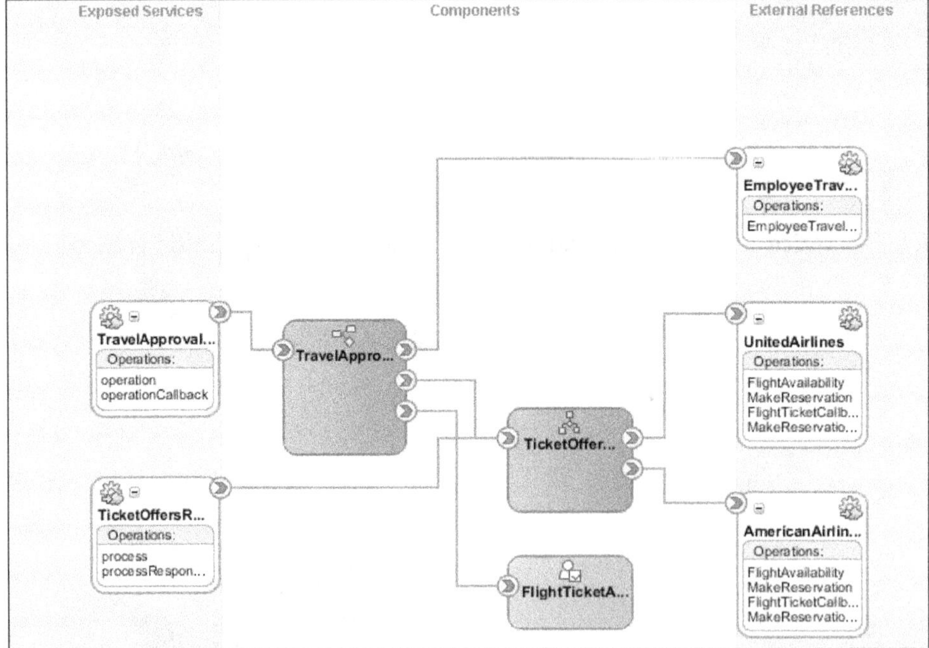

Now we double-click the `FlightTicketApproval` human task to open the SOA Human Task Editor. Then we click on the **Assignment** tab and edit the stage to assign the task to a static user `weblogic`.

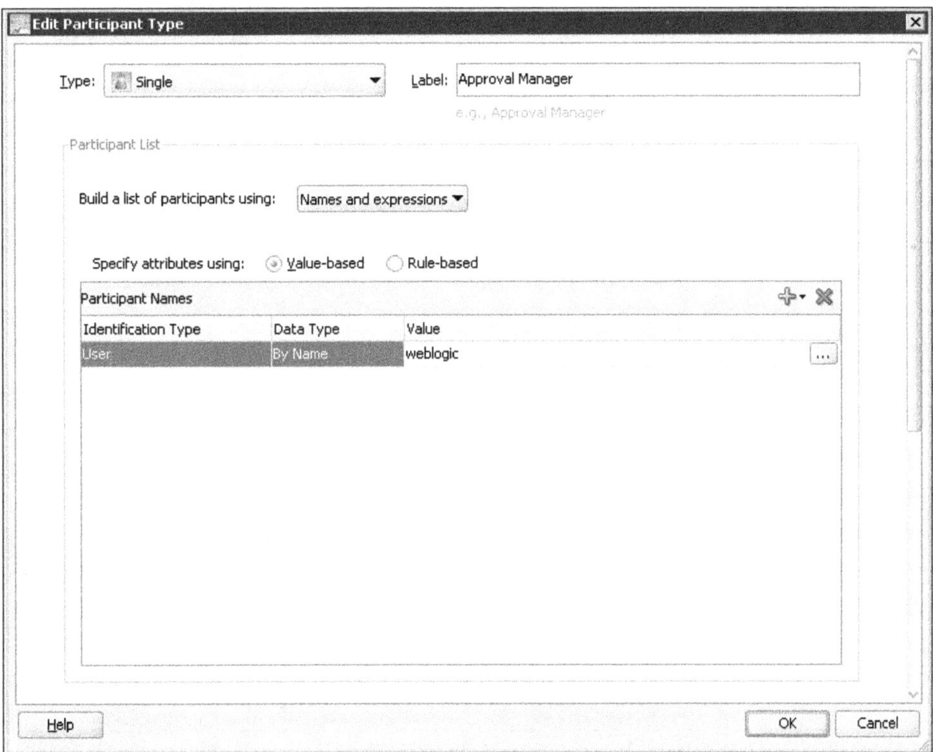

We click **OK** to close the dialog. We also close the SOA Human Task Editor and save the project.

Adding a second BPEL process

If the Approval Manager approves the selected flight ticket, the next step of the process is flight ticket reservation. For this, we will create another BPEL process. We open the SOA Composite Editor and drag-and-drop a **BPEL Process** service component to the **Components** swim-lane of the composite diagram. The **Create BPEL Process** dialog opens.

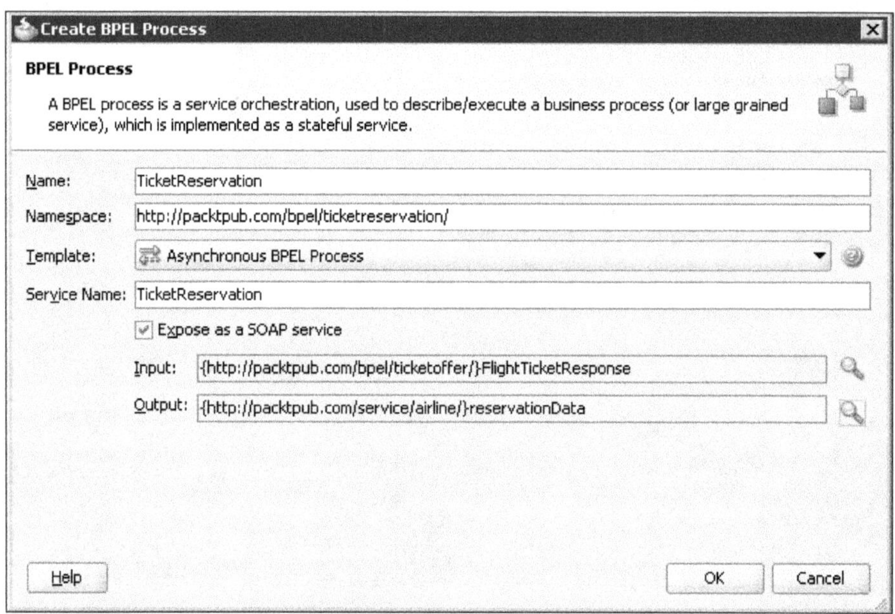

We set the process name to `TicketReservation` and the namespace to `http://packtpub.com/bpel/ticketreservation/`. We also set the process input and output. The process input is defined by the `FlightTicketResponseType`, which was used to define the result of the `TicketOffersRetrieval` BPEL process that we are already familiar with.

For the process output, we use the `FlightReservationType`, which contains data about the selected flight number:

```
<xsd:schema xmlns:xsd="http://www.w3.org/2001/XMLSchema"
            xmlns:tns="http://packtpub.com/service/airline/"
            targetNamespace="http://packtpub.com/service/airline/"
            elementFormDefault="qualified">

<xsd:complexType name="FlightReservationType">
    <xsd:sequence>
      <xsd:element name="FlightNo" type="xsd:string"/>
      <xsd:element name="Confirmed" type="xsd:boolean"/>
```

```
    </xsd:sequence>
  </xsd:complexType>
</xsd:schema>
```

Then we wire the new BPEL process with both airline services using the SOA Composite Editor.

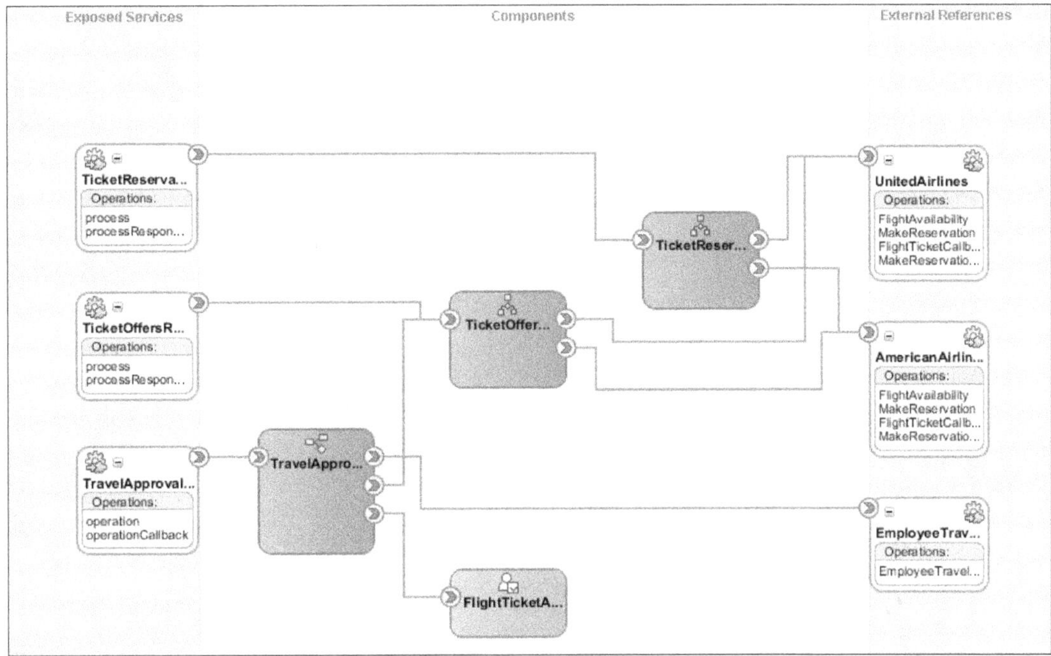

In this chapter, we will not explain how to implement the BPEL process. The following is a screenshot of the implemented BPEL process.

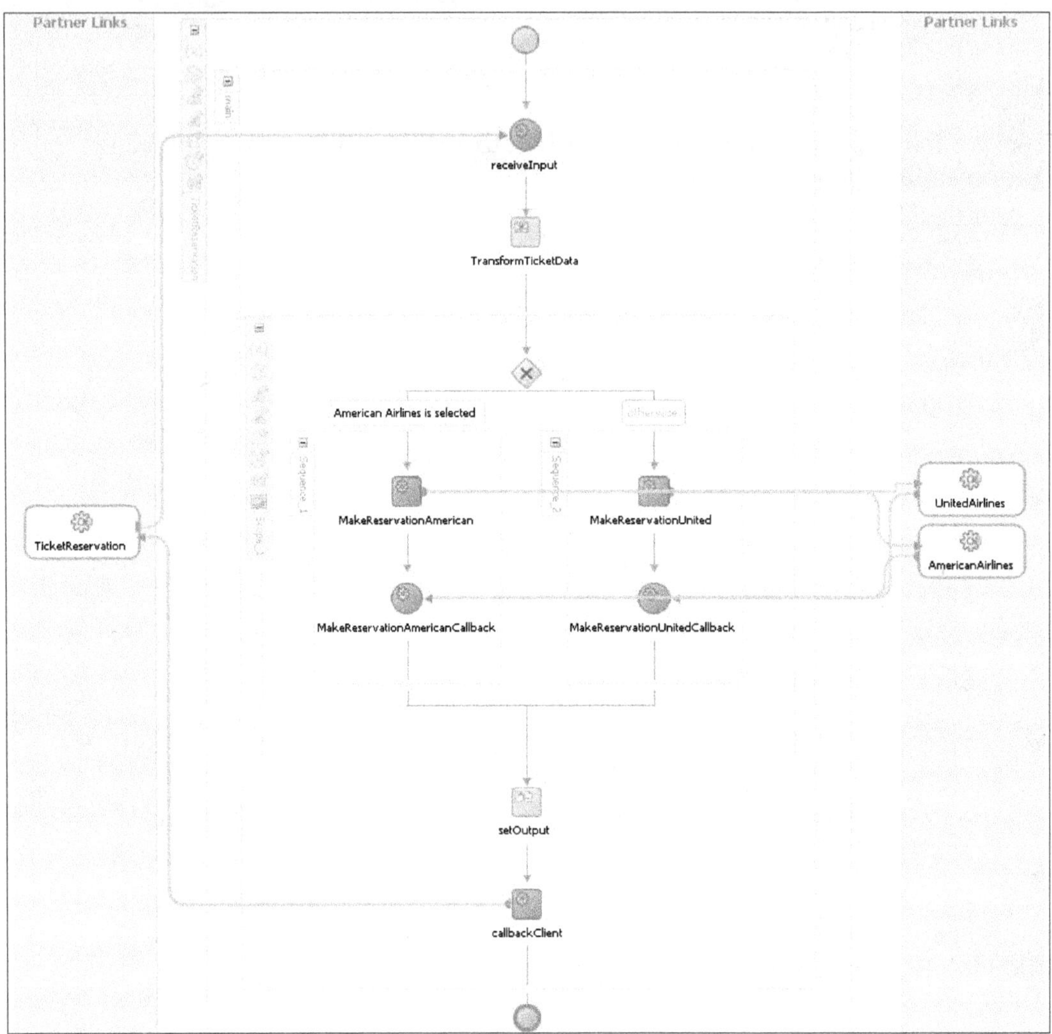

We close the BPEL Editor and save the project.

Completing the process

We open Oracle BPM Studio. As the human task defines two possible outcomes (`APPROVE` or `REJECT`), we have to add an **Exclusive Gateway** flow object to handle the outcome by taking the appropriate path. We drag-and-drop an **Exclusive Gateway** from the **Gateways** category of the **Component Palette** to the process diagram after the `Flight ticket approval` human task. We set the name of the gateway to `Task outcome?`. Then we add **Send Task** and **Receive Task** flow objects and configure them to invoke the `TicketReservation` BPEL process in a similar way as we invoked the `TicketOffersRetrieval` process. We also add another **Exclusive Gateway** flow object to merge both paths.

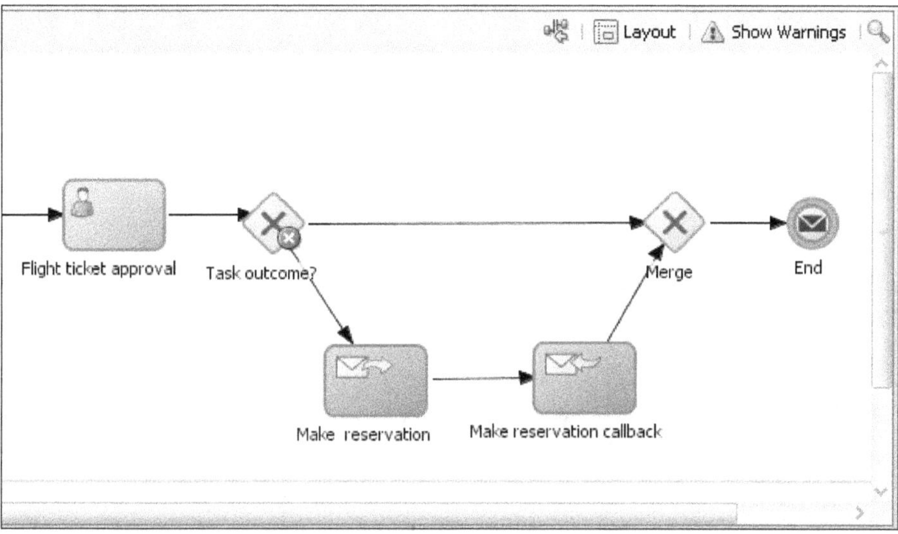

In the previous screenshot, we can see an error icon indicating that conditions for the **Exclusive Gateway** flow object are not set. We double click the transition that connects the gateway flow object and the `Make reservation` **Send Task**. In the dialog, we open the **Properties** tab and select **Condition** from the **Type** drop-down menu.

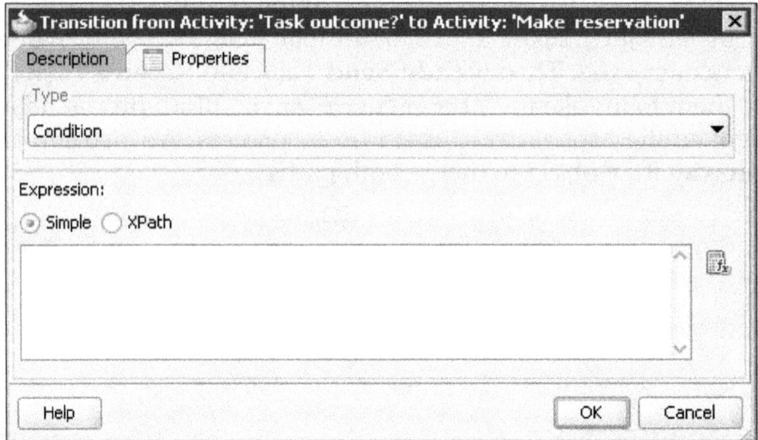

Here we can select whether we want to define simple a condition expression or use the XPath. We select **Simple** and click on the calculator icon on the right to open the Expression Editor. We enter a simple condition expression, as shown next:

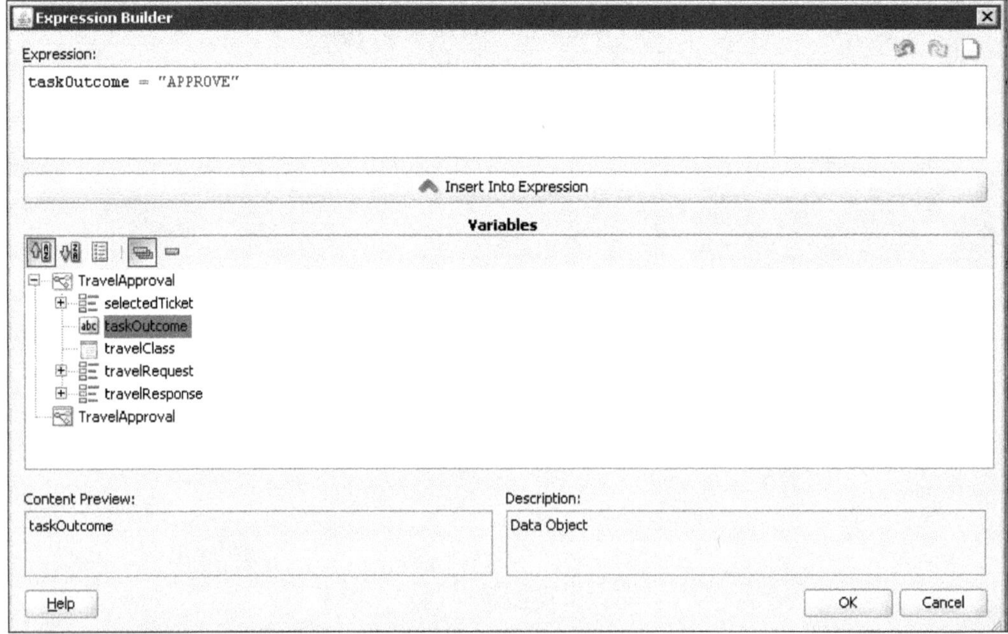

We click **OK** twice to close both dialogs. Our BPMN process is now implemented and is ready to be deployed.

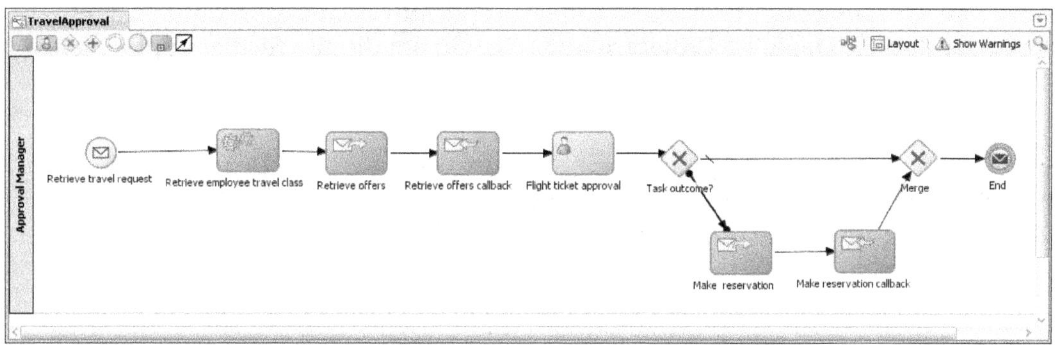

We open the SOA Composite Editor. We can see that our composite application contains four service components. The `TravelApproval` BPMN process is on the top level and uses two BPEL processes (`TicketOffersRetrieval` and `TicketReservation`) and a `FlightTicketApproval` human task. As both BPEL processes are exposed as web services, they can also be invoked from the outside world.

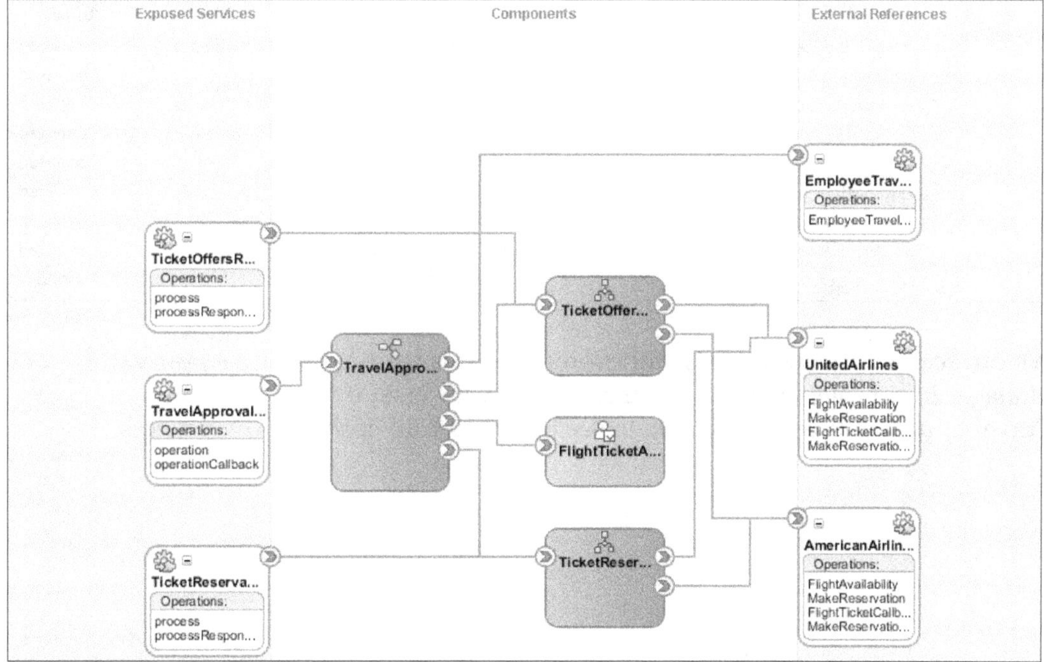

We save the project.

Deploying a BPM project

Now we can deploy our BPM project to runtime. BPM projects can be deployed in the same way as regular SOA projects. We open Application Navigator, right-click the project, and select **Deploy | Project_name**. We will not discuss further deployment steps, as this is already covered in *Chapter 4, Using BPEL with Oracle SOA Suite 11g*.

Testing an SOA composite application

Now we are ready to test our SOA composite application using Oracle Enterprise Manager Console.

Initiating an SOA composite instance

We open Oracle Enterprise Manager Console and initiate a composite instance. Then we open the instance flow trace.

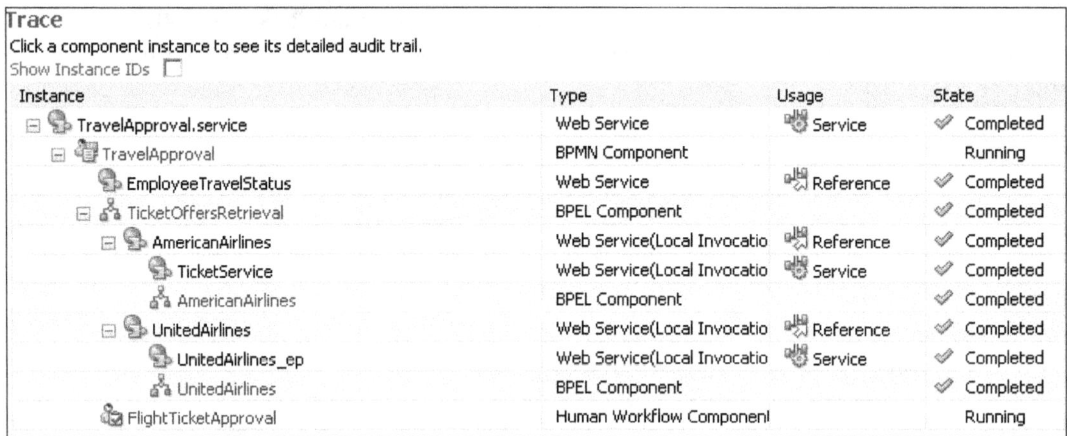
Trace

Click a component instance to see its detailed audit trail.

Show Instance IDs

Instance	Type	Usage	State
TravelApproval.service	Web Service	Service	Completed
TravelApproval	BPMN Component		Running
EmployeeTravelStatus	Web Service	Reference	Completed
TicketOffersRetrieval	BPEL Component		Completed
AmericanAirlines	Web Service(Local Invocatio	Reference	Completed
TicketService	Web Service(Local Invocatio	Service	Completed
AmericanAirlines	BPEL Component		Completed
UnitedAirlines	Web Service(Local Invocatio	Reference	Completed
UnitedAirlines_ep	Web Service(Local Invocatio	Service	Completed
UnitedAirlines	BPEL Component		Completed
FlightTicketApproval	Human Workflow Componenl		Running

We can see that the instance is still running, as it is waiting for the Approval Manager to complete the `FlightTicketApproval` task. If we click on the **TravelApproval** link, we are able to see the audit trail of the BPMN process.

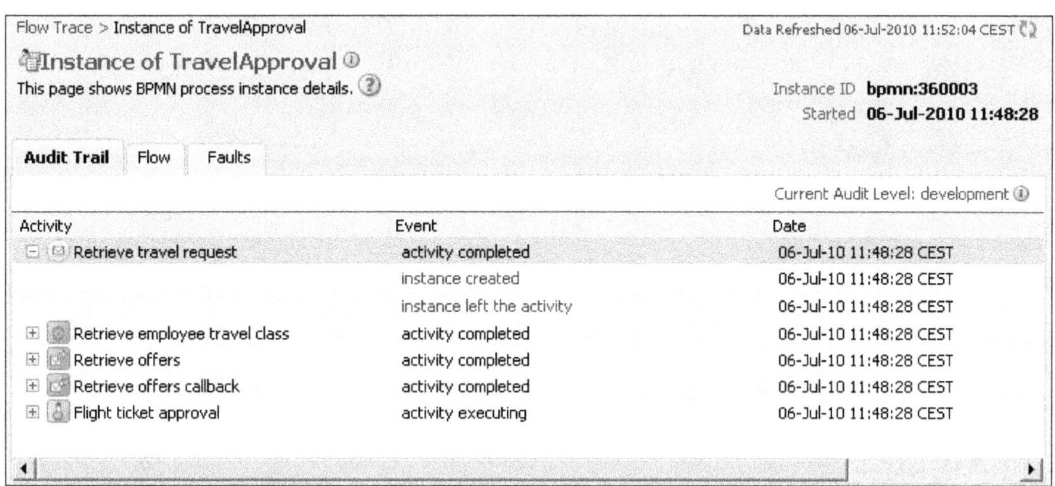

By clicking on the links in the **Event** column, we can see the values of BPMN data objects.

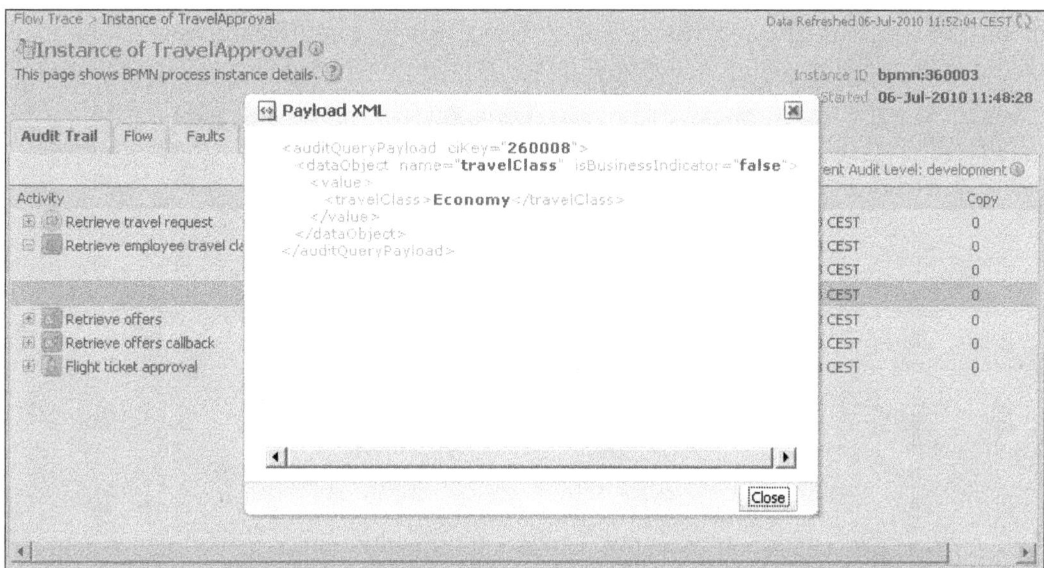

If we click on the **Flow** tab, we can also see the visual flow of the instance. All flow objects that have already been executed, or are currently running, are highlighted with green.

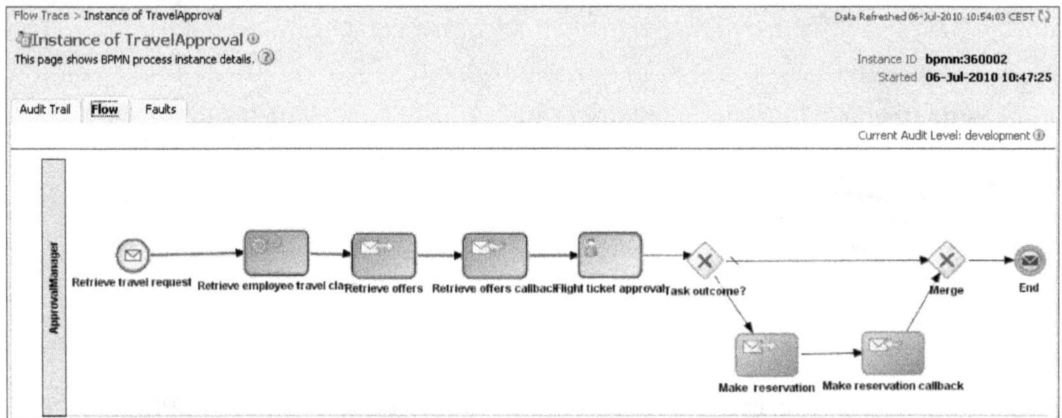

We can also view the audit trail and visual flow of both BPEL processes. The following screenshot shows the flow of the `TicketOffersRetrieval` BPEL process.

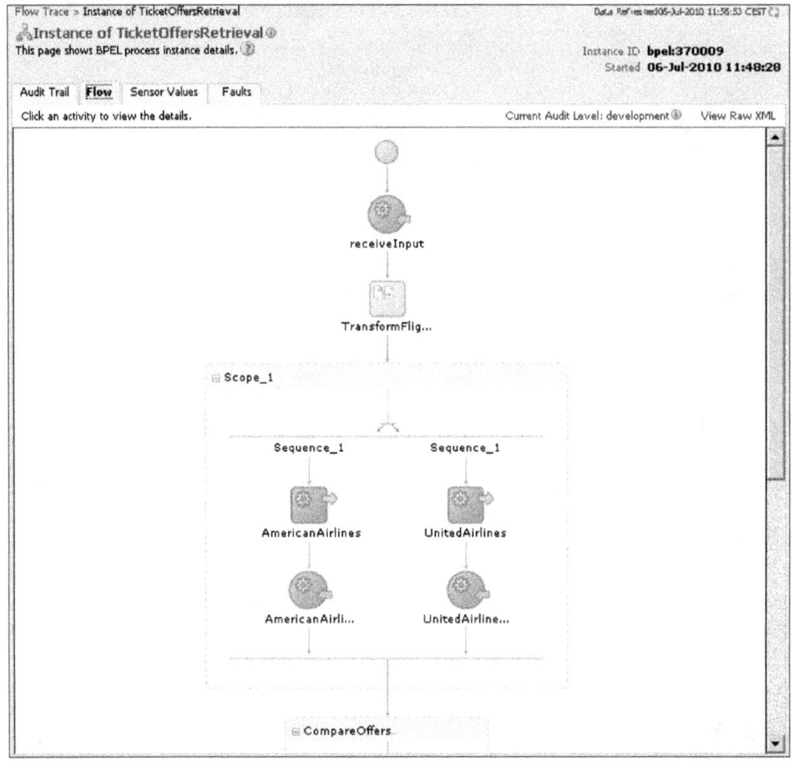

Now we open Oracle BPM Workspace to complete the human task.

Completing the human task using Oracle BPM Workspace

To complete the human task, we have to log into the Oracle BPM Workspace web application using the following URL: `http://host_name:port/bpm/workspace/`, where `host_name` is the name of the host on which Oracle BPM Workspace is installed and `port` is the port number of the SOA managed server (default is 8001). Oracle BPM Workspace is a very powerful application, allowing users to not only act on tasks, but also use the following functionality:

- Customizing the visual appearance and behavior
- Reassigning tasks to other users
- Escalating, renewing, withdrawing, and suspending tasks
- Setting the vacation period to automatically reassign tasks during absence
- Creating reports on task productivity, time distribution, and so on
- Viewing process and custom dashboards to monitor effectiveness
- Sending of notifications and alerts

In this chapter, we will not discuss Oracle BPM Workspace in detail. We will just show how to complete the task. We log into the BPM Workspace as the user `weblogic`, as the task is assigned to him. The BPM Workspace opens as shown in the following screenshot. By default, the **Inbox** view is selected and the user can see all tasks assigned to him in the **My Tasks** list. In our case, there is only one active task: `Flight ticket approval`. Remember that this is the name of the human task that we set during the creation of the human task definition.

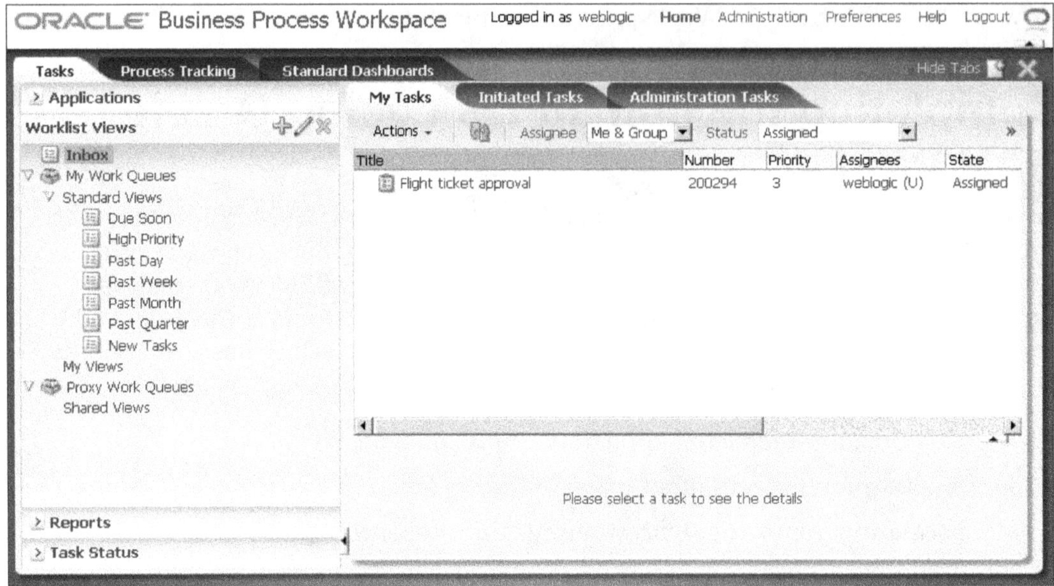

> Notice that a Oracle BPM Workspace application looks very similar to a Oracle BPM Worklist, which we are already familiar with. However, BPM Workspace provides some additional functionality, like monitoring process performance using the Dashboard.

Now we select the `Flight ticket approval` task. Notice that the human task form is not displayed at the bottom of the screen, as we did not create it. We complete the task by selecting **Approve** from the **Actions** drop-down menu. The task is completed and is removed from the **My Tasks** list.

Now we open the flow trace of the instance again. We can see, that all flow objects are highlighted, meaning that the instance has successfully completed.

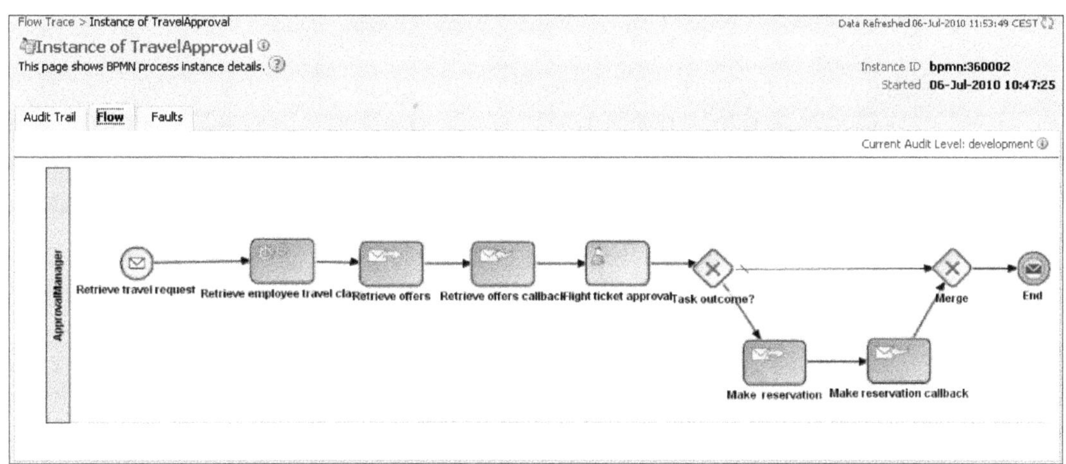

Summary

In this chapter, we have become familiar with Oracle BPM Suite 11*g*. We have described the Oracle BPM Suite architecture and features. We have discussed the importance of being able to directly implement and deploy BPMN processes, without the need to transform them to BPEL.

We have shown how to use Oracle BPM Studio, how to create a new BPM project, and how to model and implement business processes using BPMN 2.0. We have also demonstrated how a BPMN process and BPEL process service components can be used inside a single SOA composite application.

We have also shown how to deploy a BPM project and how to debug a process instance by opening the instance audit trail and the visual flow. Finally we have become familiar with the Oracle BPM Workspace application.

Index

Symbols

A

B

C

D

E

F

G

H

I

N

O

T

U

V

W

X

Y

Z

Thank you for buying

WS-BPEL 2.0 for SOA Composite Applications with Oracle SOA Suite 11*g*

About Packt Publishing

Packt, pronounced 'packed', published its first book "Mastering phpMyAdmin for Effective MySQL Management" in April 2004 and subsequently continued to specialize in publishing highly focused books on specific technologies and solutions.

Our books and publications share the experiences of your fellow IT professionals in adapting and customizing today's systems, applications, and frameworks. Our solution based books give you the knowledge and power to customize the software and technologies you're using to get the job done. Packt books are more specific and less general than the IT books you have seen in the past. Our unique business model allows us to bring you more focused information, giving you more of what you need to know, and less of what you don't.

Packt is a modern, yet unique publishing company, which focuses on producing quality, cutting-edge books for communities of developers, administrators, and newbies alike. For more information, please visit our website: `www.packtpub.com`.

About Packt Enterprise

In 2010, Packt launched two new brands, Packt Enterprise and Packt Open Source, in order to continue its focus on specialization. This book is part of the Packt Enterprise brand, home to books published on enterprise software - software created by major vendors, including (but not limited to) IBM, Microsoft and Oracle, often for use in other corporations. Its titles will offer information relevant to a range of users of this software, including administrators, developers, architects, and end users.

Writing for Packt

We welcome all inquiries from people who are interested in authoring. Book proposals should be sent to author@packtpub.com. If your book idea is still at an early stage and you would like to discuss it first before writing a formal book proposal, contact us; one of our commissioning editors will get in touch with you.

We're not just looking for published authors; if you have strong technical skills but no writing experience, our experienced editors can help you develop a writing career, or simply get some additional reward for your expertise.

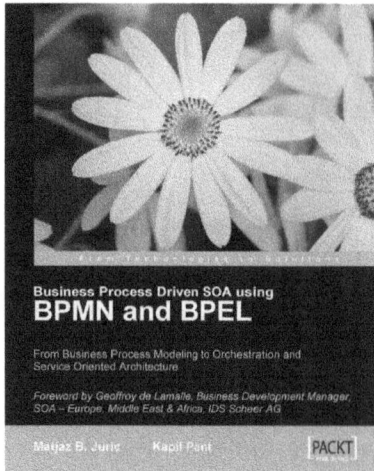

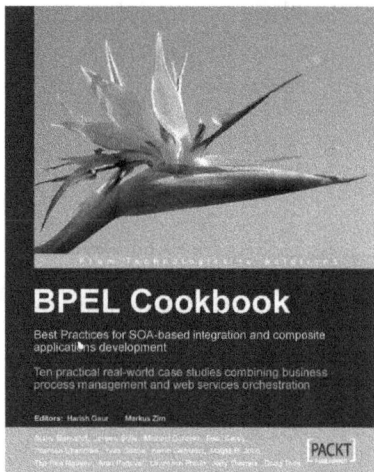

BPEL PM and OSB Operational Management with Oracle Enterprise Manager 10*g* Grid Control

Narayan Bharadwaj

BPEL PM and OSB operational management with Oracle Enterprise Manager 10*g* Grid Control

ISBN: 978-1-847197-74-0 Paperback: 248 pages

Manage the operational tasks for multiple BPEL and OSB environments centrally

1. Monitor and manage all components of your SOA environment from a central location
2. Save time and increase efficiency by automating all the day-to-day operational tasks associated with the SOA environment

---

Oracle SOA Suite 11*g* R1 Developer's Guide

Antony Reynolds Matt Wright

Oracle SOA Suite 11*g* R1 Developer's Guide

ISBN: 978-1-849680-18-9 Paperback: 720 pages

Develop Service-Oriented Architecture Solutions with the Oracle SOA Suite

1. A hands-on, best-practice guide to using and applying the Oracle SOA Suite in the delivery of real-world SOA applications
2. Detailed coverage of the Oracle Service Bus, BPEL PM, Rules, Human Workflow, Event Delivery Network, and Business Activity Monitoring

Please check **www.PacktPub.com** for information on our titles

www.ingramcontent.com/pod-product-compliance
Lightning Source LLC
Chambersburg PA
CBHW060940210326
41598CB00031B/4684

* 9 7 8 1 8 4 7 1 9 7 9 4 8 *